Growing Toward Unity

L T H

THE LIVING THEOLOGICAL HERITAGE
OF THE UNITED CHURCH OF CHRIST

Volume 1. Ancient and Medieval Legacies

Volume 2. Reformation Roots

Volume 3. Colonial and National Beginnings

Volume 4. Consolidation and Expansion

Volume 5. Outreach and Diversity

Volume 6. Growing Toward Unity

Volume 7. United and Uniting

THE LIVING THEOLOGICAL HERITAGE

OF THE UNITED CHURCH OF CHRIST

Barbara Brown Zikmund

Series Editor

L T H

VOLUME SEVEN

United and Uniting

Edited by Frederick R. Trost
and Barbara Brown Zikmund

The Pilgrim Press
Cleveland, Ohio

The Pilgrim Press, 700 Prospect Avenue
Cleveland, Ohio 44115-1100, U.S.A.

Printed in the United States of America on acid-free paper

10 09 08 07 06 05 5 4 3 2 1

Library of Congress Cataloging-in-Publication Data
The living theological heritage of the United Church of Christ /
Barbara Brown Zikmund, series editor.
p. cm.
Includes bibliographical references and index.

Vol. 1, Ancient and Medieval Legacies ISBN 0-8298-1064-1
Vol. 2, Reformation Roots ISBN 0-8298-1143-5
Vol. 3, Colonial and National Beginnings ISBN 0-8298-1109-5
Vol. 4, Consolidation and Expansion ISBN 0-8298-1110-9
Vol. 5, Outreach and Diversity ISBN 0-8298-1111-7
Vol. 6, Growing Toward Unity ISBN 0-8298-1112-5
Vol. 7, United and Uniting ISBN 0-8298-1113-3

In memory of and
in grateful appreciation for
the life and ministry of
Charles Shelby Rooks
1924–2001

Contents

The Living Theological Heritage of the United Church of Christ

Remember me, O L*ORD, when you show favor to your people; help me when you deliver them; that I may see the prosperity of your chosen ones, that I may rejoice in the gladness of your nation, that I may glory in your heritage.*

Psalm 106:4–5 (NRSV)

The United Church of Christ is a microcosm of the history of Christian theology. Although the UCC was not officially "born" until 1957, it draws upon a long-standing and rich theological legacy. A living theological heritage has shaped, and continues to support, its common life.

Unfortunately, a perception exists that the UCC is without any roots, that it is unsure about its faith. Lutherans quote the works of Martin Luther; Methodists revere the ideas of John Wesley; Episcopalians have the divines of the Church of England. But members of the United Church of Christ often seem uncertain about their theological heritage and identity.

The United Church of Christ was created out of a mid-twentieth-century ecumenical passion to heal the divisions of the Christian church. Its focus was on the future, not on the past. Nevertheless, it has a remarkable theological and historical legacy. This volume, and others in this series, offers resources from Congregational and Christian history and German Evangelical and Reformed traditions, along with many hidden histories, to leaders and members of the United Church of Christ and to the wider society. We hope that these materials will strengthen the denomination and inform those seeking a better understanding of the past and present life of the UCC.

For example, New England Congregationalism leaned on the theological insights of key English separatist thinkers in the late sixteenth and early seventeenth centuries. Participants in American frontier religion developed six theological principles to guide their Christian witness. The theological work of John Nevin and Philip Schaff shaped and reshaped the German Reformed Church. German Evangelical immigrants brought with them a theology forged by a European church-union movement. Few people know this heritage, and when they look for more information, it is difficult to find the sources.

In the late 1980s the Office for Church Life and Leadership and the Board for Homeland Ministries of the United Church of Christ authorized *The Living Theological Heritage of the United Church of Christ.* They designed this series of seven volumes to enable the United Church of Christ to recover its theological past and strengthen contemporary faith and practice. The series is offered to the churches and their members to enable them to move beyond their theological inferiority complex and to claim their heritage.

• • •

The series brings together key materials that undergird UCC faith and practice. A team of thirteen editors, guided by an editorial board of seven, presents these volumes as a quarry of resources to be mined by the churches for years to come.

The design of each volume does three things:

First, it gathers together important materials that have shaped the theological identity of the United Church of Christ — ancient christological discourses, sixteenth-century treatises by Reformation theologians, the Heidelberg Catechism, writings and sermons from colonial Congregationalism, the Cambridge Platform, mission statements, popular hymns, prayers, official ecumenical materials, resolutions from wider church meetings, minority reports, and even protest literature. Some of the materials are obvious and known, some are fugitive, and some are new discoveries. The editors chose all of them, from the first century to the twentieth century, not simply because they are part of the historical record, but because the editors believe that these documents have shaped the theological identity of the UCC.

Second, each volume contains brief introductions to individual documents or groups of source materials, giving the reader background information needed to understand what is printed. Who wrote it? When was it written? Why was it written? What was the result? These document introductions help make the materials understandable in and of themselves.

Third, each volume has one or more introductory essays to highlight broader insights and theological interpretations of the materials. Obviously, any selection of documents can distort by highlighting some things and excluding others, but the editors have attempted to make the selections as inclusive as possible. The introductory essays, written by the editors, weave the materials into meaningful patterns and gather up the collective wisdom of the UCC to make it more accessible in the present.

• • •

The Living Theological Heritage of the United Church of Christ has seven volumes.

Volume 1, *Ancient and Medieval Legacies,* grounds the theological life of the United Church of Christ in the search for unity and theological clarity within the ancient and medieval church. As a Protestant denomination, why should the UCC concern itself with pre-Reformation theology and history? Because not to begin with the early church betrays its understanding of Christian unity. This volume explores the themes of unity ("united"), ecclesiology ("church"), and Christology ("Christ") from the time of Jesus to the Reformation. It highlights the fact that the United Church of Christ stands in a long line of faithful Christians who have sought to understand and name their faith from the first century to the present.

Volume 2, *Reformation Roots,* explores the theological legacies of the United Church of Christ found in the sixteenth-century Protestant Reformation. From reformers like Erasmus, Zwingli, Luther, Calvin, English separatists, and the irenic leaders of the Palatinate, the UCC has forged its theological core. Volume 2 provides a collection of Reformation materials especially meaningful to the United Church of Christ.

Volume 3, *Colonial and National Beginnings,* examines the development of early Congregationalism and German Reformed theology. It lifts up the ideas and concerns that motivated colonial thinking and demonstrates how they evolved with the migration and increasing diversity of the population.

Volume 4, *Consolidation and Expansion,* documents the story of the Christians and the German Evangelicals on the American frontier and tracks later developments in Congregational and German Reformed history. It illustrates how the Christian movement brought together Methodists from North Carolina, Baptists from New England, and Presbyterians from Kentucky. It reveals the contributions of German Evangelicals on the Mississippi frontier. At the same time, it follows the development of German Reformed and Congregational faith and practice as the nation matured and people migrated west.

Volume 5, *Outreach and Diversity,* brings together a mix of materials flowing from the mission outreach of all of these groups. It also explores the experiences of minority and immigrant communities. The call to evangelize, educate, and serve stretched the theological mind of those groups that later created the UCC. African American contributions, encounters with indigenous peoples, social witness, and new immigrants raised new theological issues and encouraged a pattern of theological engagement with the world.

Volume 6, *Growing Toward Unity,* celebrates the long-standing commitment of the UCC to an ecumenical vision and the search for Christian unity. It steps back from the complex history of peoples and ideas documented in the earlier volumes to examine the vision of Christian unity that eventually gave birth to the United Church of Christ. It is a theological heritage that takes seriously the prayer of Jesus "that they might all be one."

Volume 7, *United and Uniting,* documents the evolution of the United Church of Christ's theological identity from 1957 to 2000. It looks at more than four decades of UCC life and gathers up its theological treasures. It recognizes that the theological journey of the UCC has been wide-ranging, one that has produced a distinctive living theological heritage. It also invites the UCC to become more theologically self-conscious.

• • •

We hope that *The Living Theological Heritage of the United Church of Christ* will enable those who are members of the UCC to find new courage to speak with pride about their UCC faith and theological inheritance and will give those who are not members of the church a clear understanding of this unique community of Christians.

Acknowledgments

At the beginning of the Living Theological Heritage project there were three editors for volume seven. The two remaining editors, Frederick R. Trost and Barbara Brown Zikmund, dedicate this volume to Charles Shelby Rooks, who did not live to see its completion. The editors are also indebted to four associate editors: Yvonne V. Delk, Rosemary McCombs Maxey, Teruo Kawata, and Olgha Sierra Sandman. These associate editors gathered materials to show how African Americans, American Indians, Pacific Islander and Asian Americans, and Hispanics contributed to the theological heritage of the United Church of Christ. Project research assistant Virginia H. Child made an almost overwhelming task manageable by maintaining document files, scanning hundreds of pages and serving as a central repository for three years. Additional thanks go to United Church of Christ archivists George Hing and Bridgette Kelly. And finally we thank our spouses, Louise Hermann Trost and Joseph Zikmund II, for their patience and support during a very long project.

Barbara Brown Zikmund
Series Editor

PART I

Becoming One Church

The birth of the United Church of Christ in 1957 is truly a remarkable event, an astonishing achievement inspired by the Holy Spirit of the triune God; the result of more than fifty years of ecumenical hope and twenty years of work and prayer. The founders of the United Church of Christ truly believed that the Church of Jesus Christ is one, bringing together in a single body people of all nations, tongues, and races. Human limitations and human conflicts repeatedly fracture the church into many groups, but those who labored to create the UCC profoundly believed that the central calling of the Church of Jesus Christ is unity — which is a gift of God. The union of the Congregational Christian Churches and the Evangelical and Reformed Church is a step towards the fulfillment of Christ's prayer in the Gospel of John, "that they may all be one." For the United Church of Christ that vision remains an ongoing challenge.

Claiming an Ecumenical Vision

This effort to claim church unity had a rocky history (see vol. 6). In 1957, however, those involved in the formation of the United Church of Christ were filled with hope. Although challenges remained, the uniting General Synod embraced the "Basis of Union with Interpretations" with optimism and a sense of purpose (see vol. 7:1). Through the creation of the United Church of Christ, its leaders sought to "preserve unity of heart and spirit" with those who had gone before, as well as "with those who now labor with us."

This ecumenical vision shaped the new church, pushing it to move beyond denominationalism. Leaders stated that "unity lies in holiness," and that "the more the church grows into 'Christlikeness' " the more its oneness will become apparent. The United Church of Christ was making the "impossible possible." Each of the uniting churches was "bringing its best." Its future would "be measured by how profoundly and with what deepening devotion" it was able to get God's work done in this world (see vol. 7:2).

Testifying to the Faith

Although some people felt that they could not affirm their "oneness" in Christ until after a constitution was written and approved, the first major accomplishment of the new denomination was not a constitution, but a Statement of Faith. At the uniting General Synod in 1957, a commission was formed and charged to write a Statement of Faith, presenting its draft in 1959. The commission heeded advice recommending that the statement make use of historic language, while sustaining "theological freedom" and sounding a word of Christian hope (see vol. 7:3).

The Statement of Faith of the United Church of Christ sings with the dynamic voices of the saints who have come before us, looking to a future marked by Christian hope. Following the lead of Roger Shinn, the member of the commission who drafted the initial version, it celebrates the "deeds of God," even as it is grounded in classic Trinitarian theology. It lifts up the ways in which God creates, redeems, and sustains the world and calls those who share in Christ's baptism and eat at his table to the struggle for justice and peace and to the cost and joy of discipleship (see vol. 7:4).

When the draft of the Statement of Faith was published, reactions were mixed. Letters in the new *United Church Herald* were enthusiastic and critical. "Continuing Congregationalists," who resisted the formation of the United Church of Christ lamented the statement's failure to emphasize Congregational principles (see vol. 7:5). Others rejoiced that the statement expressed classic Christian beliefs in words that could inspire modern Christians. People outside the United Church of Christ offered praise for the statement, calling it a significant theological accomplishment — a deeply meaningful confession of belief connected to historic creeds and platforms, but cast in compelling contemporary language.

The Statement of Faith attempts to articulate the faith of the whole church. Given the diversity and dynamic mix of traditions and ethnic groups in the United Church of Christ, this is difficult. Yet, it has endured and evolved. Twenty-five years after its creation, one black UCC leader noted that African American UCC members sometimes "hear" the Statement of Faith differently. Black experience affords a distinctive perspective on salvation, Jesus Christ, the Holy Spirit, the church, and the promises of God. Although the statement has served the church well, some communities of faith within the UCC also use other texts and actions to express their faith (see vol. 7:6).

Furthermore, the Statement of Faith was written before there was much awareness about "inclusive language." It repeatedly refers to both God and humans in masculine terms. By the 1970s feminists and others took exception to its exclusivity. In 1976, Robert V. Moss, the second president of the UCC, revised the statement to make it more "inclusive." He retained words that expressed the humanity of Christ in the classical tradition, while altering words about God and humanity. The "Moss version" is widely used and debated, although it was never endorsed formally by General Synod. While it helped resolve some of the language problems, it presented new and challenging theological issues (see vol. 7:7).

As the United Church of Christ approached its twenty-fifth anniversary, many people thought that it was time to produce a new "Statement of Faith." The Office for Church Life and Leadership (OCLL) engaged in a process to find more inclusive ways for the church to "testify to its faith." The result was a new "doxological" version of the Statement of Faith, which addresses God rather than making statements about God. Through words of praise and thanksgiving it testifies to the work of God in the world and provides a creative way to keep the beauty and central convictions of the original statement. At the same time it avoids some of the linguistic and theological problems found in the original version and its later revisions (see vol. 7:7).

In addition to these English revisions, the UCC Statement of Faith has also inspired a hymn and been translated into several other languages. Protestants in Germany were very interested in the development of the United Church of Christ, and a German translation of the UCC Statement of Faith was widely circulated after 1969. As the Spanish-speaking population of the nation increased, a Spanish translation was produced, serving the multicultural life of new UCC congregations and reflecting historic ecumenical relations with churches in Latin America, such as the Mexican Congregational churches and the Evangelical and Reformed Synod of Honduras (see vol. 7:7).

The United Church of Christ Statement of Faith stands in a long line of creeds and confessions in Christian history. Unlike some doctrinal statements, however, it is affirmed by the UCC as a "testimony," not a "test" of faith. Christians with wide-ranging perspectives about God, Jesus Christ, the Holy Spirit, and the church are challenged to "make it their own" in many cultural contexts.

Forming Faithful Structures

At the first General Synod in 1957 a commission was also chosen to draft a constitution for the United Church of Christ. It was a special time of testing, because so much early resistance to the union revolved around governance questions.

The "Basis of Union" was drafted ten years before the union was consummated. Many of those who were resistant to the union feared that the new church would limit congregational freedoms among Congregational Christians, so a set of "Interpretations" was added to clarify polity issues. Legal challenges in the courts further tested the ways in which money, property, and power would be used and protected in the new church.

Writing a constitution for the United Church of Christ was a demanding task, because the United Church of Christ brought together two very different ecclesiastical organizations. On the one side was the General Council of the Congregational Christian Churches, serving the needs of local congregations who jealously guarded practices that preserved local congregational independence. In the Congregational and Christian traditions individual congregations had come together in fellowship to form denominational structures for mission and outreach, but local congregations had no *legal* obligations to each other. Congregations could accept or reject the actions of other churches or their General Council as "guided by the Holy Spirit."

The ecclesiastical form of the Evangelical and Reformed Church was different. Local congregations in the E and R Church sent representatives to wider church meetings with the understanding that actions taken there became binding on every local congregation. The Evangelical and Reformed Church made decisions like the national government of the United States. When Congress or the General Synod passes a law, or votes a resolution, once the law is signed by the president, or the resolution is approved by the General Synod, citizens or church members cannot reject it.

This approach meant that when the General Synod of the Evangelical and Reformed Church voted to become part of the United Church of Christ, all E and R congregations were expected to become part of the new church. The General Synod was, in Evangelical and Reformed polity, authorized to speak for all the congregations. For Congregational Christian congregations, however, the issues were far more complicated. The General Council of the Congregational Christian Churches could speak only for itself. Although the *General Council* of Congregational Christian Churches had united with the General Synod of the Evangelical and Reformed Church, each local Congregational Christian congregation still had to vote to "belong" to the UCC.

Given this reality, the wording of the new constitution was crucial. Congregational Christian people wanted to be sure that their congregational traditions were adequately honored and protected. If they did not find such protection in the proposed constitution, they might postpone their vote, or even vote "no."

The Constitutional Commission worked for two years. To ease the fears of Congregational Christians, the constitution contained a paragraph about "the autonomy of the local church" as "modifiable only by its own action" (Article IV, Paragraph 15 in the pre-2000 constitution: Article V, Paragraph 18 in the 2000 constitution). However, the paragraph immediately preceding the "autonomy paragraph" also emphasized the mutual "God-given responsibility" of local churches for the wider church and vice versa. And the paragraph that followed reminded the church that the "actions, decisions and advice" coming from one part of the church "should be held in highest regard by every local church."

The heart of the constitution, however, is stated in the preamble. It emphasizes the centrality of Jesus Christ as "sole Head" of the church. It reminds all of the churches that each generation is called to "make the faith of the historic church and the insights of the Protestant Reformers" its own (see vol. 7:8).

Douglas Horton helped the United Church of Christ interpret its new structures theologically. If Jesus Christ is the head of the church, all those who share that confession are family. Christ provides a perfecting influence on church structures. Furthermore, the Word of God in the Scriptures, and the presence and power of the Holy Spirit sustain the work of the church in the world (see vol. 7:9).

In 1959, when the commission brought its draft of the proposed constitution to the General Synod, there were many questions. Committed to answering every question, the Synod did not act, but scheduled "an adjourned session" for a year later. Finally, in 1960 the constitution and bylaws were approved and sent to conferences and local congregations.

Growing together into unity, including the adoption of a constitution, was something former Evangelical and Reformed congregations had experienced after their union in 1934 (see vol. 6:53, 65–69). They were prepared to welcome the ways in which the new constitution would clarify how their life in the new denomination would be ordered. For Congregational Christian congregations, however, the new constitution became "a test." CC leaders who had worked for many years to bring about the "union" or "merger" (as they sometimes called it) made the case that congregational freedoms would not be compromised by an affirmative vote. They encouraged congregations to "join the UCC." A small minority of CC leaders argued that the constitution destroyed "congregational principles," or that the UCC was not a good way to affirm Christian unity (see vol. 6:79–83 and vol. 7:10).

Convincing the former CC churches to "join" was only one small part of the organizational challenges facing the new denomination. There were many national bodies to be merged and restructured. There were new regional conferences to be organized.

As the United Church of Christ moved into the 1960s, new social issues claimed its attention, yet concern for constitutional and structural issues persisted. In 1961 a Long Range Planning Committee appointed by the General Synod set forth a list of issues likely to confront the UCC in the coming decade. Many of them were structural. In 1967, a Committee on Structure drafted a "Statement of Purpose and Mission for the UCC," and two years later it reported on organizational problems that continued to undermine the effectiveness of the UCC. Its statement reminded the church that "The authority of the whole is the self-imposed willingness of each part to co-operate with the rest and to undergird and support the responsible leadership of those who represent the larger fellowship" (see vol. 7:11).

Some churches or denominations rarely worry about polity and structures. For the UCC, however, concern about structures, especially among Congregationalists who often define themselves largely in terms of polity, can become obsessive. As a consequence UCC understandings of order and identity remain at once inspiring and vulnerable and are revisited again and again. Newcomers join the United Church of Christ and bring with them preconceptions about the ways they expect authority and power to work in the church. When things do not match their expectations, leaders are forced to explain once again the unique mix of theology and polity that is uniquely present in the United Church of Christ.

Blending Traditions

From the very earliest conversations about a "united church," advocates insisted that the new denomination should seek to preserve its living theological heritage, bringing faithful convictions from the past to bear on the creation of a new future. There were moments when leaders in the Evangelical and Reformed Church sought clarification about the "free church" tradition. There were times when Congregational Christians seemed to forget that their history is filled with cooperative or "conciliar" experiences. Through it all the hope and the dream remained that the effort and prayer surrounding the achievement of one small church union in 1957 might be the beginning of a larger unity.

As people lived together within the United Church of Christ, they were in some respects understandably anxious. Yet the story of the UCC is not a blending of church traditions with centralized authority with those that insist upon local autonomy. What is exciting is that the UCC discovered how to bring together two different ways of perceiving the church, although it was not easily achieved. There were many arguments as the church struggled with its ecclesiology and with the theological meaning of its life together. There were those who cherished "an organic view of the church as a compact integrated people" and there were those who cherished "the tradition of functional responsiveness to the needs of the world." In the United Church of Christ these two spirits were able to "confront each other creatively and refuse to be smothered for the sake of a superficial harmony" (see vol. 7:12). It is true that there were those who challenged the dichotomy on biblical and theological grounds, believing that a compact and integrated people can act responsibly in the world. Indeed, the love of Christ compels them.

Looking back years later, many people gratefully celebrated the fact that the UCC was a "merger of two kinds of churches." Objectively, the UCC does not make sense, because the social, cultural, and religious contrasts it contains are not a natural match. The UCC gradually came to experience unity in diversity by trusting God in Jesus Christ. But the way to unity was not placid. It was rough and uneasy at times. It is probably true to say that the story of the United Church of Christ is a story of trusting God and gradually coming to trust one another.

The United Church of Christ was not created, nor is it sustained by compromise — or even by ignoring or tolerating differences. It depends upon "reconciliation." It trusts in the capacity of very different people, with very different interpretations of the gospel, to recognize in each other the historic faith. It flourishes when it is able to make, as the preamble puts it, "this faith its own in reality of worship, in honesty of thought and expression, and in purity of heart before God" (see vol. 7:13).

Claiming an Ecumenical Vision

1. The Basis of Union:
"Article II: Faith"

(1957)

The Basis of Union with Interpretations was the document that the General Council of the Congregational Christian Churches and the General Synod of the Evangelical and Reformed Church developed and affirmed to unite the two denominations to form the United Church of Christ (see vol. 6:77 and 84). Its "Article II: Faith" expresses the content and meaning of the faith held generally by the members of the two uniting churches. The Basis of Union "Faith" statement is not considered a substitute for a confession of faith that might have been used by any congregation. Nor is it a substitute for the more ample statement that the two churches planned to develop after union (Basis of Union Article IV, section F). In both cases, however, the statements are understood to be a testimony, and not a test, of faith.

Source: "Article II: Faith" from "The Basis of Union with Interpretations," *GS Minutes 1957,* Appendix 30, 174.

II. Faith

The faith which unites us and to which we bear witness is that faith in God which the Scriptures of the Old and New Testaments set forth, which the ancient Church expressed in the ecumenical creeds, to which our own spiritual fathers gave utterance in the evangelical confessions of the Reformation, and which we are in duty bound to express in the words of our time as God Himself gives us light. In all our expressions of that faith we seek to preserve unity of heart and spirit with those who have gone before us as well as those who now labor with us.

In token of that faith we unite in the following confession, as embodying those things most surely believed and taught among us:

We believe in God the Father Almighty, Creator and Sustainer of heaven and earth and in Jesus Christ, His Son, our Lord and Saviour, who for us and our salvation lived and died and rose again and lives for evermore; and in the Holy Spirit, who takes of the things of Christ and shows them to us, renewing, comforting, and inspiring the souls of men.

We acknowledge one holy catholic Church, the innumerable company of those who, in every age and nation, are united by the Holy Spirit to God in Christ, are one body in Christ, and have communion with Him and with one another.

We acknowledge as part of this universal fellowship all throughout the world who profess this faith in Jesus Christ and follow Him as Lord and Saviour.

We hold the Church to be established for calling men to repentance and faith, for the public worship of God, for the confession of His name by word and deed, for the administration of the sacraments, for witnessing to the saving grace of God in Christ, for the upbuilding of the saints, and for the universal propagation of the Gospel; and in the power of the love of God in Christ we labor for the progress of knowledge, the promotion of justice, the reign of peace, and realization of human brotherhood.

Depending, as did our fathers, upon the continued guidance of the Holy Spirit to lead us into all truth, we work and pray for the consummation of the Kingdom of God; and we look with faith for the triumph of righteousness and for the life everlasting.

2. Coming Together:
"Toward a United Church of Christ" and "Each Brings Its Best"

(1955, 1956)

S.[Samuel] D. Press and James E. Wagner

Samuel D. Press (1875–1967) was an Evangelical and Reformed/UCC minister who graduated from Elmhurst College and Eden Theological Seminary, with other studies at the University of Berlin. He served as a pastor and district president of the Evangelical Synod in Texas and played a key role in the formation of the Evangelical and Reformed Church (1934). It was his 1938 telegram to Truman Douglass of the General Council of the Congregational Christian Churches on behalf of the Evangelical and Reformed Church's committee to explore closer relations with other churches that asked, "What about a rapprochement between our two communions looking toward union?" (see vol. 6:70).

In his graduate studies Press had studied under Adolf von Harnack. He was on the faculty at Eden Theological Seminary for more than forty years (1908–51), serving as Eden's president (1919–41). He did not believe that the "oneness of the church" required organizational unity, but argued that "churches weaken their common message by their separate claims." His 1955 article in The Messenger, *the magazine of the Evangelical and Reformed Church, is a strong, supportive statement of the long-anticipated union.*

James E. Wagner (1900–1985) was a Church of God/Evangelical and Reformed/UCC minister educated at Findlay College (Ohio) and

Sources: S.[Samuel] D. Press, an excerpt from "Toward a United Church of Christ," *The Messenger* (November 29, 1955), 7–8. James Wagner, an excerpt from "Each Brings Its Best," An Address to the General Council of the Congregational Christian Churches, Omaha, Nebraska, June 26, 1956.

Lancaster Theological Seminary. Wagner was a local church pastor in several congregations in Pennsylvania (1922–53) and president of the Evangelical and Reformed Church (1953–61). During the last four years of his E and R presidency, he was also co-president of the United Church of Christ.

Wagner was not part of the early discussions about a union between the Evangelical and Reformed Church and the Congregational Christian Churches, but he became supportive and eloquent in his advocacy of the United Church of Christ. His 1956 speech to the General Council of the Congregational Christian Churches in Omaha, Nebraska, seeks to reassure apprehensive Congregational Christian leaders that the Evangelical and Reformed Church has "never even remotely assumed that its 'way of life' could be or should be imposed upon the United Church of Christ."

Toward a United Church of Christ

A Divine Creation

The oneness of the church so intrinsic to the nature of the church does not, then, refer to her empirical form of existence primarily, but to her spiritual essence. Neither the witness of the prophets concerning the messianic church nor the testimony of the apostles concerning the church which came into being through Christ relates to individuals, but to the church. What constitutes the primary datum are not individuals as such, but the church as a divine creation.

The early Christians did not proclaim to the world: "We are Christians" — others gave them that name; or "We are saved," which might carry the implication that only the others are lost. The message of the early Christians to the world was *Ecclesiam habemus* — we have the church: that for which the centuries waited has now become a fact. The commonwealth of nations is no longer a dream: it is here; it exists in Jesus Christ. Something has happened in him through his mediatorial work on Calvary, where he died for all: the barriers of race, nationality, class, and social status, which kept men apart, have been broken down; the disintegrating forces of sin have been conquered; a new power — the power of a divine love, the integrating power of holiness from above — has created a new humanity, a fellowship of folk who are at one on the deepest level of life.

As followers of Jesus Christ, we in the church recognize it to be our mission to make the truth known to the world. But truth is never factious; it does not lend itself to be used as party or denominational label; it does not acknowledge this or that school of thought. Therefore the world cannot evaluate as truth our divided witness presenting itself in so many conflicting versions. The churches call men to be baptized into the name of Jesus Christ, into his death and resurrection, that they might receive the forgiveness of sin. But how can men be brought to believe in our message of forgiveness of sin as long as they who proclaim it do not know how to hold their divergent interpretations in the bond of peace?

The churches weaken their common message by their separate claims; they hinder the divine truth by seeking to provide or to restrict the human channels for the operation of the sovereign, almighty grace of God. All the churches acknowledge and praise Jesus as their Lord, but in their conflicts they more often follow their own wills and obey their own opinions.

If denominationalism is justified as an end, then the grace of the gospel is no longer pure grace, that is, the *sola gratia* proclaimed by Paul and the Reformers, but becomes in some sense a human achievement, thus annulling grace. For grace cannot be a part as in a pact or in a contractual relation. That would be a compound of merit and reward, and not grace. Grace is sovereign, or it is not grace. We cannot earn it, we can only accept it as a gift; it is not compounded of human and divine activity, but it is the creative dynamic of the whole. We do not build the kingdom of God by our efforts and achievements individually or corporately, but the kingdom as the rule of God over our lives through the Holy Spirit in the church builds eternal life into the structure of our souls. The Holy Spirit, the Spirit of Jesus Christ, is the sole and true dynamic of all Christian activity in the life of the individual believer as well as in the work of the church.

Therefore, the true basis of spiritual unity lies in *holiness.* The more the church grows spiritually, grows in grace, into Christlikeness, the more her oneness will become apparent; her unity will shine through her diverse empirical forms. The more the church grows in the knowledge of our Lord Jesus Christ, that is, theologically, the deeper her creed goes, the clearer, the more earnest her confession — her espousal of the truth and righteousness of the gospel — becomes, the more her catholicity will manifest itself. The more our theology, our spiritual understanding, fathoms the depth of divine grace and the depth of human need, the more the universal outreach of the church of Christ, the world-encompassing mission of Christianity, will be realized.

If there were a dogma in the church which would spell death to a soul crying out of deepest anguish, then that dogma would have to give way to love; for the sake of saving one single soul, the church would have to relinquish her creed. But there is no such doctrine in the gospel: it has only words of eternal life, a message of salvation for all who believe. This does not mean that we subordinate truth to human need, but it does mean that truth provides the abundant life, that life in which all the needs of man are met. Grace and truth are *one* in Jesus Christ. They must remain one in the church if the church is to remain united. The grace of the gospel is rooted in truth; and the fundamental truth, the final law of the kingdom of God, is *mercy.*

Each Brings Its Best

. . . The outside unbelieving world will be skeptical of the possibility of thus bridging the historical abyss between two traditions apparently so divided on basic theory.

Some of our sister-communions, still bound by the weight of their own traditions of polity and vocabulary, may share that skepticism.

Ours will be, therefore, all the more, the wondrous opportunity to demonstrate in our time, and in this country for the first time, that this "impossible possible" can be done, and that, further, in church government as in life

Our little systems have their day,
They have their day and cease to be,
They are but broken lights of Thee,
And thou, O Lord, art more than they.

The real worth and validity of this union in the sight of God will eventually be measured by how profoundly and with what deepening devotion we set about getting God's work done in this world. If by the witness of our united churches the world's brokenhearted find hope and healing, the grieving have the comfort and consolations of grace made real, the aged discover that "at evening time it shall be light"; if young men and women are wisely guided in the choices they must make and strengthened when they have chosen "the hard right against the easy wrong"; if men and women in the midst of life's struggle are made "strong in the Lord and in the power of his might"; if the imperatives of God's justice and love are brought effectually to bear on the relationships of men in our workaday world and of nations wrestling with the promise and the peril of power — that is, not in devising new and grandiose schemes for making the world better, but in doing better the age-old ministries to which priest and prophet have always given themselves — then time and the event and the silent whispers of the Eternal God will confirm our present faith that the establishment of the United Church of Christ was doing his will.

Testifying to the Faith

3. Statement of Faith:
Commission Report

(1959, 1957)

Commission to Prepare a Statement of Faith, John C. Bennett

Article IV, F of the Basis of Union states, "If and when the Basis of Union is regularly adopted, the General Synod shall appoint a commission composed of an equal number of representatives of the two uniting communions to prepare a statement of faith based in principle upon Article II of this document (see vol. 7:1) which shall be submitted for approval to the General Synod, Conferences, Associations and Congregations. This statement shall be regarded as a testimony, and not as a test, of faith."

In June 1957 the UCC General Synod elected thirty persons (fifteen from each of the two uniting communions) to serve on the Commission to Prepare a Statement of Faith. Of the membership, five were women, and six were laity. Elmer J. F. Arndt (1908–69), a professor at Eden Theological Seminary, was elected chair, and Douglas Horton (1891–1968), former minister and secretary of the Congregational Christian Churches, was vice-chair.

The commission held three meetings (October 1957, May 1958, and January 1959). At the first meeting the members sought to deepen their understanding of the theological heritages of the Congregational Christian Churches and the Evangelical and Reformed Church. At the second meeting they reviewed a draft statement based upon individual

---

Sources: "Statement of Faith," *GS Minutes 1959,* 27–28. John C. Bennett, "Memorandum on the Statement on Faith of the United Church of Christ," to the Commission to Prepare a Statement of Faith, typescript, UCC Archives, box B-133.

statements that each of them had written (twenty-three statements were reviewed).

Discussion at the second meeting clarified the thinking of the commission, which decided that the final statement ought to be one that (1) could be used liturgically and (2) was written in contemporary language. At the end of the second meeting four members of the commission were asked to write new drafts based upon the discussion.

In January 1959 the four drafts were reviewed and the commission settled on one that it found to be "different from the traditional models." It was revised, endorsed by the commission, and submitted to the 1959 General Synod for adoption.

The final draft was written by Roger L. Shinn (b. 1917), an Evangelical and Reformed/UCC minister educated at Heidelberg College, Union Theological Seminary in New York and Columbia University. After serving in the military during World War II he was on the faculty at Vanderbilt University and then called to be professor of ethics at Union Theological Seminary in New York (1959–85). Shinn authored many books and essays on theology, education, and mission in the church. He was involved with the development of the innovative United Church of Christ curriculum, interpreting its importance in The Educational Mission of Our Church *(1962) (see vol. 7:47).*

Shinn wrote several books about the Statement of Faith and its theology. He points out that it does not avoid modern language. It uses simple subject-verb sentences, includes symbolic expressions, avoids Latinisms and Elizabethan forms in favor of common words found in contemporary speech and words that recall the thought and language of the Bible [Shinn, Confessing our Faith *(1990), 26–28].*

During this process, another commission member, John C. Bennett (1902–95), a Congregational Christian/UCC minister educated at Williams College and Mansfield College (Oxford, England), who taught at Pacific School of Religion (1938–43) and was professor, dean, and president of Union Theological Seminary in New York (1943–62), wrote a memorandum to the commission. Bennett was a keen observer of church and society and author of many books, such as Christian Ethics and Social Policy *(1950). His memorandum highlights the debate within the commission about the language that the new denomination ought to use to give testimony to its faith.*

United Church of Christ Statement of Faith

We believe in God, the Eternal spirit, Father of our Lord Jesus Christ and our Father, and to his deeds we testify:
He calls the worlds into being,
creates man in his own image
and sets before him the ways of life and death.
He seeks in holy love to save all people from aimlessness and sin.
He judges men and nations by his righteous will
declared through prophets and apostles.
In Jesus Christ, the man of Nazareth, our crucified and risen Lord,
he has come to us
and shared our common lot,
conquering sin and death,
and reconciling the world to himself.
He bestows upon us his Holy Spirit,
creating and renewing the Church of Jesus Christ,
binding in covenant faithful people of all ages, tongues, and races.
He calls us into his church
to accept the cost and joy of discipleship,
to be his servants in the service of men,
to proclaim the gospel to all the world and resist the powers of evil,
to share in Christ's baptism and eat at his table,
to join him in his passion and victory.
He promises to all who trust him
forgiveness of sins and fullness of grace,
courage in the struggle for justice and peace,
his presence in trial and rejoicing,
and eternal life in his kingdom which has no end.
Blessing and honor, glory and power be unto him. Amen.

Memorandum on the Statement of Faith of the United Church of Christ

Part One — Some General Observations

The statement should not be a theological essay that discusses the many-sided problems discussed in the first meeting of this Commission.

It should be kerygmatic rather than apologetic without using either word.

It should make use of historic language, partly because this language is the language of the Church and partly because the fact that it obviously calls for interpretation makes room for much theological freedom. Contemporary language is likely to be taken too literally or univocally. There is a kind of freedom under the ancient creeds which should not be lost.

We should on the one hand seek to express the faith of the Church rather than our own present opinions and on the other hand avoid insincerity and irrelevance by stressing those things which we hope to appropriate or hope to have our children appropriate.

Part Two — The Range of the Statement and Some Suggestions for Contents

(Note: I retain the words "We should affirm etc." in order to make clear that I am not attempting even to suggest final wording.)

We should identify the United Church in terms of assumptions about the Church as an essential element of Christian faith and doctrine. It is under the lordship of Christ and not under its own authority. It is part of Christ's universal Church. It emphasizes continuity in terms of community with the Church of the New Testament but leaves open many matters of structure and government to be determined by contemporary needs. It is under the guidance and judgment of the Word of God which comes to it through the Scriptures.

We should make clear in what sense the Scriptures are the medium of authority, affirming the centrality of the Word of God which they mediate and avoiding any absolutizing of the Bible as a book. We should recognize the necessity of subjecting the Bible to free scholarly criticism. We should also make clear that Christianity is not a system of ideas that can be detached from the events in which God has acted to reveal himself and to redeem humanity, supremely the life, death and resurrection of Jesus Christ.

We should declare our faith in God as Father, Son and Holy Spirit without identifying that faith with particular interpretations of the Trinity. We should emphasize belief in God as Creator and Lord, as Judge and Redeemer, as the one who emphasizes belief in God as Creator and Lord, as Judge and Redeemer, as the one who transcends the cosmic and historical process known to us and yet who demonstrates in Christ his loving identification with us in our weakness and sin.

We should emphasize both sides of the Christian understanding of man, his creation in God's image as the symbol of his dignity and the radical nature of his sin. His sin is universal and persistent and in disguised forms may appear on the highest levels of his life. We should distinguish our position from a sentimental optimism about man and from a hardened doctrine of total depravity. We should affirm the present consequences of redemption in human life and make room for the idea of "common grace" which redeems men apart from their conscious relation to Christ.

We should affirm faith in the divine forgiveness, in justification by grace through faith, and relate this to the possibilities of the renewal of the person without suggesting a *secure* type of santificationist doctrine. We should affirm the responsibility of the Christian and of the Church for the institution of society, for the costly effort to realize justice and freedom and peace in the life of nations without identifying any social structure with the Kingdom of God.

There should be a statement of the Christian hope that points toward the fulfillment of the person in spite of death and to the ultimate realization of the Kingdom of God.

4. Statement of Faith: *"Brief Introduction"*

(1959)

Elmer J. F. Arndt

Elmer J. F. Arndt (1908–69) was an Evangelical and Reformed/UCC minister educated at Tulane University, Eden Theological Seminary, Washington University, Union Theological Seminary in New York, and Yale University. Arndt taught at Eden Theological Seminary (1929–69). Arndt chaired the Evangelical and Reformed Council on Social Action and taught courses on social ethics. In the 1960s he chaired the UCC Theological Commission. Later in his life he was an observer at the Second Vatican Council and represented the UCC at the Consultation on Church Union (COCU).

As chair of the Commission to Prepare a Statement of Faith (1957–59), Arndt wrote a "Brief Introduction to the Statement of Faith" "to indicate some of the basic themes which underlie the Statement of Faith." He points out that the Statement uses seven sentences in the present tense to testify to the ongoing activity of God from creation to the promise of eternal life. Arndt's introduction is not an "official interpretation," but was offered as a guide for individual use.

Source: Elmer J. F. Arndt, "A Brief Introduction to the Statement of Faith," small pamphlet 1959, UCC Archives.

A Brief Introduction to the Statement of Faith

In form, the Statement of Faith is a recital of the mighty acts of God framed between the profession, "We believe in God," and the closing doxology. The seven sentences state God's creative and saving acts to which we testify. In each of the sentences, God is the subject followed by an active verb indicating what he has done, is doing, or will do "for us and our salvation."

Through the use of the present tense, the Statement suggests the ongoing activity of God, which links past and present together and continues into the future. God "*calls* the worlds into being, *creates* man in his own image, and *sets* before him the ways of life and death." In this way, the Statement indicates the divine creativity as continuing action, rather than as a happening in some distant past. God both "calls the worlds into being" and sustains in being what he has made. He both creates man and sets before him "the ways of life and death," so that he may exercise his freedom knowingly rather than in ignorance. Creation and providential order are intimately associated. Likewise God *"seeks"* (which is to say he has sought and continues to seek) "in holy love to save all people" and "he *judges*" (again, past and present) "men and nations by his righteous will."

But God "has come to us" in Jesus Christ and "shared our common lot." His coming to us in Jesus Christ is an historical event, the memory of which is cherished by the Church. That act has occurred; what, however, God did in Christ, namely, conquered sin and death and reconciled the world to himself, he continues to do. Therefore, the Statement uses *conquering* and *reconciling*. These examples indicate the significance of the verb forms throughout the Statement.

The seven sentences are cumulative in meaning. Each successive sentence carries forward, as well as adds to, the testimony of the preceding ones. Thus the recital, beginning with God's creative activity, continues through his seeking "to save all people" and judging "men and nations" to his coming to us in Jesus Christ, his gift of the Holy Spirit, his calling into the Church, and reaches its climax in his promise of "eternal life in his kingdom which has no end."

The Statement opens with the words, "We believe in God." Since this momentous declaration of belief, trust, and commitment is made by a fellowship, the use of "We" rather than "I" underscores its corporate character without making it any less personal.

We believe in "the everlasting God" (Isaiah 40:28), who is Spirit (John 4:24). He is "the Father of our Lord Jesus Christ and our Father." Thus the Statement identifies God in whom we believe. He is the One in whom

Jesus believed, to whom he was loyal, and in whom he hoped. God is he whom we also address as Father, confident of his fatherly relation to us. If we testify that God is our Father, we do not limit God's fatherhood to any group of men. God wills that men look to him as Father; but too often human beings are hostile to God in spite of his fatherly goodness to them. The statement of belief that God is "our Father" is an invitation to our fellowmen to join with us as we, following our Lord, say: "Our Father."

In the teaching of Jesus, the fatherhood of God involves the distinctively Christian ethic. The reason Jesus gave for his saying, "Love your enemies and pray for those who persecute you," is "that you may be sons of your Father who is in heaven; for he makes his sun rise on the evil and on the good, and sends rain on the just and on the unjust" (Matthew 5:44–45).

The Statement of Faith, in common with the classical Christian confessions, testifies to God's deeds. It is God-centered. We believe in the living God who acts, and our testimony concerns what he has done, is doing, and will do for men: God creates, seeks to save, judges, shared our life in Jesus Christ, bestows his active presence on us and within us, calls us to be his people, and promises renewal and favor now and the fulfillment of the new life he bestows. God's acts are the basis for describing him as the Creator, Savior, judge, and Sanctifier. The one God reveals himself to us as Father, Son, and Holy Spirit.

As the variation in the form of the fourth sentence suggests, God's coming to us in Jesus Christ is his decisive and central deed in relation to us men. The incarnation in Jesus, "the man of Nazareth" who is the Christ, "our crucified and risen Lord," is the heart of the Christian faith. The Statement declares that God has come to us in one who was genuinely human and who shared the conditions of our human existence, "one who in every respect has been tempted as we are" (Hebrews 4:15). Jesus Christ is "our crucified and risen Lord," the humiliated one who is "designated Son of God in power according to the Spirit of holiness by his resurrection from the dead" (Romans 1:4). We belong to him.

In Christ, God conquered and conquers sin and death, breaking their power over men. In him, God reconciled and reconciles the world to himself. "Therefore, if anyone is in Christ, he is a new creation; the old has passed away, behold, the new has come. All this is from God, who through Christ has reconciled us to himself and has given us the ministry of reconciliation; that is, God was in Christ reconciling the world to himself, not counting their trespasses against them, and entrusting to us the ministry of reconciliation" (2 Corinthians 5:17–19). This is the very essence of the good news, the gospel from the beginning of the Christian movement.

God continues his ministry of reconciliation begun in Christ by bestowing "upon us his Holy Spirit" who is God present among and within his people. The Holy Spirit creates and renews "the Church of Jesus Christ" in which "faithful people of all ages, tongues and races" are bound in covenant. Thus we testify to our conviction that the Church is a divine creation always dependent on the presence and activity of the Spirit of God. In its own understanding of itself, the Church is not primarily an association of people for the cultivation of religious and ethical interests. Rather it is a fellowship constituted and maintained by divine action. Therefore its first responsibility is to God. Its chief concern is to be faithful to its mission. It is the fellowship of people which is always being created and renewed by the Spirit, and consequently looks to the Spirit for direction and vitality. As the preceding sentence set before us the content of the festivals of Christmas, Good Friday and Easter, so this sentence reminds us of Pentecost.

God "calls us into his Church." This sixth sentence speaks of God's call to each of us. We testify in this sentence that our decision to join the company of Christian people is a response to God's call to us. God has called us — each one of us personally — to be "fellow citizens with the saints and members of the household of God" (Ephesians 2:19) and to his service in harmony with the mind of Christ.

The final sentence recites God's promises "to all who trust him." He promises to those who are cut off from fellowship by their guilt that great gift of love, namely, forgiveness. He promises the abundance of his divine favor, grace sufficient for all our needs. He promises courage in the struggle for justice and peace, for these goals are his will. He promises his own presence in times of trouble as well as in times of prosperity. He promises eternal life, which is not only indestructible but also a life of such quality that in it our essential nature is fulfilled. It is a life of uninterrupted communion with God and unbroken fellowship with his people. To us, God gives now the foretaste of eternal life and promises the completion of the new life.

The seventh sentence ends with the triumphant words: "his kingdom which has no end." In these words the Christian hope sounds its assured conviction. God's kingdom, which seems so remote, so easily defied with seeming impunity, so removed from the real world, is affirmed to be the enduring and indestructible reality. Here sound "the loud voices in heaven" saying, "The kingdom of the world has become the kingdom of our Lord and of his Christ, and he shall reign forever and ever" (Revelation 12:15).

Unlike the Apostles' and the Nicene Creeds, the Statement of Faith includes, in the context of God's deeds, a sketch of Christian living. As the recital of God's deeds states the acts of him in whom we believe, so the statement of our vocation suggests the Christian way of life. God calls us into his Church "to accept the cost and joy of discipleship"; to serve him "in the service of men" — which is the way of neighbor — love; "to proclaim the gospel," which is the mission of the Church; to be loyal to God's order in the midst of human disorder by resisting "the powers of evil"; to share in the redemptive suffering and humiliation as well as the joy and victory of our Lord by sharing "in Christ's baptism" and eating "at his table" and joining "him in his passion and victory."

The clause "to share in Christ's baptism" carries a number of associations. It suggests Jesus' dedication to the kingdom of God. It also suggests baptism "in the name of Jesus Christ for the forgiveness of your sins" (Acts 2:38). It points directly to Jesus' use of baptism to refer to his crucifixion, "I have a baptism to be baptized with; and how I am constrained until it is accomplished" (Luke 12:50); and his probing question to James and John, "Are you able to drink the cup that I drink, or to be baptized with the baptism with which I am baptized?" (Mark 10:38).

The Christian moral life is described in a way which keeps vividly before us the life of Jesus, "the pioneer and perfecter of our faith." Without any sentimentality, the basic nature of love of God and love of neighbor is suggested. The "joy of discipleship" is explicitly stated as is also its "cost." The Christian life is clearly understood in terms of social responsibility, active resistance to evil, and participation "in the struggle for justice and peace." The inseparably personal and social character of the Christian ethic, the inseparable responsibility to God and service to men, the inseparable mission "to proclaim the gospel to all the world" and to be the spokesman for God's order of righteousness are clearly indicated.

The insistent demands of the Christian way are joined with the recognition of the blessedness of the Christian life in the fellowship of the Church and in the service of the crucified and risen Christ in the world. God not only promises forgiveness but also his favor — "fullness of grace" — "courage in the struggle for justice and peace" — "his presence in trial and rejoicing," and "eternal life in his kingdom which has no end." The blessings he bestows are for the here and now as well as for the future, for the pilgrims on their way as well as at journey's end, which is the fulfilment and the consummation of the hope we cherish.

The Statement of Faith is a testimony to "the faith commonly held" in the United Church of Christ. It is not a "test"; indeed, it is not a body of theological definitions. Rather it declares in words of our own time basic Christian and biblical affirmations and convictions.

The Statement is not intended to be a revision of or a substitute for the ancient creeds and confessions and covenants of the Protestant Reformation.

It is commended to the church for use in congregational worship and for study. To the extent that it is used in the churches to testify to our common faith in congregational worship, the Statement will prove its value. Our prayer is that the Statement of Faith does provide a proof of words through which the people in the churches can testify with integrity to their faith before God and men and by which they will be more firmly established in the faith and united in one fellowship.

5. Statement of Faith:

Objections

(1959)

Harry W. Johnson

Harry W. Johnson (1890–1973) was a Congregational minister educated at Chicago Theological Seminary. He served pastorates in Congregational churches in Wisconsin, Wyoming, and Oregon (1915–30), and during the Depression he became a "pastor at large" for the Intermountain Conference of the Congregational Churches (1930–37), later serving as its superintendent (1937–55). In the mid-1950s he became the first executive secretary of the National Association of Congregational Christian Churches (NACCC), an association founded by Congregational Christians opposed to the union that gave birth to the United Church of Christ, with offices in Boise, Idaho. Upon his retirement, the NACCC offices moved from Boise, Idaho, to Wauwatosa (Milwaukee), Wisconsin.

Johnson's reaction to the United Church of Christ Statement of Faith reflects the views of many Congregationalists who resisted the formation of the United Church of Christ (see vol. 6:79–83). Writing in The Congregationalist, *the NACCC monthly journal, he asserts that the Statement of Faith "sounds the death-knell of everything Congregational."*

Source: Harry W. Johnson, "A Statement or a Denial?" from *The Congregationalist* (July 1959), 7.

A Statement or a Denial?

The statement of faith proposed for adoption by The United Church of Christ sounds the death-knell of everything Congregational.

Reciting together a selected list of the "deeds" of God is not a characteristic mode of expression of the Pilgrim spirit. It becomes even less so when those "deeds" of God which have been selected for recital are couched in the language of doctrinal authoritarianism.

The "gathered Church" is not there.

The covenant between believers, entered into freely to form the Church, is not there.

Indeed, the local Church, which in Congregationalism is THE CHURCH, has been completely submerged from view.

The manhood of The Master is not there. The teachings of Jesus are not there. Yet these teachings are the heart and core of the Christian message to the world. On the centrality of these teachings there has been general agreement among us as Congregationalists, whether we be "liberals" or "conservatives." The teachings of Jesus are so true, so relevant, so basic, and so eternal that the greatness of such a Teacher has filled our hearts with grateful loyalty, and our minds with wonder. Herein, and here alone, is the true foundation for Christian unity. Yet, from His day to ours, men have sought to explain His wonderful greatness by offering to us man-made doctrines as to who this Teacher was.

These man-made doctrines have, in this statement of faith, crowded out both the teachings and the Teacher.

Not the Congregational Way

Whatever else it is, this is a document that would dislodge the Jesus of history, and His teachings from their rightful place at the center of the Christian message.

It also brushes into the discard [pile] every distinctive emphasis which we, as Congregationalists, have been offering to Protestant thinking in the last four hundred years.

The adoption of such a statement would commit The United Church of Christ to a complete denial of the Congregational Way, — the way of "Ye Lord's free people" who have "joyned themselves by a covenant of the Lord, into a church-estate, in ye fellowship of ye gospell" ("Plimoth Plantation" — Bradford).

6. Statement of Faith:

Black Perspectives

(1984)

Lawrence Jones

Lawrence N. Jones (b. 1921) is an African American Congregational Christian/UCC minister educated at West Virginia State College, the University of Chicago, Oberlin School of Theology, and Yale University. He worked with the Student Christian Movement (1957–60) and was chaplain at Fisk University (1960–65). He was a professor at Union Theological Seminary in New York (1965–74), serving as dean (1971–74) and then moved to become dean of the School of Divinity of Howard University (1975–91). As the United Church of Christ marked the twenty-fifth anniversary of the adoption of the Statement of Faith, UCC leaders recognized that African Americans had had little influence upon the drafting of the original document. In order to understand how black UCC members felt about the statement, Jones was asked "to describe the consciousness and context" within which blacks hear and use the Statement of Faith. His presentation was part of the annual midwinter meeting of UCC executives in February 1984.

Source: Lawrence Jones, an excerpt from "A Statement to UCC Executives in Orlando, Florida," February 12, 1984, typescript, UCC Archives.

Reflections on the Statement of Faith

It is appropriate that we should be reflecting upon the Statement of Faith this quarter of a century after its formal adoption. A creed is by definition a brief and succinct statement of religious belief or confession of faith. Clearly, one of the purposes which called forth the 1959 Statement of Faith was to take account of changing theological understandings, as well as the contexts within the life of the church and the society out of which those understandings emerged and were understood. Much water has gone over the dam since the placid days of the Eisenhower presidency. This statement was issued just as the crisis in the cities intensified, followed by the civil rights revolution, the Vietnam War, the era of Kennedy, Nixon, and Ford and the presidency of Ronald Reagan. These twenty-five years have seen basic changes occurring in values thought to be inscribed upon the very fabric of the Universe and certainly upon the American character. A sexual revolution has taken place, marriage and the nuclear family became less and less an option for young men and women, radical changes began to affect the lives of individuals via changing industry, technology, nuclear weapons, ecological deterioration, a shrinking world community, wars and rumors of war, and insurgent clamorings and disruptions by the marginalized and poor of the world for recognition of their legitimate claims for a humane and just life. Challenges to education as an assured access to middle-class existence have been launched. Studies in the humanities and in the liberal arts have been declining. Moreover, in the specifically religious sector there has been a steady hemorrhage in the membership of some mainline denominations and a rising appeal of the electronic churches — if their revenues are any index. Beyond this, there has been after an initial surge of commitment to the claims of social justice, a steady erosion of enthusiasm for these concerns among American Protestants. If national trends are authentic landmarks, a majority of the American people are in support of efforts to assign responsibility for the presence of the poor and the marginalized to these victims themselves and to somehow stigmatize them as being immoral for being poor. These are some of the ethical, social, political, and economic contexts within which the statement of faith must be heard anew.

Now let me shift the terms of the discussion to the Black members of the United Church and seek to describe the consciousness and context within which they now hear this statement of faith. Some of the observations I will make will be specific to Blacks but a number of them will be generalizations which would obtain for others as well.

1. The predominance of male nouns and pronouns would certainly be challenged by females but I will leave that matter to others to address.

2. The phrase in the second affirmation "to save all people from aimlessness and sin" would be understood in radically different ways than in 1959. For many black people it is not sin as a category but specific manifestations of sin in systems and persons that need to be taken account of. Sin become incarnate in racist attitudes, structures of oppression, marginality, invisibility, powerlessness, and exclusion. That is what they would wish to be delivered from. The aimlessness and meaningless that the experiences engender are the inevitable progeny of such incarnate sin. Sin as understood conventionally refers to individual morality. Blacks have come more and more to appreciate the demonic as it is manifested in systems and structures, not excluding those in religious institutions.

3. Blacks assign a more activistic role to Jesus Christ than the Statement of Faith assumes. Blacks, who know no other helper, see in Jesus the incarnation of God himself and they believe that his basic identification is with the poor, the marginal, and the oppressed. They see him as the advocate, ally in confrontations with evil, source of guidance and illumination, companion in suffering, strength of individual life, a true liberator whose death was not only a triumph over evil but over specific manifestations of evil. They would see Jesus as a source of hope and as the ultimate guarantor that the justice of God will prevail and that those who love and serve him will not finally be left to the machinations of evil persons and systems. Christ is also a source and incarnation of power, a counterpoise of human pretensions to ultimate sovereignty in creation. This Jesus is not only concerned for the individual but for the community and he wills not only individual salvation but as stated in his first sermon he is concerned for the "least of these," equally with all more privileged others. It is Jesus who finally is advocate and contenter [*sic*] for justice and peace in the world.

4. In a similar way, the Holy Spirit is perceived as being engaged as the presence of God in the affairs of individuals and communities. The Holy Spirit is the one who empowers the good; who enables faithful witness; who communicates the intention of God and provides guidance in life's dark places and crossroads decisions. The Holy Spirit is the source of courage in the presence of danger; the final guarantor of the presence of God. In some mysterious way he is the pro-active expression for the presence of Jesus Christ and God.

5. With respect to the church Black Christians would see it not only as the arena of God to accomplish all things enumerated but something more. They would want seriously to see the church, not only as a manifestation of the people of God but as an earthen vessel which is at once both a source of promise and yet stands under judgment of God. They would see the church as the place where racism frequently and persistently raises its head and in which structures become the servant of racist attitudes. It would see the church, too, frequently accompanying the powers in the larger societies which make for suffering, injustice, and war. They would want in a creed some word concerning the judgment of God upon the church and upon its apostasy. They would want the church to be perceived as living out its life within the world which closes in on every side — a world in which unemployment, poor housing, drugs, alcohol, poverty, and hopelessness are constant companions of vast numbers of marginalized persons. They would want something to be said in creed about the world as the creation of God which has been deformed by men but which he loves nonetheless.
6. The paragraph which delineates the promises of God has some different meanings for Blacks and particularly for the young. Here again, God is viewed as being an initiator as well as a responder to the initiatives of men and women. Many young people are experiencing conversion these days; to them it is God who did it and they do not view their salvation as the result of their action only. They know what it is to be delivered from sin, sexual promiscuousness, drugs, and other manifestations of the hedonistic life. They see God, not only as forgiving, but as delivering, and empowering, and companioning, and as praiseworthy. They see victory manifested in this life and affirmed through personal and communal encounters with God. They would take hold of the two aspects of faith: *fiducia* as faith in a God who has shown himself to be trustworthy, and faith as a series of propositions about him. The propositions are in large measure framed, as they always have been for blacks, out of their experience with and of him. The propositions of faith are confessions of relationships. . . .

7. Statement of Faith:

Versions and Translations

(1976, 1982, 1973, 1969, 2000)

Robert V. Moss, Office for Church Life and Leadership,
Mary Louise VanDyke, Hanns Peter Keiling, Dámaris Vélez

The United Church of Christ Statement of Faith was criticized by continuing Congregational Christians (see vol. 7:5) and heard differently in the African American community (see vol. 7:6). As awareness of inclusive language increased in church and society during the early 1970s the masculine language of the statement also became more and more problematic (see vol. 7:31). In 1975 the Office for Church Life and Leadership (OCLL) began a study to decide whether a new Statement of Faith ought to be drafted.

Robert V. Moss (1922–76), an Evangelical and Reformed/UCC minister who was professor and president of Lancaster Theological Seminary (1957–69), became the second president of the United Church of Christ in 1969. Moss served on the original Commission to Prepare a Statement of Faith (1957–59). In 1976, as OCLL was asking local churches to consider the question of a new statement, Moss was hospitalized with a terminal illness. During the last few weeks of his life he wrote a revision of the Statement of Faith. The "Moss Version" was circulated widely, and in 1977 the General Synod commended it to the church for further study.

Sources: Robert V. Moss, "United Church of Christ Statement of Faith," 1976. *Book of Worship: United Church of Christ* (New York: United Church of Christ, Office for Church Life and Leadership, 1986), 513. "The Executive Council approves for distribution for use in the United Church of Christ in connection with the Twenty-fifth Anniversary the following version of the Statement of Faith," *Executive Council Minutes,* 1981. Mary Louise VanDyke, "On God the Spirit We Rely," *The Hymnal of the United Church of Christ* (Philadelphia: United Church Press, 1974), hymn no. 149. Hanns Peter Keiling, "The Statement of Faith in German," from *Die Entstehung der "United Church of Christ" (USA) Fallstudie einer Kirchenunion unter Berücksichtigung des Problems der Ortsgemeinde* (Berlin: Lettner-Verlag, 1969), 175–76. "Declaración de Fe de la Iglesia Unida de Cristo," translated by Dámaris Vélez, 2000.

The Office for Church Life and Leadership (OCLL) continued its work on the Statement of Faith, and in 1981 the General Synod asked that an "interim version" of the statement be prepared for the twenty-fifth anniversary of the United Church of Christ the following year. At the same time the General Synod endorsed UCC participation in an ecumenical effort to produce a collaborative Statement of Faith with other interested denominations. The collaborative effort never materialized, but soon thereafter a "Doxological version" of the Statement of Faith was made available to the church.

Since 1981, therefore, three versions of the UCC Statement of Faith are commonly found in the United Church of Christ. All three appear in the UCC Book of Worship *(1986).*

The UCC Statement of Faith has also taken other forms. In 1973 Mary Louise VanDyke wrote a new hymn for the United Church of Christ Hymnal *(1976). "On God the Spirit We Rely" celebrates the importance of testifying to God's deeds and sets to music some key phrases of the UCC Statement of Faith. It is also significant to note that the entire organizational arrangement of hymns in the* United Church of Christ Hymnal *(1976) follows the structure of the UCC Statement of Faith.*

The United Church of Christ Statement of Faith was respectfully studied and used by the Evangelical Church of the Union (EKU) in East and West Germany, especially after the EKU-UCC "full communion" votes of 1980 and 1981 (see vol. 7:69) The EKU looked to modern statements of faith such as the Barmen Declaration of the German Confessing Church (1934) to give guidance and to inspire courage in the church. It found the UCC Statement of Faith particularly intriguing. Hanns Peter Keiling (b. 1939), educated at the Kirchliche Hochschule in Wuppertal, Heidelberg University, Eden Theological Seminary, and the University of Göttingen, wrote a history of the United Church of Christ, Die Entstehung der "United Church of Christ" (USA) *(1969). In this book, which introduced many Germans to the UCC, he included a translation of the 1959 Statement of Faith. Keiling's German translation was acclaimed and used widely in EKU congregations in both East and West Germany.*

By the year 2000, the United Church of Christ and the population of the United States had grown to incorporate many Spanish-speaking people. Dámáris Vélez, a native of Cayey, Puerto Rico, served as secretary at Euclid Avenue Congregational UCC, Cleveland, Ohio (1993–98) and joined the administrative staff of the national UCC offices in 1998. In 2000 Vélez translated the UCC Statement of Faith into Spanish.

United Church of Christ Statement of Faith
Adapted by Robert V. Moss

We believe in God, the Eternal Spirit, who is made known to us
in Jesus our brother, and to whose deeds we testify:
God calls the worlds into being,
creates humankind in the divine image,
and sets before us the ways of life and death.
God seeks in holy love to save all people from aimlessness and sin.
God judges all humanity and all nations by that will of righteousness
declared through prophets and apostles.
In Jesus Christ, the man of Nazareth, our crucified and risen Lord,
God has come to us
and shared our common lot,
conquering sin and death
and reconciling the whole creation to its Creator.
God bestows upon us the Holy Spirit,
creating and renewing the church of Jesus Christ,
binding in covenant faithful people of all ages,
tongues, and races.
God calls us into the church
to accept the cost and joy of discipleship,
to be servants in the service of the whole human family,
to proclaim the gospel to all the world and resist the powers of
evil,
to share in Christ's baptism and eat at his table,
to join him in his passion and victory.
God promises to all who trust in the gospel
forgiveness of sins and fullness of grace,
courage in the struggle for justice and peace,
the presence of the Holy Spirit in trial and rejoicing,
and eternal life in that kingdom which has no end.
Blessing and honor, glory and power be unto God.
Amen.

United Church of Christ Statement of Faith in the Form of a Doxology

We believe in you, O God, Eternal Spirit,
God of our Savior Jesus Christ and our God,
and to your deeds we testify:

You call the worlds into being,
   create persons in your own image,
   and set before each one the ways of life and death.

You seek in holy love to save all people from aimlessness and sin.

You judge people and nations by your righteous will declared through prophets and apostles.
In Jesus Christ, the man of Nazareth, our crucified and risen Savior,
   you have come to us
   and shared our common lot,
   conquering sin and death
   and reconciling the world to yourself.

You bestow upon us your Holy Spirit,
   creating and renewing the church of Jesus Christ,
   binding in covenant faithful people of all ages,
   tongues and races.

You call us into your church
   to accept the cost and joy of discipleship,
   to be your servants in the service of others,
   to proclaim the gospel to all the world
   and resist the powers of evil,
   to share in Christ's baptism and eat at his table,
   to join him in his passion and victory.

You promise to all who trust you
   forgiveness of sins and fullness of grace,
   courage in the struggle for justice and peace,
   your presence in trial and rejoicing,
   and eternal life in your realm which has no end.

Blessing and honor, glory and power be unto you.
Amen.

On God the Spirit We Rely

On God the Spirit we rely;
To his great deeds we testify;
All worlds are his, all mankind shares
Creation's pow'r and the choice it bears.

His love shall guide, his judgments stay,
His righteous will direct our way.
He shares our humble, human frame;
His resurrection we proclaim.

Thus bound in covenant, we search
For ways to serve him through his church;
By serving man where'er is need,
Our lives from self and death are freed.

His help we seek to face our time;
Through trial we trust his grace divine;
Man's justice, peace, O Church defend;
Help shape God's kingdom without end.

Erklärung des Glaubens

Wir glauben an Gott, den ewigen Geist, den Vater unseres Herrn Jesus Christus and unseren Vater, und wir bezeugen seine Taten:

Er ruft die Welten ins Dasein,
schafft den Menschen nach seinem eigenen Bild
un zeigt ihm den Weg des Lebens und den Weg des Todes.
Er sucht in heiliger Liebe alle Menschen zu retten
von Ziellosigkeit und Sünde.
Er richtet Menschen und Völker nach seinem gerechten Willen,
verkündet durch Propheten und Apostel.
In Jesus Christus, dem Mann von Nazareth, unserem gekreuzigten und auferstandenen Herrn,
kam er zu uns
und nahm teil an unserem Los,
überwindet Sünde und Tod
und versöhnt die Welt mit sich selbst.
Er verleiht uns seinen Heiligen Geist,
schafft und erneuert die Kirche Jesu Christi,
vereint in seinem Bund glaubende Menschen aller Zeiten, Sprachen und Rassen.
Er ruft uns in seine Kirche,
damit wir Opfer und Freude der Nachfolge bejahen,
damit wir seine Diener sind im Dienst an Menschen,
damit wir das Evangelium aller Welt verkünden und den Mächten des Bösen widerstehen,
damit wir teilhaben an Christi Taufe und an seinem Tische essen,
damit wir mit ihm verbunden sind in seinem Leiden und in seinem Sieg.
Er verspricht allen, die ihm vertrauen,
Vergebung der Sünden und Gnade die Fülle,
Mut im Kampf für Gerechtigkeit und Frieden,
seine Gegenwart in Anfechtung und Freude
und eweges Leben in seinem Reich, das kein Ende hat.
Ihm sei Lob und Ehre, Ruhm und Macht. Amen.

Declaración de Fe de la Iglesia Unida de Cristo

Creemos en Dios, el Espíritu Eterno, Padre de nuestro Señor Jesucristo y nuestro Padre, de sus obras testificamos:

Dios llama los mundos para que existan, creo al ser humano a su imagen y semejanza, y puso ante el y ella los caminos de la vida y la muerte.

Dios en su santo amor busca salvar a toda persona de la perdición y el pecado.

Dios juzga al ser humano y a las naciones por medio de su justa voluntad declarada a través de los profetas y los apóstoles.

En Jesucristo, el hombre de Nazaret, nuestro Señor crucificado y resucitado, Dios ha venido a nosotros y nosotras y ha compartido nuestra suerte, venció el pecado y la muerte y reconcilió al mundo para si mismo.

Dios nos concedió el Espíritu Santo, que crea y renueva la iglesia de Jesucristo, y une en un pacto de fidelidad a personas de todas las edades, idiomas y razas.

Dios nos llama como iglesia para que aceptemos el precio y la alegría del discipulado, para que seamos sus servidores al servicio del ser humano, para proclamar el evangelio a todo el mundo y resistir los poderes del maligno, para compartir el bautismo de Cristo, comer en su mesa, y unirnos a Jesús en su pasión y victoria.

Dios promete a toda persona que confia en Jesús el perdón de los pecados y la plenitud de su gracia, valor en la lucha por la justicia y la paz, su presencia en las tristezas y en las alegrías, y vida eterna en su reino que no tiene fin.

Bendición y honor, gloria y poder sean dados a Dios.

Amén.

Forming Faithful Structures

8. The Constitution:

"Preamble"

(1960)

The Basis of Union stipulated a process by which the United Church of Christ would prepare both a Statement of Faith and a Constitution. During the pre-union period a Joint Committee to Study Basic Doctrine suggested a paragraph related to doctrine to inform the preparation of both documents. The paragraph was basically a revision of the Basis of Union, Article II "Faith" (see vol. 7:1):

> *The faith we confess is that faith in God which the Scriptures of the Old and New Testaments set forth, which our spiritual fathers expressed in the ancient creeds (such as the Apostles', Nicene, and Chalcedonian creeds), to which they gave utterance in the confessions and covenants of the Reformation and later times (such as Luther's Small Catechism, the Augsburg Confession, the Heidelberg Catechism, the Westminster Confession, the Covenants, and Statements of Faith). In the freedom inherent in the Gospel, we acknowledge our dependence upon the Holy Scriptures, our kinship with those in the history of the Church who have given various accounts of the nature of the faith, and our continual obligation to give fresh and valid expression to the faith which informs us.*

This paragraph was seriously considered by the Commission to Prepare a Statement of Faith, but it decided that its work was not to refine a statement of doctrine. Its minutes noted that the mode and expression of the Statement of Faith it planned to present to the General Synod was

---

Source: "Preamble to the Constitution of the United Church of Christ," *GS Minutes 1960,* Appendix 31.

to "point to God's work," and not to "define against heresy." The UCC Statement of Faith was an "act of union."

For this reason the Commission to Prepare a Statement of Faith recommended the above "revision of the 'Faith Article' from the Basis of Union" to the Commission on the Constitution. The Constitutional Commission reviewed the revision carefully. When it completed its work, the "Preamble to the Constitution" that it presented to the General Synod in 1959, and which was formally adopted at the special "adjourned session" of the second General Synod in 1960, built upon the "faith article." The Preamble to the Constitution offers a way of anchoring and interpreting the set of beliefs that is stated narratively in the UCC Statement of Faith.

Constitution of the United Church of Christ

Preamble

1. The United Church of Christ, formed June 25, 1957, by the union of the Evangelical and Reformed Church and The General Council of the Congregational Christian Churches of the United States in order to express more fully the oneness in Christ of the churches composing it, to make more effective their common witness in Him, and to serve His kingdom in the world, hereby adopts this Constitution.

2. The United Church of Christ acknowledges as its sole Head, Jesus Christ, the Son of God and the Saviour of men. It acknowledges as brethren in Christ all who share in this confession. It looks to the Word of God in the Scriptures, and to the presence and power of the Holy Spirit, to prosper its creative and redemptive work in the world. It claims as its own the faith of the historic Church expressed in the ancient creeds and reclaimed in the basic insights of the Protestant Reformers. It affirms the responsibility of the Church in each generation to make this faith its own in reality of worship, in honesty of thought and expression, and in purity of heart before God. In accordance with the teaching of our Lord and the practice prevailing among evangelical Christians, it recognizes two sacraments: Baptism and the Lord's Supper or Holy Communion.

3. The provisions herein define and regulate the General Synod and those instrumentalities of the United Church of Christ which are recognized, established by or responsible to the General Synod, and describe the free and voluntary relationships which the local churches, Associations, Conferences and ministers sustain with the General Synod and with each other. The pattern of relationships and procedures so described is recommended to local churches, Associations, Conferences and ministers, to enable them more effectively to accomplish their tasks and the work of the United Church of Christ.

9. Theology:

"The Head of the Church" and "The Bible and the Holy Spirit"

(1962)

Douglas Horton

Douglas Horton (1891–1968) was a Congregational Christian/UCC minister educated at Princeton University, in Europe at Edinburgh, Oxford, and Tübingen universities, and at Hartford Theological Seminary. After serving in parish ministry in Connecticut, Massachusetts, and Illinois (1915–38), he became minister and secretary of the General Council of the Congregational Christian Churches (1938–55). Horton was professor and dean at Harvard Divinity School (1955–59) and a Protestant observer at the Roman Catholic Second Vatican Council (1962–65). After the United Church of Christ Constitution was voted at the 1960 UCC General Synod Horton wrote a book entitled The United Church of Christ *(1962), carefully interpreting each paragraph of the constitution. The preamble begins: "The United Church of Christ acknowledges as its sole Head, Jesus Christ, the Son of God and the Saviour of Men . . . looks to the Word of God in the Scriptures, and to the presence and power of the Holy Spirit. . . . " Horton believes that the centrality of Jesus Christ, scripture, and the Holy Spirit are the "fundamental characteristics of the United Church."*

Source: Douglas Horton, "The Head of the Church" and "The Bible and the Holy Spirit" in *The United Church of Christ: Its Origins, Organization and Role in the World Today* (New York: T. Nelson, 1962), 44–50.

The Head of the Church

> The United Church of Christ acknowledges as its sole Head, Jesus Christ, the Son of God and the Saviour of men.

So begins the second paragraph of the Preamble to the Constitution, and so the United Church is marked not only as Christian but as Christian in the mainstream of the church's tradition.

When Jesus Christ is called the sole Head of the Church, Christianity's extraordinary paradox is touched upon, because Jesus Christ is the very man who lived in Palestine almost twenty centuries ago, a Jew, a carpenter, a preacher of the love of God who for his preaching died an agonizing death on a Roman cross and is yet alive today in a mystical but real way, speaking no words, making no appearances, invading the physical world not at all, and yet exerting an enormous influence on those who are sensitive to his presence. This is a strange belief because it is at once historical and not historical; it binds two worlds together. It has had more to do with giving Western man such decency as he has achieved than any other single force. When this Jesus Christ is called the Son of God, the intimation is that God through him has entered into human life; and when he is called the Saviour of men, it is indicated that through this contact men have come to realize that the Creator of the universe has sufficient concern for them to keep them in his care forever.

The Constitution now proceeds:

> The United Church of Christ . . . acknowledges as brethren in Christ all who share in this confession.

This was not always so. When our fathers of the Reformation read of "Antichrist" in the Epistles of John, the word reminded them not of Satan or any other members of the spirit world — though these were regarded as being the close collaborators of Mr. Against-Christ (as the Greek title might be translated into American) — the only figure that rose in their mind was that of the Roman pope. When they read in their Bibles that Jesus had said, "Many shall come in my name, saying, 'I am Christ'; and shall deceive many," they thought they knew the chief contemporary representative of the group our Lord had in mind and could have given any man his address in the Italian capital. And now the United Church of Christ calls the Pope its brother — along with all others who believe that God was in Christ reconciling the world to himself.

This is an illustration of the fact that it is dangerous to belong to a living church. The danger lies in the possibility of growth. When one puts himself into the hands of a creative God, one cannot be certain how one will come out. One's philosophy may be changed, one's attitude toward life, one's ethics.

That which imparts growth to the church, the matrix of its life, is the Christ of whom we have spoken. Slowly but inevitably as the centuries progress he converts every secondary thing within the church into conformity with his own gracious intent. All the forms of thought, of worship, and of structure that are found within the church are subject to his perfecting influence. He and his people, united in love, alone constitute the real being of the church (its *esse,* as the theologians are likely to say), and no *forms* of belief and action, though they may belong to its well-being (its *bene esse*), do. Christ in the midst of his people is the same yesterday, today, and forever; all shapes of response to his presence are subject to change as his loving will becomes more perfectly understood.

This is the occasion for the difference between the attitude of the United Church of Christ today and that of its Protestant forebears to the Roman Church. Granted that there are profound divergences between the ways of the Roman Church and those of the United Church, granted that no method of reconciling those ways has as yet been conceived or is at the moment conceivable — nonetheless, because Roman Catholics, too, lift up Christ as the sole head of the church, the United Church of Christ approaches them not as old enemies but as brethren with whom Christ can make all things new.

And so the United Church of Christ looks toward the Eastern Orthodox Church and to all other churches which profess and call themselves Christian.

The Bible and the Holy Spirit

The Constitution says:

> The United Church of Christ . . . looks to the Word of God in the Scriptures, and to the presence and power of the Holy Spirit, to prosper its creative and redemptive work in the world.

This is a carefully written sentence which repays a careful reading; it relates the Bible and the Holy Spirit to each other and speaks of them as together a force in the world.

When we speak of the Word of God in the Scriptures we mean God's utterance, his expression of his will. The very word, *word,* stands, after all, for something marvelous. Here I am, setting down various words for the pages of a book and there you are, good reader, separated from me perhaps by continents and by numbers of months or years which I cannot guess — and yet, thanks to the words, we are able to share the same ideas and know part of each other's minds. When words are used by a genius in language their power seems almost magical. To read, for instance, the simple words of Homer describing Hector's leave-taking of his wife and infant before he goes out to the conflict finally fatal to him is to relive the poet's pathetic admiration for his hero after three thousand years; it is, after all, something, to be compelled to brush away a tear by the writing of a man who lived before the dawn of recorded history. This is the *mana* of the word; it reaches from mind to mind and, when it comes from a master, reaches deeply. But the Word of God in the Scriptures is something that comes from before history itself, recorded or unrecorded; it is spoken in historical settings but tells of God's will, which is from everlasting to everlasting.

The Word of God in the Scriptures, however, is more than an ordinary word: it is God's expression of his will. By his word he created the world:

> By the Word of Jehovah were the heavens created,
> And by the breath of his mouth all their host.

By his word, God sustains the whole world and in the long last assures the consummation of his purposes:

> So shall my Word be which goeth forth from my mouth; it shall not
> return unto me void,
> For it shall have done that which I desired,
> And shall have accomplished that for which I sent it.

This Word of God can be understood by some men and from them others can learn its meaning. It came to the prophets as something to be announced. Jeremiah found that even when he fought against speaking it, there was that within him which, like a creative thought in a thinker's mind, demanded utterance.

> The Word of the Lord has become for me
> a reproach and derision all day long.
> If I say, "I will not mention him,
> or speak any more in his name,"
> There is in my heart as it were a burning fire
> shut up in my bones,
> And I am weary with holding it in,
> and I cannot.

This is the Old Testament idea of the Word; it was God's expression of himself in the world, in the underlying forces of the world, and in the mind of man. The New Testament brought the meaning of the Word to its fullness:

> The Word became flesh and dwelt among us, full of grace and truth.

In Jesus Christ, the Word was a person; this was God's supreme expression of himself. When the Constitution speaks of God's Word in the Scriptures as the force behind the church's creative and redemptive work in the world, it points to all those ways in history, epitomized in the Scriptures, in which God has made his character known. In those ways he has spoken (used the vehicle of the Word) to the United Church of Christ, and it is as a direct response to his Word that this church exists and goes about its work. It is as much his creation, as fully a carrier of his purpose, as were the heavens and the earth in the beginning; it is the extension of his Word in Christ—and it is good to belong to a church when it is such.

The Constitution refers to God's Word as being spoken in the Scriptures; it does not equate the Scriptures with the Word of God, as if everything in them were his own truth. The United Church of Christ does not regard the writers of the Bible as having been protected supernaturally from reporting events erroneously or setting forth inadequate and untrue philosophies. It is said in the Book of Joshua (10:12–14), for instance, that:

> Joshua . . . said in the sight of Israel, "Sun, stand thou still . . . " and the sun stood still . . . and did not hasten to go down for about a whole day. There has been no day like it before or since.

This is plainly folklore, most interesting to any hearer, but imaginative beyond the limits which a modern historian would impose upon himself.

> Happy he who taketh and dasheth thy little ones against a rock!

This line from an imprecatory Psalm (137:9) hardly identifies its author as one who knows the loving Will of God. One cannot say that it and other biblical passages like it set forth the Word of God. And yet the Bible as a whole has been a mine in which diamond after diamond of insight into God's ways has been discovered.

The United Church of Christ through its scholars approaches the Bible as any literary critic approaches any book. Every line is investigated until everything about it that can be known is known. The historians are called in, and the experts in language, the students of the sacred books of other religions (so that comparison may be made), and the archaeologists, who can support or question or supplement the writers of the Bible from their delvings into the sands that cover the remains of ancient biblical civilizations. And, after all is said and done, after the Bible has been laid on the laboratory table and all the instruments of modern scientific investigation have been employed to get at the truths it contains, it still speaks to us the Word of God; the man Christ Jesus, quivering on the cross outside the walls of Jerusalem and telling by his very agony what God is willing to endure if only his people will accept his love and live by it, is, if anything, more clearly limned today than ever. In the pages of the Bible, better understood now than in the past, though not magically, God speaks to the United Church of Christ and to us all.

Linked in the Constitution to the mention of the Word of God in the Scriptures is the reference to "the presence and power of the Holy Spirit." This is as it ought to be, for no person would know he was hearing the Word of God unless God himself marked the word for him. A contemporary playwright speaks of "the glow of the soul" which occurs when one encounters any event which he feels to have been caused by the direct hand of God. That glow may be said to be itself the result of God's touch. The religious thinkers of yesterday who wrote in Latin called this the *testimonium Sancti Spiritus internum* or the inner witness of the Holy Spirit, for "Holy Spirit" is the name we give to God when he comes to us in this way. God speaking with one voice at these two points — through the historical record of the Scriptures and in the mind of the reader by his Holy Spirit — causes the moment of illumination in the life of any man or any church. It is to the Scriptures and to the Holy Spirit that the United Church of Christ looks, and asks others to look, as it goes about its creative and redemptive work in Christ.

10. Voting:

To Join or Not to Join

(1960)

Fred Hoskins, Neil H. Swanson Jr.

The campaign to get local Congregational Christian churches to vote on the UCC Constitution and become members of the United Church of Christ went on for several years. Fred Hoskins (1906–66) was a Congregational Christian/UCC minister educated at Yale Divinity School. After serving in pastorates in Connecticut, Iowa, and Illinois (1928–56), he became minister and general secretary of the General Council of Congregational Christian Churches (1956–61) and one of the co-presidents of the UCC (1957–61). Later he was on the faculty at Chicago Theological Seminary (1961–64) and served as a pastor in New Jersey (1964–66). Hoskins played a key role in reassuring laity and clergy that they had nothing to fear from the UCC.

Neil H. Swanson Jr., executive secretary of the National Association of Congregational Christian Churches (an association formed by congregations voting not to become part of the UCC) wrote an "Open Letter to all Congregational Ministers . . . " (1960). His letter asks clergy if they want to preserve "Congregational Principles." He admits that some people might not think this is important. However, if they do think that it is important they need to ask three questions: "1. What kind of Christian unity do you want?" "2. Does the proposed Constitution preserve Congregational principles?" and "3. What kind of Church do you want?" Swanson's questions reflect the concerns that informed the thinking and voting in many Congregational Christian congregations in the early 1960s.

Sources: Fred Hoskins, part of a letter inviting churches to join the United Church of Christ. *United Church Herald,* July 14, 1960, reprint, no page. Neil H. Swanson Jr., "What Kind of Christian Unity Do You Want?" an excerpt from "An Open Letter to All Congregational Ministers" (offprint rubber stamp dated June 15, 1960).

Why Join the United Church of Christ?

. . . Again, you have asked me to state briefly why any of us should want to be party to the United Church of Christ. All I can do is submit a part of my own testimony.

1. I want to be a part of the United Church of Christ because my religious life is being enriched by acquaintance, partnership, study and prayer with the Evangelical and Reformed Church brethren. It is occurring in much the same way that my life has been enriched in marriage to a wonderful woman. Renewal and horizon-capture are common experiences throughout the uniting communions.

2. I want to be a part of the United Church of Christ because it is providing my local church better church school materials than Congregational Christian churches (and the Evangelical and Reformed Church, I dare say) by themselves ever had or could have. There are parallel advantages in the fields of evangelism, social action, church extension, higher education, health and welfare, overseas missions, human emergency services and a church magazine, to cite a few examples.

3. I want to be a part of the United Church of Christ because it is an adventure in doing something positive to show that Christ's church is one. Talk about "Oneness of Spirit" is easy and cheap. But it doesn't mean a thing until the oneness is demonstrated in the church that people can see.

4. I want to be a part of the United Church of Christ because I believe that it can be more effectively relevant to the times, the problems and the duties imposed upon us by Christ than can be either the Evangelical and Reformed Church or the Congregational Christian churches separately and independently.

5. I want to be a part of the United Church of Christ because I believe God's hand is helping shape it to serve his gracious ministry of love. I am certain that at many points and times we who are working in the United Church are misunderstanding and frustrating his will and may God forgive us, but that his hand is in it I am absolutely confident.

What Kind of Christian Unity Do You Want?

The first point to be made in regard to this question is that there are many types of Christian unity. I happen to be a strong believer in Christian unity, but I do not believe in the type of unity represented by the "United Church of Christ." It is an oversimplification to identify only two types of Christian unity, but for our present purposes this may suffice. On the one hand there is the concept that Christian unity can best be expressed by organic structural unification of churches into one united church. On the other hand there is the concept that Christian unity can best be expressed by fellowship between and among free churches. I believe in fellowship, and I am opposed to organic unity.

I do not think there is much question that the "United Church of Christ" moves in the direction of organic unity. One of the major motivations for its development is the hope that it will constitute a major step in the direction of a united church. Therefore, those who believe in organic unity will be likely to support the "United Church of Christ." But those who believe in the Congregational principle of freedom with fellowship will be likely to oppose this new denomination.

Incidentally, I believe that those who use the phrase "that they may all be one" to imply that Jesus supported the idea of organic unity are distorting its meaning. When these words of Jesus are read in their full context, they obviously refer to the spiritual relationship of a person with God. The words which immediately follow the phrase are sufficient to make this clear: "that they may all be one; even as Thou, Father, art in me, and I in Thee."

From the very outset of my acquaintance with the "Basis of Union," my major reason for opposition to the "United Church of Christ" has been my opposition to organic unity. I believe that this union does constitute a major step toward the organic unity of all Christians. Since I do not believe in this goal, I cannot take a step in this direction.

11. The Future of the Church:

"Statement of Purpose and Mission"

(1967)

By the mid-1960s the constitution had been in effect for four or five years. During that time new national UCC instrumentalities were created by merging mission boards and other church agencies from the uniting denominations into "united boards." These new bodies were "recognized" by the United Church of Christ as agencies for the work of the church. In addition a number of new national UCC instrumentalities were "established" to carry out other ministries in the name of the United Church of Christ. Regional synods and state conferences merged, and many local congregations became more comfortable with their "UCC identity."

At the same time, the weaknesses and limitations of some of the new UCC structures also became evident. Vested interests and unanticipated events continued to sharpen UCC polity. The UCC struggled with the incertainties of its internal life while at the same time the violent events of the 1960s were shaking the foundations of the society into which it was being called.

In 1965 the General Synod appointed a nineteen-member Committee on Structure to consider what structural changes should be made to strengthen the life of the church. The committee did its work carefully and also drew up a "Statement of Purpose and Mission of the United Church of Christ" to guide its work. The 1967 final revision of the statement appears in the report of the Committee on Structure to General Synod.

Source: "Statement of Purpose and Mission of the United Church of Christ, Final Revision — January 20, 1967," from the Report of the Committee on Structure, *GS Minutes 1967,* 175–76.

Statement of Purpose and Mission

This Statement was prepared for the use and guidance of the Committee on Structure. It does not purport to express the views of the United Church of Christ or any part thereof other than the Committee on Structure.

The United Church of Christ was formed, according to the preamble to its Constitution, "in order to express more fully the oneness in Christ of the churches composing it, to make more effective their common witness in Him, and to serve His kingdom in the world." Although that is true, it is so inclusive that it fails to suggest the shape and style of the church to which it refers. As the Committee on Structure pursues its assignment to study services and interrelationships in the United Church in order to make its structure more effective, we must be clear about its character and its mission. It is a church of pioneering spirit which seeks to serve God in terms which are relevant to the changing times. Form and structure are essential, but from time to time they will change and may even die. They must always be subservient to mission.

United by our allegiance to Jesus Christ, we take for ourselves the purpose to be his witnesses, to proclaim the gospel, to make disciples of all nations, and to work for peace in the world, for justice among men, and for the acknowledgment of God's sovereignty over all. The commission is from God; the field of action is the world and all its people. The tasks to be undertaken and the methods to be employed take shape both in loyalty to Christ and in response to the changing world. It is the inevitable and indispensable tension between that loyalty and that response which makes it both difficult and imperative to define the purpose and program of the United Church.

It is our purpose through worship, stewardship, education, and evangelism to celebrate the presence of God in life, to sustain and strengthen a community of faith, and to equip its members for mission.

It is our purpose through witness, service, influence, and action to declare that God is at work in the world and to be his servants in the service of men, to meet human need, to undergird institutions of freedom, to preserve human values, and to effect the social change required to secure justice and freedom for all men.

It is our purpose through reflection, research, experimentation, and review to discover the needs of a changing world and to develop ministries to meet them, not in disregard of the past or in affection for novelty itself, but to serve God's purpose in the present and to break new trails of obedience into the future.

It is our purpose through ecumenical councils, consultations on union, and partnership in action to work for unity wherever possible and to continue to be a uniting as well as a united church, not because we trust in strength of numbers, but because we disavow sectarianism and seek the most effective way to do God's will in the world.

Since both our knowledge of God's will and our understanding of men's needs are imperfect, there are natural differences in judgment and in expression among those who share a common Christian loyalty. Therefore, the United Church of Christ means to provide room for the sincere witness of Christian believers who may differ widely in their understanding of God's will in specific situations. The Church must provide for corporate actions which its responsible bodies may take but must respect the integrity of those who dissent and the right of individuals to dissociate themselves from such actions.

The United Church consists of local churches, Associations, Conferences, General Synod, and the various Instrumentalities. Neither the national bodies, the Conferences, nor the Associations exercise authority over a local church. The local church is the basic unit of the United Church. The Associations, Conferences, and national bodies are created or recognized as instruments of mission. The United Church includes them all in a fellowship of freedom and responsibility, and all of them together bear mutual responsibility for the whole mission.

For its structure and program the United Church relies, not on hierarchical authority, but on full and effective communication between the several parts so that each one can make its decisions in the light of its responsibility to and for the whole. The achievement of its purposes requires a structure of interrelationships which provides freedom through order, flexible enough to accommodate differences of understanding in a democratic process of decision making yet strong enough to assure mutual support and faithfulness. The authority of the whole is the self-imposed willingness of each part to co-operate with the rest and to undergird and support the responsible leadership of those who represent the larger fellowship. The structure of the United Church needs to be more clearly defined in order to deepen the sense of loyalty and to strengthen the financial support of and by the several parts. Associations, Conferences, national bodies, and the specialized ministries which are provided should be seen as the outreach of local churches, and each local church and specialized ministry should be understood as the expression of the whole Church.

Blending Traditions

12. A New Church:
Two Anxieties

(1963)

Robert W. Spike

Robert W. Spike (1923–66) was a Baptist/UCC minister who served as pastor of Judson Memorial Church on Washington Square in New York City (1949–56). Educated at Denison University, Colgate Rochester Divinity School, and Columbia University, he was on the staff of the Congregational Christian Board for Home Missions (BHM) (1956–58) and the United Church Board for Homeland Ministries (UCBHM)(1958–63). In 1963 he became director of the Commission on Religion and Race of the National Council of Churches of Christ (1963–66), organizing the participation of more than forty thousand white Protestants in the "March on Washington" (1963). As someone new to the United Church of Christ Spike — through his article in the Christian Century *(1963) — was able to address the lingering anxieties about the United Church of Christ among many UCC members.*

Source: Robert W. Spike, an excerpt from "The United Church of Christ: In Search of a Special Calling," *Christian Century,* February 20, 1963, 234–35.

Two Anxieties

. . . Two anxieties began to emerge in the days of final debate over the United Church constitution. These anxieties do not reflect present fixed positions or parties; on the national level at least, there prevail a remarkable degree of harmony and a great desire to consolidate the union. But these anxieties do represent real positions, and the tension between them has to do with the significant difference between presbyterial and congregational polity.

In this case at least, the tension is not fundamentally between centralized authority and local autonomy. The Evangelical side of the Evangelical and Reformed Church was notably congregational in heritage, and the Reformed Church, though more presbyterial in organization, participated in that general congregational orientation which in actual practice characterizes most of Protestantism. On the other hand, many of the agencies of the Congregational Churches, particularly the home and overseas boards of missions, were far more centralized administratively than were the comparable agencies of the Evangelical and Reformed Church. To some extent the extreme autonomism of the continuing Congregationalists has been a reaction against this aspect of Congregational practice; the most bitter expressions of hostility from this group have been directed against the leadership of the national boards. The antimerger Congregationalists tend to misinterpret the union as another step in already overextended centralism.

The real tension has instead been between those who cherish an organic view of the church as a compact, integrated people and those who cherish the tradition of functional responsiveness to the needs of the world.

This assertion in no way implies that the Evangelical and Reformed peoples had no missionary spirit or that Congregationalists were without a doctrine of the church. To a certain extent the idea of union was congenial to so many in both wings of the United Church because of the excesses of both emphases. "Our German Reformed Zion," as John Williamson Nevin, one of the great leaders of the 19th-century Mercersburg movement, referred to it, was strong because of its high doctrine of the church and because it was small enough to foster deep familial ties and commonly accepted disciplines, but it tended also to be insulated from the world and to be too dependent on common national background for its unity. Congregationalism, closely linked to early American thought patterns that produced much of the nation's public philosophy, in the past century often was too open to the various winds blowing across the secular society. It tended to assimilate liberal gentilities too easily, too uncritically.

Evangelical and Reformed constituents have generally desired a broader church experience and larger encounter with the world; Congregational Christians have generally desired a deeper and more ordered churchmanship. But, in the process of union, many on both sides discovered how deeply they held and cherished the ethos of their own tradition. Close up, high churchmanship began to look like inflexibility and a too easy identification of the General Synod with *the* Church. Responsiveness to the times began to look like dilettantism and highhandedness on the part of the mission boards.

The two anxieties remain, but they are now in working harness and are no longer pulling against each other. The future of the United Church of Christ will be very largely affected by the degree to which these two spirits confront each other creatively and refuse to be smothered for the sake of a superficial harmony.

13. A New Church:

"The UCC: A Merger of Two Kinds of Churches"

(1986)

Reuben A. Sheares

Reuben A. Sheares (1933–92) was an African American UCC minister educated at Talladega College (Alabama), Colgate Rochester Divinity School, Roosevelt University (Chicago), and Chicago Theological Seminary. After serving several pastorates in New York and Tennessee (1959–63), he worked in metropolitan mission for the Southern California and Southwest Conferences UCC, (1963–65). He was secretary for urban church development for the United Church Board for Homeland Ministries (UCBHM) (1965–67) and associate executive director of the Community Renewal Society (Chicago) (1967–73). When the Office for Church Life and Leadership (OCLL) was created in 1973, Sheares became its executive director (1973–88). Later he was pastor of the Congregational Church of Park Manor, Chicago (1988–92).

Sheares did not grow up in the UCC, and as a newcomer he had great appreciation and enthusiasm for its capacity to live with differences. At a 1985 symposium sponsored by the Connecticut Conference UCC entitled "UCC Theology: Yesterday, Today, Tomorrow," Sheares describes significant social, cultural, and religious differences between the Congregational Christian Churches and the Evangelical and Reformed Church. Following "conventional wisdom," he says, most people would think, "the differences were so deep, so profound and so basic, that there was

---

Source: Reuben A. Sheares, an excerpt from "The UCC: A Merger of Two Kinds of Churches," a presentation given at a symposium entitled *UCC Theology: Yesterday, Today, Tomorrow,* sponsored by the Connecticut Conference UCC, October 1985, 5–12 [typescript].

no way in which these folks, being so different, could ever really have had anything to do with one another." Yet, "The union came!" For Sheares the UCC is a case study of how union is possible among people who are theologically, and in other respects, very different.

The UCC: A Merger of Two Kinds of Churches

. . . My hunch is that almost every one of us has a sense of the differences, and it might not really matter whether or not the differences as we describe them are objectively true or not. I think one of the things that simply was there throughout the negotiations was the realization that the stereotypes of one another abounded and, in a variety of ways, were exaggerated. And yet, if you strip it all away, the affirmation that there were differences was real; the differences often ran very deep. There were, in that sense, two different churches. Yet the union came!

Now one of the reasons I said to you that the story of the United Church of Christ inspires me and challenges me is that, for all of my life, I have been concerned with the way in which we deal with differences. I've been aware of the fact that in perceiving difference we tend to judge the differences. If things are different, then some things must be better than the others. They just can't be different. It just seems like you have to have a value judgment. If you've got two things, one is better than the other. Or the other way we tend to think is that one has to be inferior to the other. Consequently, when differences are judged and valued, the best way of responding to them almost flows naturally from the way in which the differences are perceived. So that, if you are wrong, I have got to correct you, duty bound. The Lord expects it. Or can I say it another way? That is, "You're really wrong, and you really need to repent."

I wonder what it takes to get to the point where the realization, under certain circumstances, is that we're different and that both of us might be right and both of us might be wrong, maybe at the same time. The fact of differences in the history of the United Church of Christ has inspired me because it keeps saying to me that it really is possible to encounter differences and still find the point of unity. It is still possible to be different—diverse—and yet be one. You don't see many signs of that anywhere in the world. One inspiration for me in the church is that the United Church of Christ itself is a living example of the fact that it might be possible to deal creatively with differences. The union came!

At the uniting General Synod a message was sent to the churches over the signatures of the Co-Presidents and the Co-Secretaries of the church. "This union has been made possible," said the message to the churches, "because the two companies of Christians have held and hold the same basic beliefs, that Christ and Christ alone is the Head of the Church. From Him derive the understanding of God as Father, the participation in the same Spirit, the doctrines of faith, the influence toward holiness, the duties of Divine worship, the apprehension of the significance of baptism and the Lord's Supper, the observance of church order, the mutual love of Christians and their dedication to the betterment of the world. To be drawn to Him is to be drawn to one another, and to acknowledge Him as Head is to feel pain in the dismemberment one from the other." And so the union has come!

The message also went on to say, "Now two classical polities of Christian history have adjusted themselves to each other through union in such a way as to leave intact and effective the excellence of each. Differences in ecclesiastical procedure, which in sundry places and times have occasioned tensions and disorders, are appointed a secondary place and divested of evil effect."

There's a sense in which the message declares a perspective of the mothers and fathers that the differences, as important as they tend to be, were all on the secondary level. Looking at that which is primary, or that which is indispensable, they were not really two different groups of people. They were not really two different churches. They agreed that Christ and Christ alone is the Head of the Church. To be drawn to Him is to be drawn to one another. To perceive the unity in Jesus the Christ is to feel pain over the dismemberment or the separation or the division that exists within the Body of Christ.

Now the mothers and fathers at that point probably were being too simple. Because surely for a union to come, we need a lot more than agreement that Christ is the Head of the Church. Don't you need a whole bunch of stuff? Most of you are aware of the fact that the union took place, obviously before there was a Constitution and Bylaws of the church. It's weird! Did any of you watch the playoffs when the St. Louis Cardinals played the Los Angeles Dodgers — for the National League Championships? Do you remember the role reversal in the first two games? Take my word for it! The Dodgers acted like the Cardinals and the Cardinals acted like the Dodgers. That was the role reversal, OK? We like to deal with stereotypes. One thing always strikes me as I read the documents of the union and the negotiations and the different positions that were taken. This is the discovery that, as often as not the Evangelical and Reformed people acted like the

Pilgrims. If you are looking for the people who had the open Spirit, or who were willing to be Abrahams, it wasn't any of those Congregationalists, it was those Evangelical and Reformed people, and you get surprised! The people who for various and sundry reasons wanted to do the Constitution and Bylaws before the union were the Congregationalists.

The point I'm making is that the union was indeed a spiritual union and a theological union before it became a political union. Can you ever learn to be inspired by men and women of faith who are willing to trust God, and trusting God and Jesus the Christ, are willing to trust each other in the Church? "To be drawn to Christ and to be drawn to one another." Within Christ there may be all kinds of differences, and all kinds of things that divide us and all kinds of issues that have to be hassled, but within that commitment to Christ you've got a foundation upon which we can build and within which we can resolve. When I read the documents, I don't know but that I might be making the mothers and fathers of the United Church of Christ more noble than they've been. You know, it's the same thing I do with those biblical people. Maybe I do tend to make them larger than life, but as one son who comes after them I must say to you that I am inspired and indeed challenged by their devotion to God in Jesus the Christ. They were Christians, and they were willing to die, on that basis. It is as if they were really moving by faith more than by sight. And so the union came!

In the General Synod of 1960 when the Constitution and Bylaws were presented and indeed, adopted, James Wagner, who was then one of the Co-Presidents of the United Church of Christ, observed something that I think all of us need to remember. He observed that throughout their work, especially in the shaping of the United Church of Christ, they were never fully able — they were never absolutely free — to do what it was they thought they really needed to do. And that to which he pointed was the litigation that had occurred. As Gunnemann has pointed out, the arguments that were necessary in court, in a sense, set limitations on what the United Church of Christ could be, especially as we got into the nature of authority, the nature of freedom, and the nature of the relationship between the parts of the church and the whole of the church. The discouragement occurred along with the kind of realization that every time you thought you had clarity, somebody muddled it. It just got foggy. Just test your own spirit; how often do you climb up to the top only to roll back down? Once? Twice? What is it that allows you to keep on going when it looks as if everything isn't for you? Do you see the discouragement, my friends? It wasn't easy. That's why I get inspired from it, because I know that being "church" isn't easy. They persevered because they believed. Together they believed that what they were about was within the will of God for the church. In the final analysis, they were willing to trust in God. And so the union came!

Any number of the issues before the church were resolved. I like the language that Gunnemann uses to talk about it because it challenges me, even as it inspires me. I used to have trouble with all of the compromises that were made. But Gunnemann wants to use the language of reconciliation. I suppose for the life of the church that's the word I want to appropriate — the word "reconciliation." To make the affirmation, the union of two different churches or two kinds of churches, especially if you have been set apart, does require reconciliation. It isn't just compromise. And it isn't just toleration. Reconciliation is so necessary! I hear all kinds of stuff about the United Church of Christ being very tolerant, and I like that because some of my best friends need to be tolerated. But it seems to me that we have learned to ignore each other by tolerating each other. One of the ways in which we do that is even in the process of saying something like, "Well, in the United Church of Christ anybody can be whatever they want to be, and it doesn't matter." See, I think that's a little stiff. I think that something is missing. I think it is true that nobody is going to curse people who talk about their belief, but I think that in the life of the church we are to take each other seriously because it does matter what you believe. And what you believe matters to the whole of the church. I do have to take you seriously in order to help you to repent so that both of us can increasingly find a unity in the grace of God, a unity in the power of God. There is a need in a church like ours for reconciliation and not simply compromise.

To achieve reconciliation you do have to argue. For twenty years the United Church of Christ and its antecedent expressions had to find ways to argue with those who were of varying opinions. And I like the arguments! This is a church that isn't willing to say, "Well, we don't want to hurt your feelings, therefore, we will deny the Lord." That's easy. The net result was a church struggling to know and do the will of God. And so the union came!

The ecumenical commitment of the mothers and fathers needs to be commented upon. They chose the name, the United Church of Christ, because they said it expressed a hope as well as a fact. Do you remember the way in which they articulated the hope that this United Church of Christ would be a uniting as well as a united church? Part of what I think was very, very strong — as Gunnemann and others have pointed out — was apparent on both sides of the union. There were persons on both sides who were moved out of the sense of the ecumenical call, the ecumenical challenge confronting the church. I think they may have realized the relationship between that ecumenical challenge and the capacity of the church to be a faithful instrument of mission in the world.

So the question is, "How can a church take seriously enough an ecumenical vision in the way in which it shapes its life?" My answer to that is simply this — I think that for the United Church of Christ of the past and the United Church of Christ now in the present, the ecumenical question has become the denominational question. Those of you who received, for example, the recent "Baptism, Eucharist, and Ministry" document realize that one of the questions asked is, "Can you recognize in this expression the historic faith of the church across the ages?" Increasingly, even within the denomination, the question we are having to ask each other as we encounter each other is the question, "Can we recognize in each other, in the midst of our diversity, an expression of the historic faith across the ages?" I think that is the genius of the union. It isn't that you've got the whole truth; but the part you've got you've really tapped. But don't forget that you don't have it all. You really have tapped in, in a sense, when you believe in asking of each other the question of recognition of the faith — because it takes all of this and all of us to make the whole. And yet, it is still more than all of us together. It's the analogy of the Body of Christ in the twelfth chapter of 1st Corinthians, the whole and the parts; and yet it is simply in Jesus the Christ.

I find the United Church of Christ to be challenging. Our diversity today is much broader than it was at the time of the union. There is ferment with the Lord as people are making their advocacies. It seems to me that the mothers and fathers would smile out of their ecumenical vision. Because they would say that this church — that they wanted to see formed — which would be uniting as well as united, is the microcosm of the whole Church Universal.

Can it be done? Can the world believe? Can anybody believe that it can be done — that you can take all of this diversity, separate it and focus it in the church? Is this the question to which the United Church of Christ seeks to be an answer?

Amen.

PART II

Engaging the World

The United Church of Christ is the result of an ecumenical vision rooted in the conviction that God's church is already "one." By moving quickly to develop a classic but contemporary Statement of Faith and by producing a new Constitution in its first years of union, the United Church of Christ affirmed a unity of faith and order. Furthermore, as congregations, regional associations, synods and conferences, and national instrumentalities created new forms and structures to carry out their common mission, they realized that becoming "one" church is not an event, it is a process.

The early twentieth century had been a time of theological change and renewal within Protestantism in the United States. Congregational Christians, who had been deeply involved in the nineteenth-century Social Gospel movement, were sobered by the horrors of two world wars and the Great Depression. The Evangelical and Reformed Church, which affirmed its indebtedness to pre-Reformation Catholicism in the Mercersburg movement and remembered its concerns for racial justice on the nineteenth-century frontier, moved into mainstream religious life. By the early 1930s four traditions had become two denominations committed to an ecumenical vision and confident that the church had a responsibility to engage the world. When fundamentalism led some Protestants to retreat into biblical literalism, these traditions insisted that Christians are called to witness in deed as well as word and to seek after the Kingdom of God and God's righteousness in the world.

Confronting Injustice

In the 1920s the National Council of Congregational Churches adopted a "Statement of Social Ideals," and in 1934 they established a Council for Social Action (CSA). The council was created because Congregationalists were "stirred by the deep need of humanity for justice, security and spiritual freedom and growth, [and] aware of the urgent demand within [the] churches for action to match [the] Gospel."

Social concern within the Evangelical and Reformed Church was deeply rooted in the heritage of German and Swiss Pietism and in the commitment of the Reformed tradition to the sovereignty of God over society as well as the soul. In 1913 the Evangelical Synod of North America created a Commission on Common Welfare, later renamed the Commission on Christianity and Social Problems. Shortly thereafter the German Reformed Church in the United States appointed a Committee on Social Service. Following the formation of the Evangelical and Reformed Church these two committees met together to form the E and R Commission on Christian Social Action.

Even before the consummation of the United Church of Christ in 1957, the social witness of the two churches was closely linked. In 1949 they began cosponsoring the magazine, *Social Action,* which had been started by the Congregational Christians in 1935. After the union they joined together to create the Council for Christian Social Action (CCSA) of the United Church of Christ.

In the late 1950s theologians were concerned with how the message of love in the gospel of Jesus Christ related to the need for justice in the world. Social gospel liberalism and pacifism were inadequate. Yale Divinity School UCC theologian H. Richard Niebuhr made that clear with his often quoted statement about the inadequate theology of liberal Protestantism, with its beliefs that "A God without wrath brought men without sin into a kingdom without judgment through the ministrations of a Christ without a cross" [*The Kingdom of God in America* (1937, 1959 edition), 193].

The writings of theologians in the Reformed tradition, like Karl Barth and Emil Brunner, and in the Evangelical tradition, like Reinhold Niebuhr, argued for renewed belief in a transcendent God, who judges and loves humanity, and who enters into history through Christ and the Holy Spirit. When this classic theology combined with the legacy of the social gospel movement, the result was what some scholars call a "chastened liberalism." It affirmed God as sovereign and loving, the Bible as central but not inerrant, sin as real but overcome by grace, Christ as God's incarnate Word, and the Christian life as called to justice under the guidance of the Holy Spirit (see vol. 7:14).

Within this theological climate in 1959 the new UCC Council for Christian Social Action drafted a document of great significance for the future of the United Church of Christ. The "Call to Christian Action in Society" spelled out what it meant to be a Christian in the world. It acknowledged that "God as revealed in Jesus Christ is the ruler of all human affairs" and that "men live as members of one family under God." It challenged UCC members and churches to pray and work for changes in four areas: race relations, international relations, political life, and culture. It specifically advocated for peace, justice, the United Nations, the Universal Declaration of Human Rights, the control and reduction of armaments, and the relief of human misery. It offered a critique of the excesses of "American culture" in the light of Christian understandings of work, the environment, and family life. It focused upon the need for changes in race relations and political power. Christians needed to dedicate themselves to "seek justice for all" and "to love their neighbors not only in word but in deed" (see vol. 7:15).

The "Call" generated excitement in the early years of the United Church of Christ. It challenged churches and members to "do something" to change the world. Although some church people were hesitant or uneasy about whether churches should get involved in political issues, the leadership of the UCC was unambiguous. In 1959, John Bennett, dean at Union Theological Seminary in New York City, wrote in the *United Church Herald* that churches should not enter into partisan conflicts, but they should "influence the moral sensitivities, the scale of values and the conscience of the community as a whole." "Churches, from distinctively Christian motives, should support those positions that are based on a broad sense of justice and on a public conscience that unites citizens of different religious commitments."

Yet there were UCC members who worried that if the church became too involved in social and political issues, its evangelistic vocation would be compromised. They feared that faith and worship might become secondary.

Leadership in the UCC insisted that social action and evangelism were both faithful responses to the gospel of redemptive love. "Evangelism expresses this love for the brother whom we have seen, Christian social action for the brother whom we may or may not have seen." The church is called to witness to the good news in both "quiet and flaming deed," "in relationship to one person at a time and in behalf of all who suffer" (see vol. 7:16).

By the early 1960s the realities of racial injustice in the United States gave these words even deeper meaning. As the third General Synod gathered in Denver, Colorado, in July 1963, racial rioting and unrest were tearing the country apart. Ben M. Herbster, newly elected president of the United Church of Christ, spoke out. He asked the synod to set aside its ordinary business in order to "face the present crisis in our country and in our churches, and agree on action that cries out to God to be undertaken." He deplored the way in which blacks were treated, economically, politically, and socially. It was, he said, "a blight from which we must be saved," because "all of us stand condemned before the bar of Christian judgment." He insisted, "We shall betray our Lord if we take no action now" (see vol. 7:17).

The Executive Council and the General Synod took action, calling for a denomination-wide commitment to racial tolerance and advocacy. They urged local congregations to welcome blacks into their worship and to call pastors "without any restrictions as to race, class or ethnic background." They reminded the entire church that conferences and associations, which in some cases had been racially segregated, were no longer acceptable under the UCC Constitution.

The United Church of Christ struggled to bring its words and deeds together. Advocating "courage in the struggle for justice and peace," it attracted people who had given up on the church. Being a Christian actually could make a difference, and people wanted to know more.

At the same time, some UCC members and local leaders continued to question the social activist agenda. They yearned for "the good old days" when there was no controversy.

Controversy, however, did not go away. Although it was bitter and unpleasant at times, controversy was welcomed. An argument was made that controversy within a community of faith protected freedom and unmasked falsehood; that controversy was needed to keep a healthy balance between totalitarianism and indifference. In short, there was "no better way to protect freedom than to exercise it," and there was "no better way to avoid conflict than to welcome the possibility of controversy." Without controversy, differences of opinion could be reduced to matters of "taste," or labeled "treasonous betrayal." In the midst of controversy people prayed that they might be "faithful to the vision," while at the same time prepared "for the darker days of doubt" (see vol. 7:18).

The 1963 General Synod was a pivotal event in the life of the United Church of Christ. Recognizing that conference delegations to the General Synod were almost exclusively white, national leaders of the United Church of Christ invited ten leading UCC African American clergy to attend the synod as honorary delegates (voice without vote). Their influence and the decisions made at that synod positioned the United Church of Christ to create new institutional structures to address many aspects of the racial crisis.

Individuals also got involved. Robert (Bob) Spike, director of the Commission on Religion and Race of the National Council of Churches of Christ, mobilized UCC people and thousands of others to participate in the 1963 "March on Washington." Southern pastors called church members to open their doors and hearts. UCC clergy worked in voter registration drives in Mississippi, supported black education at places like Tougaloo College, and raised funds for the Delta Ministry. In a few short years hundreds of northern activists were dramatically changed by their participation in freedom rides, sit-ins, and marches (see vol. 7:19).

Martin Luther King and the civil rights movement shaped the United Church of Christ profoundly. By 1966, however, many young blacks questioned King's non-violent philosophy, embracing the new race-conscious ideology of "Black Power." In July 1966 an ad hoc group of black clergy from predominantly white denominations and historically black denominations met in New York City. They discussed the reactions of white clergy to black power and the way that the slogan was being distorted and misused by both whites and blacks. They drafted a statement and raised ten thousand dollars to publish it as a full-page advertisement in the *New York Times.* Forty-eight black clergy signed the statement about black power; four of them were UCC.

The statement began, "We, an informal group of Negro churchmen in America, are deeply disturbed about the crisis brought upon our country by historic distortions of important human realities in the controversy about 'black power'." It noted that when people use the words "power" and "Christian conscience" they are speaking about a "gross imbalance." White people assume that they are "justified in getting what they want through the use of power," but they think that blacks must "make their appeal only through conscience." "As a result the power of white men and the conscience of black men have both been corrupted." This has created "a situation where conscienceless power meets powerless conscience."

This statement, drafted by the National Conference of Negro Churchmen (NCNC) (later renamed the National Conference of Black Churchmen [NCBC]), was the first carefully reasoned pronouncement on black power to get international publicity. It contained sections addressed to public leaders, white clergy and laity, black citizens, and the mass media. It insisted that love is not the opposite of power, but that love needed to be the controlling element in power. It lamented the fact that as long as white Christians continued to "misinterpret Christian love," justice would be "subverted." Black and white church people read the statement with interest. The editors of the UCC *Social Action* magazine asked three white UCC national leaders to respond in their December 1966 issue (see vol. 7:20).

In October 1966 a group of forty-five "Negro Clergymen of the UCC and Workers with Principally Negro Constituency" met in Washington, D.C., to focus specifically upon how the United Church of Christ was dealing with what they called a "world in revolution." Speaking for the "racially dispossessed," they asserted that growing urban unrest was "rooted in the frustrations and yearning nourished by a century and more of delayed justice." Their statement lamented the "moral impotence" of the church, the continued racial discrimination within the church, and the misuse of power in both church and society. It asked local congregations, associations, conferences, boards, ecumenical commissions, creators of worship resources, and all "white brethren" within the UCC to work for interracial community. In return the forty-five UCC leaders who drafted and signed this specifically UCC statement listed nine distinct ways in which they pledged to do their part to meet the goal of interracial community. Charles Earl Cobb, new denominational executive for the Committee for Racial Justice Now, interpreted the statement to the wider church in *Social Action* magazine (see vol. 7:21).

The 1966 Washington meeting also led to the formation of a new grassroots caucus of UCC African American leaders known as "Ministers for Racial and Social Justice" (MRSJ). It was dedicated to advance the cause of racial justice and to strengthen African American leadership in the UCC. In 1967 it worked to elect Joseph Evans, a black Chicago pastor, as national secretary of the UCC.

Two years later, in 1969, James Forman and the National Black Economic Development Conference disrupted the work of several New York City UCC offices and presented the UCC Executive Council with four major economic demands outlined in what was called the "Black Manifesto." Although many people in the UCC were sympathetic to black requests for economic power, the Administrative Committee of the Executive Council deplored the Manifesto's implied endorsement of violence as "offensive to a Church committed to human brotherhood."

Feelings ran high. Black UCC leadership met with the Executive Council and convinced those in charge to let James Forman speak directly to the upcoming 1969 General Synod. He did, and his presence stimulated extensive debate about the responses of several UCC instrumentalities to the programs and the actions of the National Black Economic Development Conference. Few of the demands of the Black Manifesto were ever met, but the tactics used by Forman and the NBEDC sounded a note of urgency that shaped the future social witness of the United Church of Christ and several other predominantly white Protestant denominations. In 1969 the "Committee for Racial Justice Now," created at the 1963 General Synod, was voted a permanent national instrumentality, the Commission for Racial Justice (CRJ). The commission was charged "to provide leadership in mobilizing the membership of the Church to work for justice and reconciliation among persons and groups, in the area of race, both within the Church and in society in general."

As the General Synod of United Church of Christ took actions and passed pronouncements during the 1960s, some UCC members became increasingly troubled. In some instances, if they did not agree with a pronouncement passed by the General Synod, they felt betrayed. It was misleading, they said, to assume that all members of the United Church of Christ supported General Synod votes.

It had always been difficult in the United Church of Christ for local church members to understand how the actions of General Synod related to their views. Recognizing this, in 1959 the General Synod had passed a "Statement on Pronouncements" upholding the importance of Christian witness on issues where opinions differed. It said that although the General Synod was "the most widely representative body of the United Church," the authority of its utterances and enactments was dependent on their "fidelity to the Word of God." The Statement on Pronouncements insisted that no member of the UCC was "bound" by the action of any synod or instrumentality. Yet, it also reminded the church that the finest hours of Christian witness often came when a few "stood for what the multitude denied or decried."

During the controversies of the 1960s church members listened carefully to the voice of the General Synod, even when they did not agree. In order to help everyone remember the relationship of synod actions to local churches, in 1969 the General Synod reaffirmed its 1959 "Statement on Pronouncements," recognizing the freedom of the General Synod to act in its own name without permission from the wider church. UCC members expressed gratitude that the voice of the United Church of Christ was able to ring out where other denominations were forced to remain silent (see vol. 7:22).

There still were times, however, when controversial pronouncements and resolutions were proposed and some UCC members took exception. They reminded the General Synod that faithful Christian men and women sometimes hold opposing positions in good conscience. They argued that the church needed to speak out to name the problems of the day, to educate, to encourage Christian witness, and to help people take personal action. However, they believed that the church should not act for the Christian at the top, but demand that Christians act for themselves at the crossroads of their lives (see vol. 7:22).

Reshaping Mission

The majority of the United Church of Christ was exhilarated by the expanded activist image of their church. UCC members saw social action as an authentic human response to the grace of God, not an arrogant assumption that sinful humanity could save the world. Grounded in its chastened liberalism, United Church of Christ leaders knew that human sin and systemic evil could never be overcome simply by human effort. They embraced the ongoing struggle for justice and peace, not because they imagined that their pronouncements and actions would save the world but because of their profound awareness of the power of evil in the world, and their deep faith in the redemptive power of God in Christ. In so doing they reclaimed the biblical and theological conviction that Christians are called to action as a grateful response to the gospel, because they have been claimed and enabled to be agents for salvation by God.

Emboldened by this conviction, the United Church of Christ asked with new urgency, "What is the mission of the church in a world come of age?" Allen O. Miller, a professor at Eden Theological Seminary, answered this question with four phrases: evangelical witness, suffering service, responsible stewardship, and church unity. As the church awakes to the needs of the world, he wrote, it is forced to "search its own soul to discover who it really is and whose it is . . . " (see vol. 7:23).

For many Christians this search called for old-fashioned "Evangelism." After all, at the end of Matthew Jesus said, "Go therefore and make disciples of all nations, baptizing them in the name of the Father and of the Son and of the Holy Spirit" (Matthew 28:19 NRSV). The popular evangelist Billy Graham was calling thousands of churched and unchurched people to find personal salvation through belief in Jesus Christ.

The United Church of Christ did not reject this traditional evangelistic message, but it asserted that discipleship requires more. When some texts of the Bible are isolated from the whole and rigidly interpreted to concentrate attention on the destiny of the individual soul, to the neglect of the Bible's wider concerns for human needs and the human future on earth, something is wrong.

In 1966 the United Church of Christ had two engagements with what was later called "New Evangelicalism." Representing the UCC and the United Church Board for Homeland Ministries (UCBHM), Willis E. Elliott attended the World Conference on Evangelism in Berlin, Germany. Billy Graham and Carl F. H. Henry, founding editor of the sponsoring publication, *Christianity Today,* led the meeting.

Later that year Elliott and Graham had a formal exchange where Elliott articulated the discomfort most UCC people had with Graham's version of "biblical evangelism." Popular evangelicals, said Elliott, work from a kind of "scribal mentality," which narrows the gospel. The Bible, "with its jungle manifolds of meaning, its rich and unsystematic imagery, its pulsating, untidy, and unfinished life" is actually a resource for new forms of discipleship and evangelism, as well as for the old (see vol. 7:24).

The United Church of Christ took the Bible seriously even when critics argued that activism was undermining Christian conviction. Very early in his distinguished ministry committed to racial justice and civic service, Andrew J. Young, a young UCC clergyman working for the Southern Christian Leadership Conference, made the case that "demonstrations" were an authentic way for contemporary Christians to translate faith into action. "We should thank God daily for demonstrations," he wrote, because they may be "the witness through which God reveals history" (see vol. 7:25).

The United Church of Christ was energized by the turbulence of the 1960s. It knew that God was present amidst the turmoil, joy, and pain of society. People struggling to be faithful to the gospel wanted to bear witness to God's love in the world (see vol. 7:26).

By the early 1970s this conviction began to bear fruit in more focused denominational programs and national priorities. In 1972 the "Deering Conference on Faith and Its Corporate Expression" called the United Church of Christ to a "joyful sharing of the Christian Story." Denominational leaders wrote, "Evangelism must ultimately spring out of our experience of the gospel, as persons and as communities of faith, if it is to have any integrity and to be effective." In response the General Synod passed resolutions upholding its conviction that the "church's word-in-deed" had to be contextualized (see vol. 7:27).

Gabriel Fackre, professor at Andover Newton Theological School, wrote soon thereafter, "Evangelism is the joy and task of sharing the tale of the deeds of God." It is "telling" and it is "doing." Christians cannot choose between evangelism and social action. Evangelism that changes persons must always be companion to social action that changes structures. Such word-deed evangelism is rooted in the biblical story found in Acts, calling Christians to look to God in Jesus Christ — where the deed of God is one with the word of God (see vol. 7:28).

The journey of the United Church of Christ during its first fifteen years was a rough journey. It was marked by theological vision, organizational consolidation, action, and controversy. Gradually its understanding of Christian commitment and discipleship stretched and matured. By 1973, the United Church of Christ had emerged as a progressive denomination committed to social action. Robert V. Moss, former president of Lancaster Theological Seminary and the second president of the UCC, celebrated its work, but warned against "idolizing this Church, which we love and in which we share." He reminded the UCC that its "polity and church life are a gift of God. They are to be held in trust and nurtured for the good of the one fellowship for which Jesus prayed." He said, "We cannot necessarily assume that God intends our form of church life for the whole church, or that God does not have more light to break forth out of [God's] word" (from a speech delivered to the 1973 General Synod, "A Message for the Pilgrims").

Confronting Justice

14. Justice and Love:
"The Problem of Justice and the Power of Love"

(1959)

Reinhold Niebuhr

Reinhold Niebuhr (1892–1971) was an Evangelical and Reformed/UCC minister born in Missouri, who attended Elmhurst College and Eden Theological Seminary. He later earned two theological degrees from Yale Divinity School. From 1915 to 1928, he was the pastor of Bethel Evangelical Church in Detroit, Michigan, where he wrestled with the plight of working-class people and wrote his Leaves from the Notebook of A Tamed Cynic *(1929), (see vol. 4:65). For over thirty years he taught Applied Christianity (Ethics and Theology) at Union Theological Seminary in New York City (1928–60). While immersed in a rigorous academic career that included teaching and many scholarly publications he remained actively involved in the Evangelical and Reformed Church and supported the formation of the United Church of Christ (see vol. 4:61 and vol. 6:65 and 66).*

Niebuhr is considered by some to be the most influential twentieth-century theologian. Promoting what came to be known as a theology of "Christian Realism" in Moral Man and Immoral Society *(1932) Niebuhr wrote that human efforts to achieve good are always compromised by the ambiguity of political and social institutions (see vol. 5:39). He claimed that both religious and secular liberalism had yet to discover the difference between individual morality and the morality of nations. In his book* The Nature and Destiny of Man *(1941) he explored individuality, conscience,*

Source: Reinhold Niebuhr, excerpt from "The Problem of Justice and the Power of Love," *United Church Herald*, January 1, 1959, 12–13, 34.

sin, pride, human responsibility, and the transparent character of original righteousness.

During the early years of the United Church of Christ, Niebuhr wrote in a United Church Herald *article that "a 'Christian' approach to every problem of the community must include not only the moral demand of the 'love' commandment but Christian interpretation of the human situation which affirms the universality of the inner contradiction in men and the consequent prevalence of self-love."*

The Problem of Justice and the Power of Love

Christians of our day are undoubtedly too complacent about their ability and inclination to establish either brotherhood or justice either within the nations or between the nations. We are living in a highly complex society in which brotherhood within a nation is preserved by measures of justice, which carefully weigh competing claims and adjudicate conflicting interests.

Minimal Rights

The question, in domestic politics, is how much surtax the wealthy must pay in order to provide social security for the poor; how much the economic life should be regulated in order to prevent centralization of power and wealth; how much the Federal government should intervene in order to guarantee a Negro minority within a state even the most minimal rights of citizens and to prevent them from being consigned to "second-class" citizenship because of prejudices arising from race, color and "previous condition of servitude," i.e., the onus of slavery, long since abolished but still a potent force in forming the mores of communities.

In foreign policy we have to decide whether we have given adequate weight to the desire of the "colonial" peoples for independence since they desire and need their national independence, but not all are prepared to maintain their health without tutelage. We must decide whether to support the new state of Israel or whether it is necessary to appease the Arab world in order to prevent its adhesion to the Communist bloc.

On these and many other issues, including the paramount issue of how much we can trust the Russians and their "new look," we need discriminating intelligence in weighing the various competing factors and conflicting claims. It is obvious that even the most vital Christian faith does not offer us a panacea for the solution of all these problems.

What does it offer? The Christian faith is not primarily an ethic but it contains an ethic. This ethic makes love the final norm of human existence. Jesus defined the norm in the double "love" commandment: "Thou shalt love the Lord thy God with all thy heart and all thy soul and all thy mind" and "the second which is like unto it, thou shalt love thy neighbor as thyself." About these two commandments, Jesus said they contain "all the law and the prophets." If the Christian faith were only an ethic, the double "love" commandment would most perfectly define it.

But the Christian faith not only defines the ultimate norm of life as love, it also discloses the human situation in its starkness; and to that disclosure belongs the fact, perfectly expressed by the Apostle Paul, that "there is a law in my members which wars against the law that is in my mind."

There we have the two dimensions of human existence: the law of love is the norm but the law of self-love is the universal fact of human existence. We may know about the law of love "in our mind" but we are betrayed "in our members" into self-regard. This is the inner contradiction in human nature to which the Christian gospel addresses itself.

We must add one further detail to this Christian diagnosis. It is that the double "love" commandment does not guarantee that those who profess the love of God necessarily have the capacity or inclination to love their neighbor. The Johannine Epistle puts the matter succinctly: "If a man says he loves God and hateth his neighbor he is a liar; for how can he love God whom he hath not seen, if he loveth not his neighbor whom he has seen?"

The Christian gospel is an answer to this situation of self-contradiction in human nature. The final answer is the assurance of God's forgiveness in Christ and, through that assurance, there proceeds ideally the "grace" to love the neighbor. For love cannot be demanded as a duty. It can only be the fruit and response to the love which has been shown us. Such in briefest outline is the gospel answer to the final predicament of man.

All efforts to establish community and to maintain tolerable relations between various communities must be approached by the Christian in terms of the framework of meaning which the gospel discloses.

We have suffered for a long time, particularly in America, from an inadequate description of the whole Christian gospel which reduced it to an ethic and consequently approached every situation in the community with the simple affirmation that the problem of justice or injustice in review could be solved if only men loved one another as Christ bade them to do.

This kind of Christian moralism is irrelevant because both experience and biblical insights refute the idea that ideal love of the neighbor is a simple possibility, particularly in the collective relations of men. Our task in the community is rather to find instruments and structures of justice which will make our love effective against the hazard that we and others are motivated by self-love rather than love.

A proper Christian interpretation of the labor movement, for instance, will regard the dangers of new centralization of power in its organization but will also recognize that it was a necessary instrument of justice which established the equilibrium of social power by which the Western world was saved from the monstrous injustices of early industrialism. If these injustices had prevailed the Marxist indictment against capitalism would have proved true and the Marxist-inspired rebellion would have taken place everywhere, as it did take place in Russia, China and the decaying feudal structures of the East.

In short, a "Christian" approach to every problem of the community must include not only the moral demand of the "love" commandment but Christian interpretation of the human situation which affirms the universality of the inner contradiction in men and the consequent prevalence of self-love.

If this second element is lacking, Christian "politics" degenerates into sentimentality and every problem is assumed to be solved by the statement that men ought to love one another more. The real problem is how to give the love of the neighbor scope in spite of the hazards of self-love. If this task is fully analyzed it will be seen that love must be transmuted into justice before becoming effective in any relations of the community outside the family. Even in the family, which has been the seed-pot of community from the earliest time to the present, love must avail itself of calculations of justice if it is to remain viable.

A mother of more than one child must decide what she regards as a "just" distribution of the common resources of the family. Any obvious unfairness toward one child will have catastrophic results. In the relation between husband and wife, the modern family stands under the obvious necessity of constantly reassessing the position of the woman in the home and in the community because many factors in technical civilization have given her a potential freedom and equality which were not granted in agrarian civilizations and which cannot be denied now.

It is rather interesting, incidentally, that the religious community has lagged behind the secular community in granting women equal rights because traditional religious mores have been more powerful than the ultimate challenge of the "love" commandment: "In Christ there is neither male nor female."

If justice must be the servant of love, how does it distinguish itself from love? The most primary distinction is that there is calculation of rights in justice while there is none in love. Love in its pure form is heedless and unprudential. "Love seeketh not her own, is not easily provoked, beareth all things, believeth all things." This Pauline description of heedless love is classic but few Christians realize that it represents a pinnacle of the spiritual life which is not frequently experienced in even the most ideal mutualities of our modern family existence.

But the very genius of justice is calculation. We calculate the competing claims of our children in the home. We adjudicate the conflicting claims of nations and groups to decide which claims are "right." In adjudicating these claims, we avail ourselves of certain standards, usually the standards of equality and liberty, which are directly related to love.

Liberty is a standard of justice because love wants to affirm the right of the other to be "an end in himself," to be a self, to have ideals, ends and goals which I must respect even though I do not share them and though they may run counter to my interests.

Equality as a transcendent principle of justice has a long history. It would seem that it was introduced into Christian thought by the Stoics and there are Christian theologians who think it ought to be discredited for that reason. But it is neither Stoic nor "modern" in its origin. It is rather the almost instinctive principle of love, when love begins to calculate.

My fellow man has a claim upon me. How much of it should I grant? As much of it as would make his opportunities equal to my own. Of course, equality cannot be regarded as an absolute principle of justice. It is only a regulative one. Men are not created equal. They have different gifts, needs, capacities and ambitions.

Absolute equality would destroy a community as surely as absolute liberty would. Yet it is significant that our conscience is uneasy about race relations because we know that prejudice prevents the Negro child from having "equal" opportunities with our children. And our conscience is uneasy about the status of colonial peoples because they resent the inequalities of power and privilege which we take for granted. . . .

15. Christian Action:

"Call to Christian Action in Society"

(1959)

Council for Christian Social Action

Early in the twentieth century the Federal Council of Churches adopted a document known as the "Social Creed of the Churches" (1908). Many congregations in the traditions that came together to form the United Church of Christ had been actively engaged in social activism since before the U.S. Civil War. Their denominations had formally cooperated on several ventures before 1957 and therefore UCC leaders moved quickly, after the uniting General Synod, to prepare a new statement to help the United Church of Christ engage the social order. The newly created UCC Council for Christian Social Action (CCSA) sent out questionnaires and received suggestions from more than three hundred social action leaders. It drafted the "Call to Christian Action in Society," challenging congregations and their members to pray and work for changes in race relations, the role of nations, political life, and culture. The "Call" was first published in Social Action *magazine and later adopted by the 1959 General Synod. It is generally considered the most formative document in shaping the distinctive United Church of Christ commitment to social action.*

Source: "Call to Christian Action in Society," Appendix 13a, *GS Minutes 1959,* 171–75.

Call to Christian Action in Society

Half a century ago the four communions which now form the United Church of Christ joined with others in the Federal Council of Churches to proclaim the Social Creed of the Churches. They summoned the churches to stand for such ideals as the abolition of child labor, the release of workers from employment for one day in seven, the protection of workers from occupational hazards, and the right of employers and employees to organize. Many of these ideals of the churches are now embodied in the social legislation of our nation. This "Call to Christian Action in Society" is an attempt to discover what the Lord requires of us today.

1. The Gospel is the Good News of what God has done and is doing in the world. In Jesus Christ God entered the arena of human history, grappled with the principalities and powers of evil, won a victory over those powers, and made manifest his love and gracious purpose toward all men. In grateful response, the Christian seeks to tell the story of God's action in ways which are persuasive for the men and women of our day.

2. At the same time, the church responds to God's saving act by seeking His will in all human relationships. For God as revealed in Jesus Christ is the ruler of all human affairs — nations, social orders, institutions. To Him belong our souls and bodies, our possessions and cultures, our churches and communities.

3. God has made us to live together in community. Without love of neighbor there is no love of God. Without service to men there is no service to God. We live, we rise, we fall as members of one family under God.

4. We confess the pride and greed which separate us from God and from each other. Before God we repent of our smugness and sloth, our absorption with self and neglect of neighbor. The judgment of God lies upon us and all our affairs.

5. We rejoice in many signs of the power and grace of God in the events of our time. People are asking recognition of their God-given worth. Barriers between races, classes, and nations are being brought down. We are thankful that God is stirring his people against injustice and oppression.

I. The World of Nations

6. We live in a world of nation states, constantly growing in number. This world has become so interdependent and interrelated that nearly every

action has an appalling number of relations and effects. The power struggle is therefore greatly intensified, particularly between communist and noncommunist states.

7. Deeper than the divisions, however, is mankind's essential unity under God. Deeper also are the common danger, the common need, the common hope. Nations must therefore develop a larger measure of mutual confidence through more creative use of peaceful methods for relieving international tensions.

8. In the contemporary situation each nation will inevitably seek to maintain military force at a level considered necessary to national security. We must, however, avoid the militarization of United States foreign policy. We should strive for the development of an effective and enforceable body of international law.

9. We therefore call upon our churches and their members to pray and work:

10. For peace, justice, and the welfare of all nations and peoples;

11. For the United Nations as a major resource for the settlement of disputes, for peaceful change, and for economic and social development;

12. For a full implementation of the Universal Declaration of Human Rights;

13. For creative sharing among nations of persons, ideas, and skills;

14. For deeper awareness of the problems, legitimate interests, and fears of other peoples, especially those in the newer nations and in nations under communist rule;

15. For effective international control and reduction of all national armaments, including the testing of nuclear weapons;

16. For the use of our wealth, personal resources, and trade policies in a world-wide attack upon human misery;

17. For a clearer demonstration through our own national life that both order and justice can be achieved under free institutions;

18. For the extension and strengthening of the world-wide Christian community, that it may help to provide spiritual foundations for a world community, combat ignorance, superstition, and traditional social evils, and serve as a reconciling fellowship among all peoples.

II. American Culture

19. Our cities rise higher. Our suburbs spread afar. Streams of people move from place to place across the land. Astounding inventions provide abundance of goods, swiftness of communication, miracles of healing, and relief from many burdensome tasks. Opportunities for educational and cultural enrichment are multiplied.

20. In the midst of this abundance, we are beset by much that is trivial, dehumanizing, and vulgar. Prodigious plenty tempts us to selfish indulgence while millions of people in our land and abroad live in want. Private consumption has reached unprecedented levels while public services on which all of us depend are starved. Concentrations of power, controlling the channels of information, beguile masses of people into unthinking conformity and slavish striving for goods that do not satisfy. Much of our leisure time is devoted to forms of entertainment and escape that dull us to the world's need. We are tempted to love things and use people when we should love people and use things. And even in the midst of crowds our lives are often empty, anxious, and alone.

21. Now as always God calls us to a new life that offers genuine meaning, faith, and community. He sets before us goals that are higher than comfort and success. He summons us to develop our capacities for mental and spiritual growth. He frees us from our bondage to the networks of opinion and taste. He saves us from calling good evil or evil good. He searches the streets of our cities and the by-ways of the countryside not for the church that takes pride in its popularity, its wealth, or the splendor of its buildings — but for the church that does justice and seeks truth, that cares for people and loves the Gospel, lifting up family, community, and world.

22. We therefore call upon our churches and their members to pray and work:

23. For a deeper understanding of the Christian meaning of daily work;

24. For the participation of Christians in organizations of farmers, labor, management, the professions, and other vocations, encouraging democratic procedures, wise practices, and concern for the public interest;

25. For fuller appreciation of the role, rights, and responsibilities of both organized labor and management in the democratic functioning of an industrial society;

26. For policies that safeguard the well-being of the farmer and the farm family as well as the interest of the general public in the efficient production of abundant food and fiber;
27. For the conservation and development of the earth's resources for the benefit of mankind now and in the future;
28. For economic institutions and practices which provide meaningful work, serve human needs, eliminate blighting poverty, prevent unemployment and harmful inflation, and bring about more equitable sharing in the goods and services which our productivity makes possible;
29. For action to strengthen the family and counteract the forces making for family disorganization;
30. For the support and expansion of necessary public services such as schools, transportation, and health programs;
31. For increased educational and cultural opportunities for all;
32. For more effective programs of education and action in church and community on the meaning and effect of alcoholic beverages, narcotics, and gambling;
33. For the provision of adequate social services for special groups such as the young, the aging, the handicapped, the mentally ill, and the victims of alcohol and drugs;
34. For the protection of migrant workers and their families;
35. For the admission of more immigrant refugees and their integration into the American community;
36. For better methods in the treatment and rehabilitation of those convicted of offenses against the law;
37. For the use of leisure time in creative avocations, in wholesome recreation, in strengthening family life, in enrichment of human culture, and in service to church and community.

III. Race Relations

38. Jesus Christ as Lord and Shepherd of all men requires us as his followers to repent of those violations of brotherhood and justice which create separation, tension, and conflict between men of different races and to manifest — within the Church, the Body of Christ, and within the community of nations — acts worthy of such repentance.

39. We therefore call upon our churches and their members to pray and work:

40. For the elimination of pride and prejudice from our hearts;

41. For the end of racial segregation and discrimination in our communities — in church life, in housing, in employment, in education, in public accommodations and services, and in the exercise of political rights;

42. For the alleviation of poverty, ignorance, illness, and all other handicaps which are aggravated by unequal opportunity and by segregation imposed by law or custom;

43. For the furtherance of human rights throughout the world and respect for all men as persons created in the image of God.

IV. Political Life

44. God holds political life under his providence and judgment. It is the area in which men and nations make some of the most fateful decisions of our time. In this process controversy and compromise serve important and necessary functions.

45. We therefore call upon our churches and their members to pray and work:

46. For the support of effective, representative, and responsible government;

47. For active participation of Christians in political life as voters, workers in parties, candidates, office holders, and civil servants;

48. For the critical evaluation, within the fellowship of the church and in the perspective of the Christian faith, of the policies and practices of candidates, office holders, and political parties;

49. For a church with bonds of Christian fellowship so strong that it dares to discuss and act upon civic and political issues.

50. For maintaining the independence of the churches and the state, and for creative cooperation between them.

Dedication

51. To these tasks we dedicate ourselves in the name of God who calls us to seek justice for all his children and to love our neighbor not only in word but in deed. In him is our confidence and our trust.

16. Social Action:
"Revolution and Renewal"

(1963)

Gerald J. Jud

Gerald J. Jud (b. 1914), is a Congregational Christian/UCC minister who served as general secretary of the Division of Evangelism and Renewal for the United Church Board for Homeland Ministries (UCBHM) in the 1960s. He was educated at Yale University and was one of the authors of Ex-Pastors: Why Men Leave the Parish Ministry *(Pilgrim Press, 1970). In a 1963 article "Revolution and Renewal" in* Social Action *magazine Jud argues that the church has "two ears." With one the church listens to the world, and with the other the church listens to individuals on their personal faith journeys. In the church, therefore, Christian social action and Christian evangelism must work together out of their mutual obedience to the vision of the gospel. In 1976 Jud founded the Shalom Mountain Retreat and Study Center in the Catskill Mountains in New York State.*

Revolution and Renewal

In the little Texas town where I grew up there was an old man who when asked how he was doing always gave the same reply, "Just living." It was plain to all that his reason for existence was vague and his joy almost nil. Yet paradoxically he manifested a great interest in staying alive. He frequented doctors' offices, and when medicine shows with their fake

Source: Gerald J. Jud, "Revolution and Renewal," *Social Action* (January 1963): 13–18.

remedies came to town he always bought whatever was offered for the ills of the body. But both before and after the latest remedy his response was always the same, "Just living."

Today, in this revolutionary age, some people wonder whether the church is not like that old man who had lost his reason for existence and his joy but nevertheless was preoccupied with his continued existence, eagerly trying fake nostrums in the wistful hope that something might help. Of course, the answer to this wonderment is to be found in the deeds of the church, in its stance toward and involvement in the revolutions now engulfing us. Unfaithfulness and irrelevance are the marks of a church preoccupied with her own existence, desiring survival at all costs. Faithfulness and relevance are the marks of a church deeply aware of her reason for being and creatively alive in her service and witness in the world.

Revolutions

Rapid social change characterizes our time. We speak rightly not of revolution but of revolutions. These revolutions are social, political and economic. They permeate every area of the church's life and the life of each individual.

The *urban revolution* is foremost among the revolutions of our time. Within the next decade 90 million new people, half of them coming from rural areas, will be living in the cities.

Mobility is a towering mark of our time — families on the move, work communities fractured, long-range commuting, old class lines disappearing and new ones emerging. Such mobility fosters rootlessness and loss of personal identity.

The *mass media* have a food-blender effect, homogenizing these depersonalized, uprooted masses. To use another figure, people increasingly look and act as though conformity — the fear of being different — submerges the individual. Even desires are mass-produced. The old ways and satisfactions are dying, and the ersatz replacements are not filling the inner void.

The *electronic* revolution promises to change the meaning of "work" as we have known it. Automation and cybernetics accelerate their speed in reshaping man as a worker. New leisure is promised, but it has an ominous corollary in the threat of emptiness. The presses step up their output of books on loneliness.

Minority groups symbolized by the young Negro rise to claim their rights. Sit-ins, pray-ins, ministers in jail, a stubborn governor refusing to yield to law and order, the quiet courage of Mr. Meredith and little Negro children attending once completely segregated schools — all of these point to the racial revolution in our time.

Then the problem is compounded when we add international politics to these revolutions — Cuba, Algeria, Berlin, the seething continent of Africa and the ferment of Asia, inequities and strivings to be equal, starvation and struggles for supremacy. Revolution! Change! Challenge! And in the midst of it all stands the church of Jesus Christ. Her response reveals whether she is "just living" or is serving the living God.

Revolution and the Person

These revolutions not only affect man in the mass, but impinge upon individuals one at a time. We are born one at a time, suffer one at a time, find or fail to find meaning one at a time, die one at a time. In the midst of these swirling revolutions the person cannot exist in a vacuum. He has to make some kind of response. One description of our age is "the age of anxiety," and probably the central reason for this anxiety is man's present inability to respond creatively in this revolutionary age. Feeling the impact of revolution upon him, experiencing the death of old meanings and the failure to find adequate new ones, he represses his fears and loses himself in great busyness.

Man in his solitariness and in his need confronts the church. Does the church in this day of revolutions have anything to say to him in his solitariness? Are there deeds to be done which enflesh the word? If she has good news for this man and communicates it in word and flaming deed, then the church is not "just living."

The Two Ears of the Church

The church has two ears. With one she hears what is going on in the world, "where rise the cries of race and clan," where human beings act and react to the gales of the new solitary struggles for identity. With the other ear she listens to the agony of man on his pilgrim journey through this world.

Evangelism is the communication of the gospel of Jesus Christ under the power of the Holy Spirit to the end that men may confess Christ as Lord and walk in faithfulness to him. This faithfulness is expressed in the world.

Christian social action is also the witness of the church in the world. Its objective is justice and peace. And like evangelism it is centered in a compassionate concern for persons.

The Need for a Living Relationship between Evangelism and Christian Social Action

Christian social action and evangelism have so much in common that in vision they are hardly separate at all. Any organizational separation of the two at the national, state, or local level must not be permitted to frustrate their mutual obedience to that vision.

Under this strong conviction an experimental conference was held this past summer at Deer Hill, the conference and retreat center of the New York Conference. Two members from the national Christian social action staff and the four members of the national evangelism staff, together with twenty-four pastors, a seminary professor, and a process researcher, lived together for ten days in very close dialogic relationship. Under the general heading of "The Relationship of the Word and the Deed" we allowed ourselves to be addressed by a cluster of crucial questions. The social ethics teacher was with us as "disturber of the peace," the researcher observed the process to interpret the dynamics. We were a worshipping community, a searching, seeking, open-ended community, desirous of grasping more fully the meaning of faithfulness in our time.

Through our life together, certain feelings about the relationship of evangelism and social action emerged.

Some Things We Know

1. Both social action and evangelism are ideally faithful responses to the gospel of redemptive love. Evangelism expresses this love for the brother whom we have seen, Christian social action for the brother whom we may or may not have seen.

2. Both are dependent on dialogue. Evangelism listens to the affairs of the solitary human heart and, when that heart opens, witnesses to the good news. Social action listens to the noises of the world and having listened does the costly deed in the interest of justice. Though we know that there can be no authentic speaking without listening, evangelism and social action are tempted to talk without first listening. Yielding to this temptation results in ineffectual propaganda rather than in reconciling witness.

3. Evangelism and social action are both dependent on the word becoming flesh. Both call upon the church to "put your deeds where your mouth is." The word of the gospel is that "The Word became flesh and dwelt among us." The primary witness of the church is in the living language of deeds in costly relationship to persons one at a time and in costly

action in society as a whole, Social action and evangelism are alike dependent upon dogmatics and apologetics as they manifest themselves in preaching, lecturing, writing and all of the intricacies of the mass media. But while there is heavy dependence upon these imperatives still we know that both social action and evangelism must move beyond sermons, pronouncements and neat phrases to involvement with persons who in their uniqueness stand in need of the good news.

4. Both are involved in compassionate risk. Words are cheap. It is easy to speak idealistically, with judgmental overtness, but it is dangerous and costly to permit such words to become flesh. It is one thing for evangelism to talk glowingly about salvation, it is another to take the risk of listening to one human soul, of entering into his suffering, and of striving to relate the good news to his condition. It is an easy thing to draw pictures of the just and peaceful society but quite another matter to do the compassionate deed in behalf of the downtrodden and the sinned against. Unlike the evangelistic deed the social action deed involves not one person but the structures of society. It is the deed done for racial justice, fair housing, equitable employment and education, peace and good will in the world.

5. Both social action and evangelism are dependent upon Christian community. Some hold that the days of the residential church are over. I believe very strongly that it will remain the primary center of power for the church's witness in the world. The faithful and effective witness of both evangelism and social action is an expression in the world of meanings which are experienced and celebrated in the local Christian community. Too often the local church cancels out by her deeds what she says with words. She has little to say to the world if in her own life she does not, both silently and dramatically, act out those truths which she proclaims to the world.

6. Together, evangelism and social action need to stand in great openness before the Lord in these days, to discover the forms of witness and to receive wisdom and courage. Though the local church will remain the key source of strength and power because of the revolutionary aspects of our time new forms of witness need to emerge. They will likely depend on the residential church for support, but they must be free of its traditional trammels. What forms these new ministries will take we do not know. But if we seek with great diligence, if we pray with openness, and if we have the kind of receptivity and willingness to give up old forms and ways if new and better ones become apparent, then the way will be found. The gospel does not give us a blueprint but provides a relationship, a foundation and a backdrop upon which and against which we can work out the

ministry of our respective lives and churches. And in our time our faithfulness involves a willingness to be led by the Spirit to change and to sail uncharted seas.

We look with great interest to such experiments and acts of faithfulness as are manifest in the Christian Faith-and-Life Community in Austin, Texas, as it ministers to university campus, clergy, and laity; the Detroit Industrial Mission as it seeks to find significant new paths in industrial evangelism; the Church of the Savior in Washington, D.C., as it searches out relevant forms of witness in the world; and Koinonia Community of Americus, Georgia, as it seeks to bear witness to the reconciling power of Christ in a strife-torn area of the Deep South.

The Church Called to Faithfulness in a Revolutionary Age

The church, whose good news is the good news of redemptive love, is called now to witness to this good news in both quiet and flaming deed, in relationship to one person at a time and in behalf of all who suffer. The path of faithfulness is also the way of renewal for the church in our time, a church that is not "just living" but is afire with good news, full of relevant words and deeds for the individual and for the world.

17. The Racial Crisis:

"Remarks on the Present Racial Crisis"

(1963)

Ben M. Herbster

Ben M. Herbster (1904–84) was pastor of Zion Evangelical and Reformed Church in Norwood, Ohio, for thirty years. In 1961 he was elected the first president of the United Church of Christ and reelected to a second four-year term in 1965. Herbster's dedication to racial equality, expressed in his speech to the 1963 General Synod, changed the history of the United Church of Christ. Under his leadership during the 1960s the United Church of Christ created new structures and strategies to deal with pressing racial challenges facing the nation and the churches.

Herbster was also deeply committed to the ecumenical movement: in addition to participating in conversations leading to the formation of the UCC (1957), he attended the constituting Assembly of the World Council of Churches in Amsterdam (1948), and three subsequent WCC assemblies in Evanston (1954), New Delhi (1961), and Uppsala (1968). As the president of the UCC he exercised leadership in the Consultation on Church Union (COCU) and other national and international ecumenical organizations.

Source: "Ben M. Herbster's Remarks on the Present Racial Crisis," *GS Minutes 1963,* Appendix 10, 132–35.

Remarks on the Present Racial Crisis

Amid happenings that are at once both ominous and pregnant with potential for good, I make bold to ask for the special privilege of setting aside the ordinary business of this General Synod in order that we can face the present crisis in our country and in our churches, and agree on action that cries out to God to be undertaken. Few times in our lives have we faced a greater responsibility than we face now. I believe we dare undertake nothing else until we have acted with faith, courage, and vision, and I trust with unanimity, in terms of the need of the hour. The situation present across America, the way in which in our society our Negro brethren are treated, economically, politically, and socially, constitute a blight from which we must be saved. This blight must be eradicated; eradicated now.

The demonstrations which sometimes have enflamed into riots and have taken place in two score cities across the country are much upon our minds. But the deep-seated prejudice and discrimination with which our Negro brothers are treated is not much better in the rest of the country than in these places where violence has erupted. All of us stand condemned before the bar of Christian judgment. The issues at stake are not only moral and ethical, but they have their unmistakable implication for us as followers of Jesus Christ. We shall betray our Lord if we take no action now. Beyond all this, we need to pray to God for forgiveness, for the way in which, in our nation and in our churches, we have allowed this deep wound to fester.

We should remember that we are not embarking upon a hopeless task in fighting for racial justice. Important changes for the better in race relations have taken place, especially within the last ten years. Public transportation has been desegregated by law if not always effectively in the South. School desegregation has begun and is now being accelerated all over the country. Higher Education is open to all citizens who can qualify for it. Barriers of discrimination in public places have been torn down in many parts of the country. We must express our indebtedness to the persons who have led in effecting these changes in the church and in society. We can take some encouragement from the record.

We here can also be encouraged by the knowledge that the United Church of Christ has been able to achieve a great deal in furthering racial equality. Our drive for racial justice that began over one hundred years ago when New England Congregationalists led in the Abolition Movement and then organized the American Missionary Association has never faltered. We have supported efforts to provide social justice for our Negro brethren in higher education, in open covenants for housing, in fair employment practices, to name only a few. But we must face the fact that the changes that have taken place as a result of our efforts are pitifully few in comparison with those that must yet take place. We dare not become complacent.

Certainly this General Synod will not adjourn without speaking out prophetically, boldly, courageously, and in compassion so that in the minds of the members of the United Church of Christ, and in the Negro community there will be no questions as to where we stand. We shall not only call our people to law and order, but to justice and brotherhood. We shall back our pronouncements with our lives, that by our action in the church and the community our stand shall be evident. To do less than this would be to forsake our responsibilities and to be unworthy of our Lord.

On July 5, 1963, words and resolutions are not enough. We have had too many words that changed too little. We must act, and we must act now.

1. That action must begin in our own lives. We must uproot intolerance, bigotry, and prejudice; and we must replace them in our own hearts with good will and the determination to strike down immediately the barriers which divide men on account of race. Furthermore, we must make it plain to our neighbors and our co-workers that our own lives have been changed and that from here on we shall stand for brotherhood.

2. Our church life must also be transformed. Segregation in churches must be stopped at once. Our churches, which are really God's, not ours, must be open to all people. How can anyone of us set himself to bar His brethren and ours from His church? Who gave us that right? The Associations and Conferences of the United Church of Christ must be fully integrated. The Constitution of the United Church of Christ provides for integration at all levels. We must carry out its provisions for racial equality. Furthermore, the United Church is not utilizing to the full the contribution that its Negro members can make to its work and life. We must give them their share of leadership opportunities and responsibilities.

Some of our church-related institutions are segregated. We cannot tolerate this condition. The purging from our life of prejudice and discrimination must begin in the House of God.

3. We must mobilize the manpower and the means of the church for racial justice. The present crisis demands that we shall be ready to meet needs wherever they arise and whenever the opportunity presents itself. In such a fast-moving situation as the one we face, we must keep our program and our resources flexible. To this end we should name a committee of non-national staff persons who are trusted throughout the Church and have competence in this area. Then we must give to that committee the power to make decisions as to how the resources of the Church will be used in the effort to secure social justice and racial equality both at home and

abroad. If this plan is adopted the Council for Christian Social Action and the Division of Church Extension of the Board for Homeland Ministries have offered Dr. S. Garry Oniki to serve as executive coordinator in this.

In most instances the actual implementation of the work undertaken would be committed to one of our existing agencies (The Board for Homeland Ministries, the Board for World Ministries or the Council for Christian Social Action) so thus money can be conserved for actual program needs. Where projects would be undertaken by the committee itself experienced staff could be borrowed on a temporary basis from the Instrumentalities. The program which this committee shall project could include but need not be limited to:

a. Mobilization of the whole membership of the church, to join where possible with our Protestant, Roman Catholic, and Jewish brethren, on a community basis, to meet the needs of the situation on the local level.
b. Providing of bail bonds for those who are arrested as they demand social justice.
c. Providing legal defense for such persons.
d. Providing economic aid to persons who lose their jobs because of their participation in activities in behalf of racial quality.
e. Providing financial aid for institutions whose support is threatened by those who oppose an "open policy" of service.
f. Mobilizing the United Church of Christ, its individual members, congregations, associations, and conferences to press for the adoption of legislation to guarantee civil rights.
g. Extension of the program of voter registration.
h. Providing other emergency or long-term help, the need for which only the future will reveal.

All of this work, and more than we can now outline, should be undertaken in cooperation with the National Council of Churches, State and Local Councils of Churches, the National Conference on Religion and Race, and other interreligious and community groups.

4. We should challenge our people to bring an emergency special offering of funds to cover the cost of this program. With the consent of the Board for World Ministries the General Synod should recommend that the first of these offerings be received this fall instead of the S.O.S. offering. The setting of a date for the second offering should be left to the Executive Council. The responsibility to raise these funds should rest with each congregation and each member of the church under the direction of

the Stewardship Council. (We can borrow against these offerings in order to set the work forward immediately.) We should receive an offering on this coming Sunday evening, here at General Synod, as the beginning of this fund. Congregations and individuals who want to add to this fund before next fall will be able to do so by sending their contributions to the Treasurer of the United Church of Christ, 297 Park Avenue South, New York 10, New York.

5. Most important of all we should call upon all the people of the United Church of Christ to pray that justice and good will shall prevail, and then to work in order to make the fulfillment of that prayer possible.

One of the happy factors in this effort is that it fits in so well with the emphasis which we shall be asked to approve for the years 1964–65, "The Church and Urbanization." This effort will complement that effort for in most cases it is in urban areas where the Negroes are most seriously disadvantaged.

Two years ago I stood before you when you committed unto me the responsibility of the office of President and said, "I pledge to all of you that we shall not be content as long as there are any disadvantaged people. We shall work, pray and strive that all men shall have a decent chance at life." This challenge that I bring to you at the beginning of this General Synod is but the sequel of that promise. I pray that this General Synod will have the vision and the courage to support a program something like the one I have outlined to you and then have the persistence and the will to carry it into action that a new day shall dawn within the Church and within the nation. To fulfill this determination we must constantly rely upon the strength which comes alone from God. In His Spirit let us make our decision.

18. Controversy and Prayer:

"Controversy: An Instrument of Freedom," and "A Prayer for These Days,"

(1963, 1962)

Buell G. Gallagher, John C. Bennett

Buell G. Gallagher (1904–78) was a Congregational Christian/UCC minister who graduated from Union Theological Seminary in New York, studied at the London School of Economics, and later earned a doctorate from Columbia University. His book American Caste and the Negro College *(1938) helped to guide the church's thinking about race. During the 1930s he was active in the formation of the Council for Social Action of the Congregational Christian Churches. As a progressive white academic leader he served as president of the historically black Talladega College (1933–43) and was president of The City College of New York (1952–61, 1962–69). Gallagher understood the importance of controversy, having led City College through the "McCarthy era" when fear of communism threatened many civil liberties. His article, "Controversy: An Instrument of Freedom," is based on an address he gave to the Anti-Defamation League's Pacific Southwest Regional Board, December 17, 1961.*

John C. Bennett (1902–95) was a Congregational Christian/UCC minister educated at Williams College and Mansfield College (Oxford, England) who was on the faculty at Pacific School of Religion (1938–43) and was professor, dean, and president of Union Theological Seminary in New York (1943–62). Bennett taught and wrote many books on Christian ethics and theology, but always stayed connected to the church and its social witness. "A Prayer for These Days" is a good example of his pastoral sensitivity.

Sources: Buell G. Gallagher, "Controversy: An Instrument of Freedom," *Social Action* (February 1963): 27–29. John C. Bennett, "A Prayer for These Days," *Social Action* (February 1962): 31.

Controversy: An Instrument of Freedom

The right to differ without rancor is fundamental to any form of free inquiry. Indeed, it is basic to a free society. Unless men can differ without malice, differences become malicious and men who differ resort to malicious devices. "Mutual insult with impunity" may be an overstatement of a desirable goal, but it points us in the right direction.

My thesis is that the possibility of controversy is essential to freedom. And since I would not associate myself with any society other than a free society, I gladly welcome the possibility of controversy.

Not that there is any positive virtue in controversy for its own sake. Other things being equal, I am a man of peace, preferring a peaceful atmosphere preserved by peaceable men. And that is precisely why I insist that controversy must always be an open possibility. If the controversy which is natural in a free society were to be outlawed, then differences of opinion would be regarded as bad taste at best — and, at worst, as treasonous betrayals. In such a world, the notion of controversy itself would have become controversial and therefore taboo.

Possibility of Controversy Essential

On the contrary, I hold that the only issue which is not open to controversy is whether controversy is permissible. There is no other way to maintain and to promote freedom than to exercise it. If freedom is to be real, the possibility of advancing new ideas or old ideas must always be present. The possibility of controversy being open, needless controversy can be avoided.

There is a second reason why controversy must always be an open possibility. In the words of John Milton, "Controversy being permitted, falsehood will appear more false, and truth more true." If controversy were only a means of maintaining freedom it would justify itself; but when it is seen also as a means of unmasking falsehood and of clarifying man's understanding of truth, the method of controversy takes on pragmatic dimensions of strength.

In the third place, free controversy is the only method known to man whereby the heavy hand of forced conformity may be lifted while at the same time creative energies are released. There are two, and only two, methods of avoiding controversy. Neither of them is acceptable. The first method is, by force and compulsion to declare that only one position is acceptable and that all must accept it. This is totalitarianism — whether in government or in religion or in education. The result of denying the possibility of controversy is a monolithic political state buttressed by a monolithic religion and served by a monolithic education. Uniformity of thought, of belief and of practice is demanded. Controversy is forbidden. The working tools of such a society are force and fear. The accusations of treason, heresy and subversion blanket the political, religious and educational life of the people. Controversy is forbidden. The police state becomes a reality.

The second and equally objectionable method of avoiding controversy is indifferentism. Nobody argues because nobody cares. This position holds that all ideas are equally acceptable, all moralities equally viable, all practices to be suffered with equal indifference. Under this alternative, one may think, believe, and act entirely as he pleases — provided only that he is ready to be completely indifferent to what others do and say and think. Thus, where all points of view are regarded as equally valid, there is no controversy; but anarchy is perilously avoided only by a quality of individual and group forbearance which, if successful, prevents all enthusiasms and results in a specious social blandness — a society where naively mediocre persons with suspended judgments are alternately horrified and bored at the notion of a passionate espousal of any cause or adherence to any set of values. The working tools of such a society are studied indifference and cultivated ennui and foppishness, in the actual and potential drying up of all creative impulses, the decay of art and morality, and the falling apart of the political structure.

Twin Evils

Totalitarianism and indifferentism are twin evils, so closely related to each other that with the passing of a single night, a society may move from one to the other.

The easy transition from indifference to tyranny and back again from tyranny to indifference is possible mainly because both of these methods lack the only ingredient which defeats them both — namely, they recognize no legitimate place for controversy in the affairs of men. Without the possibility of controversy, there is no way to break the repetitive cycle of vice following viciousness.

There is no better way to protect freedom than to exercise it. There is no better way to avoid conflict than to welcome the possibility of controversy. The free minds of free men will never submit either to the pressures of conformity or to the hysterias of fear. Unbowed and uncowed, free men will stand in the integrity of their freedom.

A Prayer for These Days

Lord God Eternal,

Have mercy upon the peoples of the world
whose fate hangs in the balance;

May they be delivered from those whose hearts are hardened
by faith in systems which they seek to impose on others,

and may they be delivered from those who assert their will
with reckless disregard of the consequences for humanity.

May those who call upon thy name be guided
by thy love for all thy children,

and may those who deny thee know, in spite of their denial,
the pressure of thy providence and thy judgment.

We ask for ourselves faithfulness, wisdom, and courage;
may we commit ourselves afresh to thy will for us.

Guide us as we work;

Help us to remain faithful to the vision
that in our best moments has led us.

Prepare us for the shocks that come to us from new knowledge
or from hearing unexpected convictions and opinions.

Prepare us for the darker days of doubt;
of frustration, of despair.

Help us as we live with one another,
that each of us may be thoughtful and forbearing,
that we may listen to one another,
that we may see in ourselves the habits of feeling and of doing
that give pain to others and cause them to stumble.

Be thou the light of our life. Amen.

19. Time for Action:

"A Report on a Pilgrimage to Selma"

(1965)

Roy F. Alberswerth

Roy F. Alberswerth (b. 1916) is an Evangelical and Reformed/UCC minister educated at Blackburn College, Elmhurst College, Eden Theological Seminary, and Union Theological Seminary in New York. He was the pastor of Faith-Salem United Church of Christ in Florissant, Missouri, in the mid-1960s. Late in the evening on March 9, 1965, he received a phone call inviting him to join Christian clergy from all over the country by traveling to Alabama to stand in solidarity with African Americans seeking basic civil rights. Alberswerth explained later, "I knew that the time had come for more than an occasional sermon about the 'brotherhood of man' and the 'fatherhood of God.' . . . It was time for action! It was time to stand up for what I believed." At 6 o'clock the next morning he was on a plane bound for Selma. From his pulpit the next Sunday, March 14, 1965, Alberswerth preached, "In Selma, Alabama, I experienced the Church like I have never experienced it before." It was a remarkable day, he concluded, because in Selma "We had borne a visible witness to the Christian faith, and to our best hopes for our nation. . . . We hoped, that in some small measure we had helped the Church also see its tremendous potential, its opportunities and its grandeur in our time." Alberswerth later served as Southeast Association Minister in the Wisconsin Conference UCC.

Source: Roy F. Alberswerth, excerpt from "A Report on a Pilgrimage to Selma, Alabama in March 1965," *On the Way* (Summer 1997): 19–21.

A Report on a Pilgrimage to Selma

. . . I need to say something about the practical reasons for going to Selma. One of the great deeds of our faith is to "witness." But it has been somewhat corrupted by the courtroom. We think now of a witness as someone who simply stands up and tells what he or she knows. But to "witness" in the New Testament sense is much closer to what Civil Rights workers mean by the word "demonstrate," that is, to "put your life where your mouth is!" That's to demonstrate. To demonstrate your faith and your hope — that is the hard thing in the world for me, and I know for all of us. To give visible evidence that the whole nation is involved in the events in Selma, and that the Church of Jesus Christ does care deeply about what happens to people; particularly the oppressed.

Secondly, a very practical reason: Civil Rights workers in the South have known for a long time that police will rarely attack whites. So one of the purposes for having white ministers in Selma is the very practical method of putting them at the front of the march. And all of us in our group were very delighted to hide behind the skirts of the nuns, for they were in the front row. It was a tremendous experience for the Civil Rights workers to see those grand ladies who normally are seen only in institutions of learning and in hospitals, standing for what they believed. And equally impressive was the fact that two of the sisters were Negroes. When introduced in Brown's Chapel, the Negro pastor called them "holy women" to which they immediately replied, "We're no holier than you are." It was a tremendous thing for the Negroes of Selma to see Catholic sisters — members of their own race.

I want to now tell you how we arrived, and a little about the city. Selma, Alabama is a city of 29,500 persons, of which 14,400 are white and 15,000 are Negro. But the voting roll, that is the listing of registered voters, shows 99% are white; 1% are Negro. There is a huge air base in Selma, but of course, we did not land there. We landed at the smaller Municipal Airport. The terminal building was locked up, so we couldn't get in. I thought this might be the last chance to call home, and indeed it was.

We were greeted as we came off the plane by a number of Negro men and women who were our chauffeurs. We were assigned to the cars that were lined up and made our way to Brown's Chapel, which has now become so famous. I suppose it might become one of the shrines of freedom of the future. We noticed on the way that the drivers were extremely careful, that is, they were over-cautious. I learned from Civil Rights workers, that laws in some Southern states are on the books primarily to be used against Negroes and whenever the police want to use them. Sometimes they are never enforced at all, and never against whites. So at stop signs we stopped longer than we really needed to. We moved along, not too slow, not too fast, and for our own protection the cars kept close together.

We had received instructions about our own personal conduct, and a few warnings: We were not to use any words that were uncomplimentary; we were to do only what we were asked; and, we were never to separate ourselves from the larger group or go off in a group of less than six persons. You see, it was the night before we arrived that Rev. Reeb had been slugged in Selma. We arrived without incident at Brown's Chapel, which fortunately is located on the edge of town near the airport. We went into the Chapel and there at about 9 o'clock the young people — teenagers, 15 to 19 — were singing, making speeches, and generally conditioning themselves for the march. Here I was introduced to the remarkable way one is conditioned for non-violence. Later on, more of the adults came in until the church was packed and people were surrounding the church on the outside. They could hear what was going on through the open windows. I've never seen a group so disciplined in my life, and yet the discipline was not obvious. I've never seen young people so attentive to the instructions of older people. The Civil Rights movement in the South is primarily made up of the young and the old for a very practical reason. The wage earner does not get into the demonstration because he or she will lose their job. So it is the sons and daughters and grandparents that take up the burden of demonstrating for freedom. Certainly there were those who were in their middle years, but not many at all, and I'm told, this is usually the case. So in the church, when enthusiasm ran a little bit farther than it should have, it was only a clap of the hands of an older Negro that brought complete silence. Hence, we were conditioned. We needed to be conditioned, too. This was the most moving service I have ever been in. It went on for two and one half hours. We were to purge ourselves of any resentments, of any hatreds we harbored. We were reminded by the Civil Rights leaders that we could not demonstrate for the dignity of all men if we were going to degrade or smear the dignity of some men. All of the demonstrators were encouraged to think of the genuine nature of those who were, in those moments, their opponents. We were to think of the Chief of Police as a man created in the image of God, and consider that under other circumstances, his genuine person might come forth. At the same time, as we purged ourselves of our hatreds and resentments, the service of music, prayers, and speeches was to give us backbone, courage!

I was so tremendously impressed by the faces of the Negro demonstrators. The look of hope and eagerness seen there, the light of freedom in their eyes. It was the hope that must have been in the eyes of our forefathers when they came to this country — a hope that knows it cannot be stopped, a hope that can only be fulfilled by non-violent action. Such courage, such confidence! Standing next to me as we entered the street was a tall, young man. I think he was the same one whose picture was in Life magazine. I'm quite sure it was, because I recognized the shape of his bandage. He had been slugged during Sunday's confrontation, but got out of the hospital immediately to participate in the demonstrations on Monday and Tuesday, and was back on Wednesday. He was only one among many who were saying over and over again, "the only way you'll ever stop us is by shooting us down, because we know what is rightfully ours and we'll demonstrate until we have it. . . . "

20. Black Power:
"Reflections on . . . "

(1966)

Alford Carleton, Truman B. Douglass, Ray Gibbons

The "Statement by the National Committee of Negro Churchmen," which appeared in the New York Times *on July 31, 1966, was signed by forty-eight black clergy, four of whom were UCC. It was not a United Church of Christ document, but it was reprinted many times. (See* Black Theology: A Documentary History, 1966–1979, *ed. Gayraud S. Wilmore and James H. Cone [Maryknoll, N.Y.: Orbis Books, 1979], 23–30.)*

The statement was taken seriously by many UCC people, black and white. The UCC-sponsored magazine Social Action *asked three top UCC leaders to respond to the statement. Their brief comments reflect the deep commitment to racial justice of many whites within the UCC.*

Alford Carleton (1903–83) was a Congregational Christian/UCC minister who graduated from Hartford Theological Seminary. He served as a missionary in Turkey (1924–27) and Syria (1929–53), returning to the United States in 1954 to head the American Board of Commissioners for Foreign Missions (ABCFM), the foreign missionary board of the Congregational Christian Churches. After the formation of the United Church of Christ, he became executive vice president of the United Church Board for World Ministries (UCBWM) (1957–70).

Truman B. Douglass (1901–69) was a Congregational Christian/UCC minister who graduated from Union Theological Seminary in New York. After serving churches in New Jersey, California, and St. Louis (1926–43),

---

Source: Alford Carleton, Truman B. Douglass, Ray Gibbons, "Response to the Statement on Black Power published in the *New York Times* on July 31, 1966," *Social Action* (December 1966): 38–40.

he became the executive vice president of the Congregational Christian Board for Home Missions (BHM) and its successor, United Church Board for Homeland Ministries (UCBHM) (1943–68), influencing its social justice commitments. He was also involved in the earliest conversations about church union in St. Louis with Samuel Press and others that led to the formation of the United Church of Christ (see vol. 6:73).

Ray Gibbons (b. 1903) is a Congregational Christian/UCC minister educated at Oberlin College, Oberlin School of Theology, Union Theological Seminary in New York, and Columbia University Teachers College. After pastorates in Maine and Massachusetts (1928–43), he served as director of the Council for Christian Social Action (CCSA) of the Congregational Christian Churches (1944–57) and director of the UCC Council for Christian Social Action (CCSA) (1957–67). Gibbons played a key role in the development of the "Call for Christian Action in Society" (1959) (see vol. 7:15).

Response to the Statement on Black Power

Editors Note:

We invited executives of three UCC Boards to respond to the statement on Black Power published in the New York Times on July 31, 1966. This statement was introduced as follows:

"We, an informal group of Negro churchmen in America are deeply disturbed about the crisis brought upon our country by historic distortion of important human realities in the controversy about black power . . . we are impelled by conscience to address at least four groups of people in areas where clarification of the controversy is of the utmost necessity. We do not claim to present the final word. It is our hope, however, to communicate meanings from our experience regarding power and certain elements of conscience to help interpret more adequately the dilemma in which we are all involved." The four groups addressed were: (1) the leaders of America: power and freedom; (2) white churchmen: power and love; (3) Negro citizens: power and justice; and (4) the mass media: power and truth. . . .

To Restore Rational Basis

In a situation as complicated by conscious and unconscious prejudices as is anything to do with race, the problem of reaching rational rather than emotional solutions is nearly insuperable. The fact that emotions are as real as "reasons," and that rationalizations are emotional before they are "reasonable" means that great care must be taken in the choice of language in which to discuss issues. Then some term like "power" that is supposedly a neutral term pops up as a slogan, and the search for the vocabulary of rational discussion is on again. There would be, of course, no issue of "black power" were there not "white power" in existence — in existence so long and so pervasively that it has been taken for granted. The statement by the National Committee of Negro Churchmen is an admirable attempt to recognize facts, and to restore the discussion of the facts to a rational basis in spite of the emotional impact of good words turned into slogans and hurled into the conflict.

ALFORD CARLETON, Executive Vice-president
United Church Board for World Ministries

Justice Disturbs Peace

Most of the protests against "black power" fail to take note of the prior existence of "white power."

Church people for a long time have tended to ignore the issue of power — except when the balance of power to which they have been accustomed is disturbed. Yet the rough approximations to justice — which are the most that seem achievable in this world of imperfection and sin — all depend on some equitable sharing of power. The question of the distribution of power is a more fundamental issue in our society than the distribution of wealth. Indeed, wealth has ethical significance mainly as a symbol of power. It is the control of other people's lives — making decisions for them, determining the limits within which they operate as free persons — that is the great offense against Christian ethics.

The supreme ethical offense which many of us are coming to recognize realistically is the fact that the white man, because of the biological accident of being white, has been the determiner of the destiny of people of other skin colors, not only in this country but throughout the world.

We have been slow to recognize that power unethically held is as bad as power unethically seized. All our conventional codes favor the status quo. The person or group who moves to adjust the balances in favor of a more equitable distribution of power is automatically a disturber of the peace. Well, he is! All change disturbs somebody's peace. But in God's political economy justice is more fundamental than peace. Enduring peace is possible only on the basis of a fair measure of justice.

Until there is a voluntary yielding of white power (which seems wholly unlikely) there will be need of organizing black power. As sinful men we are subject to man's inherited, built-in prejudices against fundamental changes in the status quo.

TRUMAN B. DOUGLASS, Executive Vice-president
United Church Board for Homeland Ministries

A Countervailing Force

I cannot become greatly aroused about the cry of "black power." What really disturbs me is the failure to recognize the existence of "white power." For one thing there is a great deal more of it. Choose any criterion you please — per capita income, educational advantages, freedom of residence, upward mobility — it is the whites who have the power. Not only do they have the power but it is the whites who misuse it. Whites stole Africans for American slavery, exploited their labor, smashed their family life, and ground them into abject servility. It is whites who wall blacks into the ghetto, who provide superior schools in white suburbs and vociferously object to more taxes for inner-city schools, who vote into office those who suppress riots with police power instead of preventing riots with remedial measures. It is the whites who put property above people, who establish criteria of pseudo success, putting spending "for that which is not bread" above humane considerations. Against such ersatz culture, discerning students and fellow Christians from abroad rightly rebel. It is for such hollow mockery white power has spent itself.

Not only do whites have the power and misuse it but it is the whites who have most to gain by the development of "black power." It might help redeem white power from its own destruction. If Negroes developed power more nearly commensurate with their numbers, their needs, and their possibilities, this power might provide a countervailing force, corrective of white power, and so establish a greater possibility of justice for all. This redistribution of power might offer the possibility that white power would be redirected toward higher values and more humane goals. There is no certainty that such will be the result, but even the possibility becomes a reason for white power to rejoice in the growth of black power. It might redeem white power from its total corruption — a possibility devoutly to be wished.

RAY GIBBONS, Executive Director, CCSA

21. Black Power:

"Washington Consultation Statement" and "Now More Than Ever: The Church Is Challenged"

(1966, 1966)

Washington Consultation of Negro Clergymen of the UCC and Workers with Principally Negro Constituency, Charles Earl Cobb

Forty-five United Church of Christ clergy, most of them black, met at Plymouth UCC in Washington, D.C., October 18–20, 1966, to discuss mutual concerns, problems, and opportunities in the United Church of Christ. They were troubled by the lack of progress within the UCC toward racial inclusiveness and freedom of opportunity. Not only did the group issue a statement, it organized an ongoing advocacy group within the United Church of Christ known as UCC Ministers for Racial and Social Justice (MRSJ), and it developed strategies to support racial justice and expand the presence of African Americans in the leadership of the UCC. The Steering Committee behind the "Washington Consultation Statement" was Edwin R. Edmonds (Dixwell Avenue Church, New Haven, Connecticut); Robert R. Johnson (St. Albans Church, St. Albans, New York); W. Sterling Cary (Grace Church, New York); Arthur D. Gray (Park Manor Church, Chicago); Robert D. Sherard (Corona Congregational Church, Corona, New York); George Gay Jr. (Gregory Congregational Church, Wilmington, North Carolina); Martin Duffy (Vernon Heights Congregational Church, Mt. Vernon, New York); Channing Phillips

Sources: The Washington Consultation of Negro Clergymen of the UCC and Workers with Principally Negro Constituency, "Statement to the United Church of Christ," *Social Action* (December 1966): reprint. Charles Earl Cobb, an excerpt from "Now More Than Ever: The Church Is Challenged," from *Social Action* (December 1966): 12–22.

(Lincoln Temple, Washington, D.C.); and Charles E. Cobb (Committee for Racial Justice Now, New York).

Charles Earl Cobb (1916–98) was an African American Congregational Christian/UCC minister educated at North Carolina College and Howard University. After a long pastorate in Springfield, Massachusetts, in 1966 he became executive director of the Committee for Racial Justice Now and the executive director of the Commission for Racial Justice (1969–85). In a 1966 article in Social Action *magazine, "Now More Than Ever: The Church Is Challenged," Cobb outlines past ways in which African Americans have challenged the church and describes the frustrations of young blacks in the mid-1960s that led to the black power movement. He also reports on the Washington, D.C., meeting of UCC Negro clergy and its call to the United Church of Christ to face the facts of the social revolution.*

Statement to the United Church of Christ

No one can be unaware that the world in which we live is a world in revolution. Everywhere the winds of discontent are blowing against the status quo. Moreover, the revolution we face is not one but many.

For the racially dispossessed the revolution is rooted in the frustrations and yearning nourished by a century and more of delayed justice. We talk a great deal about the American way and the Free World but are strangely blind to a sterner truth; the impossibility of achieving a Free World through a segregated society.

We, a group of United Church of Christ clergymen, concerned with predominantly Negro congregations, are deeply disturbed over the failure of the United Church of Christ to be the servant church in the world and particularly its failure to be a servant in the world by reflecting in its own life as well as in its efforts in the world, a community free of racial and class prejudice and discrimination. We are unanimous in support of racial justice for reasons over and above self interest. We are equally concerned about the welfare of the nation. We are morally obligated to confront ourselves and our white brothers with the requirements of our Judeo-Christian Faith. We cannot and will not be equivocal with the ethical and moral principles involved.

First we are alarmed over the increasing moral impotence of the church. Whenever an instrumentality, publication or conference takes a stand upon the issues of race, open housing, economics or politics a hue and cry goes up throughout the land.

Who authorized them to speak for the church? The answer is clear: the New Testament authorizes them to speak for the church. However inadequate his words the Christian must speak for God, to himself, to the church and to the world, or his speaking is in vain. It is better to speak and be wrong than to remain silent and safe.

Our refusal to face controversial issues for the sake of harmony, or the budget or fellowship has no support in the New Testament or the Old. The prophets and apostles took no opinion polls and granted no equal time. Their "thus saith the Lord" was spoken without fear, favor or consensus.

Next, we are appalled by the racial discrimination within the church. Discrimination and attitudes of prejudice manifest themselves throughout the length and breadth of the United Church of Christ. This is significantly revealed in a study made by the Committee For Racial Justice Now in 1966 on non-white employment within the Instrumentalities. This condition is also shown as we look at the composition of policy-making boards and commissions of the church. It is again revealed in the meager employment and use of non-whites on the Conference and Association levels. Discriminatory practices are also noted as we look at the faculties, staffs and student bodies of our predominantly white colleges, universities and theological seminaries. Tokenism is also evident in Church Extension. The absence of open pulpits and memberships is further evidence of discriminatory practices and prejudicial attitudes. A report prepared for the Urban Church Advisory Committee by the Department of Research documents prejudicial attitudes that are current in the United Church of Christ.

Thirdly, we are concerned for the use and racial misuse of power within the United Church of Christ as well as in the social order. If the United Church of Christ is to be the Beloved Community and become an instrument for social justice, our inner and outer architecture must agree. . . . In order to achieve that full community, we believe the time has come to maximize the collective power of clergy and members of predominantly Negro churches to influence the structure, policy and program of the United Church of Christ towards that end.

We Call Upon

1. Our churches to include commitment to interracial community and racial justice in membership vows and training, to instruct pulpit committees with a clear mandate for pastoral search without reference to race,

and to initiate exchanges and mergers between white and Negro congregations, with the goal of eliminating segregation in the churches. We call upon all churches to join their Lord in the establishment of a truly human society. To this end we urge them to work aggressively for interracial and inter-class urban and suburban communities, to mount programs to establish decent housing, quality integrated education, job opportunities and job training programs, adequate annual income for all citizens, and to work for international justice and peace.

2. Our Associations to develop and to enforce similar standards of interracial commitment in (a) ordination of ministers and (b) acceptable standing of churches in the United Church of Christ, (c) to promote those congregational exchanges recommended to churches as a matter of urgent priority.

3. Our Conferences, especially through their staff and boards of directors, to take affirmative action to recommend qualified Negro clergy for every available pulpit and other staff positions and carefully to assess rejection of Negro candidates, to seek out qualified Negro representation on all decision-making bodies of the Conference, to develop and commend standards for membership training, staff selection and interracial church goals for congregations and Associations.

4. Our Boards for Homeland Ministries and the General Synod to give priority to new mission projects which explicitly gather interracial and inter-class congregations committed to Christian reflection and concerted community action, and to finance such projects adequately and patiently when self-support is slow in coming; to include in its regular budget provisions for a United Church of Christ program for racial justice which does not therefore depend on occasional and unpredictable free-will offerings; to bring the historic concerns of our American Missionary Association for a "society without caste" north of the Mason-Dixon Line.

5. Our Consultations on Church Union to seek only those ecumenical unions which can shape themselves around a mission in the world which is thoroughly interracial and interclass in intent, strategy, structure and forms of worship.

6. Our Commission on Worship, Divisions of Christian Education and Evangelism, and other appropriate groups to develop and to promote the use of worship resources — forms of prayer; preaching, hymns, sacraments — which honor and draw upon the rich religious resources of Negro congregations and Negro history, in order to help overcome those barriers of cultural and religious style which tend to separate us and to prevent the establishment of genuinely and permanently interracial churches.

7. Our white brethren in the United Church of Christ to work with us for fully interracial life in church, school and society. At the same time, we lay upon their conscience those spurious efforts at token integration which are patronizing and finally alienating, as seen in those who would admit Negroes into white churches but never urge whites to join Negro churches, who proudly open the door of segregated suburbs to a few prosperous Negroes but show little concern for the plight of the poor in slum housing, who would allow Negro children to be bussed into white neighborhood schools but never allow their own children to be sent to Negro neighborhood schools, who fear Black Power but never complain of the ancient inequities wrought by generations of White Power. Interracial community is our goal, but anything less than a peer relationship is degrading to those of both races.

We Pledge Ourselves

1. To organize for the achievement of these ends, to accept whatever group discipline is necessary, to delegate responsibilities for addressing those individuals and groups with critical power of decision in the church, and to seek primarily from our own constituents and churches the necessary finances for this.
2. To develop and to promote qualified Negro nominations for church leadership positions throughout the United Church of Christ.
3. To develop and to promote whatever direct or indirect political action techniques may be necessary and consistent with Christian ethics to eliminate racism within all United Church of Christ institutions.
4. To develop resources for mutual aid, including financial, for our fellow members who suffer or risk serious loss in the course of pursuing these purposes.
5. To explore fully, and to develop if feasible, a clergy union committed to minimal standards of church racial and interracial policies for pulpit, membership, and outreach, with sanctions against churches and pastors supporting or promoting racist activities.
6. To develop those worship resources we have commended to the church at large, resources which mirror the Negro tradition but which can and must enrich the total church life if our fellowship is to become fully interracial.
7. To support whatever consolidations of Negro economic and political power may prove necessary to force a change in America's racial inequity in housing, jobs, schools, access to all cultural advantages and in political

self-determination, and those which may be necessary to assert a pride and dignity so long denied by a white society.

8. To review periodically the performance and achievement toward implementing these goals and actions, and to issue a progress report on accomplishments and failures to each general synod in the most effectual manner.

9. To develop as a last resort procedures for withdrawal and reorganization of churches and clergy of the United Church of Christ committed to interracial community and to racial justice, if the denomination fails to renew itself as a community committed to a kingdom without caste and showing this in its own church life.

Now More Than Ever: The Church Is Challenged

"Black Power" Concept Emerges

This new approach by these militant young men manifested itself on a Mississippi road during the Meredith March for Freedom in the cry, "Black Power," from the lips of Stokely Carmichael. Across the length and breadth of the land there was a response to this cry, both positive and negative, fanned to a white heat by news media whose motivation yet remains a question mark.

The positive response came principally from Negroes because, from the lowest to the loftiest, each knew what Stokely Carmichael was talking about, whether they could explain it or not. Even those Negroes who were horrified at Stokely's articulation were so because of their own vested interests and the possible implications of the term, even though they knew what he meant.

Stokely Carmichael himself spells it out to some measure in the September 1966 issue of *Ebony* magazine, saying:

(a) Black Power is a black declaration of independence.

(b) Black Power is a demand that black and white people recognize and actualize the existing power potential of black Americans.

(c) Black Power is an attempt to instill pride in black Americans.

(d) Black Power is a developing program that will ultimately be defined in action by black Americans.

(e) Black Power is not an end, but a means to the transformation of American society.

(f) Black Power is a call, perhaps a last call, to the black middle class to come home. It is a demand that the black haves make common cause with the black have-nots so that all blacks, haves and have-nots, can have more.

There are few Negroes and few whites who could disagree with these definitions or goals. Only when one's effort to expand on them, is mingled with emotions born of frustration, deprivation, denial, or fear, does the possible negative connotation that is inherent become most evident.

Negatively the response has run the gamut; and the civil rights movement itself has become fragmented, with some of the major segments of it calling for isolation of other major segments. President Johnson, who had been responsible for more civil rights legislation than any president in history, panicked and in his panic saw fit to warn the Negro community of the most obvious fact, stating ominously "that the Negro community only comprised 10 percent of the nation's population." Harold Howe, U.S. Commissioner of Education, who had honestly set out to implement the law as it had been passed, became apologetic and suffered Congressional abuse, getting little assistance from the nation's resources — judicial, legislative, executive, or population-wise. Congress became recalcitrant; liberals became indistinguishable from the conservatives, consequently killing pending civil rights legislation for 1966 and "gutting" civil rights legislation already passed. Liberals literally quaked, conservatives became belligerent. And, perhaps most shattering of all, the church for the most part was ominously silent.

The Church Is Challenged Anew

Our thesis here is that the church once again is in the midst of a significant period of turmoil and unrest. And, if it responds to the need and meets the challenge as it has so courageously done in the past, it stands upon the threshold of its fincst hour.

When one views the historical church, it has always been at its best in crisis — particularly when that crisis has had at its center human dignity and freedom. But first the church must search its own soul, come to terms with itself, and realize to what extent it contributes to tensions and crises by ignoring or even denying human dignity through fear, intimidation, hostility, ignorance, or lack of commitment.

It is safe to say that a large number of those who make up the so-called white backlash, who retain and sustain segregated substandard education, who maintain rat-infested inner-city ghetto housing, who are now withholding assistance from the civil rights organizations, are church people.

The President of the United Church of Christ, addressing the Executive Council in Cincinnati, October 1966, said:

> I have one concern at the moment, and that is that many people within the church will use the militancy that has developed in the Negro community and the fragmenting of Negro leadership because of differences of opinion concerning this militancy, as an excuse to withdraw from the effort. . . . Civil rights is one of the areas where the church can continue to make its influence felt for justice, for righteousness, for compassion, and for reconciliation. Unless we are able to stand here, we will not be worthy of standing any place.

One could change President Herbster's last sentence and say that "unless the church is able to stand here, it will be unable to stand anywhere."

22. General Synod:

"Pronouncements"

([1959] 1969, 1971)

General Synod, John Esch

In 1957 the Uniting General Synod elected a twenty-four-member Executive Council (composed of twelve people from each of the uniting churches) to tend to the interim organizational details of the new denomination. During the two years when special commissions were at work drafting the UCC Statement of Faith and the UCC Constitution, the Executive Council formalized financial matters, encouraged ecumenical relationships, appointed a nominating committee, and dealt with practical issues.

One of its recommendations, approved by the 1959 General Synod, concerned the way in which all members of the United Church of Christ should understand "pronouncements" made by the General Synod or its instrumentalities. The recommendation emphasized that pronouncements speak only for the body that makes them, and as such, although they are morally binding, they are not legally binding on other parts of the church. This was difficult for people to understand. Debates over General Synod actions continued, and ten years later when people needed a reminder about the meaning of pronouncements, the 1969 General Synod reaffirmed its earlier 1959 "Statement on Pronouncements."

Some delegates, such as John H. Esch (1921–83), a prominent businessman and General Synod lay delegate from Zion United Church of

Sources: "Statement on Pronouncements adopted by the Second General Synod," *GS Minutes 1959,* 79, and *GS Minutes 1969,* 164. John H. Esch, Sheboygan, Wisconsin, Statement to General Synod, *GS Minutes 1971,* 208.

Christ in Sheboygan, Wisconsin, questioned the usefulness of pronouncements. In a statement to the 1971 General Synod Esch argued that the "church must speak out in a loud voice" to help individual Christians take action, but the United Church of Christ should not take actions on issues where church members are divided.

Statement on Pronouncements (1959)

When the Church or any of its Instrumentalities exercises a prophetic role in society, criticizing its complacency, judging its evils, and otherwise attempting to bear a Christian witness concerning issues on which opinions differ, no responsible group of Christians can hope to escape the penalty which the prophets and reformers have always incurred.

It can be hoped only that their Christian integrity will not be questioned just because the word they speak may be an unpopular one, and that they themselves are clear as to the nature and limits of the authority their utterances possess. To this end the Executive Council registers the following observations:

The General Synod, even though numerically and geographically the most widely representative body of the United Church, can claim authority and representative character for its utterances and enactments only in the measure of their inherent truth and fidelity to the Word of God.

A Church agency speaks only for itself, not for the whole fellowship, except as members of that fellowship concur or their assent is won by the weight of what is spoken.

An utterance of the General Synod or of any of its agencies binds no member of the United Church except as he is convinced and his commitment secured by what he accepts as the rightness of the utterance itself. This is axiomatic for the freedom of the Christian man.

The General Synod and its Instrumentalities, however, are composed of ministers and lay members whose devotion, interest and competence have been recognized in their selection by their fellow members to serve in such bodies; and their utterances and enactments therefore merit, even from those who disagree, respect and serious consideration.

Every agency is urged, in published announcements of its views, to make clear the authority on which its statement is based in a way to avoid any misunderstanding of other bodies in the matter.

Any agency which takes a position on an issue on which views diverge may serve to evoke creative exchange of thought and may, and frequently does, serve the Lord of the Church by stimulating the mind and pricking the conscience of the Church, its individual members, and of those outside the Church as well.

Because the Church agencies are composed of ministers and lay members chosen by their fellow members to serve where they do, we should thank God for the creative intelligence they exercise as followers of Christ in the discharge of their responsibilities, and judge their corporate word and deed as testimonies offered by them to us and the world in good faith.

We must remember always that many, if not most, of the Church's finest hours were when it stood for what the multitude denied or decried, and that the continuing symbol of the Church's faith and witness is a cross.

Statement to General Synod

I am deeply grateful to the Synod for the opportunity to speak. These remarks were prepared for the presentation on Friday.

When I was a boy I was intrigued by Aesop's fairy tale of the blind men and the elephant, and as a man I have tried to remember his lesson. You will recall that Aesop told of the blind men who sought to understand the appearance of an elephant. One, judging the elephant by his leg, assumed that an elephant must be something like a tree. Another determined from the trunk that an elephant was like a serpent. The third felt the elephant's side, and thought that an elephant must be like a wall. Each attempted to judge an elephant from where he stood, and in each case it was not possible to get a complete picture from that position.

There is a great temptation to direct the thrust of the Church in the direction that our personal opinions dictate in the various complex social, economic, and political issues of our day. It is easy to overlook the effect of our action on those who in good faith hold to contrary positions. As we face these issues during this General Synod, I would like to suggest that we stand back from our position of personal posture to try to get a larger perspective.

If there is anything that is obvious, it is that the lay membership of our denomination is diverse. We are urban, suburban, and rural; we are Democrats and Republicans. In economic philosophy we are liberals, conservatives, and all points in between. We are hawks and doves. We have a diversity of regionalism, race, and vocation. We have really only one thing in common and that is our Christian faith.

We have been schooled to understand that this common bond transcends all diversity, and that all these differences disappear when we gather into the Lord's House to worship. Within our Christian fellowship we have been taught to seek the Lord in our own way, and to respect the sincerity and integrity of others in our fellowship.

So long as this bond of faith is strong we have Christian communication throughout all of our diversity. It is little wonder that the great commission of our Lord is to teach and preach his gospel of love.

When General Synod or church officials take positions in the secular issues of the day — Vietnam, selective conscientious objection, free trade, Angela Davis, abortion — we separate ourselves from those who hold other positions in good faith. We fracture our solidarity with a different break on every issue. We speak here in General Synod as if we were God from the mountain top, proclaiming ourselves right and others within our fellowship to be wrong. Often we speak on subjects on which we are ill equipped to judge.

The result is that Christian men and women, like this speaker, holding opposing positions in good conscience feel separated. We sometimes feel that our gifts to God are being misappropriated to promote objectionable causes, and that somehow our Church has become a political party. Our loyalty is weakened. We are deprived of some of the joy of giving. The result is a double tragedy — a weakened Church and orphaned Christians.

You may rightfully ask if I am suggesting a Church that is not relevant, a return to the monastery, faith without good works. I do not think that this is the alternative.

I feel very strongly that the Church must speak out in a loud voice of concern for the problems of our day. We must confront each congregation and each church member with the triple challenge:

1. The obligation of the Christian to understand these complex problems as best he can;
2. The certain knowledge that no Christian can profess to be one and escape his obligation to seek a solution to these problems;
3. The responsibility for personal action, to seek to contribute to resolving the problem within his sphere of influence.

This means simply that the Church does not tell him how to think, but it demands that he does think on these things. The Church does not tell him what to do, but it tells him he must do something. The Church does not act for him at the top, but it demands that he act for himself at the crossroads of his life.

In summary, I would urge this General Synod to consider these suggestions:

1. Our strength is in our common faith.
2. Our threat comes from divisiveness.
3. Our obligation is to emphasize our unity, and to refrain from contributing to division.
4. Our hope for unity lies in avoiding "right or wrong" decisions on social issues on which Christians can have opposing viewpoints, in favor of a recommendation to all members that:
    a. Each issue be studied;
    b. Each Christian carefully seek a path of personal action;
    c. No Christian can deny his obligation to act.

The result will be

1. A Church with Christians sensitive to the needs of the world,
2. Resolved to do their share
3. And joined by a common bond:
    The love of God
    and membership in a whole Church—
    The United Church of Christ.

Reshaping Mission

23. Rethinking Mission:

"What Is the Mission of the Church . . . ?"

(1962)

Allen O. Miller

Allen O. Miller (1912–99) was an Evangelical and Reformed/UCC minister who was educated at Lafayette College, Yale Divinity School, and Yale University. He taught theology at Eden Theological Seminary for more than fifty years, beginning in 1946. Along with many members of the United Church of Christ Miller was clear that the ultimate reason for church union was mission. His 1962 article in the United Church Herald *acknowledges that many Christians harbor a "hidden arrogance" when they talk about a post-Christian world, as if at some earlier time the world had been Christian. He believed that "the proper name for the world into which [Christians were] being sent" was a "come of age" world. The "Light of the World" comes into this age to cast "in bold relief the truth about [humankind], and to cast judgment." He then asks, What is the mission of the church in this world come of age?*

Source: Allen O. Miller, an excerpt from "What Is the Mission of the Church in a World Come of Age?" *United Church Herald,* January 25, 1962, 22–23.

What Is the Mission of the Church?

. . . What is the mission of the church in the world come of age? There are actually two prior questions: (1) Whose mission and to whom? and (2) What or who is the church?

The church dare not lose sight of the truth about its existence, namely, that it has been gathered and is being sent by its Lord. A chosen people is nothing apart from the One who chooses them. The church's mission is God's mission. His love and righteousness are not only its central message but the motivating power and the ultimate goal of its existence. By God's love the church ministers and for God's righteous kingdom, coming to earth as it is in heaven, it spends itself.

Moreover, just as people are singled out to bear this mission, so people are the object and purpose of it. Some people are called out of the mess that all of us are in so that they may be renewed in their being and become the salvagers of the others — all the others.

Divine Ordination

The church is the community of those who "body-forth" the spirit of Christ in the world. Obviously, it is this understanding of the church that the Protestant Reformers attempted to recover in the sixteenth century and that is the foundation of the "Lay Life and Work" movement in the United Church of Christ. One is constrained, however, to insist upon some careful verbal clarifications. If, indeed, the people (laos) are the church, their churchmanship is Christian ministering. But who, then, are the clergy, the people we used to call ministers? Do we still have to distinguish between unordained and ordained ministers?

We suggest that the church can never make the lay movement a going concern until it invests the lay people with the reality of their Christian calling as divine ordination. Baptism and/or confirmation, when properly understood, constitute precisely this initiation into the people of God and ordination to a ministry to the world. Once this is clearly affirmed and seriously implemented, the distinctive role of the pastor of a congregation of ministers comes into focus.

The Epistle to the Ephesians spells it out in the phrase "called to equip the people of God for the work of the ministry," i.e., called to exhort and to instruct, to nurture and to discipline the fellowship of believers who minister to the world in which we all live. For this specialized ministry the church has rightly required special training and commitment and marked the office with a "second" ordination.

Four words identify the sweep of the church's ministry to the world: (1) Evangelical witness — the concern of those who have been witnesses to bear witness, to carry the good news of God's gracious acceptance and forgiveness to all the hungry and broken of mankind.

(2) Suffering service — the concern to implement the gift of the revolutionary spirit of redemptive love for persons in the social, economic and political structures of our life.

Witness and service, like the systole and the diastole of the heartbeat, define the church of Jesus Christ, committed to the full task of ministering to the world coming of age — both in breadth of inclusiveness and in depth of renewal.

(3) Responsible stewardship — the acknowledgment that the natural world, as well as mankind, belongs to God and that it is given to us for our use in the service of our common needs and to the glorification of his holy name. Economics (the literal translation of oikonomia, commonly translated stewardship), thus identified as our servant and not our master, becomes the basic instrument for carrying forward both the church's witness and its service.

(4) Church unity — again an acknowledgment that, since we all belong to the one and only Lord Jesus, we can do no other than accept his gift in openhanded and open-hearted gratitude. In a time when the church could be content to serve one nation, one race or one economic class and ignore all the others, it could also afford the luxury of specially designed and patented theologies and polities to fit some provincial segment of the world.

"The world come of age," however, has its own brands of provincial loyalty and partisan devotion, but they do not match up with the prefabricated designs of the churches. In the same period of reawakening that has sharpened the church's concern for the world, it has been forced to search its own soul to discover who it really is and whose it is, emerging from hiding behind the many masks of theological controversy and competing polities.

An insightful prophet, Dietrich Bonhoeffer, prescribed for the world come of age "Christianity without religion." True Christianity will abolish the distinction between the sacred and the secular, will break down the wall between the sanctuary and the world, will tear away the veil between the saved church and the lost world.

The Christian church has itself come of age, too late to become the religion of a world that by revolution is outgrowing religion, and needs to be helped to achieve a mature existence. The world's people need to be helped to help themselves and to help one another, not to be forced again into benevolent slavery no matter how charitable the tyrant may claim to be. The world's people need to be set free. The church must decrease that the world for which Christ died may increase.

Dynamic Remnant

It is imperative, in our time, that Christianity become utterly what its Lord is — a Christer, a suffering-servant. It may no longer be the spiritual imperialist who emasculates the world and is hated for it, nor the paternalistic dispenser of "cheap grace," to whom the world becomes beholden and who is despised for it. This dynamic remnant of Christian people will function as the incognito Samaritan, the Christ unawares, the minister of "costly grace." The reborn church of Jesus Christ will leave a man or a woman "a new being" with no more and no less than a sense of gratitude, which, not knowing whom to thank, he or she will find ways to express to others in the form in which it has come, i.e., by costly grace. Love, Christian love, comes "for free" but, because it changes us inside, our entire life becomes the price that is exacted in the service of love.

The churchmanship demanded in this hour is neither Roman Catholic nor Protestant, neither Jewish nor Greek, it is simply Christian. Bonhoeffer says:

> Men go to God when they are sore bestead,
> Pray to him for succor, for his peace, for bread,
> For mercy for them sick, sinning or dead:
> All men do so, Christian and unbelieving.
> Men go to God when he is sore bestead,
> Find him poor and scorned, without shelter or bread,
> Whelmed under weight of the wicked, the weak, the dead:
> Christians stand by God in his hour of grieving.
> God goeth to every man when sore bestead,
> Feedeth body and spirit with his bread,
> For Christians, heathens alike he hangeth dead:
> And both alike forgiving.

24. Biblical Interpretation:
"What Is the Scribal Mentality?"

(1966)

Willis E. Elliott

Willis E. Elliott (b. 1918), a Congregational Christian/UCC minister educated at Houghton College, Winona Lake School of Theology, Southern Baptist Theological Seminary, Northern Baptist Theological Seminary, and the Divinity School of the University of Chicago was on the evangelism staff of the United Church Board for Homeland Ministries (UCBHM) during the 1960s.

Early in 1966 Elliott attended a World Congress on Evangelism in Berlin, Germany, led by popular evangelist Billy Graham and sponsored by the conservative evangelical magazine Christianity Today. *Later in the year, Elliott pressed the planning committee for the Triennium of the National Council of Churches of Christ, U.S.A. in Miami Beach (December 6–7, 1966) to invite Graham to the meeting. The invitation was extended, but the committee insisted that Elliott and Graham engage in a formal exchange. In preparation for their encounter, Elliott prepared a paper entitled "Beyond the Old and the New Evangelism" and sent a copy to Graham. Elliott lauded Graham's evangelistic work, but he also articulated the discomfort many people had with Graham's version of "biblical evangelism."*

"What Is the Scribal Mentality?" is part of Elliott's speech at the Miami Beach meeting. Elliott, a biblical scholar, laments the contemporary polarization between the "verbalists" who ran the World Congress on

Source: Willis E. Elliott, an excerpt from a summary of "Beyond the Old and New Evangelism," a paper prepared for the NCC General Assembly, December 6, 1966. This excerpt is part of a typescript summary prepared for the *Living Theological Heritage* by the author and used with his permission.

Evangelism earlier that year and mainline "actionists" who tend to neglect scripture. Reflecting the United Church of Christ openness to the Spirit in its understanding and use of scripture, he warns of the dangers of "the scribal mentality."

What Is the Scribal Mentality?

1. The scribal party in any religion **takes the religion's sacred text(s) more seriously than the living context** within and beyond the community. The text is held, as it were, so close to the eyes that what is seen beyond its edges is of secondary import and must be shaped to conformity with the text.

Of course for us Christians, the classical instance of scribalism must ever be "the scribes" who, unable to force Jesus into conformity with their reading of Torah, were one factor leading to his Roman execution. In Jesus, God was doing a new thing — and the scribes could not, or would not, see it, their tunnel vision being on the text, their myopia keeping their eyes too close to it. (As an old professor of the Bible in its original languages, I cannot be accused of having my eyes too far from the text!)

Scribes, biblicists, bibliolaters study more to teach than to understand. Therefore, they have more interest in proof-texts than in contexts (literary, historical, contemporary).

2. Again, the scribe not only sees **all things through his book;** he also **intrudes his book into all things.** For example, the Congress statement's section on race condemns racism (called "racialism") "in the name of Scripture and of Jesus Christ," in that order; and "the biblical unity of the human race" makes an overclaim for the Bible; and no other factor than the Bible is credited, in the statement, with any part of the American public's rising sensitivity to racial injustice. One form of Bible-abuse is over-elevation of it, exploiting its content sometimes at the cost of deflecting its intent.

3. Again, the scribe **prefers yesterday**, is antiquity-oriented, distrusts the new. Jesus, "not like the scribes," gave priority to the new without prejudice against the old (Matthew 13:52). The Lord's Prayer is future-oriented and the scribes hated him.

4. The scribe's over-claim for his book is that it is **errorless.** For a few years after my teenage conversion, I tried to defend this stance, which is so useful in cultic competition and so comforting to those who yearn for certainty and move toward preachers who pander to this yearning. But

gradually I became aware I was fighting reality, and one by one surrendered the artful dodges I had used to "defend the Word of God." When I became a seminary teacher of biblical languages, in some students I was up against the elaborate chicanery and legerdemain I had come to see, in my former self, as intellectual dishonesty and moral turpitude. Myself freed from the prison of the perfect book, I was able to unlock the prison doors in others — an achievement for which I was "let go" more than once.

Our Lord spoke of gnats and camels. The Bible's errors are gnats, its truths are camels; but the scribal mentality, in its ideological infallibilism, makes camels out of gnats.

5. Again, the scribe **sees things the size he thinks his holybook sees them**, "straining out the gnat and swallowing the camel" (for which disproportion Jesus called them "blind guides" [Matthew 23:24]). Said Harold John Ockenga at the Berlin meeting, "the **Bible** is our authority. . . . We're here because we believe in the **Bible**." Derivative authority, yes. But the Lord Jesus Christ is the Christian's central and primary authority. We trust him for our identity and destiny, our continuity, our intersection-point of God/man/world. We trust him (not any book) for the power of resurrection life, of internal coherence, of service and witness.

Does the gap seem small? Not when we see how differently the old and new diagnose and prescribe for the here-and-now wounds of the heart and of the world, how differently they see and use the same book.

6. Again, the scribe's adulation for his book distorts his vision, his perspective, his sense of proportion, his judgment, and even seduces him into **using his book for non-seeing**: he sees not at all, or only dimly and small, what he thinks his holybook does not see. I say "he thinks," for the scribe is a double eisegete, reading into his book both what is not there and occlusions to what is there. The Bible does not exclude "the world," which however was absent from the Berlin gathering's booktables, which were loaded with how-to books about getting "the soul" to heaven — an otherworldliness that is biblical, but not to the exclusion of thisworldliness. The scribe, his book, and his church — all need to be sprung from the prison of his prejudicial non-seeing.

7. Again, the scribe **uses the silences of his book** as a sword against uncomfortable environing realities and a shield against disturbing environing responsibilities. *Argumentum e silento* falsely assumes that Scripture's silences are blanks to be filled in however the preacher chooses. The fact that it is a centuries-long discredited hermeneutic method does not deter the scribe. Two recent instances on the divide between the old and new evangelism:

> " . . . Jesus commanded us to go into all the world and preach the Gospel to every creature. He did not command us to go into the world and organize a peace corps or civil disobedience demonstrations. He did not resort to law or coercion as a means of improving society."
>
> —March 2, 1966, *Christianity Today*

> " . . . The commission of the Church is not to reform society but to preach the gospel."
>
> —from one of the plenum Bible studies at the Berlin meeting

In both instances the absence of a command to is converted into a command not to. Just before the Berlin meeting, I saw a set of Red Chinese "gospel" tracts in which Jesus' "silences" had been slyly filled in with quotations from Chairman Mao and Karl Marx. While those Communist pamphlets and the two scribal instances were equally violation of truth and literary canons, I consider the latter more dangerous to the Christian mission in the world.

Of course the scribe makes negative use of Scripture's silences only to oppose what on other than scriptural grounds he rejects. For what both Scripture and he reject, he can quote the Bible.

On the American frontier two centuries ago, the "Christian" movement produced the slogan, "Where the Bible speaks we speak, where the Bible is silent we are silent." That was biblicistic, but it did provide some protection from the form of Bible-abuse I am here exposing, viz., **not** being silent where the Bible is silent.

Chinese ignorant of the Gospels wouldn't know that Mao and Marx were being sneaked in. Biblical literacy — knowing the contents of the canon, the whole Bible — is one's only defense against the scribes' slipping their ideological negatives into Scripture's silences. At the Berlin meeting, scribe after scribe sounded good (right in what they were affirming) until I asked myself, when hearing a negative and knowing it was not biblical, "Where did *that* come from? Is it only unbiblical, or antibiblical?"

8. Again, closely allied to the unscrupulous **insertion** of the scribe's spins where the Bible does not speak is his **omission** of attention to passages disturbing to his mentality. In the Berlin meeting, after each speech I asked myself "What did he leave out, and why?" Of course every believer is selective in the sense of having a canon (scriptures frequently used) smaller than **the** canon (i.e., the whole Bible). But the scribe is **structurally selective**, imposing his thought-system on the Bible, whose materials are highly unstructured. Not content to let the Spirit speak through Scripture's profusion, the scribe quarries it to build his foundation,

fells its timber to build his house, and transplants into his orderly garden its flora. . . .

The New Reading Fits the New Age

There is a way of salvation from the scribe's contorted and procrustean "way of salvation" abuse of the Bible. It is this: one can surrender the scribal longing for a tidy and comprehensive system and the scribal fascination with "harmonizing" the biblical data into a single structure and system. The "hard" physical sciences and the "soft" human sciences have humbly surrendered their lust for tidy, comprehensive paradigms; the computer is rapidly diminishing pride in our brain-power; and the electronic environment is transforming us all into impressionists.

The good news for Bible-reading is that the Bible, with its jungle manifolds of meaning, its rich and unsystematizable imagery, its pulsating, untidy, and unfinished life, fits into the form of consciousness now emerging. Our children's apperceptive patterns are closer to the Bible than are ours, and their children's will be closer still. This is not a question of biblical **head**-knowledge, which has been declining; some of the scribes who tried to trap Jesus were superior to him in that. Rather, it is a question of **heart**-openness to a fresh understanding of the Word through the psyche of the new age, in contrast to the "soul" of the old and the scribal mentality burdened with the need for reeducation.

Whole new vistas of preaching and teaching the Bible are opening up to us if our eyes do not remain scribally blinded against binocular seeing of the Bible as it really is and of these vistas as gifts of the Spirit. God wants now to free his Word from scribal slavery to structure and system.

25. Mission in Action: *"Demonstrations"*

(1964)

Andrew J. Young

Andrew J. Young (b. 1932) is an African American Congregational Christian/UCC minister who was educated at Howard University and Hartford Theological Seminary. After his ordination he served Congregational Christian churches in Georgia until he went to work for the Youth Division of the National Council of Churches of Christ (1957–61). In 1961 Young joined the staff of the Southern Christian Leadership Conference (SCLC) and became a key associate of Martin Luther King Jr. He was increasingly convinced that nonviolent demonstrations are a powerful "twentieth century Christian witness." Later in his career he served as a member of the U.S. House of Representatives from Georgia (1973–77), U.S. ambassador to the United Nations (1977–79), mayor of the city of Atlanta (1982–90), and co-chair of the 1996 Olympic Games.

Demonstrations: A Twentieth-Century Christian Witness

Whenever a man realizes that he is a child of God some sort of demonstration is inevitable. Conditions in this world are such that in the moment of realized sonship, man must act. This is what is happening across the globe at present: men are becoming aware of their innate worth and dignity and

Source: Andrew J. Young, an excerpt from "Demonstrations: A Twentieth-Century Christian Witness," *Social Action* (May 1964): 5, 10–12.

are demanding that they be accorded the same respect accorded the persons of highest earthly stature. What we are witnessing is a moment of mass self-discovery.

Thousands of heretofore bland creatures of the earth are suddenly repeating en masse the proclamation of Martin Luther, "Here I stand." Willingly they submit to violence and intimidation rather than retreat into the cloisters of inferior status. A civil reformation is in process, and young secular saints are shaking the political foundations of our society much in the same way that George Fox, John Wesley, or John Calvin shook Christendom during the Protestant Reformation. . . .

"Soul Force"

The success of the Montgomery Protest taught Negroes the power which is resident in the human soul. They were introduced to "soul force." They learned that jail could be a place of Christian refuge, for when a man is jailed for doing what is right his body in jail is a powerful witness against the evil which placed him there.

Having learned of the power of the human soul, students began aggressively to challenge the inconsistencies in our democracy. These challenges brought forth all of the subterranean hatred which is present in the slave system, and America began to exorcise the demons of prejudice. As Martin Luther King Jr. says, "segregation is like a sore, and it must be opened to the light that it may be purged of impurities and thereby healed." This is the second stage of demonstrations.

God Is at Work

The suffering of innocent students, Christians, willingly volunteering themselves as living sacrifices was as powerful a witness in America as was Stephen's martyrdom to Paul, for the men and women of good will began to rally and, for the first time in many years, America began the search for national salvation. The separation of her citizens evidenced her separation from God, and the sickness of her soul spewed forth the world over, via Telstar. This was perhaps the most powerful Christian witness ever made — in magnitude if not in depth. God is certainly at work in this crisis leading men out of their own hatred.

The fruits of this witness seem forthcoming, for once faced with the problem in such an inescapable way the Congress of the United States began to draft legislation which might provide for the healing of the body politic. Social science has indicated that behavior changes soon result in attitudinal changes, so our government began the amendment of our codes to regulate inhuman behavior against fellow human beings.

A New Mode of Evangelism

This should be recognized as a new mode of evangelism. We began to see the relationship when so many people, young and old, found new faith and meaning in jail with their pastors. Certainly such public attempts to "break down the dividing wall of hostility" must be celebrated as the work of Christ in the world.

Sin in high places is definitely the problem of the church in an essentially urban culture. The difficulties of our society are so pressing that normal patterns of reform are ineffective. Negroes faced with the threat of automation are not apt to be patient with inadequate education which is not preparing them for an automated society; and so, demonstrations will become more and more dramatic. They will take diverse forms, but in each there will be a cry against injustice. The demonstrations themselves will not always be as neat and dignified as college students reading Shakespeare at lunch counters, but the message will be the same, "Things are not right."

Confronted, Will We Hear the Message?

Rome, at the height of her moment of greatness, found herself challenged by inequities within her midst. Christians then demonstrated at the stakes of the Colosseum, singing hymns as they burned, but Rome could not hear their message. Now America is confronted with many of the same problems with the added advantage of having them dressed in black and demonstrated aggressively by millions. The evils against which they demonstrate are not their problems. These are America's problems. Schools would be a problem for twentieth-century America even if no Negroes existed, and so would jobs. Regional concentrations of political power, whether they resulted from racial discrimination or changing rural-urban population ratios would make government ineffective in times like these. The Ku Klux Klan is not a result of race hatred, but of the fact that Amcrica has never shared her vision of democracy with the poor and insecure working classes; nor has the church witnessed to the fact that all are one in Christ Jesus.

We should thank God daily for demonstrations, and we should encourage, plan, and participate in them whenever possible. They may very well be the witness through which God reveals the course of history.

26. Beyond Rivalries:

"Do We Really Mean One Mission?"

(1960)

Truman B. Douglass

As the merged mission boards of the United Church of Christ took shape in the 1960s many people were hopeful that the future mission work of Christians around the world could express the unity of the Gospel more effectively. Truman B. Douglass (1901–69), an executive for Congregational Christian and later United Church of Christ mission boards, challenged the churches to leave behind their petty rivalries and take the unity of mission seriously. Douglass was a Congregational Christian/UCC minister who graduated from Union Theological Seminary in New York. After serving churches in New Jersey, California, and St. Louis (1926–43), he became the executive vice president of the Congregational Christian Board for Home Missions (BHM) and its successor United Church Board for Homeland Ministries (UCBHM) (1943–68). He was also involved in the earliest conversations between Congregational Christian and Evangelical and Reformed church leaders in St. Louis. His commitment to mission was personal and his leadership institutionally important during the formative years of the United Church of Christ (see vols. 6:73 and 7:20).

Source: Truman B. Douglass, "Do We Really Mean One Mission?" *United Church Herald* (December 24, 1960), 11, 30.

Do We Really Mean One Mission?

. . . I recall a remark by Margaret Mead, the anthropologist. "Today," she said, "in order to understand a teen-ager it isn't enough merely to have been one." That is true. It requires an act of will, an act of creative imagination.

This is true also of the Christian mission. Many acts of disciplined and informed thought and creative imagination are required if we are to understand the character and dimensions of the church's mission in our time.

. . .

[Today] It is in a setting of such complexity and in the midst of forces of such tremendous dynamism that Christians are to find their task and carry forward their mission.

That mission, despite the great variety of forms and ministries in which it is expressed, despite many frontiers — tangled, moving, interlacing — where the missioners do their work, is one mission.

It is one mission because it has its source in one God, who is the Creator of the world and of man, who has made man in his image and who redeems man by continually reminding him of this divinely given image and calling him to fulfill the whole meaning of his own selfhood.

It is one mission because it is carried on in the name of the one Christ. We think of him in different ways and try to express our thought of him in diverse creedal forms. But in all this diversity there is a large element of common affirmation: that in Christ we have seen the character and purpose of God in terms of an actual man dealing with the hard stuff and the agonizing perplexities and pains of this actual world. In Christ's compassion, obedience, self-abandonment, victory over evil and the life-denying forces of existence, we have seen not only what God is but also what man is intended to be. And what Christ has shown us by his teaching, life, death and victory is gospel — good news — for all people and it is to be made known everywhere in the world.

There is one mission because there is one community of Christians — one People of God — one church. This is a difficult thing to say in a time when there are these multitudinous churches, many of them claiming to have the whole truth and implying by their claim that the others do not have it.

27. Evangelism:

"A Statement of Commitment"

(1972)

Deering Conference on Faith and Its Corporate Expression

During the 1960s the United Church of Christ and many mainline Protestant denominations sought to balance the responsibility of Christians to act in society with the expectation that Christians are called to evangelize the world. The United Church of Christ insisted that action and proclamation were united as "word in *deed—speaking in the midst of doing," rather than as word* and *deed. The "Deering, New Hampshire Conference on Faith and Its Corporate Expression" produced a statement by participants that became the basis for a grassroots evangelism movement later carried forward by the United Church Board for Homeland Ministries (UCBHM). The statement helped UCC leaders and members see new ways of "marrying word and deed."*

Source: The Deering 1972 Conference on Faith and Its Corporate Expression, "A Statement of Commitment," in *Evangelism for a New Day* (February 1976), newsletter published by the United Church Board for Homeland Ministries.

A Statement of Commitment

The Deering Conference on Faith and Its Expression calls the United Church of Christ to a joyful sharing of the Christian Story in the decade of the '70s. We believe the time has come to fling our faith in the air in ways that are true to our style and history.

At the heart of that heritage there is a drama of what God has done, is doing and will do. The chief Actor "calls the worlds into being, creates man in his own image, and sets before him the ways of life and death." From the beginning, the creature with the human face falters, and curves inward away from Maker and neighbor. The pull of conscience, the laws of nature, and the lessons of history do not turn around. A patient God calls a people, Israel, to share his dream of shalom, a vision of peace and freedom among God, humankind, and nature. In the exodus from Egypt he enacts liberation, and in the pointing of prophets he beckons toward reconciliation. We continue as killers of the dream.

"In Jesus Christ the man of Nazareth, our crucified and risen Lord, he has come to us and shared our common lot." In him, hope happens and shalom comes to be. The powers of evil meet their match, mercy covers our guilt and the future is opened. A new people is born to celebrate the deeds of God and to participate in the Spirit's ever-fresh stirrings of liberation and reconciliation. That Body is turned toward the future looking for the new things God will do, and the time when his full Kingdom will be. "Blessing and honor, glory and power be unto him!"

Evangelism is the sharing of this tale of hope. For the United Church it is a special kind of sharing. As the Word became flesh and dwelt among us, so an authentic human word about God must be embodied. More than word and deed, true Storytelling is word in deed, speaking in the midst of doing. We testify to salvation not in tent or temple but on the road in our own journeys toward freedom, justice and peace. We believe in action evangelism and seek to explore new ways and models of marrying word and deed.

To share the dream and saga of God is to call for commitment and to expect the birth of new things. The Word that goes forth does not return barren. When healthy seeds are planted in good ground, we look for these green shoots in the soil of the '70s:

- New Persons who know *shalom* in their deepest being, people who have been turned around, who have seen visions and made decisions.
- New behavior from the people of God that fearlessly confronts the systems of injustice, empowers the powerless, and ministers to the victims on today's Jericho roads.
- New strength and growth for the church. As the Spirit added daily to the early church, we look and work for that increase that God can give. In that time, and now too, the Host invites to the table "people of all ages, tongues and races." And we view the strengthening of the Body as growth of new communities around centers of need and vitality, as well as the infusion of new life in our congregations.
- New joy in the Lord of the church and the world that celebrates the things he has done, is doing and will do.

Paul declares, "I live . . . yet not I, but Christ . . . lives in me" (Gal. 2:20). So too, we believe that we are not our own. Our words and deeds are by his grace and power. We discern his Spirit working in our time and seek to be his agents of reconciliation and instruments of liberation. We pray for his coming in our midst, so that the old may dream new dreams and the young may see new visions.

28. Word-in-Deed Evangelism:

"Evangelism and Social Action: Either/Or?"

(1974)

Gabriel Fackre

Gabriel Fackre (b. 1926) is an Evangelical and Reformed/UCC minister educated at Bucknell University and the University of Chicago Divinity School. After serving churches in Illinois and Pennsylvania (1949–60) he was called to the faculty at Lancaster Theological Seminary (1961–70) and Andover Newton Theological School (1971–96). While teaching he served as a consultant to the United Church Board for Homeland Ministries (UCBHM) on evangelism.

Fackre is the author of numerous books on theological topics, including The Christian Story *(1978–), a series of volumes on basic systematic theology. He represented the United Church of Christ in the Lutheran-Reformed dialogue leading to the 1997 "Formula of Agreement" (see vol. 7:110), and he also served as a member of the UCC Theological Panel on Jewish-Christian Relations that produced the "Message to the Churches" (see vol. 7:108). His 1974 article "Evangelism and Social Action: Either/Or?" builds upon the idea of "word-in-deed" evangelism developed in the Deering "Statement of Commitment" (1972) (see vol. 7:27).*

Source: Gabriel Fackre, "Evangelism and Social Action: Either/Or?" *Evangelism/Social Action* (1974): 6–14.

Evangelism and Social Action: Either/Or?

The title "Evangelist" appears after the names of a number of entries in the archives of New England Congregationalism. The biography of one records his commissioning to found three churches "in the interior counties." Another is credited with "abolishing atheism in southern Iowa." Another is described as instrumental in the conversion of a large number of the inhabitants on one of the Sandwich Islands.

The histories of these evangelists mention some other interesting facts: one started the first abolition society in his territory; one was what we would call a "community organizer" on the most agitated social issue in his location — temperance; one was a leader in the struggle against the exploitation of Polynesians by the sandalwood traders of the mid-Pacific.

This wedding of evangelism and social action sounds like an anachronism because the divorce of the two has become commonplace in much contemporary church life. So much so that the great-grandchildren of these Congregational pioneers, and the heirs of a Wesleyan tradition that also married word and deed in the mines and factories, have to be reminded of the faith of their fathers and mothers. The assumption of separation is now so deep-rooted that the best-known evangelist of our time, Billy Graham, can sever the tie with one swift stroke: "I am a New Testament evangelist, not an Old Testament prophet."

What are the grounds for the historic union of evangelism and social action, and what is the nature of this bond? The alliance is based on kindred purposes and a common biblical root. Let us examine each.

Evangelism is the joy and task of sharing the tale of the deeds of God. It is telling the story of what God did, is doing, and will do to fulfill the vision of a world reconciled, *shalom.* At its center is the evangel, the Good News that the powers of sin and evil have been overcome in the life, death, and resurrection of Jesus Christ. Evangelism is the communication of this *kerygma* to those who haven't heard it — therefore, getting the story *out.*

Evangelism, however, is a special kind of storytelling, one that connects the biography of God with our own autobiography. The saga of God does not let us alone. It upsets, exhilarates, and calls for decision and commitment. It wheels us about from one direction to another, a turn (*epistrophe, metanoia*) we describe as conversion.[1] Evangelism, therefore, is getting the story out that turns people around.

1. For a detailed study of the meaning of conversion see Gabriel Fackre, "Conversion," *Andover Newton Quarterly* 14, no. 3 (January 1974).

Christian social action takes its stance from the story. Its fundamental reference point is the ultimate vision of *shalom* toward which the narrative thrusts, that realm of God in which swords are beaten into plowshares, wolf and lamb lie down together, the lame walk, the blind see, the naked are clothed, the hungry are fed, the prisoner is liberated, justice is done, and peace is made. Social action is one expression of *diakonia,* servanthood, the human deed that witnesses to the divine deed, that Kingdom in which all tears shall be wiped away, and there shall be the liberation and reconciliation of all things. It is that form of *diakonia* that deals with "the principalities and powers," the systematic, structural forces that seek to kill the dream. Social action is the struggle to bring social power to bear on social issues and institutions in the light of the vision of *shalom.*[2]

Action Evangelism

Why have New Testament evangelists engaged in the business of Old Testament prophets? The answer is found in the story the evangelist has to tell. It is the saga of the acts of God moving toward a world liberated and reconciled. How can such a tale be told without pointing to that kingdom? "The end pre-exists in the means," said Emerson. Most of all is this true for Christian storytellers. The great end toward which the story moves, one which has entered our history in Jesus Christ, must be manifest in the witness of the evangelist. A deed of *shalom* is integral to a word about *shalom.* The *medium* of acts of liberation and reconciliation testifies to the *message* of liberation and reconciliation.

How clearly this can be seen in the evangelism of the first evangelists! The chronicle of their work is not called the *Talks* of the Disciples but the *Acts* of the Apostles. From the first evangelism sortie after the birth of the church (Acts 3:1–10) to the close of the books of Acts, the first apostles of the Good News demonstrated their message in deeds of healing as well as words of hope. And this acts evangelism, action evangelism, was viewed by them as a divine accreditation of their mission as well as an imperative for it. The signs and wonders of shalom in which bodies as well as souls were liberated from the powers of evil were seen to be confirmation by the Holy Spirit of the world they preached.

In the long history of evangelism and mission the Holy Spirit has empowered evangelist successors to Peter and Paul, Priscilla and Tabitha, to both do *and* tell the Good News, to so unite word with deed that the

2. Themes developed in three essays in *Social Action* 36, no. 4 (December 1969).

witness becomes a word-in-deed.[3] *How* they manifest this empowerment to heal bodies as well as souls varied according to the gifts and challenges of time and place. That they were called to do so was never in question. On some occasions storytellers bound word to deed after the fashion of William Booth's social service/evangelism. On other occasions doing and telling became partners in the social action/evangelism of Toyohiko Kagawa. Throughout, the great redemption in which bodies as well as souls, society as well as selves, were liberated and reconciled, was attested to by the word-in-deed witness of Acts evangelists.

Of "Principalities and Powers"

In the Acts charter of evangelism faithful witness to the Gospel takes the evangelist regularly into the arena of the "principalities and powers." Thus Peter and John encountered the power structure, a political-military-ecclesiastical complex, which, taking offense at both their words and deeds, jailed them. How often in the history of evangelism has this same scenario been acted out. Thus in the annals of the German Reformed Church in America appears this record of an evangelistic effort among native Americans by a group from Bethlehem, Pennsylvania: "In proportion to the success of the mission among the Indians grew almost a wicked prejudice against it, and opposition to it, among the white settlers of the province. . . . The loss the whites sustained in not having the Indians under their control, as formerly when they were accustomed to taking unlawful liberties and advantages of them, by defrauding them of their just due for labor, by imposing liquor upon them . . . was considered by them a serious loss. . . . In ascribing the cause of the change in life and morals of the Indians to the missionaries, they sought by every stratagem to get rid of them. . . . All kinds of false charges were brought against the missionaries. They were accused of being enemies of the government; as being secret papists and traitors; as being in alliance with the French in Canada to furnish arms and ammunition to fight the English. In December, 1744, they were brought before the magistrate for examination; and still later, they were cited to appear before the governor himself . . . at length such oppressive

3. A formulation of the meaning of "Word-in-deed" evangelism is found in "A Statement of Commitment" worked out by a group of clergy and lay evangelists in 1972. It appears in *Evangelism for a New Day,* edited by Frances Eastman and Theodore Erickson (New York: United Church Board for Homeland Ministries, 1972), 28–29. It is the premise underlying the *Evangelism Training Manual,* a six-session training program for lay evangelists in a local congregation (New York: United Church Board for Homeland Ministries, 1974), mimeograph, developed by grassroot evangelism leadership in the United Church of Christ. When the word "evangelist" is used in this article it has reference basically to this kind of people's evangelism activity, clergy and lay, rather than to the professional evangelists.

laws were passed in reference to them, and such restrictions laid upon them, that they could no longer care for their missionary work. In the beginning of the year 1745, they were compelled reluctantly to leave the converted Indians to themselves; and Mr. Rauch and his companions, not without receiving insults from the mobs on the route, found their way back to Bethlehem."[4]

The apostles' expectation of the imminent closure of history precluded the careful strategizing and organizing we associate today with social action. Our engagement with power structures is executed in a different frame of reference, one that must dissociate the calendar error of the evangelists' apocalypticism from the perennial relevance of their eschatology. The continuing impact of the vision of the coming *shalom* means that we in our time are called and empowered by the Holy Spirit to do deeds of *shalom* with the resources and perceptions God gives us in this context. These resources and perceptions press us into the same arena of the principalities and powers to call them to accountability before the lordship of Christ and the judgment of his kingdom. One of the most powerful contemporary currents of this kind of eschatological evangelism that calls powers and principalities, as well as persons, to repentance is found in Third World mission theory and practice. In Latin America, for example, it can be seen on a spectrum that runs from the Protestant Orlando Costas to the Roman Catholic Gustavo Gutiérrez.[5]

Does Christian social action reach toward evangelism in the same way that witness in word fulfills itself in company with deed? The Acts paradigm would certainly suggest it. The proclamation of the story comes on the heels of an act of *shalom* (Acts 3:11–26), and in the midst of the court confrontation with the powers that be (Acts 4:5–12). Why should Christian mission press us beyond a Wordless deed as much as beyond a deedless word? There are two reasons:

The first has to do with the grounds for Christian social actions: witness to the vision of *shalom* is at the center of the story told by the evangelist. Social action gets its mandate from the kingdom of God, and, by the power of that future working in our world, sets up signs and pointers to the liberation-and-reconciliation-to-be. As testimony to this fulfillment, seen in its first fruits, Jesus Christ, the Christian activist is constrained to say *why* these deeds are done. At the very least, those engaged in social action should be "ready to give reasons for the hope that is in them." And

4. Henry Harbaugh, *The Fathers of the German Reformed Church in Europe and America,* vol. 1 (Lancaster: Sprenger & Westhaeffer, 1857), 383–84.

5. See Orlando E. Costas, *The Church and Its Mission: A Shattering Critique from the Third World* (Wheaton, Ill.: Tyndale House, 1974), and Gustavo Gutiérrez, *A Theology of Liberation,* trans. and ed. Sister Caridad Inda and John Eagleson (Maryknoll, N.Y.: Orbis Books, 1973).

when they become agents of the Spirit's miracle of humanization, today's activists, as Peter and John, are called to interpret the social act, and thus tell the story.

The second reason bears upon the fulfillment of the intentions of social action itself. A few years ago, Joseph Hromadka, the Czech theologian, reported a new interest by Marxists in the Christian faith. The Marxists told him that socialism had solved to their satisfaction the problems of systematic injustice. However, they found that the human beings in the new society appear to be so subject to corruptions and apathies that the system itself was being endangered. So, they expressed curiosity about how the Christian community changed *persons,* and asked Hromadka to lecture to them at the University of Prague on the subject of prayer.[6]

Structural Change Not a Guarantee

Structural change does not of itself guarantee a new society. The tiny tower of the human spirit is rooted in, but rises above the social, economic, and political systems with which change agents deal.[7] The impulses emanating from that spirit can either subvert or enhance the changes effected by social action. They can also empower or erode the drive of social action. Therefore, a form of mission that addresses itself to those spiritual heights (and depths) should be seen by the action agent as an important ally in the task of social action. An evangelism that changes persons is companion to a social action that changes structures.

The opening to evangelism in the mainstream churches in the 1970s is related to a growing realization of these two factors. Denominations that have plunged into socially oriented mission in the 1960s experienced resistance to this thrust by many in their constituencies. Some of this resistance sprang from a demonic racism and war-mongering and had to be faced down. Some of it, however, rose from ignorance of the Word that spawned the social deed. And some of it was the result of an uneasiness that the Word itself had been censored from mission by overzealous activists interested only in the deed. As a consequence, there emerged a concern for a more full-orbed mission that blended faith and action, word and deed.[8]

---

6. Described by Donald Miller in Allen Miller, ed., *Reconciliation in Today's World* (Grand Rapids, Mich.: Wm. B. Eerdmans, 1969), 28.

7. The tower figure is Reinhold Niebuhr's. See his *Nature and Destiny of Man,* vol. 1 (New York: Charles Scribner's Sons, 1945), 17, 157 and *passim.*

8. Attempts to put word and deed together are to be found in the *Evangelism Training Manual* mentioned previously, the *New Life Mission Manual* produced by the Board of Discipleship, United Methodist Church (Nashville: Tidings, 1974), and *Resources for Developing an Evangelistic Life Style* from the American Baptist Churches (Valley Forge, Pa.: Judson, 1972).

To this response to the church's silent majority was added a developing awareness by social action protagonists of the insights noted by Hromadka. Basic social change in our society requires changed persons as well as changed structures. (The perversion of this new sensibility also occurred in the wholesale retreat into neomysticism and neopietism by a significant number of 1960s activists.) Out of the convergence of this consciousness-raising with regard to the personal dimension and a rediscovery of the interpretive word, there grew a variety of endeavors to bring together evangelism and social action.

Singularity and Unity

The partnership in the process of formation cannot violate the integrity of each commitment. Paul viewed the church as a body with many parts (1 Cor. 12, Eph. 4, Rom. 12). Now, as then, some have the spirit's gift of evangelism, some are healers, some prophets. This is the grain of truth in the Graham bifurcation noted above. There is a unique function of telling the story that turns people around. And there are people who have a talent and call to exercise this gift. There is a special function of encountering prophetically the powers, and doing deeds of mercy and justice. And there are people who have a talent and mandate for this social action. Some are tellers and some are doers.

But if we are faithful to the holistic vision of Acts then we must affirm that neither of these functions can be fulfilled unless it is joined by the other. The deed must buttress the word of the evangelist for the story to go forth with power. And the word must support the deed of the social actor for the story to be done in its completeness. Indeed, the special gift of the teller will be in the foreground in evangelism, and the unique talent of the doer up front in social action. But the environment for each is constituted by the witness of the other.

The maturation of each ministry entails the growth of the evangelist toward the capacity to do as well as tell, and the activist toward the ability to speak the word as well as enact it. This is the message of 1 Corinthians 13, which calls the gifts described in the twelfth chapter beyond their particularity into love interrelationships with, and learning from, the other parts of the body of Christ. The goal of such interpenetration is the kind of evangelist and activist described in Acts, they bring healing, prophecy, proclamation, and the call to commitment together.

Most of us have a good deal of growing to do. We are still children who see the goal of full stature in Christ (Eph. 4:13), the call to a full mission, but find it all we can do to exercise the gift we do have. Growth from our infant witness means, in its earliest stages, first steps toward the other members of the body. The simplest one is the decision to honor the differing gift of another: the evangelist who affirms the presence and role of the activist, the activist who accepts the importance and gift of the evangelist.

"You do your thing. I'll do mine," is not venturing far out, but it is a movement beyond an old polarization in which one denied the significance of the other, and sought to exterminate the other. Beyond this minimal act of mutual accreditation there is the reaching out for partnership in mission. Thus an evangelism task force and a social action commission in a congregation, or state conference, or national church, join together to plan for ways in which each can undergird the work of the other. The achievement of a giant step in growth would be the mutual fructification that equips each with the gifts of both so that evangelism and social action are carried out according to the acts rhythm of the apostles.

The holism of the first apostles is grounded, finally, not only in their Gospel but also in their Lord. Action evangelism and evangelical action take their pattern from the incarnate Word, Jesus Christ. Here is the deed of God that is one with the word of God. Word-in-deed mission has its source in the word made flesh. The Incarnation itself is manifest in the career of Jesus in which acts of healing, encounter with the powers and principalities, proclamation of the Good News, and call to decision are fused together. Thus in the central chapter of the Christian story, the enfleshment of God in Jesus Christ, and its expression in the saga of that Nazarene, is laid the groundwork for that gestalt of mission lived out by the apostles in their time, and sought by us in ours.

PART III

Keeping the Church Strong

The United Church of Christ began as a unique blend of ecclesial traditions and assumptions, rooted in the proclamation of the good news of Jesus Christ expressed in word and sacrament. To be sure, it trembled in the face of racial injustice in the 1960s. Yet, it sought to be the church, continuing its day-to-day life of worship and witness. Members of congregations gathered for prayer and sermon and song, laity and clergy engaged in debate over how to sustain congregational vitality, leaders developed a theology to affirm authorized ministry and wider church oversight. As a servant people, the church worked to pass its faith on to the next generation.

Christians worship. And they pray. This is self-evident, and yet as the activist agenda of the United Church of Christ expanded in the 1960s, there were times when the church was tempted to ignore the centrality of worship in its common life. Although the Basis of Union affirmed the importance of public worship, and the Statement of Faith reminded church members that Christians are called "to share in Christ's baptism and eat at his table," these crucial elements did not always receive enough attention.

Early Congregationalists had a profound concern for preaching, for baptism, and for faithful participation in the Lord's Supper. But by the middle of the nineteenth century, Congregationalism developed an individuality and a privatism that sometimes ignored theological reasons for communal worship. Similarly, the frontier Christian movement, originally committed to democratize church life and simplify liturgy, showed signs of declining vitality in worship.

Within the Evangelical and Reformed Church, German, Swiss, and Hungarian ethnicity and piety sometimes cultivated an unhealthy individualism. Yet, the church-centered worship traditions present in the Palatinate Liturgy, the Heidelberg Catechism, alongside a progressive Lutheran heritage, kept its focus on word and sacrament. The Mercersburg movement, although a minority voice in the revivalistic climate of the mid-nineteenth century, prevented the Evangelical and Reformed Church from ignoring the importance of the sacraments.

Enabling Worship

In 1961, the new Constitution of the United Church of Christ set up a Commission on Worship "to pursue a scholarly study of worship and give leadership to the United Church of Christ ministers and church in the conduct of worship, corporate and personal, . . . " by drawing upon the "treasures of the historic and universal church." The Commission on Worship was deeply influenced by the wider ecumenical liturgical renewal movement. It argued that weekly services of "Word and Sacrament" ought to be "uniformly observed" in all Christian churches and prepared a model "Lord's Day Service" (1966) for the United Church of Christ (see vol. 7:29).

Local response to the "Lord's Day Service" was mixed. Many pastors and laity in congregations within Evangelical and Reformed traditions welcomed it as a new, ecumenically based resource. Others, mostly within the Congregational and Christian traditions, resisted the idea that sermon and sacrament belonged together in weekly congregational worship. They argued that such a practice diminished the importance of preaching, and that focusing on the "table" sacrament relegated baptism to a secondary status. The UCC Commission on Worship was caught between an emerging ecumenical consensus about the unity of word and sacrament, and longstanding "free church" resistance to formal liturgical practices. By the mid-1970s the UCC had produced a loose-leaf set of worship resources known as *Services of the Church* (1969) and a new denominational hymnal — *The Hymnal of the United Church of Christ* (1974). Experimentation and innovation using banners, brightly colored vestments, modern music, and dance also enriched UCC worship in many places (see vol. 7:30).

Concern to strengthen congregational worship came not only from the ecumenical liturgical movement, but also from a widening understanding of social justice within the United Church of Christ. In 1977, the General Synod asked the Office for Church Life and Leadership (OCLL)"to develop, if feasible, a book of worship for the United Church of Christ using inclusive language."

This was ironic. Suddenly the social justice agenda, which had sometimes led members of the United Church of Christ to ignore or diminish the importance of worship, became a driving force for creative liturgical work. With the rise of the women's movement the nature and significance of language in Christian worship emerged as a central principle in UCC liturgical and theological efforts (see vol. 7:31).

Furthermore, thinking about the sacraments began to change. Instead of debates about "What is a sacrament?" Or "Who or how Christians should baptize or partake of bread and cup?" Christians began to ask, "Why sacraments?" Within the United Church of Christ there was a new awareness of how Christian vocation, community, and authentic discipleship are nurtured by the sacraments (see vol. 7:32).

Preaching remained central in the United Church of Christ, calling Christians to faith, freedom, justice, and equity. When it was strong, it spoke about gift as well as command. The most faithful preaching in the United Church of Christ dug deeply into scripture and invited the faithful to listen to the biblical story. "In the Bible, obedience takes the form of listening," and the preacher must operate among those who both "yearn to listen" and "dread to listen" (see vol. 7:33).

The *UCC Book of Worship* (BOW) (1986), released after several years of testing, was a solid piece of liturgical and theological work. It drew resources from biblical material, ecumenical history, and the unique traditions of the United Church of Christ. It gave careful attention to the contemporary context of worship and struck a balance between ordained and lay leadership, leaving room for variety and innovation. It encouraged the use of music and the arts and followed the "Common Lectionary." Although the *UCC Book of Worship* closes its introduction with humble words suggesting that "like all books of worship" it is "transitional literature," it embodied some carefully developed and strongly held principles (see vol. 7:34).

The book had its critics, but over the years BOW has become widely used and appreciated by pastors and congregations within and outside the United Church of Christ (see vol. 7:35).

As the *UCC Book of Worship* became a highly respected liturgical resource, plans developed to publish a hymnal filled with fresh hymnody, inclusive language texts, and materials for and from the growing ethnic communities of the church. The selection of music, words, and worship materials for *The New Century Hymnal* (TNCH) (1995) was very controversial. Although the guidelines used in the preparation of the hymnal call the church to "sing" its faith, not "debate it," theological debates generated by the *UCC Book of Worship* and *The New Century Hymnal* were both passionate and lively (see vol. 7:36).

Some observers of the United Church of Christ argue that between 1957 and 1977, the UCC became so deeply involved with the problems of "a suffering and bleeding world" that it lost its "ecclesiastical self-understanding" and failed to sustain authentic worship practices. Others believe that in the midst of its social witness, the United Church of Christ actually found a new and contextually strong theology to revitalize and focus its worship. Only the passage of time will determine which analysis is more accurate.

Affirming Congregations

The 1961 Constitution of the United Church of Christ states that "The basic unit of the life and organization of the United Church of Christ is the local church" (Article V, Paragraph 9). Life and vitality in the UCC flow from the bottom up, rather than from the top down. Church unity, centered in Christ is grounded in local churches, "composed of persons who, believing in God as heavenly Father, and accepting Jesus Christ as Lord and Savior, and depending on the guidance of the Holy Spirit, are organized for Christian worship, for the furtherance of Christian fellowship, and for the ongoing work of Christian witness" (Article V, Paragraph 10).

In the early years of the denomination, as the churches embraced their new affiliation — and in the case of the Congregationalists, actually voted to "join" the UCC — there was lively conversation about the importance of local congregations. Church leaders knew they could not take the local congregation for granted. Local communities of faithful Christians were understood to be servants, carrying on the faith entrusted to them and opening themselves to new possibilities for discipleship in the contemporary world (see vol. 7:37).

By 1963 the Theological Commission of the UCC did some serious thinking about the role of the laity in the ministry of the church. Whereas "lay ministers" were sometimes designated to serve local congregations in emergency situations, the commission reminded the UCC that Christ calls the *laos,* the whole people of God, to ministry. "The ministry of the laity is not to be set over against the ordained ministry; nor is the ordained ministry a matter of status." All Christians are involved in "maintaining the ministry of the church in its wholeness" (see vol. 7:38).

Unfortunately during the 1960s, the activist stance of the United Church of Christ sometimes appeared to neglect the local church. Observers wondered if the "local congregation" was becoming obsolete. In spite of those worries, vital congregations continued to flourish and in some cases local churches became active agents for social change. A subcommittee of the Long Range Planning Committee appointed by the General Synod (1963) studied the situation and issued a "Statement on the Role of the Local Church in the Total Life and Mission of the Church" (1965). It reaffirmed the importance of local, congregational life, but also reminded each congregation of the need to "encourage and support the emergence of new forms of mission through its denomination." It also reiterated the responsibility of the denomination to help the local church be "renewed, empowered and equipped as a form of mission in its particular place" (see vol. 7:39).

In 1967 and in 1971 delegates at the General Synod voted a special denominational emphasis or priority to strengthen the "Local Church in God's Mission" (1967) and the "Local Church in Life and Mission" (1971). Church members and denominational leaders affirmed and celebrated the value of local communities of faith (see vol. 7:40).

With or without such a special priority, from its beginning the UCC has recognized local churches as treasures in "earthen vessels." The United Church of Christ affirms the ministry of local congregations because it believes God continues to call Christians "into the [local] church to accept the cost and joy of discipleship." At the same time there have been periods of dis-ease and bewilderment, particularly in some urban and rural areas where it has been a struggle to maintain congregational life.

Authorizing Ministries

As the United Church of Christ sought to renew and strengthen the local church liturgically, theologically, and in its public vocation, it looked more intentionally at the nature of the ministry itself. According to its constitution, the UCC "recognizes that God calls the whole Church and every member to participate in and extend the ministry of Jesus Christ." It seeks to "undergird the ministry of its members by nurturing faith, calling forth gifts, and equipping members for Christian service." However, the UCC also "recognizes that God calls certain of its members to various forms of ministry in and on behalf of the church for which ecclesiastical authorization is required." Ecclesiastical authorization is given through "ordination, commissioning, licensing, granting either ordained ministerial standing or ordained ministerial partner standing and other acts of authorization" (Article VI, Paragraphs 20–21).

The ministry of the church is the continuing ministry of Jesus Christ. All Christians are called to ministry through their baptism. However, although there is one ministry in Christ, there are diversities of gifts. Many forms of service are celebrated, as long as they support the ministry of the church of Jesus Christ.

Early in its history the Christian community "ordained" its leaders. "By prayer and the laying on of hands," servants of word and sacrament were set apart for the equipping of the saints for their varied ministries in the world. In the United Church of Christ, an "ordained minister" is "one of its members who has been called of God and ordained to preach and teach the Gospel, to administer the sacraments and rites of the Church, and to exercise pastoral care and leadership" (Article VI, Paragraph 23).

Understandings of the meaning of ordination in the United Church of Christ vary. The UCC recognizes there are some of its members who have been given special gifts for ministry. These *charisms,* or gifts of God, are given for the benefit of the whole community and usually require special education, study, and experience. Those ordained are not considered better or more holy than others. Indeed, they are servants of the servants of God so that faith might be nurtured and the church might fulfill its calling to witness to Jesus Christ.

Ideally, the church understands that all baptized Christians bear responsibility as members of the servant community. Ordained leaders are stewards of the "identity" of the community through word and sacrament. Laity are stewards of the "vitality" of the community witnessing and working in the world. The church seeks to respond to God's saving love that redeems "all people from aimlessness and sin," understanding word and sacrament as the means of grace keeping the community alive, and ministries of the laity to each other and the world as action keeping the community alert.

Official policies and practices related to ordination in the United Church of Christ seek to preserve both dimensions of ministry. For example, in 1969, the UCC Council for Church and Ministry wrote that although "ministry represents persons designated by the church to fulfill specific functions," it is more than merely function, it is "representational." An ordained person represents the church, because "in the ordained person, Christ personifies his call to all people" (see vol. 7:41).

Ordination is always an act of the church, celebrating the ministry of the whole church. Individuals, congregations, and the wider church covenant with each other for the sake of Christ's ministry, even as one person accepts a specific calling (see vol. 7:42).

Before 1957, ordained ministers in the Evangelical and Reformed Church were members of "synods," not of local churches. However, in the United Church of Christ, Congregational Christian practice prevailed. Clergy in the UCC are members of local congregations and hold ministerial standing in "associations." Seminaries, conferences, associations, and home congregations share responsibility for nurturing "in care" students. Local committees on Church and Ministry provide oversight and ongoing support for congregations and clergy.

Theology and procedures related to "authorized ministry" in the United Church of Christ respect both tradition and contemporary need. The *United Church of Christ Manual on Ministry* has been a work in progress, going through many editions. In 1977 a new updated *Manual,* published by the Office for Church Life and Leadership (OCLL) and revised and expanded in 1986, summarized UCC perspectives and procedures related to ministry (see vol. 7:43).

Scholars and church leaders repeatedly debate the meaning of ordination and the importance of biblical and historical traditions. Furthermore, UCC involvement in worldwide ecumenical conversations about baptism, eucharist, and ministry have challenged the United Church of Christ to define more clearly its understanding of ministerial vocation (see vol. 7:44 and 106).

To practice "ministry" as an authorized church leader is an awesome responsibility. It must begin with dismantling the claims of the world and move to energize a new community. The one who is ordained is functionally "set apart," but that status implies no spiritual or moral excellence. Yet, clergy are also looked to as theologians for the church, "providing the intellectual formulation of Christian experience both as cosmic Event and personal encounter" (see vol. 7:45).

Finally, in the wider ecumenical world, an emerging theological consensus about leadership in the churches focuses upon the historical "threefold" pattern of ministries named in the early church (deacons, elders, and bishops). Although the United Church of Christ remains uncomfortable with the idea of "bishops," it has come to see how conference ministers and wider church bodies exercise "oversight," thereby carrying on historic patterns of episcopé in new ways (see vol. 7:46 and 106).

Passing on the Faith

The traditions that united to create the United Church of Christ hold education in high value. Church leaders founded colleges, nurtured theological seminaries, and established Sunday schools because they believed that Christians have a responsibility to understand their faith and to pass it on to the next generation.

The Evangelical and Reformed Church and the Congregational Christian churches began working together on Sunday school materials long before the 1957 union. In 1952 they launched a major curriculum project bringing together scholars and experts in biblical studies, theology, and educational methods. Using the latest information about human development, they thought deeply about Christian beliefs and Christian nurture. The resulting *UCC Curriculum* (1964) was an exciting breakthrough in Christian education (vol. 7:47).

Amidst the social activism of the 1960s, however, passing the faith on to the next generation was a severe challenge. During these years the United Church of Christ published (with other denominations) the award-winning *Youth Magazine.* Unfortunately, many young people were increasingly disillusioned with Christianity and its relevance in the world. At the General Synod in 1971 youth delegates spoke out about their loss of confidence in the church (vol. 7:48).

Parents and educators debated the question, "Will our children have faith?" Some people called for a return to classic "Bible study." Others wanted tighter moral education. Yet, assumptions about authority and values were changing rapidly. Teaching "morals" in an increasingly pluralistic society is complicated. UCC educators argued that moral education depended upon cultivating relationships and called for teachers and mentors grounded in their own faith with a passionate commitment to justice (see vol. 7:49).

As the United Church of Christ matured it also became more aware of the importance of the arts in Christian life and practice. Not all worship or education is verbal or formal. The local congregation is a community that sustains faithful Christians in the present, even as it shares a "hope of timeless promise" (see vol. 7:50).

In the end, however, the strength and humble faith of the church includes more than worship, vital congregations, properly authorized ministry, or quality Christian education. The integrity of the church lies in the capacity of its members, under the guidance of the Holy Spirit, in prayers and in selfless deeds, to share the astonishing good news that God is in Jesus Christ. Amidst earth's crucifixions and contradictions, reconciliation takes place. Light shines in darkness. Darkness cannot overcome it. Although UCC membership statistics declined from their highs in the late 1950s, the responsibility of the United Church of Christ to stay true to its vocation remains. The church continues to be called to nurture faithful liturgy; generous congregational life; thoughtful, compassionate leadership; and the vocation of all the baptized to offer their faith to one another and to the next generation.

Despite weakness and disappointment, setback and arrogance, and a lack of courage that tempts the church in every generation, UCC members continue to be called to a ministry of peace, reconciliation, and justice in the world. Confessing a belief in Jesus Christ in simple words and honest deeds, they "share in Christ's baptism and eat at his table." They "join him in his passion and victory." They follow "Jesus who calls us into an active faith; Jesus who challenges us to grow spiritually, journey constantly, question always and serve others continually" (see vol. 7:51).

Enabling Worship

29. The Lord's Day Service: *"An Interpretation of . . . "*

(1964)

[Horton Davies]

Early in the 1960s the UCC Commission on Worship, made up of eighteen pastors, laypersons, and several recognized scholars in worship and theology, produced "The Lord's Day Service." It is a new liturgy, respecting the liturgical traditions of Congregational Christian and Evangelical and Reformed worship, but also greatly influenced by the growing ecumenical conviction that authentic Christian worship should involve weekly services of word and sacrament. According to the commission minutes, "An Interpretation of The Lord's Day Service" was written by Horton Davies.

Horton Davies (b. 1916) is a Congregational Christian/UCC minister born in England and educated at the University of Edinburgh and Oxford University. After serving as a pastor in a London congregation, he went to South Africa where he was a professor at Rhodes University (1946–53). He returned to Britain to teach at Oxford University (1953–56) and came to the United States in 1956 to become a professor at Princeton University (1956–84). Davies has written many books documenting the history of worship and theology: Christian Worship: Its History and Meaning *(1957),* Worship and Theology in England, *five volumes (1961–75),* The Worship of the American Puritans, 1629–1730 *(1990), and his autobiography,* A Church Historian's Odyssey: A Memoir *(1993). In the*

Source: [Horton Davies], "An Interpretation of the Lord's Day Service," in *The Lord's Day Service with Explanatory Notes* (Philadelphia and Boston: United Church of Christ Press, 1964), 31–35. [A manuscript copy of this in the UCC Archives indicates that it was written by Horton Davies.]

early years of the United Church of Christ his scholarly contribution to the work of the UCC Commission on Worship was highly valued.

An Interpretation of the Lord's Day Service

The Lord's Day Service is the work of the Commission on Worship appointed by the United Church of Christ and has been produced by members of that commission representing complementary traditions of liturgical and free worship.

An attempt has been made to provide an ordered structure of worship that will do justice not only to the historic pattern of Christian worship, but also to the comprehensiveness of our common response to the gospel of Christ and to the ecumenical consensus of convictions on worship in our time. It is recommended that this structure, or that of the similar structure of "An Order for Morning Worship," be uniformly observed, with such variations as are provided for freshness. The supplementary use of free prayer, silent prayer, or bidding prayers is welcomed as long as it does not break the basic order and the progression of the service.

The Structure of the Service

The Lord's Day Service falls into two related parts, corresponding to the origins of Christian worship in the synagogue and in the upper room. The first part is essentially a service of the word, consisting of praise, prayers, the reading and exposition of Scripture, the affirmation of faith, and the offertory — the climax of the Service of the Word, and the beginning of the Service of the Upper Room.

The second part of the service derives from the upper room and, in the primitive church, the Lord's Supper was joyfully celebrated every Lord's Day. It recalls, not only in words but in prophetic and symbolic acts, the four actions of our Lord who *took* the bread and wine, *blessed* them, *broke* or poured them, and *gave* them to his disciples, as the anticipation of his sacrifice on the cross and his Messianic Banquet in eternity, through which he would unite his disciples to himself, incorporating them in his mystical body, the church, and granting them forgiveness by the Father's acceptance of his obedient sacrifice and eternal life by his atoning death. This is the *visible* and dramatic demonstration of the gospel of Christ, as the reading and preaching of the word of God in the first part of the service constitute the *audible* demonstration of the same gospel.

Both parts of the service belong together, and we hope that the full service, including both the sermon and the Lord's Supper will become the pattern and norm of the worship of the United Church of Christ each Lord's Day. Until that becomes customary, however, we desire the first part of the service to retain its character as antecommunion, so that the preached gospel will look forward to the sacramental gospel, which is its completion.

The Principal Aims

In its approach the Commission on Worship has had five principal aims. The first, as indicated, was to stress the unity of word and sacrament, of sermon and supper, in line with the ecumenical movement, the modern liturgical movement, and the ancient practice of the church before it was splintered into Roman Catholic, Orthodox, and Protestant fragments.

Second, because we believe in the priesthood of all believers, and hence in the active vocal participation of the congregation in the several prayers as well as the praises, we have provided prayers in which all may join and responses in the consecration prayer of the communion which emphasize this privilege.

Third, because we believe that Protestantism, in its Anglican and Reformed traditions, has overstressed the introspective and penitential note in piety to the loss of the gladness of the people of God in worship, we have given the element of adoration precedence over the element of confession and thus set forth Christ's victories as being far more significant than our failures. In the same spirit we wished to make clear that while we commemorate the death of our Lord on the cross in the Lord's Supper, it is the risen and exalted Christ with whom we have communion. For this reason we have included an account of the risen Christ breaking bread with his disciples, as recorded in the Gospel of Luke.

Fourth, because we believe that the prophetic actions of our Lord in breaking the bread and pouring out the wine, symbolizing in advance his broken body and spilled blood, take us to the heart of the mystery of our redemption, we do not want them to be obscured by being placed in the midst of the prayer of consecration. For this reason we have caused them to be repeated when the warrant of the institution of the Lord's Supper is read, that it may be realized that we were commanded to do this in remembrance of Christ.

Finally, since it is the august function of the Holy Spirit to take the things of Christ and make them ours, we have included in the prayer of consecration a solemn invocation of the Holy Spirit to "bless . . . us and these thy gifts of bread and wine that in this holy communion of the body and blood of Christ we may be made one with him and he with us and that we may remain faithful members of his body until we feast with him anew in thy heavenly kingdom." It is the Holy Spirit, not we, who consecrates and blesses the Lord's Supper to our use and growth in grace.

The Order and Progression of the Service

The Lord's Day Service begins with the recognition that all of our worship is a glad response to God's gift to us of Christ Jesus, the Word made flesh. The opening hymn and sentences of Scripture strike the note of adoration. By a natural transition we proceed to a confession of our own unworthiness of the divine generosity of grace, and thence to a plea for forgiveness. This is assured to us positively by the promises of Christ's gospel, and our gratitude finds renewed expression in the Gloria in Excelsis or other form of praise. Thus the first movement of worship, as preparation, is completed.

God's forgiven people are now ready to receive the divine message of the criticism and comfort of the word in the Scriptures in lessons from the Old and New Testaments to which, as a congregation, we sing or speak a brief response. These lections may be prefaced by the collects for the day, which are very suitable in congregations that regularly have readings from Gospel and Epistle, while other congregations may prefer a prayer for illumination to ask for hearts prepared to receive the instruction of God's word. The sermon follows the lessons, since it is intended to be the exposition and application of the revelation of God to his people. To this the appropriate response is the affirmation of the fullness of our faith by the recital of either a historical and ecumenical creed (the Nicene or the Apostles') or of the Statement of Faith of the United Church of Christ in contemporary language. Thus the second movement of worship, that of the building up of our faith, ends.

The third movement of worship, the celebration of the compassion of Christ, begins with the prayers of intercession. In these we remember the church throughout the world, and pray for peace, for the nations including our own, for the sick and sorrowing, for the troubled, for ourselves and our families, and as our Lord bids us, for our enemies. Room is also provided for additional common intercessions and for personal intercessions offered in silence. The third movement of worship ends with the offertory, a token of our total response in commitment to the work of Christ and the church in the world.

The fourth and prolonged climactic movement of worship is the Holy Communion itself, which now follows. Too subtle for pedestrian analysis this mystery includes at least five aspects: thanksgiving, commemoration, communion, sacrifice (Christ's and ours), and the anticipation of eternity in the Messianic Banquet. For the communion part of the service the elements of bread and wine are included in the offertory brought to the communion table by the representatives of the people, symbolizing that these products of God's gifts and man's labors are to be made the means of our communion with him.

As adoration marked the beginning of the first part of the service, so does the record of the risen Christ breaking bread with his disciples, and the note of glad welcome is sounded: "Beloved, this is the joyful feast of the people of God." The people's response is a reminder of the privilege and call to Christian unity.

Immediately we are ready to begin the great prayer of consecration together. It opens with the familiar responses common to almost all of Christendom. Then follows a great catalog of heartfelt thanksgiving for creation, for the old and the new dispensations of God, for the mighty redemptive acts of God in Christ, for the Holy Spirit and the church, ending with the *Sanctus* and the *Benedictus qui venit* said or sung by the people recalling that our praise is linked with that of the whole church triumphant in heaven and militant upon earth. From joy the mood changes to solemnity as we recall the upper room and the anticipated sacrifice and the duty of the church to bring it to remembrance. Then the Holy Spirit is asked to sanctify both the people and the elements of bread and wine that they may be the means of our incorporation into Christ until the Messianic Banquet is celebrated. The final response of the prayer is the solemn affirmation of the people's oblation of themselves in obedient loyalty, thanking God that they are his representatives in the world, and all is concluded in the saying together of the Lord's Prayer.

Then follows the reading of the Pauline warrant for the celebration of Holy Communion, with the great symbolic manual actions which annihilate the time between the Last Supper and this Lord's Supper.

The climax of the service is reached with the distribution of the consecrated bread and wine. The service ends with a prayer of thanksgiving and, like the Last Supper, with the singing of a hymn or the *Nunc Dimittis,* followed by the final blessing.

Thus have Christ's covenanted people been renewed and reinvigorated by the hearing of the word and the celebration of the Lord's Supper.

Conclusion

The Commission on Worship sends out The Lord's Day Service as the first fruits of its continuing work in providing forms of worship suitable for all occasions in the church's corporate life and for private and family devotions. It will be tested in all of our congregations as an experimental liturgy. Members of the commission will be glad to consider all constructive suggestions that may be offered for its improvement.

This order of worship is sent to the churches of our faith and order with the hope that it will glorify God and edify his people.

30. Resources for Worship:

Services of the Church *and the* Hymnal of the UCC: *"Introductions"*

(1964–69, 1974)

After the publication of "The Lord's Day Service" (see vol. 7:29), the Commission on Worship, under the leadership of Louis H. Gunnemann (see vol. 7:32) prepared "Services of Word and Sacrament I and II" (1967). The first service made small revisions to "The Lord's Day Service," while the second service sought to use more modern language. A few years later, a collection of "Services of the Church" (1969) was published in a unique notebook format with services for Sunday morning and evening, Baptism/Confirmation, Communion, Weddings, Ordination/Installation, and Funerals. The notebook also included a Lectionary and Collects for the Christian year. Rather than a book of worship, the commission decided that the notebook would encourage pastors and worship leaders to insert their own prayers and liturgies. They believed that this was a more authentic way for the United Church of Christ to support the worship life of local congregations.

In the 1970s, in collaboration with the Division of Publication of the United Church Board for Homeland Ministries (UCBHM), the United Church of Christ Hymnal *(1974), was published. The new hymnal includes common texts for a core of widely used hymns designated by the Consultation on Ecumenical Hymnody. At the same time it emphasizes its identity as the* Hymnal of the United Church of Christ *by organizing*

Sources: An excerpt from the "Introduction" to *Services of the Church* (Philadelphia: Division of Publication, United Church Board for Homeland Ministries, the Executive Council and the Commission on Worship, 1964–69), 1–2. John Ferguson and William Nelson, eds., an excerpt from the "Introduction," *The Hymnal of the United Church of Christ* (Philadelphia: United Church Press, 1974), 9.

its table of contents around the seven sentences of the UCC Statement of Faith.

Unfortunately, its size and its language limited its usefulness. First of all it contains only 386 hymns and pieces of service music, a major reduction from the 592 hymns/service music in the Pilgrim Hymnal *of the Congregational Christian Churches and the 559 hymns/service music in the* Hymnal *of the Evangelical and Reformed Church. Second, it is an odd shape and does not fit easily into the pew racks in many UCC churches. Furthermore, by the time it was published in 1974 growing concern about inclusive language in hymns and liturgy made it unacceptable to many UCC leaders and members.*

Services of the Church

Services of the Church is for the assistance of the people in their corporate worship. When the church is at worship the people of God give public expression to the faith that shapes their lives. By their common actions and words they symbolized the oneness of their life in Christ.

At the heart of the corporate life of the people of God is the Service of Word and Sacrament. While this service may be used at any time, it is the chief service of the church for weekly worship. Other services are provided for use on those occasions of a congregation's life that also call for the celebration of God's presence and his work on man's behalf. Some of these, such as baptism, confirmation, marriage, ordination, and burial, mark the transition points of life where the celebration of God's presence and work expresses the singular meaning of our personal and corporate existence. . . .

The grouping of the services in pamphlets and their inclusion in a ring binder make the book adaptable to a variety of situations and uses. Ministers will find it to be a convenient service book which allows the insertion of other materials and of new sections as they become available.

Beyond its practical intention the format of *Services of the Church* clearly conveys the view that the development of liturgical materials is an ongoing task. What is offered in this book is not normative but indicative. The services are in many respects quite traditional. At the same time they include important developments that have resulted from ecumenical endeavors in worship during the past quarter century. Responsible liturgical work requires faithfulness to the historical patterns of Christian worship, but it also requires deep sensitivity to the nature of the human situation today. It is hoped that these services, carefully prepared to show the great tradition of the Christian faith, will enable congregations and pastors to lay a firm foundation for new steps in the development of forms and materials that express the same faith in times of change and stress. . . .

An Explanation for the Order of the *Hymnal of the UCC*

. . . Most hymnals, including the *Pilgrim Hymnal* and the Evangelical and Reformed *Hymnal,* are arranged in the order of the church year, by categories reflecting the content of the texts, or alphabetically. The Hymnal Committee decided early that this hymnal should follow the theological order of the Statement of Faith of the United Church of Christ. For this reason, the user of this hymnal may not find certain hymns where he expects to find them, except, of course, in the alphabetical index. The Statement of Faith has a natural progression which can be stated as follows:

Affirmation of the character of God and his actions.

Proclamation of what God has done and does for his people.

Our responsibility for what we are called to be and do as a result of what God has done.

Our assurance, as set forth in the promises of the gospel.

Doxology, the climatic affirmation of the Faith.

31. Inclusive Language:

"National Guidelines," "A Conference Statement," "A Personal Reflection"

(1980, 1983, 1985)

Office for Church Life and Leadership,
Wisconsin Conference UCC, Davida Foy Crabtree

The United Church of Christ first addressed the question of inclusive language in a General Synod "Resolution on Inclusive Language" (1973). The resolution promoted education about language, requested that the language of the UCC Constitution and Bylaws be revised to be inclusive, and stipulated that all new printed materials published or officially used by the "agencies of the UCC" use deliberately inclusive language. In 1977 a General Synod "Overture on Inclusive Language" asked the Advisory Commission on Women in Church and Society to develop guidelines for inclusive language about people and for "utilizing a multiplicity of ways of referring to our relationship with God and that which we experience as God." It also asked the Executive Council to ensure that inclusive language guidelines were being followed in all UCC publications. And finally, it started the process to create a new official UCC hymnal that would "follow the guidelines for intentionally inclusive language."

Sources: *Inclusive Language Guidelines for Use and Study in the United Church of Christ* (New York: United Church of Christ, 1980), 1–2. Wisconsin Conference UCC, "Statement on Inclusive Language," June 1983. Davida Foy Crabtree, "Authority and Faithfulness: Inclusive Language Issues — Rock, Water, and Word" a presentation given at a symposium, *U.C.C. Theology: Yesterday, Today, Tomorrow,* sponsored by the Connecticut Conference UCC, October 1985, 105–10 (typescript).

The Inclusive Language Guidelines for Use and Study in the United Church of Christ *(1980) explain why and how language relating to God, the church, and people need to be changed. It addresses problems of language in historical materials, in hymns and worship resources, and in religious education texts, and the problem of copyrights. It offers many practical suggestions.*

Conferences and local congregations struggled with the issue. In 1983 a Committee on Inclusive Language in the Wisconsin Conference UCC prepared a statement on inclusive language. Although the Annual Meeting never formally passed the statement, it was sent to associations and congregations and commended for their study, affirmation, and use.

Davida Foy Crabtree (b. 1944) is a UCC minister educated at Marietta College, Andover Newton Theological School, and Hartford Seminary. In 1973, after founding the Prudence Crandall Center for battered women (New Britain, Connecticut), she became minister and director of the Greater Hartford (Connecticut) Campus Ministry (1976–80) and later senior minister of the Colchester (Connecticut) Federated Church (1980–91). She served as conference minister of the Southern California Conference UCC (1991–96) and has been conference minister of the Connecticut Conference UCC since 1996. During the 1970s Crabtree was a member of the national UCC Executive Council and an early recipient of the Antoinette Brown Award (1977), given to two outstanding UCC clergywomen at each General Synod. Crabtree's presentation at a 1985 symposium, "UCC Theology: Yesterday, Today, Tomorrow," sponsored by the Connecticut Conference UCC, focuses on the issue of inclusive language.

Inclusive Language Guidelines for Use and Study in the United Church of Christ

Language — What Is It?

We humans have been described as the "rational animals" and as the "speaking animals" as a means of distinguishing us from other species. The ability to speak and to reason are, indeed, essential human characteristics, but both are based upon an even more profound capacity. That capacity is "the ability to generate and use symbols, the ability to create representations of actuality."[1]

According to James Britton, British educator and linguist, language is a "highly organized, systematic means of representing experience, and as such it assists us to organize all other ways of representing."[2] As a system of symbols, language both describes our reality and shapes it. We "think" in English as well as speak it, and early learning specialists tell us that before speech there is perception but no conception.[3]

It has been stated: "We cannot deny that language both reflects and shapes understanding, behavior, and faith. It is a tool created to facilitate the way in which we relate to each other, to our culture and to our past, present and future. Language is, and must be, a living tool which changes and develops as our understandings and knowledge expand. Our theology should shape our language rather than being shaped by it."[4]

Bias in Language — What Is It?

A society in which sexual or racial discrimination is traditional will employ a language in which that bias is reflected. Changes in the language to correct such bias can both reflect changes in the society and at the same time produce such changes. If women and ethnic racial groups are to be acknowledged as full human beings and partners with men and white people in the fullness of Jesus Christ, we must, as a church, confront language bias and as a church act as a continual force for human liberation, salvation, and healing. Change occurs slowly and only through the commitment of the many who begin to demonstrate new vision and new behavior. Such commitment will produce new ways of speaking about the movement of God in history as that power which has liberated and freed us all from the bondage of the past.

1. James Britton, *Language and Learning* (Baltimore: Penguin Books, 1970), 14.
2. Ibid., 21.
3. Ibid., 190.
4. Source unknown.

Sex Bias

The National Council of Teachers of English says, "Sexism occurs in language when words, phrases, or particular usages either reflect or promote a cultural tendency to use sex as the basis for judging and classifying people in matters unrelated to actual sex difference."[5]

This phenomenon results in several major difficulties.

1. When the masculine pronoun is used more regularly than the feminine to describe the generic, there is an implication that things masculine are superior (or at least normative) to things feminine.
2. When masculine nouns or pronouns are used in the generic sense, the hearer or reader assumes they describe the masculine and does not necessarily transfer the meaning to include the feminine or the characteristics of the feminine.
3. Often our words and images involve implicit as well as explicit stereotypes. The images we use to describe how women or men respond to life situations may reinforce traditional concepts of sexism or may create new images that begin to diminish old myths and establish creative ones that are freeing.

Race Bias

In powerful ways, words and images also connote as well as denote stereotypes about racial and ethnic groups. Perpetuating such stereotypes, particularly in educational materials, has been found to be destructive of white children's positive attitudes toward other groups, and certainly damaging to the self-image of racial and ethnic children themselves. The extent of this is demonstrated in the famous Doll Study by sociologist Kenneth Clark, which was a major factor in the 1954 Supreme Court decision striking down separate but equal education.

It is essential that we portray racial and ethnic groups both as victims of history and as strengths within the culture. Such groups must not always be seen as the poor or as being subservient. While leaving room for failure and human struggle, we must ensure that images other than those of victims are portrayed.

---

5. *Guidelines for Confronting Attitudes That Penalize Women* (New York: National Council of Teachers of English, 1974).

Statement on Inclusive Language

Where there is life there is growth and adaptation. This is true of language as of other living things. Societies do not stand still, and neither should the languages that serve them. Emerging sensitivities are no longer at ease with the use of conventional language that excludes women and other groups of our society in the expression of the universal human experience. Within the Christian community, our liturgy must reflect a deep concern for the whole people of God, language that is just to male and female, to all races, and to people of diverse cultures and circumstance; language that is faithful to the full range of our knowledge, experience, and understanding of the God who has drawn near to us in Jesus Christ.

A powerful tool of communication, language in worship ought to be used with great care, and precision. Modern studies have established that language performs an important role in how individuals perceive themselves, others, and God. The range of symbols and images in our language determines the scope of religious understanding and practice among the people of God. If this range of symbols is limited, so will be our understanding and practice. Language in worship ought reflect our historic and emerging experience of God, with all the richness, care and reverence we can bring to the task. We believe that this will require an expansion of our language about God so that we are not limited to male imagery.

The lack of inclusive language in prayer, in liturgy, and in daily living is not only an issue of faithfulness to the biblical story; it is a profoundly pastoral concern as well. The careful use of language is an expression of love for God and neighbor. As our language begins to change, we shall have to be nurtured into the richness of new expressions. This can be an exciting moment in our life together, as we explore biblical images and ideas that have been hidden or ignored for centuries. . . .

Because any change has far-reaching implications, we know that more study and reflection are necessary. We offer our proposals with the belief that all members of the Wisconsin Conference of the United Church of Christ can work together in our congregations in the exploration and use of new language and in the study required to root our language on the solid biblical foundations of our faith. We affirm that language is a gift from God. We . . . pray for God's guidance in renewing and empowering our language so that it can more effectively communicate to the hearts and minds of all God's people.

Rock, Water, and Word

Language is action. It is action that sculptures and changes our environment as inexorably as flowing water carves a rock. By the words we speak we declare ourselves, we establish relationship, we signal our worldview and our values.

When I was little, my parents always told me that sticks and stones could break my bones, but names would never hurt me. Yet to this day, I wish the other kids had thrown sticks and stones, for the names they called me stayed with me for years and years, shaping and molding my consciousness of myself, even to the core of my identity. Human beings are sculptured by words and by the language in which they think just as surely as rock is carved by water.

I daresay, we all know this truth. If we didn't know the power of language, we wouldn't believe in the importance of preaching, wouldn't be Christians affirming that the Word became flesh, wouldn't be so engaged in the current theological debate.

I want to begin by saying that inclusive language is not the issue; exclusive language is. The continued use of language for humanity or the divine in a way which excludes or denigrates women's life experiences and women's reality, and which is based in sexist (or for that matter, racist) presuppositions — that is the issue. Today I want to identify and begin to elucidate several theological issues arising from this tension within our faith community. Because of the nature of this symposium, I will not be addressing current translation debates, nor the practical issues of the rendering of specific words in a more inclusive manner.

The first and fundamental issue that exclusive language raises is: Who is God to us, and how do we know? Our advocacy of inclusive language is based in a conviction that God is beyond our knowing, that every one of us has access to a bit of the knowledge of God, and that one of the tasks of the faith community is to open ourselves up in as many ways as possible to the experience of the divine. That was the way Jesus' teaching functioned: creating metaphors and drawing on constructs from life that opened up the God-experience, making it accessible to any person.

There are three historic sources of authority for Christians. Some of us place in highest regard the Bible, some the tradition of the church, and some the believer's experience with God. These three ways have coexisted for centuries, sometimes peacefully, often at odds. Our present debates in the UCC represent in part just one more flare-up of an ancient enmity among these three, an enmity based in our inability to hear, to understand, and to honor one another.

We have in the present debates an opportunity to overcome some of that enmity both in the way we conduct ourselves and in the way we frame the issues. I do not mean by this that we must avoid confrontation and conflict. Rather, I mean that we must face directly into the conflict, state it as clearly as possible, and risk loving one another in the midst of it.

Debates about inclusive and exclusive language have been a gift to the Church, for they have forced us back to this fundamental question, "Who is God, and how do we know?"

God is spirit. And when we attempt to speak of God, we inevitably use metaphor and image. Yet metaphors and images must retain their fluidity and resiliency to function theologically. As soon as they ossify, they become idols and make us into idolaters. Masculine language for God is idolatrous now. Though it may once have been a flowing metaphor, the fact that people fight for its retention demonstrates its idolatrous nature.

This first question challenges us to stretch our sense of God and to open ourselves to the many ways of knowing God through experience, tradition, and Bible.

Following upon the first, I have to ask the second question: "Whose tradition?" When we speak of the tradition of the church, we must question who participated in forming that tradition. And I ask you, how many women were at Jamnia when the rabbis closed the canon? How many women were at Nicea or Chalcedon? What woman can you name as a Mother of the Church? I have my days when I am tempted to say that women's exclusion from the tradition totally invalidates its authority. But that would not be entirely fair. That tradition authentically represents the thoughtful consensus of the (albeit male) leadership of the Christian church in that time. Its authority is limited by its exclusiveness, but not totally invalidated.

Ironically, the very faith they sought to interpret and to encapsulate becomes their judge. The faith of Jesus of Nazareth was a simple yet profound faith which showed forth dramatically in inclusion and empowerment. The poor and outcast, the despised and powerless, yes and even women, were definitively and dramatically included in the teachings and the ministry of this Jesus. That the Christian Church was so quick to shed its inclusiveness and its empowerment of all people is a matter of history. It is a source of embarrassment and shame, and should bring us up short whenever we believe we are faithfully representing the gospel. All of us have blinders and filters on the eyes God gave us.

This second question reminds us that the issue of power and participation is a valid Christian criterion for weighing authority, if not authenticity. Authority and faithfulness live in tension with one another.

A third issue presses in upon us, and this pushes us to the edge of our ability to communicate. There are some I have encountered within the United Church of Christ who insist that we must use the same words or we do not share the same belief. And so I ask, do we mean the same thing when we say the same words? Is it possible that the same substance can be meant when we use different words? Take the Trinity. I contend that "Father," "Son," and "Holy Spirit" are just one way of speaking of the three "persons" of the Trinity. The use of those specific words does not make one of us more of a trinitarian than another who chooses to use a longer formulation to point to the same reality. The determination of the Baptism, Eucharist, and Ministry document that the traditional formulation must be used in baptism comes frighteningly close to the institution of a magic formula. To suggest as some have, that the words, "in the name of the Father, the Son, and the Holy Spirit" are required for a baptism to be authentically Christian implies that the words themselves (not the reality to which they point) have a mystical power. And that, few of us are prepared to accept.

The fourth theological dimension of exclusivist language centers in the Bible's role in our life. Is the Bible authoritative because it is the Word of God? Or is it authoritative because it points to, reveals, conveys, makes possible the experience of the Word of God? And if we believe it points to the Word of God, what do we do when the words it uses block the evangelical task? Historically, the believing community has substituted new words, added to the text, translated into common language, and sought to allow the text to reveal rather than obstruct the dynamic power of the Word of God. We cannot allow the Bible's reduction to the status of a quaint museum piece or to that of a false god in our time. We must insist on its life and its liveliness!

Every theological issue has pastoral implications. This one implies both pain and joy. Because language is coextensive with personality, changing language can be very threatening. The issue can be painful in pastoral ministry, for both pastor and laity. Yet it can also be a source of joy as some who have been unable to hear the word of God are now set free to receive it.

It is my conviction that the Christian Church already is and will continue moving toward fully inclusive expression of our faith. But we live between the times. And so the pastor must find the truly compassionate blend, on the one hand, of leadership that encourages and challenges people to new concepts and images of God and new relationship with the triune God, and on the other, of pastoral concern that respects their spiritual journeys. It is, let us be clear, a truth that will never please everyone.

Language sculptures and changes the church as inexorably as flowing water carves a rock. By the words we speak we declare ourselves, we establish relationship, we signal our worldview and our values. In the United Church of Christ, we have begun to declare ourselves for justice — not only justice for women, but justice in our portrayal of God. Inclusive language restores right relationship with God. It saves us from outrageous idolatry and puts us in our place. Inclusive language signals our acceptance of the value Jesus placed on women's participation in his movement, as Christ-bearer, as disciples, as first witnesses to the resurrection, as partners in the evangelical task. The patriarchal worldview signaled by exclusive language will remain for a long time to come, but if we are to be a United Church of Christ we can have nothing to do with its perpetuation.

32. Baptism:

"A Sacrament of Christian Vocation," "Child of Blessing, Child of Promise"

(1985, 1981)

Louis H. Gunnemann, Ronald S. Cole-Turner

Louis H. Gunnemann (1910–89) was an Evangelical and Reformed/UCC minister educated at Mission House College, Mission House Theological Seminary, and Princeton Theological Seminary. After serving pastorates in Iowa and Indiana (1935–52) he became a faculty member at Mission House Theological Seminary (1953–62). In 1962, when Mission House joined Yankton School of Theology to create the United Theological Seminary of the Twin Cities, Gunnemann became dean and professor, serving until his retirement in 1974. Gunnemann chaired the UCC Commission on Worship during the 1960s when it produced The Lord's Day Service *(1964) and* Services of the Church *(1969). Later he was a member of the committee that worked on the* Hymnal of the United Church of Christ *(1974) (see vol. 7:29–30).*

During the 1980s Gunnemann was highly respected as a senior scholar of United Church of Christ history and worship. His books, The Shaping of the United Church of Christ *(1977) and* United and Uniting: The Meaning of an Ecclesial Journey *(1987), are widely used as texts in history and polity courses. In 1985 he was one of the founding co-editors of* Prism: A Theological Forum for the United Church of Christ *(see vol. 7:59).*

Sources: Louis H. Gunnemann, an excerpt from "Baptism: Sacrament of Christian Vocation," *On the Way* (Winter 1985–86): 13–19. Ronald S. Cole-Turner, "Child of Blessing, Child of Promise," *The New Century Hymnal* (Cleveland: The Pilgrim Press), Hymn #325. Words Copyright © 1981 Ronald S. Cole-Turner. Used by permission.

In 1985 Gunnemann gave two presentations on the sacraments that were published in the Wisconsin Conference UCC theological journal On the Way: *"Eucharist — Sacrament of Christian Discipleship" and "Baptism — Sacrament of Christian Vocation." In each he "reconsiders" the place of the sacraments in the life of the church. He argues that two recent developments were inviting the UCC to rethink the sacraments: first, the tendency of modern society to distort the Gospel by privatizing sacraments, and second, the growing ecumenical desire to relate the sacraments to the renewal of the whole human community. "For many generations," he writes, "the meaning of the sacraments has been characterized in terms of 'what' they accomplish, and 'how' they accomplish certain benefits for the believer — always related to the individual. Today the questions of 'what' and 'how' are giving way to the question of 'why?' "*

Ronald Stephen Cole-Turner (b. 1948) is a United Church of Christ minister who has been a professor of theology at Memphis Theological Seminary (Tennessee) and at Pittsburgh Theological Seminary (Pennsylvania). He wrote the hymn "Child of Blessing, Child of Promise" for the 1982 baptism of his daughter, Rachel Elizabeth. It was first published in the hymn supplement Everflowing Streams *(1980).*

Baptism: Sacrament of Christian Vocation

I

. . . Why does the Church in these critical times continue this religious ritual which is not only often accompanied by mushy sentimentality but is also among many people so little understood? An illustration of the problem is given by Laurence H. Stookey in his book, *Baptism: Christ's Act in the Church:*

> Early in this century, a baby born in England, Lucille by name, was taken by her maternal grandmother to the local Wesleyan Chapel to be baptised. Lucy's father, a sturdy Anglican, was skeptical about the whole proceeding since the Church of England does not regard Methodist clergy as being in the Apostolic Succession. So he took Lucy to the Anglican parish church where she was baptised again. Now Lucy's mother was a convert to the Salvation Army and didn't think much of either the Wesleyans or the Anglicans. So she took

> Lucy to the local citadel for presentation under the banner of blood and fire — the Salvation Army's counterpart to baptism.
>
> In time the family emigrated to the midwestern United States. The community they moved into had neither an Episcopal church nor an Army citadel; so the family attended the Methodist church. As a teenager, Lucy joined a class of those preparing to take the vows of church membership. Now it happened that the pastor was one of those mavericks who looks upon the practices of his own denomination with disapproval, and regards the baptism of infants as a misguided tradition. He therefore decreed that all in the class had to be *truly baptised* at the font on the day of their vows. Lucy's mother discovered what was afoot and said: "Absolutely not. Three times is enough for anyone." But Lucy was a good psychologist and knew that once her mother was seated in the church she would not make a scene. When the rest of the class went to the font so did Lucy.
>
> Now it came to pass that some years later Lucy fell in love with, and married, a Southern Baptist — but not without a pledge from him that she need not be baptised yet again. He agreed that she was quite sufficiently initiated into the Church, and all was well — until they moved to a community where they attended a Baptist church that was in need of a pianist. Lucy loved to play, and seemed to be a providential gift to the congregation. But, ruled the deacons solemnly and steadfastly, unimmersed hands may not play the Lord's song for us. And so, for the fifth time, Lucy was initiated into Christ's Church.[1]

While that account is an extreme example of confused thinking, mixed motivation and practice in the Protestant use of baptism, it does illustrate the all-too-common reality of the strange admixture of folk religion, superstition, denominational parochialism, and a limited understanding of the New Testament in today's baptismal practice. A recent personal experience underlines the confusion; and this is an incident in a congregation of the United Church of Christ. I was asked to participate in the baptism of a child of the pastor by preaching and reading the baptismal liturgy. As we gathered about the font with the family, I began to read the liturgy. At the appropriate time the pastor, who wanted to do the act of baptism, took the child, uncovered the font and placed his hand in it. At that point I realized that the font contained no water. This did not stop the pastor who went through the motions of placing his hand three times on the child's head.

---

1. H. Stookey, *Baptism: Christ's Act in the Church* (Nashville: Abingdon, 1982), 11–12.

What does baptism without water mean? Is the symbol of water essential to baptism? If it is not, is any symbol of importance? These are questions to be considered seriously today.

Over against that picture I am pleased to draw one out of another recent experience when we worshipped in a nearby Lutheran church where the Sacrament of Baptism was being celebrated that day. The striking aspect of that service was its liturgical and Gospel integrity. For the first time in decades we heard a baptismal sermon linked directly to the focal event of the service. Based on 2 Corinthians 4:7–12, the sermon interpreted in simple and direct fashion the relationship of Christ's life and death to the life of the child being baptised; and, of course, to the lives of all baptised persons. There was nothing sentimental in that message; it was, in one sense, starkly realistic about the nature of suffering and death in life in Christ; but at the same time it was comforting and reassuring in its underlining of the magnificent promises of the Gospel. It was a powerful, moving time of worship in which the entire congregation, as well as the parents of the child, were helped to see the power of this sacrament.

There are signs of significant and serious addressing of the meaning of baptism for our time. The most important of these directs us to the theme of the Sacrament of Christian Vocation. To this we now turn.

II

To speak of Baptism as the Sacrament of our Vocation (calling) is not to attempt a new definition. It is, rather, to lift up an accent or theme running all through the New Testament teaching. Christians are a *called* people. The Gospel accounts of Jesus' ministry underline this in every event and every teaching. Further, the presupposition of the Pauline epistles is the called community. In writing to the Church in Rome, in Corinth, in Ephesus, the apostle addressed those "called to be saints."

Strangely, however, most baptismal liturgies make no reference to "call"; although, in some respects the concept is implicit. The accent falls, rather, upon the gifts of grace in the relationship with God in Christ, signed and sealed in the act of baptism for the benefit of the individual; and further, upon the sign and seal of forgiveness and incorporation into the Church. In this way baptismal liturgies even today underline the benefits of baptism for the baptised person. The fact is that these liturgies represent the "religionizing of the Gospel" which became a marked feature in the Church of the third and fourth centuries and thereafter. Religion's focus is always upon the benefits to be derived from a relationship with God.

But the *focus of the Gospel* is upon liberation from the bonds of self-serving religion and, at the same time, upon a new life given and realized in answering *God's call.*

Religion asks: "*What* happens when I become a Christian, that is, what is there in it for me?" "*How* does it happen?" And through the centuries much of the Church's energy has been given to answering such questions. In the process, the Church took charge of the spiritual pilgrimages of all who sought assurance. In so doing, as is well known, the authority and power of the Church grew and baptism became a means of establishing ecclesiastical domination of human life. The sacraments, not only Baptism and the Eucharist, but the others of the Medieval Church became instruments of control and oppression.

The Protestant movement of the sixteenth-century Reformation did set up a powerful counterforce to these religionizing aspects of the Church's life. To learn that one is justified by grace through faith according to the promise of the Gospel was to be liberated from ecclesiastical oppression. To know baptism as the sign of grace, unlimited by human pretension, and to know that by baptism one enters the realm of new life by the power of the Spirit—to know these things was to know the power of baptism.

But the threat of "religionizing" the Gospel was not removed by the Reformation. It continued in new ways to be exhibited in the misinterpretation of the Gospel, limiting the free grace of God, devising new forms of control of human destiny. The Protestant accent on the freedom given by the Gospel was changed into the ideology of human autonomy, thus seeming to counter the "tyranny of the ecclesiastical hierarchy" with the "tyranny of the individual." By the eighteenth century it was already clear that new forms of religion, though subtly designed, were undercutting the power of the new life in Christ.

Religion, as we have said, accentuates the *benefits* to be secured in a relationship with God. The Gospel calls for a renunciation of that kind of use of God, and for a surrender to the life Christ gives. It is the recapturing of that insight and teaching that we seek to express in calling Baptism the Sacrament of Christian Vocation.

III

Baptism became a major theme of theological discussion in the churches in large part because of the work of the Faith and Order movement, beginning in the third decade of the present century. That movement, incorporated into the World Council of Churches shortly after World War II, has exerted continued pressure on the churches to re-think baptismal theology and practice.

It was in this context that the United Church of Christ made its first and, in my judgment, most important statement about baptism. In the Statement of Faith, adopted in 1959, the sacraments (as Roger L. Shinn has said in *We Believe: An Interpretation of the United Church of Christ Statement of Faith*) are put in a "context that is strange to many churchmen."[2] That context is the "mission of the Church." And Shinn points out that baptism is "the symbol . . . of an entrance into the missionary community that continues Christ's reconciling ministry and shares in his death and resurrection."[3] That is what we say when, in the words of the Statement of Faith, we confess (acknowledge) that we are "called to share in Christ's baptism, eat at his table, and join him in his passion and victory."

"Called to share in Christ's baptism" — this is our Christian vocation. It is ironic that this understanding of baptism was not given expression in the two baptismal liturgies produced by the United Church of Christ since 1959. I confess to some embarrassment about this because its absence in the baptismal liturgy in *Services of the Church* (1967) was produced by the UCC Commission on Worship of which I was a part. It is also disappointing to note that the new baptismal liturgy to be published next year gives only a hint of the Gospel concept of baptism as the sacrament of vocation. "To share Christ's baptism" is a theme that should have prominence in our liturgical material, not only for the sake of consistency but also as an expression of our ecumenical responsibility, especially since the publication of the BEM documents.

It should be noted that in the "Order for Baptism to be Administered With the Rite of Confirmation" (in the 1967 *Services of the Church*), there is this powerful passage: " . . . baptism is the sacrament through which we are united to the Lord Jesus Christ and given part both in his offering of himself and in his conquest of evil. It is the visible sign of an invisible event: the reconciliation of men to God . . . "[4] This is a clear expression of the point in the Statement of Faith. It is, of course, true, that in part of our tradition the emphases upon vocation in God's mission is made in confirmation, not in baptism. But failure to include it in baptism has weakened the meaning of that sacrament and has made confirmation more important. (The problem related to the misunderstanding and misuse of confirmation will come into our discussion later.)

---

2. Roger L. Shinn, *We Believe: An Interpretation of the United Church of Christ Statement of Faith* (Philadelphia, Boston: United Church Press, 1966), 105.

3. Ibid., 106.

4. *Services of the Church* (Philadelphia, Boston: United Church Press, 1967), No. 3, 13.

"Called to share in Christ's baptism" — the phrase, as you know, derives from the Pauline teaching, especially in Romans 6:4. — "We were buried therefore with him by baptism unto death, so that as Christ was raised from the dead by the glory of the Father, we too might walk in newness of life." An additional facet of meaning is derived from Jesus' words in Mark 10:38–40: "With the baptism with which I am baptised you will be baptised." To share that baptism is not primarily to receive personal benefits; it is, rather, to enter a new calling, a new vocation, a new life, characterized by self-giving rather than self-seeking, shaped by a life that brought hope to the hopeless, and strength to those who were weak and ill. All the marks of the baptism we are called to share with Christ are evidence of a new and different realm of human existence in which self-advantage is renounced for the sake of the other. This is the import of Christ's baptism at the hands of John. For there he identified himself with the outcast, the needy, the sinners, with those who made no claim on God but awaited Divine mercy. For Christ's baptism gives shape to the mission of the Church. And that is the shape of the vocation (calling) signed and sealed in our baptism.

What does this mean for the practice of baptism in the United Church of Christ? We cannot deny that our baptismal practices are often lacking in emphasis upon vocation. We live in that part of the world where privatistic Christianity effectively seals itself off from the needy, the oppressed, and the outcast. Denominational church life for its own survival demands of us the wisdom, resources, and energy required so desperately for a needy world. Can we move beyond the pressures of self-serving religious life to the life to which Christ calls? We need new and vital images of Church life if the mission of justice, peace, and reconciliation is to be accomplished. That is possible, I believe, by a faithful and responsible use of Baptism as the Sacrament of Christian Vocation. What is necessary?

The liturgical and educational life of the Church must be organized around the full meaning and practice of baptism. It must cease being an occasional religious rite, available upon request and at the convenience of those seeking it. As the Sacrament of Christian Vocation it is a rite to be used with the utmost seriousness and planning; it must be kept at the center, not the periphery, of the Church's worship and nurture. This will require re-education and continuing nurture of adults, youth, and children. It means:

a) Re-thinking the meaning of the relationship between baptism and confirmation. Two errors in confirmation result from a misunderstanding of baptism. First, confirmation is seen as the "rite of joining the Church." As such, it implicitly denies the meaning of baptism as "incorporation into the Church which is Christ's body." It further withholds from the baptised child all of the needed nurturing of faith — a nurturing usually delayed until puberty. Second, confirmation instruction is primarily designed as a means of generating faith through knowledge. The early Church understood instead: "Credo ut intelligam" ("I believe that I may understand"). Confirmation instruction should focus upon training for the Church's mission.

b) Re-consideration of the appropriate time for baptism — a consideration involving aspects of family life now rarely considered, especially in view of the change in family structures in this time.

c) Re-conceiving the role of the family relationship in the nurture of faith, thus moving the major responsibility from the "educational process" to the "nurturing process."

Conclusion

It is in this emphasis upon Baptism as the Sacrament of Vocation that the Church will be able to address the problems of community, justice, peace, and reconciliation in our time. Faithfulness to this vocation is not an assurance of success or security for the Church. To be a faithful witness of God's presence and work in the world is to risk all known securities.

Child of Blessing, Child of Promise

Child of blessing, child of promise,
baptized with the Spirit's sign;
With this water God has sealed you
unto love and grace divine.

Child of love, our love's expression,
love's creation, loved indeed!
Fresh from God, refresh our spirits,
into joy and laughter lead.

Child of joy, our dearest treasure,
God's you are, from God you came.
Back to God we humbly give you;
live as one who bears Christ's name.

Child of God your loving Parent,
learn to know whose child you are.
Grow to laugh and sing and worship,
trust and love God more than all.

STUTTGART 8.7.8.7.

33. Preaching:
"Listening as Proper Human Business"

(1989)

Walter Brueggemann

Walter Brueggemann (b. 1933) is an Evangelical and Reformed/UCC minister educated at Elmhurst College, Eden Theological Seminary, Union Theological Seminary in New York, and St. Louis University. He was professor and dean at Eden Theological Seminary (1961–86) and on the faculty at Columbia Theological Seminary (Decatur, Georgia) (1986–2003). For more than three decades his books and essays have been widely read in the church: The Land *(1977),* The Prophetic Imagination *(1978),* The Creative Word *(1982),* Hopeful Imagination *(1986), and* Interpretation and Obedience *(1991). Brueggemann is a biblical scholar who uses biblical theology, especially the thought of the Hebrew prophets, to inform and challenge the practice of contemporary ministry. His speaking, writing, and teaching emphasize "God's purpose for the world, articulated in the grand themes of the saving narratives and the prophetic promises" calling the world to "come to freedom, justice, and equity."*

Listening as Proper Human Business

Evangelical preaching takes as a central theme the will and purpose of God for creation, for humankind, and for the church. The biblical tradition asserts that God wills well-being for the world that is radical and enduring, well-being wrought through joyous obedience. God's purpose for the

Source: Walter Brueggemann, an excerpt from *Finally Comes the Poet: Daring Speech for Proclamation* (Minneapolis: Fortress Press, 1989), 79–81.

world, articulated in the grand themes of the saving narratives and the prophetic promises, is that the world should come to freedom, justice, and equity.

Biblical articulations of God's purpose, however, do not stay with grand themes. The will of God is more precisely articulated in quite concrete commandments that require and demand specific actions in the service of the grand vision. The dynamic of biblical faith requires that the command should always be re-articulated for specific times, places, and circumstances.[1]

The Bible and the memory of the church is a long procession of voices that claim to speak the voice of God, or that claim to be faithful interpreters of the voice of God. The address of God to Israel, echoed through so many human voices, asserts the ways of conduct that make life possible, that make available communion with God and peace with neighbor. God's address to Israel, variously mediated, is not a heavy-handed coercion, but a gift that makes wholeness possible. The command of God and its mediation are indeed a gift of God's grace; we are made privy to the foundational requirements whereby God's good will is offered to us.[2] In the moment of preaching, it is the high call of the preacher to join the long procession of human voices in the tradition: to dare to utter what can be known about the will and purpose of God, about the costs and requirements that make joy, peace, and well-being possible in the world.

It is not a surprise to church people that the preacher should speak about the will of God, even to dare to speak about command. Popular religion in our midst, however, has greatly reduced the notion of obedience, so that it has become either a virtue too much celebrated or a burden too much dreaded.

On the one hand, our distorted notions of obedience are lifeless because they are too much taken for granted, and too well known, as though the mind of God is fully exposed. Conventional notions of "God's will" understand the commands to guarantee not only the delight of God's company but also happy family, secure economy, and prosperous life. Obedience as guarantee is a misunderstanding that works for those who find life good

---

1. On "rearticulation" in recent scholarship, see Joseph W. Groves, *Actualization and Interpretation in the Old Testament* (Atlanta: Scholars Press, 1987). See Claus Westermann, ed., *Essays on Old Testament Hermeneutics* (Richmond: John Knox Press, 1963), on which Groves bases much of his argument. Gerhard von Rad, in *Studies in Deuteronomy,* SBT 9 (Chicago: Henry Regnery Company, 1953), and in many other places has seen that much of Israel's law is interpreted, preached law.

2. On the foundational character of the commands, see Walter Brueggemann, "The Commandments and the Liberated, Liberating Bonding," *Journal for Preachers* 10, no. 2 (Lent, 1987): 15–24.

and equitable and whole.[3] Such a distorted notion, however, does not want to probe or notice the unavoidable ambiguity present in ethical certitude or to live with the demand of God that outruns convention. On the other hand, our distorted notions of obedience are lifeless because they are discerned only as dread censure, as world-denying prohibition. The commands are therefore old-fashioned, heavy-handed, and only for those who live in fearful anxiety. For the rest, they are outmoded and superseded.[4]

The preacher may be tempted either to sound the nonnegotiability of the command, or to abridge the gospel into a therapeutic mode that requires nothing. The live command of God, however, must be spoken faithfully by the preacher against both of these distortions: command as guarantee, and command as censure — on the one hand too eagerly embraced, on the other too carelessly scuttled. In the midst of such embrace and scuttling, the commandments persist, the voice insists, and the preacher must speak.

Even when the commandments are misunderstood as guarantee or as censure, God's voice of command nonetheless continues to haunt us. We are haunted by this voice that has called us to be. The voice of command is and continues to be a sovereign voice, a voice that addresses us anew when we embrace too easily. It is a voice that addresses us persistently and relentlessly, even when we scuttle. We are haunted not only by the voice of command that seems to be at the root of our very life. We are also haunted by our yearning to be addressed, by our need to listen. We are created for listening. It is our proper business. We are made for communion, but the communion for which we are formed is not that of mindless camaraderie. It is a communion with the one who has hoped us and made us and summoned us and who waits for us. This one who is so active before us and for us and with us, is one who cares and governs.

Our life consists in coming to terms with that one. We yearn to come to terms by listening. In the Bible, obedience takes the form of listening. The obedient life is one in which Israel listens, attends to, and responds to the voice of God. The preacher, who comes late to this traditioning processing of witnesses and interpreters, operates among those who suspect that they must listen if they are to live, who yearn to listen, who dread to listen.

---

3. On the question of "goodness," see Mary Gordon, *Men and Angels* (New York: Random House, 1985), 200: " 'How I hate the word "goodness." What an obstacle it is to the moral life,' said Jane. 'Do you find goodness and morality incompatible?' Anne asked. 'Of course not. But the term "goodness" has been so perverted, so corrupted, it now covers only two or three virtues when there are hundreds.' "

4. On false notions of freedom generated by the Enlightenment, see Colin Gunton, *Enlightenment and Alienation* (Grand Rapids: Eerdmans Publishing Company, 1985). See especially Gunton's utilization of Iris Murdoch's *The Sovereignty of Good* (London: Methuen, 1985), and her notion of "obedience to creation." The argument of Gunton and Murdoch is that freedom is always dialectically related to obedience. It is the dialectic that must be recovered in the ethical reflection of the church.

34. Book of Worship:

"Theological Guidelines That Informed the Development of . . . "

(1986)

Thomas E. Dipko

Thomas E. Dipko (b. 1936) is a United Church of Christ minister educated at Otterbein College, United Theological Seminary (Dayton, Ohio), and Boston University. He also studied at the Ecumenical Institute in Geneva, Switzerland. After serving pastorates in Massachusetts and Pennsylvania (1963–84), Dipko was conference minister of the Ohio Conference UCC (1984–92) and executive vice president of the United Church Board for Homeland Ministries (UCBHM) (1992–2000).

In 1979, following the 1977 General Synod request that the Office of Church Life and Leadership (OCLL) explore the development of a new book of worship for the United Church of Christ using inclusive language, Dipko joined a ten-person committee to envision and develop the book. After many meetings, he was invited to become the primary drafter of the text, following guidelines established by the committee. In 1983–84 draft services and resources were circulated as test documents, and the UCC Book of Worship *(BOW) was finally published in 1986. The "Theological Guidelines That Informed the Development of the* Book of Worship*" reflect the careful historical, theological, and practical work of the* Book of Worship *committee guided by OCLL staff.*

Source: Thomas E. Dipko, "Theological Guidelines That Informed the Development of the *Book of Worship*," in *The Symbols, Space, and Sanctity of the Place of Worship* (New York: United Church Board for Homeland Ministries with the Fellowship of UCC Architects, 1986), 5–9.

Theological Guidelines That Informed the Development of the *Book of Worship*

The Office for Church Life and Leadership, at the time of the publication of the *Book of Worship,* invited me to summarize the theological guidelines that were used by the committee that prepared the contents of the book. The ten persons on the committee, ably assisted by three members of the staff of the Office for Church Life and Leadership, began their work in 1979. Their mandate originated in a General Synod action in 1977 which reads tersely as follows: "The Eleventh General Synod of the United Church of Christ directs the Executive Council to request the Office for Church Life and Leadership to develop, if feasible, a book of worship for the United Church of Christ, using inclusive language."

1. The first guideline, simply stated, is that "Christian" worship, by definition, is worship centered in the life, death and resurrection of Jesus Christ as witnessed to us in holy scripture. Said another way, Jesus Christ is the Christian Tradition with a capital "T," while all our derivative traditions that center in him are traditions with a small "t." Ignatius of Antioch, a theologian of the early church, affirmed this in these words: "To my mind it is Jesus Christ who is the original documents. The inviolable archives [of the Christian faith] are his cross and death and resurrection and the faith that came by him." The *Book of Worship,* in seeking to be faithful to this guideline, is a response to Jesus' promise, "And I, when I am lifted up from the earth, will draw all people to myself" (John 12:32 NRSV). It strives to be Christocentric without being Christomonist; it respects fully the place of Jesus Christ within the trinitarian understanding of the nature of God.

2. The second guideline, in the words of Harry Emerson Fosdick, is that we worship God in the beauty and duty of holiness; that is to say, for Christians, worship cannot be separated from ethics. Liturgy, "the work of the people of God," includes not only what we do when we gather for what is narrowly called "worship," but all that we do as persons baptized into the life, death and resurrection of Jesus Christ.

Karl Barth speaks of the inseparable relationship of worship and ethics in this way:

> In its New Testament form, Christian ethics is never concerned only with the requirements of an abstract private morality, but always with instructions for the edifying of the community. It is not only in worship that the community is edified and edifies itself. But it is here first that this continually takes place [that is, in the gathered worship

> of the congregation]. And if it does not take place here, [in assembled worship], it does not take place anywhere. If the [congregation] does not edify itself here, it certainly will not do so in daily life, nor in the fulfillment of its witness to the cosmos.[1]

This unitive relationship between worship and ethics is expressed frequently in the various services. For example, the second Service of Word and Sacrament begins with the prophetic words of Micah 6:8, calling us "to do justice, and to love kindness, and to walk humbly with our God." Near the end, a petition is offered to God in these words: " . . . that whether we are gathered or scattered, we may be the servant church of the servant Christ" (BOW, 75).

3. The third guideline is that we dare not confuse our human language about God with the being of God in the mystery of who God is. Clement of Alexandria once wrote, "The Divine Being cannot be declared as it is; but as we who are fettered to the flesh were able to listen, so the prophets spoke to us."[2] The introduction to the *Book of Worship,* in a similar way, reminds us in the words of the book of Hebrews (13:8) that " 'Jesus Christ is the same yesterday, today and for ever.' but the language, customs, and historical situation of the people of God are continually changing" (BOW, 7). It was with this conviction in mind that John Williamson Nevin, a great theologian of the Reformed Church, once remarked, "No [book of worship] was considered to be of perpetual force."[3]

Humility is a wise virtue when we assess the language of worship. In Paul's letter to the Romans (8:26), we find the apostle owning the limitations of human words in reference to prayer. "Likewise the spirit helps us in our weakness," writes Paul, "for we do not know how to pray as we ought, but that very Spirit intercedes for us with sighs too deep for words." This humility concerning the relevance and the relativity of human words is expressed in the Book of Worship in a special way in a prayer included in a service for a person who is dying. The prayer contains the petition, " . . . you hear our cries through lips unable to speak. Hear with compassion the yearnings of your servant, and the prayers that we would offer had we the words" (BOW, 362).

4. The fourth guideline further develops the significance of the limitations of human language. Briefly stated it is this: truly inclusive language is more than a matter of aesthetics; it is a matter of integrity and justice;

---

1. Karl Barth, *Church Dogmatics,* IV/2, trans. G. W. Bromily (Edinburgh: T. & T. Clark, 1962).
2. The Ante-Nicene Fathers, II, *Stromata,* II, XVI, 363.
3. John Williamson Neven, "Historical Vindication of the New Liturgy," in *Catholic and Reformed: Selected Theological Writings of John Williamson Nevin,* ed. Charles Yrigon Jr. and George H. Bricker (Pittsburgh: Pickwick Press, 1978), 317.

it is an issue of ethics. Words that "exclude" persons today, even though they did not have that intention in some earlier era, are words of injustice "now." This is so not only with regard to gender, but also with respect to distinctions of race, class and physical or other disabilities.

When this guideline is applied to language about God, it quickly becomes apparent that the church has ignored the rich metaphors of the Bible in which the feminine in God is celebrated. At times this happens because our translations of the Bible are less than accurate. For example, we read in Deuteronomy 32:18: "You were unmindful of the rock that begot you, and forgot the God who gave you birth." William Holladay, an Old Testament scholar, points out that the first part of that verse can mean parenting by either a father or a mother. The second part, however, is "womb" language, and clearly refers to one who is experiencing labor pains. Yet we read in the Jerusalem Bible: "You forgot the rock who begot you, unmindful now of the God who *fathered* you." In the New Testament we find similar shifts to male language where the Greek text does not warrant it. We read in Romans 8:28: "We know that in everything God works for good with those who love him." However, have you ever noticed the footnote at the bottom of the page? There we discover that the word "him" has been substituted for another word. The Greek text actually says, "We know that in everything God works for good with those who love *God.*" There is no "him" in the verse.

The biblical witness to the feminine in God is expressed in many of the services in the *Book of Worship.* In the wedding service, the great prayer of thanksgiving for holy communion includes these words: "Blessed are you, O God our Creator. From the womb of your being you brought forth worlds. Into mere dust you blew the breath of life, creating men and women to bear your likeness in the world" (BOW, 342).

In relation to Godhead, the word "Lord," which is the usual translation of the tetragram or "high name" for God in the Old Testament, is expressed diversely as "Holy One," "loving God" or in other ways consistent with the context. Likewise, references to Jesus Christ affirm his gender where that is appropriate, but also express his familial relationship within the Trinity in diverse ways. In the first order of Word and Sacrament, we find the prayer: "We give you thanks, Holy One, almighty and eternal God, always and everywhere, through Jesus Christ, the only one begotten by you before all time, by whom you made the world and all things" (BOW, 45).

Great care has also been taken in the *Book of Worship* to make references to the people of God as inclusive as possible. Words like "black" and "dark" are not used as symbolic words for evil. In the service of Tenebrae, used during Holy Week, the title has been retranslated more accurately to express what the Latin term intends. Consequently, it is not a service of "darkness," but a service of "shadows." In relation to gender, the place of women in the history of salvation is cited along with the role of men. In the marriage service, thanks is given to God "for Adam and Eve, for Sarah and Abraham, for Joseph and Mary, and for countless parents whose names we do not know" (BOW, 338). In a more universal way, the great prayer of thanksgiving in Service of Word and Sacrament II includes the words: "We offer you our praise for women and men of faith in every age who stand as witnesses to your love and justice" (BOW, 70). In the services for healing, the words consistently remind us that each of us is in some measure "disabled," and that every human being is continually in need of God's healing grace. The language seeks to celebrate God's embrace of the entire human family, with all its diversity and need.

5. The fifth guideline is that worship, liturgy, is in truth the "work" of the whole people of God, and not only of those who "lead" the people of God. That is to say, Christian worship is not passive — it is a participatory action. It is not the domain of a priesthood separated from the people of God, but a function of the royal priesthood of the whole people of God. Dom Gregory Dix has cautioned that the dominance of worship by religious specialists has historically coincided with the periods of corruption in the life of the church. John Williamson Nevin and Jonathan Edwards shared that point of view. Nevin, in describing the liturgical reformation of his day, commented, "We were carried gradually beyond [a book of forms for the minister only] and came to feel more and more the meaning of worship in its proper congregational view."[4]

In the *Book of Worship,* every effort has been made to include laity not only in the corporate participation of those who sit in the pews, but in the leadership of worship as well. Some of the services do not require the presence of an ordained minister, and those at which an ordained minister properly presides call for the partnership of lay leaders in appropriate roles. Various parts of the services are often written in a way that permits them to be led by any baptized Christian. The words of pardon, for example, in the Services of Reconciliation, read: "In Christ's name, and as one with you in the church, I declare to you: your sins are forgiven" (BOW, 273 and 286).

6. The sixth guideline is that liturgy is the response of total persons to the loving initiative of God. Worship addresses the intellect, but not the intellect alone. There is a rightful place for the sensate, symbols, movement and preeminently, for music. Joseph Gelineau, a Roman Catholic liturgical

---

4. Ibid., 340.

reformer, echoes Martin Luther with his claim, "the Christian liturgy was born singing and has never ceased to sing."[5]

The services in the *Book of Worship* make rich provision for touching, breaking and pouring, embracing, eating, washing, anointing, dancing and singing. Appreciation is expressed for the place of the arts in directing our attention to God. All this is done with the awareness that any of these things can be abused as surely as the more cognitive practices of the church can be abused. Gelineau's wisdom is cited in the introduction. He puts all these affective and cognitive human responses to this one test:

> The signs [through which the liturgical arts are expressed] are not there to reflect our own light. Neither are they themselves a source of light. They refract into our bodily and worldly existence a light that comes from elsewhere. They are not there to be seen but to see by. They are there to open our eyes to other things.[6]

7. The seventh guideline is that worship is both here and now and then and there — that is to say, worship at its faithful best is ecumenically catholic! It is timely precisely because it is respectful of time, and cherishes continuity with the church across the ages. We are indeed surrounded by a great cloud of witnesses. We are neither victims of amnesia inventing liturgy as though we were the "first" Christians, nor are we victims of "nostalgia" seeking to imprison liturgy in the confines of one culture or century. Philip Schaff, a scholar of the Reformed Church, gave this counsel in 1852 as the Reformed Church sought to publish a new book of worship:

> The new liturgy ought not to be shaped simply after modern models, reaching back no farther than the Reformation. . . . The general basis of the work should be "the liturgical worship of the Primitive Church, as far as this can be ascertained from the Holy Scriptures, the oldest ecclesiastical writers, and the Liturgies of the Greek and Latin Churches of the third and fourth centuries."[7]

The committee for the United Church of Christ *Book of Worship* took this counsel very seriously. We began with the assumption that the Bible is the church's primary liturgy book. The services in the *Book of Worship* are filled with imagery unapologetically taken from the Bible, illumined by

---

5. Joseph Gelineau, "Music and the Singing of the Liturgy," in *The Study of Liturgy,* ed. Cheslyn Jones et al. (New York: Oxford University Press, 1978), 440.

6. Joseph Gelineau, *The Liturgy Today and Tomorrow,* trans. Diana Livingstone (London: Darton, Longman and Todd, 1979), 121.

7. *Catholic and Reformed,* 327.

the experience of the church across the centuries, and cast in the idiom of our own time.

8. The eighth guideline is that worship at its fullest includes both Word and Sacrament. This ideal is affirmed by the vast majority of churches today even though few churches have an impressive track record in implementing the ideal. Often, where holy communion is celebrated weekly on the Lord's Day, the preaching of the word takes a subordinate place. Where the sermon has risen to predominance, holy communion is celebrated only occasionally and often in an abbreviated order. The *Book of Worship,* in keeping with the witness of the primitive church and the teaching of Calvin and Luther, holds both Word and Sacrament together in a unified order.

It also provides for a more biblically sound balance in the holding together of the cross and the empty tomb, the crucifixion and the resurrection. The second Service of Word and Sacrament, for example, includes a resurrection acclamation just prior to the sharing of the bread and cup. The leader says: "Alleluia! Fear not, I am the first and the last and the living one." The people, continuing the words from Revelation 1:17–18, respond: "I died, and behold I am alive for evermore. Alleluia!" (BOW, 73).

9. The ninth guideline is that liturgy is both a recalling (*anamnesis*) and a calling (*vocatio*). We remember God's great deeds "for us and for our salvation" in order to take our place in the line of witnesses who then tell the story. The introduction to the *Book of Worship* explains the connection this way: "Christian worship is more than a passive response to God's revelation. . . . It both announces the good news of God's love for all the world and invites all people to share God's saving embrace" (BOW, 1). In the second service of Word and Sacrament this relationship is expressed in a petition: "Through this meal, make us the body of Christ, the church, your servant people, that we may be salt, and light, and leaven for the furtherance of your will in all the world" (BOW, 71–72).

10. The tenth guideline is that liturgy today is in truth the liturgy of the church of Pentecost. Throughout the *Book of Worship,* a conscious effort has been made to heighten our awareness of the place and power of the Holy Spirit. In the first service of Word and Sacrament, at the prayers of the people, one of the sets of responses begins with the leader saying: "Holy Spirit, our Comforter," and ends with the people answering: "Receive our prayer" (BOW, 42). Every service of holy communion includes an invocation of the Holy Spirit on the gifts of bread and wine and on the worshiping community. In the orders for Christian discipleship, references to the presence and work of the Holy Spirit are frequent. "Come, Holy

Spirit" is a refrain that assures us again and again of God's invisible, immediate presence in the church and in our individual lives.

11. The eleventh guideline is that for Christians, liturgy is cosmic in the scope of its concern. It touches upon the whole creation and recognizes the sanctification of time itself. Matthew Fox and others are rightly challenging us today not to set a theology of redemption over against a theology of creation. It is one and the same God who created the universe and pronounced it good who also became incarnate for our redemption in the person of Jesus Christ. The *Book of Worship* affirms God's grace in both divine actions. In the prayers for holy communion, the baptismal prayers, the order for the Vigil of Easter and consistently through the book, the goodness of creation is affirmed and human responsibility for the stewardship of the natural world is asserted. In the first service of Word and Sacrament, God is asked, "Restore the earth with your grace that is able to make all things new" (BOW, 48). The calendar itself is called into the service of the gospel through the use of the liturgical seasons and principal Christian holidays. The introduction to the *Book of Worship* rightly reminds us that "Christians, from the New Testament age to the present, regard time not only as a product of nature but also as a parable of God's saving action in human history" (BOW, 19).

12. Finally, the twelfth guideline is that Christian liturgy takes history seriously, but anticipates the "not yet" of God's consummation of all things in Christ at the end of time. The consequence of this eschatological anticipation is not the devaluation of history, but the elevation of history to its more than mundane significance. Christians read history not only as an account of the past, but as a foretaste of what God yet has in store for the human family and for all of creation. We therefore say boldly, "Christ has died, Christ is risen, Christ will come again."[8]

One result of taking history seriously in this way is that we do not take the liturgy of any one generation so seriously that we absolutize the worship customs of a given period. The introduction to the *Book of Worship* closes with this wise counsel:

> This *Book of Worship,* like all other books of worship, is transitional literature. It seeks to provide a small span in the bridge that will traverse and link the worshipping church of the twentieth century with the church of the past and the church of the twenty-first century. To the extent that it serves faithfully in this endeavor, it deserves careful study, prayerful reflection, and imaginative use. (BOW, 27)

---

8. See Robert Adolfs, O.S.A., *The Grave of God: Has the Church a Future?* trans. N. D. Smith (New York: Harper & Row, 1966.)

As I conclude this review of the twelve theological guidelines, I want to share with you a prayer that many on the committee found helpful and sobering as we completed our work. It is taken from the Presbyterian Worship Book.

> Almighty God, you have no patience with solemn assemblies or heaped-up words to be heard by [our neighbors]. Forgive those who have written prayers for congregations. Remind them that our words will pass away, but that your word will last and be fulfilled; through Jesus Christ our Lord. Amen.

35. Book of Worship:

A Response

(1988)

Chalmers Coe

Chalmers Coe (b. 1922) is a Congregational Christian/UCC minister educated at Yale University and Yale Divinity School. After serving pastorates in Connecticut and Massachusetts (1945–56), Coe became a faculty member at Hartford Theological Seminary (1956–60). In 1960, however, he returned to local church ministry and for more than twenty years was senior pastor at First Congregational UCC in Columbus, Ohio (1960–83). In retirement he has taught at Phillips Theological Seminary, Trinity Lutheran Seminary, and the Pontifical College Josephinum (Ohio). Coe was vice chair of the UCC Commission on Worship (1960–67).

After the UCC Book of Worship *was published in 1986 the theological journal* Prism: A Theological Forum for the United Church of Christ *asked several people to critique and evaluate the new resource. Coe examines the "Services of Word and Sacrament" in detail. His commentary on "Word and Sacrament I" reflects both the pleasure and the dissatisfaction of many local pastors with the book.*

Source: Chalmers Coe, an excerpt from "The Services of Word and Sacrament: A Theological Commentary," *Prism* (Spring 1988): 33–37.

The Services of Word and Sacrament: A Theological Commentary

The most effective, and the most pointed, way of assessing the Services of Word and Sacrament is not, I think, to compose a general summary of their eucharistic teaching (which it would be difficult, if not impossible, to do), but to review them from beginning to end. Our business is principally with the analysis and evaluation of content, although structure and style also have theological significance and cannot well be avoided.

And so at once to Service I.

1. The *Greeting,* more especially the first of the printed three greetings, raises an issue which inevitably affects the theology of the sacrament: that of impersonality in the Godhead. "The Creator, the Christ, and the Holy Spirit" commits the congregation to no belief that "whatever else God is, God is at least personal." Our nouns and pronouns are, of course, deficient in what might be called the "personal neuter." Failure to use one gender or the other results, however, in a style of worship that might as well be addressed to what Mr. Graham Greene, in his latest phase, is willing to call the Noosphere. Which may satisfy Mr. Greene, but will be unacceptable to most Christians.

2. The *Sentences of Adoration* begin, as they so often (and so puzzlingly) do in our church, with "Our help is in the name of the Holy One," etc. A biblical quotation, no doubt, but perhaps unduly need-entered for the purpose at hand. The other sentences are doctrinal, or historical, or biblical, and as such are in a sense unexceptionable.

They contain, however, not one line of adoration. "Holy, holy, holy, Lord God of hosts" would have been better, although of course "Lord" would be regarded as shockingly indecent in certain quarters.

3. With the invitation to the *Confession of Sin* we come to a serious theological issue. Granted, Christians acknowledge their wickednesses to the God whom they already know to be gracious. Nevertheless, is it not conducive to complacency for them to dwell on the fact before the words of confession have passed their lips? Are we encouraging that idolatrous reliance on cheap grace to which they are all too prone? Liturgical precedent to the contrary notwithstanding and there is much of it — does not the initial bland assertion of God's willingness to pardon seem a bit like pulling gently at the divine sleeve as if to remind God how inappropriate it would be to ignore past promises and assurances? That "God, in whose presence we gather, promises us grace" is undoubtedly true. It is better said, however, after we have recited the many evidences of our culpability. As matters now stand, the subsequent *Assurance of Pardon*

is repetitious and therefore almost anticlimactic — particularly with the Reformed "I declare to you" so sadly omitted.

Perhaps it is a matter of accent, or balance. For the alternative invitation, although it too includes the reminder that "God, who is faithful and just, will forgive our sins," and does so before the people have begun to list their faults, starts with a blunt "If we say we have no sin, we deceive ourselves, and the truth is not in us."

Most of the alternative *Confession* itself is a reprint of a confession in the *Lutheran Book of Worship.* It is admirably terse, frank, and monosyllabic. What a disappointment, then, to turn back to the first *Confession* and find sin reduced to a failure "to respond fully to your gracious presence in our lives." (Where else, one wonders, could that gracious presence be?) It would appear that, on the whole, we have done rather well, thank you very much, and may congratulate ourselves on our performance. And yet there remains a distance to go: not "fully" have we responded. It is highly regrettable. Nevertheless, reassurance comes posthaste: "Through Jesus Christ you have offered us new life," as if we need not feel too badly after all about our lack of perfect response. Thus far, the first *Confession* seems more a method of slapping ourselves on the wrist than of pouring out penitence for our Eve-like, and Adam-like, revolt. How astonishing, then, and how unaccountable, are the following words: "We confess that we are captive to sin, that our sin binds us with false pride." It is as though some stalwartly orthodox member of the group of writers, rightly objecting to the reduction of sin to a lack of responding "fully," had insisted that the old vigorous language about bondage and captivity and pride be introduced at all costs. And yet the appearance of it seems abrupt, imprecise, and without adequate preparation. And it is followed by the dark saying that the "wrong we do is made worse by the good we leave undone." How, in the words of Nicodemus, can these things be? Wrong is wrong, and cannot be made worse by anything. We return to a petition for forgiveness; and with a strangely archaic word — "anew" — this *Confession* lurches to its conclusion.

4. An *Act of Praise* ensues. One choice, the Gloria in Excelsis, contains the predictable removal of sexist and monarchical language, but does so at the sacrifice of precision and coherence: "heavenly king," abhorrent to many, becomes "heavenly God," a redundancy; "God's only begotten one" takes the place of "God's only begotten son" (we are left in some uncertainty as to what kind of being Jesus is); and "you alone with the Holy Spirit [are] in the glory of the triune God," which suggests that Jesus Christ and the Holy Spirit have somehow been made to associate with an

independently existing triplicity, and therefore that the Godhead consists not of three persons but of five.

5. As for the *Reading of Scripture,* the commission has been commendably anti-Marcionite: the Old Testament is included as a matter of course. One might reasonably ask, however, what provision can be made for readings from Acts and from Revelation when the only lessons from the New Testament are Epistle and Gospel. (The traditional solution of some churches, according to which readings from those two works are introduced as "*for* the Epistle," seems a bit arbitrary.) And the exhortations "Listen for the Word of God in ______" and "Listen to the Gospel of Jesus Christ according to ______" are ill chosen. "Hear the Word of God in ______" is simpler and better. "Listen for," in the first case, implies that the Word of God just might be heard as the lector proceeds, but that you cannot be sure. "Epistle *lesson*" and "Gospel *lesson*" are unnecessary: "Epistle" and "Gospel" are enough.

The *Sermon, Affirmation of Faith,* and *Prayers of the People* call for no comment.

6. But why *Concerns of the Church?* The title is nothing but a pietistic term for the old "announcements" and provides an excuse for that chitchat which masks itself as warm informality and indulges our Protestant penchant for garrulity. This, it may be objected, is no theological point. But it is: the trivia upon which we choose to comment disclose what we believe to be of overriding importance. God loses out to the bake sale, the flea market, the car wash, and the picnic. Would it not be just as easy to give out this information after the Benediction or before the first hymn? Or even cancel the car wash?

7. The *Offertory* is an event which ought to be quite straightforward. Not so: "The people may express their dedication . . . through dance, and other acts." As for the "other acts," perhaps the less said the better; we may discreetly be left to our speculations. Dance conjures up visions of seventh-grade girls in tutu and ballet slippers, improvising to a piano reduction of "Jalousie." In the Doxology, note the pathetic, embarrassing "in flesh born low."

8. We come now to the *Communion Prayer* as such, preceded by its invitation. The Sursum Corda makes no compromise: the word "God" is rattled off like rapid-fire bursts from a machine gun; "the Lord" would be a slavish concession to masculinity and monarchy.

Pages 45 and 46 are the heart of the service. It is here that the framers had to come to terms with issues that have daunted liturgical authorities for centuries. Have they done so successfully? I shall examine only the first prayer.

We begin, as is most proper, with *thanksgiving;* as Alexandria did (unlike Antioch), the prayer includes thanksgiving for created nature. Commendable enough — the modern urban world is all too far removed from its rootage in the land. But the achievement is rendered less effective by the moralistic, sententious reference to our "vision of the day when sharing by all will mean scarcity for none." Good newspaper reporters would resent having this sentiment called journalistic; it is not journalistic, it is trite.

Remembrance follows, notably of God's covenant with Israel and of those who have gone before us in the faith. The prayer soon drifts off, however, into additional thanksgivings — for the call to reconciliation, for the divine promise of fidelity, and for the inclusiveness of God's summons to the table — and subsequently drifts back again to remembrance, this time of Jesus. More thanksgivings follow, notably for the presence of the Spirit. A truncated Sanctus, Benedictus, and Hosanna bring this section to a close. The Hosanna, be it noted, is for "the one who comes," not for "he who comes."

Anamnesis comes next, the remembrance of the night of betrayal. "Jesus," not "he," took bread, although the proper name is already in the previous sentence and need not be repeated. He gave it not to "his" but to "the" disciples. "In the same way also the cup," the beginning of a new sentence, omits "He took," and therefore has no subject, and therefore is not English.

The prayer goes on, appropriately enough, to *oblation* and *epiklesis.* The *epiklesis* is curiously reticent: it says nothing whatever about the Holy Spirit's acting upon the elements in such a way that, as we receive them, we may know that we are receiving Christ himself. The emphasis is entirely on the church's Spirit-given power to be the "champion of peace and justice in the world." The theology is, to say the least, incomplete, and the sacramental realism of the later words of administration — "Take and eat, this is the body of Christ" — cannot repair the oversight.

We should be deeply grateful to the authors for omitting the miserable "Ministering to you in his name, I give you this bread," which succeeds only in calling attention to the minister's role, and at exactly the wrong moment. And we may be similarly grateful for what must have been a stubborn resistance to the practice of asking the members of the congregation to keep the bread in their hands so that all may make their communion together. This absurd and flamboyant custom, which robs the individual of a suitable moment of private devotion in the midst of a corporate act, is a direct violation of one of the most solemn of all New Testament injunctions. Jesus did not say, "Take and hold"; he said, "Take and eat."

One final comment about the Communion Prayer, taken as a whole, may be appropriate. The persistent avoidance of the words "he," "his," and "him" for Jesus is, in the final analysis, not only clumsily done but also docetic. If the "scandal of particularity" is inherent in our holy religion, the fullness of the Incarnation requires that the Savior be either a woman or a man. The New Testament is unambiguous about the manhood of Jesus. Any effort, therefore, to avoid the implications of this fact is in effect to deny the Incarnation, and is as heretical as the claim of many long ago that Jesus did not really die.

9. The *Prayer of Thanksgiving* is unfortunate in two respects. First, to speak of Jesus' presence "in the simplicity and splendor of this holy meal" is to call excessive attention to our evaluation of, or response to, an objective act which has just occurred. It is atmospheric. It is subjectivist. The focus is not on God but, cloyingly, on the quality of the service we are now concluding. Second, the hope that God's universal church may be a "rainbow of hope in an uncertain world" is simply mawkish.

10. Service I ends with a lovely version of the Nunc Dimittis. There follows, before the *Benediction,* what is called a *Commissioning.* In spite of the fact that my honored and respected friend, Horton Davies, the most learned liturgical scholar in our church, first arranged it more than twenty years ago, I have never liked it. The job of the church, once the communion is over, is to thank God briefly, to receive a final blessing, and — to go home to lunch. This dragging-in of more commandments is out of place, and no argument that the service lacks ethical point without it will persuade me to the contrary. "Go forth into the world to serve God with gladness." Do we really need to be told to do it? Can't something be left to the imagination? . . .

36. The New Century Hymnal:

"Theological and Ecclesiological Strengths of . . . " and "The Language of Faith and . . . "

(1997)

Daniel Johnson, Richard L. Christensen

The first effort of the United Church of Christ to produce an official hymnal to replace the Congregational Christian Pilgrim Hymnal *and the* Hymnal *of the Evangelical and Reformed Church began in the late 1960s. However, by the time the* Hymnal of the United Church of Christ *(1974) was published it was unacceptable to many UCC members, in part because it did not use intentionally inclusive-language (see vol. 7:30). Within a few years the General Synod (1977) passed an "Overture on Inclusive Language" suggesting the need for a new inclusive language hymnal, and by the late 1980s the United Church Board for Homeland Ministries (UCBHM) was urged to proceed with the project. After many years of work* The New Century Hymnal *(TNCH) was published in 1995.*

Controversy surrounding The New Century Hymnal *was intense. At the 1993 General Synod there was a lively floor debate about the use of the word "Lord" in hymnody. The work of the hymnal committee was challenged and the role of the UCBHM staff questioned. Soon after TNCH was published, Confessing Christ, a group founded in 1993 to encourage*

Sources: Daniel Johnson, "Theological and Ecclesiological Strengths of *The New Century Hymnal,*" in Richard L. Christensen, ed., *How Shall We Sing the Lord's Song: An Assessment of The New Century Hymnal* (Centerville, Mass.: Confessing Christ, 1997), 35–39. Richard L. Christensen, an excerpt from "The Language of Faith and *The New Century Hymnal,*" in Richard L. Christensen, ed., *How Shall We Sing the Lord's Song: An Assessment of the New Century Hymnal* (Centerville, Mass.: Confessing Christ, 1997), 32–34.

theological dialogue (see vol. 7:72), held a consultation in 1996 in Boylston, Massachusetts, and subsequently published a book How Shall We Sing the Lord's Song: An Assessment of The New Century Hymnal *(1997).*

Daniel Johnson (b. 1940) is a UCC minister educated at North Park College, American Academy of Art (Chicago), William Jewell College (Liberty, Missouri), and Andover Newton Theological School. During his ministry he has served pastorates in Massachusetts, Connecticut, Illinois, Ohio, and Maine (1970). He also taught UCC history and polity at Yale Divinity School and Eden Theological Seminary. Johnson is a musician and a member of the committee that did most of the work to develop The New Century Hymnal. *His twenty-one "Theological and Ecclesiological Strengths of* The New Century Hymnal,*" presented at the 1996 consultation, set forth the rationale for most of the decisions made surrounding the hymnal. He celebrates the hymnal's return of the Psalter to the liturgy, its inclusion of new hymns and music from a variety of ethnic traditions, and its responsiveness to the Christian feminist critique of the language of faith (see vol. 7:31 and 65).*

Richard L. Christensen (b. 1945) is a UCC minister initially educated at Lehigh University and Lancaster Theological Seminary. After serving pastorates in Ohio and Pennsylvania (1970–80 and 1983–88), teaching for three years in Botswana in south central Africa (1980–83), and doing further graduate study at Union Theological Seminary in Virginia (1988–92), he became a faculty member at Phillips Theological Seminary, Tulsa, Oklahoma (1992–98). Since 1998 he has been on the faculty at Lakeland College, Wisconsin.

Christensen was the editor of How Shall We Sing the Lord's Song *and his presentation at the 1996 Confessing Christ consultation on TNCH, "The Language of Faith and* The New Century Hymnal,*" summarizes the theological critique of TNCH. He outlines various ways in which he believes that it eliminates or distorts "classical Christian language for the Trinity" and how it refuses to acknowledge that "Jesus of Nazareth was a particular person of the male gender." Christensen and other critics of TNCH insist that Christians can and should use a variety of terms and forms in worship and prayer, but they are troubled with the language of the TNCH because they believe that it is inconsistent with the Christian story.*

Theological and Ecclesiological Strengths of *The New Century Hymnal*

1. We are living in a new era of hymn-writing creativity, and like many recently published hymnals *TNCH* includes many new hymns which give authentic contemporary voice to the Christian faith.

2. *TNCH* restores the Psalter to the UCC. That's an important part of our Reformed legacy. Until now we have had only a small sampling of psalms as responsive readings in our predecessor hymnals.

3. *TNCH* is fully compatible with the Revised Common Lectionary. That's an important linkage with the whole Church and an act of ecumenical responsibility. The Lectionary index is proving helpful to many pastors and lay leaders for choosing hymns for any given Sunday in the Church Year.

4. *TNCH* places new emphasis on the sacraments. This hymnal offers more hymns for Holy Baptism than any predecessor hymnal. The Trinitarian naming of God is fully employed both hymnodically and in the Order for Baptism in the liturgies. TNCH has an intentionally large section for Holy Communion. This too is an attempt to compensate for an "ecclesiological deficit" from the past, and to make a significant UCC statement about the Real Presence of Christ in the Eucharist (e.g., Hymn 348).

5. Some *TNCH* texts are accurate translations from ancient texts rather than alterations of familiar texts (e.g., Hymn 440). Note also Hymn 118, "Of the Parent's Heart Begotten," which accurately translates Prudentius' fourth-century Latin text *Corde natus ex parentis.*

6. Predecessor hymnals avoided hymns sung regularly in racial "minority" congregations. *TNCH* deliberately includes many such hymns due to the conviction that Christianity is for the whole world, not just for the American white middle class.

7. *TNCH* dares to explore boldly the theological boundary between traditional orthodoxy and the feminist critiques of that orthodoxy which have emerged toward the close of the twentieth century. Critics damn *TNCH* for this, but time and wise discernment will tell whether *TNCH* moves faithfully toward new ways to sing the Christian faith. Early and strident naysayers are only early and strident. *TNCH* has dared to rework language for people and language for God because such reworking has become a theological priority for the United Church of Christ over the last two decades. Though much is written and discussed about such reworking of language, most recently published liturgies and hymnals stop short of bold exploration of new possibilities. The hymnal committee had few

models or tested examples from which to work, and found it necessary to create theological and language guidelines.

8. The additional images for God in *TNCH* texts are drawn from the Bible. The committee was intentional about creating a hymnal in which dependence on the Bible would be clear and obvious. The Theological Guidelines state, "Father is one way to envision God, but God is also seen biblically as Creator, Mother, Builder, Rock, Mystery, Love, Breath. . . . " These seven images were meant to guide and encourage the poets and hymn-writers to whom textual revision was assigned and indeed they found many more: Flame, Strength, Wind, Lamb, Word, and Light are some of the biblical images by which God may be sung.

9. The Advent 1995 issue of the Consultation on Church Union's *In Common* describes as "radical and refreshing" *TNCH*'s "approach to power and gender language." This brief comment contrasts with comments from within the UCC, warning that TNCH will jeopardize our relations with COCU and with other denominations. I would ask those who worry about other denominations' reactions to our new hymnal whether those denominations worried about UCC opinion of their new hymnals.

10. *TNCH* puts into the hands of the worshiping congregation the liturgies of the UCC *Book of Worship* for the first time. The *Book of Worship* is too expensive to be purchased by our congregations for every worshiper. Liturgy belongs to the people and must be available to the congregations.

11. For congregations accustomed to freer ways of worship, the Worship Resources (Nos. 816 through 880) offer many options, old and new, for prayer and the leading of worship.

12. The first options in *TNCH* for the ecumenical creeds (No. 881 and No. 883) are reprinted from the English Language Liturgical Consultation revised texts (*ELLC* 1988). This is important ecumenically.

13. As far as I know, the background sketch of the hymn or its writer on each page is unique to *TNCH.* Previously we depended on a hymnal companion for this kind of information.

14. The way *TNCH* is organized (see Contents pages) reveals the hymnal committee's understanding of the United Church of Christ thirty-eight years into its life: following conformity to and provision for the full Church Year, the next two sections organize the hymns according to the well-known structure of the World Council of Churches, dividing hymns between Faith and Order, and Life and Work.

15. You will find no separate category for children and youth. One very young person who spoke up at a hymnal forum advised that such a category was unnecessary segregation. We agreed, and included hymns

traditionally associated with children and youth wherever they fit in the overall design of the hymnal.

16. Any who resist or reject *TNCH* are advised that the three predecessor hymnals of the UCC remain available in print. And congregations are free to choose any hymnal anyway. Critics need not proceed on the assumption that *TNCH* is the only new option open to congregations. This point is offered not as a strength of *TNCH,* but as an example of UCC diversity, one of our strengths as a denomination.

17. Much has been said about the reduction of use of the title "Lord" in *TNCH.* Notice that in the early Christian confession "*Iesus Christos Kurios,*" we have transliterated the first two words, but translated the third into all the languages on earth. Does "Sovereign" not mean precisely the same reality as "Lord"?

18. The joining of the two names "Jesus" and "Christ" is itself a confession of faith identifying God particularly in Jesus of Nazareth. *TNCH* constantly affirms this confession of faith.

19. Is the gender of Jesus compromised when he is sung as "Child" of God? The third-century *Apostolic Tradition of Hippolytus* didn't think so. Does our salvation depend upon the atoning sacrifice of a male? Does our salvation not depend upon the atoning sacrifice of the Word made flesh? Critics mistakenly think *TNCH* is embarrassed about the gender of Jesus; in hymn after hymn *TNCH* clearly confesses the incarnation of Christ in one specific human being in whom "Now the light of God revealed . . . through the Child of human face" (Prudentius, Hymn 118, v. 3).

20. Brian Wren's hymn "Bring Many Names" (Hymn 11) is quickly becoming a modern favorite. To be sure, its fourth and fifth verses risk the unorthodoxy of a God in process and change (but for incarnational reasons). But more importantly, this hymn teaches that the Christian faith is not shackled to one vision or one perception of the Holy One. Rabbi Sandy Eisenberg Sasso's book for children, *In the Name of God,* brilliantly and simply teaches the same truth from a Jewish perspective, and I urge critics of *TNCH* to read Rabbi Sasso, and to sing Hymn 11 with a congregation learning to love it.

21. Finally, and perhaps most important: any hymnal is for singing our faith, not for debating it. I have yet to find a perfect hymnal, and I have some experience with our faith and with our music. *TNCH* provides a very large collection of hymns, and any congregation can find many hymns in it for the singing of our faith in ways both old and new. Praise God!

The Language of Faith and *The New Century Hymnal*

. . . While it is true that the variety of Christian theology is endless, it is not limitless. We cannot simply make up new terms just because they suit us. That is defining the faith from our own experience rather than recognizing the grace that comes to us from beyond ourselves, grace that startles us and transforms our own experience. It shatters our lives, and we find that the things we trusted in, the things that we depended on, pale in comparison. We find that the things we thought determined our lives no longer do. That is the judgment and grace of the gospel.

I don't want to be misunderstood here. This is not to say we cannot use a variety of terms and forms in worship and prayer. Indeed, for a richer worship life we should use a variety. But they should be terms that are consistent with the Christian story. As I noted earlier, all we have to do is go through the Psalms (for example) and we will find a rich variety of language for God. I would like to come to a conclusion by suggesting four false premises which seem to me to underlie *TNCH,* several of which I have already alluded to. The first false premise is one that underlies much of contemporary church life, and it is the idea that it is only our own personal experience that defines the faith of the Church. When we change the wording of hymns because it does not square with our own experience, that is a quite a-historical stance, and if Christianity is anything, it is a historical faith. This idea tends to deny there is something outside our experience which comes to us and transforms our experience. This premise makes for fragmentation and tends to deny unity. Our unity is in Christ, not in our own personal experience. The real question here is this: Does Christianity have any historical integrity? If we answer "no," then Willis Elliott is right and we are starting a new religion. If the answer is "yes," then we need to be sure that the expression of the faith is essentially what the Church has proclaimed through the ages.

The second false premise is related to the first. That is, the attempt to get rid of hierarchical language is based on the notion that we need no authority over us, that we need nothing outside ourselves. There is a pop song heard often these days called "A Hero Lies in Me." The words of the song go something like this: "When you think all hope is gone, look inside yourself and be strong, and you will learn the truth that a hero lies in you." This is the epitome of New Age Pelagianism. Every time I hear that song on the radio I think how hopeless a song it is for people who are poor or marginalized and have a sense of powerlessness. The hymnal does not go to that length, but there are a number of places where the words of the hymns have been changed to put the emphasis on human actions rather than on God's initiative.

The third false premise is the idea that the hymnal was intended to be a prophetic book. I would argue with that and say it should be more of a pastoral book. I have heard hymnal committee people say they wished to produce a book that every person could sing without taking offense. I suspect if *TNCH* were truly prophetic, it would offend everybody.

The fourth false premise is this: that changing language will lead to more just and equal treatment of those who have been marginalized and abused. This simply does not take sin seriously enough. As I noted before, people can misuse language to back up their actions, but even if we don't have the language, we will simply find other justifications for what we do. It is more often true that we act our way into a way of thinking than it is that we think our way into a way of acting. Language and culture work together in that people have attitudes and act in ways that bring about a change in language. Twenty years ago, we did not decide to start calling the person heading a committee a chairperson and then afterward begin to see women chairing committees. No, women were becoming more evident in leadership and finally becoming more recognized for their gifts and many people concluded that the language had to change. We cannot change familiar language by decree and expect people to embrace it wholeheartedly. We will just meet resistance.

I have been made particularly aware of the significance of language lately because of my acquaintance with a young man in Tulsa who is a member of the Yuchi Indian tribe. He is learning the Yuchi language, because there are only twenty-two people in the world who speak it, and they are all getting up in years. He said to me, "I have to learn the language, because if we lose our language, we lose our ways. And if we lose our ways, we lose our way." Imagine having the responsibility for the continuance of an entire way of life. We have a responsibility for the integrity of the Christian witness. We must be careful to maintain that integrity in a world that twists and manipulates language to suit its own narrow purposes. However we choose to use the new hymnal, I hope we will seek to maintain that integrity.

Affirming Congregations

37. Congregational Life: *"Servants of the Church"*

(1960)

Roger Hazelton

Roger Hazelton (1909–88) was a Congregational Christian/UCC minister educated at Amherst College, Chicago Theological Seminary, the University of Chicago, and Yale University. He was on the faculty at Olivet College (1936–39), Colorado College (1939–45), Andover Newton Theological School (1945–57) and (1965–78), and Pomona College (1957–60). Hazelton was the dean of the Oberlin Graduate School of Theology (1960–65).

In his 1960 United Church Herald *article, "Servants of the Church," Hazelton celebrates the role of the laity. Laity are servants of the church which is itself a servant; laity means ministry, so there is no difference between ministers and laity; laity and clergy in the ministering community (the church) do not minister to themselves; and laity should let the church be shaped by its God-given purpose. He concludes by reminding readers of what Jesus said about salt, yeast, and light: "Christ calls us all to life within the church—a salty, yeasty, and radiant sort of life."*

Source: Roger Hazelton, "Servants of the Church," *United Church Herald,* December 15, 1960, 12–13, 30.

Servants of the Church

It would be wrong to take this title, "Servants of the church," as meaning that the church itself is to be the object of our service. Our job then, whether as laymen or ministers, would be merely to keep the institution going and growing, its organizations lively and its operations financially sound.

According to this view, what would be expected of us is just what would be expected of any "good worker" in any successful enterprise in twentieth-century America — that we should be fully serviceable to the institution that commands our effort and loyalty, giving our time and talent and treasure to the running of that to which we belong.

Frightening Ignorance

I hasten to say that I do not think for a moment that this is the intention behind this frequently used phrase. But all the same this point of view does show up with alarming frequency in what we call laymen's work. What is wrong with such a notion is that it betrays a frightening ignorance of the nature and purpose of the church itself. For what we all need is not so much a "shot in the arm" to work harder for something whose existence and importance we can take utterly for granted. We need and need mightily a keener, surer sense of what we have to do and to be as members of that strange and wonderful community, called and guided by the spirit of God, that we know as the Christian church.

Working for the church is by no means an end in itself. If we are only good "organization men" we cannot be the servants of God's everlasting kingdom. We must know whose we are, whom also we serve. Something as drastic and decisive as that is required of every one of us.

We cannot take the church for granted because we cannot take the reign of God for granted in our kind of world. Isn't there something just a bit ridiculous about assuming that we in the church are simply doing what God wants done? Is the church we are asked to serve only a piece of the world, more of the same, or is it a colony of heaven and an outpost of eternity?

Actually, when you come to think of it, the life of the church is always a double life — a life that is visible, organized, budgeted, social, institutional, and a life that is invisible, mysterious, hid with Christ in God. We serve the church best if we serve the cause the church is meant to serve. And we should never forget the hidden, eternal dimensions of our service in which to act is to believe and to work is to pray.

Yes, the church's life is always a life lived on two levels at once and this makes our servanthood, like that of Jesus Christ himself, a risky and difficult affair. The church exists to preach the gospel and hand down the faith to coming generations, but it must not suppose that God has nothing new to tell us or that our job is merely one of churchly self-preservation or churchly self-expression. We Christians live in two orders, two sorts of community, two dimensions of being, one earthly and the other spiritual. And there must be no doubt as to which is finally the more important.

My first point, then, is that we are servants of a form of life in the world that is itself a servant. The institution called the church is actually the instrument of God's intention to love the world back into fellowship with himself.

Church Loyalty

Loyalty to the church is nothing unless it is even more a loyalty to him who makes and endlessly remakes the church according to his will, declared unto mankind in Jesus Christ our Lord. The task within the church is nothing less than that of saving and making whole the common life of man in God's own name and by his gracious governing power. That is what we are doing, or should be doing, when we plan new buildings, serve communion, raise budgets or go to meetings. And it is our deepest faith that there is open to us a gift equal to our task, that in our working for the church we may become coworkers with the Lord of the church, in whom and through whom and by whom are all things.

My second point is that in the church laity means ministry. After all, this is the real intent behind the affirmation that we Protestants like to make of "the priesthood of all believers." Not that everyone can be his own priest; that is plainly false. This is something we can only do for each other. Forgiveness, healing, helping, teaching, encouraging — these are things that happen between persons within a community of acceptance and understanding. What a priest does is to lift up the needs and hopes of his fellow worshipers into the presence of the high and holy God.

This is what each one of us does for the others in the church, as well as what each of us has a right to expect will be done for him by all the others. That is what membership in a common body means and is. Not that priests are unnecessary but that all of us are priests is the plain meaning of this central principle in our Protestant faith.

Protestant Principle

So, far from distinguishing professionals from nonprofessionals in the service of the church, these words "laity" and "ministry" mean much the same thing and apply to each and all of us. In a very real sense everyone is a layman before God: there are no special privileges or advantages, from the view point of the gospel, by which one group of Christians can be set off against another. The layman may think that clergymen, by virtue of training and experience, are or ought to be more adept and dedicated in living the Christian life than he can ever be. But we clergymen know better.

We have learned too much from laymen about the claims and promises of the way of Christ, about the cost and joy of discipleship, to suppose that our professional status in the church gives us any head start or potential toe hold on righteousness. If anything, our clerical role makes Christian living more difficult; we are handicapped by our vested interest in the church, by the fact that we are "front men," symbols of a way of life that no man or woman can worthily represent in its fullness, and by the further fact that since our knowledge of the gospel is presumably greater our awareness of how far our lives come short of its demands and rewards is necessarily greater too.

I cannot make a way of life into a way of making my living without a kind of constant and insidious treason to my Lord. And to get some sort of reality and downright honesty into my effort to live that life, I must come out of the sanctuary, step down from the pulpit and learn how "to wait on the street corner, or walk about the steel mill, or sit in the office or the board room, speaking, listening, thinking, participating with the layman in his effort to hear, to understand and to live by the word of God."

And if "laity" defines what we all are before God, "ministry" defines what we all must do for him. It means, of course, the same thing as service — being serviceable to the purposes for which God has fashioned and maintains his church. But let us look a bit more closely at this idea of service or ministry.

The surest thing about the Christian life is that nobody can bear his own burden but must carry someone else's burden. This is as far as can be imagined from the attitude that was expressed once: "We are all here on earth to help others; what on earth the others are here for I don't know." No, the motto of the kingdom of God, of which the church of Christ is the frontier outpost, is this: "Your life and death are with your neighbor." That is the deepest meaning of the word "love" and it makes ministers of us all in Christ's name. We Christians do our suffering and rejoicing together. That is why laity means ministry, and cannot mean anything else but ministry.

All of this goes back to our understanding of the church. It was Truman B. Douglass who said that laymen spend so much time doing church work that they never get around to doing the work of the church. Well, almost never. It all depends on what you mean by "church." Let me try to say what I mean by it. I mean the ministering community set down in the midst of other communities, the community launched into being by Jesus Christ who came not to be served but to serve, and to give his life a ransom for many. It is the community in which the first shall be last and the humble exalted, where suffering is triumph and burden-bearing is joy.

Ministering Community

It is the community where men and women and children are gathered out of many nations, tongues and races, and are bound and kept together not by the cozy human warmth of those who fear solitude and crave support but by the infinitely costly, caring, daring action of God in Christ — an act the name of which, the only possible name, is simply love.

What is the church? The church is that gathering together and tethering of human life, that humbling and gentling of life, by which the love of God for us becomes our love for one another — and not a sticky, clinging sort of love either, but a kind of ministering gratitude and praise and overflow and adoring answer to him who first loved us. That is the church and we are all members of it, as members of the body of God's loving purpose in the world of things and persons where our Christian lot is cast.

And the work of the church, in which we all share according to the variety of our needs and gifts, is the carrying on and greatening of that mode of community that entered history in Jesus, the community of love serving men and of men serving love. Such community is always being threatened by forces deep and dark within the very flesh of man, but it has a way of breaking in and. through them into visible reality, into the world where we are most at home. And if you ask what this can have to do with cranking mimeograph machines or working your way down a telephone list, the answer is that it has everything to do with such "church work," but only so long as its main purpose is kept clear. So long as we remain servants of him who came to be the servant of all, so long as our only question is not "Who am I" but "Whose?" church work will always be the work of the church.

That is my third point — that as a ministering community the church does not minister to itself (that would be a contradiction in terms) but to the world God sent his Son to save. And do not be misled; we are all in the world and the world is very much in the church. When St. Augustine wrote about the two cities, the earthly and the heavenly, mingled in the world, or when Jesus spoke of the wheat and the weeds growing together till the consummation of his Father's kingdom, they had this truth very much in mind. Just as there is something shockingly indiscriminate in God's love for us, so there must be the same charitable, generous concern within our love toward others. We are ministers, every one of us, precisely because we are the people of God.

God-Given Purpose

Let me express my fourth point as briefly and simply as I can, then try to spell it out a bit in various practical ways. The point — or better, the principle — is this: let the church really be the church. Let it become what it truly, deeply is. Let its programs and procedures be stirred and shaped by its perspective and God-given purpose, that of ministering to all people everywhere by the power of the love that worketh in us. "But how?" someone is sure to ask. "What guidelines can be set up?" Let me mention just a few.

For one thing, there is the old pesky problem of denominationalism; what are we going to do about that? Fortunately we in the United Church of Christ are already working on it. We shall fail miserably if our new ordering of churchly life becomes merely one more denomination added to the old. But if we can make plain the oneness of our faith in God who makes us one, then instead of increasing confusion and disorder in the household of God we shall be able to bring wholeness and renewal to it. But again, how? Certainly not by any spectacular feat of social engineering on our part, but by becoming pliable and serviceable to the moving of God's spirit.

So while no denomination — not even a merger of denominations — can be the church, it is through denominational and interdenominational channels that the work of the church in our time must and therefore can be carried on. Our guideline with respect to denominationalism should be: "Use it, but don't let it use you." And remember that it is not bigness but oneness that makes the church the church.

Or there is the matter of religious growth and success in the life of the church today. Without doubt it is fashionable and popular to be a church member. Everybody's doing it. Religion fits snugly into the American way of life. Indeed most people, if the truth were told, find it hard to distinguish religious faith from patriotism. The point is that we churchmen are having things our own way, much too much our own way, and as a result the cutting edge of our message and the sting of our mission have gotten lost.

The words written by Thomas à Kempis centuries ago apply to us: "God has now many lovers of his heavenly kingdom, but very few bearers of his cross." Christianity is not a success story; the cross is not anybody's "dish of tea"; and the piety that would make this mistaken identification is nothing so much as a kind of blasphemy and idolatry, in fact, anything at all but Christian faith. "Woe to you," said Jesus, "when men speak well of you." Let us stop being among those who make religion their God instead of God their religion. We must restore something of that quality of pilgrimage and commitment that belongs to faith when it is most itself. . . .

38. Laity:

"The Ministry of the Church and 'Lay Ministers'"

(1963)

In the United Church of Christ from time to time when a local congregation cannot find a qualified ordained minister to call as its pastor, laypersons are authorized to take on leadership responsibilities as "lay ministers." Theologically, this designation is confusing. As a consequence, early in the 1960s the General Synod asked the UCC Theological Commission to look into the status and understanding of "lay ministers."

In a report to the General Synod (1963) the commission notes that " 'lay ministry' should be considered in relation to the church's ministry, the ordained ministry and the ministry of the laity." Care needs to be taken to distinguish between the ministry of the laity and the "lay minister." The ministry of the laity is grounded in the ministry of the whole church of Jesus Christ, whereas the ministry of a "lay minister" is a ministry of leadership by a layperson in the church in a specific place under "specialized and exceptional circumstances."

Source: "The Ministry of the Church and 'Lay Ministers'," an excerpt from the "Report of the Theological Commission," in *Advance Reports to General Synod 1963,* 77–78.

The Ministry of the Church and "Lay Ministers"

Jesus Christ is the minister in the church. From his ministry, all ministries of the church are derived; on his ministry, all ministries of the church are dependent; to his ministry, all ministries of the church are instrumental. Thus, all the ministries of the church other than that of Jesus Christ are derivative, dependent and functional. The only one essential ministry in the church is the perpetual ministry of the risen and ever-present Lord himself, as T. W. Manson wrote.

The context in which alone the ministry of the laity, the "lay minister" and the "ordained minister" can be fruitfully discussed is the nature and mission of the church, as that nature and mission is given to it by Christ himself. Christ has given the total ministry — derivative from, dependent on and instrumental to his ministry — to the whole church. The ministry of the laity is not to be set over against the ordained ministry; nor is the ordained ministry a matter of status. Within the total ministry of the church, there are differences of function and certain ministries are representative of the church's total ministry. In the New Testament, the most important factors for such functional ministries as apostles, prophets, teachers, healers and interpreters (1 Cor. 12:27–30) are that the individual should have the necessary gifts and that those gifts should be recognized by the church.

The standard for our understanding of the church's ministry is our understanding of the ministry of Jesus Christ. As Professor [Robert] Paul wrote in his paper: "If this is the source of all ministry within the church, then the call of the laos — the whole People of God — is to live redemptively and kerygmatically within the world, i.e., to live in a way which not only helps to redeem humanity, but also in a manner which actively proclaims that redemption in Jesus Christ. Indeed, this would appear to be the meaning and intent of the Sacrament of Baptism, which deserves to be regarded as the special sacrament of the People of God's consecration to a ministry of witness."

Since all Christians are involved in the total ministry of the church, all are involved in maintaining the ministry of the church in its wholeness, whether exercised within the church or in society. If the church's ministry is to be fulfilled in the world, then the work of ministry, the "building up of the body of Christ" by the means of grace we receive through the church alone, has to be carried on. Provision for nourishing the inner spiritual life is the concern of Christian laymen as well as of ordained ministers. The need for the church to maintain its own inner life arises both from its recognition that it lives by grace ever newly given and from its recognition that without daily renewal it cannot fulfill its mission in the world.

In such a perspective, we view both the ordained ministry and the ministry of the laity. They are not mutually exclusive roles. They are comprehended in the ministry and mission of the church. To quote Professor Paul again: "Normally, the main concern of those whom God has called to be ordained is with building up the faithful within the church so that the members may engage more fruitfully in the world. Similarly, the principle concern of those whom we think of as 'laymen' is to be witnesses in secular society: this is where God the Redeemer is able to use their gifts best in the service of his Kingdom."

39. The Local Church:

"The Church Faces Its Own Crisis" and "The Role of the Local Church"

(1963, 1965)

Shirley E. Greene, Long Range Planning Committee

In the early 1960s as the nation responded to the racial crisis, local congregations struggled to clarify their identity and mission. In 1963 (August 27–29) the Department of the Church in Town and Country, in the Division of Church Extension of the United Church Board for Homeland Ministries (UCBHM) held a convocation entitled "The Church and Culture in Crisis" at Heidelberg College (Tiffin, Ohio).

Worship, speeches, and discussion groups wrestled with the social upheavals of the day and their relationship to local churches. Shirley E. Greene (1911–96) was a Congregational/UCC minister educated at Dartmouth College, Chicago Theological Seminary, and the University of Chicago. After serving churches in Indiana and Illinois and working for the National Farmers Union (1954–57), he served on the staff of the UCBHM (1957–64). Later he worked for the National Council of Churches (NCC) (1964–68). Greene's lengthy presentation on the relationship of the church to culture concludes with words about change.

Several years later, as the Long Range Planning Committee of the UCC addressed challenges facing local congregations, an ad hoc committee was appointed to explore the role of the local church. Its "Statement

Sources: Shirley E. Greene, an excerpt from "The Church Faces Its Own Crisis: In Relation to Community and Culture," from *The Church and Culture in Crisis* (St. Louis: Department of the Church in Town and Country, Division of Church Extension, United Church Board for Homeland Ministries, 1963), 64–65. Ad Hoc Committee on the Local Church, "Statement on the Role of the Local Church in the Total Life and Mission of the Church," a typescript attached to the Minutes of the Long Range Planning Committee, May 7–8, 1965.

on the Role of the Local Church in the Total Life and Mission of the Church" was attached to the May 7–9, 1965, committee minutes. The ad hoc committee was J. William Arnold, R. Elizabeth Johns, Gerald J. Jud, James W. Lenhart, and Richard L. Ford, chair.

The Church as Change Agent

I will begin this summary by stating categorically that there are four ways in which a church (or any group) may respond to change: We can ignore it; resist it; accept it; or mold it. Of course, our reactions are never wholly unitary or consistent, either as individuals or as groups. I speak, however, in terms of major types of response.

Stupidly to ignore the changes taking place in the culture of town and country is to condemn ourselves to the worst form of irrelevancy, a charge which is already being hurled with painful accuracy against us at many points.

Stubbornly to resist the trends of the times is a sure formula for suicide. Change is as inevitable as the tides of the sea. We may stand fast on the rock of traditionalism until the sea of change rises and engulfs us. We will not turn that tide back.

Blindly to accept all the changes coming our way from a society essentially oriented to secular science and technology, is to be guilty of apostasy in its worst form. It is to repudiate the role defined for the Church in our Lord's Great Commission, and to relinquish the moral initiative which justifies the Church's claim to be the witnessing Body of Christ.

This leaves the Church with but one live option, one stance which it can legitimately assume in the face of revolutionary change and crisis. The Church must enter dynamically and creatively into the stream of flux and change, to mold trends in the direction of those values, those attitudes, those practices which it understands to reflect God's will for men as revealed in Biblical teaching and most especially, in the life and teachings of Jesus Christ. The Church, in short, must become a "change agent" in its own right.

The role of change agent involves a degree of commitment to serious study, thought, analysis, evaluation and value projection quite beyond anything presently characteristic of most of our constituency in the United Church of Christ — either laity or clergy. We will probably have to look to the atomic scientists, the ideological communists, or the Holy Rollers for samples of the kind of single-minded commitment to which our Lord is calling us as agents of change after the pattern of the Divine Will.

To do less is to deny the calling of the people of God and to repeat the betrayal of Peter who, in a moment of crisis, swore "I do not know the man!"

To accept this role involves risk. In our involvement with the culture, we may get contaminated at times by the radioactive wastes cast off by a secularized society. We may even get blown up by the explosive qualities of the struggle among conflicting secular ideologies for domination over the minds of men. . . .

Statement on the Role of the Local Church in the Total Life and Mission of the Church

In the polarization of conversation about the local church, two widely separated views have emerged. On the one hand there is the view that the congregation as we know it is obsolete, destined for disappearance. On the other hand is the view that there is nothing basically wrong with the church as an institution and that no change in structure or outlook is either needed or anticipated.

It is the consensus of this committee that neither of these views adequately appraises the situation. Rather, leadership of the churches, lay and clerical, needs to take seriously the crucial questions, relative to the call to mission and the structure of mission in the world, and it must come to terms with the fact that we live in a new age. The relevance and role of the local church require careful redefinition.

Here in our judgment are some of the basic presuppositions underlying a creative critique of this problem:

I. Presuppositions about the Local Church

1. The institutional church as we know it is presently structured for mission with its primary dependence on the local parish.
2. The entire mission of the wider church is heavily dependent on this form for recruitment and financial undergirding.
3. The local church is the primary means for—
    a. Equipping Christians for mission in the world through "memory" (Biblical theology and Christian education).
    b. Creating a "community of reflection" on witness in the world.

c. Providing corporate worship.

d. Ministering to persons and families in private life.

e. Being a sign of God's "for-manness" in the world.

II. Presuppositions about the World

Secularization and urbanization are the striking marks of the new age in which we live. Secularization proceeds as there is a breakdown of closed world views. Thus increasingly a diversity of ways of looking at the world emerges and a new tolerance is evidenced. Anonymity, nobility, pragmatism, and "this-worldliness" characterize this process and constitute the milieu in which the life of the local church is set.

Urbanization provides a context for this new style of living. The secular world is the urban world. Secular man is urban man. This new life style is further accelerated and shaped by scientific and technological advances, high mobility, cosmopolitanism, and economic concentration.

Secularization and urbanization, as we experience them, create for us a new crisis in the erosion and collapse of widely accepted religious and ethical norms.

III. Theological Presuppositions

Part of the difficulty in our local church life reveals that "our theological slip is showing." Too often, people have been brought to a conviction of Jesus Christ as personal Saviour with a resultant pietism of a private religion and deity rather than being related to the God already incarnate in the world.

The witness of the Old Testament is that God is for man and against all that shackles man and keeps him from being fully man. This God is personal but not a private God. He is God of all creatures and all men and in all the worlds in which man lives.

In Jesus Christ this "for-manness" became flesh, and Christ is to be found on the altar of human need. A man in Christ must be a servant in the world. And the church of Jesus Christ must be a servant church, participating in God's mission to man, freeing him to be fully human. Christ is the new Adam — the new man — and his description of the kingdom is the vision that calls the church and to which the church calls the world.

IV. Critique

Granted that the institutional church as presently structured for mission is primarily dependent upon the local parish, and granted that in the foreseeable future this dependence will continue, we must then hear God's call for constant renewal in this shape of the church. Perhaps this call may come most clearly to us by asking penetrating questions relative to our presuppositions:

1. How adequately are we equipping Christians for mission?
2. In what sense is there within the local church a "community of reflection" on our witnessing in the world?
3. How relevant is our worship in lifting up both world and Word?
4. How effective is our ministry to persons in family and private life?
5. In what sense is the local church a "sign" that God is for man in all the worlds in which man lives?

V. Summary

We are affirming the local church as crucial for mission. It lives in response to the God who calls it into being and who calls it forth to servanthood in his world. It is in the local church that the Word is encountered, celebrated, reflected upon, and authenticated in a "living out" into the world. The local church does not exist in isolation. It is nurtured in the faith and experience of the historic church, and it lives in relationship to the ongoing Christian community. But the most meaningful thrust of its life in this time is toward a loving and prophetic involvement in the world in which it is summoned to live as God's pilgrim people.

The local church must continue to proclaim the Gospel, celebrate the past and present acts of the Living God, nurture the life of its people and seek to experience true community in Christ.

It is recognized that the local church is presently well equipped and structured to minister to the family and to persons in the private sector. The church must not lessen but rather strengthen and make more effective this vital area of its ministry.

The church should also be sensitizing and preparing its people for ministry in the world. It will ask its people, not only to come, but even more importantly, to go; not merely to come to, but to go out into. It will equip its people to participate in the life of the world in such ways as will deal relevantly with the issues of human existence. It will deploy its people out into community and institutional life, helping them to see this as a meaningful extension of their churchmanship.

While individual Christians must continue to bear witness to their Lord in all aspects of life, the community of believers must discover corporate ways to make the Gospel relevant to all the worlds in which modern man exists. A local congregation will think not only in terms of individuals, but in terms of the corporate structures in the world where decisions are made and values are determined which affect man's life. It will be flexible enough to restructure itself for its own ministry to its immediate community and the larger, diverse society in which it is set. It will develop new forms and strategies aimed at penetrating the worlds of work, leisure time, and public life. Instead of using its people in the organizational work of the local church, it will minimize internal "housekeeping" and develop task forces on issues and needs in the community. Thus, the local church will seek constructively to engage the world around it in direct action and service.

But the very nature of the local church sets some limits on the amount and extent of its involvement. Increasingly, our ministry to the world must be done in cooperative ways developed along total community and ecumenical lines. Also, the local church will encourage and support the emergence of new forms of mission through its denomination, that things it cannot do may be done through a denominational focus and penetration. On the other hand, the denomination itself will help the local church to be renewed, empowered and equipped as a form of mission in its particular place. Instead of an estrangement between church structures, there may be an "alongsidedness" of local church, denominational agencies and . . . cooperative and ecumenical ministries.

40. Strengthening and Celebrating the Church:

The Local Church Priority

(1971, 1971, 1986)

Franklin W. Thomas, Grant E. Harrity, Ruth Duck

In the late 1960s and early 1970s when the General Synod adopted priorities to channel national resources for the support of the local church, new appreciation and enthusiasm for local leadership and mission grew. At the General Synod in 1971 a layperson, Franklin W. Thomas, from Atlanta, Georgia; and a pastor, Grant E. Harrity, from Allentown, Pennsylvania, gave personal testimonies about the importance of the local church — challenging the General Synod, national instrumentalities, and conferences to give local churches new attention and assistance.

Ruth Duck (b. 1947) is a UCC minister educated at Rhodes College (Memphis, Tennessee), Chicago Theological Seminary, University of Notre Dame, and Boston University School of Theology. She was a local pastor in Wisconsin (1975–84) and has been a faculty member at Garrett Evangelical Theological Seminary (Evanston, Illinois) since 1989. Duck is co-editor of Bread for the Journey *(1981),* Everflowing Streams: Songs for Worship *(1981), and* Flames of the Spirit *(1985). Twelve of her hymns are in* The New Century Hymnal *(1995). "God, We Thank You for Our People," written in 1986 for a family reunion, celebrates the importance of family and community.*

Sources: Franklin W. Thomas, Atlanta, Georgia, speaking on "Strengthening the Local Church in Life and Mission," *GS Minutes 1971,* 198. Grant E. Harrity, Allentown, Pennsylvania, speaking on "Strengthening the Local Church in Life and Mission," *GS Minutes 1971,* 201–2. Ruth C. Duck, "God, We Thank You for Our People."

Thomas: Strengthening the Local Church in Life and Mission

Speaking from the perspective of a layman who was literally born in the church, and one who has assumed church responsibilities at various levels ranging from youth ministry through Association Moderator (you see, I'm now a "life begins at forty," latter-day young adult), I see today's local church either finding a way to meet human needs or going out of existence.

It is no longer a question of whether the church is in God's world or of God's world, the church must come to recognize that it is God's world! Our local churches, as God's world, have a responsibility to the unlovely as well as the lovely — to the haves as well as the have-nots. The saved as well as the unsaved are a part of God's world, and if God's world already is perfect, then why do we need the church?

One local church I know about strengthened its life and mission through struggling and succeeding in maintaining a viable ministry in a racially changing neighborhood. But this was not accomplished through being satisfied with token black representation in its membership. That church had to move from token black membership to considerable black membership.

Another local church with which I am familiar effected a resurgence of life and mission by recognizing its over-dependency upon its staff of clergymen and upon the related Conference staff. This particular church decided, wisely, to reexamine its full program, to study the makeup and needs of its broad community, and to utilize its findings in its search for a new minister. Clergy-laity partnership was developed as a welcome substitution for clergy domination.

The local church will be strengthened if it can come to know and understand that black power and lay empowerment are no more undesirable than "the power of the gospel." Life in the local church cannot become sufficiently fulfilling without development of the role, involvement, and influence of blacks and nonwhites, youths, laywomen and laymen to their fullest potential!

I want to see the local church, all local churches, prove by their actions that God's world is a world of love and caring rather than a world of demagogy and hatred. The local church has a commission to lead people — all people — to Christ.

I want to see the local church mature to the point that decisions about its program and operations are reached through responsible lay involvement rather than as a result of clergy domination. The local church is going to have to make up its mind whether or not it wants to "look right" or to "be right." This, I submit, will be faced up to and dealt with realistically when at least the majority of the individual members in our local churches decide and demonstrate in their day-to-day living that loving things and using people is not only un-Christian, it is ultimately self-destructive. The local church must believe in and exemplify the principle that people are to be loved, and things are to be used!

Christ, our Lord, did not say to Simon Peter: "If you love me, feed my black sheep, or feed my white sheep, feed my chosen sheep, or feed my ordained sheep." Jesus said, "If you love me, feed my sheep."

The local church must, in every respect, be God's world.

Harrity: Strengthening the Local Church in Life and Mission

Described by many as hopelessly outdated, attacked and condemned as an irrelevant anachronism, the local church still remains a strong and active institution in God's witness among men. Though bloodied and bruised, the local church is still the vital instrument through which the mission of the church finds its fullest expression.

Recognizing this, let us hope that at this session the General Synod will seek new ways and means to help the local church perform its task more effectively. We all know what the problems are, so let's not spend all of our time analyzing and dissecting our difficulties and shortcomings. Rather let us, by positive and concrete actions of this Synod, move to strengthen our local church witness so that the entire church may go forward in fulfilling the tasks set before all of us.

No matter what is said about us, we local church pastors do have some confidence left. We do have faith. We have the willingness and desire to work hard. We have an abundance of deeply committed people in our congregations eager to work through the structure of the local church. We do preach sermons. We do meet with our youth. We do make calls. We do raise ever larger sums of money in order to keep us all going. We do stand up for the right things in our communities. We do make sacrifices. In short, those of us in the local churches are far from being down and out.

But we do need some encouragement and recognition. At this General Synod you must make clear to us in no uncertain terms that the priority of the local church is really of major concern to you. You must proclaim loud and clear — and all local churches and pastors must hear your voice — that the parish church is still at the heart and soul of the Christian ministry. For too long it has been the local church that has borne the brunt of what's wrong with the church. At this point in time our pastors and people need a pat on the back for many jobs well done. Your response to this need can do wonders for the church.

We also need more help and support from you in our efforts to make your pronouncements meaningful to the lives of our people. Our Synods and Conferences, Boards and Instrumentalities have been long on making statements but short on how they should be implemented on the local level. We are the ones who are in daily contact with the people — and with the non-Christian, the sub-Christian, the misinformed Christian, the bigot, the racist — and we try our best to present the Christian gospel to all. But high-sounding pronouncements from the ivory towers must also be accompanied by some practical, down-to-earth suggestions as to how they might be implemented in our local communities.

And when we do get into trouble in trying our best to do what you want us to do, then you must make it clear to us above all doubt that we have your unqualified support in our agonies. This support must be in word and in deed. To set before us goals without proper assistance to carry them out is to put us where David put Uriah. We cannot survive that circumstance.

Finally, we need your help in a crash program that will help us develop a more effective parish life. This General Synod should seriously consider the funding of new experimental programs in local churches which may serve as prototypes for new forms of ministry. What are the alternatives to the centuries-old Sunday morning worship hour? Are there churches willing to experiment in new worship concepts? Cannot new and exciting youth ministries be developed within the parish? Certainly we can afford to subsidize such experiments in our churches, the results of which may enrich the ministries of us all.

And what about a new hymnal one of these years? And new responsive scriptures in modern English? And new church school curriculums that honestly recognize that most of our church schools are small in size, staffed by teachers who do not have degrees in higher education? And a program to help the local parish reverse the trend of declining church membership?

We need new tools, new ideas, and new approaches. What worked before won't work now. Help us, through experimentation, to find out what really will work in this day and age.

In a moment you will see a film. In many ways it will be a depressing picture of the local church today. It will make you think. It will also make you feel sad about the state of affairs in our churches today. But as a local church pastor I want to say this final word. If this General Synod honestly seeks to help us do our job, we will give you the talent, the commitment, and the faith to keep God's word alive among men.

God, We Thank You for Our People

God, we thank you for our people,
roots dug deep with-in the soil,
hardy spirits rich in loving,
strong for struggle, bold for toil.
Faithful Rock of generations,
you whom parents' parents praised:
Here in hope as we remember
may our song to you be raised.

Thank you, God, for gentle pleasure:
lessons learned and secrets told,
hopes and memories saved as treasure,
passed to young ones by the old,
Pranks and glories, songs and stories,
food by loving hands prepared.
God, we bless you for your presence
in our tears and laughter shared.

Still we must confess before you,
sometimes, Savior, we have failed;
though we worship and adore you,
sometimes love has not prevailed.
Tempers racing, devil chasing,
hearts estranged by ice or flame
You transform by ways forgiving.
Grace amazing! Grace, your name!

By your Spirit of creation
keep us bold for risking still,
eager in anticipation,
ever strong to do your will.
Bind us close to one another,
sharing life and death and birth,
Welcoming as sister, brother,
all your children on the earth.

HOLY MANNA 8.7.8.7.D

Authorizing Ministries

41. Ordination:

"Ordination: Stance and Circumstance"

(1969)

Council for Church and Ministry

Ministry: The Journal of the Council for Church and Ministry *was the successor to* The Minister's Quarterly *(1945) and* Theology and Life *(1958). In June 1969 a special issue of* Ministry *examined "ordination," stating that the meaning of ordination was the "sum of several cumulative factors . . . and should be defined in relationship to:*

- *the nature and mission of the church;*
- *the laos — the whole people of God;*
- *the structure of the social order;*
- *the needs and sufferings of humanity;*
- *the ministry begun in Jesus Christ;*
- *the new tools for healing that God places in our hands."*

The Council for Church and Ministry first offers a "Functional Introduction" based on the UCC Constitution, and then it suggests a more "flexible approach" by describing ordination as "a representational advocation." The council states that it is dedicated to keeping ordination "in creative tension with the several sources that gave it birth and give it relevance." Furthermore, the council acknowledges its indebtedness to Robert S. Paul for helping it describe an "advocate" or "representational" understanding of ordination.

Source: Council for Church and Ministry, "Ordination: Stance and Circumstance," *Ministry: The Journal of the Council for Church and Ministry,* UCC, June 1, 1969, 8–9.

Ordination: Stance and Circumstance

A Functional Introduction

Out of the scriptural injunction that all things be done decently and in order, the free churches have taken a pragmatic and functional stance on the priesthood. We of the Council for Church and Ministry must develop flexibility while defending the functions and standards of our office.

Ministries are not orders established as original creations in the church. Instead ministry represents persons designated by the church to fulfill specific functions.

Christ came to minister to the world, and his body, the church, was instituted to continue his work. Ordination and ministerial standing must be seen within the institution striving to be a complete body. All members share the ministry of that body.

Within the mission of the laos, the whole people of God, individuals are ordained to a representative role by specific congregations. The ministerial representatives assume functional responsibilities as priests and prophets, shepherds and counselors, teachers and preachers.

The Council for Church and Ministry must relate its pastoral standards to new manifestations of specialized and secularized ministries. Our office will not and cannot dictate decisions for the associations of a free church. We will, however, strive to maintain both our standards and our flexibility.

Our standards are outlined by the constitution and by-laws of the United Church of Christ and by the "Manual on the Ministry," although these statements codify practices existing at the time they were written and must remain open to the changing dimensions of our profession.

While attempting to honor the diversity of our mission, we suggest the following norms for ministerial standing:

Standing shall be continued without question for all those whose pastoral ministry is fulfilled in the residential parish, as full-time officials in associations, conferences and denominational or interdenominational councils of churches, as teachers of theology or as missionaries abroad or at home, and all those retired from these positions.

Standing shall be continued for those ministers who serve in secular employment not included above and who meet these two requirements: they somehow fulfill the pastoral role in counseling or teaching, and they exercise an accountable and responsible relationship to a congregation or association.

Accordingly, a man who sells insurance and carries on a planned program of ministry within the insurance community should remain in full standing. Each situation must be judged by our standards and by its own uniqueness.

Having changed the former phrase "set apart" to "set into," we hopefully herald an era of new excitement in the ministry among all Christians. Knowing not where our Lord will lead us, we do know where we must begin. We will only be able to meet tomorrow's needs by remembering the roles we are called to fill and ordaining to those functions today all those — but only those — prepared to profess an old story anew.

*A Representational Advocation**

Ordination is a singular expression of a corporate task — it is the whole ministry of the church represented in a specific individual. The one ordained is not set apart but set within the total ministry of the church.

The ordained should be to the church what the church should be to the world. Traditional phrases such as "intercessor for and servant of the people," "proclaimer of and agent for reconciliation," "preserver of and contemporary interpreter of the historical faith," mark the vocation of the community instituted by Christ and the apostles.

The Christian enters the community of faith and accepts these functions in his baptism and confirmation. As general ordinations, baptism and confirmation affirm God's grace for us and also our responsibility for the world Christ came to save.

The general ordination of the laos in baptism and confirmation centers on the individual. This person must work out for himself the implications of his call to the ministry. A diplomat and a housewife share the same call and the same promise, but the vocational implications will be unique to the personalities and situations involved.

Ordination to the ministry approaches Christianity from precisely the opposite direction. While beginning and centering on a single person, it points to the whole ministry of the church.

As Robert Paul states: "It is a churchly act, not because this man and his vocation are chosen for special ecclesiastical dignity or because his work is mainly within the church, but because this vocation brings before the whole company of Christ's people what its own corporate vocation is within the world."

Instead of setting someone apart from other Christians, ordination should emphasize his essential unity with the church and its mission. In the ordained person, Christ personifies his call to all people.

---

*We are indebted to Dr. Robert S. Paul for his advocate approach to ordination, but relieve him of responsibility for our adaptation.

Considering this representational view of the ordained ministry, we should explore further its implications for persons completing theological training and considering ordination and for persons ordained but not engaged in leadership positions within the institutional church.

First, apart from what the individual and the institution identify as the nature and status of ordination, non-ecclesiastical issues impinge on our definitions. For young men, the greatest impingement is their Selective Service status. For good or ill, present laws exclude seminarians and ordained men from military service. However, they do not exclude seminary graduates, priests incognito or Christian servants in the world.

Ordination entitles persons to certain rights and privileges in the secular realm. Consequently, a person's decision to be or not to be ordained should recognize that the social order has a preconceived image of what ordination means.

Second, it is virtually impossible to impose on the tradition and polity of free churches fixed and arbitrary standards defining the nature and status of ordination. In the United Church of Christ, where decision-making on issues related to ordination resides in associations, it is not surprising that definitions vary from place to place and even from time to time within the same association.

Third, the Council for Church and Ministry assumes responsibility for consulting regularly with the associations on matters pertaining to the establishment and maintenance of ministerial standing.

We advocate the representational role of the ordained clergy because we recognize the unresolved issues confronting the several associations. We believe this representational definition provides a viable guide for candidates and their advisors.

Potential candidates should not be discouraged from seeking ordination for the wrong reasons. Too many seminarians see ordination as a divisive and unnecessary feature of the church. Advocating a representational ministry, we affirm an ordination relating to and epitomizing the mission of all Christians — an office established not to single out individuals but to lift up the corporate ministry of the church.

Furthermore, associations must face continuing questions of standing for ordained persons in non-ecclesiastical vocations. We affirm that ordination cannot be renounced if a man continues to be a representative of the ministry of Christ.

If a man is convinced he is serving a representational ministry for the church, tangible signs should authenticate his conviction. A minister should be in fellowship with the church. The lack of participation in and through a local church or association suggests a deficiency in the representational role we expect of the ordained.

We contend that ordination represents to the church its ministry to the world — a ministry apostolic in its character and total in its commitment. To that end we have pledged ourselves, and we invite others — called of the Spirit — to join us in its pursuits.

42. Ordination:

"Charge to a Church" and "You Are Called to Tell the Story"

(1976, 1991)

Robert Y. Johnson, Ruth Duck

Ordination in the United Church of Christ is a three-way or four-way covenant between an individual who has been called and approved for authorized ministry, a local congregation, and an association (or conference acting as an association). If the ordination involves authorization for some specialized ministry or chaplaincy, ordination may become a four-way covenant.

In most ordination services, the ordinand is charged to accept the responsibilities of her or his ministry. In a similar fashion, the congregation, or special calling body, is also charged to take its obligation seriously. "Charge to a Church," written by Robert Y. Johnson, a retired pastor who served churches in Connecticut, Massachusetts, Maine, and Wisconsin, appeared in the "Platform" column of A.D. Magazine *in the mid-1970s.* A.D. Magazine *was a 1972 merger of the* United Church Herald *and* Presbyterian Life.

Ruth Duck (b. 1947) is a UCC minister educated at Rhodes College (Memphis, Tennessee), Chicago Theological Seminary, University of Notre Dame, and Boston University School of Theology. She was a local pastor in Wisconsin (1975–84) and has been part of the faculty of Garrett Evangelical Theological Seminary (Evanston, Illinois) since 1989. Duck is co-editor of Bread for the Journey *(1981),* Everflowing Streams: Songs

---

Sources: Robert Y. Johnson, "Charge to a Church," *A.D. Magazine* (May 1976): 24. Ruth C. Duck, "You Are Called to Tell the Story." Words Copyright © 1991 by GIA Publications, Inc. All Rights Reserved.

for Worship *(1981), and* Flames of the Spirit *(1985). Twelve of her hymns are in* The New Century Hymnal *(1995). Duck wrote the text for "You Are Called to Tell the Story" in 1991 for the ordination of a longtime Presbyterian friend, Elizabeth Caldwell. It seeks to "set ordained ministry in the larger context of the ministry of the whole people of God."*

Charge to a Church

You do not "have" a minister, nor does a minister "have" a church. Rather, together you have a mission. A church devoted to itself alone is like a snake that tries to swallow its own tail — it consumes instead of multiplies itself.

You call yourselves lay people, but you are also ministers. Your minister, though ordained, is also a layperson. As fingers and thumb coordinate for a firm grasp of their object, so must you and your minister function severally and together as one of God's hands stretched forth to serve.

Inside your church speak your own truth with care and encourage others to do the same. Though your truth must ever fall short of the whole truth, your witness to it will enable others to know you better. Silence may be misinterpreted as indifference, which is more damaging than hostility.

Also bear your witness outside the church in words and deeds; our fellowship must not be an army that flees from a victory we've already won. An obedient servant leaves outcomes in wiser hands.

When you remember each other in your prayers you make straight a highway for the coming of the Lord into your midst. Dissension frustrates the gospel and the most dedicated ministers as well. More important than a new organ, a new building, or anything else that money can buy is the warmth of your mutual love. If you must choose between a warm stable and a cold cathedral, let there be no doubt in your minds as to where the Christ is more likely to be born.

If you pray also for your ministers behind their backs, you will be less likely to speak harshly of them from the same location.

Temper your pastoral expectations with common sense. It is possible, but improbable, that your chosen leader will be equally adept as pulpiteer and organizer, private counselor and public prophet, fund-raiser and priest, administrator and model for the young. One fire cannot heat all irons; many buds must be pruned if the few best are to flower.

A minister with an itch for visibility may be evading the more demanding disciplines of study, prayer, and outreach, of sitting up all night with a drug addict or a man whose wife has died. Satan runs to and fro across the land; his popularity takes a high polish.

Demand from your ministers their best and spare them not, but set them free to define the shape and style of their ministry, for what you expect of them and what God expects are not necessarily the same. Tell them what you desire of them, then see that the means are available whereby they can fulfill your desires, for responsibility without power breeds resentment. Their best friends are honest critics, not flatterers, though a pat on the back in season cheers them on.

Call them when you need them, but don't ask them to treat your pet peeve as though it were a mature Christian conviction. A pastor's life is often a series of interruptions, and its most precious possession is time.

Minister to your pastor by sharing your miseries and failures no less than your joys. Let your pastor prove to be worthy of your confidence. A pastor is shock-proof; he or she can help you or refer you to another who may.

Know that the ones you have called to serve you are burdened with a guilt peculiar to the calling, for they dare to stand for more than they are. They are constrained week after week to live with visions and mysteries our poor clay can neither embody nor communicate. Torn between that which is desirable and that which is possible, when the best is done, they can but sigh, "Lord have mercy on me, a sinner."

Bear with patience the ecstasy of ministry, which sometimes feels like a woman in travail, probing the frontiers of new births of the spirit. The secret treasure in this very earthen vessel is the assurance that if God can use a body like me, he can use anybody. Be kinder to your servant than the servant is to self.

Accept with grace the occasional empty cup of sacrifice, for mountain tops do not exist apart from dark valleys.

Grant your leader seasons of refreshment and times for further education, travel, and recreation; a string stretched too taut yields poor music. Since we must be persons before we can be parsons, see that there is leisure and privacy for the enjoyment of family and for doing nothing.

As for sermons, remember that the Word truly preached is from the Spirit to minister and congregation alike and that our best judgments are in this life ambiguous. Try to glimpse beyond what is said to the spirit of what is meant, for the hearing of the Word requires no less effort than the speaking.

You Are Called to Tell the Story

You are called to tell the story,
passing words of life along,
Then to blend your voice with others
as you sing the sacred song.
Christ be known in all our singing,
filling all with songs of love.

You are called to teach the rhythm
of the dance that never ends,
Then to move within the circle,
hand in hand with strangers, friends.
Christ be known in all our dancing,
touching all with hands of love.

You are called to set the table,
blessing bread as Jesus blessed,
Then to come with thirst and hunger,
needing care like all the rest.
Christ be known in all our sharing,
feeding all with signs of love.

May the One whose love is broader
than the measure of all space
Give us words to sing the story,
move among us in this place.
Christ be known in all our living,
filling all with gifts of love.

JULION 8.7.8.7.8.7.

43. Manual on the Ministry:
"The Pastor's Code"

(1977)

Office for Church Life and Leadership

After the Office for Church Life and Leadership (OCLL) was created in 1973, it began developing a new expanded Manual on the Ministry *(MOM). Existing practices were not always consistent in the UCC, and therefore association and conference "committees on Church and Ministry" desired more guidance.*

The new 1977 Manual on the Ministry *(MOM), later revised and expanded in 1986, began with an important essay on "Historical and Theological Perspectives." It sets forth the biblical foundations for UCC understandings of ministry and their historical legacies. It describes the various ways in which Congregational, Christian, Evangelical, and Reformed traditions define and support authorized leadership. It asserts that although in theory there were differences prior to the formation of the UCC in 1957, "actual practice was quite similar." The* Manual on the Ministry *(MOM) names the ongoing tensions between understandings of ordained ministry that focus upon Word and Sacrament, and views of ordained ministry embedded in local congregational life. Its clear guidelines around "in care" and "ordination" seek to cultivate consistency without imposing national regulations. "The Pastor's Code" is a good example of the practical capacity of the MOM to articulate high standards for authorized ministry in the United Church of Christ.*

Source: "The Pastor's Code," *A Manual on the Ministry: Perspectives and Procedures for Authorizing Ministry in the United Church of Christ* (New York: Office for Church Life and Leadership, 1977), 14.

The Pastor's Code

My Ministry

I have been called by God to be a minister of the Lord Jesus Christ. I have sought to prepare myself spiritually, intellectually, and physically to offer professional ministerial leadership to the Church. I seek to model my ministry after the servant ministry of Jesus Christ.

Freedom of the Pulpit

I am called to study, interpret, and proclaim the gospel of Jesus Christ given to us in Scripture and revealed by the Holy Spirit. This congregation expects to be challenged and nurtured by the Word of God, and I attempt to speak the truth in love and with courage in my preaching and teaching.

Pastoral Leadership

I have been called and have prepared myself to preach and teach the gospel, to administer the rites and sacraments of the Church, to provide pastoral care, and to offer leadership in the community, that this congregation may be empowered and enabled for effective ministry and mission.

I will seek to regard all persons with equal love and concern and undertake to minister impartially to the needs of all.

I will hold as sacred all confidences shared with me.

I will stand with those who risk personal well-being because of actions taken in response to their Christian convictions.

I will share the leadership of this congregation with others selected for this purpose and will honor the democratic process in administering the life of this congregation.

I will, upon my termination and departure as pastor, sever my pastoral relations with this congregation, recognizing that all future pastoral functions should be fulfilled by my successors.

Support for Ministry

I will take responsibility for encouraging adequate standards of compensation for all professional and lay employees of this congregation.

I will interpret to the congregation my need for adequate time for physical and spiritual renewal, recreation, and vacation.

I recognize my need for continued growth in ministerial competence and will work with the congregation to develop a plan and the provision of time and money for continuing education and will participate in such education.

I will interpret to the congregation the role of my family in the life of the congregation and will seek to protect my family's privacy and our need for time together.

I recognize the need for regular assessment of my work as pastor and leader of the congregation and will work with the leaders of the congregation to make provision for this. Should divisive tensions threaten our life together, I will join in seeking the counsel of the Conference or Association Minister and/or the Association Committee on the Ministry.

Partnership in Ministry

I believe that the ministry and mission of God's Church depends upon the leadership and labor of both ordained ministers and lay persons. All of us bring our particular skills and gifts, our faithfulness, our strengths and weaknesses to offer in creative and joyful response to the Christian gospel. We worship and work together to become ever more fully and faithfully God's people in this place.

I will stand in a supportive relationship with my colleagues in ministry, offering and receiving counsel in times of need.

I recognize that I am a part of the larger faith community which is the United Church of Christ and will strive to be a responsible participant in Association, Conference and denominational decisions, programs, and actions.

I recognize that the United Church of Christ is a part of the Church Universal and will strive to be a responsible participant in ecumenical activities in order to strengthen the witness and mission of the Church everywhere.

44. Ordination: *"Biblical Foundations" and "Traditions"*

(1987)

Clyde J. Steckel

As the United Church of Christ became more intentional about its theology during the late 1970s (see vol. 7:57) a consultation on ministry, theology, and polity was held near Madison, Wisconsin, in the spring of 1979. Papers from the consultation were published in New Conversations *(Fall 1979). A few years later the faculty at Eden Theological Seminary wrote a paper entitled "A Perspective on Ordination" (1983). Also, in 1983 the Constitution and Bylaws of the United Church of Christ were amended, leading the Office for Church Life and Leadership (OCLL) to revise and update the* Manual on the Ministry *(MOM) (1986) (see vol. 7:43). OCLL felt that it was important to "codify the emerging vocabulary of a 'covenantal' polity" and to recognize the "greater commonality of practice among associations and conferences."*

Response to the revised Manual on the Ministry *was mixed. On the one hand people were pleased that it articulated and regulated a maturing polity and theology about ministry in the UCC. On the other hand, some wondered if the UCC needed to be more open and supportive of Spirit-led understandings of ordination.*

Clyde Steckel (b. 1928) is a Congregational Christian/UCC minister educated at Butler University, Chicago Theological Seminary, and the University of Chicago. After a short time in a parish in Indiana (1950–51), he was a hospital chaplain and campus minister in Illinois and Minnesota (1954–70). As a faculty member at United Theological Seminary of the

---

Source: Clyde J. Steckel, excerpts on "Biblical Foundations" and "Traditions" from "Ordination in the United Church of Christ," a typescript dated October 1, 1987, in the UCC Archives, 1–9.

Twin Cities (1970–93), he served as its academic vice president and dean (1979–88). Since 1989 he has been co-editor of Prism: A Theological Forum for the United Church of Christ, *the theological journal started by UCC seminaries. In 1991 Steckel drafted the background paper on "Ecclesiology" that informed UCC restructuring in the 1990s (see vol. 7:138).*

Steckel's 1987 paper, "Ordination in the United Church of Christ," offers a careful summary of the biblical foundations and historical traditions behind UCC views of ordination. His paper also comments on contemporary ordination issues: the impact of the ecumenical movement, the expectations of nontraditional students, and the growing regulatory role of the Manual on the Ministry *(MOM).*

Ordination in the United Church of Christ

Biblical Foundations

While the Bible seems filled with texts on what to believe and how to act, it does not as clearly prescribe how the church should be organized, nor does it mandate particular offices, ordained or otherwise. That has not deterred our ancestors in the faith, however, or even some contemporary interpreters from finding such prescriptions.

Three groups of texts have been employed to argue that the Bible sets norms for church offices: Those describing the emergence of the priestly, prophetic and kingly offices in ancient Israel; texts referring to the offices filled and fulfilled by Jesus Christ (pre-eminently in the Pauline, Johannine and Matthean communities); and those fragmentary late New Testament and early patristic texts which describe the emergence of formal offices in the early Christian communities.

Each of these groups of texts has its own history of interpretation and relative interpretive weight in the history of the churches. In the modern era of historical-critical interpretation, the texts from ancient Israel[1] are generally not viewed as normative for contemporary church practice, except as they illuminate the history of promise and fulfillment. (Biblical literalists and communities viewing themselves as the true Israel would

1. The books of 1 and 2 Kings and the writings of the prophets give glimpses of the prophetic vocation and message. The books of Leviticus and 1 and 2 Chronicles set forth the priestly view of history centered on the tabernacle and the temple. And the historical books, along with eschatological and apocalyptic sections in the prophetic books, portray the Davidic Monarchy and the messianic age which will succeed it.

not share this view.) These texts point forward thematically, and are useful in deepening our understanding of the way the church came to interpret Jesus Christ and itself in continuity with his ministry. But these texts from ancient Israel are not a plan of church government or offices.

The texts interpreting Jesus Christ,[2] often employing the language of priest, prophet and king (Messiah), show how the early communities deepened their grasp of the meaning of their faith by examining ancient Jewish texts. The Protestant reformers, particularly Martin Luther and his followers, sought to reclaim these offices for Jesus Christ from a medieval western church where priests and kings, at least (not so many prophets) abounded shamelessly where only Jesus Christ had the right to serve, mediating between God and creation, ordering all things for good. It was less clear, however, where the new churches fit in this theological scheme. Were they Christ's living embodiment in the world? The reformers were nervous about such a claim, since it seemed at the root of medieval Catholic excesses. Were the churches no more than communities of witnesses to a completed heavenly drama of salvation? That seemed too severely limited, especially in light of the experience of corporate worship, preaching and the eucharistic meal. And what about the ministers or pastors leading the churches? Were they in any sense representative? Did they stand in the place of Jesus Christ? *In theory* the reformers rejected such an interpretation. But *in practice* (and increasingly in theory in subsequent centuries), such interpretations were fostered; (more about this Protestant ambivalence later).

Today in liberal Protestant and Catholic communities there is less theological queasiness about claiming to be Christ's living embodiment in the world. Perhaps the sense of a collapsing Christian triumphalism makes that claim less troubling. In these same communities, however, it is my impression that, of the three historic offices, the prophetic office is strongly (often unambiguously) affirmed; the priestly office is affirmed but carefully qualified to eliminate traditional theories of mediatorship; and the kingly office is either quietly avoided or openly rejected because of the horrors of triumphalism. (While these theological "corrections" may indeed be welcomed in the broad sweep of Christian history, they have not always helped theological education and formation, where students and pastors are eager to be prophets, ambivalent about being priests, and certain they should eschew governance or administration.)

---

2. A priestly interpretation of Jesus is set forth clearly in Hebrews and John. Prophetic allusions are scattered through the gospels. The Kingly or messianic understanding of Jesus appears in a more ambiguous way in the synoptic gospels, openly in the Johannine writing and Pauline literature, and cosmically in Revelation.

As long as Christian communities continue to reflect on their mission in the world — what is the church called to be and do? — these central Christological themes will continue to be formative. Christology cannot, however, provide specific guidance on the ordering of the church, beyond holding the church to its priestly, prophetic and ruling tasks. Forms of government, offices (ordained and otherwise), rules and procedures must all be grounded elsewhere.

The third group of biblical texts studied for their ecclesial guidance are those which hint, in all too fragmentary ways, at the emergence of formal offices in the earliest communities[3] — how the apostles and other specially gifted leaders (prophets, teachers, healers, etc.) seemed to be replaced in the second generation by deacons, elders and bishops. The Acts of the Apostles, Paul's letters, and the pastoral epistles are the sources of these tantalizing fragments. The Didache, the Shepherd of Hermas and other early patristic texts add further information about these developments.

Reforming theologians, particularly, have searched these texts for evidence that their proposed changes are faithful to the "New Testament Church," and that the ecclesiastical establishment they oppose has become corrupt. Modern critical scholarship, however, has made it abundantly clear that even in the first generation, Christian communities were already incredibly diverse in theology, worship and organization. If one seeks scriptural precedents among these texts for one's own polity, they can be found. But so can warrants for many other polities. Local autonomy, connectionalism, hierarchies, and radically communitarian practices seemed to flourish side-by-side. Happily? It is hard to tell, but there they are!

In addition to these corrosive effects of modern scholarship, contemporary ecumenical dialogue on issues of ecclesiology and ministry (e.g., the COCU Consensus; *Baptism, Eucharist and Ministry*) has further shaken the Protestant Reformation fixation with a supposedly biblical ecclesial practice. It becomes clear that the catholic traditions — Roman, Eastern, Anglican — claim their own scriptural grounding, but follow a quite different principle regarding the ordering of the church and its offices, namely, that in its history, the Spirit leads the church into forms of governance and offices which meet the needs of the moment, which need not be specifically grounded in the scriptures, but which must only meet functional criteria. Hyperactive Protestant sensitivities quickly detect the iron hand of "tradition" in this view. But a genuine commitment to ecumenical dialogue requires at least some hesitation before rushing to that judgment.

3. These texts include the Acts of the Apostles, 1 Corinthians, Ephesians, and 1 and 2 Timothy.

These are particularly difficult matters for the United Church of Christ, where polity issues have held center stage. Questions of belief, worship, even moral action have not claimed our attention as persistently as organizational issues. This makes us a bit of a puzzle to some of our ecumenical partners. We become, I blush to say, very "traditional" when asked to consider the office of the bishop, or to consider delegating powers to bodies beyond the local church. Our prized openness, our love of diversity suddenly fade away. One seldom hears the word "never" in UCC circles, except on such issues as these.

If the United Church of Christ in our own time is to hear the witness of these scriptural texts about church order and offices, we will first need to repent of our organizational fundamentalism, to cease reading our own organizational forms into these texts, and then, to consider their meanings with a chastened spirit.

I cannot claim for myself a sufficient degree of such repentance and chastening to be more than suggestive about what we might hear in a fresh encounter with these texts. But my suggestions are along these lines: the gifts of ministry are rich and diverse, distributed widely in communities of faith. Many gifts are distributed to some members and mysteriously — tongues, healing, prophecy, inspired preaching, ecstatic prayer, martyrdom. Other gifts are both granted to and expected from all — service, worship, proclaiming the faith, love. Aptitude and experience will not be the same for all. But all are called to receive and exercise these gifts. Beyond these charismatic and baptismal gifts, some are called to lead the communities in special and continuing leadership roles — those who organize and resource the servant ministries (deacons); those who teach and preside at the table (elders); and those elders who care for groups of local communities, while perhaps continuing to lead one of them (bishops). Early in the history of these offices, ceremonies developed that included anointing and/or the laying on of hands with prayer. Perhaps other gifts were also liturgically confirmed in this or some other fashion. But we cannot tell. Though not a matter of great emphasis in these texts, there was undoubtedly a strong belief that the Spirit was vividly present in such acts.

As we seek in the United Church of Christ to be guided by the scriptural word on these matters, I would further suggest that, from these late New Testament and patristic texts, ordination seems to be employed primarily for standing leadership roles, where organizational, leadership, teaching and liturgical activities predominate. Because they are included among the baptized, the ordained are also called to serve, worship, proclaim and love. And, occasionally, the ordained may also be specially gifted by the Spirit, but that is not a prerequisite for ordination. More than that, however, we cannot draw from these ancient texts without drifting into proof-texting.

Traditions

While the United Church of Christ affirms the primary authority of the scriptural witness, it also claims its continuity with the faith of the ancient church as expressed in the ecumenical confessions, and with its antecedent Protestant Reformation traditions. I will not linger over the meaning of ordination in the time of the ancient ecumenical councils. While some developments toward a sacramental theology of priesthood took place in the ancient period, it was not until the late Middle Ages that a fully developed priestly theory of ordination became dominant.

The Protestant Reformation traditions comprised within the United Church of Christ agreed in rejecting the sacramental theology of ordination, since all believers belong to the priestly office of the church. In practice, however, these Reformation churches (except for some of the radical groups) continued to appoint pastors or ministers, to specify their personal, confessional and educational qualifications, and to install them liturgically with the laying on of hands and prayer. These were certainly not ordinations in the late medieval Catholic sense; more a combination of our contemporary rites of ordination and installation. And our Lutheran and Reformed ancestors agreed that such ordinations were, strictly speaking, functional and not sacramental. The Church does not need ordained ministers in order to be the Church. They did believe, however, that God called leaders to these roles for the well-being of the church.

Beyond these fundamental agreements, our Lutheran and Reformed ancestors employed different words and images for the ordained office. Since for Luther and his followers, the proper preaching of the Word and administration of the sacraments constituted the true Church, pastors were defined by these most sacred duties. And the shepherding connotations of pastor following the lead of our true shepherd, Jesus Christ, led to the pre-eminence of that title in the Lutheran tradition. Subsequently, in Lutheran pastoral theology, the prophetic, priestly and kingly offices filled by Jesus Christ were understood to define the duties of the ordained pastor.

In the earliest Reformed view, there were four ordained offices in the church — pastor, teacher, elder, and deacon. Calvin and his followers believed that these offices were mandated by the scriptures. The pastor preached, led worship, and shared the duties of oversight or discipline with the elders. Teachers were responsible for proper education in faith and morals for all ages. Elders ruled in the church and community. Deacons served in the church and in the community for all in need. Early in Reformed history, the pastoral and teaching offices became combined, though even as late as some of the early New England Puritan settlements, there were still separately ordained and installed teachers in local churches.

While the influence of these Lutheran and Reformed ordination perspectives continue to dominate our UCC rituals and theology, we should not neglect the contributions of the radical reformers (especially Baptists, Independents and Quakers) and the contributions of 19th-century American revivalism, as mediated through the Christian tradition in the Congregational Christian churches, to our understanding of ordination. Both of these historical movements shared the conviction that the Holy Spirit came upon those who were to preach, pray, or lead, giving them the power or insight which they needed. This ordination by the Holy Spirit could indeed be recognized and confirmed by the community, but it could not be conferred. No ritual, no curriculum could give the Spirit, only the Spirit could give itself. This view makes for a less orderly and livelier church. The influence of this viewpoint today may, at least in the UCC, seem limited to the charismatic movement. But our emphasis on the personal experience of faith in our procedures for in-care status and ordination surely bears the stamp of this Puritan and revivalist heritage. And we do expect spiritual depth in our ordained leaders, along with academic and practical competence.

45. Ministry:

"A Note on the Practice of Ministry" and "Theologian, Presider, Manager"

(1978, 1983)

Walter Brueggemann, Browne Barr

As the United Church of Christ refined its polity and became more intentional in its thinking about clergy, the writings of Walter Brueggemann and Browne Barr enriched understandings of ministry and helped pastors clarify their roles in the church.

Walter Brueggemann (b. 1933) is an Evangelical and Reformed/UCC minister educated at Elmhurst College, Eden Theological Seminary, and St. Louis University. He was professor and dean at Eden Theological Seminary (1961–86) and was on the faculty at Columbia Theological Seminary (Decatur, Georgia) (1986–2003). Brueggemann's writings invite many clergy to look at scripture and ministry in new ways: The Land *(1977),* The Creative Word *(1982), and* Hopeful Imagination *(1986). In his book* The Prophetic Imagination *(1978) Brueggemann highlights the stance of the Hebrew prophets and the ministry of Jesus of Nazareth, to remind clergy and laity that the task of prophetic ministry is to evoke an alternative community. It is a stance that informs all of life, that penetrates numbness, and that moves into the future. Furthermore, the practice of ministry involves personal mourning on the way to joy.*

Browne Barr (b. 1917) is a Congregational Christian/UCC minister educated at Grinnell College and Yale Divinity School. After serving

---

Sources: Walter Brueggemann, "A Note on the Practice of Ministry," in *The Prophetic Imagination* (Philadelphia: Fortress Press, 1978), 109–13. Browne Barr, "Minister: Theologian, Presider, Manager," an excerpt from *High-Flying Geese: Unexpected Reflections on the Church and Its Ministry* (New York: Seabury Press, 1983), 31–35.

pastorates in Connecticut (1943–53) he returned to Yale to teach preaching and pastoral theology (1953–60). He became senior minister of the First Congregational UCC of Berkeley, California (1960–77), and professor and dean of San Francisco Theological Seminary (1977–83). His thinking reflects a deep respect for the calling of the preacher as pastor and teacher, as well as a high concept of the ministry of the laity. One of his books, High Flying Geese: Unexpected Reflections on the Church & Its Ministry *(1983), looks carefully at the natural patterns of leadership exhibited in geese and sets forth some helpful insights about the functional role of clergy and the importance of the theologian to the church.*

A Note on the Practice of Ministry

First let me summarize the argument. Something new happened in history with the Exodus and the Moses movement. On the one hand, Moses intended the dismantling of the oppressive empire of Pharaoh and on the other hand he intended the formation of a new community focused on the religion of God's freedom and the politics of justice and compassion. The *dismantling* begins in the groans and laments of his people; the *energizing* begins in the doxologies of the new community.

The Moses movement is too radical for Israel, however, and so soon there is an attempt to counter the new history of energy. The old history of Pharaoh is continued in the monarchy of Israel. The monarchy, with its interest in self-securing, is effective in *silencing the criticism* and *denying the energizing,* but the kings never seem able to end the prophets. The prophets of Israel continue the radical movement of Moses in the face of royal reality. On the one hand, *Jeremiah practices the radical criticism* against the royal consciousness. He does this essentially by conjuring a funeral and bringing the grief of dying Israel to public expression. He does this to penetrate the numb denial of the royal community which pretended that things must go on forever. On the other hand, *Second Isaiah practices radical energizing* against the royal consciousness. He does this by conjuring an enthronement and bringing the amazement of rebirthed Israel to public expression. He does this to penetrate the weary despair of the royal community, which assumed things were over forever.

Jesus of Nazareth, a prophet, and more than a prophet we argue, practiced in most radical form the main elements of prophetic ministry and imagination. On the one hand, he practiced criticism of the deathly world around him. The dismantling was fully wrought in his crucifixion, in which he himself embodied the thing dismantled. On the other hand, he practiced the energizing of the new future given by God. This energizing was fully wrought in his resurrection, in which he embodied the new future given by God.

Second, this note is concerned with the practice of ministry. Without this note the entire discussion lacks the concreteness appropriate to discussions of the prophetic. Without precluding peculiar ministries in special places, it is presumed that the practice of ministry is done by those who stand in conventional places of parish life and other forms of ministry derived from that model. We cling to the conviction that prophetic ministry can and must be practiced there, although many things militate against it. First, the ministry is consumed by the daily round of busyness that cannot be ignored; perhaps that daily pressure may be reduced but it cannot be ignored. Second, the ministry most often exists in congregations that are bourgeois, if not downright obdurate, and in which there is no special openness to or support of prophetic ministry.

Other things can be said as well and I have tried to say some of them in this book. I have tried to say that prophetic ministry does not consist of spectacular acts of social crusading or of abrasive measures of indignation. Rather, prophetic ministry consists of offering an alternative perception of reality and in letting people see their own history in the light of God's freedom and his will for justice. The issues of God's freedom and his will for justice are not always and need not be expressed primarily in the big issues of the day. They can be discerned wherever people try to live together and worry about their future and their identity. So these urgings come from our study:

(1) The task of prophetic ministry is to evoke an alternative community that knows it is about different things in different ways. And that alternative community has a variety of relationships with the dominant community.

(2) The practice of prophetic ministry is not some special thing done two days a week. Rather, it is done in, with, and under all the acts of ministry — as much in counseling as in preaching, as much in liturgy as in education. It concerns a stance and posture or a hermeneutic about the world of death and the word of life that can be brought to light in every context.

(3) Prophetic ministry seeks to penetrate the numbness to face the body of death in which we are caught. Clearly, the numbness sometimes evokes from us rage and anger, but the numbness is more likely to be penetrated by grief and lament. Death, and that is our state, does not require indignation

as much as it requires anguish and the sharing in the pain. The public sharing of pain is one way to let the reality sink in and let the death go.

(4) Prophetic ministry seeks to penetrate despair so that new futures can be believed in and embraced by us. There is a yearning for energy in a world grown weary. And we do know that the only act that energizes is a word, a gesture, an act that believes in our future and affirms it to us disinterestedly.

In a society that knows about initiative and self-actualization and countless other things, the capacity to lament the death of the old world is nearly lost. In a society strong on self-congratulation, the capacity to receive in doxology the new world being given is nearly lost. Grief and praise are ways of prophetic criticism and energy, which can be more intentional even in our age.

Third, as I reflect on ministry, and especially my ministry, I know in the hidden places that the real restraints are not in my understanding or in the receptivity of other people. Rather, the restraints come from my own unsureness about this perception. I discover that I am as bourgeois and obdurate as any to whom I might minister. I, like most of the others, am unsure that the royal road is not the best and the royal community the one which governs the real "goodies." I, like most of the others, am unsure that the alternative community inclusive of the poor, hungry, and grieving is really the wave of God's future. We are indeed "like people, like priest" (Hos. 4:9). That very likely is the situation among many of us in ministry and there is no unanguished way out of it. It does make clear to us that our ministry will always be practiced through our own conflicted selves. No prophet has ever borne an unconflicted message, even until Jesus (cf. Mark 14:36). Thus the Beatitudes end in realism (Luke 6:22–23). Also, it reminds us again that such radical faith is not an achievement, for if it were we would will it and be done. Rather, it is a gift and we are left to wait receptively, to watch and to pray.

Perhaps our own situation credits what we have suggested here. We ourselves shall likely move in and out, precisely because of our poor capacity to grieve the death in our own lives and to be amazed at the new futures. We are not more skilled in that than all the other children of the royal community, and therefore we must engage in the same painful practices of becoming who we are called to be. I have come to think there is no more succinct summary of prophetic ministry than the statement of Jesus "Blessed are you that weep now, for you shall laugh" (Luke 6:21), or, more familiarly, "Blessed are those who mourn, for they shall be comforted" (Matt. 5:4).

Jesus' concern was, finally, for the joy of the kingdom. That is what he promised and to that he invited people. But he was clear that the rejoicing in that future required a grieving about the present order.[1] Jesus takes a quite dialectical two-age view of things. He will not be like one-world liberals who view the present world as the only one, nor will he be like the unworldly who yearn for the future with an unconcern about the present. There is work to be done in the present. There is grief work to be done in the present that the future may come. There is mourning to be done for those who do not know of the deathliness of their situation. There is mourning to be done with those who know pain and suffering and lack the power or freedom to bring it to speech. The saying is a harsh one, for it sets this grief work as the precondition of joy. It announces that those who have not cared enough to grieve will not know joy.

The mourning is a precondition in another way too. It is not a formal, external requirement but rather the only door and route to joy. Seen in that context, this is not just a neat saying but a summary of the entire theology of the cross. Only that kind of anguished disengagement permits fruitful yearning and only the public embrace of deathliness permits newness to come. We are at the edge of knowing this in our personal lives, for we understand a bit of the processes of grieving.[2] But we have yet to learn and apply it to the reality of society. And finally, we have yet to learn it about God, who grieves in ways hidden from us and who waits to rejoice until his promises are fully kept.

Minister: Theologian, Presider, Manager

. . . The minister or priest is one who nurtures and frees the total ministry of the Body of Christ. In recent years, however, the ministry of the laity has been so emphasized that the minister's particular place has often been obscured. Have you noticed that in some Protestant circles the article "the" in reference to "ministry" has been done away with almost altogether? "*The* ministry" as a particular and defined vocation in the church is lost

---

1. At the level of individual personality this is the argument of George A. Benson, *Then Joy Breaks Through* (New York: Seabury Press, 1972). He begins his last chapter in this way: "The transformation of all time and the Christian prototype of joy is the resurrection of Christ" (123). And his entire book is about the meaning of the cross on the way to life.

2. In a way that is enormously helpful and a bit deductive we have been helped greatly by the research of Elisabeth Kübler-Ross, *On Death and Dying* (New York: Macmillan, 1969). See my discussion of her paradigm in relation to the faith of Israel, "The Formfulness of Grief," *Interpretation* 31 (1977): 263–75.

in a vast cloud of "ministries," all appropriate for the Body of Christ—street ministry, prison ministry, campus ministry, hospital ministry, senior citizen ministry, and so on ad infinitum — but where, O where, is *the* ministry?

Is one ordained as a sort of vocational appointment to any one of these ministries? If so, then why should not any Christian person be ordained who seeks to follow Jesus Christ and to see Christ and to act for Christ in every aspect of life including vocation? Sometimes it is argued that the difference lies in the time clock and that ordination presupposes "full-time Christian service"! However, I suspect that "*part-time* Christian service," whatever that may be, might have even more need for the sustaining grace ordination may provide. Or again, it is proposed that the difference lies in education: so in some branches of Protestantism ordination is offered as though it were an ecclesiastical endorsement of an academic degree in theology. Or again, it often appears that the difference between ordained and unordained leaders in the church is a matter of personal spirituality or personal morality. The minister must "set an example," and thus there is fostered a kind of discrimination as profoundly offensive to the Body of Christ as racism, sexism, or ageism.

How can we possibly have a vigorous shared ministry until we establish the work of the ordained clergy with some consensus and clarity? Many ministers in the Reformed tradition have been ordained, according to the words of the ritual, "to preach the Gospel, administer the sacraments and bear rule in Christ's church." Ordination is thus defined functionally. Is this not the burden of 1 Corinthians 12, where the differing functions of various members of the Body of Christ are described? Ordained persons have a particular function on behalf of the whole body, the whole formation. Specialized education and intense preparation are required because persons ordained are entrusted with the special function, which I suggest is the responsibility of caring for the "formation," for the "structure." Thus they are charged with maintaining the *identity* of the church and with its *preservation* until Christ comes again. This is a holy office, to be sure, but still an office, a service, "something performed . . . for another," as Webster defines it.

To preach the Gospel and to celebrate the sacraments is to bring Christ to memory's present and to reenact his saving work until he comes again. Surely we can understand Luther's reported amazement that God had entrusted the *continuity* of the Church to *the* ministry: God's gift to his church, Luther called it. That continuity, that identity and preservation are not necessarily provided by any number of *general* ministries, however pivotal and relevant and difficult and self-sacrificing they may be. That identity and continuity are not protected even by ministries of evangelism or mission save as they are specifically exercised through both Word and sacrament. Honest public media evangelists do not claim that function for themselves and candid Christian critics of their work would despair if the identity and continuity of the Body of Christ reposed in their attaché cases.

If the ordained minister is, as we are urging, a "breed set apart," let it be clear that it is a *functional* setting apart and not one based on spiritual or moral excellence. Indeed, the supposition that it is a spiritual or moral category rather than a functional one undercuts the function, because in believing this, other Christians begin to suppose that the validity of the Gospel and the efficacy of the sacraments depend upon the moral character or intellectual preparation of the ordained person.

The question is not who is good enough to preach the Word and to celebrate the sacraments, but rather, could anyone be wicked enough to nullify the grace of God there set forth. Furthermore, when it is supposed that the minister's character or intellect is an absolute qualification for this function in the church, we have the unseemly spectacle of ordained persons reacting to that supposition with grotesque pretensions of piety to support the contention or even more grotesque acts of impiety to deny it. . . .

Theologian

The community of faith . . . needs the professional theologian, one who has been allowed time to become deeply acquainted with Scripture and history, with the Story of the people of God. The church needs the perspective of the scholar and the service of persons who are acquainted with the intellectual formulation of Christian experience both as cosmic Event and personal encounter. Congregations everywhere today are starved for professional leaders who have had the opportunity for disciplined study of Christian doctrine, of other religions and philosophies and of the condition of persons and society. As Kenneth Phifer maintains, "Christian worship needs to be truly catholic and authentically contemporary" (*A Protestant Case for Liturgical Renewal* [Philadelphia: Westminster Press, 1965], 19). Amen! Thus someone in the church must be charged with its direction who is by profession a competent theologian. The Christian theologian is appointed to reflect on Christian experience and tradition and offer the church perspective and direction. . . .

Many of the decisive moments in the history of the church have been times when God has raised up a theologian who has cried out, "I have the nagging feeling we're doing something wrong!" The church lays this responsibility upon a person when it lays hands upon her or him in ordination. The fulfillment of this responsibility requires much more than intellectual preparation, but it does require that! Examination for ordination should seek to discover if the candidate is prepared intellectually as well as spiritually to assume the responsibility as theologian in the church and to grow in the exercise of it. But ordination itself is a "setting apart" for a function and not a badge of superior piety or of a greater intensity of Christian commitment.

Where and how is that functional responsibility employed by the ordained person as against the unordained theologian? It is employed only where a body of believing persons requires the preaching of the Word and the celebration of the sacraments for its identity and preservation. . . .

46. Ministry:
"Episcopé or Oversight"

(1998)

Randi Walker

Randi Jones Walker (b. 1952) is a UCC minister educated at the University of New Mexico, the School of Theology at Claremont (California), and Claremont Graduate School. After serving pastorates in California (1983–92) she has been on the faculty of Pacific School of Religion, Berkeley, California, since 1992.

In December 1998 Walker was asked to address a Joint Placement Conference of the United Church of Christ and the Christian Church (Disciples of Christ) in Orlando, Florida, regarding the question of "oversight," or episcopé.

Her lengthy paper is divided into four parts: personal reflections about the concept of episcopé, a short history of the conference minister in the United Church of Christ and the regional minister in the Christian Church (Disciples of Christ), some theological reconstructions of episcopé for possible use, and an examination of the theological content of episcopé for contemporary ecclesiology. The last section of the paper suggests that visitation, "the disturbing intrusiveness of love into business as usual in the church," and oversight, "bringing the view of the larger church into the local scene," stand at the heart of episcopé.

Source: Randi J. Walker, an excerpt from "Episcopé," an address given to the Joint Placement Conference of the United Church of Christ and Christian Church Disciples of Christ, Orlando, Florida, December 4, 1998, 10–12.

Recovery of the Theological Content of Episcopé in Our Ecclesiology

The first aspect of episcopé I wish to lift up for you is visitation and the Presence of God. Episcopé is really the disturbing intrusiveness of love into business as usual in the church. In a world where most symbols have diluted meanings, where memory of their meaning is not passed on from generation to generation, it is important for the symbolic presence of God in episcopé to be lifted up. In individual episcopé, such as a conference or regional minister, that person (in her or his office) serves as a symbolic representation of Christ. In collective episcopé, such as an association, the gathered churches are a symbolic representation of the Apostles.

Visitations of Regional and Conference ministers and of Associations to local churches, while they may carry some of the disturbing baggage of spying, simply remind the Church of the disturbing power of a visitation from God, a visitation of love, honest, open, caring but challenging, a reminder of things that it is in our nature to forget. But in my work as a historian, I have found no more powerful thing church leaders can do to strengthen the churches than to visit them with love. The first visit from the Home Missionary Society Superintendent to the congregations in Illinois in 1873 had surprisingly powerful results:

> By the end of the year nearly every church will have been visited. The plan is this: special prayer and visitation of members are the preparation for one. A day is then given, with each church, to visiting in the forenoon; service for salutation, conference and prayer in the afternoon; and to addresses on Home Evangelization in the evening. Great good has followed. Weaker churches have been encouraged, the strong stimulated, and all have felt the quickened pulse of church communion.[1]

Symbolic signs of a visitation from God can all be accomplished by either personal or collegial episcopé.

I would suggest the following three things as especially good symbolic signs of God's presence in the community. Confirmation or Baptism, times when people are sacramentally incorporated into the Body of Christ are good times for episcopal visitation. Representing the wider church, the Association or the Regional or Conference minister remind people that the presence of God is not just present in the local church but also in

---

1. The Forty-Seventh Report of the American Home Missionary Society for Annual Meeting, May 7, 1873 (New York: The American Home Missionary Society, 1873), 74.

its connections to other churches. Communion is another such symbolic sign. Sharing the same bread and cup, unity in the confession of Christ's teaching, life, death, resurrection, and coming again, strengthen a church beset by secular concerns. For the church to continue to understand its center in Christ, being "in communion" with its episcopé is essential. In the communion service, the Association, or the Conference or Regional minister sits with that congregation as Christ or as the Apostles, and once again passes down the tradition, re-presents the love of God to them. Finally in ordination, laying on hands, healing and anointing, recognizing and confirming what God has done for the people as they call forth leadership. Any such visit in the work of episcopé should include, as the Home Mission Superintendent quoted above included, preaching, communion, and prayer with the people.

The other main task of episcopé, oversight, depends on visitation for effectiveness. In one sense this is obvious. Effective oversight depends on having a view of things. However, in episcopé this is a deeper spiritual matter. This is a view not tailored to human measurements. While no human being can claim God's view, the visit of a conference or regional minister, or of the churches of an association, to a congregation is a symbolic reminder of the presence of God and should have the character of love. Greek has several words that relate to visiting. As a historian for instance, I am interested in the root word for history — ἱστωρεω (historeo) to visit with the purpose of coming to know. That is not the purpose of a visit of episcopé. The visit of episcopé is a visit for the purpose of unity (of the congregation and among the larger body of churches), a visit to observe with care. The visit of episcopé brings the view of the larger church into the local scene; it conveys a sense of the whole to the parts. Doris Lessing in one of her novels, I think it was *Shikasta,* used an apt phrase, the "Substance of We Feeling." The function of episcopé is to renew the substantial reality of the Body of Christ, another reason why communion is such an important part of such visits.

Though the renewal of this sense of the Body of Christ is one of its primary purposes, oversight in episcopé is the service of *unity,* not *uniformity.* The authority of episcopé is not something granted by an organizational chart, but by the relationships within the Body of Christ. One scholar, Archie Smith Jr.,[2] reminds us that by baptism we are siblings by choice, not by kinship. We are responsible for our relationships with each other in the household of God. Such a household model of authority is rooted in

2. Archie Smith Jr. and Gill Gorell Barnes, *Navigating the Deep River: Spirituality in African American Families* (Cleveland: United Church Press, 1997).

the ancient church's origin in the household — the *oikos* — rather than in the polis, or political sphere. Within the *oikos,* even though certain persons were granted certain kinds of authority by law, in reality, the household was sustained by a system of relationships based on the decision to love and trust, or the obligation to care. The Christian bishop was considered the *pater* or *mater*[3] *familias.* The power of Christian episcopé lies in bringing love to bear on the affairs of the church, the essence of the presence of God.

The task of serving the unity of the church has received particular attention in our ecumenical conversations, especially since the beginning of the Consultation on Church Union and the Lima meeting of the World Council of Churches Faith and Order Commission. That body's consensus document, *Baptism, Eucharist and Ministry* has become the theological starting place for many churches' considerations of episcopé. The important Paragraph 23 of the Ministry section reads as follows:

> The Church as the body of Christ and the eschatological people of God is constituted by the Holy Spirit through a diversity of gifts or ministries. Among these gifts a ministry of *episcopé* is necessary to express and safeguard the unity of the body. Every church needs this ministry of unity in some form in order to be the Church of God, the one body of Christ, a sign of the unity of all in the Kingdom.

Notice that the form is left open. Within the United Church of Christ, and I believe in the Disciples churches as well, the recovery of the gift of episcopé in our churches will be a collaboration between the people who hunger for a visitation from God, a sign of their unity in the body of Christ, and you who hold this precarious office.

In our churches so sensitive to the intrusion of episcopé on congregational prerogatives, it is I think necessary to maintain the ambiguity of collegial and personal aspects of it. Though the current ecumenical conversations about episcopé seem to call for hurry in this matter, lest we let a moment slip by, it takes time and great love to reshape a ministry for a time unlike any we have ever seen.

I close with this ancient message of Paul to the leaders of the Church in Corinth:

---

3. There is evidence of woman bishops in the earliest Christian inscriptions. For further information see Karen Jo Torjesen, *When Women Were Priests: Women's Leadership in the Early Church and the Scandal of Their Subordination in the Rise of Christianity* (San Francisco: Harper and Row, 1993).

You show that you are a letter of Christ . . . written not with ink but with the Spirit of the living God, not on tablets of stone but on tablets of human hearts. Such is the confidence that we have through Christ toward God. Not that we are competent of ourselves to claim anything as coming from us; our competence is from God, who has made us competent to be ministers of a new covenant, not of letter but of spirit; for the letter kills, but the Spirit gives life. (2 Cor. 3:3–6 NRSV)

Passing on the Faith

47. The United Church of Christ Curriculum: *"Educational Principles"*

(1961)

The story of the United Church of Christ curriculum began in 1947 when educators from the Congregational Christian Churches and the Evangelical and Reformed Church, anticipating union, began to cooperate in their planning and production of materials for Christian education. Congregational Christian publications were called the "Pilgrim Series," while the Evangelical and Reformed Church published the "Church and Home Series." During the 1940s and 1950s the two series overlapped frequently.

By 1952, the two denominations began serious planning for a radically new joint curriculum. They gathered information from local congregations, collected the latest research on educational methods and human development, and engaged the best biblical and theological scholars. Christian education was increasingly important as church attendance increased and Sunday schools expanded to serve the Baby Boom generation.

Initially a planning seminar was convened under the direction of a Congregationalist, Harry T. Stock, and a member of the Evangelical and Reformed Church, Franklin I. Sheeder, to ask basic questions: What in the Christian faith demands and makes possible education? When a theologian talks about the Christian faith, does it make sense to people in local congregations? How do biblical descriptions of human nature

---

Source: An excerpt from the 1961 revision of "A Statement of Educational Principles As Seen in the Light of Christian Theology and Beliefs" made available to writers and editors in 1957, Appendix A in Roger Shinn, *The Educational Mission of Our Church* (Boston and Philadelphia: United Church Press, 1962), 150–57.

compare with the insights of educational psychology? What are the best teaching methods for different age groups?

By 1957 the planning team developed a "working paper" to guide editors and writers in the project — "Theological and Educational Principles Basic to the UCC Curriculum." This Principles statement, "representing a consensus emerging through years of discussion and activity," guided authors, even as it continued to be revised. In 1964, carefully written texts, combined with teaching suggestions based upon the most recent understandings of human development and presented in artistically designed formats, were published as the United Church of Christ Curriculum.

The many years of planning, designing, writing, editing, and testing offered local congregations state-of-the art educational materials for all ages. Although Sunday school teachers sometimes complained that it was difficult to teach the new curriculum, nearly everyone agreed that the UCC Curriculum *was a major educational and theological accomplishment.*

Theological and Educational Principles Basic to the United Church Curriculum

The Task of Christian Education Grows Out of the Nature of the Church

The Christian church is the fellowship of those persons, living or dead, who have responded to God's forgiveness and power freely given in Jesus Christ and have committed themselves to spreading this good news of God's love throughout the whole world and into every walk of life. The church is both an historic and a contemporary community. It confesses Jesus Christ as Lord. It bears witness to God's grace and love by acknowledging God's call to his people to live individual lives worthy of his name, to work for a just society, to proclaim his Word to all men. This historic and living church is not properly said to have a mission; this worshiping and witnessing church is a mission. Because the church believes that God has created man in his own image, it recognizes people's universal need to realize that they have been created by God and are in relationship with God, whether or not they are consciously aware of this fact, whether or not at any given moment they are at peace with God or have spurned his love. Because the church has also experienced God's saving grace and power in restoring people to right relationship with him, it seeks ever to share the message of this grace with all the world. Through its witness as a community, through the witness of individual members' lives, through the proclamation of God's word in all possible ways, the church seeks to enable men to hear its good news, enter the community of Christ's followers, participate creatively in its life, and fulfill its mission.

The church has always recognized teaching as one form of proclamation and witness, and has regarded it as one of its ministries. Teaching that fulfills Christian mission can help to provide conditions suitable for fostering the development of trust in God and outgoing concern for fellowmen. Such teaching takes place wherever the Christian fellowship is functioning effectively. Relationships within the home, the planned educational program of the local church, the work and worship of the total congregation, the activity of the Christian fellowship in the local and world community—all are potential locales for Christian teaching.

The task of Christian education, therefore, is to draw individuals into the reality of the Christian fellowship and to nurture them in the Christian faith and mission so that, by accepting with gratitude and obedience God's forgiveness and power for new life, they will be enabled to mature as Christian persons and will become faithful participants in the mission of the church.

Christian Beliefs Shape the Task of Christian Education

For Christians, taking part in the life and faith of the Christian community is the primary way in which we come to know God. Central in the life of the community is Jesus Christ in whom God has shown his grace and has given it both as forgiveness and as power. By accepting God's gift, man can be made whole and thus receive power to live a new life. The Bible contains the record of this unique activity in history. It is man's record of what God has done, is doing, and eternally stands ready to do for man. In the light of it we hear God speak to us, and we interpret his saving activity in our lives and in the world today.

The basic theological ideas, or beliefs, of the Christian tradition spring from God's Word to man as we know it from the Bible and from man's continuing response to the Word in faith. Such ideas or beliefs try to describe in *words* our *experience* of God's activity in the world. To develop and maintain the integrity and basic meaning of the faith, Christian beliefs must be adequately understood. They are an essential part of the content of Christian education. They also have important implications for the *nature* of Christian education.

God

Christian belief concerning God holds that God is more than we can ever know or imagine, but through his revelation of himself we know him as sovereign and righteous Spirit whose basic nature is love. In our day-to-day experiences of the world about us, of other people, and of ourselves, we see both creation and destruction, continuity and discontinuity, order and disorder. As Christians we look at these experiences through eyes of faith. We interpret them in the light of God's revelation of Jesus Christ and his continuing presence in the Holy Spirit. We find in them evidence of God at work in his activity of creating, sustaining, judging, and redeeming.

We confess that we understand only partially the depths of the mystery and glory of God. Therefore, even in the face of the ambiguities with which life confronts us, we have faith that God's love is sovereign and that he can be depended on to act in accordance with his own established purposes. Although he does not will the evil that exists in the world, in his sovereignty he can use even evil for his good purposes.

Implications for Christian Education

1. Because God is the Creator and Preserver of heaven and earth, all knowledge of the world is, to some extent, knowledge of God's activity and purpose. For this reason, Christian education can make use of all valid knowledge that is relevant to its task. This general knowledge, however, will be interpreted and understood from the perspective of God's redemptive act in Jesus Christ.

2. Because God is greater than any human experience or conception of him, no human knowledge of God can ever be complete. No experience of God's reality can ever be comprehensive or final. Throughout our lives, in ways consistent with our capacities at every age, we must seek to know God and his will for us more fully. Both increased knowledge of God's ways of working and heightened awareness of the unresolved mysteries of the universe should evoke in Christians a continuing spirit of awe, reverence, humility, and grateful adoration of the Lord of all being.

3. Because the distinctive Christian revelation of God is most readily made known through sharing the life of the community of believers in Jesus Christ, Christian education needs to help draw people into the community of faith and guide them in making its work and revelation their own.

Man

Christian belief concerning man reflects the biblical view of man as a spiritual unity of body and soul, rather than the Greek view of him as a dualism of mind and body. This Christian conviction grows out of the Old Testament affirmations that man is created "from the dust," meaning that he is a physical being; that he is created "in the image of God," meaning that he is endowed with the potentiality of responding to God and shares in the ongoing process of creation; and that he is created "male and female," meaning that he has been given capacity and responsibility for entering into relationships with others. These three affirmations have important implications for understanding man's limitations and possibilities.

God is the Creator, man is the creature. The creaturely character of man's existence sets limits within which he must live. He is bound to time and place. He is wholly dependent upon God and owes his life's allegiance to the sovereign Lord. Yet his creation in God's image also makes him capable of carrying on creative, purposeful, and moral activity; thus he can be held responsible for his own behavior. How he develops as a person will depend on his relationships with God, with his fellowmen, and with the world. These relationships result from and are affected by the manner in which he chooses to exercise his God-given freedom.

Man can use his freedom to acknowledge his dependence on God and enter into sustaining, constructive relationships with him. He can also use his freedom to reject God and deny God's sovereignty, thus cutting himself off from a vital relationship with his Creator. In exercising his freedom, man is never completely free, but is limited by the changing circumstances of his life and the very finiteness of his situation as a creature. Yet man is ever unwilling to admit that he is limited. His pride, obstinacy, and defiance in so refusing cause him to deny that God is sovereign, thereby leading him to try to save himself by relying upon his own resources for controlling life to his own satisfaction. The result of this refusal is separation from God and the bringing of God's judgment upon himself. Man's condition in being thus alienated from the source of his personal existence and sustenance is the reality underlying the Christian doctrine of sin.

Because he sins, man's capacity for responsible, creative, spiritual growth is stunted. He is bound to the limitations of his own desires, being alternately driven and blocked by fear that these will not be satisfied. He is filled with anxiety. Life becomes a burden, instead of a joyous fulfillment of the potentialities for which he was created.

Man's anxiety is further deepened by the inescapable prospect that death will cut him off. This threat may cause him to despair of the worthwhileness of life itself. To this condition of ever-present anxiety, brokenness, and potential despair, the gospel of Jesus Christ is addressed.

Implications for Christian Education

1. Man has been created as a spiritual unity of body and soul. If the Christian faith is to make an impact on his total being, it must confront him at all levels of age and experience and in all aspects of his personality.
2. Man's freedom is a gift of God. But man's capacity to exercise this freedom responsibly depends fundamentally upon his relationship with God and is affected to a large degree by his relationships with others. Many people play a part in the development of any one individual and his relationships. Education in the Christian community, therefore, will be carried out in the wide span of relationships at home, in the life of the church and church school, and in other associations.
3. Since man is created a physical and spiritual being, his freedom can be exercised only within the framework of his physical and spiritual limitations. Parents and teachers, therefore, should use all available valid insights into man's physical and psychological development that help in understanding his capacities and limitations for learning.
4. Since man has real freedom, education which fosters his true development as a person cannot be forced upon him. It must be offered in the kind of relationship between teacher and pupil which enables both persons to respond freely and honestly to each other and to the content of the educational situation. Relationships of trust which foster the person's free and genuine response are especially important in education in the Christian community.
5. Since God has made man free that he may, by his own choice, dedicate himself to the purposes of his Creator, it follows that the goals of Christian education must be selected in the light of God's will and purpose for man, and that the means to these goals must be worked out in the same light. When a person acknowledges his dependence upon God and lives in consciousness of that dependence, he is enabled to grow in wholeness and integrity.
6. Because man must continuously seek to learn God's will for him if right relationship with God is to be renewed and sustained, Christian education will aim to help people develop a practice of prayer which opens the person to God's guidance and purpose for him.

7. By the very nature of human existence, all people are involved in interaction and relationships with other persons. Such interaction and relationships may be helpful or harmful, constructive or destructive. Therefore, Christian educators are concerned about the kind of relationships which are developed among persons.

Jesus Christ

God is Redeemer as well as Creator, Sustainer, and judge of mankind. The heart of the Christian gospel is the proclamation that, while man continues to be sinful, God has shown his grace and has given it both as forgiveness and as power in Jesus Christ. God's forgiveness calls men to repent, to turn again to God; his gift of power enables men to live a new life. This good news has been disclosed in the person of Jesus Christ in such a fashion that it cannot be separated from his person and work. It provides Christians with a once-and-for-all sufficient revelation of God's power and love, enabling all who respond in faith to enter into a loving and trustful relationship with God, and requiring them to make the good news known to all men for the salvation of mankind and the transformation of the world.

How God accomplishes redemption in Jesus Christ has important implications for our understanding of Jesus Christ. In the first place, Jesus of Nazareth spoke and acted as a man among men, addressing himself to the condition and needs of people around him. As a man, his function was to reveal God to men and to direct men to God. He did so from the perspective of that which was best in the Judaic tradition. The quality of his life reflected a relationship with God heretofore unknown and never equaled or surpassed. In his teachings and actions, in his ministry and death, and in his resurrection, the content of the gospel was revealed. In Jesus Christ we see at their fullest the possibilities that are opened to man when his right relation to God is restored. For this reason, Christians have declared that Jesus Christ is truly human.

In the second place, the good news of God's forgiving love was revealed in the life, death, and resurrection of Jesus the Christ. In Jesus Christ, God both judged sinful men and took the initiative in reconciling them to himself. Those who in repentance accept his sacrificial love, who respond in faith, are given the power to live as children of God. They are redeemed. The experience of the death and resurrection of Jesus was the turning point in the lives of the apostles. Through the power released by God's revelation in Jesus Christ, the apostles' allegiance to Jesus the man was transformed into allegiance to God in Christ. As a result, their lives began to reflect

God's power at work in them as it had been in Jesus Christ. For this reason, Christians have also declared that Jesus Christ is truly God.

Implications for Christian Education

1. The aim of Christian education is to nurture all persons within the fellowship of the church so that they will be enabled to perceive and accept God's forgiveness and power for new life as revealed in Jesus Christ, and so grow in wisdom and in power, becoming true sons of God and intelligent, committed disciples of Jesus Christ. Teaching is one essential form of proclaiming the gospel.

2. In and of itself, Christian education cannot restore a right relationship between mankind and God. It can, however, point out man's need of such relationship, stimulate his desire for it, and in general help to provide the setting for man's positive response to God's seeking. The teacher who is dedicated to guiding each pupil to know God more fully can be a powerful and sustaining influence in the life of the individual pupil and, as such, a channel of God's grace.

3. The most effective Christian educators will be those who are deeply aware of the reality of God's forgiving love and new power. Such personal experience frees them to enter into the kind of creative relationships with others which are basic to effective education.

4. Christian education seeks to establish and guide relationships which disclose and demonstrate God's forgiveness, love, and power among persons or groups of persons, wherever they may be — in the home, in the church, or in the community.

The Holy Spirit

The Holy Spirit is the name given by Christians to God as they perceive his working in the world of men. The Christian church declares that the Holy Spirit guides, heals, and empowers men. He works among us in ways beyond our knowing; he makes demands beyond our expectations. We believe in faith that he creates and sustains the fellowship in Christ through which knowledge of God is deepened and through which man's new life, given by God in Christ, is purified and ennobled.

We perceive the presence of the Holy Spirit in the community of faith: "Where two or three are gathered together in my name, there am I in the midst of them." Members of this community share its common life in prayerful trust that the Holy Spirit may there work in their lives.

The Holy Spirit also manifests himself to the individual. Through his working, he continually transforms our lives, awakening dormant capabilities, setting new directions of the self, vitalizing members of the community into new fullness of devotion to human brotherhood, restoring the deep joy of life lived in right relationship with God.

Implications for Christian Education

1. Confidence in the work of the Holy Spirit undergirds the task of Christian education. The Spirit, not the educator, converts and transforms man. Therefore the educator cannot manipulate the lives of others to "make Christians" or to assure high morality or integrated personalities. The educator invites others to share in the life of the community of faith in the trust that the Spirit may there work in their lives.

2. As a community of faith, the Christian family provides an important context for the working of the Holy Spirit. In the intimacy of family life, the child comes in contact with the meaning of God's redemptive love insofar as he experiences such love in the lives of parents and other members of the family.

3. Persons who enter into the life of the church should find there a fellowship which, moved by God's love, welcomes and accepts them. The educator is concerned that, through a wealth of unfolding experience, each person will learn to identify himself with the Christian fellowship of believers and to share in its purposes, its worship, its beliefs, and the fruits of the Spirit, which it seeks to foster and support. Thus persons become responsible members of the community through which they meet God working redemptively. . . .

48. The Faith Crisis:
The Synod Debate

(1971)

Kay White

The 1960s were filled with many events that challenged the political and social order. Many young people, in particular, were deeply disturbed by racism and social problems. In 1971 the UCC General Synod invited synod delegates to share personal testimonies about "The Faith Crisis: Recovering and Renewing a Living Experience of God's Promise for Humankind." A woman student, Kay White, from Indianapolis, Indiana, calls the "Faith Crisis" on campus "the 'Faith Cop-out' — something that has been attempted but given up." She says that institutional forms of faith from the past do not serve her needs and she asks the church to help her find herself and her faith in God.

The Faith Crisis

The "Faith Crisis" can be more eloquently expressed on campus as the "Faith Cop-out" — something that has been attempted but given up.

Students are preoccupied today with society's demands and expectations, neither of which include a living faith in Christ. Society teaches that the dollar replaces faith and gives substance to our hopes and makes us certain of realities. A vast majority of students today are in colleges for the basic reason of the almighty dollar — personal monetary gain and not knowledgeable gain. A living faith in Christ is not a prerequisite for

Source: Kay White, Indianapolis, Indiana, speaking on "The Faith Crisis," *GS Minutes 1971,* 166–67.

economic security and rewards. Students are not pushed or guided to seek an understanding with Christ, they "cop-out" and exhaust their energies before Christ is given a chance as society overshadows individual and emotional needs with economic needs. Advertisements for affluence surround us every minute of the day. Advertisements for faith in the form of human models are scarce, lying dormant, not growing and not meeting the challenges they are faced with today. Society's affluence offers more glamorous ways of occupying time spent away from work, pushing aside the role of the church as a place for fellowship, sharing and worship. The glamorous society receives the enthusiasm while the church lives in dreams of the past.

Society does not encourage us to seek an understanding of ourselves, but it forces us to seek a place for ourself in society. The church does not provide a role for us in society or the benefits that are associated with being socially acceptable. Instead of working together, the church and economic society are in competition with each other for each person's time and energies. The preoccupation of today's students lies in the demands of society.

Institutional forms of faith which once were depended upon do not serve my needs today as a student and member of society. My needs are manifested in meeting the demands of society and coping with its problems. I am searching for myself in a world that is struggling in much the same way. For the church to be effective in helping me find myself and faith in God, it must offer more than rituals and structure. I need a place to express, share and develop my faith. I need a place that is not strange, and archaic, where I can feel as though I am being listened to as well as a place to listen. I need a place where I can get to know Christ and forego the formal introductions. I need a place for a running dialogue with people of the same concerns, ideas, and uncertainties that I experience. I need a place that does not depend on established people who are settled down in a community. I am a transient person who is growing and changing, doubtful and confused. I need a place that will also grow, change and erase my doubts and confusion so I can become a strong person of strong faith to help develop a strong community that will be the basis of the stability of a strong world.

49. Youth:
"Why We Don't Teach Them Morals"

(1978)

Gaylord Noyce

Gaylord Noyce (b. 1926) is a Congregational Christian/UCC minister educated at Miami University (Ohio) and Yale Divinity School. After teaching in Istanbul, Turkey, and serving UCC parishes in Massachusetts and North Carolina, he taught for over thirty years at Yale Divinity School (1960–94). Deeply committed to the relationship between the church's proclamation and its public witness, Noyce was among the first of the "Freedom Riders" who ventured into the South to accompany African Americans in their struggle for civil rights in the early 1960s. In his writing and teaching, he influenced several generations of divinity students at Yale as they confronted the challenges and heartaches of pastoral ministry. Drawing on his expertise as a professor of pastoral theology, Noyce outlines five principles of moral education to which Christians must pay serious attention.

Source: Gaylord Noyce, "Why We Don't Teach Them Morals," *A.D. Magazine* (March 1978): 10.

Why We Don't Teach Them Morals

"Why don't you teach them morals?" a frustrated mother asked the advisor of her son's church youth group.

In a nearby Bible chapel there is a fast-growing youth club with a no-ifs-ands-or-buts style of teaching right and wrong. Moreover, the mother knows that her own son is unchallenged by either the "fun and games" or "serious discussions" in the youth group at her own UCC church.

Working with many seminary students who are youth advisors, I hear similar questions from the parents of their charges.

"Teaching morals" in a pluralistic society is a problem for parents, public-school teachers, and Christian educators alike. An authoritarian or sectarian mentality tempts us in spite of our better judgment. Some teachers avoid stubborn moral ambiguities by saying certain things are always right and others absolutely wrong.

Our teaching problem in the church arises from five principles to which Christians must pay serious respect.

1. *Christian faith at its center is not a set of moral regulations spelled out like so many embellishments on the Ten Commandments.* Our faith provokes in us profoundly moral concerns. We are given by God's grace a way, a Torah. But at our roots, we Christians know, instead of a restricting law, a liberating joy in the God we meet through Jesus.

St. Paul went so far in his experience of legalistic religious interpretations as to say, "The law is dead." It is freedom in Christ that creates our loyalty to God, and it is our love of neighbor that seriously probes all questions of personal virtue and social justice.

2. *The Bible is more of a storybook about God's way with us than it is a cookbook of rules for proper behavior.* It is through our celebration of the story that Christians are made whole by God's grace rather than through the personal virtues we cook up from the rules.

3. *Moral character is a quality of persons, not a function of machines.* We do not aim at programming our children and youth for automatic reflexes that make them perform in flat "moral" patterns of routine respectability. Rather, we want them to be loving, creative persons with an inner freedom showing through in a zest for life. That means taking the risk of less respectability and traditional piety for the sake of a richer sense of relationship with God and an inner commitment to the lively fabric of human community.

4. *We should hold to a pattern of integrity not for fear of punishment or of disapproval from others or of losing a reward, but from an inner conviction that it is simply the good to which we are committed.* "I couldn't

live with myself if I did that," a mature person might say. Many adults never mature that far. They find morality in laws and in the disapproval of others. When they can do for their own advantage what is unjust or deceitful, without danger of punishment or disapproval, they will. They do not reflect seriously on what is simply right, just, or true — to put it another way, on God's hope for the human community. This is the moral immaturity of Watergate.

5. *Moral reasoning depends on an ability to recognize the difference between private desire and moral obligation, between personal wants and a more objective rightness or goodness that can lay claim on us.* St. Paul exhibited that ability when he wrote that he could "will the good" but that he found himself doing evil because of his own selfish inclination.

This says to the teacher or parent in each one of us that our aim for moral maturity in our own family and church life will include a strong sense of selfhood and responsible relations to others. Much broader and deeper than obedience, we call this character.

Merely enforcing rules that one church or teacher proclaims as the law of God forecloses personal reflection and practice in moral decision-making. It leaves open the possibility of retarded moral development or of moral cynicism if the student later questions these particular "Godly" rules. Promoting unthinking obedience is really the opposite of teaching morality.

Yet participatory moral development does not allow good leaders to play a nonpartisan role on moral questions. We need parents, teachers, and advisors of character and passionate conviction about justice and generosity, what is right and what is good.

Moral reflection that leads to active commitment is one of the most characteristically Christian and spiritually essential lessons that we can teach and learn.

50. Art and Music:

"Resolution on the Church and the Arts" and "Like a Tree beside the Waters"

(1977, 1992)

General Synod, James F. D. Martin

Although the proclamation of the Christian faith requires words, and the United Church of Christ is especially sensitive to the importance of inclusive language (see vol. 7:31 and 73), the members of UCC congregations know that their faith is grounded in the Word beyond words. Architecture, poetry, liturgy, stories, dance, choirs, organs, and other artistic expressions of Christianity all bear witness to this Word. They "open us to new ways of understanding both personal and public life and give us insight and energy to act in love and justice for the sake of the Holy." The 1977 General Synod "Resolution on the Church and the Arts" affirms the importance of the arts and urges support for the "UCC Fellowship in the Arts."

Music, especially hymns, remains the most common art form in local congregations. James F. D. Martin (b. 1953) is a UCC minister educated at Illinois State University and United Theological Seminary of the Twin Cities. Since 1980 he has served as pastor in four different UCC congregations in Wisconsin. His 1992 hymn "Like a Tree beside the Waters" was written for the 125th anniversary of the United Church of Christ at Campbellsport, Wisconsin.

Sources: "Resolution on the Church and the Arts," *GS Minutes 1977,* 58–59. James F. D. Martin, "Like a Tree beside the Waters," *The New Century Hymnal* (Cleveland: The Pilgrim Press), Hymn #313. Words Copyright © 1994 James F. D. Martin. Used by permission.

Resolution on the Church and the Arts

WHEREAS, we are heirs of the Biblical inheritance of art, of the God who created form out of chaos and who put life and breath into the dust of the earth, of David who danced before the ark and sang songs of faith, of Miriam who sang songs of joy, of Jesus who drew pictures in parables and raised the common elements of our lives to a symbolic and sacred use, and of John who revealed a new vision of heaven coming to earth;

WHEREAS, the Church through the ages has been a patron and preserver of the arts and the artists;

WHEREAS, the United Church of Christ firmly believes in the development of the whole person as a cultural, social and political being;

WHEREAS, the potential for magnificent creative activity exists within and among each of us;

WHEREAS, we believe that the arts are a prophetic and effective channel for the mediation of God's judgment and grace for the redemption of the world; we are drawn into a work of art, we experience its transforming power; the arts open us to new ways of understanding both personal and public life and give us insight and energy to act in love and justice for the sake of the Holy.

RESOLVED, That the 11th General Synod of the United Church of Christ affirms the contributions of art and artists that enrich the quality and the vitality of life in our Church and world. We recognize that artists illuminate the symbols by which the religious dimensions of life and experience are made known. Also, that they enable the people of God to experience and express the living and liberating power of God, and to renew, sustain, and transform people in a new sense of themselves as persons and in relation to each other in community

RESOLVED, That we encourage freedom to bring to creative expression the religious dimension of our life which nurtures community;

RESOLVED, That we urge the United Church of Christ, through its instrumentalities, publications and church-related institutions (educational, welfare, health, etc.) to recognize further and support the arts:

RESOLVED, That we urge local churches to:

1. Encourage the expression of all forms of art,
2. Examine their use of physical space in order to consider sharing space available with the community's artists.
3. Support and expand the number of artists in residence both in the Church and in the community.

4. Struggle for justice for the artists in our society.
5. Support arts agencies and councils, municipal governments, and school districts, at state and local levels, to the end that no one be denied opportunities to create and experience art, because of barriers, e.g., circumstance, class, race, sex, income, or remoteness;

RESOLVED, That we encourage all members of the Church, laity and clergy, to open themselves to the power and dynamics of the contemporary arts.

We encourage seminaries and colleges related to the Church to take seriously aesthetic ways of knowing and communicating through art the judgment and grace of God in their curricula and degree programs.

We encourage the judicatories of the Church to recognize and support certain churches as having special ministries to and with artists.

We support and urge membership in the United Church of Christ Fellowship in the Arts.

Like a Tree beside the Waters

Like a tree beside the waters,
nurtured by your loving care,
We, O God, your sons and daughters,
your enduring witness bear.
In each passing generation
may your voice of love be heard.
Bless, we pray, this congregation
with your holy, living Word.

Like a tree beside the river,
drawing life from holy streams,
Fill us with your love forever;
recreate our hopes and dreams.
Through the storms of life sustain us
by the wisdom of your grace.
May the changing of the seasons
find us in your warm embrace.

We, beside the living waters,
drink from your eternal life.
Give to all, your sons and daughters,
faith that rises over strife.
O Living God, most glorious,
strengthen us for life today.
By the hope of timeless promise
guide your church upon the Way.

SILVER CREEK and HYFRYDOL 8.7.8.7.D

51. A Personal Testimony:

"Who Do You Say That I Am?"

(1996)

Mary Gafner

Mary Gafner (b. 1946) is a licensed lay minister in the Southwest Wisconsin Association UCC and a graduate of the Wisconsin Conference Lay Academy. She and her husband are dairy farmers, and she has served UCC congregations in Monticello, Wisconsin, since 1990. Her personal testimony about Jesus is an honest statement made by someone who celebrates the fact that "Jesus makes my life a bit uncomfortable. Jesus bids me to act and forgives me when I don't. Jesus fills me with his presence."

Who Do You Say That I Am?

The question of "Who is Jesus?" has been screaming at me for the past few months. Its shout and persistence have crept into every facet of my life: prayer time, telephone conversations, family visits; it is the memo listing things to do. It has crept into driving time, chore time, husband and wife time and all time. The thought has not left me.

I wanted to say something deep and theological about Jesus, but the thoughts didn't come. I wanted to stand before you a visionary, but the images eluded me. Instead, I stand before you: you, who I consider faithful, committed and knowledgeable. I stand before you naked with a simple faith and an almost child-like perception of who Jesus is. I am not going

---

Source: Mary Gafner, "Who Do You Say That I Am?" *On The Way* (Summer 1996): 36–39.

to apologize for my naivity [*sic*] and innocent stance, because for today, this is Who I Am! I have a faith that is foundational, if not fundamental, and it is more than just a little conservative. I have a faith in Jesus Christ that reduces me to tears when singing the song:

> For what earthly reason did the Heavenly Father send down
> His Son?
>
> To suffer rejection and pay for crimes he had not done.
>
> For what earthly reason did the Heavenly Father send down
> His Son?
>
> That one earthly reason was me.

I have a faith that seeks understanding and a heart that struggles with some of the lessons Jesus taught. I have a faith that is thankful for the humanness of Jesus. The voice from the Garden of Gethsemane: "Father, if you are willing take this cup from me" is the same voice I heard in my mother, ill with cancer, as she and I stood arm in arm, basking in the red and golds of autumn. I still hear her whispered plea: "It is so beautiful here, I don't want to die!" And I am thankful for the response that whispered to our souls, "Not my will be done but yours." It was a call to trust God in all matters whether of life or of death.

I have a faith in Jesus that is strong enough to welcome new ideas and understandings. Much has been said of late about the historical Jesus, contemporary faith, and the divinity of Jesus. I love history and these new views concerning Jesus are fascinating to me. Finding out who the Jesus of history is through interpretations of theologians like Marcus Borg, John Dominic Crossan and Burton Mack is truly a treat. Marcus Borg and Dominic Crossan have some wonderful insights, many of which I can relate to. But Burton Mack I'm not so sure about.

The wedding of traditional and contemporary views isn't difficult for me. God has always chosen to reveal to us those things we are supposed to know — and the time in which we are supposed to know them. Jesus is God's revelation.

So . . . I know who Jesus is. He is the Son of God and the Son of Man. He is the Crucified and Risen Lord. He has come "to save all people from aimlessness and sin. God judges all people and nations by his righteous will. He promises to all who trust in him, forgiveness of sins and fullness of grace, his presence in trial and rejoicing" and a home with Him in the eternal kingdom. I also know that in order to have a relationship with God I have to have a relationship with Jesus.

But these are all just words. Jesus, for me, is alive in every sense of my being. To know Jesus is to feel his touch, to inhale his fragrance, to hear his words, to taste his presence and to see the work of God on this earth.

Have you not felt a light breeze dance across your skin and ruffle your hair as you soak in the beauty of creation? Have you not felt the sun warm on your face? Have you not experienced the kiss of a child, the hug of a friend or the caress of a lover? Have you not felt the certainty of answered prayer? Have you not inhaled the sweet smell of freshly cut grass, a spring shower, freshly baked ginger cookies, or the pungency of marigolds or the sweetness of lavender? Have you not heard the voice of Jesus say, "Your sins are forgiven, go and sin no more," or "Come to me, all who are heavy laden and I will give you rest"? Have you not heard "I am going to prepare a place for you, if it were not true would have not told you so"?

Have you not tasted Jesus' presence in the sweetness of the wine and the flavor of the bread? Have you not seen Christ's work in the hammer of those who build for Habitat, or those who labor for the youth of Sunburst? Have you not seen Christ's work in the mission fields around the world, or in the dedication of those who strive to make the gospel known in creative and innovative ways through the teaching ministry? Have you not seen Christ's work in the healing of Mother Teresa, in the persistence of Civil Rights activists, in the Heifer Project, SERVE, GRAM, the Gideons, and others?

This is to know Jesus!

But can you also not feel the cold hand of a child with no mittens and the tugging on your sleeve of a street urchin begging for a quarter to ride the bus? Have you not felt, at some time, the sting of inequality or injustice in your own life? Have you not smelled the inner city, the garbage dumps of Egypt, or the sick rooms of the lonely or destitute? Have you not heard, "Feed my sheep," or "For when did we see you hungry and feed you, thirsty and gave you something to drink? . . . When did we see you a stranger and invite you in? . . . When did we see you needing clothes and clothe you? When did we see you sick or in prison and go visit you? . . . I tell you the truth, whatever you did for the least of these my people you did it for me"? Have you not heard "Go into all the world and tell the good news to all creation"?

Have you not tasted the vinegar of sour words spoken at someone's expense? Do we not still cry "crucify! crucify!" at new ideas? Have you not tasted the salty tears of disappointment and the hurt of overpowering grief and loss? Do you not see the child left out of play on the playground? Do you not see the bondage of gang participation? Do you not see the abuse of men, women and children, the abuse of drugs and alcohol? Do you not see the pitfalls and pits of society? Jesus does! To see these things is to know who Jesus is.

To see all these things and more is to recognize the living God: Jesus who calls us into an active faith; Jesus who challenges us to grow spiritually, journey constantly, question always and serve others continually. Jesus makes my life a bit uncomfortable. Jesus bids me to act and forgives me when I don't. Jesus fills me with his presence. Jesus guides me. Jesus loves me and answers my prayers. Jesus is the living God.

So I stand before you, naked, with my simple faith, and my belief in Jesus Christ, the Crucified and Risen Savior. The question now remains for you to answer. "Who do you say that I am?"

PART IV

Doing Theology

The Preamble to the Constitution of the United Church of Christ states that the UCC "claims as its own the faith of the historic Church expressed in the ancient creeds and reclaimed in the basic insights of the Protestant Reformers," and that it "affirms the responsibility of the Church in each generation to make this faith its own. . . . "

During the prolonged union negotiations between the Congregational Christian Churches and the Evangelical and Reformed Church major theological controversies did not arise. All parties agreed that theologically the new church would draw upon the legacy of the ancient church and the sixteenth-century Reformation, and that there were fresh and vital ways by which twentieth-century Christians might make this faith their own. The UCC Statement of Faith (1959) set a tone that enabled the new denomination to articulate its convictions by celebrating God's deeds and calling Christians into action (see vol. 7:3).

Developing a Theological Center

The United Church of Christ was theologically confident at its birth, but not particularly theologically self-conscious. UCC writers described the common biblical roots present in the life of the new church. They accepted various theological viewpoints in an irenic spirit and without fanfare (see vol. 7:52). Members of theological faculties, as well as pastors and many lay leaders, shared a common respect for Christian doctrine. They could not conceive of the church without it. Yet, other themes claimed attention, alongside deepening social issues. Although the diversity of the United Church of Christ was admired and people were inspired by the evolving and passionate presence of the UCC in society, there were critics. They charged that the UCC was little more than a social-action group, effective perhaps, but theologically undiscerning. They insisted that the UCC took theology "for granted." They pointed to a fuzzy ecclesiology. Criticisms, some of them loving, persisted. In response the UCC reminded its critics that the vocation of the church is foremost "to tell the Christian story to people in winsome ways" (see vol. 7:53), while affirming the rich theological heritage of the church.

Although the theological life of the UCC was surely imperfect and incomplete, over time it became more articulate.

In 1982 the UCC *Leader's Box* defined theology as "what is believed about God and all that is related to God." It claimed that theology draws upon the Bible and tradition, and also on personal experience and the contemporary life of the church. Theological identity is not simply a matter of substance. It is shaped by a process. It takes the form of "theological dialogue in search of the Word of God in the contemporary setting" (see vol. 7:54).

By the 1970s many United Church of Christ leaders spoke about their church as finding its theological voice in an action-reflection lifestyle (see vol. 7:28). This sometimes led to a paradoxical identity grounded in faith expressed in "contradictory impulses" (see vol. 7:55).

For this reason when asked about what they believed, UCC members felt comfortable lifting up key phrases embedded in the history and practice of their traditions. They insisted that the prayer of Jesus "that they may all be one," stood at the core of their commitment to church unity. They affirmed "in essentials unity, in nonessentials diversity, in all things charity." They asserted that faith statements are "testimonies rather than tests of faith." They grounded their faith in the hope that "there is yet more light and truth to break forth from God's Holy Word." And they affirmed "the priesthood of all believers" alongside the principle of "responsible freedom." For the United Church of Christ theology was a journey rather than a static possession (see vol. 7:56).

On this theological journey the church hears many voices; it sings many songs. It is marked by a long line of confessions and covenants through time. From one generation to the next the call is to embrace the journey, to love the theological challenge that is always present, and to celebrate the gospel.

Clarifying Theological Identity

During the late 1970s, however, the various ad hoc patterns of theological affirmation used by the United Church of Christ were becoming increasingly inadequate. In 1971 the General Synod wrestled with what it called the "faith crisis" and the Office for Church Life and Leadership (OCLL) launched "faith exploration" programs. Soon a group of UCC leaders came together to reflect about the nature of "sound [theological] teaching" in the church. They were critical of the UCC, concerned that it was "excessively accommodated to cultural values and perceptions." They "initiate[d] a new discussion" to lead "the whole church in a new act of faithfulness." For many it was an exciting time of "theological ferment," prompted by internal forces and influenced by growing interest in "liberation theologies" (see vol. 7:57).

At the same time, theologians in the UCC pressed for theological clarity. UCC theologian James Gustafson wrote about the need to reclaim a "theocentric" or "God-centered" worldview (see vol. 7:58). In 1983 a paper, drafted by a small group of UCC seminary faculty and eventually signed by thirty-nine theological education colleagues from all over the country, was sent to the UCC Executive Council. The "Letter from the Thirty-nine" theological educators warned that the United Church of Christ was facing a "Most Difficult and Urgent Time." It agreed with UCC president Avery Post that there was a "theological deficit" in the church and a "void in sustained, disciplined reflection." It called for "an articulation of faith in the life and witness of the church" to "faithfully witness to the bedrock truth of Jesus Christ in our common life" (see vol. 7:59).

The Executive Council responded with a statement entitled "Theological Renewal in the United Church of Christ" (March 1984). It celebrated the "explosion of theological expression" in the church. Not only were the theological educators calling for disciplined reflection, there was a renewed interest in spirituality, a new Council on Racial and Ethnic Ministries (COREM); a Committee on Pluralism; an emerging ecumenical theology around issues of baptism, eucharist, and ministry; and several other venues "involved in theological study and action."

Soon thereafter, the seven "closely related" seminaries of the United Church of Christ launched a new theological journal, *Prism: A Theological Forum for the United Church of Christ* (Fall 1985). Its editors challenged the entire church to enter into "clearheaded . . . thinking and disciplined speech" about theology.

At the same time, the Office for Church Life and Leadership (OCLL) convened a "Theology Work Group" of eleven people to explore the "Theological Foundations in this United Church of Christ" (June 1985). The work group set out to describe how the United Church of Christ does theology. It did not pretend to offer a definitive word, but shared its work as "a catalyst for further discussion and conversation" in regional theological convocations held throughout the country (1985–86) (see vol. 7:60).

Some people began to suggest that the UCC needed a new theological "book of creeds and platforms," like Williston Walker's *Creeds and Platforms of Congregationalism,* or a new Statement of Faith. In that conversation the vision for what became *The Living Theological Heritage of the United Church of Christ* (1995–2004) was born. It would not be a collection of "authoritative documents," but a multivolume library of resources to inform and nurture theological maturity in the UCC. The living theological heritage of the UCC was vibrant, rich, and diverse, but most people did not know how to access its treasures.

Other grassroots theological developments emerged. In 1977 a small group of pastors and laity, involved in an anniversary celebration of the Evangelical Synod of North America in Chicago, recognized the need for more intentional intellectual work in the UCC. They organized the Biblical-Theological-Liturgical Group (the "BTL Club," as it was affectionately called), which met yearly to share papers on the authority of scripture, the sacraments, confessions, and other theological topics. In 1979 at its meeting in East Petersburg, Pennsylvania, the group issued a statement calling the United Church of Christ to overcome its "acculturation" and to listen only to the one Word, Jesus Christ (see vol. 7:61).

Subsequently, the "BTL Club," in collaboration with a new group seeking to contemporize the legacies of nineteenth-century Mercersburg theology (see vol. 3:26, 28 and vol. 7:68), convened the first "Craigville Colloquy" (1984). Meeting on the grounds of the old "Christian campground" on Cape Cod, it became the first of many yearly Craigville Colloquies dedicated to providing opportunities for grassroots theological work, always with an ecumenical component, within the framework of the UCC Constitution. Craigville sought to do theology "from below," bringing together people from different theological perspectives in an effort to articulate common concerns. The first "Craigville Colloquy Letter" (1984) praised God for the "theological ferment" in the church and called the UCC to ground social witness in its biblical heritage and Christological center (see vol. 7:61).

Even as the Office for Church Life and Leadership (OCLL) convened the "Theology Work Group," and the seminaries launched a new journal, and the "BTL Club" joined with the Mercersburg Society to sponsor Craigville Colloquies, the United Church of Christ was touched by the wider "charismatic movement." During the faith crisis of the 1970s some UCC people became enthusiastic about revitalizing worship to focus upon the immediate religious experience of the Holy Spirit. The charismatic movement was often criticized for ignoring society while seeking escapist ecstasy, but UCC Charismatics insisted that oneness with the Spirit naturally supported the historic social commitments of the UCC. In 1977 the United Church of Christ Charismatic Fellowship was organized (see vol. 7:62).

Theological concerns within the United Church of Christ were also stimulated by the serious debate around human sexuality that took place at the 1977 General Synod. After the Synod vote on *Human Sexuality—A Preliminary Study* (see vol. 7:98), a minority caucus made up of delegates who voted against the *Sexuality* report organized a new special-interest group, the United Church People for Biblical Witness (UCPBW). Although the UCPBW was born as a protest against the sexual license that its leaders perceived present in the sexuality study, the UCPBW stated that it wanted to be "a positive force for biblical accountability, reformed practice, and spiritual renewal within, rather than against the United Church of Christ."

For the next two synods the United Church People for Biblical Witness (UCPBW) urged the General Synod to reclaim what it believed to be a more orthodox understanding of scriptural authority on sexuality issues. When the UCPBW was unable to accomplish this goal, it decided that reform from the top down was a lost cause. Therefore, in late 1983 when UCPBW leaders met in Dubuque, Iowa, to discuss the future of their renewal work in the United Church of Christ, they reorganized to form a new organization committed to work from the "bottom up" to change the theological stance of the UCC. Taking a new name, "Biblical Witness Fellowship" (BWF), its leaders drafted the "Dubuque Declaration" (1983), summarizing their traditional or orthodox theology. BWF turned to some of the writings of UCC theologian Donald Bloesch at Dubuque Theological Seminary to support its stance, and it invited all like-minded UCC congregations to join the BWF by affirming the "Dubuque Declaration" (see vol. 7:63).

Theological ferment in the UCC took many different forms in the early 1980s. While those who lamented the decline of traditional theology formed the UCPBW and the BWF, in 1980 a group of UCC social activists organized a group called "Christians for Justice Action" (CJA) to promote justice issues within the UCC. In 1985, drawing upon the words of the prophet Isaiah (Isaiah 58), CJA invited the UCC to recognize its preoccupation with the church rather than God's ministry, its misplaced anxiety over falling membership statistics, its failure to challenge church members to grow, and its tendency to equate prosperity and happiness with the gospel. CJA read the words of Isaiah with new passion, calling the UCC to return to the cost and joy of discipleship at the core of its identity and mission (see vol. 7:95).

About the same time the General Synod also took several additional actions to strengthen the theological identity of the church. In 1985 it declared justice and peace to be church priorities for the next four years, and it passed a pronouncement, "Affirming the United Church of Christ to be a Just Peace Church" (1985). Work leading to the pronouncement had begun in 1981 and led to the publication of a small study book entitled *A Just Peace Church* (1986), reminding everyone that making peace and doing justice are the God-given tasks of all Christians (see vol. 7:64).

The culture of the United Church of Christ was changing. Alongside increased racial and ethnic diversity more and more women were attending seminaries and becoming ordained as pastors and teachers. With its rising exposure to women's leadership and its expanded awareness of the need for inclusive language the 1971 General Synod passed several progressive pronouncements advocating for women in church and society (see vol. 7:85 and 86). Feminist theology embraced a diversity of methods and began to rethink Christian theology. Christian feminists, "stretched by the more radical expression of women's experience of the transcendent," developed new views of power and value based upon models of participation, mutuality, and solidarity (see vol. 7:65).

By the end of the 1980s the United Church of Christ was clearly more theologically aware and had done some important things to clarify its theological identity. It had moved from theological self-critique and "ferment" to claim new theological self-confidence. Although it did not follow conventional patterns, the United Church of Christ was beginning to "come of age" theologically.

Living with Theological Diversity

Maintaining the "theological health" of the United Church of Christ was a challenge. Yet, as the denomination matured it found a variety of ways to sustain its Christocentric conviction that its life was a gift from God and not a human accomplishment, even as it embraced theological diversity. The apostle Paul had written that "there are varieties of gifts, but the same Spirit; and there are varieties of services, but the same Lord; and there are varieties of activities, but it is the same God who activates all of them in everyone." The United Church of Christ was seeking to live out its calling confident that "To each is given the manifestation of the Spirit for the common good" (1 Corinthians 12:4–7, NRSV).

Theological vitality in the United Church of Christ took many forms. Drawing upon the historic theological legacies of the Reformation, the United Church of Christ continued to recognize the value of traditional theology and liturgy (see vol. 7:66). At the same time the United Church of Christ applauded the activist conviction that the "name and power of

Jesus Christ is indissolubly linked to the two-fold struggle for a new person and a new society" (see vol. 7:67).

Although the United Church of Christ valued the work of many of the sixteenth-century Protestant reformers, it also appreciated the ways in which nineteenth-century Mercersburg theology reminded the church of its "catholic" identity. During the early 1980s, the "Mercersburg Society" was formed to study and reappropriate the sacramental and liturgical insights of John Williamson Nevin and Philip Schaff and provide new opportunities for contemporary UCC clergy and laity to learn about the Mercersburg theological tradition (see vol. 3:26, 28, 33 and vol. 4:88, 90). Those who sought to nurture the Mercersburg perspective through common prayer and contemplation leading to "concrete action in the life of the Church and the world" founded the Order of Corpus Christi (see vol. 7:68).

In 1981 the United Church of Christ further stretched its theological self-understanding by adopting a "Resolution Toward a Covenant in Mission and Faith" with the Evangelical Church of the Union (EKU) in both East and West Germany. The year before, the EKU, one of the UCC "ancestors in the faith," had acknowledged "the integrity of the faith and mission of the United Church of Christ" and voted "Kirchengemeinschaft" (the shaping of full community, or full communion) with the "members, ministers and sacraments" of the United Church of Christ (1980).

The United Church of Christ response to the EKU reflected a deepening of historic ties. During the 1930s, Eden Theological Seminary had granted an honorary degree (in absentia) to Martin Niemoeller, who had been imprisoned in a concentration camp in Germany for his theology and his resistance to National Socialism. Not long thereafter, the president of the seminary, Samuel Press, observed that the Confessing Church in Germany (of which Niemoeller was a leader) was training its pastors "for martyrdom." "Kirchengemeinschaft" was born of such a spirit of faith, rooted in the biblical story and taking the violence, fractures, and needs of the world seriously. The United Church of Christ response to the EKU in 1981 was a sign that it saw itself linked in vital ways to other Christians seeking to be authentically present in the world and developing sound teaching for the "global village." In "full communion" the UCC came to live less "nationally" and more and more "globally" (see 7:69).

Other ecumenical relationships further expanded UCC theological horizons. The church continued its participation in the Consultation on Church Union (COCU), which went back to 1962. The long-standing relationship with the Christian Church (Disciples of Christ) found new expression. The response of the United Church of Christ to the World Council of Churches

Faith and Order document on *Baptism, Eucharist and Ministry* and the involvement of the United Church of Christ in dialogue with Lutheran and Reformed churches also deepened UCC theological self-confidence (see vol. 7:107, 105, 106 and 110).

Rediscovering theological foundations and responding to theological and cultural diversity took many forms. It meant that the UCC became more intentional about its desire to be the "church" — a complete community of Christ's people. General Synod actions and local church life during the 1980s reached out to people who were oppressed, marginalized, and different, giving new voice and recognition to: African Americans; women; gays, lesbians, and bisexuals; people with handicapping conditions; the poor; people from Spanish-speaking cultures; Asian and Pacific Islanders; and Indigenous peoples (see vol. 7:83, 84, 116, 89, 98, 97, 133, 128, and 120).

The affirmation of gays and lesbians in the UCC was extremely difficult for some members of the church to accept. There were those who found the situation intolerable. They summarized their unhappiness in the "Dayton Declaration" (1991), stating that it was time for "faithful members of the Church of Jesus Christ to call into account the leaders of an organized church that calls itself Christian." The Dayton Declaration asserted that UCC leaders were guilty of altering the wording of scripture, advocating unbiblical sexual practices, denying the right to life, and rejecting the Great Commission. Writers of the Dayton Declaration asked the Biblical Witness Fellowship (BWF) to mobilize local churches to reject recent actions. They accused current United Church of Christ leaders of leading the church into "apostasy" (see vol. 7:70).

This was a painful time in the United Church of Christ. National leaders had difficulty understanding how their efforts to open the doors of the church to be more fully the body of Christ in the world were equated with "apostasy," or departure from the church. It was a period of soul searching and, as is often the case, a time of attempting to attain greater theological clarity.

The theological energy that had generated the BTL Club, Sound Teaching, the Mercersburg Society, the Craigville Colloquies, the Order of Corpus Christi, the UCC Charismatic Fellowship, the Letter from the 39 Theological Educators, the UCC Theology Project, and the new theological journal *Prism* did not wane. As the 1980s gave way to the 1990s the United Church of Christ found fresh ways to nurture its theological life and sustain its Christocentric core, while remaining open to remarkable diversity.

In 1993 the General Synod passed a document "Toward the 21st Century: A Statement of Commitment." Using four key theological phrases it affirmed the calling of the United Church of Christ to be "a church attentive to the Word," to be "a church inclusive of all people," to be "a church responsive to God's call," and to be "a church supportive of one another" (see vol. 7:71).

That same year, a convening committee for a new group, calling itself "Confessing Christ," invited local UCC leaders and members to gather in three regional conversations. They suggested that clergy and laity needed to "engage in dialogue about the meaning and importance of the heritage of the United Church of Christ, the dangers present in its erosion, and its place in the new century." Confessing Christ took as its theme the central statement of the 1934 Barmen Declaration (developed by the Confessing Church movement in Nazi Germany). "Jesus Christ, as he is attested for us in Holy Scripture, is the one Word of God which we have to hear, and which we have to trust and obey in life and in death" [Arthur Cochrane, *The Church's Confession under Hitler,* 254]. Its organizers believed that there was a growing need to gather people together who loved the church "neither to 'weep bitterly' over the Church (which would be theologically irresponsible)," nor "to pound upon others (which would be uncharitable)." Rather, they invited Christians to "confess Christ" — to honor our shared baptism in Christ and to see how "dialogue with one another and with those who believed before we were born, can reform the life of the Church for the sake of its vocation in the world." They called for regional centers to encourage thoughtful, joyous, and imaginative theological work (see vol. 7:72).

During 1993 the Office for Church Life and Leadership (OCLL) also updated the *UCC Inclusive Language Guidelines* and suggested that the "persistence" of the language issue in the church might be "a sign" that God is "prompting us to see it as more than a passing notion." Language "allows all God's people to readily recognize the dignity of their having been created in God's image." The updated guidelines challenged individuals, groups, local churches, and other church bodies to commit themselves to an "Inclusive Language Covenant" and to seek ongoing respectful dialogue on issues of language (see vol. 7:73).

Many congregations, pastors, and teachers throughout the UCC enthusiastically affirmed the diversity of the church's life. Trusting in the Spirit, articles and sermons explored the power of language, inviting faithful Christians to "listen" and reminding them that "self-righteousness was the bane of both interpersonal and international relations" (see vol. 7:74 and 75).

Reaching Out in Mission

In the midst of the challenges of the 1990s, the United Church of Christ kept its balance. It drew upon the thought of its founding leaders and sustained the dynamic interplay between confession and action. As the UCC was born, a small paperback book entitled *The Faith We Proclaim* (1961) summarized the "doctrinal viewpoint generally prevailing in the Evangelical and Reformed Church." It reflected the belief that the church witnesses to God's mighty acts in the history of the world and proclaims its faith in grateful response to those acts. Thirty years later the "mission and the message" of the church that it set forth remains fundamentally the same. God is in Christ "reconciling the world . . . " (2 Corinthians 5:19). The church "testifies to God's deeds" through its ministry to the needs of society. In so doing it upholds "the reality and sovereignty of God's order." "The church cannot be itself unless it ministers to the world" (see vol. 7:76).

Furthermore, ministering to the world flows from covenants inherited from the past. As it reaches out, the United Church of Christ recognizes that it stands before God's mercy seat, and its hope is in Jesus Christ who "transcends all memories." In 1977, Joseph Evans, the third president of the UCC, called the church to a bold faith. "This boldness should make us dedicate the United Church of Christ to being a missionary instrument in the hand of God to bring about a commonwealth of love and justice in the world" (see vol. 7:77).

There were still those who believed that the United Church of Christ was not "theologically serious," that its theology was merely "a series of ad hoc opinions usually added on to some practical concern," or that it used theology to "justify positions already taken for other reasons." When confronted with these criticisms the widely respected UCC theologian and ethicist Roger Shinn commented that "ad hoc theology is not entirely wrong. If God meets us in the midst of all the events of life, it is as likely that an urgent human demand will lead to a theological insight as that theology will lead to actions" (see vol. 7:77).

The United Church of Christ "does theology" its way. In its nearly fifty years of existence it has found and clarified its theological center and embraced its growing diversity. Its theological work, however, has not been done as "internal housekeeping." When true to its mission, it worries about the future of the world, not the future of the church. It works to claim a new vision and to seek "justice with each move." When the United Church Board for World Ministries (UCBWM) celebrated its 175th anniversary it sang about its calling to build "justice as the bulwark of the peace that God would give." When a National Conference on Mission, sponsored by the United Church Board for Homeland Ministries (UCBHM), produced the "Houston Statement on Mission" (1987), it affirmed the call and commitment of the church "to join oppressed and troubled people in the struggle for liberation" and "to work for justice, healing and wholeness of life" (see vol. 7:78).

At about the same time the United Church Board for World Ministries (UCBWM) refined its emerging understanding of mission as "partnership" — drawing upon biblical images of unity and interdependence. Around the world, as well as at home, the United Church of Christ sought to ground its theology of mission in mutual sharing as well as in mutual acceptance. As overseas churches became increasingly self-reliant and independent, they began to invite the United Church of Christ into relationships of trust and to share commitments to unity and common mission. The historic "mission boards" no longer existed as "agents" of mission for the church, but became channels for shared fellowship and work in the world (see vol. 7:79).

So what is the theological stance of the United Church of Christ? While it is difficult to summarize in classic terms, it remains grounded in the Christocentric affirmation that Jesus Christ is the Head of the church. It is fed and cultivated by grassroots faithfulness and controversy. It encourages and supports diversity without compromising its integrity and it ultimately works for justice and peace in the world. It is capable of risk for the sake of the truth of the gospel. It is also grounded in the mystery of life and knows itself to be a reflection of that mystery.

In the United Church of Christ, with all its diverse viewpoints, it can be said that theology begins in wonder — not the wonder of disinterested science, but the wonder of deep concern and personal involvement. This wonder leads to the conviction that Christian theology is "a confession of what God has done, of what God is doing, and of what God promises yet to do." The United Church of Christ longs for theology that is biblically informed and contemporary; theology that remembers the "underlying divine-human encounter of revelation and response." It seeks a theology that empowers Christians to act in the world in Christian freedom, not because they believe they can redeem the world, but because they have glimpsed the mystery that God in Christ loves the world and never tires of summoning the church to witness to the redemption of the world in both word and deed (see vol. 7:80).

Developing a Theological Center

52. Basic Theology: *"What Does It Mean to Be a Christian?"*

(1962)

William L. Bradley

William L. Bradley (b. 1918) is a Congregational Christian/UCC minister educated at Oberlin College, Andover Newton Theological School, and the University of Edinburgh. He was on the faculty at Hartford Theological Seminary (1955–66) and spent the rest of his career working for the Rockefeller Foundation and the Hazen Foundation. His book The Meaning of Christian Values Today *(1965) addressed many of the same issues he examined in his* United Church Herald *article on Christian theology. Bradley gives a good summary of the general theological stance of the United Church of Christ at its founding.*

Knowing What It Means to Be a Christian

Christianity burst upon the Western world in a brief, climactic moment of history and in a very short period of time transformed its whole culture.

Five thousand years of Near Eastern civilization preceded the thirty-odd years of Jesus' life and yet those five millenniums are as nothing compared with the brief ministry of this man and the apostolic age that followed soon upon his death.

Source: William L. Bradley, "Knowing What It Means to Be a Christian," *United Church Herald,* November 15, 1962, 8–9, 23.

Historic Task

Since that time Christianity has been engaged in the task of understanding, interpreting and implementing the gospel of Jesus Christ, which was preached and spread throughout the ancient world by the early church.

In the course of the centuries that have followed, the church has developed a body of doctrine that is intended both to retain the essential truth about God's revelation in Jesus Christ and to make relevant this message for every generation as it takes over the continuing task.

Men and institutions being what they are, it is inevitable that disputes should arise and that some should use theology merely as a weapon of attack or defense rather than as an instrument of evangelism. Nevertheless, theology and theologians have an honorable record of accomplishment and it is noteworthy that nineteen hundred years after the death of its founder Christianity should still be able to proclaim to the world that it has the same Lord, the same faith and the same baptism as had that little company of apostles who knew Christ as their risen Saviour.

We should note this during this time of ecumenical discussions among the great Christian groups around the world. For it is first as Christians that we come together and only secondarily as members of distinctive denominations. It is always in this context that we should discuss theology, for it has two functions to perform, both of which are essential to the life of the church.

The one is conservative: it seeks to preserve in a recognizable form the essential and distinctive message or witness of the Christian faith. In this role, theology takes the form that is commonly classified as dogmatics. Here theology is charged with the responsibility of instructing Christians in the basic doctrines that together form a rational, coherent system.

These doctrines have to do with the nature and activity of God, the Trinity, the person and work of Jesus Christ, the role of the Holy Spirit, the nature and destiny of man, the nature of the church and the kingdom of God. Christians need to know what it means to be a Christian, not only in terms of their responsibilities and possibilities as the children of God. Without systematic theology, Christianity would inevitably have been reduced to a way of life not unlike that of Confucianism.

The other function of theology is the dynamic: it seeks to interpret the timeless message of the gospel in terms that are relevant and compelling to each generation as it comes upon the scene. It has to make its impact upon human culture. This it does through what is known as apologetics.

The task of apologetics is more difficult and more fraught with danger than that of dogmatics because here a Christian is always threatened with the possibility of translating the faith into terms that will alter in a radical way the central truths he seeks to preserve. Yet it is essential for theology to engage in this aspect of its role, for otherwise Christianity remains the private wisdom of the few rather than the public message of God's redemption for all the world to hear.

Usually, a theologian must choose which of these roles he as an individual will assume, for it is difficult if not impossible for one man to do both. Having made the choice, he will always thereafter be tempted to maintain that his is the better — nay, even the only proper — role in the theological task of the church.

Within the past five years, a revival of theological interest has occurred at the same time that the popular schools of neo-orthodoxy and existential theology have lost ground to newer forms of liberalism.

Confused Layman

The layman seeking to understand theology may be confused by the debate between theologians, for often he is unable to understand why the issues are considered important in the first place. Is it not enough that men should try to do as Jesus would do in their situation, living by the Golden Rule and turning the other cheek whenever possible?

What is the background of this continuing discussion? It centers about controversies between modern schools of theology. Protestantism has not had a commonly shared theological standpoint since the middle of the last [nineteenth] century. At that time the orthodoxy that characterized most denominations was shattered by the impact of revolutionary changes in man's outlook on the world in which he lived.

Our great-grandparents could assume that the Bible is literally true in every respect, that the creation of the world actually followed the pattern depicted in Genesis, that the sin of our flesh-and-blood ancestor, Adam, is transmitted from parent to child and that the Bible provides a blueprint for the end of the world and the kingdom of heaven.

Then came Darwin, Hegel and Marx, to be followed by Freud. With the tools of literary criticism Biblical scholars discovered sources that lay behind the Biblical accounts. Men ceased to believe in original sin and they no longer looked forward to the second coming of Christ in the old way.

The result was a very healthy theological development, which we know as liberalism. Liberal theology turned men's attention to Jesus the human being and to his teachings, particularly those of an ethical kind. It inspired a humanitarian approach to people and their problems and was responsible for many necessary social reforms. It took liberalism to do something about the poverty of the working man, to banish child labor, to create decent standards for women and to open men's minds to the possibilities of a good life for all men here on earth.

Liberalism's Temptation

But liberalism was always in danger of casting its thought in terms of human values and naturalistic ideas of inevitable progress. That is, it could hardly avoid the temptation of replacing the sovereignty of God with the sovereignty of man. It thought too highly of the inherent possibilities of human nature, not to mention evolutionary progress, and so closely identified man with Jesus Christ as to lose sight of the classical Christian distinction between Redeemer and redeemed.

In stressing the humanity of Jesus it often forgot — and in some cases even denied — his divinity, thereby making theology only one of man's many possible philosophies.

In reaction to liberalism there arose an orthodox revolt known as fundamentalism or Biblicism. Essentially a rearguard action against its more popular and open-minded opponent, it was disturbed lest the central truths of Christianity be lost. These were usually conceived to be the inerrancy of Scripture, the doctrine of the virgin birth of Christ, the substitutional theory of the atonement (interpreted literally in this case to mean that Christ paid off man's debt to a wrathful God by giving his life on the Cross as a substitute for sinful man), and the second coming of Christ to herald the end of the world.

There are many shades of fundamentalism and in recent times there has been a division between the more open-minded scholars and the anti-intellectuals. But by and large fundamentalism has suffered because it was defensively conservative and — more important — because it substituted faith in a set of statements about God for faith in the living God. In our fellowship fundamentalism plays a minor role today, as it has in the past.

Far more important as an alternative to the liberalism of the twenties and early thirties has been a theological viewpoint that is inaccurately termed neo-orthodoxy. The expression has this in its favor, that it shows the intention of the group to restore those elements of the traditional faith that had been blurred or lost by liberals. However, it is impossible to define neo-orthodoxy more exactly than this, for there is no single representative point of view to which all can assent. Karl Barth and Paul Tillich have often been bracketed under this label, but they have been in basic disagreement for two decades.

Neo-orthodoxy has an affinity with liberalism. One must have come through liberalism to qualify for this type of thought. It really is a criticism of liberalism by former liberals. Reinhold Niebuhr, for example, is commonly called neo-orthodox. Yet his social views, as well as his openness to science and allied disciplines, are in the best liberal tradition.

What chiefly characterizes neo-orthodoxy are its realistic appraisal of man's capacities and limitations and its emphasis upon those differences between Jesus Christ and ourselves, which enable him to be our Redeemer. Also significant are its belief in a divine self-revelation of God in Christ as contrasted with a perfectly natural revelation of God in nature and in human culture, its feeling of identification with the church as a unique institution and its critical attitude toward liberalism's emphasis on the authority of religious experience. Neo-orthodoxy also rejects the characteristically liberal distinction between the spiritual and material aspects of existence.

Neo-orthodoxy has been with us for a generation and its leaders have left an indelible mark on Protestantism. It has been a healthy and necessary reaction against the optimism of the Protestant churches before the crises of this century had shown us how easily men of education and culture can become demonic.

Existentialism is a more recent trend in theology that has begun to arouse in some members of the neo-orthodox group the same kind of anxiety that certain liberals had displayed a generation earlier. It is as closely related to neo-orthodoxy as is the latter to liberalism. Its terminology is somewhat the same and it depends to a certain extent upon common sources — particularly the writings of Søren Kierkegaard. In fact, men like Barth have been strongly influenced by existential thinkers. But whereas neo-orthodoxy attests that the historical revelation of God in Christ is the central affirmation of Christianity, existential theology finds the locus of the gospel in subjectivity or man's inwardness.

Neo-orthodoxy starts with God's revelation of himself; existentialism is concerned almost exclusively with man's coming to a condition of self-awareness.

Fundamental Decisions

It is occupied primarily — almost entirely, it would seem — with that area of man's life wherein he makes decisions of life-and-death significance. The fundamental decisions that men must make, if ever they become aware of the fact, deal with loyalties or allegiances.

If my loyalty is first of all to material possessions, then the meaning of my existence is to be found in these material goods and what I do with them and they to me. If my loyalty is first of all to my country, then the deepest meaning of my life is to be found in my identification of myself with my nation and its manifold involvements for me. If my loyalty is first of all to myself, then my existence is to be understood in terms of what I do and how I behave as an object of my self-love.

If my loyalty is first of all to God, then the meaning of my existence is to be found in the way in which whatever is fragmentary (temporal existence) can be endowed with eternal significance by the grace of God who stands apart from me and yet somehow enters into my existence.

Those who criticize existential theology usually do so on the ground that it reduces historical Christianity and the historical Jesus to ultimate irrelevance, just as an early rival of Christianity, Gnosticism, did centuries before. Unless existential theologians are able to meet this criticism, they must ultimately give way to a theology that does not endanger this primary aspect of our faith.

Everyone has a theology, whether he knows what it is or not. In our fellowship the majority of laymen are liberal, though in the suburbs there are increasing numbers of people — usually recent graduates of colleges in which religion departments are staffed by the younger theologians — who might be termed orthodox. Fundamentalism is not wide-spread among us and is usually found in areas where that viewpoint predominates across denominational lines. Existentialism is too new to have shown any influence among the laity.

It is hard to classify our ministers by their theology. Perhaps it is fair to say, however, that because our churches give the minister so little opportunity to study and keep pace with theology, most ministers reflect the point of view that prevailed in their seminary days. This means that there will probably be more liberals among the older men than the younger and that among the younger ministers, those who are in the liberal group will be so because their seminaries had not been as greatly influenced by Barth, Brunner, Bultmann, Tillich and Niebuhr as had others.

It is true to say that almost none of the seminaries that our ministerial students ordinarily attend have been unaffected by the theological revolution of the last fifteen or twenty years. This is due not only to the fact that the younger teachers will have felt the influence of neo-orthodoxy and existentialism, but also because the older men keep pace with theological debate and are influenced by it. Thus there has developed, for example, what is known as neo-liberalism. And as a matter of fact, many of the so-called neo-orthodox teachers are more liberal in their viewpoints than are some ministers who sat at their feet years ago when they were just beginning to formulate their ideas.

What lies ahead for theology? It appears that we shall not in the near future witness any such giants as Barth, Bultmann, Tillich or the Niebuhrs. The concern now is less for systems than for a theology of the church. Individual thinkers, therefore, are set within the context of the living church; no longer do we consider them independently of the historic faith they seek to elucidate.

Furthermore, there is increasing momentum among scholars to correct or modify the excessive claims of Biblical theology, which imputed to key theological words more than was warranted. A healthy interest in linguistic, literary, archeological and philosophical studies is the order of the day in our seminaries. Thus there is no school of theology that is now dominant. The liberal spirit (but not the theology of liberalism) has made all schools out of date.

53. A Word Picture: *"The UCC: A Beautiful, Heady, Exasperating Mix"*

(1975)

Oliver Powell

Oliver Powell (1912–2003) was a Congregational Christian/UCC minister educated at New York University and Union Theological Seminary in New York. After starting a new church in Evanston, Illinois (1940–44), he became secretary for young people's work at the Board of Home Missions (BHM) of the Congregational Christian Churches (1944–50). In 1950 he returned to pastoral ministry, serving churches in Massachusetts, Illinois, and Washington, D.C. (1950–71) and finally rounding out his ministry as associate conference minister for the Boston Metropolitan Association of the Massachusetts, Conference UCC (1971–77). In retirement he did interim ministry in Colorado, Massachusetts and Washington (state).

Powell was deeply involved in the formation of the United Church of Christ, serving on the Statement of Faith Commission and on several hymnal committees. He was an active advocate for justice in church and society around issues of race and sexual orientation. His "word picture of the histories, the people, the diversities that are the UCC" appeared in A.D. Magazine *(1975) and was repeatedly quoted by UCC members when they tried to describe the UCC to outsiders. Powell writes that UCC people consider themselves "God's people," "a believing people," "an independent people, but bound by covenants," "a whole people (but not quite) united in diversity," and "a church in the world."*

Source: Oliver Powell, an excerpt from "The United Church of Christ: A Beautiful, Heady, Exasperating Mix," *A.D. Magazine* (September 1975): 39–48.

We Are a Believing People

The United Church "is a teller of the Christian Story. . . . We have to get it straight ourselves before we can get it out."

Gabriel Fackre

There never has been a greater piece of nonsense than the notion that it doesn't make much difference what a person believes. Christianity, some people say, is a *doing* kind of religion, and particularly in a time like ours. With so many evils to be tackled and so much healing and reconciling to be done, spinning your wheels over a lot of theology is a waste of precious time.

The truth, of course, is the other way around. It matters enormously what a person believes. It matters enormously what kind of understanding a congregation has of the Christian faith. Everything we do or leave undone depends ultimately on what we fundamentally believe about people and issues and what we believe the purposes of God have to do with them.

Straight off let it be clear that the United Church puts a high premium on believing. It stands in the mainstream of Christian theology. Before it is anything else, it is a proclaimer of the gospel, the good news of the love of God made plain in the life, death, and resurrection of Jesus Christ. It is a teller of the Christian story.

The believing that underlies everything the United Church is and does has its roots in the story it is called by God to tell. And its task is just that: to tell the Christian story to people in winsome ways, not to persuade them to accept correct doctrine.

As we have said, it is the story of a particular people, of the God who created them, who entered into covenant with them, who tried several times unsuccessfully to rescue them from self-destruction and who, finally, because of such deep love for them, came into their crazy, mixed-up world in the person of Jesus of Nazareth. In his resurrection they learned that God's will and purpose for the world was stronger than death itself.

In fact, they were convinced that Jesus wasn't dead after all and that somehow he had empowered them to finish what he had begun with them. They were to go into the world with the message that new life was a gift, that it was available to everyone, and that nothing could ever separate them from the love of God.

This is the story that the United Church believes and is commissioned to get out into the world. But, as Gabriel Fackre has put it, we have to get it straight ourselves before we can get it out.

This story is the faith commonly held among us, to use familiar language. We may use a variety of ways to express it. We may recite the Apostles' Creed or a simple statement of faith growing out of the life of our own congregation. Often we stand and say together the Statement of Faith of the United Church of Christ, never as a test of the correctness of our faith, but as a living, eloquent testimony to it. . . .

The more you know the United Church, the more you sense its strong affinity for contemporary society. You can feel it, for instance, in the Statement of Faith. People are comfortable with it, in part, because it has a traditional ring. Yet it avoids the kind of frayed, tired language that lulls rather than ignites. "He has come to us and shared our common lot," it says of Jesus. This is a fresh way to talk about the Incarnation. There is a statement about saving people from aimlessness that has an up-to-date feel for where many people are these days. And, who knows, to keep faith with where people will be tomorrow may require us to amend the Statement from time to time in order to keep it close to the ever shifting human situation.

Clearly the stance of the United Church is toward the world. All its doors and windows open onto it. The church believes that God loves the world as much as he loves the church, and so, the members are required to serve the world in God's name.

Because this is so, three things, in particular, follow:

• Taking the world seriously, as it does, the ultimate rationale for the very being of the United Church is its mission. It is simply not correct to say that the church has missions (and certainly not so-called "benevolences," implying ecclesiastical charity, that is the wrong concept entirely). Nor is it accurate to say that the church has a mission program, as though it were one more activity to be carried on along with everything else — buying office supplies, repairing the roof, paying the organist, putting on a bazaar. The only thing that makes sense is to say that the church of itself, by its given nature, is a mission.

"As fire exists by burning," said the noted church leader D. T. Niles, "so the church exists by mission."

The mission of the church is local. It embraces the members of a congregation and their immediate neighbors. It serves its community. It brings strategies of healing to broken and diseased situations. It reconciles differences, enabling and empowering those who have been put down and dehumanized by unjust forces.

The mission is nationwide. It reaches beyond the boundaries of parish life to serve other people in 50 states through the work of the Board for Homeland Ministries and other national agencies.

The mission is global because the church of Jesus Christ is global. Through the Board for World Ministries the United Church prosecutes God's mission on six continents and the far-flung islands of the seas.

The mission is astonishingly varied. Whether carried on by local congregations, conferences, or national instrumentalities, it appears in the form of schools, hospitals, agricultural stations, social-service centers, books and journals, homes for children, youth-serving agencies, homes for the elderly, chaplaincies on campuses and in prisons, new strategies for churches in transitional communities, counseling centers, summer camps and conferences, television and radio programs, street ministries, night ministries, apartment-complex ministries.

The mission is mobile and flexible, ready to deal with emergency needs as they arise. The 17/76 Achievement Fund is typical. It is aimed at meeting the urgent needs of six black colleges in the South and of a number of overseas schools in order that they may pursue in full strength their unique and historic venture in quality education.

• Taking the world seriously, as it does, the United Church becomes involved in the issues and dilemmas of current social history. Its people become active in efforts to redress injustices and to correct costly, criminal blundering. They help to reconcile differences between opposing factions. Above all they unite in efforts to reshape society in God's vision of peace and order for all people.

The degree to which the United Church becomes involved in complex and often controversial issues is, and probably always will be, a source of tension. But by and large the United Church has demonstrated uncanny skill in knowing when to tighten the tension (because the judgment and justice of God demands it), and when to release it (because the reconciling spirit of Christ prompts it).

• Taking the world seriously, as it does, the United Church insists on bringing it into the center of its worship, which is, of course, the beginning and the ending of its life.

In its prayers it holds up the fragile hopes and eroded confidence of people who seek the renewing of their faith and courage at an impasse along their pilgrimage.

In its music it tries to sing its way into the hearts of believers who long for help in their unbelief.

In its preaching of the good news it tells again the beautiful, often bruised and blood-stained story of the God who indeed "has come to us and shared our common lot."

It tells of the birth, there in a smelly cow-barn in a little up-country town. It tells of the life, shared with fishermen and tradespeople and domestics in the marketplaces and backyards of Galilee. It tells of the death, mindless, savage, ignominious. It tells of the resurrection, the new life now possible to people who in the face of contrary and persuasive evidence can accept the acceptance of God who accepts them even when they are most unacceptable to themselves!

Nicodemus, steeped in the Jewish law, paid a call on Jesus one night to talk about religion, hoping that through a series of rational questions he would get some sensible answers.

Jesus listened to him politely and respectfully. Then he stood Nicodemus on his ears by referring him, of all things, to the wind. Listen to it, he said. "You hear the sound of it, but you do not know where it comes from, or where it is going. So with everyone born from spirit" (John 3:8, NEB). So with the United Church of Christ.

54. The Leaders Box: *"Theology in the UCC"*

(1982)

Office for Church Life and Leadership

In 1982 the Office for Church Life and Leadership (OCLL) developed a new resource for Christian education — a box filled with 8½-x-11-inch cards on many topics related to the life of local congregations. Topics were presented on cards (back and front) and color-coded to related subjects. Cards on "theology in the UCC," the "nature of the church," "belief," and "faithfulness" summarize theological ideas in the UCC in a way that is accessible to local lay leaders. Each card ends with a set of questions designed to encourage and support small-group discussions.

Theology in the UCC

Theology states what is believed about God and all that is related to God. It is reflection on our experience of who God is and what God is doing. Theology makes belief understandable for those who believe, guiding their behavior. It also informs those who do not believe. The purpose of theology is to understand who God is, what God is doing and what this implies for our actions. Theology is the theory out of which we plan and carry out our ministry as Christians.

Source: "Theology in the UCC," *Leaders Box* (New York: Office for Church Life and Leadership, 1982), A-43.

The process by which individuals or groups or churches develop a theology is called "doing theology," or "theologizing" or "theological reflection."

If in reading the definitions above you disagreed with what was said, responded with, "Yes, but . . . ," or wondered what was meant, you are in touch with the problem of describing theology in the United Church of Christ.

Any attempt to proclaim what the theology of the United Church of Christ is or what the United Church of Christ believes will be met with assorted responses: it is wrong; it doesn't go far enough; it goes too far; it omits something important: it is confusing. There is no official theology *of* the United Church of Christ, but there is theology *in* the United Church of Christ.

Yet, we make significant efforts to state what it means to be related to God. Individuals, churches and the denomination have found it to be important to be centered around the Statement of Faith of the United Church of Christ.

Sources of Theology

Attempts at theology emerged very early in the life of the Church. This was one way to eliminate the likelihood of distortions. Early Christians wanted to be able to share their beliefs with others and to have their actions be informed by their beliefs. Today we still are concerned with theology in order to be clear about what we believe, to be able to share our beliefs with others and to be faithful in our lives.

There are at least four sources of theology:

- *the Bible.* It is the primary source of our understanding about God and the things of God. It is in the Bible that we find very basic information that is a foundation of our understanding the kind of God in whom we believe.

- *the tradition.* Knowledge about God has increased throughout the ages. Creeds, doctrines and statements of faith are part of the tradition of the Church which informs our theology.

- *the experience of the contemporary and ecumenical church.* We acknowledge that God is still being made known to us and to people who are our contemporaries. For example, liberation theology, black theology and feminist theology are attempts to discover and articulate new insights about God and the ways of God. We discover that we need the perspectives of people from other cultures, backgrounds and experiences for a full theological understanding.

- *personal experience.* All Christians can describe their experience with God and the meanings and conclusions they reach because of their experiences. Sometimes these experiences help us understand what other sources mean. Sometimes the theological perspective which we have developed helps us interpret the meaning of our experiences. There are times when our experiences call into question a portion of our theology and force us to see a new insight God is revealing. The Bible, tradition and many personal experiences lead to the belief that God is the source of our knowledge and understanding about God. They also support the belief that the Holy Spirit is an active participant in our theological processes and formulations. Not everyone agrees with this theological statement, however.

The Substance of Theology

The product of doing theology or theologizing is theology: substantive statements about God and the things of God. The forms have varied through the ages. For some it has been enough to say, "Jesus is Lord." For others, such as professional theologians like Thomas Aquinas or Karl Barth, it has taken volumes and volumes to say it and then it was never complete.

Some of the familiar ways in which the substance of theology is set down are in creeds (Nicene Creed, Apostles' Creed), catechisms (Heidelberg Catechism, Evangelical Catechism), covenants (Salem, Mayflower), platforms (Cambridge), statements of faith (United Church of Christ), declarations of faith, confessions of faith and sermons.

For some individuals and churches the content or substance of theology is all-important. Thus, some churches have theological formulations or beliefs to which members must agree. These churches are variously called confessional, creedal or doctrinal churches.

Other churches, including the United Church of Christ, do not have set beliefs which members are required to accept and which serve as a test of faith. The constitution of the United Church of Christ insures the rights of each local church to " . . . formulate its own covenants and confessions of faith . . . " (Article IV, paragraph 15).

The United Church of Christ Statement of Faith, for example, is not an authoritative statement to which members are required to give allegiance. Rather than being a test of faith, it is a testimony of faith which informs, instructs and inspires the members, local churches and national bodies of the United Church of Christ.

The Methodology of Theology

In our tradition the process of theology as well as the substance of theology gives us our theological identity. "Theology in the United Church of Christ" is experienced through theological dialogue in search of the Word of God in the contemporary setting. This theological dialogue is faithful and sensitive to the four sources of theology identified above, but does not attribute sole authority to any one of them. Indeed, the constitution of the United Church of Christ states:

> The United Church of Christ acknowledges as its sole Head, Jesus Christ, Son of God and Savior. It acknowledges as kindred in Christ all who share in this confession. It looks to the Word of God in the Scriptures, and to the presence and power of the Holy Spirit, to prosper its creative and redemptive work in the world. It claims as its own the faith of the historical Church expressed in the ancient creeds and reclaimed in the basic insights of the Protestant Reformers. It affirms the responsibility of the Church in each generation to make this faith its own in reality of worship, in honesty of thought and expression, and in purity of heart before God (Preamble, paragraph 2).

Of course, there are core theological assertions assumed by all in the United Church of Christ: there is a God; God has been made known through Jesus Christ: the Holy Spirit is present today; the Church is an instrument of God. Even with these statements, however, there are some who would take exception with the way they are formulated. The content of theology is essential to the Church, but it is not the content of theology which gives the United Church of Christ its theological identity or uniqueness. Rather, it is our theological methodology.

Our theology emerges as we talk together around questions like: Who is God? What is God doing? What is God calling us to be and do now and in the future? Informed by the Bible, tradition, experiences of the contemporary and ecumenical church and our own experiences, and trusting in the presence and guidance of the Holy Spirit, we seek the truth. We live our lives and carry out our ministries on the basis of our insights about the truth.

Creedal churches tend to begin with a well developed body of formulated belief and then interpret and ask theological questions about life situations. Non-creedal churches tend to begin with life situations and raise questions about what can be believed. In the United Church of Christ we work toward gaining a theological understanding of the situation in which we find ourselves.

Critics, within and beyond the denomination, point out that our situational orientation keeps us from dealing with core theological questions that have proven valuable for the Church in the past. These include:

Who and what is God?

Who is Jesus Christ?

Who is the Holy Spirit?

What is humankind?

What are good and evil?

What is sin?

What is atonement?

What is revelation?

What are the nature and purpose of the Church?

Implications

The numerous implications from the understanding of theology are crucial for the way we live together and seek to be faithful in the United Church of Christ. Some of the implications are:

We all need to be responsible partners in the theological dialogue and interaction. Each part of the United Church of Christ — local church, association, conference, seminary, national body — needs to contribute its best insight and understanding to the dialogue. Each needs to immerse itself in the Bible, the tradition, personal experience and the experience of the contemporary and ecumenical church. Each needs to listen carefully to the other partners in the dialogue. Each must avoid the arrogance of believing it alone knows the truth. We need to create more settings in which the partners engage one another in theological dialogue and interaction. Our natural inclination is to join only those who already share the same understanding or stance that we have. If we believe the Spirit of God gives us the truth as we engage the sources of theology and the partners in the church, then we are called to more vigorous and open dialogue within the United Church of Christ.

Theological dialogue in search of the truth belongs to all of us, lay people and clergy alike. No one can do theology for us. We have to be a partner in the enterprise.

The role of professional theologians is crucial. Their role is not to do for us or for the church. Their role is to do the disciplined work of biblical exposition and interpretation, to teach us the tradition and its meaning, to make us aware of the present theological ferment occurring in the contemporary and ecumenical church. They pose the issues, clarify the questions, provide us with the insight and information, formulate positions and possibilities and challenge us with implications for decision and action. They do not, however, authorize the truth for us.

- The weakness of our way of doing theology is that it makes us prone to neglect the historical questions and affirmations of the Church. The tendency is to begin with an issue (for example, sexuality, peace, poverty) and to seek out theological understandings relevant to it. The danger is that the specifics of the situation will prevent our grappling with the broader and more fundamental questions of the meaning of Christ, the meaning of the Church, the meaning of the creation. Some people within our church are calling for the development of theological position papers which wrestle with fundamental doctrinal matters. This call reflects a sense of inadequacy of always making the contemporary situation the starting point in the theological enterprise.
- We are prone to have a low opinion of ourselves theologically because we don't seem to be as clear as the confessional churches about what we believe. We can take heart in the recognition of our strengths. We are skillful in engaging one another theologically. Equally important is the seriousness with which we value the Bible, tradition, the experience of the contemporary and ecumenical church, and our own experience.

Questions

- What is theology? What is its relation to Christian living and action?
- What are the four sources of theology? Which seems more important to you? To your church? How is each relied upon in your church?
- What are the roles of pastors, laity and theologians in theological growth?
- What are the ways in which your church is engaged in ongoing theological dialogue with other partners in the United Church of Christ?
- How are theological dialogue and growth fostered in your church? How satisfactory is this? What are ways in which greater emphasis could be given to this?

55. Identity:
"Paradoxical"

(1982)

Scott S. Libbey

Scott Libbey (b. 1929) is a Congregational Christian/UCC minister educated at the University of Iowa and Chicago Theological Seminary. After serving as a pastor in Iowa (1954–59) he became director of Christian education and youth ministry for the Iowa Conference UCC (1959–61) and director of educational programming for the United Church Board for Homeland Ministries (UCBHM) (1961–69). He served as conference minister of the Nebraska Conference UCC (1969–71), conference minister of the Iowa Conference UCC (1971–85), and executive vice president of the United Church Board for World Ministries (UCBWM) (1985–94).

As the United Church of Christ approached its twenty-fifth anniversary in 1982, and UCC leaders debated about the "theological ferment" of the early 1980s, people continued to say that the UCC still was searching for its identity. Libbey disagreed. "We have discovered our identity," he writes in A.D. Magazine *(1982), "—but we don't know it." It doesn't fit expectations, it is not a given static thing, and it finds expression in a lifestyle filled with creative paradoxes.*

Source: Scott S. Libbey, "Our Identity Is Paradoxical," *A.D. Magazine* (June 1982): 22.

Our Identity Is Paradoxical

Have we discovered our purpose, our identity in the United Church of Christ during these 25 years? The conventional answer is "No," and continues: "That is one of our great needs — to find our identity." I am convinced, however, that part of our 25th anniversary reflections should consider a different kind of response to that question. I am inclined to think that we have discovered our identity — but we don't know it! I see three reasons why we don't know we are already discovering our identity:

1. We don't recognize the identity that is emerging because it does not fit our expectations.

2. Our UCC identity is not a given, static "idea"; rather, it is a developing, changing energy that moves a pilgrim people.

3. Our UCC identity is expressed in a surprising new lifestyle — a dynamic, moving interaction of creative paradoxes.

The emerging shape of this distinctive identity of the United Church of Christ grows out of the catalytic chemistry of basic affirmations such as these:

- We are a deeply rooted people — and we are an uprooted people.
- We are churches — and we are part of the church.
- We respect and honor individual integrity — and we are committed to responsible community.
- We are free and we are bound.
- We strengthen our own churches — and we give ourselves to others with diaconal abandon.
- We cherish particular traditions — and we welcome independent diversity.
- We are fiercely denominational — and we are explosively ecumenical.
- We are firmly Bible-centered — and we are openly Spirit-directed.
- We find grace in the gifts of the Sacraments — and we find the gifts of grace within the secular.
- We are intentionally local — and we are responsibly global.
- We value personal piety — and we strive for public justice.

Is this not the United Church of Christ — born in and growing in "reforming traditions" — a changing pilgrim people?

I believe the United Church of Christ is a covenant community, affirming in life and faith these contradictory pulses: systolic/diastolic; breathing in and out. There are forces that appear to be counterforces but which, in fact, participate in shaping the creative surprise that is the United Church.

56. Identity:

"Who We Are, What We Believe"

(1980–98)

Beginning in 1980 the United Church of Christ developed and used a simple flyer to promote and identify the United Church of Christ. The flyer was basically a legal sheet of paper folded into four panels, which could be placed in pew racks, mailed in an envelope or given to prospective members. Although it was revised slightly in 1991, 1993, and 1998, it remained the basic identity piece about the United Church of Christ for over twenty years.

Entitled Who We Are, *the flyer reprints the Preamble to the Constitution (see vol. 7:8) and the Statement of Faith (see vol. 7:7), explains the origins of the UCC and describes its Christian, Reformed, Congregational, and Evangelical characteristics. Under the banner "What We Believe" it summarizes UCC theology by highlighting significant phrases commonly used to express the theological commitments of the United Church of Christ.*

Source: Excerpt from "What We Believe," in a pew rack pamphlet entitled *United Church of Christ: Who We Are, What We Believe* (New York: United Church Press, 1980–98).

What We Believe

The preceding description can be amplified by significant phrases commonly used by Christians, which express the commitments of the United Church of Christ.

• *That they may all be one (John 17:21).* This motto of the United Church of Christ reflects the spirit of unity on which the church is based and points toward future efforts to heal the divisions in the body of Christ. We are a uniting church as well as a united church.

• *In essentials unity, in nonessentials diversity, in all things charity.* The unity that we seek requires neither an uncritical acceptance of any point of view nor a rigid formulation of doctrine. It does require mutual understanding and agreement as to which aspects of the Christian faith and life are essential.

The unity of the church is not of its own making. It is a gift of God. But expressions of that unity are as diverse as there are individuals. The common thread that runs through all is love.

• *Testimonies of faith rather than tests of faith.* Because faith can be expressed in many different ways, the United Church of Christ has no formula that is a test of faith. Down through the centuries, however, Christians have shared their faith with one another through creeds, confessions, catechisms, and other statements of faith. Historic statements such as the Apostles' Creed, the Nicene Creed, the Heidelberg Catechism, the Evangelical Catechism, the Augsburg Confession, the Cambridge Platform, and the Kansas City Statement of Faith are valued as authentic testimonies of faith.

In 1959, the General Synod of the United Church of Christ adopted a statement of faith prepared especially for the United Church. Since that time a revision was made by Robert V. Moss, president of the United Church of Christ, 1969–76, and recommended for use by the Eleventh General Synod, 1977. Another revision, in the form of a Doxology, was affirmed by the Fourteenth General Synod (1981). Both revisions use inclusive language. . . .

• *There is yet more light and truth to break forth from God's Holy Word.* This classic statement assumes the primacy of the Bible as a source for understanding the good news and as a foundation for all statements of faith. It recognizes that the Bible, though written in specific historical times and places, still speaks to us in our present condition. It declares that the study of the Scriptures is not limited by past interpretations but is to be pursued with expectancy for new insights and help for living today.

• *The priesthood of all believers.* All members of the United Church of Christ are called to minister to others and to participate as equals in the common worship of God, each with direct access to the mercies of God through personal prayer and devotion.

Recognition is given to those among us who have received special training in pastoral, priestly, educational, and administrative functions, but these persons are regarded as ministers — servants — rather than as persons in authority. Their task is to guide, to instruct, and to enable all Christians to do the work of ministry rather than to do the work of ministry for us.

• *Responsible freedom.* As individual members, we are free to believe and act in accordance with our perception of God's will for our lives. But we are called to live in a loving, covenantal relationship with one another — gathering in communities of faith, congregations of believers, and local churches.

Each congregation or local church is free to act in accordance with the collective decisions of its members, guided by the working of the Spirit in the light of the Scriptures. But it is also called to live in a covenantal relationship with other congregations for the sharing of insights and for cooperative action.

Likewise, associations of churches, conferences, the General Synod, and national boards and agencies of the United Church of Christ are free to act in their particular spheres of responsibility. Yet all are constrained by love to live in a covenantal relationship with one another and with the local churches in order to make manifest the unity of the body of Christ and thus to carry out God's mission in the world more effectively.

The members, congregations, associations, conferences, General Synod, and national instrumentalities are free in relation to the world. We affirm that the authority of God as revealed in Jesus Christ, and interpreted with the aid of the Holy Spirit, stands above and judges all human culture, institutions, and laws. But we recognize our calling both as individuals and as the church to live in the world:

- ministering to its needs
- contributing to the welfare of all
- being enriched by those aspects of culture that help to make human life more human
- working through institutions and supporting laws that reflect God's just and loving purposes for the world
- seeking justice and liberation for all

This is the challenge of the United Church of Christ.

Clarifying Theological Identity

57. Theology: *"Toward the Task of Sound Teaching"*

(1978)

In 1976 the Office for Church Life and Leadership (OCLL) convened a seminar of minister teachers and conference and instrumentality leaders to "reflect on the theology of the United Church of Christ, particularly as it relates to the faith and ministry of the church." The group "gathered out of a sense of urgency in the church." They believed that the 1960s had produced defining moments for the UCC, but in the chaos many Christians seemed to have lost their connection to biblical teachings and tradition. The seminar sought "to articulate those substantive concerns pressed upon us by our theological tradition," and "to initiate a process of engagement and exploration" involving the whole church.

The "Seminar Report: Toward the Task of Sound Teaching in the United Church of Christ" was drafted by six people (Walter Brueggemann, Paul Hammer, Frederick Herzog, Ralph Quellhorst, Henry Rust, and Clyde Steckel). Between July and September 1977 it was sent to thirty other people for critical response and revised accordingly. "Sound Teaching" was distributed throughout the United Church of Christ, and it also was translated into German. Within a year a German response to "Sound Teaching" was received by the UCC-EKU Working Group, which was engaged in "full communion" discussions with the Evangelical Church of the Union in East and West Germany (see vol. 7:69).

Source: "Liberation Affirmation," an excerpt from a typescript *Seminar Report: Toward the Task of Sound Teaching in the United Church of Christ* (New York: Office for Church Life and Leadership, United Church of Christ, 1978), 5–7. Also published in Frederick Herzog, *Justice Church: The New Function of the Church in North American Christianity* (Maryknoll, N.Y.: Orbis Books, 1980), and Joerg Rieger, ed. *Theology from the Belly of the Whale: A Frederick Herzog Reader* (Harrisburg, Pa.: Trinity Press International, 1999).

The Seminar Report is divided into four sections: (1) The Historical Context: 1957–77, Two Decades of Church Life, (2) The Present Context, (3) A Liberation Affirmation, and (4) Implications of Sound Teaching.

The first section briefly sketches the twenty-year evolution of UCC advocacy, noting that "responsive action has tended to precede and take precedence over theological reflection." Unfortunately, in this situation the church often identifies with dominant cultural values and "the teaching office of the ordained minister" is "reduced to public relations, efficient organization and supportive comfort."

The second section suggests ways in which the teaching office in the church might be strengthened through renewed attention to confessions of faith, through greater awareness of how UCC polity shapes and reshapes faithfulness, and through respectful accountability between clergy and laity.

The third section, entitled "Liberation Affirmation," makes strong, biblically grounded affirmations about God, the church, and ministry.

The fourth section spells out the implications of sound teaching for understanding and using the past, for the pastoral office and for ethical decision making.

Toward the Task of Sound Teaching in the United Church of Christ

Liberation Affirmation

The United Church of Christ is at a turning. Harsh issues of sound teaching are emerging that we can no longer dodge. Church and society are caught in increasing conflict. In this situation, God calls upon us to give a new account of our hope lest we be "tossed to and fro and carried about with every wind of doctrine" (Ephesians 4:14).

The following emphases appear especially pertinent:

God is Justice. God is struggling with the poor, the outcast, and the lost for a just life. In Jesus Christ, God takes sides with the poor. God "has put down the mighty from their thrones, and exalted those of low degree" (Luke 1:52).

Faithful teaching excludes the unsound teaching that God is on our side, that of a rich and powerful nation. The meaning of life does not consist of a national defense of wealth, but of struggling with God for justice among all peoples. As a sociopolitical and socioeconomic institution, the church is implicated in the evils of the state. It is called to serve God, not the free enterprise system. Today, racism is the most powerful means of "capitalism" to denigrate human beings into non-persons. Sexism today is its most powerful means of assigning persons the status of minors. We need to work for alternate sociopolitical and socioeconomic models. New forms of "socialism," including responsible public ownership of the means of production, are live options also for us.

Church is Justice Covenant. The church is people called in covenant to join God's struggle for the new age of justice. Jesus Christ as embodiment of God's justice is our only motivation in the struggle for justice, "Seek first the kingdom of God and God's justice, and all other things shall be added to you" (Matthew 6:33).

Faithful teaching excludes the unsound teaching that the church can transform the nation when it allows itself to be co-opted by the powers that be. Attacked by increasing secularism in our Western nations, the church is called to be in constant conflict in various ways with principalities and powers that legitimate injustice. God is at work in all nations to create a more just life. But God's embodiment in Jesus Christ, and not the American way of life or Manifest Destiny, is the clue to human destiny. It is Jesus Christ who calls and directs his people in the conflict.

God is Life. God is battling death as the enemy of justice. In Jesus Christ, God provides the power of life over death. "I am the resurrection and the life" (John 11:25).

Faithful teaching excludes the unsound teaching that we ultimately control life in our technological culture. With our vast technological know-how, we can cause death a million times over in our "laboratories" without the majority of the people even being aware of the murder. Totalitarianism is not always discernible by outward emblems or uniforms. It also rules in the cover-up of our "death industry." Christian faith opposes the death dealings of our culture as well as other cultures.

Church is Life Covenant. The church is people drawing upon God's vast creativity in human life. Jesus Christ is Good News as empowerment for sharing the goodness of life — conquering the destructive evils of civilization. "Do not be conformed to the world, but be transformed by the renewal of your mind, that you may prove what is the will of God, what is good and acceptable and perfect" (Romans 12:2).

Faithful teaching excludes the unsound teaching that the task of the church is to critique culture without showing how to keep together a civilization. The church can be engaged with culture without being co-opted by culture as court chaplain of civil religion. Culture has no right to become the value framework that determines the way of life in Christ. God's rule is to be embodied in culture. Both collectivism and individualism work against God's rule. The church is people working for an obedient culture in keeping with God's will — an unending task.

God is Spirit. God forms in us a conscience accountable to justice and life for true worship. In Jesus Christ, the meaning of life is worship in spirit and truth. "God is Spirit, and they that worship must worship in spirit and truth" (John 4:24).

Faithful teaching excludes the unsound teaching that everyone is an autonomous individual free to do his or her own thing. Worship is first of all God ministering to us, calling us to be daughters and sons. Becoming daughters and sons in turn involves worship of God that overcomes race, sex, and class domination, making us sisters and brothers. Re-creation of people through the Spirit affirms the value of each person. God brings each a vision of life abundant. That life issues in the discipline of piety in each individual Christian. Human beings become persons where the Spirit of justice reigns.

Church is Spirit Covenant. The church is people responding in obedience to God's Holy Spirit as empowering Presence in history. In Jesus Christ, God continues to draw near as Immanuel, God with us, so that the church can be a community of true worship among all people. "By the mercies of God . . . present your bodies a living sacrifice, holy and acceptable to God, which is your proper worship" (Romans 12:1).

Faithful teaching excludes the unsound teaching that ministry and polity are merely incidental to the life of the church. God in ministry to the poor, outcast, and lost, battles to order human history for the sake of justice and life. Ministry and polity of the church become means of sharing in the struggle in a revolutionary as well as an orderly way. The ministry of Word and Sacrament embodied in just polity seeks to evoke faithfulness to God's action in the lives of all people. The teaching office of the church, responsible for discipline and transformation, invites people to present their bodies as a living sacrifice in the struggles of history.

58. Theology:
"A Theocratic Interpretation of Life"

(1980)

James M. Gustafson

James M. Gustafson (b. 1925) is a Congregational Christian/UCC minister educated at Northwestern University, Chicago Theological Seminary, and Yale University. After serving as a pastor in Connecticut for a few years he taught on the faculty at Yale Divinity School (1954–72) and at the University of Chicago from 1972 until his retirement. Among his books, Treasure in Earthen Vessels *(1961) and* Theology and Christian Ethics *(1974) were popular among clergy.*

When Gustafson was asked to contribute an article to the Christian Century *(1980) series "How My Mind Has Changed," he suggested that the subtitle for his essay ought to be "How My Thinking Has Been Developing." He was not interested in revisiting what he had said in the past, but wanted to reflect about the guiding convictions that informed his intellectual journey.*

For Gustafson the idea of "theocentricity" is central to his life and work. From early interests in choices related to the value of human life, to later writings on culture and the place of natural piety in ethics, Gustafson sustains a conviction that "life must be conformed to that ordering activity of God which we cannot fully know." His theocentric orientation concludes that "relativism without relation to an ultimate object degenerates into religious subjectivism."

Source: James M. Gustafson, excerpt from "A Theocentric Interpretation of Life," *The Christian Century,* July 30–August 6, 1980, 755–56.

A Theocentric Orientation

. . . During this period I have found myself making a move that the generation of my teachers made in the 1920s and 1930s. Religion had become terribly subjective; its object, God, seemed to be left out. My perceptions of a great deal of religious activity in the past two decades is that it is highly instrumental — not for the purpose of honoring God and offering gratitude to him, but for the purpose of inducing subjective states in humans. Even the great Christian theme of redemption has been reduced to a psychological principle: you are accepted. By whom? On what basis?

And, as has been the case so often in Christian history, religion becomes instrumental to moral ends chosen for other than religious reasons. When we give the examples of anticommunism and nationalism, all of us cheer and say Amen. But the same principle has been at work in movements for radical social change. The most vulgar form is the "pray-in"; the sophisticated forms are more profoundly theological: a moral end or a moral interest becomes the hermeneutical device for interpreting the Bible or theological themes that can be grounded in the Bible. If we can find a way to make religion or God serve our subjective ends, whether they be to help us feel better or to change the world, we use them.

Certainly religion in all times and all cultures has had utility value: in the biblically grounded religions of the West, however, the ultimate end has been theocentrically oriented, turned toward an objective reality. Moses and the prophets, Jesus and Paul, Augustine and Thomas Aquinas, the great 16th century Reformers, the Puritans, Jonathan Edwards and others — they were correct in the primary intuition that religion deals with the relations of humans and the world to God and to his purposes. Those rebels against religious subjectivism earlier in our century — Barth and Brunner, Wieman and H. Richard Niebuhr and others — had a similar primary intuition, and it was correct.

I have, since adolescence, been persuaded that cultural and historical relativism was more valid than the efforts to shed our various layers of skin so that we could achieve pure disinterestedness, rational autonomy in morality, and pure objectivity in other areas of knowledge. No doubt my growing up in an immigrant sectarian religious community contributed to that opinion, as did my service in Burma and India during World War II, studies of sociology and anthropology as an undergraduate, my reading of Troeltsch under the aegis of a great teacher, James Luther Adams, and other things. It was H. Richard Niebuhr's *The Meaning of Revelation* that made more theological sense to me than the process theology that dominated the

Federated Theological Faculty of the University of Chicago in my years as a Bachelor of Divinity student.

I am somewhat amused that Roman Catholic theologians, a lot of Protestants, and sociologists of religion are only now learning about sociology of knowledge and its significance for theology, about "historical" mentalities and such things. Different persons and different groups are not, in that terrible current term, "in phase" because they are the bearers of the cultures and beliefs from which they come. But when persons begin to call any set of symbols — any beliefs which give meaning and coherence to life — a "theology," I wish they would instead talk about the functional equivalents to theology. (I suppose, though, that if philosophers are no longer lovers of wisdom, theologians no longer should be expected to be thinking about God.)

Surely all religions do function to provide meaning to experience; descriptively there is nothing wrong with that. But surely in the Western religious traditions those meanings relate all things to God, and when the properly descriptive becomes the basis for prescriptions for religious life, the reduction transforms Christianity and Judaism almost to the point of unrecognizability. Relativism without relation to an ultimate object degenerates into religious subjectivism; i.e., there are no bases for making judgments about the adequacy of religious views other than how satisfying they are to those who share them. When relative traditions do not test themselves by more generalizable criteria, they become defensive, smug and incorrigible. . . .

59. Theological Ferment:

"A Letter from Thirty-nine . . . "

(1984)

As concern about the theological health of the United Church of Christ developed during the early 1980s, thirty-nine UCC faculty members teaching in theological education signed and sent a letter to the Executive Council of the UCC. The letter stated its concern that theology in the UCC was "utilitarian" and without "sustained, disciplined reflection on the condition of the church."

"A Most Difficult and Urgent Time," as the letter came to be called, describes how public issues, ecumenical relations, and ecclesiological decisions need more attention, suggesting that the unity and the faithfulness of the church is endangered. It calls for a moratorium on reformulations of doctrine and worship already under way, and urges the leadership of the church to constitute a new "body of theological leadership and reflection" — to express the "central faith affirmations" of the church, and to show "how these affirmations might nurture and discipline the concrete practices" in the church. Faculty who signed the letter had no "preconceived notions" about where the process might lead, but they felt a "dire need" for a better "articulation of faith in the life and witness of the church."

Source: "A Most Difficult and Urgent Time" (a letter from thirty-nine UCC theological faculty dated Reformation Day 1983), later published in *New Conversations* (Spring 1985): 2–3.

A Most Difficult and Urgent Time

We regard this time in our church as a most difficult and urgent time, and we urge that a special action be taken in response. We affirm that the United Church of Christ is a vehicle of God to live a peculiar life and bear a peculiar witness at this time in the church universal and the world. But in important ways, we judge our church to be ill-prepared for that life and witness due not only to an "ecclesiological deficit" (of which President Post has spoken), but due to a void in sustained, disciplined reflection that can claim the assent of the church.

Across the spectrum of opinion in the United Church of Christ there is a tendency for theological thought to be utilitarian, in the service of programmatic ends, without sustained, disciplined reflection on the present condition of the church. What is needed, we believe, is a sustained rethinking of our theological tradition (as reflected in the various traditions behind the United Church) to see how that tradition can be reappropriated in faithful and fresh ways as a discipline and resource for our life and faith.

1. The need for reappropriating the tradition in critical reflection as discipline and resource seems to us to be evident in a variety of areas, including the following:

a) *Public issues* which range from questions of national security, peace and human welfare, to questions of sexuality. It appears to us that our current modes of thinking about these questions are largely pragmatic and ideological (across the spectrum of opinion) and that we need to pause to rethink the shape of these issues in light of our theological inheritance.

b) *Ecumenical relations* which specifically concern conversations with the Disciples of Christ (on which the church seems not to know its own mind), but which also touch the larger questions related to world Christianity, third world churches and the conciliar movements (national and worldwide). It appears to us that our postures on these issues tend often to be by happenstance without the discipline and guidance offered to us in our theological tradition. We believe that a reconsideration of the historic and confessional roots of our church would greatly serve the mind of the church in these confused and conflicted areas.

c) *Ecclesiological decisions* concerning the character of our church. These include current explorations of worship resources, language practices, lifestyle and modes of accountability in the church. It appears to us that much of our decision-making in these areas is made variously on grounds of "pragmatism," "liberalism," "conservatism," "pluralism," which are inappropriate to the church of Jesus Christ. While valuing diversity in our church, particularly as it includes representation of diverse groups in our society, we urge a sustained reconsideration of our common faith to see if together we might discern the mind of Jesus Christ in ways that will move us past the ideological posturing in which we are much engaged.

2. We view the void of sustained, disciplined theological reflection at the center of the church's life as risky because:

a) *The unity of our church is endangered.* Disunity may by some take the form of schismatic departure. By others it may take the form of indifference, alienation and loss of participatory affiliation.

b) *The faithfulness of our church is endangered.* Lack of faithfulness may be reflected in a series of subjective judgments (under the guise of autonomy or pluralism) which are in fact not acts of obedience to Jesus Christ.

3. On this spectrum of issues (no. 1 above) and for these reasons (no. 2 above), we urge the Executive Council (acting for the General Synod) and our Conference ministers to place on hold all reformulations now underway in doctrine and worship and to constitute a body of theological leadership and reflection responsible for assisting the local congregations, associations, conferences, national officers, and instrumentalities in developing teaching consensus which would:

a) express the central faith affirmations of our church as reflected in the confessional and platform heritage of the various historical elements of our church, and,

b) indicate how these affirmations may nurture and discipline the concrete practices of the contemporary church.

4. We make this urgent appeal without prejudgment about the outcome and without preconceived notions where the process may lead. We offer the proposal at this crucial time in our church out of responsibility commonly entrusted to us as teachers of the church. From the perspective of our vocation as teachers of the church, we urge and affirm that a critical refocus on the gifts and claims of the gospel as mediated through our history of confessions, creeds, and platforms may be a source of unity, fidelity and energy for our church. Sound Teaching (1978) already tried to invite the church to take the necessary steps in this direction. There have been other

similar efforts calling attention to the dire need. It is now the time for decision.

We submit this proposal prayerfully and respectfully, out of our deep love for the church. We yearn for an articulation of faith in the life and witness of the church that may claim the assent of the church precisely because it faithfully witnesses to the bedrock truth of Jesus Christ in our common life.

60. Theology Work Group: *"What Is Theology?"*

(1985)

In the midst of growing interest and concern about theology in the United Church of Christ in the early 1980s, the Office for Church Life and Leadership (OCLL) launched a project funded by the Family Thank Offering entitled "Theological Foundations in the United Church of Christ." The project invited eleven people to be part of a Work Group to address three primary questions: (1) What is theology and why is it important to the church? (2) How does the United Church of Christ do its theological work? and (3) How can theological work be strengthened?

The Theology Work Group met three times during 1984. It "embodied many of the differences, disagreements, distrust, dissension, dissatisfaction, and diversity present in the UCC."

> *It reflected some of the tensions between clergy and laity, local church and national instrumentalities, denomination and seminaries, theological traditions and liberal struggles, theology generated by grassroots movements and theology generated from the institutional centers of the church, and tensions between those whose faith is rooted in the European Reformation and those with cultural roots in Africa, Asia, the Pacific islands, North, Central and South America.*

The complete report (1985) of the Theology Work Group contains eight short sections covering the importance of theology, the way it emerges in the UCC, historical and contemporary influences, and future directions. Each section is arranged in two columns: one presenting descriptive

---

Source: Theology Work Group, "What Is Theology?" in *Theology and the United Church of Christ* (New York: Office for Church Life and Leadership, June 1985), 11–12 [typescript in the UCC Archives].

observations and conclusions about theology in the UCC and the other offering commentary growing out of the group discussion. The core of the report is found in the section entitled "What Is Theology?"

What Is Theology?

Description:

Theology is a word about God.

Whenever we speak about God, whenever we try to name for ourselves or communicate to others our experiences, questions, or speculations about God, we are doing theology, being theologians. Theology is something we all have and do as we reflect on our faith and deepest commitments.

Theology is also a specialized branch and discipline of knowledge that has been culled through the ages, the province of scholars and teachers, pastors and religious seekers who specialize in the study of religion. Some of us bring special gifts, training, and knowledge as theologians.

Theology, in its universal sense, grapples with ultimate questions, matters of "life, death, and destiny" (Roger Shinn). Theology joins us with people of all religions and deep commitments who seek to understand their lives in reference to God and the things that are eternal.

Comments:

It has been said around the UCC: "You can't do theology by committee." We're not sure whether that is true or not, but we do know that it is not easy. Coming to a common mind, finding words we could all agree upon was difficult.

We started with our individual voices, our particular theological approaches, passions, and perspectives. We examined our points of resonance and dissonance. We worked in small groups composing and writing sections of this paper. We worked together adding, deleting, revising, reworking. In the end, Barbara Gerlach was the writer, gathering our thoughts into one hand.

Any consensus involves compromise. We each gave a little here, demanded a little there.

This section on What Is Theology? reflects our attempt to grapple with theology as universal and particular, as substance and process, as the work of all the people and the specialized work of professional theologians, as engaging heart as well as mind.

Some of our most heartening agreements came over the sources of theology. We all agreed that Christian theology is formed in the dynamic interaction of the words of the *Bible,* the traditions of the *Church,* the presence of the *Spirit,* and questions and insights of our *life-experience* in the world. We all agreed that Scripture is foundational

Theology, in its specific manifestations, is rooted in and shaped by particular communities of faith. *Christian theology* grapples with ultimate questions in light of *God* revealed in the life, death, and resurrection of *Jesus Christ,* and known to us through the primary witness of *Scripture,* the *traditions* of the Christian Church, the guidance of the *Holy Spirit* and the illumination of *human experience.*

Theology in the United Church of Christ is a "beautiful, heady, exasperating mix" which defies easy description. We are a Church which worships in seventeen different languages. We are a people with roots in the European Reformation, in Asia and Africa, in North and South America. We are also a United and uniting Church, knitted and joined together by Jesus Christ who has made us one and broken down the dividing walls (Ephesians 2:14). Theology in the United Church of Christ moves between the many and the one. The unity we find and seek in Christ is not uniform, but large-spirited, ecumenical, and diverse.

to our understanding of who Jesus Christ is. But we also found among us different ways of interpreting and understanding Scripture. We observed how some of our theological differences in the United Church of Christ arise from different ways of understanding our theological sources. Some of us draw more heavily on the words of Scripture; others on the leading of the Spirit. Some of us put more emphasis on the traditions of the Church; others on the authority of their experience.

As we struggled to finalize this section of our paper, it was clear that we never found wording that fully satisfied all of us. Some of us were more at home with the words in the description section of our paper. Others preferred the language that emerged from our first meeting: "the source of theology is God, centered in Christ. Scripture is the primary and foundational witness for our faith. The traditions of the Church and human experience inform and validate the substance of Christian belief." Some of us saw the Spirit as a distinct source of theology; others of us saw the Spirit working through Scripture, tradition, and experience. Some of us saw human experience as a significant source for theology; others questioned the choice of that word, observing that we also "experience" God in the Bible and the traditions of the Church.

There is no doubt that our Work Group and our paper would have benefited from another face-to-face meeting to examine more fully and articulate more clearly how we understand the sources of theology and how these sources interact in the formation of a variety of theological perspectives in the United Church of Christ.

61. East Petersburg and Craigville:
"A Declaration" and "A Letter"

(1979, 1984)

The Biblical-Theological-Liturgical Group (BTL Club) met regularly after 1977 to share papers on theological topics. At one of its meetings, held in East Petersburg, Pennsylvania (1979), it issued a brief statement listing "forces that today seek to contest our loyalty to Jesus Christ, both inside and outside the Church." The statement became known as the "East Petersburg Declaration."

A few years later the "BTL Club" and the Mercersburg Society (see vol. 7:68) launched a series of grassroots colloquies to further stimulate theological work in the United Church of Christ — weeklong events that have continued annually. The first Craigville Colloquy (1984), celebrating the fiftieth anniversary of the "Barmen Declaration" of the Confessing Church in Germany in 1934, issued a "Witness Statement" by a near-unanimous vote of the 160 colloquy participants. The statement echoes the witness of Barmen, declaring "Jesus Christ as the one Word of God" and setting forth common affirmations on authority, faith, the church, polity, and justice. At the same time it acknowledges that there are ongoing ambiguities and rejects all forms of cultural accommodation that offer false hope and security to the church.

Sources: "East Petersburg Statement," 1979 [typescript from Gabriel Fackre]. "The Craigville Colloquy Letter, May 16, 1984," as published in *New Conversations* (Spring 1985): 9–10.

East Petersburg Statement

Brothers and Sisters:

Grace and peace to you who share our common life in the United Church of Christ. We are moved to speak to you out of our struggle this week with matters of authority and faithfulness in that Church. Meeting in the shadow of the towers of Three Mile Island heightens our sense of the urgency and magnitude of the claims of the One who is that final authority, and who calls us to that faithfulness.

Our deliberations have made us profoundly aware of the forces that today seek to contest our loyalty to Jesus Christ, both inside and outside the Church:

- the civil religion that tempts us to mute the uncivil Word of truth we may be called to speak
- the techniques of management and manipulation on which we have relied in the Church that have elbowed aside biblical preaching, sound theological teaching, living worship and sacrament
- the latest wisdom of this world that regularly beguiles us from our fundamental norms of Scripture and Tradition — timid and temporizing leadership in times that cry out for bold proclamation and fearless deed
- the loyalty to our private fiefdoms of parish, caucus, and bureaucracy that denies our first allegiance to Jesus Christ and erodes our larger ecclesial life together
- our captivity to the comforts and idolatries of a bourgeois Protestantism that shuts our eyes and closes our mouth before misery, tyranny and untruth.

Sisters and brothers, this bondage must not be. The acculturation of our beloved Church is an agony to us. On Golgotha and Easter morning Jesus Christ has freed us from this captivity. Let us be what we are! As pastors and teachers in this faith community, we own again our common covenant: to listen only to the one Word, Jesus Christ; to tell only this Story of the liberating and reconciling deeds of the triune God.

We invite you, together with us, to look for, hope for, pray for, and, work for a time of empowerment by the Spirit who breaks the prisoners' chains and makes the wounded whole.

The Craigville Colloquy Letter

Grace and Peace:

On the 50th anniversary of the Barmen Declaration we have come together at Craigville to listen for God's Word to us, and to speak of the things that make us who we are in Christ.

We praise God for the theological ferment in our Church! When such life comes, and light is sought, we discern the Spirit's work. The struggle to know and do the truth is a gift of God to us. So too are the traditions that have formed us — Congregational, Christian, Evangelical, Reformed, and the diverse communities that have since shaped our life together. We give thanks for the freedom in this family of faith to look for ever-new light and truth from God's eternal Word.

Thankful for the vital signs in our midst, we know too that our weaknesses have been the occasion for God's workings among us. To make confession at Craigville is also to acknowledge our own part in the confusions and captivities of the times. The trumpet has too often given an uncertain sound. As the people of God, clergy and laity, our words have often not been God's Word, and our deeds have often been timid and trivial. Where theological disarray and lackluster witness are our lot, it is "our own fault, our own most grievous fault."

Yet we trust God's promises. Mercy is offered to those who confess their sin. Grace does new things in our midst. Blessing and honor, glory and power be unto God!

In our deliberations we have sought to honor the ties that bind us, and to learn from the diversities that enrich us. We gladly speak here of the affirmations we can make together, and the judgments we share.

Authority

Loyal to our founders' faith, we acknowledge Jesus Christ as our "sole Head, Son of God and Saviour" (Preamble, Para. 2, The Constitution of the United Church of Christ). With Barmen we confess fidelity to "the one Word of God which we have to hear and which we have to trust and obey in life and death" (Barmen, Art. 1). Christ is the Center to whom we turn in the midst of the clamors, uncertainties and temptations of the hour.

We confess Jesus Christ "as he is attested for us in Holy Scripture" (Barmen, Art. 1). As our forebears did, we too look "to the Word of God in the Scriptures" (Preamble, Para. 2). Christ speaks to us unfailingly in the prophetic-apostolic testimony. Under his authority, we hold the Bible as the trustworthy rule of faith and practice. We believe that the ecumenical creeds, the evangelical confessions, and the covenants we have made in our churches at various times and places, aid us in understanding the Word addressed to us. We accept the call to relate that Word to the world of peril and hope in which God has placed us, making the ancient faith our own in this generation "in honesty of thought and expression, and in purity of heart before God" (Preamble, Para. 2).

Affirmation

According to these norms and guides, we call for sound teaching in our Church, and so confess the trinitarian content of our faith. Affirming our Baptism "in the name of the Father, and of the Son and of the Holy Spirit" (Matthew 28:19), we believe that the triune God is manifest in the drama of creation, reconciliation and sanctification. Following the recital of these mighty acts in our Statement of Faith, we celebrate the creative and redemptive work of God in our beginnings, the covenant with the people of Israel, the incarnation of the Word in Jesus Christ and the saving deed done in his life, death and resurrection, the coming of the Holy Spirit in church and world, and the promise of God to consummate all things according to the purposes of God. In the United Church of Christ we believe that the divine initiatives cannot be separated from God's call to respond with our own liberating and reconciling deeds in this world, and thus to accept the invitation to the cost and joy of discipleship.

Church

Our faith finds its form in the Christian community. We rejoice and give thanks to God for the gift of the one, holy, catholic and apostolic Church, gathered by the Holy Spirit from the whole human race in all times and places. That Church is called to share the life-giving waters of Baptism and feed us with the life-sustaining bread and wine of Eucharist: to proclaim the Gospel to all the world: to reach out in mission by word and deed, healing and hope, justice and peace. Through Baptism the Church is united to Christ and shares Christ's prophetic, priestly and royal ministry in its servant form. We rejoice that God calls some members for the ministry of Word and Sacrament to build up the Body and equip the saints for ministry in the world. We rejoice that God calls the laity to their threefold ministry, manifesting the Body of Christ in the places of work and play, living and dying.

We confess that although we are part of the Body in this Church, we are not the whole Body. We need always seek Christ's Word and presence in other communities of faith, and be united with all who confess Christ and share in his mission.

Polity

We confess our joy in the rich heritage of the Congregational, Christian, Evangelical, and Reformed traditions and the many diverse peoples who compose the fabric of the United Church of Christ. We are a "coat of many colors" and we give thanks for this diversity. We affirm the value of each voice and tradition that God has brought together and that our unity in Christ informs our faith and practice. In these days together, we have been reminded of the search for unity amidst the marvelous diversity in the United Church of Christ. We acknowledge that our diversity is not only a precious gift of God but that it is sometimes the source of hurt, frustration and anger.

God is gracious. Through God's grace we are able to embrace in forgiveness and to reconcile divisions. In covenant we are continually being called to be present to and for one another. In covenant we are being called to acknowledge that without one another we are incomplete, but together in Christ we are his Body in which each part is honored.

We have not yet reached agreement in our discussions regarding the governance of the Church. We acknowledge a need to develop further our polity, to hold together in mutual accountability all the various parts of our Church. We affirm that the Christian community must conform its life and practice to the Lordship of Jesus Christ and dare not heed the voice of a stranger. We affirm that in the United Church of Christ the Holy Spirit acts in powerful ways as the communities of faith gather for worship and for work, in local churches, in the Associations, in the Conferences, in the General Synod, and in the Instrumentalities and Boards. As a servant people, the prayer on the lips of the Church at such times is always: "Come. Holy Spirit!"

Justice

We have not reached agreement on the meaning of peace with justice. We confess however our own involvement with the injustices present in our society. We acknowledge our need to embody God's eternal concern for the least and most vulnerable of our neighbors. This shall require a renewed commitment to the study of the biblical teachings on justice and a fresh determination to do the things that make for peace.

We invite you to join us in reconsidering the meaning of Jesus' call and the summons to the Church to preach good news to the poor, proclaim release to the captives, enable recovery of sight to the blind, set at liberty those who are oppressed, and proclaim the acceptable year of our Lord.

Where justice is compromised and the rights of the weak sacrificed to the demands of the strong, the Church is called to resist. Christ stands alongside those deprived of their just claims. We pray for ears to hear God's voice resounding in the cries of those who are victimized by the cruel misuse of power. God's tears are shed also amidst the indifferent. We share with each of you the ministry of reconciliation. We ask you to consider thoughtfully the meaning and implications of this high calling in the world God loves and to which Jesus Christ comes as the embodiment of hope, the messenger of love, and the guarantor of the divine intention that the bound be set free from the unjust yoke.

In response to the witness of the Holy Scriptures and the example of Jesus Christ, we beseech our government at every level to be steadfast and persistent in the pursuit of political, economic and social justice with mercy and compassion. We are of a common mind, inviting you to join us in the urgent pursuit of those longings that compel a just peace in the nuclear age. Where justice is withheld among us, God is denied. Where peace is forsaken among us, we forsake Christ, the life of the Church is compromised, and the message of reconciliation is gravely wounded. Let us bear witness to the truth in this.

Ambiguities

We acknowledge with joy that new light is yet to break forth from God's Word. This bright light is a gift for the nurturing of our lives as Christians. At the same time, it is our experience that this vision of the Church is often blurred and incomplete. "For now we see through a glass, dimly" (1 Corinthians 13:12). Where our vision is unclear and the voice of the Church uncertain, we are urged not to indifference or compromise, but to our knees; to repentance, to prayer, and an earnest quest, seeking together the way of Christ for us.

We acknowledge with gratitude that in Christ every dividing wall of enmity or hostility is broken down. How do we celebrate this when we are tempted to ignore, avoid or resist some members of the community? Is not such resistance a contradiction of love of neighbor? As brothers and sisters in Christ we are summoned to address one another with humility knowing that our words and actions are subject to the judgment of God. Are we not to trust God to reconcile divisions among us, and when there has been separation or hurt to lead us back to one another as a shepherd searches for the flock? Can we afford to be any longer apart from the promise of the Gospel? Are we not to live this promise in the brilliant light of God's redeeming ways with us? God is faithful and just. Trusting in that faithfulness and the enormity of divine grace, surely we may bear the tension of the paradoxes of salvation not yet fully realized.

Rejections

Ours is an age of a multitude of gods and we are tempted on every side to cling to a false message and a false hope. This is a dangerous path and it is no stranger to any of our congregations. Idolatry can tempt us and lull us to sleep; it offers us false comfort and false security. We ask you to consider with us the idolatries of our time and to reject all that denies the Lordship of Jesus Christ.

We reject "the illusions of self-liberation" (WARC, II, 2, p. 12). With the framers of the Barmen Declaration, we reject the false teaching that there may be "areas of our life in which we would not belong to Jesus Christ, but to other lords; areas in which we would not need justification and sanctification through him" (Barmen, Art. 2).

We reject the racism and sexism that demean our lives as those created precious in the sight of God.

We reject materialism and consumerism that put things in place of God and value possessions more than people.

We reject secularism that reduces life to its parts and pieces, and relativism that abandons the search for truth.

We reject militarism that promises "security" by means of a nuclear balance of terror, threatening God's creation with destructive "gods of metal."

We reject identification with any ideology of the right or the left "as though the Church were permitted to abandon the form of its message and order to its own pleasure or to changes in prevailing ideological and political convictions" (Barmen, 8:18).

We reject cultural captivity and accommodationism as well as the notion that we can turn aside from the world in indifference, for we remember that "the earth is the Lord's and the fulness thereof" (Psalm 24:1).

We urge the Church in each of its parts to prayerfully consider the meaning for our times of Paul's admonition in Romans 12:2: "Do not be conformed to this world but be transformed by the renewal of your mind, that you may prove what is the will of God, what is good and acceptable and perfect." Pray that God will help the United Church of Christ discern the things we must reject as well as the things we must affirm, that to which we say "no" and that to which we give our glad assent.

Life Together

For the health of the Church and the integrity of our witness and service, we urge clergy and laity to gather in timely fashion for prayer, study, and mutual care. We encourage the mutual support of clergy for one another in their ministry, and ask the theological faculties to maintain communion with students beyond the years of their formal study. We ask Church and Ministry Committees to nurture Christian love and concern for seminarians during the course of their preparation for ordained tasks in the Church. We hope that retreats and periods of rest, reflection and spiritual renewal will become part of our life together in each Conference, and that the teaching ministry might be affirmed by laity and clergy to the end that our congregational life and our mission be anchored deeply in Scripture and informed generously by the urgent realities of our time.

Doxology

To the truth of the Gospel that has sustained and emboldened the Church in each generation, we too say "yes." With grateful hearts, we affirm the gift of faith present in the United Church of Christ — evangelical, catholic, and reformed — which we are being called to live out in these fragile and bewildering times.

While the way ahead is not always clear to us, we dare to hope and rejoice, believing that we belong to our faithful Saviour, Jesus Christ, our "only comfort in life and death" (Heidelberg Catechism, Ques. 1). We seek to hold together worship, discipleship, proclamation and service, Word and world.

As our forebears have done, we too declare that we shall tread this path with all who are "kindred in Christ" and "share in this confession" (Preamble, Para. 2). We invite you to walk with us in this way.

In Christ,
The Participants in the Craigville Colloquy,
Craigville, Massachusetts, May 16, 1984

62. UCC Charismatic Fellowship:

Purpose and Theology

(1977, 1978)

During the 1970s many churches in the United States were influenced by a spiritual renewal known as the "charismatic movement." A small group within the United Church of Christ participated in this movement and in October 1977 the United Church of Christ Charismatic Fellowship (UCCCF) was organized. The purpose of the UCC Charismatic Fellowship reminds the UCC of the outpouring of "God the Holy Spirit" on the church. Its theological framework recognizes the "word and deed" understanding of ministry in the United Church of Christ; the importance of the Bible, the Kansas City Statement of Faith, and the Heidelberg Catechism, the power of Jesus' Baptism in the Holy Spirit, and the gift of the Holy Spirit to individual Christians.

Source: The United Church of Christ Charismatic Fellowship "Statement of Purpose" (1977) and "A Theological Framework" (1978) [UCC Archives Post Papers Box 12, File folder 15].

The United Church of Christ Charismatic Fellowship: Statement of Purpose

"To bring to the attention of all within the body of believers the outpouring of God the Holy Spirit upon all flesh by God the Father and God the Son, the one eternal, infinite God of the universe; to encourage and strengthen members of the United Church of Christ through the fellowship of praise, prayer, edification and mutual sharing of the present day Pentecost; to upbuild Christians by relying upon the power of the Holy Spirit for the glory of Christ Jesus and for the extension of His Kingdom on earth; to promote love, peace and purity among those within the United Church of Christ and all other Christians in a truly inclusive ecumenical spirit."

UCCCF: A Theological Framework

I. We affirm the "Word and Deed" concept of the United Church of Christ's wholistic ministry, while emphasizing our task as developing the spiritual life of the Christian as God's primary agent of renewal in the Church and in Society.

II. We affirm our denomination's biblical roots grounded in the Power of the Holy Spirit for creating and renewing the Church of Jesus Christ. (As expressed in the Kansas City Creed of 1913 and the Heidelburg Catechism.)

III. We claim the Power of Jesus Christ's Baptism in the Holy Spirit as a continuing reality in the Church, awaking the spiritual Gifts of Ministry.

IV. We *believe* that the Baptism in the Holy Spirit empowers Christians to experience the reality of a personal relationship with Jesus Christ, both as Saviour *and* Lord!

63. United Church People for Biblical Witness: *"Scriptural Primacy" and "The Dubuque Declaration"*

(1979, 1983)

Donald G. Bloesch, UCPBW Board of Directors

After the General Synod vote on Human Sexuality: A Preliminary Study *(1977) (see vol. 7:98), representatives of those who had opposed the report argued that the report presented views that were in conflict with the traditional and historic teachings of Christianity. After the Synod they met with denominational leaders to determine if concerns expressed in the "minority resolution" could be carried out within the existing structures of the UCC. They were not satisfied.*

Therefore, in April 1978 they convened a convocation in Philadelphia and came to the conclusion that the problems in the UCC were much bigger than human sexuality. They asked, "What is the ultimate authority for faith and practice in the United Church of Christ?" In order to pursue that question they organized a new special-interest group — the United Church People for Biblical Witness (UCPBW), electing Barbara Weller, a laywoman, as chair, and Armand Weller, a pastor, as secretary.

Under the Wellers' leadership the UCPBW began publishing a newsletter, The Witness, *and preparing a study book,* Issues in Sexual Ethics *(1979) (a response to the* Human Sexuality *study). The organization found the theological insights of Donald Bloesch (b. 1928), an Evangelical*

Sources: Donald G. Bloesch, an excerpt from "Scriptural Primacy," in *Essentials of Evangelical Theology,* vol. 1 (New York: Harper and Row, 1978), reprinted in Martin Duffy, ed., *Issues in Sexual Ethics* (Souderton, Pa.: United Church People for Biblical Witness, 1979), 32–34. "The Dubuque Declaration" adopted by the Board of Directors of the United Church People for Biblical Witness, Dubuque, Iowa, November 17, 1983. Later reprinted in *New Conversations* (Spring 1985): 17.

and Reformed/UCC minister teaching at Dubuque Theological Seminary, Dubuque, Iowa (1957–93), especially helpful. Bloesch was the son of an Evangelical pastor and educated at Elmhurst College, Chicago Theological Seminary, University of Chicago, Oxford, Tübingen, and Basel. The author of many books, including Essentials of Evangelical Theology *(1978) and later a seven-volume systematic theology called* Christian Foundations *(1992–2004), his writing on "scriptural primacy" was reprinted in the UCPBW study book* Issues in Sexual Ethics *(1979).*

Bloesch explains how the Protestant reformers recovered the authority of scripture that had been overwhelmed by tradition in the medieval church. He also criticizes more recent liberal neo-Protestant theology, with its emphasizes on individualism and accommodation to culture. Ultimately, Bloesch argues, "final authority is not Scripture but the living God himself as we find him in Jesus Christ."

The United Church People for Biblical Witness (UCPBW) worked hard to promote its understanding of biblical authority by presenting several resolutions at subsequent General Synods. By 1983, failing to change the national church, the UCPBW launched a new strategy to renew the UCC. Instead of trying to get alternative resolutions passed by General Synods the UCPBW issued "A Call to a Confessing Fellowship" and reorganized itself as a grassroots renewal organization, the "Biblical Witness Fellowship" (BWF). In late 1978 at a meeting in Dubuque, Iowa, it drafted a new confessional statement — the Dubuque Declaration — and invited local congregations and leaders to endorse it when they joined the BWF.

Those who drafted the Dubuque Declaration view it as a declaration about the Christian faith in relation to contemporary challenges facing the United Church of Christ. The declaration does not seek to split the UCC. It remains deeply rooted in the Basis of Union and the Constitution of the UCC (see 7:1 and 8). Its six points focus upon six threats that more traditional members of the UCC judge to be undermining the faith of the church.

Scriptural Primacy

In concluding this section on Scriptural primacy, we must bear in mind that the ultimate, final authority is not Scripture but the living God himself as we find him in Jesus Christ. Jesus Christ and the message about him constitute the material norm for our faith just as the Bible is the formal norm. The Bible is authoritative because it points beyond itself to the absolute authority, the living and transcendent Word of God. Against both fundamentalism and the old Catholicism we do not conceive of the authority of Christian faith in heteronomous terms. Our authority is not an external standard that impresses itself upon the soul, but a Word from God that enters into the depths of the soul and creates its own response. As Forsyth put it:

> The authority in theology is not external to the matter it works in. It is spiritual. It is inherent in the fontal fact, and connate to the soul. It belongs to the revelation as such, and not to any voucher which the revelation created, like a book or a church. It is an authority objective to us in its source, but subjective in its nature and appeal.[1]

We must go on to affirm, however, that the absolute authority of faith, the living Christ himself, has so bound himself to the historical attestation concerning his self-revelation, namely, the sacred Scripture, that the latter necessarily participates in the authority of its Lord. The Bible must be distinguished from its ground and goal, but it cannot be separated from them. This is why Forsyth could also say: *"The Bible is not merely a record of the revelation; it is part of the revelation. It is not a quarry for the historian, but a fountain for the soul."*[2]

Jesus Christ is the one who speaks, the message of the Bible is the word that he speaks within history, and the church is the mouth through which he speaks. Just as the church is subordinated to the Bible, so the Bible in turn is subordinated to Jesus Christ, who embodies the mind and counsel of God. To put it another way, the church is the phonograph by which we hear the voice of Christ on the record, the Scriptures.[3] To carry the illustration further, it is the Holy Spirit who sets the phonograph in motion. The authority of the Bible is operative within the context of the church by the action of the Spirit. Where these analogies fall down is that

1. P. T. Forsyth, *The Principle of Authority* (London: Independent Press Ltd., 1952), 396.

2. P. T. Forsyth, *The Gospel and Authority,* ed. Marvin Anderson (Minneapolis: Augsburg Publishing House, 1971), 25.

3. Another pertinent illustration is the church as the lamp, the Bible as the light bulb, and Christ as the light, the light comes to us only through the vehicles of the light bulb and the lamp, but apart from the light these have little value.

Christ is free to speak his Word in a slightly different way for every age and culture, though he remains faithful to the Word that he uttered once for all in the history of the biblical revelation.

[P. T.] Forsyth points to this higher criterion within the Bible, the canon within the canon, when he says: "The gospel of God's historic act of grace is the infallible power and authority over both church and Bible. It produced them both. They both exist for its sake, and must be construed in its service."[4] The ruling criterion of the Gospel, however, must not be construed as referring only to particular sections of Scripture, but it is either implicit or explicit in the whole of Scripture.

The authority and infallibility* of the Bible as well as of the church are derivative, having their basis in Christ and his Gospel. We must listen to the dictates of the Bible and also to the counsel of the universal church because they have their ultimate sanction in God himself. When these authorities seem to disagree, this means that we have not really made contact with the real Word of Scripture or the true head of the church, who are one and the same. We must subject the discordant voices that we hear to Christ's self-witness within the Scriptures thereby bringing a transcendent norm to bear upon the point of contention. Yet this transcendent norm is not within our possession: to hear the voice of the living Christ is a miracle of grace which we can hope and pray for but cannot take for granted.[5]

---

4. Ibid., 17.

5. It should be bourne in mind that the voice of the living Christ cannot be divorced from either the Scriptures or the church. This voice is none other than the Word of God in the Scriptures which speaks to and through the church in every age.

*In the next section of his book Dr. Bloesch says that infallibility refers to "the doctrine or message of Scripture," to "Scripture illumined by the Spirit." He advises, "this does not mean that they [the biblical writers] were faultless in their recording of historical data or in their world view . . . " (vol. 1:65).

The Dubuque Declaration

We declare our continuing commitment to the truths set forth in the Basis of Union and the Constitution of the United Church of Christ.

We perceive an erosion and denial of these truths in our church. Because of our concern for the people of our churches and the well-being of our denomination as a member of the body of Christ, we are called by God to make this confession:

1 We confess our faith in the triune God—Father, Son, and Holy Spirit.

2 We confess that Jesus Christ is truly God and truly man. Because of our sin and estrangement from God, at the Father's bidding the Son of God took on flesh. Conceived by the Holy Spirit and born of the Virgin Mary, He became like us in all things apart from sin. He died on the cross to atone for our sin and reconcile us to God and on the third day rose bodily from the dead. He is the sole head of the church, the Lord and Savior of us all, and will one day return in glory, power, and judgment to usher in the kingdom of God in its fullness.

3 We hold that the Bible is the written Word of God, the infallible rule of faith and practice for the church of Jesus Christ. The Scriptures have binding authority on all people. All other sources of knowing stand under the judgment of the Word of God.

4 We affirm that the central content of the Scriptures is the gospel of reconciliation and redemption through the atoning sacrifice of Christ and His glorious resurrection from the grave. The good news is that we are saved by the grace of God alone, the grace revealed and fulfilled in the life and death of Jesus Christ, which is received only by faith. Yet this faith does not remain alone but gives rise to works of piety, mercy, and justice. The Holy Spirit, who spoke through the prophets and apostles, calls us today, as in the past, to seek justice and peace for all races, tongues, and nations.

5 We confess as our own the faith embodied in the great ecumenical and Reformation creeds and confessions, finding them in basic conformity with the teaching of the Holy Scriptures.

6 We confess that the mission of the church is to bear witness to God's law and gospel in our words and deeds. We are sent into the world as disciples of Christ to glorify God in every area of life and to bring all peoples into submission to the Lordship of Christ, baptizing them in the name of the Father and of the Son and of the Holy Spirit. We seek to obey this commission in the full assurance that our Lord and Savior is with us always, even to the end of the age.

64. A Just Peace Church:

"Theological Foundations"

(1986)

Susan Thistlethwaite, Editor

At the 1981 General Synod a resolution was presented calling upon the United Church of Christ to declare itself a pacifist *church. Although the Synod struck the word "pacifist" from the resolution, it did vote that the UCC become a "peace church." This label, however, was confusing, because the UCC was not one of the historic peace churches (the Society of Friends, Church of the Brethren, the Mennonites, etc.). Therefore, two years later the General Synod voted that the UCC should become a "peacemaking church."*

During the discussions, no one was exactly sure what these resolutions meant. To deal with this ambiguity, in 1981 the UCC Office for Church in Society (OCIS) appointed a Peace Theology Development Team and charged it to reflect about the meaning of peace and its centrality to UCC identity. Two years later the Team "was commissioned to consider more fully the basis and ramifications — theologically, politically, programmatically — of becoming a peacemaking church."

Over a period of three years the team met for two to three days every three to six months. By October 1984 a first draft of its work was circulated and the response to the draft became the basis for a General Synod pronouncement, "Affirming the United Church of Christ to Be a Just Peace Church" (1985). Soon thereafter the draft was revised and

---

Source: Susan Thistlethwaite, ed., an excerpt from "The Theological Foundations of the Just Peace Church," in *A Just Peace Church: The Peace Theology Development Team* (New York: United Church Press, 1986), 51–60.

published in its final version as A Just Peace Church *(1986), edited by Susan Thistlethwaite.*

There were twelve members of the Peace Theology Development Team. Susan Thistlethwaite (b. 1948), a UCC minister was educated at Smith College, Duke Divinity School, and the Graduate School at Duke University. She was an associate minister in North Carolina and Massachusetts for four years in the 1970s and taught at several colleges and seminaries from 1975 to 1982 (Duke University, Connecticut College, Mount Holyoke College, Wesley Theological Seminary, and Boston University). Since 1982 she has been on the faculty at Chicago Theological Seminary and became its president in 1998.

The section on the "Theological Foundations of the Just Peace Church" in A Just Peace Church *(1986) touches on some of the main doctrines of the church: creation, sin, the Christ, and the Holy Spirit. Later topics in the theological foundations section examine the church as a peacemaking community, the relationship between church and state, and the future of the idea of a just peace.*

The Theological Foundations of the Just Peace Church

Creation: Covenant as Friendship

In the beginning, humanity was shaped by God. Human beings are witnesses to the creativity of God, the desire of God to create and not destroy. This was declared good because we were created to be with God. God does not want to be alone. God makes room for humanity. We are thus created both with and in God by virtue of our creation by God. We are inseparably related to God.

The creation narratives of the scriptures are not in conflict with science. They describe the creation as the beginning of history. The creation anticipates what is to come: a lifelong relationship between human beings and God. God and the people of God move through history together. The bond between them deepens and strengthens over time.

In the early years of their history together, God offered the people a chance to break with the Egyptian Pharaoh and his idols of sand and to take a risk in the wilderness. Though enslaved and oppressed in Egypt, the people of God are brought out of Egypt, out of slavery, and their lives are forever changed. But God is changed too. God agrees to become their

God and to abide with them. "I will make a covenant of peace with them; it shall be an everlasting covenant with them; and I will bless them and multiply them, and will set my sanctuary in the midst of them for evermore [Ezek. 37:26]."

In entering into covenant with them, God has freely chosen to abide in the midst of them. The covenant of God with the people is a self-chosen risk on God's part in which God limits divine freedom for the sake of a true partnership with humanity. Covenant represents a form of governance of the world that is a sharing of power, not an exercise of tyrannical authority.

This is why the marriage metaphor keeps recurring to describe the relationship of God and the people of God. While sometimes these biblical images have been used to identify the male role with the role of God, the biblical metaphor of marriage can be interpreted not to signify the subordination of women but the intense involvement of God and the people. The real content of the metaphor is the learning to bond with one another — as difficult in human relations as in the divine-human relation. Our continuing encounter with the scriptures in present history makes new interpretations necessary if we are really to hear the text in the present.

The book of Hosea contains a lament of God over the unfaithfulness of Israel. Israel is imaged as God's wife. This represents the risk God is taking. In marriage one never quite knows how things are going to turn out. What is certain, though, is that the marriage will be different from anyone's expectations, and both partners will be changed by it.

This understanding challenges the concept of a solitary, self-sufficient God, who comes into covenant with everything settled. Instead, things are decided as the relationship goes along. God tells Hosea to return to his wife just as God turns again to Israel and renews the covenant, despite having said in anger, "you are not my people, and I am not your God [Hos. 1:9]."

> And I will make for you a covenant on that day with the beasts of the field, the birds of the air, and the creeping things of the ground; and I will abolish the bow, the sword, and war from the land; and I will make you lie down in safety. And I will betroth you to me in righteousness and in justice, in steadfast love, and in mercy. I will betroth you to me in faithfulness; and you shall know the Sovereign.
>
> — Hosea 2:18–20

Hosea depicts not a triumphant God, who does not get involved with the people, but a God who makes peace through participating in the lives of the people and risking even hurt and rejection. A current way of describing such a relationship is with another metaphor, that of friendship. In the scriptures, God's bonding with humanity is also described as friendship.

> But you, Israel, my servant, Jacob, whom I have chosen, the offspring of Abraham, my friend; . . . —Isaiah 41:8

The description of God's relationship with humanity as friendship expresses mutuality, maturity, cooperation, responsibility, and reciprocity. This relationship of friendship, of covenant, brings about shalom, the well-being that is peace, when the weapons of war are swept off the earth and all creatures lie down together without fear.

Furthermore, covenantal fidelity is not confined to human relationship to God. It is the totality of God's abiding with the people of God as they keep covenant with one another. As people living in friendship with God, we come to recognize the inseparable connection between knowing God and doing justice to one another.

> Did not your ancestors eat and drink and do justice and righteousness? Then it was well. They judged the cause of the poor and needy; then it was well. Is this not to know me? says God, the Sovereign one. —Jeremiah 22:15–16

The Just Peace church is rooted in this understanding of covenant. God's move to bond with us in friendship opens up the possibility that such friendship is possible on earth.

Sin: The Refusal of God's Friendship

The biblical writers are never romantic about shalom. Those who have continued to struggle for peace and justice throughout human history know as well that Just Peace does not come naturally or smoothly. They are clear that humanity finds many ways to refuse the shalom vision and to turn away from God's will for human history.

One of the ways the community refuses the reality of Just Peace is to be, as the Latin American theologian Gustavo Gutiérrez has said, a "liar society." Injustice, greed, and preparation for war are mislabeled "peacekeeping." But what is kept is not peace, but injustice and greed. The prophet Jeremiah did not mince words in identifying the sin of denying shalom.

> For from the least to the greatest of them, everyone is greedy for unjust gain; and from prophet to priest, everyone deals falsely. They

have healed the wounds of my people lightly, Saying, "Shalom, Shalom," when there is no shalom.

—Jeremiah 6:13–14; 8:11; cf. Ezekiel 13:10, 16; Amos 6:1–6

Just Peace is a responsibility for the powerful. They are held accountable when prosperity is a possibility only for a few. The well-being of a small segment is not Just Peace but is in fact the refusal to see the shalom vision in all its breadth.

Another way in which the community can refuse Just Peace, shalom, is to mortgage the future for an uneasy security in the present. Going heavily into debt to buy armaments to protect the disproportionate prosperity of a few is a related refusal of shalom.

Deficit spending has been sanctioned in contemporary economic theory, but its pernicious effects were known long before the theories of the twentieth century. Isaiah records a story of King Hezekiah, who was willing to mortgage the future of his people for excess in the present, saying to himself, "There will be shalom and security in my days [Isa. 39:8]." The prophet condemns such a narrow understanding of the well-being that is shalom. (See also Jeremiah 31:29, 30; Ezekiel 18:2.) Just Peace is not limited to a few people or to only one generation. The deficits incurred in the United States today to pay for arms buildup decrease shalom for some people through inflation and joblessness. But they also mortgage the Just Peace of the future, condemning the future generations to pay for the spending sprees of the present.

Another way to refuse the broad and deep vision of Just Peace is to confine Just Peace to religious rituals. Again it is Jeremiah who is clear in criticizing the people for finding the temple a quick and easy way to shalom (Jeremiah 7:1–10). Jesus as well condemned going through the motions of religious ritual without connecting ritual to ethical conduct (Matthew 15:1–20).

The shalom vision that the authors have translated "Just Peace" is so comprehensive that there is a great temptation to try to manage its challenge and identify shalom with a particular technology or economic theory or present gratification or even a religious ritual. Over and over through human history people have rebelled against participating in the reign of God and have refused to see and do God's will for human life.

Christ: Jesus and the Power for Change

Even though generation after generation has refused Just Peace with God, we have no cause for despair. The advent of Christ is the joyous seal of our friendship with God, a friendship described in the Old Testament as a time when God speaks peace to the people and "steadfast love and faithfulness will meet; righteousness and peace will kiss each other. Faithfulness will spring up from the ground, and righteousness will look down from the sky [Ps. 85:10–11]."

Jesus, who is our peace (Ephesians 2:14), really changed human history so that it is possible to overcome the sin of refusing shalom. Jesus, when he was on earth, participated in the reign of God in a visible, tangible way. Jesus himself performed visible signs of forgiveness and healing that made manifest that the Just Peace vision was no longer merely future but also present. Through his death on the cross and his resurrection, Jesus made it possible for Christians to participate in a real way in Just Peace. The church strives to continue to live that concrete manifestation.

But, Christians generally have looked at the coming of Christ, and hence the role of the church, in ways that are not so concrete. In one view, they have seen the coming of Christ simply as a transaction between God and Christ alone in which the sacrifice of Jesus causes God to forgive humankind's sin and offer redemption. In another view they have seen the coming of Christ in terms of personal interaction between Christ and each believer. In this view, the individual turns to God by appropriating Christ's sacrifice for the self. But in either view, the power Christ brings actually to change the world is turned away from the world and frozen in a transaction that is outside history.

It is essential for the church to maintain the tension between proclaiming the real change that Christ did make in human history, opening up through his death and resurrection the possibility of humanity's turning to God, without at the same time turning this power for change into "a noun," as Hugo Assmann, another Latin American theologian, has phrased it. The power for change is not a "noun," that is, something static, but a "verb," something in which we actively participate. The work of Christ to change the world and bring it closer to God makes possible our work as we continue to bring about Just Peace.

What the work of Christ means is that the coming of Christ is more than placating God's anger at human sin and more than an individual's heart being turned to faith. While it includes both of these things, it also means that the coming of Christ really changed human history. Humanity can overcome sin, create Just Peace. It also means that this power for change is useless if human beings do not bond together to participate in changing the world. Christ's power becomes tangible through our bonding with one another.

Today, one of the strongest images of the atonement, a word that means the reconciliation brought about by Christ's sacrifice on the cross, is the suffering and pain of the oppressed. Jesus, identified in earthly life as one who was a friend of tax collectors and sinners (Matthew 11:19), acted out the message that the power to change the world comes from human solidarity.

Table fellowship shows this clearly. People eat with their friends, those with whom they have a close relationship. Jesus, who ate with the unclean, the outcast, and those in despised professions, showed that the power to change the world comes through human bonding with the despised.

Friendship was an important part of Jesus' life. But it is clear that by friendship Jesus does not mean the easy camaraderie of clubs, social organizations, or even some churches. Jesus speaks of the love of those willing to lay down their lives for their friends (John 15:13).

As a Just Peace church, members embody not a Christ who touched history only tangentially but a Christ fully engaged in human events as the fulfillment of God's promise to befriend the people. The church is thus a real countervailing power to those forces that perpetuate human enmity, that divide and destroy human community.

The Holy Spirit: Advocate for Justice

This power for change is still available to Christians and we do not have to act alone. Jesus promised us that we would not be alone in history, that we would not be orphaned. Jesus promised God would send another, the Spirit of Truth (John 14:16–17).

"Comforter" and "Sustainer" are other translations of the Greek word for Spirit usually found in John 14. These translations reflect a view of the Holy Spirit as "persuader." The Spirit is deemed to act individualistically, privately, and indirectly.

To comfort, to sustain are actions that complement the status quo and help people to adjust to their problems. While there are times of personal crisis when the Holy Spirit does come to us to comfort and sustain, the work of the Spirit is not limited to these actions. The Holy Spirit is as fully immersed in the struggles of human history as was the one by whom the Spirit was sent, Jesus the Christ. To limit the work of the Holy Spirit only to "comforting" and "sustaining" is to reflect a view of history as harmonious and untroubled. Yet, Christians view history as troubled, an arena of conflict, of struggle, in which the hegemony of the "principalities and powers" has been ended by Christ, but in which we must still struggle finally to defeat them.

The work of the Spirit includes a genuine effort at making right what has been wrong. Thus, an important part of the work of the Holy Spirit is witness and proclamation, even confrontation with those sinful rejections of the vision of Just Peace and the attempts to subvert its establishment.

In this struggle to defeat the power ranged against the shalom vision, however, we Christians undercut our own purposes if we do not make forgiveness our first act. A crucial sign of the work of the Holy Spirit is forgiveness. The past is allowed to be past, and the new hope, new possibility, is allowed to emerge. "I will forgive their sins and I will no longer remember their wrongs [Jer. 31:34]."

The community of forgiveness means a redress of the power imbalance in which the genuine interdependence people have with one another is allowed to emerge free of the power structures that keep them apart (Mark 10:42–44). Thus, to "make peace" means to work to change the conditions that make for war. To "comfort" the poor means changing their situation and working to eliminate the conditions that keep them poor. The movement of the Spirit presses us to create the conditions of a Just Peace. . . .

65. Theological Ferment:
"Feminist Theology"

(1985)

Sharon H. Ringe

In the midst of the "theological ferment" of the early 1980s several UCC conferences held consultations, established ongoing theology groups, and encouraged pastors and laity to engage in more intentional theological conversation. The Connecticut Conference and the Central Atlantic Conference published proceedings of their gatherings in typescript form (see vol. 7:13 and 31).

A 1985 Consultation on Theology sponsored by the Central Atlantic Conference produced six papers on a variety of theological perspectives — American Indian, process theology, black theology, and feminist theology. Some of these essays were later published in Daniel L. Johnson and Charles Hambrick-Stowe, editors, Theology and Identity: Traditions, Movements, and Polity in the United Church of Christ *(1990).*

A paper on "Feminist Theology and the UCC" was written by Sharon H. Ringe (b. 1946), a UCC minister educated at the University of New Hampshire and Union Theological Seminary in New York. She was an associate pastor in New York City (1971–74), a member of the faculty at the Methodist School of Theology in Ohio (Delaware, Ohio) (1977–91), and since 1991 she has been teaching at Wesley Theological Seminary in Washington, D.C. Ringe, a biblical scholar, was also actively involved in the development of the Inclusive Language Lectionary (1983)

Source: Sharon H. Ringe, "Feminist Theology and the United Church of Christ," in *Theological Ferment in the United Church of Christ: Six Essays,* ed. Consultation on Theology of the Central Atlantic Conference, 1985, 11–14 [typescript]. This essay, slightly edited, was published in the Johnson and Hambrick-Stowe volume, 117–23.

and has taught regularly at the Universidad Bíblica Latinoamericana in San José, Costa Rica, since 1991.

Feminist Theology and the United Church of Christ

Feminist theology appears to have come of age. One clear indication of that fact is the diversity of theological methods and agenda that currently bear that label. Gone are the days when one could claim with assurance to have addressed all of the significant works in the field, or when our internal insecurity about the emerging discipline demanded an uncritical echo from each woman engaged in the field. In fact, today the label "feminist theology" covers a range of perspectives from the post-Judeo-Christian position of a Mary Daly or spokeswomen for the "womanspirit" movements, to the "revisionist" position of many of us who know ourselves to be firmly rooted in some denomination of the biblical faith. Professionally, feminist theologians approach our task as anthropologists, psychologists, historians, ethicists, biblical scholars, ministers, and theologians.

In the midst of this diversity, it is clear that the United Church of Christ and other parts of the Christian church have been most directly influenced by those of us still in some fashion within the folds of the "Christian feminists."[1] Those of us who acknowledge such a label, however, are genuinely re-visioning and not simply tinkering with the tradition insofar as our own vision has been stretched by the more radical expressions of women's experience of the transcendent. (An analogy might be the way in which the radical statement of the Black experience presented by Malcolm X has joined with the explicitly Christian perspective of Martin Luther King, Jr., to ground present-day expressions of Black theology.)[2] To attempt the definition of at least a minimal common ground, I would propose the following statement from Rosemary Radford Ruether:

> The critical principle of feminist theology is the promotion of the full humanity of women. Whatever denies, diminishes, or distorts the full humanity of women is, therefore, appraised as not redemptive ... [and] must be presumed not to reflect the divine or an authentic relation to the divine, or to reflect the authentic nature of things, or to

---

1. For an excellent anthology of such writings, see Judith L. Weidman, *Christian Feminism Visions of a New Humanity* (New York: Harper & Row, 1984).

2. See the discussion in James H, Cone, *For My People* (Maryknoll, N.Y.: Orbis, 1984).

> be the message or work of an authentic redeemer or a community of redemption. This negative principle also implies the positive principle: what does promote the full humanity of women is of the Holy, it does reflect true relation to the divine, it is the true nature of things, the authentic message of redemption and the mission of redemptive community.[3]

What this means, first of all, is that feminist theology represents a critique of "patriarchy." By "patriarchy" we mean not merely a history in which men have been dominant and women subordinate. Instead we use this term to summarize systems and attitudes of dominance that result in the structures and ideologies of racism, sexism, classism, and militarism. Our opposition to such systems of dominance is related in the second place to our sense that the "image of God" in which humankind was created (Gen. 1:27) and to which we are called (Matt. 5:43–48) gives us a quite different picture of the nature of power and value. This God whom we have come to know at times in the midst of the traditional church and at times on its edges draws us toward models of participation, of mutuality, and of solidarity with those most deeply hurt by the institutions and structures of the world, as a proper locus of both Christian confession and Christian life (what theologians of liberation call "praxis").

Without pursuing further the complexities of feminist theology or spending time in retrospective consideration of the history of feminist theology (and one might add of feminists) in the United Church of Christ, let us consider directly the intersection of this movement with the current stress-points in the theological task and vocation of the United Church of Christ.

The very definition of the topic by the Consultation on Theology of the Central Atlantic Conference suggests a lack of coincidence between the concerns of the various groups and movements from which responses have been solicited and the traditional concerns and theological business of the church. To some extent that is the case: When the formerly voiceless find a voice, it should be no surprise that there is a backlog of things to be said which others may not ever have noticed. Again to use an analogy, this is the "women's studies," "Black studies," or "peace studies" part of the reform of a school curriculum, in which new priorities and agenda are introduced. As important as it is to begin to fill these significant gaps in a curriculum, such individual courses are finally no substitute for the integration of these concerns and perspectives into the rest of the curriculum. It is similarly

3. Rosemary Radford Ruether, *Sexism and God-Talk* (Boston: Beacon Press, 1983), 18–19.

appropriate to expect that the various "theological movements" identified by the Consultation will have something new to say to concerns which are at the heart of the present theological ferment. We might well find ourselves re-visioning the very questions being considered.

One might think, for example, that the historic pluralism of the United Church of Christ would account for an openness to perspectives of feminist theologians. Indeed, that is the case. However, our style of pluralism leads to what is often only an apparent openness. As a denomination we welcome "add-ons," and as with barnacles on a ship, there is usually room for one more. Also like barnacles, however, these various add-ons rarely affect the core structure of the vessel or its course. We who are added on are taken along for the ride, but it may well not be the journey on which we intended to go. The experience of various caucuses and interest groups within the church has been one of overt hospitality, but often of minimal influence.[4] Insofar as the agenda of feminist theology challenges the very images of God at the core of our theology and worship as well as the system of "patriarchy" (as defined above) by which our society and church are organized, it poses questions to the very heart of the church's life. The prevalent style of pluralism may indeed muffle that voice in the very process of allowing it a place.

Feminist theology is at its heart contextual theology. Because of our affirmation of the importance of women's experience and the particularity of women's contexts, we tend to be suspicious of any expression of "classical orthodoxy." Our style of theological reflection is often to begin not with the content of a particular doctrine or expression, but with questions about the circumstances which gave rise to it: political and social issues, social and economic context, and the social location of the principal actors or speakers. Not only do we regularly assume the historical and cultural relativity of expressions of classical orthodoxy, but we also recognize that what passes for "orthodoxy" now was originally highly controversial, and indeed the position only of the winners in the disputes. Even while asking what it was that made these positions persuasive, we would listen too for the other voices in the discussion, which also represented a portion of the community of faith.

The perspective of feminist theology prompts similar questions to the ecumenical involvements of the United Church of Christ, and results in three affirmations. First, where there is a choice to be made between advocacy for justice and sensitivity to our ecumenical partners, a feminist

---

4. I am indebted to Yvonne Delk for this image and for her clarification of the experience of pluralism in the United Church of Christ.

perspective would tend to place priority on the former. For example, the issue of the ordination of women is reduced to little more than a footnote in the World Council of Churches statement on "Baptism, Eucharist, and Ministry" (1982), partly in the hope of broadening the consensus around the document. A feminist critique of that document would not accept such a rationale. A second affirmation is that a feminist critique would recognize the historical and cultural roots of the issues which have historically divided the church. In fact, it is precisely in their political vitality that their theological significance becomes clear. Again we would find ourselves needing to listen to the various voices in the debates, not only to those of the winners in each of the resultant groups. The consequence of such questions is a more broadly "ecumenical" methodology, more fully attentive to the universal church in its diversity and to the wider *oikoumene*. Finally, we would hold out to the church the challenge of recognizing that the ecumenical "pie" is now being sliced in new ways around issues which are of theological significance at least equal to those which resulted in the historical divisions and unions. Instead of focusing on such issues as the nature of the Trinity or of Christ's "presence" in the Eucharist, the ecumenical theological issues today tend to relate to the nature of the Christian life. Struggles around issues of racism, sexism, classism, and militarism, for example, have given birth both to new expressions of unity across historical divisions and to new divisions within denominational and confessional families.

The last of the dimensions of the discussion which we were asked to address is the call for "sound teaching" or "teaching consensus." At that point the methodological suspicion of feminist theology becomes significant, in that it recalls us to fundamental questions of meaning and underlying authority for our theological reflection. From where does the definition of "sound teaching" come? And what are its assumptions about how one knows God and discerns the social consequences of such knowing and relatedness? What is the "canon" of such teaching, and what interpretive keys allow us to move between various expressions of the faith?

Cutting across all of these stress-points which have been identified in the theological task of the United Church of Christ is the problem of the language by which theology is expressed and by which the life of the church is carried forward. "Inclusive language" is clearly a concern of feminist theology insofar as it requires the reform of all language that excludes, diminishes, stereotypes, or otherwise hurts people because of their gender, racial or ethnic identity, social circumstances, or physical condition. In addition to the obvious concern with language referring to people, language referring to God and Christ is also at issue.

The biblical witness itself calls us to accountability on the issue of language. Faithfulness to the biblical story draws us into dimensions of inclusiveness which our human anxieties would lead us to shun, in response to a God whose passionate concern is always for the outcast and oppressed, and whose own vision of the covenant always transcends human envisioning of its limits. Inclusive language involves precisely the linguistic expression of that vocation. We learn about God in the Bible primarily from accounts of God's activity, and rarely in visual images. We do learn, however, that the biblical claim is of humankind in all its variety created in God's image, and not of God made in ours. Any human pretext for naming or invoking God is met with warning, and in fact early in Israel's history, the name of God written in the text ceased to be pronounced aloud (a decision underlying the common occurrence of the word LORD to refer to God in most English translations). In short, we learn from the Bible that faithfulness demands of us both a commitment to inclusiveness on the human plane, and great delicacy in our use of any "names" or images of God that are in danger of becoming literalized into idols of our own creation and control.[5]

The two dimensions of inclusiveness, namely involving language referring to God or Christ and language referring to people, are in fact inter-related. The church has usually been very careful to affirm that God transcends all human categories, and also that such human qualities of Jesus of Nazareth as his Jewishness, his first-century setting, and his maleness are not essential to his being the Christ. What is essential in our confession of Jesus as the Christ is rather that in that specific human life we learn to know God, and also that in that human life God and humankind are reconciled such that (as Paul affirms) "neither death, nor life, nor angels, nor principalities, nor things to come, nor powers, nor height, nor depth, nor anything else in all creation, will be able to separate us from the love of God in Christ Jesus our Lord." However, it is not only what the church thinks and affirms at its best, but how it lives, which communicates its understanding of God. Just as some of its images and metaphors for God have a tendency toward literalization, and its christological confession of Jesus as the Christ lapses over into an idolizing of the man Jesus, so these human expressions and understandings become

5. *An Inclusive Language Lectionary,* Readings for Year B (Atlanta: John Knox; New York: Pilgrim; Philadelphia: Westminster, 1984), 241–48. Sallie McFague, *Metaphorical Theology: Models of God in Religious Language* (Philadelphia: Fortress, 1982), 1–29, 145–92. Robert Hamerton-Kelly, *God the Father Theology and Patriarchy in the Teaching of Jesus* (Philadelphia: Fortress, 1979), 1–81.

concretized in social structures and relationships. Virginia Ramey Mollenkott reflects on these all-too-human consequences of theological language when she summarizes her own experience of growing up in the church. "If God is always 'he' and imaged as Father, Husband, or Master, then human husbands, fathers, and employers are godlike in a way that wives, mothers, and employees are not. And the stage is set for exploitation."[6]

The church in its most careful theological reflection has of course not *intended* any such consequences. Human fathers are not the models by which we are to understand the fatherhood of God. Nevertheless, in *practice* such connections are made in people's minds and psyches, and in the church and world in which we live.

If the preceding comments make clear the importance of attentiveness to language in the church's theology, liturgy, and other literature, it should be noted that the language of English translations of Scripture must itself be reconsidered. Ambiguities in the task of translation, which can never be a simple literal rendering of the ancient languages if the resulting text is to be comprehensible, plus the importance of conveying as accurately as possible the *meaning* of the biblical witness (with its vocation to inclusiveness on the human plane and its delicacy in finding human referents to God), require that a fresh look be taken at the language in which the biblical stories are cast, lest the words and grammar themselves blunt the biblical vision. The mandate for such works as the *Inclusive Language Lectionary* can thus be found within Scripture itself, and it is confirmed in the church's vocation to faithfulness in our time and place.

The controversy which has centered on the issue of inclusive language is paradigmatic of the way in which the perspectives of feminist theology push the church and each of us to raise fundamental questions at the heart of the expression and discussion of our faith, and not simply to add a new social agenda or to include a new group in our pluralistic church. Indeed, taken to its logical limits, the critical consciousness of feminist theology might lead us out of the maze of discussions of the "ferment" or "tension" in the church, and enable us to affirm the primacy of our vocation as a "peace and justice church." By its focus on the critique of patriarchy, feminist theology participates with the church, and indeed can help to lead the church in its struggle to discern the consequences of "knowing God" for a life of Shalom (Isaiah 11:6–9). By its contextual sensitivity, feminist theology can sustain that quest without giving in to

---

6. Virginia Ramey Mollenkott, "Sexist Language: The Problem and the Cure," *Language and the Church Articles and Designs for Workshops,* ed. Barbara A. Withers (New York: National Council of Churches of Christ in the U.S.A., 1984), 14.

the attempt to identify a new point of belief or practice which would claim to be the nonnegotiable bottom line of denominational identity. A posture more consistent with feminist theology is that of "proclamation" or "confession," rather than "discipline" or "orthodoxy." In keeping with our Statement of Faith, feminist theology can support the efforts of the church to find together "courage in the struggle for justice and peace," and to know God's "presence in trial and rejoicing." With the celebration of our diverse gifts, we can move together toward a fearless proclamation and embodiment of the gospel, as we learn throughout the church more graciously to "hear each other into speech," as one theologian puts it,[7] and live together toward wholeness in our common life.

---

7. Nelle Norton introduced me to the phrase and the practice of "hearing each other into speech."

Living with Theological Diversity

66. The Calvin Synod:

Holy Communion

(1967)

Aaron Elek

Protestant denominations in the United States have a varied and rich tradition of communion liturgy. Although congregations in the Calvin Synod of the UCC (see vol. 6:41) often use a variety of communion liturgies, they agree that "the communion service of the Reformed Church in Hungary contains elements of theological dignity and adds an undefinable depth of beauty to the sacrament of Holy Communion." Hungarian Calvinist congregations usually observe the sacrament seven times annually: Christmas, Lent, Easter, Pentecost, Thanksgiving for New Bread, Worldwide Communion, and Thanksgiving for New Wine.

In 1967 the Calvin Synod of the UCC published a set of seven communion meditations. Aaron Elek (1924–95) was an Evangelical and Reformed/UCC minister who was educated at the Budapest Theological Seminary (Hungary) and Princeton Theological Seminary. He served pastorates in Hungarian E and R and UCC congregations (Calvin Synod) in Pennsylvania and Ohio (1950–89). His meditation for Pentecost, based on Acts 2:1, speaks about the "real presence" of Christ in the sacrament, a conviction held by the Reformed Church in Hungary and shared by many in the Calvin Synod.

Source: An excerpt from "It Is the Spirit That Unites," a Pentecost Communion Meditation, *The Order of Holy Communion Service and Seven Meditations* (n.p.: Calvin Synod of the UCC, 1967), 32–34.

It Is the Spirit That Unites

. . . The perennial problem of a Christian community is not so much of becoming Christian, rather than remaining as one. It is a constant challenge amidst the daily troubles of life to hold on to the precious endowment: faith, and build and preserve a new life in Christ. Without the Holy Spirit, that blessed state of mutual concern and purpose, the "unity of believers," would be a vain and hopeless effort. It is that "oneness-in-Christ" of the faithful that makes the church a redemptive community, a healing fellowship. The Holy Communion is the manifestation of such a purposive unity of believers in which the interpretation of the mystery, the spiritual feeding and assuaging of our thirst and our living-in-Him and He-in-us is the work of God's own indwelling spirit, the Holy Spirit. Ever since its inception, the church of our Lord was menaced both from inside and outside. Within the church the greatest menace was disunity and dissension. Congregations as well as denominations can be effectively hamstrung by the one truly devastating force inside the church: the lack of unity. Even today, the question whether the church will survive this age or not depends almost entirely on the spirit-created, purposeful consolidation and concord of His children. The future of the church cannot be secured by contemporary tricks, know-how, not even by the most pious planning, but by recapturing the first outpouring of the Spirit. The degree of our ecumenical progress is the true gauge of God's spirit in our hearts, and the same spirit is the sole guarantee of its continued success.

As we prepare ourselves for this kingly feast we must recall that the immediate effect of this Supper must be preserved for the days to come, otherwise it will not govern our thoughts, deeds and desires, and will not penetrate our whole life. Like a contract without the corroborating seal is invalid, so is the Communion if it lacks His Spirit. Eating and drinking is not for now, but for the days ahead when we shall see, as if in retrospect, whether we had really communed with Him or not. What is its use, if it is only a solitary experience and not a lasting taste of how good it is to live with the Lord, and in the Lord through Christ? Like the bread and wine become one with and inseparable from the body, permeat[ing] its cells, [lending] power, energy and life to it, so should God's recognized, realized, shared blessing become the very life for us through that communicating agent, which is the Holy Spirit. At the touch of the spirit the bread and wine become the very reality of Christ's presence in us by faith, and it will be the very same spirit which sanctifies this for us.

Like mortar and cement bind the bricks into one structure, the Spirit of God binds and bonds man-to-God and God-to-man and even binds man-to-man in such a way that Christ's own body, the Church of His Glory becomes visible again through the lives of His children. When the unholy faces the holy, when the sinner encounters the sacred, there are two things present for certain: the shared guilt and the mutual shame of our unworthiness. The vows we utter here, the promises we make, the pledges we plight will all be in vain unless God's own spirit will seal them for us in the ongoing movement of His own body, the church of Jesus Christ, in which we move and have our being in union with Him and with all of His own.

67. Constructive Criticism:

Balaam's Courier

(1975)

By the mid-1970s United Church of Christ General Synods had become complicated and highly political gatherings. In 1975 a group of pastors started "a non-establishment, daily news sheet [at General Synod] reflecting a radical (basic) Christian consciousness and commitment, and offering comments, perspectives, and feedback on Synod."

The newssheet was called Balaam's Courier *(B.C.), recalling the biblical story of Balaam and his donkey (Numbers 22). In that story Balaam gets angry at his donkey when it mysteriously turns off the road to avoid the judgment of the angel of the Lord standing in the road. The donkey could see the angel, but Balaam did not see it. Balaam strikes the donkey several times, until the donkey reminds Balaam that he has been a good donkey for many years and does not deserve such treatment. Finally the Lord opens Balaam's eyes so he can see the problem. The angel of the Lord chides him for striking his good animal and tells Balaam, "I have come out as an adversary, because your way is perverse before me." At that point Balaam repents of his sinful ways and does what God tells him in the future.*

Balaam's Courier, *always printed on blue paper, always poking fun and calling the church into account, and always supported by volunteer labor and free-will contributions, has offered ongoing commentary and critique at every General Synod since 1975.*

Source: "Balaam's Courier," from *Balaam's Courier*, Friday, June 27, 1975, 1.

Balaam's Courier

B.C. is published by a grass roots coalition of UCC members at General Synod — laity and clergy, women and men, youth and adults, delegates, associates, visitors, and staff who are bound together by a common perspective.

We believe that the name and power of Jesus Christ is indissolubly linked to the two-fold struggle for a new person and a new society, and that the name of Jesus Christ must be named within the world of socio-political reality.

We believe that all the patterns of dominance that permeate our structures — men over women, bosses over workers, whites over people of color, adults over youth, and our biases toward affluent life-styles, consumerism, competition, and bigness (big government, big corporations, big churches, big instrumentalities) all belong to the old order.

We believe that the church in the U.S. has lost its prophetic voice and has become the chaplain of the American nation, preaching a harmless, easy, individualistic faith, and captive to the warfare state and an exploitative economic system.

We support the alliance of people and communities working together to build a radical Christian consciousness, commitment, and action in our times. We wish to serve the Lord and serve the people by proclaiming the gospel of liberation in Christ, by articulating the ethical demands of discipleship, by working and giving ourselves for peace, justice, and freedom.

68. Mercersburg Theology:

"What Does Mercersburg Have to Offer?" and "The Order of Corpus Christi"

(1993, 1987)

John Shetler, Order of Corpus Christi

The Mercersburg theological tradition is a system of thought developed by John Williamson Nevin and Philip Schaff during the 1840s and 1850s at the Seminary of the German Reformed Church in Mercersburg, Pennsylvania. It is often considered an early manifestation of the ecumenical impulse in American Protestantism (see vol. 3:26, 28 and 33; vol. 4:88, 90; vol. 5:56; vol. 6:42). In response to the sectarian and antiliturgical revivalism of nineteenth-century frontier religion, Nevin and Schaff pressed Christians to retrieve their connections with a variety of Protestant and Roman Catholic liturgies and to ground their lives in the historic confessions.

As ecumenism gained momentum in the mid-twentieth century, along with a new sense of the importance of the church and the need for liturgical reform, a group of pastors, professors, judicatory leaders, and laity, believing in the timelessness of Mercersburg theology, founded the Mercersburg Society (1983). They also started a journal, the New Mercersburg Review, *and joined with the Biblical-Theological-Liturgical Group (BTL) to cosponsor the Craigville Colloquies (see 7:61). The Mercersburg Society holds annual convocations to present and hear papers on contemporary theology, and (since 1991), sponsors*

Sources: John Shetler, an excerpt from "Entrance into the Mercersburg Movement and Its Influence on Church Union," *The New Mercersburg Review* (1993): 22–24. "The Order of Corpus Christi, September 29, 1987," from a flyer, *Mercersburg Theology: Church Renewal for the Twentieth Century,* Zion Topics No. 3 (Blain, Pa.: Zion United Church of Christ, 1989).

Mercersburg Society Theological Forums to discuss ways in which the teachings of Mercersburg might influence the contemporary church.

John Shetler (b. 1920) is an Evangelical and Reformed/UCC minister educated at Franklin and Marshall College, Lancaster Theological Seminary, and Princeton Theological Seminary. After serving several pastorates in Pennsylvania (1945–64), he became assistant to the conference minister of the Pennsylvania Southeast Conference UCC (1964–71) and conference minister of Pennsylvania Southeast Conference UCC (1971–85). Shetler was involved in the formation of the Mercersburg Society and a strong spokesperson for the conviction of Nevin and Schaff that the church is "organic and whole." He writes that the Mercersburg view of the church encouraged the Reformed Church in the United States to enter into union with the Evangelical Synod of North America in 1934, and it sustains the ongoing ecumenical interest and commitment of UCC leaders and congregations rooted in the Reformed tradition. Within the United Church of Christ it has also been influential in the development of the Services of the Church *(1964–69) (see vol. 7:30).*

Shetler argues that the Mercersburg understanding of the ecumenical church does not emerge through a "movement downward, spread and flattened to be a humanistic organization for social reform." It is a movement "upward and inward to the center which is Christ." Congregations are able to survive only when they are part of that body; they cannot survive separately. Those who hold this "concept of the church as the Body of Christ, Evangelical, Reformed, Catholic, Apostolic, organic, developmental and connectional," affirm the ecumenical creeds as witnesses to their faith, and treasure "the Eucharist as the liturgical act from which all other acts of worship emanate."

In 1987 a group committed to Mercersburg theology founded a covenant Order within the United Church of Christ called "The Order of Corpus Christi." The Order seeks "the unity and renewal of the Church of Jesus Christ." It gathers regularly in regional chapters to worship, to be nurtured and empowered through Word and Sacrament, to study scripture and spiritual writings, and to share in the fellowship of the Order. To join, persons are guided through a novitiate and novices make final profession of vows after spiritual study, reflection, and prayer. The Order is governed by a consistory and its synod convenes to address business and elect leaders.

Although initially open only to UCC members, since the Formula of Agreement *(1997) (see vol. 7:110), membership in the Order of Corpus Christi has been expanded to embrace members of churches endorsing the* Formula.

[What Does Mercersburg Have to Offer?]

. . . What does Mercersburg have to offer to the ecumenical concept of the church? We do not see the shape of the ecumenical church being attained by a movement downward, spread and flattened to be a humanistic organization for social reform. We see the movement upward with a reformed catholic doctrine if we are wearing the ecumenical spectacles of Nevin and Schaff. The movement is upward and inward to the center which is Christ with the whole body possessing the identifying characteristics of the Corpus Christi and the local units or extremities of the body being congregations that find survival possible because they are part of that body, rather than local churches which are complete manifestations of that body of Christ that can survive whole without being related to and of necessity being a part of the whole body.

To speak in one breath of the autonomy of all the parts of a denomination and to say that such a denomination is a part of the ecumenical church is to put into one sentence two antithetical ideas. To fracture the church and to say that each fractured part is a complete and a whole live unit in and of itself is a logical and scientific impossibility unless we conceive the church to be amebic without any one form or shape. The ameba divides rather than unites. This has been the heresy of the church. This has been the story of congregationalism whether it is New England Congregationalism, the Disciples of Christ or the Baptists.

In our day Mercersburg theologians know the church to be not atomistic and individualistic, but continuous, apostolic, catholic and reformed. If we look at the word apostolic, we find one of the chief keys to the unification of the outward frame of the church. The catholic church sees its continuity in apostolic succession. The reformers were not greatly concerned about the continuation of the apostolic succession as the outward manifestation of unity. John Calvin saw that succession already broken in the Roman Catholic Church and wrote, "Their plea of uninterrupted succession is a vain pretense, unless the truth of Christ, which was transmitted from the fathers, be permanently retained pure and uncorrupted by their posterity. This succession of bishops had revolted from Christ himself" and was no longer a part of Christ's ministry. It was not the reformers who had affected a disturbance in the succession of the ministry. That succession had already been broken sometime previously and they were seeking to restore it. There was no valid episcopate or ministry in existence to which they could adhere by regular institutional succession.[1]

1. James H. Nichols, *Romanticism in American Theology* (Chicago: University of Chicago Press, 1961), 268; "The Classis of Mercersburg," *Mercersburg Review* (1849): 383, 387.

Nevin believed that the church as a whole had the reproductive powers to restore a damaged organ. Ministerial powers and functions had been communicated from the Apostles to the whole community of believers as well as to the special priesthood of those inwardly called and outwardly recognized.[2] "Our ministry is descended to us from Christ through the apostate church of Rome, but not from the Apostate Church of Rome."[3]

In these writings one can see the developmental principle and the concept of historic continuity both at work. "The Reformation was not a movement to overthrow and reconstruct the work of the church in the case of its great cardinal doctrines as already positively defined by the general councils, but to carry forward and complete that work, by going on to define and settle what had not been made the subject of action in the same positive style."

Thus one can see more clearly why our denomination was never with any consistence called Calvinist as our sister was called Lutheran. With this concept of historic continuity, the appropriate word was and is Reformed. The Reformed Catholic Church. This desire for continuity was seen in the colonial period of Pennsylvania when the people at Falkner Swamp, Skippack, Whitemarsh and Philadelphia wanted to be sure their pastor was authentic and in the proper tradition. They sent John Philip Boehm to New York to seek arrangements for ordination. They did not choose to ordain him themselves, nor did they choose to have another pastor ordain him. An appeal was sent to the Classis of Amsterdam in 1728 and after a year his credentials were accepted. He was given further examination, and on the authority of the Classis of Amsterdam he was ordained by the Consistory of the Dutch Reformed Church of New York at the hands of an ordaining minister with elders present on November 18, 1729. The letter informing Boehm and the congregations of the possibility of ordination was received with great joy 250 years ago . . . on November 4, 1729. Here is seen in the action of the Classis and the Consistory the respect for historical continuity, but also the reformed or presbyterial concept of the bishop with the authority vested in the corporate body of the Classis of ordained pastors and ordained elders with that authority passed on, in this case, to the Consistory of New York.

In Nevin's statement that the "ministerial powers and functions had been communicated from the Apostles to the whole community of believers as well as to those of the special priesthood of those inwardly called and outwardly recognized" is a seed concept closely akin to, if not the

---

2. Nichols, *Romanticism in American Theology,* 267.

3. James L. Ainslie, *The Doctrine of Ministerial Order in the Reformed Churches of the Sixteenth and Seventeenth Centuries* (Edinburgh: T. & T. Clark, 1940), 218.

same as, that of Dr. Robert Paul, a present-day United Church theologian of the classical English Congregational background, who speaks of the continuity of the Apostolic Gospel — that Gospel communicated from our Lord to the Apostles and from them through the New Testament and the Church; Orthodox, Roman and Protestant. Again we can say that it is through the church and not from the church.

In this respect the fathers of Mercersburg stand us in good stead today as we relate to the ecumenical movement in the Roman Catholic, Anglican, Orthodox and Protestant denominations. In the Consultation on Church Union we can speak on the doctrine of the church and its ministry from a position which is catholic, reformed, evangelical and apostolic. The contribution of these Pennsylvania theological giants puts us squarely in an advance position in the ecumenical church.

This same tradition draws the vertical and horizontal axes together, thereby keeping us at work among the people of the world. Christianity means the renovation of the world; there is no sphere of natural life which may not be glorified. It is a demonstration of the catholicity of the church that it aspires to convert the totality of life. Specifically, Schaff considered four spheres: politics, intellectual life, art and the social and economic order. "The career, till the whole world shall appear, transfigured with its divine spirit, and states, and sciences and arts, with all their glory, shall fall down before the altar of the Most High in full, free worship. . . ."[4]

---

4. *The Principle of Protestantism as Related to the Present State of the Church* (1845), 135 and 137; also John Nevin, "Catholicism," *Mercersburg Review* (1851): 17.

The Order of Corpus Christi

On September 26, 1987, The Order of Corpus Christi of the United Church of Christ began with a Service of Word and Sacrament, including the induction of the core members of the Order, at the Trinity United Church of Christ in East Petersburg, Pennsylvania. The Order grew out of a deep concern for the Church, reflecting many similar concerns which the Mercersburg Movement addressed over a century ago.

The Order is made up of lay persons and clergy who:

- Believe that the one, holy, catholic and apostolic church to be the Body of Christ.
- Accept the purpose, intent, and concepts as set forth in "The COCU Consensus: In Quest of a Church of Christ Uniting" as well as the "Baptism, Eucharist and Ministry" document of the World Council of Churches.
- Believe that the Church is a creedal, confessional, liturgical, sacramental, and connectional body which expresses her faith through the Ecumenical Creeds: Apostles', Nicene and Athanasian.
- As part of the Order, live in communion with others in different Christian traditions that confess the same faith in different words. They seek to serve as a model of the contemporary expression of that Christian faith.
- Are nurtured and sustained through Word and Sacrament so that their lives may be lived intentionally in the Church and the world.

Membership is open to the laity, congregations and ordained clergy who hold standing and fulfill the requirements of membership in the United Church of Christ and its judicatories.

69. The Evangelical Church of the Union (EKU): *"Kirchengemeinschaft"*

(1981)

Frederick Herzog

German immigration to the United States during the nineteenth century included both Roman Catholics and Protestants. Among the Protestants there were many immigrants rooted in unionist traditions that had earlier brought Lutheran and Reformed Protestants together in Europe, and for this reason, congregations standing in the German Evangelical Synod tradition of the United Church of Christ have great affinity with unionist Protestants in Germany.

After World War II, seven unionist Landeskirchen (regional churches) in East and West Germany came together as the Evangelical Church of the Union (EKU), carrying on a theological tradition dating back to 1817 when a union of Protestant traditions in the Prussian territories had begun. Unfortunately, with the lowering of the "Iron Curtain" and the construction of the "Berlin Wall" it eventually became impossible for the EKU to meet as one church. Two regional synods were formed, one in the German Democratic Republic [East Germany] and one in the Federal Republic of Germany [West Germany]. During these difficult times, the United Church of Christ, with its long-standing relationship to the EKU throughout Germany, was able to maintain contact with pastors and laity in both countries, and provide a valuable "link" between the two synods.

In 1975 the EKU and the UCC participated in a consultation among "united churches" from all over the world that deepened their relationship. Soon thereafter a UCC/EKU Working Group (1976) was

---

Source: Frederick Herzog, an excerpt from "What Does Full Communion Mean?" A Corporate Briefing for the United Church Board for World Ministries. Undated, 12–15 [typescript].

created, supported by the United Church Board for World Ministries (UCBWM) and the office of the president of the UCC. The UCC/EKU relationship was further strengthened in June 1980 when representatives from the UCC and both regions of the EKU met together for a theological colloquy in Berlin.

In May and June 1980, EKU Synod meetings in East and West Germany took the initiative to vote "Kirchengemeinschaft" with the United Church of Christ. "Kirchengemeinschaft" is the sharing of full community, or full communion, between churches. While "full communion" acknowledges the historic relationship between the UCC and the German union churches, it was conceived as a promising opportunity for the UCC and the EKU to embrace the future as theological and spiritual companions, committed to ministry and public witness in service to the gospel mandates.

In 1981 the UCC General Synod accepted the gift offered to the UCC by its German "overseas partners" and passed the resolution, "Toward a Covenant in Mission and Faith" with the Evangelical Church of the Union (EKU) in the German Democratic Republic and in the Federal Republic of Germany. It gave thanks for the "ecumenical moment" and "new possibilities among the pathways of global Christian witness."

After General Synod, Frederick Herzog, a member of the UCC/EKU Working Group, met with the United Church Board for World Ministries (UCBWM) to explain in detail the meaning of "full communion." Frederick Herzog (1925–95) was an Evangelical and Reformed/UCC minister born in North Dakota, where his father was a pastor to German-speaking congregations of the Reformed tradition. Shortly before World War II, he accompanied his family back to Germany. The war broke out and there was no return. Herzog endured the deep trauma of the war and began theological studies at the "Theologische Hochschule" at Wuppertal, in the Rhineland. His studies continued with the theological faculty at Bonn University and at the University of Basel (Switzerland), where he studied with Karl Barth. He later completed doctoral work at Princeton University. Herzog was on the faculty at Mission House Theological Seminary in Plymouth, Wisconsin (1953–60), and the faculty at Duke Divinity School, Durham, North Carolina (1960–95).

Herzog explains that two aspects of ecumenical history came together to produce this "full communion" relationship. On the one hand there was the existing long-standing pattern of exchange and friendship between the EKU and the UCBWM going back to 1957. On the other hand there was new inspiration flowing from the global ecumenical movement, reminding "united churches" that it is customary for them "to maintain full communion with churches belonging to the same confession as the churches from which the united churches have been formed." Herzog also asserts that the churches were brought together by "God's call for Peace in East-West relations and for Justice in North-South conflicts." He states, "this does not involve a cheapening of Faith, but a deepening of Faith," pointing out that representatives from the EKU had seriously responded to the recent UCC theological statement, Toward the Task of Sound Teaching in the United Church of Christ *(see vol. 7:57).*

Furthermore, he says, this relationship is in keeping with the "Leuenberg Concord" (1973), whereby German churches in the Lutheran, and Reformed traditions affirm that differences between Lutheran and Reformed teachings do not constitute grounds for church division. On that basis Union, Lutheran, and Reformed churches in Germany began a process leading to the formation of a new Union of Evangelical Churches (UEK) in the early twenty-first century. This development is in keeping with the Formula of Agreement *signed by many Lutheran and Reformed churches in North America in 1997 (see vol. 7:110).*

Full Communion toward More Inclusive Union?

There are a few major orientation points that aid in grasping the beauty of the step taken. The Consultation in June, 1980, was able to draw also on materials developed for the EKU-Synods by the Ecumenical Commission(s) of the EKU. Three points can best explain the events that occurred at the two Synod meetings:

(a) "The EKU notes gratefully that there has been discovered, practiced, and grown between the EKU and the United Church of Christ (UCC) in 20 years of dialogue, mutual visits, and concerted theological work full communion as elaborated by the Ecumenical Commissions."

(b) "The EKU sees neither theological, nor legal grounds that would prevent full communion between the EKU and the UCC. It is ready to acknowledge Baptism, Holy Communion, and Ordination of the UCC."

(c) "Where churches follow the mission mandate in the Proclamation of the Gospel, Administration of the Sacrament, and the testimony of neighborly love in keeping with the Scriptures all conditions for full communion are extant."

The June, 1980, Consultation of representatives of the Ecumenical Commission(s) of both EKU Synods (some twenty people) and the UCC Working Group (eight members) in Berlin underscored these points as to the entire framework of ecumenical relations in which we stand:

> "The effort toward Full Communion between the EKU and the UCC is oriented in what the World Council of Churches formulated as elementary ecumenical conviction of its member churches. Each enactment of Full Communion can be only one step toward this goal."

We have to keep in mind that especially from the EKU perspective, but also in terms of UCC understandings, all our ecumenical relationships are built into the accountability framework of the ecumenical movement as a whole. Thus the United Churches claim in the 1975 Toronto Message (to which also the UCC subscribes): "The covenant we proposed is simply to serve the purpose of bearing witness together to God's call to unity within the ecumenical movement. They are to be uniting churches on the way to unity and therefore open to all efforts serving the ultimate goal." Acknowledgement of Full Communion on the part of the EKU seeks to serve this ultimate goal of more inclusive union. It is not an end in itself. It is "tending toward Full Communion of mutually accountable churches."

Global Villagers of All Persuasions Unite!

The more inclusive unity of the church is partly imposed on us because of the global village life we have entered. Many people sense that something new is happening to us on planet earth. We are beginning to live less and less "nationally," but more and more "globally." Full Communion thus also updates us to another context of the church. Not that we had not been pressed in that direction before. But in another thrust toward the global village we are led far beyond the U.S. or Germany.

So we are not being invaded by ecumenical Martians. Rather, we are being invited in view of the new global village context to be what we claim we already are as "uniting church" (*Constitution and Bylaws,* p. 33).

It is especially in regard to the global village context that the EKU invites us to be one church across the Atlantic, though not one organization — one ecclesia, though not one denomination.

The global village is not a homey place. In the time before the global village many Christians confessed God as Maker of heaven and earth. A few years ago we began worrying about the Waste Makers who destroy the earth. More recently we fret about the Baby Makers, the scientists who produce human life in the test tube. What kind of Absolute is going to shape human life in the global village? What is the quality of life going to be?

There is increasing need that human life see itself more fully in keeping with God's life — in moderation. Many issues came into play at this point in the June, 1980, Berlin Consultation of the Working Groups. Does the covenant notion redescribe the human being? What do the Sacraments contribute to the image of the human being? Does the doctrine of justification refocus the human being and offer a new understanding of the self? The most important questions arise in view of the world's poor and oppressed. Does God, in the face of the world's poor and oppressed and human beings pitted against each other in hunger and violence, reconstitute humanity?

What Full Communion is tending toward is a new commitment of the churches to the poor and oppressed. What our churches are longing for is a new departure. That pertains to the whole range of our American way of life, from A-Z, Abortion through Zen. But that will come only through a radical revamping of our life from Abortion through Zen, from Baby Makers through Waste Makers, in learning solidarity with marginals in the global village.

Sound Teaching

The more inclusive unity is primarily "imposed" on us because of Jesus Christ's mandate that we may all be one (John 17:21)—the motto of our denomination. It is here that God's teaching reaches into our lives with great force. It is a holistic thing. If God's teaching is relevant for us in one dimension of our lives (church unity), it is relevant in all other dimensions. In this regard, the Ecumenical Commissions of the EKU have been gripped by the UCC Seminar Report, *Toward the Task of Sound Teaching in the United Church of Christ* (a translation in the German has appeared in *Okumenische Rundschau* 28:3, July, 1979).

One can critique something adequately only if one deeply loves it. In the first of his 95 theses Martin Luther (and he is one of the roots the EKU and the UCC have in common) claimed that if our Lord Jesus Christ calls us to repentance he expects our entire life to be repentance. Is the UCC still able to be a repentant church? To be church is to be constantly open to renewal by the Word and the Spirit. Where readiness for transformation does not exist, Kierkegaard's dictum pertains: "Protestantism has become nothing but mediocrity from end to end." *Sound Teaching* is aiming at renewal through new accountability in teaching among church members and the congregations. We cannot proceed on the assumption that in the Christian faith anything goes.

What teachings do we hold each other accountable for? Full communion acknowledged by a sister church makes us take a hard look at what is happening to the biblical witness as norm of our church life. The United Church of Christ "looks to the Word of God in the Scriptures, and to the presence and power of the Holy Spirit, to prosper its creative and redemptive work in the world" (Constitution, p. 2).

Is our *public witness* still in keeping with the Word of God? We are all glad over our strong justice witness as a denomination, as is the case with the Wilmington Ten, for example. But next to it there is also a mixed bag that shows how we often do not draw a sharp enough line between civil religion and church. There is one of our UCC congregations the eighth Sunday after Pentecost this year of our Lord 1980 opening up Vacation Bible School with a medley of pledges: (a) To the American flag, "I pledge allegiance to the flag of the United States . . . " (b) to the Christian flag, "I pledge allegiance to the Christian flag and the Savior for whose kingdom it stands. . . . " (c) To the Bible, "I pledge allegiance to the Bible. . . . " All this as beginning of Divine Worship! We all love our country. However, the love of God distances us from all earthly things, including flags, to stand before God's truth alone. *Sound Teaching* suggests: "The church can be engaged with culture without being co-opted by culture as court chaplain of civil religion." Do we still clearly understand the difference between church and civil religion?

Is our *personal ethic* still in keeping with the Word of God? In our local church, Pilgrim United Church of Christ in Durham, our Sunday School Class studied the UCC *Human Sexuality* report January through May, 1978. We started so early we initially had to use a few copies of the original report to General Synod — the study wasn't even in print as yet. The class as a whole never rejected the effort wholesale. Yet several authors represented varied outlooks. So as to the pluralism of views, uncertainty or ambiguity was always present. The uneasiness of the class found expression in a final comment at our last meeting by a young sister who had struggled valiantly to find some clear teaching on the subject: "I have three young children growing up in this permissive society. Out there society makes marriage less and less meaningful. I come to church with my children to find values that will make them strong not to succumb to this type of thing. But the study seems to go along the same lines as society, at least in the major emphases." I am mentioning this local experience because the local church is "where it's at" in our denomination. Our small struggling group, unable to make further headway without a clear common teaching of the truth of God as to our personal ethic, is duplicated hundreds of times over in our denomination. We are groping.

Can we begin to develop teaching(s) for the global village in an increasing mutual accountability among our churches? *Sound Teaching* "seeks to initiate a *process* of engagement and exploration which might involve the whole church." The process is certainly not an end in itself, discussion for the sake of discussion, but an attempt to "engage the whole church in a new act of faithfulness."

We are becoming more conscious of how unconscionably our modern way of life contradicts the biblical witness. We mentioned two examples where the Word of God as norm does not come through loud and clear. The new act of faithfulness points to the new experience of God in the face of the poor. The EKU/UCC encounter is moving toward this new act of faithfulness sensitizing the local congregation to its mission in keeping with God's mission. God's Word clearly taught disenthralls us from our captivity to national chauvinism or private preoccupations. There is a world out there that needs our full attention. Struggling for justice and peace in facing the world's poor we forget ourselves and thus find ourselves as a people and as persons in new community. . . .

70. Apostasy:

"The Dayton Declaration"

(1991)

In September 1991 a small group of "evangelical churches and pastors within the UCC" wrote a document they called "The Beavercreek Bottom Line." Its four statements said (in summary): (1) we seek to glorify God by making and nurturing disciples of Jesus Christ; (2) national leaders of the UCC have "set themselves against that biblical mandate"; (3) seeking change through associations, conferences, and national UCC leadership does not work; and (4) the Biblical Witness Fellowship (BWF) should reorganize to accomplish the goal of renewal in the UCC (see vol. 7:63).

The Dayton Declaration (1991) identifies disagreements with the national leadership of the UCC and challenges the Biblical Witness Fellowship (BWF) to act. Representatives of the Executive Council and the BWF met several times, but there was no middle ground. National UCC leaders, seeking to be open to the diversity of the United Church of Christ, were personally attacked. Conservative evangelical UCC laity and clergy, who thought that the core of their faith was at stake, were unable to explore alternatives. In sadness some people became convinced that it was impossible to remain within the United Church of Christ, and they departed.

Source: "Dayton Declaration," 1991 [typescript in the UCC Archives].

Dayton Declaration

Preamble

When in the course of the history of the Church, it becomes necessary for faithful members of the Church of Jesus Christ to call to account the leaders of an organized church that calls itself Christian, respect for the opinions of Christians everywhere requires that they should declare what has caused them to issue this challenge. This declaration is issued in a spirit not of hostility, but of grief. It needs to be said and said clearly.

Presuppositions

> The Faith which unites us and to which we bear witness is that Faith in God which the scriptures of the Old and New Testaments set forth, which the ancient Church expressed in the ecumenical creeds, to which our spiritual fathers gave utterance in the evangelical confessions of the Reformation, and which we are duty bound to express in the words of our time as God Himself gives us light.

This paragraph *from Article II Faith — Basis of Union of the U.C.C., 1957* binds us to the revelation of Scripture as interpreted to us by the Holy Spirit of God. Those who disregard the clear words of Scripture have taken a stand against the basis of faith of the U.C.C. "To stand against" in Greek gives us the root word for apostasy.

The faithful in any church are inclined to suffer quietly occasional offenses against the faith and against their names as Christians that take the form of foolishness or irrelevance on the part of their leaders.

But when, over time, a pattern is established by which those who lead the church have led it into apostasy, then they fall under the condemnation of God spoken about by Jude and must be called to account by God's faithful people.

Jude, the brother of the Lord, speaks of these men and women when he writes:

> They are Godless men who change the grace of our Lord into a license for immorality and deny Jesus Christ, our only Sovereign and Lord. . . . These are the men who divide you, who follow mere natural instincts and do not have the Spirit.

Offenses

Against the teachings and traditions of the Apostles, the Reformers, the founders of our denominations, and the clear and plain teaching of Scripture, many leaders throughout the United Church of Christ have in recent years:

Altered the wording of Scripture in deference to cultural fads;

Advocated sexual practices that include adultery, fornication, homosexuality, bisexuality, and pornography;

> There are numerous citations over the years to document this offense. A Task Force on Human Sexuality made a report to GS 14 which included responses from "a select group of theologians, Biblical scholars and leaders" in the United Church of Christ. One of those responses was as follows:
>
> > "No sexual activity when motivated by love is ever wicked or sinful — all sexual love, whether in or out of marriage, with or without a partner, or with a partner of the same sex, is intrinsically good."
>
> More recently (summer 1991) President Paul Sherry held a "prayer vigil" and press conference at which he asserted the rights of all private, consensual, non-commercial sexual activity between adults.

Encouraged to the ordained pastorate those who practice these forms of sexuality, all of which are explicitly forbidden by Scripture;

> The General Synod in 1991 voted to "boldly affirm, celebrate and embrace the gifts for ministry of lesbian, gay, and bisexual persons" and called upon local churches, associations, and conferences "to facilitate the ordination and placement of qualified lesbian, gay, and bisexual candidates."

Advocated a return to the ancient pagan practices of abortion, infanticide, and euthanasia, explicitly denying the basic right to life;

> The General Synod meeting in 1991 overwhelmingly defeated the *Pronouncement in Defense of Human Life* which declared that "the basic right to human life" "deserves priority over every other competing human right." Two resolutions were passed: one condemning

the Supreme Court decision banning abortion counseling at federally funded clinics, and one reaffirming support for "women in their choices."

The 1991 General Synod adopted a resolution supporting the "rights of individuals, their designees, and their families to make decisions regarding human death and dying."

GS 14 was called upon to "deplore the practice of infanticide." Instead, the Synod called for "study" of "the ethical implications of our faith."

Abortion, infanticide, and euthanasia are cut of the same cloth. As our society has demonstrated since 1973, adoption of abortion logically leads to the other two.

Denied the Great Commission to make disciples of Jesus Christ and asserted that those outside Christ are not lost, thereby reducing the mission of the Church to social work without evangelism.

David Stowe, then executive Vice President of the United Church Board for World Ministries addressed the Annual Meeting of that body in November, 1978. He noted that "Contemporary theology has moved far away from simple affirmations of Christian monopoly." He spoke glowingly of a report from an "able and effective" missionary that reported the respect that local Christians had for the Muslims in their village. "Efforts to evangelize or proselytize Muslims have been carefully avoided. In the 28 years of the school's existence, not a single Muslim student or staff member was ever converted to Christianity, while associated with the school." What might well be a cry of despair is apparently reported with approval.

GS 10 minutes record the following declaration:

"We thus seek to work with all other people in the liberation of the entire world. We have as partners not only men and women of our kindred Christian denominations throughout the world, but also those of different faiths — Jewish, Moslem, Hindu, and others — who seek the same goal as we do: the creation of a community in which all people live in freedom from injustice, hunger and fear."

71. Toward the 21st Century:
"Attentive, Inclusive, Responsive, Supportive"

(1993)

When Paul H. Sherry was elected president of the United Church of Christ in 1989 he began a process challenging the UCC to come up with a clearer sense of its mission and identity. Groups were convened throughout the church and in 1993 the General Synod passed "Toward the 21st Century: A Statement of Commitment." The statement uses four words to summarize the calling of the United Church of Christ — attentive, inclusive, responsive, and supportive.

Source: "United Church of Christ: Toward the 21st Century: A Statement of Commitment," *GS Minutes 1993,* 28–29.

Toward the 21st Century: A Statement of Commitment

We, the United Church of Christ, look toward the 21st Century with anticipation. We trust God's promises. We are eager to respond to God's call. We believe that God does have more truth and light yet to break forth from God's holy word. Thanks be to God.

A Church Attentive to the Word

BY GOD'S GRACE, WE WILL BE AN ATTENTIVE CHURCH. WE COMMIT OURSELVES ANEW TO LISTEN FOR GOD'S WORD IN HOLY SCRIPTURE, IN OUR RICH HERITAGE, IN FAITHFUL WITNESS, AND IN THE FRESH WINDS OF THE HOLY SPIRIT SO THAT WE MIGHT DISCOVER GOD'S WAY FOR US.

We are claimed in baptism as children of God, disciples of Christ, and members of Christ's church. Through sustained Biblical and theological reflection on the challenges, confusions, injustices, mercies, and possibilities that confront us, we hope to discern baptism's claim so that we might be the faithful disciples these days require.

> We want to remember whose we are. Therefore, we will be faithful in worship and study, attentive to the Word and nurtured at the Table. We will be a people of prayer.
>
> We want to be faithful disciples. Therefore, we will relate our faith boldly to all of life's demands.
>
> We want all people to know of God's gracious activity on our behalf. Therefore, we will share God's Good News so that God's way may be revealed, God's forgiveness received, and God's future affirmed.

A Church Inclusive of All People

BY GOD'S GRACE, WE WILL BE AN INCLUSIVE CHURCH. WE COMMIT OURSELVES TO BE A CHURCH FOR ALL PEOPLE AND, IN CHRIST, WE CELEBRATE, AFFIRM, AND EMBRACE THE RICH DIVERSITY OF GOD'S GOOD CREATION.

We seek to be a fully inclusive community of faith, sharing bread and cup with all who see, in Christ, the way to our common future. We believe that God desires our oneness with all people, everywhere, and we long for the day when we may all be one.

We acknowledge that we are far less inclusive than we are called to be. Therefore, we will intentionally reach out into the world and lovingly invite all to Christ, and to participate fully in the ordering of our common life.

We acknowledge that we sometimes find it difficult to accept the gifts that others bring. Therefore, we will seek to be open to those gifts, affirm them, learn from them, and, at the leading of the Holy Spirit, be transformed by them.

We acknowledge that the world in which we live is far more diverse than we have hitherto imagined. We celebrate this rich diversity. Therefore, united in Christ, we will reach toward it in anticipation of God's reign.

A Church Responsive to God's Call

BY GOD'S GRACE, WE WILL BE A RESPONSIVE CHURCH. WE COMMIT OURSELVES TO BE A CHURCH OF JUSTICE AND MERCY AND PEACE SO THAT LIVES MAY BE RENEWED, SPIRITS REVIVED, AND WORLDS TRANSFORMED.

So many of God's people suffer. So many are maltreated. God's good earth cries out in pain. Our world needs those who will pursue justice, show mercy, and seek peace. That is the church we hear God calling us to be. We want "to join oppressed and troubled people in the struggle for liberation . . . and to work for justice, healing, and wholeness of life" (UCC Statement of Mission).

We envision a world wherein "justice will flow down like mighty waters." Therefore, we will stand alongside those who hurt so that the hungry may be fed, the excluded embraced, and the creation renewed.

We envision a world wherein mercy reigns. Therefore, we will heal the sick, encourage the weary, and support the dying.

We envision a world of peace for all people, everywhere. Therefore, we will be peacemakers so that hostilities and hatreds may cease and love, mercy and justice prevail.

A Church Supportive of One Another

BY GOD'S GRACE, WE WILL BE A SUPPORTIVE CHURCH. WE COMMIT OURSELVES TO STRENGTHEN CHRIST'S BODY THROUGH RENEWED RESOLVE AND MUTUAL SUPPORT IN OUR COMMON MINISTRIES.

In the immediate days ahead, our servant church will face days of challenge. We will need dedicated pastors and teachers. We will need vibrant congregations. Only a people who share a common vision, who support each other whatever the cost, and who are committed, together, to strengthen Christ's Church for ministry will be equal to the task. We want to be that church.

> We believe that a vital church is a covenantal church. Therefore, we will be supportive of each other and accountable to each other.
>
> We believe that a vital church is a sacrificial church. Therefore, we will give sacrificially of our resources so that Christ's Church may be strengthened and God's people served.
>
> We believe that a vital church is a "united and uniting church." Therefore, we will seek to embody the oneness of Christ's church through ecumenical commitment, witness and ministries in Christ's name.

THIS WE BELIEVE AND FOR THIS WE LIVE. AMEN.

72. RENEWAL:
Confessing Christ

(1993)

Growing out of the concerns of the Craigville Colloquy (see vol. 7:61) in 1993, on the theme "Theological Standards for Ministry in the United Church of Christ," a group of sixteen pastors and teachers responded to the General Synod document on UCC commitments for the twenty-first century (see vol. 7:71). They sent out a letter to many UCC clergy and laity declaring, "We are deeply concerned . . . that the commitment to 'listen for God's Word in Holy Scripture' and 'in our rich heritage' is often neglected in our Church. . . . Central to our Church is its Trinitarian faith in Jesus Christ as Lord and Savior. . . . To that end we invite you to join us in dialogue about the meaning and importance of this heritage for the United Church of Christ. . . . " In response four hundred UCC pastors and some laity gathered in three locales around the country and Confessing Christ was launched.

Within a year (Eastertide 1994) a duly constituted Confessing Christ Steering Committee set forth the purposes of the organization:

> *Confessing Christ is an invitation to the United Church of Christ to engage in joyous and serious theological work for the sake of its worship and devotion, its public witness and the mission entrusted to the Body of Christ in the world. It is a summons to the church to examine the contents of its preaching, the substance of its teaching, and the meaning of its discipleship in dialogue with the Scriptures, in conversation with its traditions, and in the face of the many and varied crucifixions of God in Christ that occur around us every day.*

SOURCE: "Letter from Organizing Committee of Confessing Christ," dated September 30, 1993 [typescript from Confessing Christ].

> *Confessing Christ takes to heart the Preamble to the Constitution of the United Church of Christ which affirms that central to our life together is our Trinitarian faith in Jesus Christ as Lord and Savior, grounded in the authority of Scripture and faithfully expressed in the ecumenical creeds, in the confessions and covenants of our Reformation traditions, and the responsibility of every generation to critically examine this rich theological heritage as we seek to make this faith our own.*

In the years that followed, Confessing Christ gatherings took place in eight regions around the country. The movement sponsored eighty consultations on theological and ethical subjects; produced a catechism, a newsletter, books, occasional papers, and a daily prayer discipline; and hosted an Internet Website with theological dialogue.

Confessing Christ

Dear Sisters and Brothers,

We believe that the future of our Church depends on faithfulness to the one Word of the triune God, Jesus Christ, which we are "to hear and which we have to trust and obey in life and in death" (Barmen Declaration, Art. 1).

We, the undersigned, welcome the action of the 1993 General Synod affirming the proposals contained in the document "Toward the Twenty-first Century: A Statement of Commitment." We too believe in a Church faithful to the Word, "inclusive of all people, responsible to God's call, and supportive of one another."

We are deeply concerned, however, that the commitment to "listen for God's Word in Holy Scripture" and "in our rich heritage" is often neglected in our Church. We view this indifference to Scripture and debilitating amnesia as a threat to the Gospel. Central to our Church is its trinitarian faith in Jesus Christ as Lord and Saviour, grounded in the authority of Scripture and faithfully expressed in the ecumenical creeds and in the confessions and covenants of our Reformation traditions, as well as in the theological standards of the Constitution, Statement of Faith, symbol, and the living witness of our Church.

We believe we here give voice to the concerns of the often-silent center of our Church and its living theological heritage. The time has come, we are convinced, for thoughtful, joyous and imaginative theological work that undergirds our defining commitments.

To that end, we invite you to join us in dialogue about the meaning and importance of this heritage for the United Church of Christ, the dangers present in its erosion, and its crucial place as we prepare to move into the next century. We propose an initial day-long meeting to discuss these matters and the possible establishment of centers of study, prayer, and practice in various parts of the country. We envision continuing conversation at these centers where we can *reaffirm* this faith, *reclaim* its biblical roots, *retrieve* its historic resources, and think together about the controverted questions within our Church and culture in the light of this reaffirmation.

Presently, we can welcome those who share our concerns and commitments to a 9:30 a.m. to 4:00 p.m. meeting in three regions:

Pennsylvania – November 29

New England – December 1

the Midwest – December 8

In the spirit of "mutual conversation and consolation" (Luther) we invite you to join us as we listen for the clear Word we need to hear among the Babel of voices, confessing together that the Word of God is not a feeling with which we can toy or an object we dare shape according to the "devices and desires of our own hearts," but that this Word is *truth, promise, and commandment.*

In this, as in all things, let us pray for the Church and its mission, and also for one another, that we may be faithful to our calling as servants of Christ and stewards of the mysteries of God entrusted to us in the United Church of Christ. "For no one can lay any foundation other than the one that has been laid; that foundation is Jesus Christ" (1 Cor. 3:11 NRSV).

Gilbert Bartholomew, Pastor
Richard Floyd, Pastor
Gabriel Fackre, Professor
Bennie Whiten, Conf. Min.
Deborah Rahn Clemens, Pastor
Willis Elliott, Professor
Herbert R. Davis, Pastor
Charles E. Hambrick-Stowe, Pastor
Frederick R. Trost, Conf. Min.
Reinhard Ulrich, Professor
F. Russell Mitman, Conf. Min.
W. Sterling Cary, Conf. Min.
Leslie Zeigler, Professor
Theodore L. Trost, III, Stud. Theol.
Browne Barr, Professor

73. Language:

"The Inclusive Language Covenant"

(1993)

The earliest action related to inclusive language in the United Church of Christ was a 1973 "Resolution on Inclusive Language." During the 1970s and 1980s the UCC produced a number of inclusive language resources (see vol. 7:31). Yet not all UCC members agreed with General Synod actions. The majority of church leaders and members affirmed that language should not exclude people, but they continued to debate about how to deal with language referring to and addressing God.

Some people insisted that God cannot be contained in human language and therefore variety is helpful. Others asserted that historical names for God cannot be changed without altering the meaning and even the content of the Christian faith. They were especially concerned about traditional trinitarian language.

In 1989 the General Synod adopted a conciliatory resolution on "Inclusive Language." It acknowledged that "the way in which inclusive language is sometimes employed or ignored in the Church gives birth to pain or a sense of loss among us." The resolution affirmed the importance of continuing the study of inclusive language.

In response, the Office for Church Life and Leadership (OCLL) prepared How Shall We Speak: A Study Guide *(1993). It was a forty-three page guide designed to help local churches give consideration to the use of language in five study sessions. Each sessions tries to help people identify language for God: that allows for faithful testimony to God's saving and renewing presence as known through the Bible, that honors*

Source: "Inclusive Language Covenant," from *How Shall We Speak: A Study Guide* (New York: Office for Church Life and Leadership, United Church of Christ, 1993), 43–44.

the traditions and historic witness of the church, and that respects the diversity of Christian experience. The last session invites people to join with others in a covenant to use inclusive language in ways appropriate for each congregation.

Inclusive Language Covenant

We Believe

1. We believe that the imagery conveyed by language and language itself is important and that they articulate and influence our understandings of what is revealed to us about the nature and activity of God and the dignity of all God's people as created in the image of God.
2. We believe that members of each generation of the church are called upon to make a relevant and faithful witness to the substance of faith and faithfulness as revealed to us in the primacy of scripture, the teaching tradition of the church, personal religious experience, and the contexts of living which shape and express questions of faith and faithfulness.
3. We believe some people have experienced the use of language and the images they convey as barriers to acknowledging that they are created in God's own image. These people need faithful and inviting language about God which welcomes them as full and complete children of God.
4. We believe that concerns expressed in relation to inclusive language present us with both challenge and opportunity to renewed faith and faithfulness in what we say, sing, and write as a part of a Christian witness we make in both church and society.

We Covenant

5. We covenant to use language that is expansive in communicating the nature and activity of God.
6. We covenant to use language in such a way that gender, race, ethnicity, age, physical ability, educational attainment, financial status, and national origin not become word barriers to persons in recognizing that they are created in the image of God and are included among the people of God.

7. We covenant to heed and respect each other as we forthrightly confront the difficulties associated with varieties of theological language, particularly the reality that language near and dear to some is experienced as excluding by others, and as we wrestle with formulations of belief which, like the trinitarian formula, are not easily expressed in ways that are immediately or readily viewed as faithful by all.

In Honoring This Covenant

8. We will seek to include male, female, and gender-neutral language and imagery for God, taking particular care to be expansive in the language and imagery chosen so that they do not inadvertently suggest that God is exclusively associated with one gender. (Examples: "God in God's wisdom" rather than "God in his wisdom"; "O God, who watches over us as a Father and nurtures us as a Mother" rather than "O God, who watches over us as a Father.")
9. We will seek to include language that helps to avoid male-only terms in pronouns and images of people. (Examples: "people" rather than "men"; "humankind" rather than "mankind"; "Give each person a Bible" rather than "Give each person his Bible"; "chairperson" or "chair" rather than "chairman"; "forebears" rather than "forefathers"; "when you become an adult" rather than "when you become a man.")
10. We will seek to include language and imagery that are not pejorative regarding the different physical conditions and abilities of persons. (Examples: "People may stand" rather than "All stand"; "Persons with leprosy" rather than "lepers.")
11. We will seek to include language that avoids referring to the gender, marital status, race, age, or physical ability of persons unless it is specifically relevant. (Examples: "the pastor" rather than "the woman pastor"; "John, a representative from First Church" rather than "John, a blind man from First Church"; "immigrant families" rather than "immigrants and their wives and children.")
12. We will seek to include language that does not lend itself to being understood as being pejorative of persons when referring to color. (Examples: "the presence of evil" rather than "the darkness of evil"; "washed clean" rather than "washed white"; "lies" rather than "white lies"; "discriminated against/excluded" rather than "blacklisted" or "blackballed.")
13. We will seek to use language that avoids stereotypes. (Examples: the color, race, ethnicity, or physicality of persons being associated with

social status; old people as being infirm, doddering, or no longer useful; young people as being rash or important only as the future; traits of nurturing or decisiveness being assigned by gender.)

14. We will seek and enter into a respectful dialogue that engages ourselves with others to find, to create, and to use worship and educational materials and programs which further our understandings and capabilities to use language and imagery in ways that are faithfully inclusive.

74. Listening:
"Attentive to the Word"

(1994)

Mary Sue Gast

Mary Sue Gast (b. 1945) is a UCC minister educated at Michigan State University and Chicago Theological Seminary. After serving in campus ministry in Iowa (1975–78) and as a pastor in several churches in Michigan (1978–89), she joined the Indiana-Kentucky Conference UCC staff (1986–91). In the 1990s she was executive director of the Coordinating Center for Women (CCW) (1991–97), and since 1997 she has been the conference minister of the Northern California Northern Nevada Conference UCC.

Gast's essay explores the idea that the church is called to be "attentive to the Word." It was part of a series of articles published in New Conversations *on "Toward the 21st Century: A Statement of Commitment" (1993) (see vol. 7:71).*

Source: Mary Sue Gast, excerpts from "Attentive to the Word: The Improbable Community," *New Conversations* (Summer 1994): 16, 21–23.

Attentive to the Word: The Improbable Community

"By God's grace, we will be an attentive church. We commit ourselves anew to listen for God's Word in Holy Scripture, in our rich heritage, in faithful witness, and in the fresh winds of the Holy Spirit so that we might discover God's way for us." [A Statement of Commitment]

Listen. Pay attention. Attend to the Word of God.

In Latin, *audire* is the root both for the word "listen" and for the word "obey." Dorothee Soelle acknowledges that linkage between "listen" and "obey" and concludes that for Christians obedience is a "fearless listening to God." We are thus alerted that listening for God's Word is not a passive process. Truly listening for God's Word presupposes an attitude of courage and a willingness to be moved into active obedience to that Word.

Listen, fearlessly.

Each of us probably hears a little differently. When you listen fearlessly, you may hear something different from what I hear. You and I may hear differently because of our differing economic situations or because of the diverse states of our households or because of the variations between the climates of our souls. You and I may hear differently because of our genders or because of our backgrounds or because of our sexual orientations. We may hear differently because of our mental or physical limitations or strengths. But we are all called to listen, fearlessly, trusting that our auditory processes are attuned to the magnificent complexity and wondrous simplicity of the vibrant Word of God.

The Word of God lives in the words of Scripture. The Word of God is Jesus of Nazareth, who acted God's thoughts and spoke God's heart and who is the Christ, the clear articulation of God's will and promise.

"On Christ the solid rock I stand, all other ground is sinking sand. . . . "

. . . Might we as a church, as the Body of Christ, as a community of love, at least extend to one another the benefit of the doubt as we attend to the Word and find that we employ different approaches and receive differing interpretations?

"The benefit of the doubt." I once had to explain that term to a ten-year-old. It was challenging. What I said was, that when someone does something that seems to be of doubtful value, and you don't really know what their motivations were, you can give the person the *benefit* of your not knowing by assuming that they intended to do something good — that they had a good reason for what they did. Usually you give the benefit of the doubt to someone you respect, or trust, or love.

As a church might we, in the spirit of 1 Corinthians 12:3, trust that those who have declared themselves to be followers of Jesus Christ are, indeed, seeking to be followers of Jesus Christ? Even if one's attitude reflects that of Torquemada during the Spanish Inquisition — "When you are right you have the absolute duty to inflict your beliefs on others" — one might offer to others the benefit of the doubt.

In seeking to be a church attentive to the Word, can we volley the benefit of the doubt back and forth between our two genders? Across the grand canyons of our ethnic distinctivenesses? Bridging the gulfs among our theological differences? Traversing the varieties of our sexual orientations? Recognizing that granting the benefit of the doubt has a unique flavor depending upon whether you are extending that benefit from an empowered position or from a position of oppression? Acknowledging that you always display vulnerability when you offer someone the benefit of the doubt, and that battle lines become blurred? Affirming in the act of extending the benefit of the doubt that the mindset we ourselves find the most natural course, the tradition which most faithfully mediates the Word to me, is not necessarily the only course that is possible or faithful or in line with our calling to be Christians?

"This is my commandment," Jesus said, "that you love one another as I have loved you" [John 15:12]. I find it comforting to note that the people who followed Jesus then, like the people who follow Jesus now, had hardly been hand-picked with an eye toward making it easy for them to love one another. Those early disciples numbered among them stolid fishermen and upwardly-mobile types with Greek names; a revolutionary working to free Israel from Roman oppression as well as a collaborator with Rome; a woman who behaved like a scholar and a woman who took responsibility for the traditionally assigned household tasks. There were two pairs of brothers and one pair of sisters, whose presence would further complicate group life with their little in-jokes and sibling rivalries. Each person came equipped with their own prejudices and agendas. These were the folk who were told to love one another. They hadn't even chosen to be part of a group. All they had signed up to do was follow Jesus. As individuals. And there they were, stuck with one another. Just like us.

"You did not choose me, but I chose you," Jesus says [John 15:16]. And you and you and you. The people who think and act just like you, and the people with the cockeyed ideas. The polite and the crude. The polished and the jangling. And just maybe we can move from being stuck with one another to sticking with each other, to being stuck on each other, right here in the beloved community of the United Church of Christ, right now in the days advancing toward the twenty-first century.

There is a scene at the end of the film *Places in the Heart* that baffled many movie reviewers. You might remember this saga, starring Sally Field as the undauntable farm woman who, with one farmhand, was able to survive poverty, natural disasters, and social scorn. Anyway, the story seems to end and then the scene shifts to the interior of the rural church building. People are sitting in pews and singing hymns. A communion service is going on. It seems peaceful and predictable until, with a start, you notice that some of the congregation are people who died early in the movie; there are avowed enemies sitting next to one another, serving one another; poor people and rich; black, brown, and white people; power brokers and outcasts — all are gathered together. "The film is great, but what is that ending all about?" one critic wrote in bewilderment.

"I'm an insurance agent and I know what it means," muttered a member of my congregation who was reading the review in the newspaper before a church breakfast began. "Well, sure," said the youth who had passed the newspaper on to the insurance agent, "but you go to church."

You go to church. You know what it means to be an improbable community, connected in life and beyond death. You know about the welcome table.

If you are attentive to the Word, you come to know these things. They may not be what you were seeking when you first turned to the Word, but the Word, like any of the winds of the Holy Spirit, often messes up well-ordered lives and presuppositions.

Attending to the Word that all God created was good, that Jesus labored to bring God close to all people, that in the Body of Christ there is no alien sorrow, no foreign joy, we flow into being "a church inclusive of all people," "a church responsive to God's call" to "justice and mercy and peace," "a church supportive of one another" ("Toward the 21st Century: A Statement of Commitment").

Hearing the music of the Word, we begin the dance. Attending to the Word, we hear the harmonies that move us to dance into the widening circle of multiple cultures and many heritages, linking ourselves to work for justice, healing, and wholeness of life, weaving ourselves into a fabric of mutual support. Attending to the Word, we hum, strum, sing, or play the tune that has settled in our ears so that it is clear that the patterns of our movements reflect the rhythms of our convictions. *On Christ the solid rock we'll stand, Word incarnate, Word among us.*

75. Preaching:

"The Dangers of Self-Righteousness"

(1999)

William Sloan Coffin

William Sloan Coffin Jr. (b. 1924) is a Presbyterian/UCC minister who was educated at Yale University, Union Theological Seminary, and Yale Divinity School. After working for the Central Intelligence Agency (CIA) (1950–53), he went back to school and then served as campus chaplain at Andover Phillips Academy (1956–57), Williams College (1957–58), and Yale University (1958–76). Coffin is best known for his work in the civil rights movement, his involvement in draft resistance and anti-Vietnam protests, and his outspoken support for gays and antinuclear activism. As the senior minister at Riverside Church in New York City (1977–87) and president of the antinuclear advocacy group SANE/Freeze (1987–90) his sermons, speeches, and writings are widely quoted and his progressive opinions lauded by many. His sermon "The Dangers of Self-Righteousness" was preached at the First Congregational Church UCC in Berkeley, California. It appears in a slightly different version in his book, The Heart Is a Little to the Left: Essays on Public Morality *(1999).*

Source: William Sloan Coffin, "The Dangers of Self-Righteousness," a sermon preached at First Congregational United Church of Christ, Berkeley, California, February 14, 1999.

The Dangers of Self-Righteousness

The New Testament lesson is a well-known parable: "Two men went up to the temple to pray, one a Pharisee and the other a Tax Collector. The Pharisee standing by himself was praying thus, 'God, I thank you I am not as other people are, thieves, rogues, adulterers, or even like this tax collector. I fast twice a week; I give a tenth of all my income.' But the tax collector, standing far off, would not even look up to heaven, but was beating his breast and saying, 'God be merciful to me, a sinner!' I tell you, this man went down to his house justified, rather than the other. For all who exalt themselves will be humbled, and all who humble themselves will be exalted."

Just as "I'm Dreaming of a White Christmas" aspires to the status of a Christmas Carol, so Cupid, an infant in diapers, blindfolded to boot, clamors for recognition in the church.

President's Day is something else again. I've long thought that Abraham Lincoln was the President closest to the spiritual center of American history. And this year we celebrate the 200th Anniversary of the death of George Washington; he was 67 years old when he died in 1799. President's Day raises a lot of questions worth pondering in a church. Can you be a Christian patriot — or is that a contradiction in terms? What is the relationship of the flag to the cross? What, to the sole remaining super-power of the world, constitutes the greatest spiritual danger?

I think that self-righteousness is the bane of all human relations. And the point, of course, is made in the classic example of self-righteousness in the parable phrase "I thank thee Lord, that I am not as others are." We've seen a lot of that kind of self-righteousness in Washington in the course of this last year. After the tawdry White House affair was revealed, a Senator said, "I feel as if I've shrunk an inch." Well, what made him think he was an inch taller in the first place? It's not that he, Clinton, isn't a sinner, it's only that it takes one to catch one.

But self-righteousness is not only the bane of individual relations, it's also the bane of international relations. Here are fine words of an historian, Herbert Butterfield: "In the kind of world I see in history, there is one sin that locks people up in all their other sins, and fastens people and nations more tightly than ever in their predicaments, namely, the sin of self-righteousness."

Nations are really prone to smugness. All of them. For example, the French have long been inordinately proud of what they call their *mission civilizatrice,* their civilizing mission — often accompanied by the French Foreign Legion. The Swiss are quite proud of their neutrality, and not averse to the money it has brought them. There was a time when the Germans considered themselves *Bermenschen,* supermen. And the ages which the Chinese and Indian civilizations boast make many of their inhabitants feel that they have cornered the world market on human wisdom. As for the British, well:

> "In the beginning, by some mistake
> Men were foreigners all created,
> 'Til heaven conceived a nobler plan
> And there was born an Englishman.
> Conceive the difference if you can,
> had Adam been an Englishman."

But these days, we Americans are the ones who've got it bad. Time and again as the sole remaining super power, our pride-swollen faces close up our eyes. Again and again we are reminded of Ezekiel's lament over Tyre: "Your heart was proud because of your beauty; you corrupted your wisdom for the sake of your splendor."

So on this solemn patriotic holiday, let us do a little soul-searching about our own national self-righteousness. And let's start by recognizing that it has a long legacy, probably going all the way back to 1630 when, on board the Arabella, John Winthrop said in a now famous sermon, "We shall be as a city set upon a hill."

As a moral aspiration, that statement from the Sermon on the Mount was both beautiful and appropriate. But when you stop to think of it, it was fraught with dangerous implications. For "We shall be as a city set upon a hill" implied that others would look up to us, and perhaps with a gaze so admiring that eventually the world would be largely populated by frustrated potential Americans. That this has been, for many years, our view of ourselves and the world, is borne out, I think, by testimony I would like to bring you from five outstanding Americans.

In the middle of the 19th Century, Herman Melville wrote, not in *Moby Dick* which most of you are probably still trying to finish, but in a book entitled *Yellow Jacket*, "Long enough have we Americans been skeptics as regards ourselves, and doubted whether the political messiah had come. But he has come — in us — if we would but give utterance to his promptings." So, arguably, the greatest American novelist.

Fifty years later at the turn of the century, Albert J. Beveridge informed his senatorial colleagues in Washington: "God has marked the United States to lead in the redemption of the world. This is the divine mission of America."

During the war in Vietnam, when tossing his hat into the presidential ring, Bobby Kennedy said: "At stake is not only the leadership of a party or the leadership of a country — at stake is our claim to the moral leadership of the world." Aides, reading the speech ahead of time, begged him to take out that sentence, the very kind of sentiment that led us into the war in the first place. But their pleadings went in vain.

In 1984, in the course of his second inaugural address, President Reagan said: "Peace is our highest aspiration. And our record is clear. Americans resort to force only when they must. We have never been aggressors."

Well, I remember the cameras panned out at that moment over the House of Representatives, and I thought some Supreme Court Justice might roll his eyes — maybe some Senator might cough into his fist — Not at all. It was as if everybody had heard the gospel. But that sentiment would certainly come as news to Native Americans, to African Americans, Nicaraguans (where our Marines have landed 14 times in their history), to Filipinos, Cubans, not to mention Vietnamese and Cambodians; and, I dare say, it would have come as news to Teddy Roosevelt had he been leaning over the balconies of heaven the better to hear President Reagan's second Inaugural.

And finally, on the *Today Show,* Secretary of State Madeleine Albright recently declared: "If we have to use force, it is because we are America. We are the indispensable nation. We stand tall. We see further into the future." Well, that statement reminded me of some Frenchman who once said, "Ma patrie, se léve; je la prèfere assise" (My country is standing tall; I prefer it seated).

The testimony of these five outstanding Americans reminds us on President's Day that the best patriots are not uncritical lovers of their countries. "My country, right or wrong." That's like saying, "my Grandmother, drunk or sober" — it doesn't advance anything. Nor are the good patriots the loveless critics of their country. Better that they emigrate to some other place if they don't love their country. I would suggest that the best patriots — and I would say Christian Patriots can fall into this category — are those who carry on a lover's quarrel with their country, a reflection of God's eternal lover's quarrel with the entire world. It's perfectly possible both to love your country and feel compelled to stand against it.

No nation is well served by delusions of its righteousness. Every nation makes decisions based on self-interest and then defends them in the name of morality. St. Augustine warned: "Never fight evil as if it were something that arose totally outside of yourself," reflecting St. Paul's famous words, "All have sinned and fallen short." Of course, we would prefer to say, "Some have sinned and fallen short," for instance "that evil empire over there," as President Reagan used to talk about the Soviet Union; or as we talk about it these days, some have sinned and fallen. Today those who have sinned are North Korea, Libya, Iraq, Iran, and Cuba — the so-called "rogue nations." But St. Paul doesn't say *some* have sinned and fallen short, he insists that *all* have sinned and fallen short, which means if we are not one in love with all nations of the world, at least we are one in sin, which is no mean bond, because it precludes the possibility of separation through judgment. That's the meaning of the scriptural injunction "Judge not, that ye be not judged."

Today, on this President's Day weekend, let us recall that our Declaration of Independence calls for "a decent respect to the opinions of mankind" (humankind we would say today). This is something we're not showing — not when we alone with, of course, Israel maintain an embargo on Cuba.

The embargo is not toppling the dictator, it's just inflicting hardships on the people — the first victims of the dictator. We're not paying much attention to the opinions of other people when we won't even discuss the possibility of changing the sanctions in Iraq, which again, far from toppling the hated dictator, represent a form of institutionalized child abuse.

The ancient Roman Tacitus defined patriotism as entering into praiseworthy competition with our ancestors.

Why not compete with Moses and Joshua, with Washington and Jefferson? As they declared their independence — the first two from Egypt, the second two from England — why not declare our interdependence with all peoples of this world? Why isn't this a good time for Christians to remind ourselves of that great prophetic insight, that we all belong one to another, every one of us five billion odd people in this planet; that's the way God made us; Christ died to keep us that way. Our sin is only and always that we put asunder what God has joined together.

Why isn't this the moment, in our public schools for instance, at least on Fridays, after the Pledge of Allegiance to the flag? Why not ask all kids to stand up and say, "I pledge allegiance to the earth and to the flora and fauna and human life that it supports. One planet indivisible, with clean air, soil and water, economic justice, freedom and peace for all."

The United States does not have to lead the human race. It has to join it. And then, with greater humility, we can play a wiser leadership role.

I said at the outset that self-righteousness was the bane of both interpersonal and international relations. I hope you agree that individuals and nations are at their worst when, persuaded of their superior virtue, they crusade against the vices of others.

We've seen that for a year domestically. And we continue to see it on the world scene. Individuals and nations are at their best when they realize that salvation does not lie in being sinless, but rather in recognizing gratefully that there is more mercy in God than sin in us. And let Christians this weekend remind themselves of that great line of the Psalms,

"Not unto us, O Lord,
Not unto us,
But unto Thy name
Be the Glory." Amen.

Reaching Out in Mission

76. The Faith We Proclaim: *"The Mission and Message . . . "*

(1960)

Elmer J. F. Arndt

Elmer J. F. Arndt (1908–69) was an Evangelical and Reformed/UCC minister educated at Tulane University, Eden Theological Seminary, Washington University, Union Theological Seminary in New York, and Yale University. Arndt taught at Eden Theological Seminary for forty years (1929–69).

In the late 1950s, as the union of the Evangelical and Reformed Church and the Congregational Christian Churches was finally consummated, both denominations became more self-conscious about their theology. A small study book, The Faith We Proclaim: The Doctrinal Viewpoint Generally Prevailing in the Evangelical and Reformed Church *(1960), was published three years after the formation of the United Church of Christ. It was, as the title page suggests, written by "Elmer J. F. Arndt under the guidance and with the counsel of the [E and R] Theological Committee." The book affirms a deeply held view of the Evangelical and Reformed Church that the Church is called to witness to God's mighty acts (and not its own) and that faith is born in response to what God has done. But this is not an E and R book. UCC members from the Congregational Christian tradition agreed with its basic doctrines. Soon thereafter Arndt became chair of the first United Church of Christ Theological Commission.*

Arndt's description of the "mission and message of the church" summarizes the foundational theology of the United Church of Christ.

Source: Elmer J. F. Arndt, "The Mission and Message of the Church," in *The Faith We Proclaim* (Philadelphia: The Christian Education Press, 1960), 8–13.

Christians believe that God has acted in Jesus reconciling the world. In response the church is called to a mission of reconciliation.

The Mission and Message of the Church

The heart of the Christian faith is contained in the words of the apostle Paul: "God was in Christ reconciling the world to himself, not counting their trespasses against them, and entrusting to us the message of reconciliation" (2 Cor. 5:19). Reconciliation is God's gracious act in Jesus Christ by which men are brought into right relation to himself. That act has decisive importance for humanity; and the message of it is the gospel, the "good news."

The Christian church exists because God has acted to restore us, his conflict-ridden creatures, to fellowship with himself; and because he brings forth a new people in whom the hostility of man to man is overcome. This fellowship we call the church, made up of the people who are entrusted with the ministry of reconciliation, just because they have received God's reconciliation. The church carries out its mission in the knowledge that the same God who acted in Christ continues to act in the proclamation of the message.

The church's mission is to direct men to God, the Father of our Lord Jesus Christ. It truly serves men and women by keeping before them God's redemptive act. Through the fellowship offered to the lonely, it points to God, the Father, who takes us into his family. Through its declaration of hope, it directs the despairing to God, whose conquest of evil through Jesus Christ gives hope to men. Through trustful reliance on God, it reminds the anxious of God's providence. Through its trust in the divine mercy and forgiveness, it leads the guilt-ridden to God's mercy seat where forgiveness is found. By its ministry to the needs of men, it testifies to God's love. By holding before men and society the demand for justice and peace, it testifies to the reality and sovereignty of God's order. The church cannot be itself unless it ministers to the world. And it cannot be true to its ministry unless it serves God in the service of men.

The Witness to God's Mighty Acts

The church can be truly described as the community which testifies to God's deeds. It is the witnessing community, which is under obligation to give its testimony before men. Its testimony is to the whole range of God's mighty acts from his creation of "all things visible and invisible" to the climactic act of his renewal of man through Jesus Christ. It proclaims that God has made himself known to us, fulfilling in Jesus Christ his saving purpose declared through his prophets; that in the self-sacrificial love of Jesus Christ, God has declared his holy love; that he gives to us his Spirit and eternal life.

The church testifies to many acts of God; but its witness is that God's act in Jesus Christ is of decisive significance. The conviction of the Christian is that God has come to us in holy love and creative power in Jesus Christ. The church proclaims what it has found and continues to find true: In Christ, God himself comes to us, meets us, brings us into fellowship with himself and gives us a share in the goodness and power of his divine life. Christ is the fulfillment of God's saving purpose. He fulfills the knowledge of God, for the knowledge of God he gives is the knowledge of communion; and because that is so, the knowledge of God we have received through Jesus Christ is the standard by which all knowledge of God is tested. Because Christians have received fellowship with God through Christ, they are convinced that God invites us into fellowship with himself through Christ's invitation.

The witness to God's acts does not end with the divine deed in the earthly ministry, crucifixion, and resurrection of Jesus Christ. It continues with the testimony concerning what God now does within man. God's sending of Jesus has its sequel in his gift of the Spirit, who works within man to awaken faith, to renew his life, to liberate him for a life of responsible freedom, to guide him into truth, to strengthen him in goodness, and to unite him to the fellowship of faithful people.

Thus the Christian testimony takes the form of a recital of God's acts, all of them bearing upon his saving purpose, disclosing his mercy and judgment, his power and his goodness. The crown of all his acts is his coming to us in Jesus Christ who brings us with him into God's own presence, through whom we receive sonship, the Spirit, and eternal life. And to what he has done and is doing, the recital adds what he will do: he will complete the new creation he has already begun. That expectation is the Christian hope which sustains faithful people in bearing the conflicts and tragedies of life in history.

Faith: The Response to God's Acts

God, to whose mighty acts the church testifies, is active; he is, in biblical phrase, the "living God." His acts are themselves the evidence that he "is working still" (John 5:17). Thus God is neither passive nor is he so remote from us that he does not take an active part in the course of man's life.

He, who creates, renews, judges and saves, takes the initiative in disclosing himself to us. God is not one who waits passively for man the seeker to discover him. Rather he actively seeks out man in order to disclose himself. He takes the initiative in engaging us in dialogue, in offering himself for our communion, and in giving us knowledge of himself.

Thus our knowledge of God, as the Christian community teaches, is based upon God's own activity of revealing himself. He is the God who discloses himself; our knowing him is our response to his act of making himself known. Whatever importance may be assigned to the role of religious genius or insight and to reflective thought or wisdom, the crucial matter is the primacy of God's act in making himself known.

Faith, understood as trust in God, is our personal response to God's disclosure of himself. The faith of the Christian church, understood as the beliefs held about God, has its source in God's self-revelation. Faith is confidence, not in the knowledge we have gained, but in God who has come to us. The faith we hold is not the statement of our discoveries; rather it is the account of him who finds us even when we hide from him.

God reveals himself, and he who makes himself known to us is he whom we are seeking. He finds us and, when we know we are found, we know that our search is ended in a fulfillment immeasurably greater than our highest expectations.

Thus the Christian gospel is proclaimed as the good news of God's reconciling act bringing us into communion with him. It is not the report of human insight or wisdom. Indeed, if by "religion" is meant man's search for God, then the Christian gospel is not a religion but rather the end of all religion. For the heart of the gospel is that God comes to man to redeem and to renew him.

But such a sharp antithesis between man's search for God and God's search for man, as if the two were mutually exclusive, contains error as well as truth. The search for God is itself in some measure a response to God's seeking for man, God, who prompts man to seek him, is he who revealed the fullness of his grace in Jesus Christ.

God takes the initiative in giving us knowledge of himself. He is not passive, merely waiting to be found, but active in disclosing himself. Because he knows us, we know him. Our knowledge of him is not our discovery but rather the gift of his self-disclosure. Thus our knowledge of God differs in kind from our knowledge of nature gained through the use of scientific method. In seeking knowledge of nature, we, the investigators, are active and nature is passive. We rightly speak of discovering truths about nature; we do not speak of nature's "revealing" itself to us.

Although knowledge of God is different in kind from the knowledge we gain by scientific method, the church has no quarrel with science. On the contrary, the church is concerned to promote and to undergird science. Moreover, it is not true, as some honestly believe, that commitment to the Christian faith is a hindrance to scientific investigation. Rather, to hold that Christ is the principle of unity of all things provides a far more adequate basis for objectivity than does non-commitment.

The church does take issue, however, with those who deny the possibility of revelation and the validity of any knowledge of God whatsoever. Science makes no such denial, though some have wrongly thought that science either required or supported denial of the possibility and validity of any knowledge of God. Clearly such denial attacks the very foundations of Christianity. For divine revelation is the basis of the Christian faith.

Revelation at its highest and best was given in Jesus Christ. It was given in an historical person, born in the reign of Caesar Augustus and crucified under Pontius Pilate. Christians, consequently, are intensely interested in the historical Jesus: his times, his teachings, his actions and, preeminently, his person. Our vital concern does not, of course, end with knowledge about Jesus. Our goal, in the words of Paul, is, "that I may know him and the power of his resurrection, and may share his sufferings, become like him in his death, that if possible I may attain the resurrection from the dead" (Phil. 3:10–11).

77. Convictions and Actions: *"Before the Mercy Seat" and "Searching for the Centerline"*

(1977, 1984)

Joseph H. Evans, Roger L. Shinn

Joseph H. Evans (b. 1915) is a Congregational Christian/UCC minister educated at Western Michigan University (Kalamazoo) and Yale Divinity School. He was a pastor at two churches in New York City (1942–46), a short-term executive for the Connecticut Council of Churches (1946), and a pastor in Ohio and Illinois (1946–67). In 1967 he was elected secretary of the UCC, becoming the first African American to hold a nationally elected office (see vol. 7:21 for background). When the president of the UCC, Robert V. Moss, died in office in 1976, Evans was asked to finish out Moss's term. After Avery Post was elected president in 1977 Evans returned to the office of the secretary until 1983. Evans's sermon to the 1977 General Synod recalls the covenants of the Hebrew people and the Congregational tradition of local church covenants. He reminds the church that the covenant of the church is a covenant of the Spirit grounded in a Divine call that the church become "a missionary instrument in the hand of God."

Roger L. Shinn (b. 1917) is an Evangelical and Reformed/UCC minister educated at Heidelberg College, Union Theological Seminary in New York City, and Columbia University. After completing his doctoral studies he taught for a time at Vanderbilt University and was on the faculty at

---

Sources: Joseph H. Evans, an excerpt from "Before the Mercy Seat," *GS Minutes 1977,* 123–24. Roger L. Shinn, excerpts from "Searching the UCC Theological Centerline: An Address at the meeting of United Church of Christ Executives, Orlando, Florida, February 12, 1984," 6–8, 11–12 [typescript in the UCC Archives].

Union Theological Seminary in New York City (1959–85). Shinn played a key role in the creation of the UCC Statement of Faith (1959) and in the development of the UCC Curriculum (1964).

In 1984, as the UCC reflected about its first twenty-five years of history, Shinn was asked to address the annual winter meeting of UCC Executives on the topic "Searching the UCC Centerline." His presentation is personal, not scholarly, outlining aspects of contemporary culture and current religious life before asking if the UCC has any recognizable theological identity. He shares thoughts about the importance of the UCC Statement of Faith (1959) (see vol. 7:3), controversies over the UCC Curriculum (1964) (see vol. 7:47), and concerns about inclusive language in the 1970s and 1980s (see vol. 7:31 and 73). In the end he finds "a few tendencies toward a consensual center."

Before the Mercy Seat

We who depend so much upon covenants must always keep in mind how easily covenants can be debased and broken when one or the other party puts self above commonality. But more importantly, I want to remind you of the great new element that binds our covenants that is not present in the covenants of Israel, in the Old Testament times or even today. Our covenants are not based solely on obedience of a people to God, renewed year by year by an act of atonement. They grow out of a glorious new relationship with God, based upon personal confrontation and personal responsibility.

On a certain Friday, God — not the inaccessible God of the tabernacle, but God in the human presence of Jesus Christ — hung on a cross to establish that new relationship.

"At midday a darkness fell over the whole land, which lasted till three in the afternoon; and at three Jesus cried aloud, 'My God, my God, why have you forsaken me?' . . . Then Jesus gave a loud cry and died. *And the curtain of the temple was torn in two from top to bottom.*"

The inaccessible God of the Old Testament is gone. Each of us now has the privilege as well as the responsibility of standing before the mercy seat, of communing directly with *"She who wipes out."* But we have something even greater. In the life and death and resurrection of Jesus Christ who has promised us forgiveness, even before we begin our confessions. This is our new hope in Jesus Christ, which transcends all memories. And, as Paul says, "Because we have this hope, we are very bold."

This boldness should lead us into new covenants, "not of the written law," as Paul says, "but of the Spirit." This boldness should make us dedicate the United Church of Christ to being a missionary instrument in the hand of God to bring about a commonwealth of love and justice in the world. This boldness will compel each of us to understand that in the immediate future our task theologically will be the sorting out of the death and birth of idols and the evolution of our images of God — a God of empowerment; a God to whom faithfulness demands risk and commitment to global interdependence; a God that is neither male nor female, neither Black, White, Blue or Green; that to recognize and know such a God will for many be traumatic and in the process this God will in all probability keep us out of step with our times. As an in-between people we will continually be called back to the best of the past, and at the same time we will constantly be forced out in front of the times.

Searching for the Centerline

In this kaleidoscopic setting, does the United Church of Christ have a theological identity? Does it represent anything recognizable? Again, I remind you, I am asking about the theology of the church, not of the career theologians.

We start with the fact that Protestantism is so acculturated on the American scene as to have no sharp identity. It is no longer the unofficial civil religion that it once was in some regions, but it is a pretty general part of the landscape. An interesting and disturbing example is an analysis of votes in the House of Representatives on the resolution asking for a nuclear freeze. Supporting the freeze were 82.7% of the Jews, 78.7% of the Catholics, and 57% of the Protestants. (The data are from Albert J. Menendez, research director for Americans United for Separation of Church and State, as reported by Jim Castelli, *The Bishops and the Bomb* [Garden City, N.Y.: Doubleday, 1983], 178). On the basis of statements by church bodies and their leaders, we might have expected far stronger Protestant support. I do not imply that congressional representatives should take orders from their churches, but I suggest that their religious insights might have some influence on their political judgments. The evidence in this case points to a low Protestant identification.

Is the UCC different? I do not know whether there was any pattern in the voting of its members in Congress. I do not know what to make of the recent study of Minnesota Christians, reporting that UCC members "are the most apt to experience God as a distant deity who plays a minor role in their daily work." (Kenneth L. Woodward in *Newsweek* [September 19, 1983], 82, reporting on a study from the Institute for Ecumenical and Cultural Research in Collegeville, Minn.) Perhaps some of you can tell me that the study is mistaken. Or maybe you will tell me that our Minnesotans are different from the rest.

Are we an exceedingly diverse but generally acculturated denomination? Is there for us no "theological center"? Or are we like two mountains, one representing the leadership and the staff, the other representing the United Church People for Biblical Witness, both emerging from a populist plateau, with the "center line" a valley between the peaks? I think not. But an unfriendly critic might try to make a case that the UCC is not theologically serious, that its theology is a series of ad hoc opinions usually added on to some practical concern.

I remember the occasion when an executive of the National Council of Churches (not a member of the UCC) told me on the phone of a just completed committee report on a social issue, then suggested that I might write a theological foundation for it. I said that I did not know much about putting foundations under houses that were already built. Do we in the UCC improvise theologies to justify positions already taken for other reasons?

Let me for a minute or two impersonate an unfriendly critic who might point to examples of ad hoc theological statements.

Item: GS 14 (1983) asked UCC bodies to use "only authorized translations of the Bible" as scripture lessons — an action widely interpreted as a rejection of the new lectionary coming from a committee of the NCC. (Here I interrupt the critic to report that I told my own faculty that, given the polity of the UCC, I did not feel bound by the action of the Synod. But let the critic continue.) A few months later the Stewardship Council mailed clergy copies of the lectionary with a recommendation for its "trial use and response." Are these two conflicting ad hoc signals?

Item: The UCC finds it easier to speak to the government on abortion policies than to speak to its own community of faith. And there are signs of an individualistic doctrine of human nature in the stands on abortion, as contrasted to the social doctrine of human nature in most stands on public issues. Is there a commonly shared position, or are ad hoc positions invoked for convenience?

Item: In its concern for peace did the UCC invoke an ad hoc theology, close to Orwell's Newspeak, in using the term "peace church" — a term representing the honorable tradition of Quakers and Mennonites, but hardly of the Lutheran and Calvinist traditions? The problem was recognized in the shift of terminology to "a peacemaking church." But is there any theological clarity in UCC positions on military conflict as represented in attitudes toward nuclear war and revolutions against tyrannies?

The critic might go on to other examples: sexuality, economic justice, and many another case. In the plethora of resolutions coming out of the UCC, is there usually a silence on theology or an occasional invocation of biblical and doctrinal proof texts on a basis of convenience?

In replying to the critic, I have one immediate comment. Ad hoc theology is not entirely wrong. If God meets us in the midst of all the events of life, it is as likely that an urgent human demand will lead to a theological insight as that theology will lead to actions. Gustavo Gutiérrez describes theology as "critical reflection — in the light of the Word accepted in faith — on historical praxis and therefore on the presence of Christians in the world" (*A Theology of Liberation* [Maryknoll, N.Y.: Orbis, 1973], 145). He finds that conception of theology as old as Augustine. It is not the only definition of theology, but it is one valid definition. We should expect our theological formulations both to influence our social responsibilities and to follow from the acceptance of such responsibilities. We will often come upon ad hoc insights. For the sake of honesty and fidelity, we will then seek to relate them to a wider range of theological insight and tradition. That is a never-ending job. . . .

In our quarter century as a United Church of Christ, I think I see a few tendencies toward a consensual center. I think we have pretty well agreed that Christian faith has a social meaning today — a controversial assertion in some places though hardly among us, even though we argue over what the specific meaning is. I think we appreciate the importance of responsible freedom, of encouraging honest and diverse expression within the community of faith. I think we agree on the importance of self-criticism — an awareness that has made it possible for me to give this talk without feeling an obligation to commend everything in the church that is my cherished home.

I think the big theological issue ahead of us is how we locate and recognize theological authority in the community of fiat. What do we do about the Bible? What do we do about Jesus? . . .

When Yeats wrote, "Things fall apart; the centre cannot hold," he went on to say: "The best lack all conviction, while the worst / Are full of passionate intensity." That, I am happy to say, is not a description of the United Church of Christ. We have passionate convictions — not all mutually agreed on. A test, and not just a testimony of faith will be our ability to live and tell our faith, knowing our need for those who live it to tell it differently.

78. The Future of Mission:

"Standing at Future's Threshold" and the "Houston Statement of Mission"

(1986, 1987)

Paul R. Gregory, United Church Board for Homeland Ministries,
José Abraham de Jesús

Paul Gregory (b. 1922) is a Congregational Christian/UCC minister who served as the East and Southeast Asia secretary of the United Church Board for World Ministries (UCBWM) (1957–86). The hymn "Standing at the Future's Threshold" was written for the concluding service celebrating the 175th anniversary of the UCBWM in 1985.

Two years later the United Church Board for Homeland Ministries (UCBHM) held a National Conference on Mission in Houston, Texas (1987). Its "Houston Mission Statement" was later commended to "the instrumentalities, conferences, and local congregations for study" and "adoption as an instrument for evaluation of their ministries" by the General Synod (1987). Later it was translated into Spanish by José Abraham de Jesús, a UCC minister educated at the University of Puerto Rico, the Evangelical Seminary of Puerto Rico, and Andover Newton Theological School. After seventeen years in parish ministry in Puerto Rico, de Jesús became director of Hispanic ministries for the Illinois Conference UCC and since 1991 has been working in the national setting of the UCC in various capacities.

Sources: Paul R. Gregory, "Standing at the Future's Threshold," *The New Century Hymnal* (Cleveland: The Pilgrim Press), Hymn #538. Words Copyright © 1985; rev. 1994 Rev. Paul R. Gregory. "Houston Statement of Mission," *GS Minutes 1987,* 12. "Declaración de Misión de La Iglesia Unida de Cristo" (Houston Mission Statement 1987), Spanish translation by José Abraham de Jesús, 2000. Used by permission.

Standing at the Future's Threshold

Standing at the future's threshold,
grateful for God's guiding hand,
Asking no protected stronghold,
called to be a pilgrim band,
Seeking ever for new vision
of the gospel for our day,
We move forward in God's mission
with our faith to show the way.

Midst the teeming cities' millions,
witness to God's boundless love,
Reaching for each system's lost ones,
seeking justice with each move;
Grant us courage, strength, and patience
to contend with vicious power,
Lead us forward in the faith that
gives us hope in testing's hour.

Open-hearted in exchanges
with the faithful not our own,
Trusting God's way with these strangers
not to leave the truth unknown,
Joining them in shared endeavor
where we have Christ's clear command,
We have faith that calls us ever
toward this good earth's promised land.

Building justice as the bulwark
of the peace that God would give,
Making sacrifice the hallmark
of the life we're called to live:
Grant us, God, to bear our witness
to this peace in Christ, and move
Forward with our faith's own access
to the life of hope and love.

Jesus Christ, eternal Savior,
Source of life and truth and grace,
We would ask no special favor,
with the lowliest seek our place,
Know the inasmuch of serving,
have your cross as our command:
Lead us in this faith unswerving
forward as your pilgrim band.

LUX EOI 8.7.8.7 D

Houston Statement of Mission

As people of the United Church of Christ, affirming our Statement of Faith, we seek within the Church Universal to participate in God's mission and to follow the way of the crucified and risen Christ.

Empowered by the Holy Spirit, we are called and commit ourselves . . .

- To praise God, confess our sin, and joyfully accept God's forgiveness;
- To proclaim the Gospel of Jesus Christ in our suffering world;
- To embody God's love for all people;
- To hear and give voice to Creation's cry for justice and peace;
- To name and confront the powers of evil within and among us;
- To repent our silence and complicity with the forces of chaos and death;
- To preach and teach with the power of the Living Word;
- To join oppressed and troubled people in the struggle for liberation;
- To work for justice, healing and wholeness of life;
- To embrace the unity of Christ's church;
- To discern and celebrate the present and coming reign of God.

Declaración de Misión de La Iglesia Unida de Cristo

Como gente de la Iglesia Unida de Cristo, afirmando nuestra Declaración de Fe, buscamos dentro de la Iglesia Universal participar en la misión de Dios y seguir el camino del Cristo crucificado y resucitado.

Capacitados por el Espíritu Santo, somos llamados y nos comprometemos a:

- Alabar a Dios, confesar nuestros pecados, y gozosamente aceptar el perdón de Dios;
- Proclamar el Evangelio de Jesucristo a nuestro mundo sufriente;
- Encarnar el amor de Dios por todo su pueblo;
- Escuchar y dar voz de justicia y de paz a toda la creación;
- Llamar y confrontar los poderes del mal dentro y alrededor de nosotros y nosotras;
- Arrepentirnos por nuestro silencio y complicidad con las fuerzas del caos y la muerte;
- Predicar y enseñar con el poder de la Palabra viviente;
- Unirnos a Los oprimidos y las gentes deshumanizadas en su lucha por la liberación;
- Trabajar por la justicia, la sanidad y la integridad de la vida;
- Abrazar la unidad de toda la iglesia de Cristo;
- Discernir y celebrar el Reinado de Dios presente y venidero.

79. Mission:

"Partnership"

(1988)

Daniel F. Romero

Daniel F. Romero (b. 1945) is a UCC Mexican American minister educated in theology and law. He served in parish ministry in California (1970–76) and then as associate conference minister of the Southern California Conference UCC (1976–87). In 1987 he became the general secretary for mission program of the United Church Board for World Ministries (UCBWM) and in 1998 he returned to the Southern California Conference UCC to become its conference minister.

In 1988 Romero wrote that for the United Church of Christ, partnership is "a mutually agreed upon commitment by two or more church bodies to relate as parts of the body of Christ and to work together." He states that the UCBWM accepts responsibility for the nurture and maintenance of overseas partnerships on behalf of the UCC and that understandings of partnership have implications for mission. He describes the types of partnerships and the obstacles to partnerships (money, structure, and culture) (see also vol. 7:111). Romero's biblical and theological reflection and his discussion of the characteristics of mature partnerships highlight key theological and ethical issues that the UCBWM believed should inform the mission outreach of the United Church of Christ.

Source: Daniel F. Romero, excerpts on "Biblical and Theological Reflection" and "Toward Partnership" from *Partnership*, rev. copy (New York: United Church Board for World Ministries, United Church of Christ, 1988), 1–3, 5–7 [typescript in the UCC Archives].

Partnership

Biblical and Theological Reflection

The covenant which forms the basis of the new partnership between the Pentecostal Church of Chile and the United Church of Christ stresses two principles: the unity of God's people and the Church's mission in today's world. "The biblical mandate demands internal unity within the local and national church, and also the intention to unify ourselves with our brothers and sisters who confess Jesus Christ as Lord by seeking the Kingdom of God and its Justice as our final objective." The covenant affirms the identity and traditions of each partner within the broad understanding of the unity of God's church. If one affirms as the central motif of Jesus' ministry the "coming of the Kingdom of God" this then is our starting point and context for mission. In the Chilean context the goal of mission is: "to transform this sinful world built up by men following their own interests into a world based on Christian values such as truth, justice, equality, love, solidarity and unity. All of the above are signs of God's kingdom among us." The purpose here is not to define mission but to challenge us toward a partnership that broadens our context for understanding God's mission. Our understanding of the church and its witness in the world does inform how we act out that partnership.

Wilbert Shank offers the Pauline concept of the Body of Christ in developing his concepts of unity and interdependence (*God's New Economy: Interdependence and Mission*). "Just as God the Creator sovereignly made the body and breathed into it the very life of God, so God the Redeemer has sovereignly constituted the body through the action of Jesus Christ." Within an "essential unity" there are "diversities of ministry" (1 Cor. 12–14), which in the words of the Chile document "does not mean that one church becomes like the other nor that traditions should be transferred, therefore losing each other's identity." The UCC and PCC recognize the unity of the Christian church. However, the UCC in entering into new mission partnerships or reaffirming established ones seeks to come to a common understanding with partners of God's activity in the world and how that activity shapes and impacts mission. The UCBWM makes commitments, judgments and decisions based on our understanding of God's activity in the world. So do our mission partners. How much alike do we have to be to be partners? What is our tolerance level for difference?

Our mutual acceptance of partnership means replacing the historic understanding of one church as the object of mission. Churches which came into being as a result of the Matthew 28:19 mandate carried out by Western churches now join us, as Christopher Duraisingh points out, as Acts 1:8 co-witnesses, "You will receive power when the Holy Spirit comes upon you; and you will bear witness for me in Jerusalem, and all over Judea and Samaria and away to the ends of the earth" (NEB). It is not that Matthew 28:19 no longer has significance for the Church's mission but rather that those defining the mission of the Church are no longer the objects of Matthew 28:19. I refer you to Duraisingh's article in the *International Review of Mission* (October 1987 pp. 475ff.).

The parable of the Good Samaritan also reinforces the dependence model of mission. It reinforces the highly individualistic understanding of our own society. The Good Samaritan in offering assistance immediately creates a potential for dependence. The person in the ditch becomes the object of mission unable to pull himself/herself out of the ditch without help. How do we move "beyond the ditch"? We need not forfeit our charitable instincts and generosity but rather use Biblical images that reinforce partnership. Duraisingh's use of the metaphor of sharing a meal as a tool to illustrate partnership is helpful. Jesus often used the banquet imagery to characterize the inclusiveness of God's invitation to the kingdom (Luke 14:12–24). A rectangular table (traditional in the West) places the host at the head in "control" of the dinner table — good manners even suggest that you don't eat until the fork of the host is lifted. A round table with food at the center (the Chinese way) suggests a different manner of distribution and the hosts are not immediately recognizable.

It will be helpful in our discussion of partnership if we begin to lift up the Biblical images that lead us toward unity and interdependence and do not always reinforce our need to control and determine the nature of our relationship. There are abundant examples in Jesus' own life and ministry and in the early church where community not dependence is the context for mission. . . .

Toward Partnership

What are the characteristics of a mature partnership? Qualities which nurture healthy, positive relationships between people are always worth mentioning, namely, mutual trust, respect, acceptance and a sense of the spiritual unity of humankind and creation. A colleague reflecting on recent conversations with partners reports "Mutuality in mission depends on mutual acceptance and sharing; it means much more than giving or receiving because acceptance is the key to power sharing." Alongside these commendable traits are issues that are regular conversation pieces in our partnership discussions:

A. *Listening* — Partners who do not listen and hear one another are doomed to failure. Listening is an art and requires sensitivity and openness. Not everyone hears the same things in the same way. Communication among people of different cultures and languages is basic to the success of our working together. It is not enough to communicate good intentions. Structured within our life as partners must be checks and balances that help us sift through data and information for clear and common understandings.

B. *Communication* — Beyond the interaction between humans in conversation, partnership will require regular communication. How this is done effectively given the geographical distances is always a challenge. However, without the nurture of the relationship on a regular basis, it becomes stagnant. Absenteeism is not conducive to strong partnership. As partnerships grow and new structures are created, more mechanisms for communication will be needed. This carries with it important implications for mission education.

C. *Presence* — One of the issues identified in our partnership discussions with the UCCSA (South Africa) was "presence." How do we maintain a presence in order to demonstrate our solidarity? Efforts at physical presence with one another need to be made at all levels of our life together. Prayer and worship in the context of our life together was listed as an important way in which our presence is lived out. Active involvement "in being faithful where you are"; mutual exchange of personnel; congregation to congregation relationships were all listed as important ways of building solidarity.

D. *Planning* — Planning and the setting of common priorities is a crucial element of partnership. It is in our planning and strategizing together that mission will take shape. We cannot guess what our partners may or may not want or need. God's mission cannot be "planned" in isolation. Budget and finances must be part of the planning process. Agreement on evaluation and review of program should be part of the process.

E. *Decision-making* — Joint planning in the partnership context assumes patterns of decision-making with serious implications for structure. How do we structure ourselves for common planning and shared decision making? How are decisions honored and respected? How are disagreements honored without affecting the partnership itself? Power sharing implies equality as a goal — not easily achieved. I've often heard powerless groups say "No one gives up power — you have to take it." The call for an ecumenical sharing of resources is based on a theological understanding of the nature of God's creation and the distribution of resources. How we share power will ultimately test the seriousness of our willingness to act as partners.

F. *Decentralization* — A new arrangement of partnership may necessarily call for a decentralization in structure and design of mission. Regional decision making bodies may be more manageable. The United Church of Christ may find creative ways of structuring itself geographically to accommodate more decentralized mission structures. Thinking globally in terms of structure will challenge our own denominational configurations. The emphasis will be on how we as a denomination, given our present structures, might best relate to our global partners to maximize contact and communication across the whole church. I understand the Disciples and Presbyterians assign regions/presbyteries to various regions of the world where they have mission efforts.

G. *Mission Education* — It cannot go without saying that mission education becomes ever more important in interpreting to our constituencies all the marvelous decisions and programs that partnerships design and implement. The task of interpreting new and emerging agreements of partnership in itself is no easy task. At what point is there sufficient ownership to move ahead with more equitable forms of partnership? How are various constituencies made to feel part of the emerging new era of mission? The trend to want personal relationships with church people overseas offers great opportunities and problems. Our World Ministries in the U.S. will play an important role in creating the climate for the type of mutuality in mission we wish to create.

H. *Role of Mission Personnel* — One of the components of partnership is the role of our mission personnel. What role will missionaries play in partnership arrangements? Are they simply extensions of the sending partner or do they occupy a unique perspective in the partnership relationship that needs to be articulated and nurtured?

Staffing at Homebase — With the appointment of an African as Africa Regional Secretary, we have taken another step toward implementing partnership at a new level. What are implications for furthering this?

What it means to be in solidarity with the poor is a nagging question in this discussion. Is a mature partnership with third world church people an act of solidarity with the poor? If our partners are not poor themselves and not involved in actions expressing solidarity with the poor, is participating in their mission to the poor adequate? The perpetual question of faithfulness for first world Christians may precede our conversations of partnership or can be informed by more mature partnerships with communities of struggle. The United Church of Christ has not always set the best example of partnership among its own local churches, Conferences and national bodies. The same power games, financial imbalances and insensitivities exist within the family. Perhaps the development of more mature global partnerships will model for us as a church a renewed sense of participation and inclusiveness in mission.

80. Reflections on the Statement of Faith: *"The Mystery of God and Humanity"*

(1990)

Allen O. Miller

Allen O. Miller (1912–99) was an Evangelical and Reformed/UCC minister who was educated at Lafayette College, Yale Divinity School, and Yale University. He taught theology at Eden Theological Seminary for over fifty years beginning in 1946. In the early years of the UCC he reminded the church that unity was its mission (see vol. 7:23).

In 1990 Miller wrote a helpful pamphlet about the United Church of Christ Statement of Faith from a historical, biblical, and theological perspective. In his reflections on the ways in which the biblical heritage can enrich our understanding of the Statement of Faith, Miller reminds Christians that theology always begins in wonder. It is "fundamentally a confession of what God has done, of what God is doing, and of what God promises yet to do."

Source: Allen O. Miller, "The Mystery of God and Humanity," from *The United Church of Christ Statement of Faith: A Historical, Biblical and Theological Perspective* (New York: United Church Press, 1990), 35–39.

The Mystery of God and Humanity

Human beings are the only creatures on the face of the earth who are able to ask questions. Most of the time we ask for information: What is it? Where did it come from? How does it work? What is it good for? But in our deeper, more reflective moments we ask questions concerning the meaning of our existence: Who am I? Where did I come from? Where am I going? What does life mean? How may I become what I am meant to be? Why is it so?

Pastors will recognize these latter questions as the kind often asked in times of crisis by troubled parishioners standing upon the threshold of decision. Teachers will identify them as the kind asked in utter innocence, but in profound sincerity, by even the youngest children in the Sunday church school.

Theology Begins in Wonder

For young or old these questions properly lie in the realm of wonder. Wonder is akin to curiosity, but it is the farthest extreme from the disinterested curiosity of the scientist, as well as from mere inquisitiveness. There is plenty of curiosity in wonder, but it is always motivated by a deep concern and a sense of personal involvement. To encourage serious-minded wondering about the meaning of our existence, therefore, is an "invitation to theology." Moreover, when Christian faith, that is, our personal response of confidence to the grace of God in Jesus Christ, sets about to deal with these questions concerning the meaning of our life, the discipline called Christian theology is born. This is the task to which Jesus himself invites us. Theology is loving God "with our whole mind."

Our biblical heritage assures us that God is involved in everything that happens, from our most joyous occasions to our most bewildering concerns. Moreover, life confronts us with the fact that the most satisfying answers to our queries are found when we acknowledge God's involvement and accept God's purpose as final. Christian theology, therefore, is fundamentally a confession of what God has done, of what God is doing, and of what God promises yet to do. It stems from divine initiative, and is bounded by the limits of God's self-revelation. Although theology means, literally, a discourse about God, its content is more like a prayer of praise and thanksgiving than a scientific description of a matter of fact.

The theologian is correspondingly humbled by temporal limitations and heartened by eternal expectation. One knows that one is in no position to make new discoveries that would revolutionize human knowledge through one's planned experimentation. Rather, like a news reporter, one is given a "scoop" on what is actually an open secret: that God loves humankind. On top of that, God has called the theologian to the glorious task of helping each new generation, and in particular, individual persons day by day, to acknowledge the truth that God loves me too!

There is, however, a powerful temptation which confronts theological thinking. It is the perennial lure to sell our birthright of wonder for a mess of information. We are prone to forget that our knowledge of God, like all communication with other persons, is fundamentally different from the spectator's knowledge about things.

Where the natural universe is concerned, knowledge means diligent attention to a specialized area, steady improvement in the techniques of investigation, and a growing body of verifiable facts.

God, however, is unlike the universe around us because of God's unique status in relation to everything else and because God confronts us primarily in personal relationships. On the one hand, God is for Christian faith the fundamental and ultimate reality, by virtue of whose activity we account for both the world we know and our human capacity to know it and each other.

On the other hand, God is not an object to be known. God is a mysterious presence to be acknowledged. We know that God works through us from the center of our being. We know that, in Jesus, God took on a personal life, the like of which we know very well from being persons ourselves. Indeed, God and humanity are so inextricably bound together that it is next to impossible to conceive of one without the other. Christian theology, however, is not a statement about our feelings or of our beliefs about God. It is, rather, a confession of what God is and does for us, and in and through us.

Anyone who has been or is in love will have appreciation for the mysterious quality of all personal involvement.

The unique individuality of each person you meet, the unfathomable depth of creativity that is revealed in every intimate personal encounter, become an ever-recurring occasion for surprise and wonder. The more intimate the acquaintance the more speechless we are to define what it is that draws us to another person, and the more deeply we become involved ourselves in the mystery. In similar fashion, the human response that the mystery of God evokes is primarily appreciation and commitment rather than understanding or intellectual satisfaction. The divine mystery is an everlasting foe of the commonplace and the complacent. Our hearts are overwhelmed with awe and fascination. Moreover, just as we make a distinction in the English language between second and third personal pronouns for direct personal communication as against the transmission of information, we reserve a special form of personal pronoun for addressing God. The overawing mystery of God's Being calls forth the words "thee," "thou," and "thy" upon our lips.

Furthermore, we must never mistake the word "mystery" as a synonym for human ignorance — that is, for that aspect of our environment which is still unknown to us. Mystery does not belong at all to the impersonal universe of the unknown and the known. In the proper meaning of the word, mystery belongs to that dimension of personal life which involves "the hidden and revealed." The truth is that the mystery of a personal relationship is never so mysterious as when the hidden is revealed (John 21:4–14)!

In this matter, God is the perfect example. Revelation is always "self-revelation," and God's self-revelation in Christ is the most miraculous event in all history. The mystery of the revealed and the hidden is the glory of the gospel (Eph. 3:1–13) and the reason for the central significance of the sacraments (mysteria) in the life of the Christian church. How true the maxim that "Christian theology begins in wonder, and when theological thought has done its best, the wonder still remains."*

Thus we are continually being assured of the intimate relevance of Christ's gospel as well as of its eternal significance. We know the gospel's relevance by its power to evoke our wonder, and its eternal significance because the mystery is never dissipated.

Theology begins in wonder: first of all, because of the concerned curiosity that human beings have regarding their origin and destiny, and second because awe, or reverence, is the normal human response to the marvelous and the unexpected. Theology begins in wonder, but not all wonder is theological. Wonder, without faith and hope, is either sterile or pernicious. For example, wonder is pernicious when it arises in a human mind that is distorted by the use of narcotics, and sterile when it is elicited by the mushroom cloud that hung over the Japanese city of Hiroshima in midsummer of 1945. This is to say that not all that is wonderful ushers us into the mystery of divine self-disclosure. What is more important is that personal self-disclosure does not, indeed cannot, take place in a vacuum. Communication requires the responsive, personal involvement of another person.

---

*This is a paraphrase of a statement made by Professor Alfred North Whitehead regarding philosophy in its relation to scientific thought, in *Nature and Life,* University of Chicago Press, 1934.

God's Revelation and Our Response of Faith

We may assume, as an axiom of biblical understanding, that revelation always occurs in a personal encounter, as a direct disclosure of one person to another. God's purpose, whenever God reveals Godself, is to elicit our response of faith.

"Faith" is a term with several levels of meaning. The Christian faith, the faith of our forebears, usually comes down to us as a body of "beliefs." When it is received on this level, the question that people ask is: "What must I believe to be a Christian?" The answer, on the same level, is: "The articles of our creed — believe in God, believe in Jesus Christ, believe in the Holy Spirit, the one holy universal Church, the life everlasting."

Now, indeed, these are the articles that express "what Christians believe" (cf. the Apostles' Creed). Taken alone, however, they throw only a faint light upon the question that really has to be answered first: "How am I to become a Christian?" One does not become a Christian by accepting or rejecting beliefs; one becomes a Christian by "a hearty trust" in God's gracious love. (cf. Heidelberg Catechism, Q. and A. 21.) The truth is that in Christ, God reveals Godself and not doctrines about God. Therefore, faith as trust always runs one whole level of experience deeper than belief. Belief is a matter of the acceptance of ideas, to which the mind gives assent; and doubt is the corresponding rejection. Faith, on the other hand, is a question of life or death. The question, with which our very existence is confronted, is always this: "Do you accept or reject the love of God?" (cf. Matt. 16:13–26; John 21:15–19.)

Christianity, however, is a complex affair, concerned with personal relationships on several dimensions at once. The gospel incorporates, at one and the same time, a religion, a theology, and a morality.

It would be simple and neat to say that religion and theology are distinguished from each other as faith and belief, respectively, and that morality is different from both in that it involves action. Such a caricature, however, is only partially true. Doctrinal beliefs are an important part of theology, but they are not the heart of it. The heart of theology is like the heart of religion and of morality, a personal relationship. Moreover, all three express action. In fact, in our Christian understanding, theology, religion, and morality are all concerned with activity — the activity of God's holy love in human affairs.

The primary category of Christian theology is the biblical revelation, God's act in making God's will and character known through personal covenant encounter. By the same token, faith, as a "confession of confidence," our acknowledgment of the covenant claim of God, is the primary category of the Christian religion. Moreover, Christian morality is distinctive as a form of human existence in that its categories of personal freedom — and social responsibility originate in this unique covenant relation of revelation and faith.

The trouble with limiting theology to traditional beliefs is that so often these beliefs find their own expression in a monologue, in which we humans, within our own minds, sort over our doubts and our prejudices. Theological beliefs are empty if they do not re-present the underlying divine-human encounter of revelation and response. When, however, we face the fact that the whole of life involves our response of faith or unfaith to God's holy love and righteousness, we see clearly that Christian theology is a recording of our Christian church's dialogue with God through Jesus Christ. In this perspective we realize that the most important things in life, namely, God's revelation in Christ, our confession of faith, and the responsible exercise of our Christian freedom-that is, Christian morality — cannot be taught as theoretical disciplines. They need, rather, to be caught contagiously from and with others who are already participating in the divine-human covenant relationship. Hence the fellowship of the church and the home is essential to Christian nurture and discipline.

"The Mystery of God and Humankind" is the most thrilling story ever told. The Holy Scriptures of the Christian church have recorded and preserved the script of this story, in which the meaning of our existence may be discerned by those who are willing to join the cast and accept a role in the "Covenant of the Living God."

PART V

Making a Difference

The Statement of Faith of the United Church of Christ is an affirmation of the presence of Jesus Christ in every aspect of life. It is a summons to discipleship that is both joyous and costly. Celebrating God's gracious and powerful presence among the faithful, it calls Christians to action in glad submission to the gospel. As a consequence, the UCC understanding of the church (its ecclesiology) emphasizes that it is a community of service to others and that this service is rooted in the good news about God in Christ. Standing deep within the world-changing Reformed tradition, the United Church of Christ is a people called not only to keep liturgies and say prayers. It is also asked to resist the powers of evil. With other Christians, UCC members share in Christ's baptism, eat at Christ's table, and join in Christ's passion and victory. Their faith is meant to reflect the discipleship of the earliest followers of Jesus. They do not turn away from the world, but work and witness in the midst of its wonder, its sorrow, and the injustices that scar the times in which they live.

A commitment to social justice and the service the church owes to God and to neighbor is not anchored in human reason or principle, nor in human virtue or conscience. Rather, faith expressed in public witness to the gospel is a responsibility the church accepts, sometimes reluctantly, in response to its divine summons to discipleship. The United Church of Christ, like other denominations, is called to offer a reply to the fact of the Incarnation. It acknowledges in its liturgies that however bold its deeds, they are always incomplete and often marked inappropriately by self-acclaim. Invariably, the church, in the midst of its mission or its social action, is tempted to lose its way. For this reason, its commitment in faith to "social justice" and "ministries of benevolence" is best accompanied by prayer, the prayer of the tax collector in the parable Jesus tells about the pharisee and the tax collector, "God, be merciful unto me, a sinner" (Luke 18:13). The challenge that faces the church, in addition to remaining awake to its vocation, is never to forget to ask the question, "How can people of faith know the will of God so that they may do the will of God?" This question, in one form or another, never goes away.

The United Church of Christ takes this question seriously. In its most faithful moments it is inspired by the mystery that God in Christ loves the world, and acknowledging dependence upon the Holy Spirit to provide leadership in the ways of truth, it acts to make a difference in the world. It remembers that it can make a difference, only because God has already made a difference. Its witness takes many forms.

Promoting Racial Justice

For example, when the UCC Office of Communication (OC) was created in 1959, it was not a typical denominational public relations office. Under the leadership of Everett C. Parker it worked diligently to safeguard the public interest in broadcasting, and specifically to advocate for the rights of people of color and for women. In the 1960s Charles Shelby Rooks, who chaired the OC Board, and Parker made the Office of Communication (OC) a watchdog at the Federal Communications Commission, challenging the renewal of the broadcast licenses of stations that discriminated against blacks in the South. In 1969 it won a landmark case against a television station in Jackson, Mississippi. Its success in defending the "public interest" and upholding the "fairness doctrine" on behalf of viewers and listeners, rather than broadcasters, is legendary.

Christians are called to proclaim God's Word and enable the search for meaning. In its report to the 1959 General Synod the Office of Communication set forth a theological rationale for its work. "If our goal is communication of the Faith, our aim must be to lead people into the Christian community, where they may risk the actions that are the ultimate tests of faith. Ideas and institutions have a place in such communication only as they are submitted to the test of the principles, ideas, ideals and possibilities of the Word" (see vol. 7:81).

The United Church of Christ's commitment to racial justice inspired activist work in the civil rights movement in the 1960s (see vol. 7:15–19). It also undergirded a decade-long struggle to free ten unjustly imprisoned young people convicted for conspiracy and the unlawful burning of a grocery store during a 1971 racial disturbance in Wilmington, North Carolina. The nine African Americans (one a UCC staff member) and a white woman VISTA worker became known as the "Wilmington 10." In the years that followed evidence surfaced that the witnesses in the trial lied when they testified against the Wilmington 10. Other irregularities highlighted the injustice of the defendants' conviction and imprisonment. Citing the admonition of scripture, "Remember those who are in prison, as though in prison with them" (Hebrews 13:3 NRSV), the United Church of Christ committed thousands of dollars to provide bail, seek a new trial, and convince the governor of North Carolina to intervene in the case. In 1978 when the governor ignored the evidence and refused to pardon the innocent prisoners, United Church of Christ president Avery Post pledged the ongoing commitment of the UCC to racial justice. Affirming the belief that all followers of Jesus are imprisoned until all those who are innocent are free, the United Church of Christ continued to work for their freedom. Finally in 1980 the case was overturned and all charges dropped (see vol. 7:82).

Racial justice issues became more nuanced and subtle in the 1980s, but racism continued to flourish as a systemic and pervasive power in society. UCC leaders reminded the churches that "we are one people because we are reconciled to God in one body through the cross." Therefore where Asians or Blacks, Hispanics or Native Americans remained targets of racial violence and bigotry, the church confronted a severe theological problem. The "destructive symptoms" of racism, namely "poverty, crime, economic disadvantage, alienation, violence, and persecution," were a "gaping wound in the body of Christ" (see vol. 7:83).

In 1989 the General Synod passed a resolution "Challenging the Resurgence of Racism in the United States of America." It called for change because "Racism is an expression of idolatry, replacing faith in God, who created all peoples equal in the image of God, with the belief in the superiority of one race over another" (see vol. 7:84).

A few years later the national leadership of the United Church of Christ issued a "Pastoral Letter on Contemporary Racism in the Church" (1991). Noting that despite significant progress, the "pervasive and destructive sin of racism" continues to prevail in society, it called the church to provide the leadership necessary to break the cycle of racial despair and move toward a future of equality and community. "Racism," the letter proclaimed, "is the intentional and unintentional use of power to isolate, separate and exploit based on race." Love for Jesus Christ and for neighbor requires the church to challenge such idolatry (see 7:84).

Advocating with Women

Even as awareness and concern about the injustice of racism continued to inform the work of the United Church of Christ, the role and place of women became an increasingly important issue. This concern built upon the long-standing commitment of the heritage of the United Church of Christ to the ministries of women, both lay and ordained. Women preachers had been active among frontier Christians in the nineteenth century (see vol. 4:8–11). Women clergy had served as ordained pastors in Congregational churches beginning in the 1850s (see vol. 4:77–79). Women missionaries, as partners with their husbands and as single women, had enriched the mission outreach of Reformed, Congregational, Christian, and Evangelical boards and synods (see vol. 4:7 and 8). In thousands of congregations laywomen supported global mission work and worked to meet the needs of church and community within local women's fellowships and guilds.

By the late 1950s, some women and men began suggesting that "separate denominational women's structures" were out of date. A national Council for Lay Life and Work (CLLW) was formed, lifting up the importance of the laity (women and men) in the mission of the Church. During the 1960s a new wave of feminist thinking led many younger women to press the national UCC for a fresh commitment to correct injustices related to women in church and society (see vol. 7:65).

In 1971 the General Synod passed a Pronouncement on "The Status of Women in Church and Society." Affirming the belief that God makes no distinction regarding the worth of males and females and that both are equal in God's sight, it stated that "distinctions made by society which assume an inferior-superior relationship are contrary to the will of God." The General Synod went on to establish a "Task Force on Women in Church and Society" (1971) with staff support in the Office of the President of the church (see vol. 7:85).

The 1971 General Synod also passed a proposal for action entitled "Freedom of Choice Concerning Abortion." Recognizing that there are many theological and ethical factors surrounding decisions about abortion, the proposal affirmed the responsibility of all men and women to share the work of creation with God. It stressed a reverence for human life and the need to protect the weak and defenseless. It stated that the present laws prohibiting abortion were unjust and unenforceable, compelling women to bear children or to seek illegal abortions. It called for the repeal of all legal prohibitions against physician-performed abortions, so that abortion would no longer fall under "the realm of penal law," but rather become a voluntary medically safe procedure available to all women. The concern behind the proposal was to place value on "personal life and upon the quality of life, both actual and potential," and to give women "freedom with responsibility." Even as it affirmed choice, however, it also acknowledged the church's obligation to aid in the resolution of the problem of unwanted pregnancies (see vol. 7:86).

Abortion presents the church with one of the most divisive issues in our society. People of faith and compassion may have different convictions about abortion, but most concede that abortion is never an ideal solution for unwanted pregnancies. The General Synod of the UCC has agreed, but it also has consistently said that alternatives which deny women options are worse. For over thirty years, understanding abortion as a profound theological and social issue, the majority of delegates to UCC General Synods have not changed their opinions. When delegates struggle with this issue, they rarely speak of abortion as a "right," but rather as a tragic choice that is always morally ambiguous. Although in 1987 a small minority that could not condone abortion under any circumstance formed a special-interest group called "UCC Friends for Life," the majority of delegates to General Synods and most UCC members uphold the belief that not to be able to choose is even more problematic (see vol. 7:87).

As the United Church of Christ spoke out on these issues, some people felt that the UCC was becoming too "feminist," while others argued that it was not doing enough for women. In 1975 a Task Force report on the Status of Women in Church and Society pressed for more advocacy. From 1975 to 1979 an Advisory Commission on Women developed new ways to support women clergy and laywomen. In 1979 a Coordinating Center for Women in Church and Society (CCW) sought to "address the concerns of women and seek strategies to eliminate sexism in church and society." That same year the General Synod (1979) voted to support the ratification of the Equal Rights Amendment (ERA) and reaffirmed its support four years later (1983). Women in the United Church of Christ were increasingly visible in the national leadership, and in 1983 Carol Joyce Brun was elected secretary of the UCC, the first woman to hold a nationally elected office.

Throughout this period the relationship between racism and sexism in church and society became even more obvious. In 1977 the General Synod passed a "Pronouncement on Racism and Sexism" that summoned the church to continue its struggle with these issues as they "interact, intersect, and compound each other." Those who have been set free in Christ to the service of God and neighbor should be among the first to understand that "Human liberation means new consciousness of oppression and rising expectations concerning the future" (see vol. 7:88).

Unfortunately, at least as far as many women were concerned, the United Church of Christ Coordinating Center for Women in Church and Society (CCW) had remained only an administrative office under the Office of the President since its creation in 1979. In 1987 CCW's report to General Synod called the church to remember the "bent over woman" who is met by Jesus in the Gospel of Luke. Jesus tells her that she is free of her illness and able to "straighten herself up." In that spirit, women leaders in the UCC insisted that it was time for the UCC to establish an "ongoing office or instrumentality to continue the long journey toward God's intended equality for women and men," and they successfully made the case for the Coordinating Center for Women to become a permanent established instrumentality of the United Church of Christ (see vol. 7:89).

Speaking Out on Social Issues

The demands of the Christian gospel require seeing life differently, through the lens of faith, both in the local setting and in the wider society. There are times, carefully chosen, when Christians best remain silent and retreat to quiet places. But there are other moments when Christians need to speak out, lifting their voices and staking out a position on behalf of the voiceless (Proverbs 31:8).

Building upon the "Call to Christian Action in Church and Society" passed by the General Synod in 1959 (see vol. 7:15), the United Church of Christ has sought to sustain an ongoing activist stance on many social problems: such as apartheid, justice and peace in the Middle East, human rights, and generic engineering. In attempting to address these issues, theological reflection provided the foundation for action. Yet, there were also times when theological grounding for the church's social statements was merely implied or only faintly articulated. Actions were taken that only later generated theological reflection. There were other weaknesses. For example, the inability of the church to give persistent attention to labor and to the justice issues of the working class, even though many UCC members were blue-collar workers was criticized. Living with its strengths and weaknesses, the UCC has attempted to address social problems with the gospel entrusted to it. And in its most faithful moments, it has remembered that Christian discipleship depends upon God's gift of grace, vitally alive in the midst of an imperfect human community.

The witness of the United Church of Christ illustrates the interplay between theological conviction and action in the world. It is a stance suggested by the bumper sticker: "To believe is to care, to care is to do." Such movement between confession and action, word and deed, has been a consistent challenge for the UCC. UCC members know very well that they have not always succeeded in carrying out God's mission in the cities, affirming human rights as foundational to the Christian faith, or wrestling with vexing and complicated questions, such as economic justice.

The social justice commitments of the United Church of Christ come from several crucial sources: the teachings of Jesus, the reality of the cross and the resurrection, the voices of the biblical prophets, the Reformed tradition (in which the rule of Christ over politics, society, and the soul of the church is stressed), and the theology and experience of multiracial and multicultural UCC members who have courageously born witness to the gospel amidst the troubles of the world. Although most UCC congregations are not urban, many have consistently attempted to take civic life seriously. Their clergy proclaim the good news of individual salvation in Jesus Christ, speaking of God who in Christ has promised "a new heaven and a new earth" (Revelation 21:1). Drawing upon scripture, its theological heritage, and the abiding presence of the Holy Spirit, the UCC is committed to the common good and to the civic fabric of society. It is a matter of Christian obedience. It is a reflection of the church's commitment to the truth of what it confesses.

Thousands of UCC people participated in the 1963 March on Washington, for example, led in large measure by African American leaders. National Council of Churches leadership, especially former UCBHM staff member Robert (Bob) Spike, helped mobilize thousands of white church leaders. The UCC Council for Christian Social Action (CCSA) helped send many UCC clergy to Mississippi in the spring of 1964 (see vol. 7:19). UCC lay leaders and clergy worked for justice and delivered sermons at public hearings. They were confident that although the church cannot build the "kingdom of God" on earth or "pray down the New Jerusalem," it can witness to its faith that "God will transform (the) old town into New Jerusalem" (see vol. 7:90).

UCC leaders have offered fresh and inspired leadership to some of the historic city mission societies. These urban leaders have spoken about being "born again." By this they do not mean some private rebirth, but the need for all Christians to be reborn into "a radical stance toward the world and the structures of society" where they will be able to "see the face of Jesus in the faces of the suffering" (see vol. 7:91). Leaders have prayed for "those victimized by oppression, political expediency and the apathy of the powerful," while at the same time giving thanks for all communities of people "bent on justice" (see vol. 7:92).

Supported by the Commission for Racial Justice (CRJ) and the Office for Church and Society (OCIS), the United Church of Christ has resisted the temptation to turn away from the world. Bearing witness to the divine intention for a world that is both compassionate and humane, members of the UCC have spoken out, lobbied, boycotted, consoled, and prayed that the collective life of the world might become more just.

When millions of the world's people sought basic human rights, freedom to live where they wanted, liberation from oppressive governments, escape from war, and opportunity to start over, the United Church of Christ attempted to find resources within its theological and liturgical soul. Some of its members, for example, remembered biblical words about the importance of sanctuary. They recognized the role of companionship in times of danger. They responded to the grief and pain of neighbors and reclaimed an understanding of Jesus Christ as the One who brings refuge, peace, and hope. Communities of faith gathered around the communion table were reminded that Christians do not look for Christ in the nouns, but meet Christ in the verbs. "This is my body *broken* for you; this is my blood *shed* for you" (see vol. 7:93).

In 1989 the General Synod passed a "Pronouncement on Christian Faith, Economic Life and Justice." This lengthy pronouncement viewed economic justice as an issue of faith. Noting the marks of a just economy, it challenged unexamined assumptions about capitalism while at the same time recognizing the need for more accountability in healthy democratic systems. God is "not only of the past and present, but . . . of the future" (see vol. 7:94).

Convictions within the UCC on social issues, while intensely practical, have not always been unified. There have been ongoing and lively debates over the relationship between the gospel's meaning and the work of the church. Some believe that the UCC is too radical. Others think that the gospel calls for greater risks.

In the early 1980s those who feared that the UCC was losing its "missional" courage founded "Christians for Justice Action" (CJA) — an organization within the UCC looking "at human life and the decisions of our world's societies in new ways." During the "theological ferment" inspired by such grassroots developments as "Sound Teaching," "A Most Difficult and Urgent Time," the "Craigville Colloquies," and the "Dubuque Declaration" (see vol. 7:57, 59, 61, and 63), CJA did its own theological work. It lifted up the fifty-eighth chapter of Isaiah as a guide to help contemporary Christians recognize anew the dialogue between God's Word and modern experience, between reflection and practice. CJA insisted that being true to the biblical vision requires leaders to "offset" "centrist accommodations to politics within the church and the world." "Contrary to what our culture prefers from people of faith," Christians are called to choose "direct political action and expressions of outrage against injustice." This may "cause division within the church, but such is the nature of biblical witness" (see vol. 7:95).

Affirming the Wholeness of Life

The life of the United Church of Christ is a mixture of healing and activism, word and deed. Historically the church is witness to the reconciliation of the world by God in Christ. In response Christians engage in service that has been redeemed in Christ through various ministries of reconciliation. Diaconal service has always been part of the church, and the United Church of Christ has carried on that legacy, finding many significant ways to affirm healing and the wholeness of life.

When the followers of John the Baptist asked Jesus if he was the Messiah, he did not answer their question. Rather, he told them to go and tell John what they saw, "the blind receive their sight, the lame walk, the lepers are cleansed, the deaf hear, the dead are raised, the poor have good news brought to them" (Luke 7:22 NRSV). The churches that came together to form the United Church of Christ had been involved in establishing and maintaining many institutions devoted to ministries of healing, health, and welfare. Hospitals, homes for orphans and the aged, and programs of assistance for those with special physical and mental needs had been strongly supported by UCC congregations for years.

These caring ministries, however, were never separate from social witness. "The key is to affirm and spiritually unite health and welfare issues with direct services as part of *one* health and welfare mission." When this occurs, Christian love can be characterized as *total* caring (see vol. 7:96).

Consequently the United Church of Christ has looked deeply into the promise of the gospel that God's love is unconditional. It has invited Christians to reexamine biblical texts and the conditions that have caused persons to be viewed as inferior or broken. Instead of calling for pity or condemnation, the United Church of Christ has challenged common assumptions about wholeness and health and worked for change in numerous ways. Its work in two areas is especially noteworthy: (1) its ministries of advocacy for persons with handicaps (an earlier word) or disabilities, and (2) its ministries of advocacy for lesbian, gay, bisexual, and transgendered persons. In both cases, it has pressed for new thinking about all human beings and about the radical love present in the gospel. While supporting the visibility and the importance of traditional family bonds in the UCC Book of Worship "Order for Marriage," it has insisted that Jesus offers wholeness and community to all persons, and that the church must do the same.

In 1977 the General Synod passed a pronouncement on "The Church and Persons with Handicaps." It recognized the fragility of all life, it called for caring for those in need, and it challenged the church to help those who "suffer hardness of heart toward the handicapped." It suggested that suffering may not always be "the enemy to be overcome," but might actually be "a means of grace." It condemned the tendency to "locate human dignity in normality and achievement" and challenged the church to change its attitudes and actions (see vol. 7:97).

As the years passed the United Church of Christ sought to help Christians recognize that persons with disabilities (not handicaps) have tremendous contributions to make to church and society. Harold Wilke, a charismatic UCC minister born with no arms, reminded the UCC of the gospel message that we are accepted into God's love, "not by our deeds or by our being, but by the grace of God." In God, he insisted, everything is made perfect in weakness. In our weakness, we are like people in those crowds that followed Jesus. We yearn for wholeness; we need supportive companions; and we find courage in God's grace (see vol. 7:97).

In 1969 the General Synod passed a resolution on "Homosexuals and the Law." This resolution, which spoke out against antiquated laws limiting the civil rights of homosexuals, was the first in a long line of national UCC actions protecting the civil liberties of homosexual persons. After 1972, when William Johnson became the first openly gay person ordained to the Christian ministry by a major Protestant denomination in the United States, the UCC Executive Council adopted a statement to guide conferences and associations in their ordination decisions. It said that "in the instance of considering a stated homosexual's candidacy for ordination, the issue should not be his/her homosexuality as such, but rather the candidate's total view of human sexuality and his/her understanding of the morality of its (expression)." Many ordaining bodies supported the Executive Council, adding that a candidate should be considered for authorized ministry on the basis of his or her faith, biblical and theological competence, and love for the church and its ministry.

Nevertheless, by 1975 the General Synod acknowledged that many in the United Church of Christ had not "faced in depth the issue of human sexuality," and therefore it commissioned a study to explore the dynamics of human sexuality and to recommend postures for the church. *Human Sexuality: A Preliminary Study* was presented to the 1977 General Synod. It was a controversial study that defined sexuality as emotional, physical, cognitive, value-laden, spiritual, personal, and social. "Sexuality is a central dimension of each person's selfhood, but it is not the whole of that selfhood. It is a critical component of each person's self-understanding and of how each relates to the world" (see vol. 7:98).

Debates over the *Human Sexuality* study were deep and difficult. By the end of the 1977 General Synod the report had been received with appreciation and commended to the whole church for study and response. Unfortunately, the debates and vote (409 yes and 210 no, or 66 percent–34 percent) left a minority very dissatisfied. Following the vote that minority organized and returned to the next several General Synods seeking a new vote. After several unsuccessful attempts to reverse the vote on the *Human*

Sexuality study, the group evolved into a new biblical/theological special-interest group within the United Church of Christ known as the United Church People for Biblical Witness (UCPBW), which became the Biblical Witness Fellowship (BWF) in 1983 (see vol. 7:63).

Generally speaking the majority of congregations in the United Church of Christ were concerned but open about issues of sexuality. Many of them upheld the civil rights of gay and lesbian persons and did not wish to see them compromised.

The 1985 General Synod passed a resolution "Calling on United Church of Christ Congregations to Covenant as Open and Affirming (ONA)." It invited local congregations to go on record as open communities of faith, welcoming lesbian, gay, and bisexual people by adopting a "covenant of openness and affirmation," or by passing an "inclusive non-discrimination policy." More importantly the United Church of Christ developed resources and a process to help local congregations study the issue and make a decision. Among UCC congregations and clergy the issue generated lively debates, with some congregations ignoring and/or avoiding it, some finding the process destructive, some finding the process liberating, and others embracing the idea but refusing to "go on record," be "listed" or "labeled." Fifteen years after the General Synod resolution, approximately 350 "ONA congregations" were listed by the UCC Coalition for Lesbian, Gay, Bisexual and Transgendered (LGBT) Concerns (see vol. 7:98).

Many members of the United Church of Christ, laity and clergy, insist that if Jesus Christ is head of the church there can be no rationale for exclusion because of sexual orientation. By 1997 the conference ministers, acknowledging that the issue of homosexuality was still a "disputed question" among faithful members of the church, sent a letter to the church urging further dialogue, especially about the issue of same-sex blessings. In 1998 it was followed by a "pastoral letter" written by UCC president Paul Sherry that drew attention to the increase of hate crimes and expressed regret over the decisions of Christian denominations to exclude gay, lesbian, and bisexual persons from sharing in the full ministry of the church. Citing Romans 8:1, he insisted "There is therefore now no condemnation for those who are in Christ Jesus" (NRSV) and sought to offer a clear statement on what it means to be an inclusive church (see vol. 7:99).

The commitment of the United Church of Christ to health and wholeness has taken many forms during its history. It was quick to speak out about the Acquired Immune Deficiency Syndrome (AIDS) epidemic in the early 1980s and to follow through with pronouncements and resolutions leading to action. Its faith-based thinking about genetic engineering, infant formula, hospice care, mental illness, substance abuse, and national health care policies has been consistent and significant.

From the birth of the United Church of Christ in 1957, statements by its leaders and actions by its General Synods have been remarkably outspoken. When many other national denominational bodies remained tentative and/or silent, the General Synod of the United Church of Christ went on record out of its concern to make a difference and to bring words and deeds together. It has been heard in the wider society, it has allocated national resources to educate, and it has empowered staff to act in its name.

One reason for this difference is that in the UCC the General Synod is not a traditional representative body and its actions can never be viewed as a formal expression of local or regional thinking. When the General Synod gathers, although its delegates reflect the diversity and geography of the churches back home, they are not instructed or bound by the opinions of those who send them to synod. The process during each General Synod encourages every delegate to engage each issue with a fresh and open mind and to vote as she or he feels led by the Spirit (see vol. 7:22).

The results of this process are sometimes surprising, even to the delegates themselves; and the UCC General Synod finds itself taking risks, speaking to the congregations from the end of a long limb. This has been upsetting to some members of the church, but it has also turned out to be a prophetic gift. Although local congregations are not formally bound by General Synod actions, they are encouraged to respect and value the work of each General Synod. As a consequence, the actions of General Synods not only confront, but also stretch the thinking and theological work in local congregations. Many find it difficult to ignore the General Synod of the United Church of Christ, empowered by pronouncements and resolutions, as it speaks out on extremely controversial, yet vital, issues.

This form of church order is unusual. It is misunderstood regularly by the general public and even by UCC members and clergy in local congregations. The General Synod does not "speak for" the thousands of congregations that make up the UCC. It "speaks to" them. When each General Synod gathers, under the headship of Jesus Christ and guided by the Holy Spirit, it challenges all UCC members in local communities of faith to rethink again and again what it means to have "courage in the struggle for justice and peace" and to keep word and deed, faith and life, together. It further chides them to remember the prayer of the tax collector, " . . . be merciful to me, a sinner."

Promoting Racial Justice

81. Office of Communication: *Christian Motivations*

(1959)

The Office of Communication report to the 1959 General Synod states that although the UCC was "still in the process of assuming form," the church "had a voice" from its very inception — a voice that "captured public attention, aroused interest, [and] raised hopes of something wondrously new in Christianity." The report cites the involvement of the office with newspapers, magazines, radio, television, and film. It notes the importance of its educational workshops and institutes to aid "local churches, conferences and synods in their work of public interpretation." It upholds its commitment to sponsor and conduct research. The final section of the report reflects upon the ethical challenges facing religious people in an age of mass media and the theological rationale for its work.

In 1959, for various legal reasons, a separate Office of Communication, Inc. was incorporated to take legal action to safeguard the public interest in broadcasting. Office of Communication, Inc. has worked diligently for over forty years to oppose owner consolidation, promote equal employment guidelines, advocate for the recruitment of responsible future media leadership, and support technology learning centers. Its annual Everett C. Parker Lecture and its Fund for Civil Rights in the Media are highly respected by church and civic leaders committed to upholding justice in the broadcasting industry.

Source: Excerpt from the "Report of the Office of Communication," *GS Minutes 1959,* Appendix 15, 182–83.

The Rationale for the Office of Communication

threedots Within this committee the knowledge of the dichotomy of man's greatness balanced against his fallibility in the search for truth constitutes a profoundly serious element in the shaping of the public expression by the United Church of the meaning and task of the Church. The tradition of critical inquiry and discussion that is characteristic of both the Evangelical and Reformed Church and the Congregational Christian Churches receives paramount consideration in every public utterance released through the Office of Communication.

This long-term tradition of our Fellowship has direct bearing on the great dilemma posed by the mass media of communication. These media do not permit communication in the form of letting people test and argue and reach a judgment through person-to-person involvement. But they do marshall so many seemingly incontrovertible facts, they do make such a strong emotional impact, they do beat with such power and persistence on their audiences that they alter convictions and initiate actions just as surely as does personal involvement. They confront the listener or the reader with ready-made intellectual goods, just as they do with ready-made foods and cigarettes and soap. He has no more share in shaping his ideas than he has in manufacturing his material goods. A man today may know more about the world than did his ancestors, but it is doubtful if he is as sure as they were of the motivation for his personal actions.

This situation poses an ethical problem for religion that is all too apparent. It is easy for religious groups to follow the tested pattern for success and rely on the repetitive slogan and soothing formula of positive thinking, instead of attempting the hard task of expounding the absolute demands of the Gospel. Time after time religious communicators skirt the danger of manipulating people — "for their own best interest," of course.

We need great sophistication in our use of the mass media. We must not compromise our principles in the thought that we must adapt to accepted practices. Our obligation is greater than that of anyone else. Religion — almost alone — is consciously using the mass media to effect fundamental life changes. The media are dangerously personal-impersonal. The communicator can seldom, with assurance, weigh the effect of his word.

A Fellowship such as the United Church cannot, therefore, in conscience use the media of public communication to boast of its achievements, or to proclaim the superiority of its beliefs and methods, or even primarily, to persuade in behalf of those acts and institutions in which it has placed its own trust. No social institution is fully satisfying. We are mindful of our close kinship with Job, who questioned even "God's ways with man."

Our primary task in communicating is not to serve ourselves, but to serve our Lord. We are to proclaim the Word — proclaim it in the belief that man's dignity demands that he should search for the meaning of that Word; that through freedom to seek and know the truth he shall come to his own confrontation with God. Our only justifiable use of the mass media, therefore, is to fulfill the obligation of service to all God's people. If our goal is communication of the Faith, our aim must be to lead people into the Christian community, where they may risk the actions that are the ultimate tests of faith. Ideas and institutions have a place in such communication only as they are submitted to the test of the principles, ideas, ideals and possibilities of the Word.

Public communication thus poses an obligation to lead people into full vigorous and searching query about their own faith and works. In this view it is better to discuss a question, even without settling it, than to settle a question without discussing it.

The Office of Communication, in pursuit of such weighty ends, is called upon to eschew the relatively easy role of a publicity agency and to speak to many audiences in terms of their own values, needs and readiness for the Faith. Such work places an enormous load of responsibility upon the members of the Administrative Committee, who must continuously review and evaluate our public communication in terms of our commitment to the Gospel.

82. The Wilmington 10:

"Free for All"

(1978)

Avery Post

In 1970 black students in Wilmington, North Carolina, wanted to hold a Martin Luther King Jr. memorial assembly. However, when interracial fights broke out, only blacks were suspended. Early in 1971, a local UCC pastor who was trying to quell the growing threat of interracial violence asked for help. In response the UCC Commission for Racial Justice (CRJ) sent field representative Benjamin Chavis to Wilmington. Shortly after Chavis arrived more shooting and burning resulted in the death of two persons (a white and a black) and the burning of a white-owned grocery store. Chavis and nine others were charged with burning the store, with conspiracy to assault emergency personnel, and jailed. After one mistrial, a second trial was held in late 1972 where the defendants were convicted and each was sentenced to serve from ten to twenty-nine years in prison.

The United Church of Christ, convinced the defendants were innocent, posted bond for Chavis shortly after the trial. In 1973 the General Synod voted to borrow additional money to free the nine other defendants still in prison while the case was appealed. Unfortunately the appeal process did not go well. First, the North Carolina Court of Appeals affirmed the conviction and then the North Carolina Supreme Court refused to hear the case. In 1976–77, even though several prosecution witnesses admitted that they lied in the original trial, a Superior Court judge again rejected an appeal for a new trial and bail. In 1978 Wilmington 10 defenders appealed directly to the North Carolina governor, but that

---

Source: Avery Post, excerpt from "Defense of the Wilmington 10: A Case of Commitment for the United Church of Christ," *A.D. Magazine* (June–July 1978): 40.

effort also ended unsuccessfully. Finally, after nearly ten years, the Fourth United States Circuit Court of Appeals in Richmond, Virginia, overturned the convictions (1980), ruling that the constitutional rights of all the defendants had been violated in the trial.

During this long process United Church of Christ leaders, especially UCC presidents Joseph Evans and Avery Post, were steadfast in their work for justice. Avery Post (b. 1924) is a Congregational Christian/UCC minister who was educated at Ohio Wesleyan University and Yale Divinity School. After serving pastorates in Vermont, Ohio, Connecticut, and New York he became president of the Massachusetts Conference UCC (1970–77). In 1977 he was elected the fourth president of the United Church of Christ, serving three four-year terms (1977–89). In 1978, after several setbacks, Post defends the witness of the UCC on behalf of the Wilmington 10 with biblical words about freedom.

Free for All

We believe that Jesus has set us free, that he is our trail breaker, that he has broken the seal of death and shaken off the chains of bondage. So let us use our liberty and power to break the chains that bind the children of God. If we are freely born again in Christ, we will not rest until all are free.

Let us rise and go to the mission edges in the struggles for justice and liberty. Let us pray for the power to run together in the right and not grow weary.

Let our piety be that daily toughness that is both personal and public — producing the discipline and endurance required by a God who moves in us to move us out.

Jesus goes before us into Jerusalem and to the jails of our nation to every point of prejudice and injustice.

Finally, let us fulfill our commitment to our brothers in North Carolina — whether they be freed tomorrow or not for years. We are free only in the Lord who has already won the victory, and we will all remain imprisoned until we are all free.

83. Racism: *"The Unfinished Agenda"*

(1989)

Yvonne V. Delk

Yvonne V. Delk (b. 1939) is an African American UCC minister nurtured in the Afro-Christian tradition of the United Church of Christ. Born in Norfolk, Virginia, she is a graduate of Andover Newton Theological School and New York Theological Seminary. After ministries of Christian Education in Atlanta, Georgia, and in Cincinnati, Ohio, she joined the staff of the United Church Board for Homeland Ministries (UCBHM) as secretary for urban and black church education (1969–76). Later she became executive director of the UCC Office for Church in Society (OCIS) (1981–90) and executive director of the Community Renewal Society (CRS), Chicago (1990–98).

In 1989 Delk reminded the church that racism is an unfinished agenda. She calls upon the church to name it, move from denial to repentance to conversion to action, to stand with victims of racism, to make the church a political force, to speak to the economic systems under which people exist, and to give leadership to all groups opposing racism.

Source: Yvonne Delk, excerpts from "The Unfinished Agenda: Racism," *New Conversations* (1989): 40–44.

The Unfinished Agenda: Racism

The year 1940 found my mother and my father bringing me in their arms to Macedonia Congregational Christian Church for a dedication service. I was not quite a year old. This was the moment that I was to receive a name, a people, a history, a community. They understood that we needed a support community if we were able to survive the racism of the nation in which I was born. They realized that for the first twenty-one years of my life, I would live in a segregated community, attend segregated schools, worship in a church that also was broken and wounded by the stain of race.

In 1940, the facts were relatively clear and uncomplicated; the law required separation of the races and no one challenged it. The moral issue was unmistakable, and clearly visible to the rest of the country. Blacks and other people of color were kept apart by law and custom in schools, on buses, in theaters, at luncheonettes, restaurants, hotels, toilets, at drinking fountains, swimming pools, at the ballot box, in the jury box, and in the work place. Blacks were denied equal access and opportunity.

My parents knew then what the Kerner report would affirm twenty-eight years later: there existed in America two separate societies, one White and one Black, and the root cause was racism. They understood that the road that I and the rest of my sisters and brothers would travel would not be easy; that the residual effects of centuries of slavery and legal discrimination would not be erased without struggle; and further, that the hearts and minds of those who had either benefited from racism or who were blind to its effects would not significantly change in their lifetime.

They, therefore, brought me to the church, to the place where the word of God would confront and transcend the hostile forces of hate, violence, prejudice, and even the law of the land. They believed that the gospel had the power to bring together, in one transformed community, people of all ages, races, and tongues. They believed that membership in the household of Jesus Christ transformed persons to become the new creation. It was their belief and hope that the church would become that new creation and that it would use its moral and spiritual force to eliminate racism and to create a wholistic and inclusive society.

There was reason to believe that their hope was not in vain. The denomination to which they belonged had deep roots in the struggle for justice. The foremothers and forefathers had distinguished themselves by their opposition to colonialism and slavery. The American Missionary Association was established by people struggling to achieve a nation without caste or slavery. The United Church of Christ, which was formed more than a century after the establishment of the AMA, continued to embody this hope. In an address to the third General Synod our first president, Dr. Ben Herbster affirmed:

> The United Church of Christ will be able to justify all the "blood, sweat, and tears" that have gone into the effort, during these past years, only if we shall be able to achieve a new devotion and loyalty to the demands of the Gospel of Jesus Christ. Those demands include, beyond a personal commitment to the Way of Christ, also an unending effort to guarantee to all men, women, and children, here in America and to the ends of the earth, a chance to live in freedom, good will, justice, and advantage.

However, in spite of our resolve and our commitments, racism continues to impact every level of our society. It is systemic and pervasive; it is sustained in 1989 by both personal attitudes and structural forces. Asians, Blacks, Hispanics, and Native Americans continue to be the targets of racial violence and bigotry. It is therefore clear that racial justice is the unfinished agenda that the church is called to address.

The challenge before us is urgent and theological. The division of the human family because of race challenges the Church of Jesus Christ to renew its foundational commitment to the faith. God's promise to us is that we are one people because we are reconciled to God in one body through the cross. Therefore, we cannot support any pattern of subordination or domination that separates and divides. The destructive symptoms of racism continue to plague our society: poverty, crime, economic disadvantage, alienation, violence, and persecution. If we keep silent at this moment in our history we will invite despair and death for the people of God. . . .

In spiritual and biblical terms, racism is a perverse sin that cuts to the core of the Gospel message. It is a gaping wound in the body of Christ. Put simply, racism negates the reason for which Christ died, the reconciling work of the cross. It denies the purpose of the church: to bring together, in Christ, those who have been divided from one another. In the early church, it was Jew and Gentile; today, the division is based on race.

There is only one remedy for such a sin, and that is repentance. Repentance will always bear fruit in concrete forms like conversion, changed behavior, and reparation.

The church is therefore called to challenge racism in the following ways:

1. *Name it!*

The church is called to identify racism as a sin against God. We cannot afford to surrender our name, our message, and our understanding of the Gospel to those who consider themselves divinely superior. The church is called to position itself in opposition to any force or power that moves contrary to the will of God. The church cannot be silent at this moment in history. The church must regain a moral sense of urgency. A failure to do so represents a betrayal of the reconciling message of the Gospel and of the very God that has called us into existence.

2. *Move from denial to repentance, to conversion and to action.*

Whites must examine themselves, their relations, and their institutions for the ugly plague of racism. Whites have benefited from the structure of racism whether they have ever committed a racist act, uttered a racist word, or thought a racist thought. Just as surely as people of color suffer in a white society because they are Black, Hispanic, Asian, or Native American, Whites benefit because they are White. If Whites have profited from a racist structure, they must try to change it. Denial represents a refusal to see the truth, and that is no longer an acceptable response. Whites who have accepted Jesus Christ as their Lord and Savior are called to repentance and conversion.

3. *Stand with the victims of racism!*

The primary task of the church is to make theologically real and relevant a God who sides with the oppressed. In the face of society's never-ending efforts to deny the basic humanity of people of color, the church must clearly come down on the side of those who are most vulnerable. It must extend its name, its resources, its theology, its power, and its influence to stand with the victims of racism, and to join with them in the struggle for a world that is free from the plague of racism.

4. *The church must become a political force!*

The church cannot accept a Christianity that does not relate the message of the Gospel to the humanizing of the social, economic, and political structures of the world. The freedom of our children and of others in the world is dependent upon our political engagement in the struggle for justice. Political decisions decide the course of our lives from the cradle to the grave. Political decisions decide how much dirt will be in the air we breathe, the kind of education children will receive, the kind of jobs we will have, whether we will have a job, and what our pay and working conditions will be. The church should encourage and empower persons to participate in the political process. Churches in the United States have participated in Voter Registration efforts, offered educational forums, and have advocated public policies that are fair, just, and equitable for all. Political action is a necessary step toward eradicating the racism in our midst because it allows us to take responsibility for our future. To be committed to the elimination of racism means making a political commitment to make the world a habitable place for all, irrespective of race.

5. *The church is called to speak to the economic systems under which people exist.*

The 17th General Synod of the United Church of Christ will be asked to declare its understanding on the relationship between faith and economics. By affirming that our economic life is also subject to the grace and judgment of God, we explore the relationships among racism, poverty, unemployment, and unequal opportunity in our nation. We are challenged to examine a system which attains the highest standard of living for some of us while denying to others even a job. In obedience to Jesus Christ, we are called to offer economic visions, theories, and policies that are more faithful with the Gospel.

6. *The church is called to give leadership to the organization of coalitions composed of church leaders, movements of the oppressed, and support groups for movements of the oppressed for combatting racism.*

Dr. Martin Luther King showed that the way to deal with racism is to find a common vision and bring people together, to find a common task on which those of all races can work together, hold hands, and move forward together. Racism can be eliminated if we can build a people's movement across racial lines in pursuit of a Just Peace world.

The unfinished agenda is still before us. The moment is at hand for us to press on towards the goal of a new, more humane society. This is not a moment for opting out or becoming passive observers. Each of us by virtue of our baptism into the household of Jesus Christ is called to be a participant in the struggle to combat racism. We will be called upon to risk our positions and our status as we pressure institutions to change, to become the wholistic and inclusive instruments that God intends.

As I face this moment in our history, I do not feel despair. The power of that dedication moment in 1940 is still with me. The words that were proclaimed over me continue to have binding authority. The faith of my parents and those early foreparents who believed in a new community now fuel my passion and commitment for A Just Peace Church and World. The power of the resurrection experience and the religious heritage of people of all colors and races, bound in covenant to achieve a world without hatred or prejudice, empowers me to hope in the midst of the tensions that continue to haunt us. Let us, then, with Jesus Christ at the heart of our efforts, move to finish this agenda. We can and we must if we are to achieve the vision of wholeness that is promised in the Gospel.

84. The Resurgence of Racism: *A Challenge*

(1989, 1991)

General Synod, UCC Leadership

By the late 1980s much of the hope generated in the 1960s about racial justice had faded and incidents of bias-related violence were growing at an alarming rate. In such an environment people began to realize that racial problems facing society were more than prejudice, or personal attitudes towards "other people based on a categorical judgment about their physical characteristics, such as race or ethnic origin." The problem was "racism"— "the intentional or unintentional use of power to isolate, separate and exploit others . . . based on a belief in superior racial origin, identity or supposed racial characteristics." In order to raise awareness and counter the increasingly destructive power of racism the UCC General Synod (1989) passed a resolution containing a theological rationale naming racism as a sin and calling upon the church to confess that sin and work to eliminate it.

Eighteen months later national leaders of the United Church of Christ sent out a "Pastoral Letter on Contemporary Racism and the Role of the Church" (1991). The letter includes a supporting essay on definitions of racism and an analysis of various manifestations of contemporary racism, such as increasing inequities, growing intolerance and hostility, and changing demographics. It uses the terms "racial and ethnic" when describing the growing diversity of church and society. This terminology

---

Sources: Excerpt from "Challenging the Resurgence of Racism in the United States of America," *GS Minutes 1989,* 105. [UCC Leadership], *Pastoral Letter on Contemporary Racism and the Role of the Church,* small pamphlet, n.p. 1991.

develops as an alternative to the term "minority," which seems to forget that the majority of the people in the world actually belong in that category.

A long footnote on the first page of the pastoral letter defines "racism."

Challenging the Resurgence of Racism* in the United States of America

Theological Rationale

Racism is a sin and an evil that stands as an affront to the Christian faith. Racism is an expression of idolatry, replacing faith in God, who created all peoples equal in the image of God, with the belief in the superiority of one race over another. When this idolatry is expressed by those who possess economic and political power, it leads to a cruel and extensive repression of selected peoples and negation of their identity and value as given by God.

The Church is called to define racism as sin against God and is summoned to confess and work to eliminate it. The Statement of Mission of the United Church of Christ, in part, states:

> As a people of the United Church of Christ, affirming our Statement of Faith, we seek within the Church Universal to participate in God's mission and to follow the way of the crucified and risen Christ,
>
> Empowered by the Holy Spirit, we are called and commit ourselves. . . .
>
> To praise God, confess our sin, and joyfully accept God's forgiveness. . . .
>
> To name and confront the powers of evil within and among us.

---

*Racism is often equated with racial prejudice, a personal attitude towards other people based on a categorical judgment about their physical characteristics, such as race or ethnic origin. For some people, racism means any form of race recognition, especially instances in which members of privileged groups act in a manner injurious to a disadvantaged group. Others, however, reserve the term for patterns of belief that one group of humanity, based upon biological or physical characteristics, is innately superior to another and therefore a justification for exploitative differential treatment. Still others use this term to denote feelings of cultural superiority. Our definition goes beyond patterns of recognition and belief to include decisions and policies made by established and well respected institutions within society, which are predicated upon considerations of race for the purpose of subordinating a racial group and maintaining control over that group. Racism is the intentional and unintentional use of power to isolate, separate and exploit based on race.

To repent our silence and complicity with the forces of chaos and death. . . .

To work for justice, healing and the wholeness of life.

The resurgence of racism in our midst, both within church and society, serves as a challenge to our faith in Jesus Christ. Theologically, the Gospel of Jesus Christ compels us to speak out and take action against this new rising tide of racist violence and evil which threatens to engulf our nation.

Pastoral Letter on Contemporary Racism and the Role of the Church

January 18, 1991

Dear Sisters and Brothers in the United Church of Christ:

Racism, in all its overt and covert forms, is an affront to the very foundations of our faith. God created all humanity in the divine image, called us into being, and into loving relationship with all of God's children. This fundamental conviction compels us to affirm our oneness and equality with all humanity. It further compels us to identify, unmask and oppose any power which seeks to divide and separate us. As the Body of Christ we accept the mission which Jesus initiated of breaking down the dividing walls of hostility.

Despite significant progress, our church, society and world are polarized today because of the pervasive and destructive sin of racism. As a multiracial church which confesses faith in the one sovereign God who binds in covenant faithful people of all ages, tongues and races, we have a special responsibility. As a multicultural church, we are called to embrace the diversity of God's gifts to the human family and rejoice in the variety of God's grace. So important is this affirmation that the Seventeenth General Synod instructed us to develop and distribute a "Pastoral Letter on Contemporary Racism and the Role of the Church." A Pastoral Letter is an extraordinary vehicle in the life of our United Church of Christ, having been used only infrequently in our thirty year history, and on only the most acute issues.

The Seventeenth General Synod thus declared, "Racism is a sin and an evil that stands as an affront to the Christian faith. Racism is an expression of idolatry, replacing faith in God, who created all peoples equal in the image of God, with the belief in the superiority of one race over another.

When this idolatry is expressed by those who possess economic and political power, it leads to a cruel and extensive repression of selected peoples and negation of their identity and value as given by God. The Church is called to define racism as sin against God and is summoned to confess and work to eliminate it."

We view with alarm the many recent manifestations of racism as evidenced by the increase in racially motivated violence throughout the United States of America. It is all too easy to dismiss these as isolated acts of fringe groups and extremist individuals. We know that they are only visible consequences of racist attitudes which permeate most of our institutions and operating assumptions, and which many of us have accepted without critical examination. The systematic discrimination which results from racism is profoundly disturbing.

The effects of racism are found in socio-economic data showing dramatic disparities in such areas as education, income, employment status, health care, housing, crime rates, infant mortality, and drug addiction. The United States continues to be two societies, separate and unequal. These words ring as true today in the 1990s as they did over twenty years ago in the Kerner Commission Report (also known as the Report of the National Advisory Commission on Civil Disorders, published in 1968) issued during the aftermath of the urban riots of the 1960s. Poverty is worse now than it was then. There is a large and growing urban underclass in the United States, more economically isolated and socially alienated than ever before. As a result of racial discrimination, all over the United States there are "quiet riots" in the form of unemployment, poverty, social disorganization, family disintegration, housing and school deterioration and crime. These are even more destructive of human life than the violent riots of the past. Hence, we emphatically reject the notion that racism, particularly in the form of institutionalized discrimination, is a problem that no longer requires our utmost attention.

The United Church of Christ has a long tradition of confronting racism through the mission work of our national bodies, conferences, associations and local churches. We also have a painful record of discrimination — sometimes benign, sometimes intentional — against racial and ethnic persons within our own household. We call upon every member and local church of the United Church of Christ to renew our faith in the unity God intends, and to increase our commitment to stem the resurgent tide of racism in our increasingly multiracial and multicultural society. Indeed, we must challenge ourselves, our church and our society to be active in seeking new ways to welcome the gifts of people of every racial and ethnic heritage. We can begin to do this together in the following ways:

- to affirm that the God of creation has called all of humanity equally into being without limitation or discrimination based on race or ethnicity (Genesis 1:27);
- to thank God in worship and in our devotional life for the diversity of the human family and for our covenant with each other;
- to examine prayerfully, in light of our faith, our own attitudes and assumptions about race;
- to acknowledge the ways in which many of us have benefited, and continue to benefit, from the racial exclusion and exploitation of others in our political and economic system;
- to identify the attitudes, institutions and structures within our communities, including our local churches, that racially discriminate, and work to transform them;
- to seek and develop ongoing opportunities for the mutual sharing of diverse histories, experiences, cultures and spiritual gifts;
- to participate actively in the political process on behalf of public policies which result in greater justice, equality and unity;
- to establish a local church Christian education emphasis on racism and cultural diversity for persons of all age groups; and
- to create groups within our churches to challenge the contemporary manifestations of racism in church and society on a continuing basis as a faithful response to the Gospel of Jesus Christ.

As Christians, affirming our oneness in Christ, let us be fervent in our prayers and in our commitment to reconcile the false divisions which the forces of racism have nurtured among us. Let us be both repentant and merciful as we boldly stand with the victims of racism and as we change the ways in which each of us contributes to this victimization of others. In this time of challenge and change throughout the world, may God give us in the United Church of Christ the strength and the courage faithfully to seek the necessary changes so that no child of God will suffer the devastating and debilitating effects of racism. And, by grace, may we come to know the deeper unity that comes as we embrace each other and all of God's manifold gifts.

Advocating with Women

85. Women in Church and Society: *A Pronouncement*

(1971)

General Synod, Marjorie H. Likins

The denominations that came together to form the United Church of Christ had a long history of women's activism in the church. Congregational women during the last half of the nineteenth century founded independent Woman's Boards of Missions. Local women's guilds and fellowships sustained important networks for education, mission, leadership development, and spiritual nurture during the twentieth century.

When the United Church of Christ established its new national instrumentalities in the early 1960s a decision was made not to have separate denominational structures for women. Although a woman, Helen Huntington Smith (1902–71) became the executive for the new UCC Council for Lay Life and Work (CLLW) in 1963, the council existed to support the ministries of all laity in the church.

Unfortunately, during this same time period there was a growing conviction among younger women that they had special needs that were not being met by existing church structures. Some of these women became involved in the "feminist movement" and pressed the church for change, even as numerous older women who did not have work outside the home continued to find local congregational women's guilds and fellowship organizations important.

The General Synod "Pronouncement on the Status of Women in Church and Society" (1971) names the situation and makes specific suggestions for change. It states that "women have been the victims of injustice resulting from cultural patterns which have greatly restricted

Source: "Pronouncement on The Status of Women in Church and Society," *GS Minutes 1971,* 129–30.

their freedom in the performance of their sexual roles," and it calls the United Church of Christ to address a number of issues.

Marjorie H. Likins was minister of Christian Education for the Southern California Conference UCC. She spoke to the General Synod (1971) in support of the pronouncement because she was convinced that relegating women to a subordinate role was common and that the church needs to recognize cultural patterns and "take steps" to bring about change.

Pronouncement on the Status of Women in Church and Society

An integral part of our Christian faith is that God's love for all his children makes no distinction of worth between male and female. They are equal in value in God's sight; therefore, distinctions made by society which assume an inferior-superior relationship are contrary to the will of God. The right of each person to achieve his or her maximum potential as a child of God is basic to any understanding of the gospel of Jesus Christ.

We affirm the vital importance of the woman's role in the parent-child relationship; however, our society has locked most women into stereotyped roles as housekeepers and child-raisers without regard to their desires or abilities to perform other kinds of work. This has resulted in widespread discrimination in employment, job training, education, and compensation for work performed. Many a woman, sheltered by her husband's earnings and presence, never learns that discrimination exists until widowed or divorced. In great part women are excluded from better paying jobs, and in many instances they receive less pay for performing substantially the same work. Furthermore they are under-represented on church boards, in church pulpits, and on the staffs of the denomination's national and judicatory structures.

The health of the church, the family, and all institutions of our society depends on the contributions all can make; thus, to deny any group the right to fulfill its maximum potential is to deprive society of the most effective means for solving its increasingly complex problems.

Moreover, women have been the victims of injustice resulting from cultural patterns which have greatly restricted their freedom in the performance of their sexual roles. These act as restrictions upon men also, since our culture makes assumptions about what are properly "male" interests and traits and what are properly "female."

In the light of these considerations, the General Synod calls on the members, local churches, Conferences, Instrumentalities, and other national agencies of the United Church of Christ to:

1. Insist on increasing opportunities for women in theological education, ordination, voluntary roles, and employment at all levels of the church's life — as pastors, as national and judicatory staff, with equal pay for equal work, and as members and officers of the policy-making boards and agencies of the denomination.
2. Introduce into church and public school materials more information concerning the significant contributions women have made to our history and culture.
3. Offer the church as inspiration and forum to develop a social action program concerning women's rights and expectations.
4. Work toward elimination of discrimination in employment and compensation on the basis of sex wherever it exists in our society.
5. Call on the United States Senate to ratify the United Nations Convention on Political Rights of Women which is now pending before the Senate Foreign Relations Committee.
6. Work for easier access to contraceptive information and materials, and for legalization of physician performed abortions during the early months of pregnancy.
7. Commend (without necessarily endorsing every claim, style, and proposal) the movements for women's rights for their contributions towards better understanding of the economic, cultural, and social injustices which have been inflicted upon the women in our society.
8. Affirm new life styles for our children which allow boys and girls to express their essential humanity and free their vocational prospects.
9. Recognize that there are other areas not covered in this document and deserving further study, especially those pertaining to the legal implications of the Equal Rights Amendment, such as military service, divorce, legal age, and property rights.

In Support of the Pronouncement on Women

In support of this pronouncement I would like to recall the phrase from the Third World presentation this morning, "More people have been done in by the Bible," and the Jewish prayer in which the suppliant thanks God

SOURCE: Marjorie H. Likins, speaking on behalf of the "Pronouncement on The Status of Women in Church and Society," *GS Minutes 1971,* 207.

that he was not born a woman, and to recall Adam's rib, Herb's wife and John's mother to illustrate that in fact we do have a problem.

"Whole earth — whole people."

Many white women, having heard the pleas of the welfare mothers, the Indians, and the Mexican-Americans, feel white guilt so paralyzing that they cannot even express or bear to think about their own condition. I would like to suggest to my white sisters that the feeling of guilt is appropriate but it is misplaced. We are feeling guilty about the wrong thing.

Properly founded, that guilt would lie in the fact that, white and favored, educated or with opportunity for education, we have refused to press for any form of power in government or in the church which would enable us this day to alleviate and radically alter this sickness in the United States.

Furthermore, actively enhancing the myth of weakness and dependence in order that we may be supported while we raise our children and then relax for the rest of our lives, we enslave white men and make it harder for them to respond to the better part of self which demands more equitable distribution of wealth. They are afraid to give up privilege because they have dependent wives whose major occupation may be the expenditure of the family resources.

Many women delegates have asked, "Women's liberation? What is that? I'm free!" In this they are secure. The church is the central gathering place of happily married families. It does not hold working women who are raising families alone because of divorce or death. It does not hold them because it does not primarily concern itself with the needs of such people.

This pronouncement seeks to care for them. It seeks to remind us all that equal pay for equal work is not the practice of the land. It seeks to remind us that in high schools women are counseled away from decision-making vocations: "Be a nurse, not a doctor — a teacher, not an administrator — a director of Christian education, not a minister." Our high school girls are haunted by the spectre of spinsterhood if they show competence. This is not necessary. It enslaves men as much as women.

Sex roles are a product of culture. Women are encouraged to be dependent, weak, immature. Mothers educate daughters to this role. If the dominant Caucasian male has relegated the people of the Third World to subordinate roles, he has learned this life-style within the intimate structure of his own family. The relegation of others to subordinate roles begins with the relegation of women to a subordinate role and persists until it becomes a life-style habit. The church needs to recognize this and take steps to change it.

That is what this pronouncement is about. I urge you to support it.

86. Abortion:
"Freedom of Choice"

(1971)

General Synod, Robert M. Bartlett

One of the most difficult issues confronting church and society during the last half of the twentieth century has been the question of abortion. Before the late nineteenth century, abortion was regarded as a domestic matter, but beginning in 1821 Connecticut made abortion illegal after quickening. The earliest abortion laws were passed to protect women against quacks and herbalists who threatened women's health; however, by the 1950s concern to protect the fetus, rather than the woman, undergirded most antiabortion laws.

During the 1960s new thinking about abortion developed: first, physicians and public health professionals became increasingly concerned about the medical dangers of illegal abortions and the impact of laws on medical decisions; and second, women themselves reasserted their role in reproductive choice and launched efforts to remove abortion totally from the realm of penal law.

The United Church of Christ proposal for "Freedom of Choice Concerning Abortion" (1971) is one of the earliest pro-choice actions taken by a major Protestant denomination. It outlines theological and ethical factors and legislative policy, and calls for the repeal of all present abortion legislation, even as it encourages churches to expand ministries of counsel and concern related to unwanted pregnancies.

Sources: "Freedom of Choice Concerning Abortion," *GS Minutes 1971,* 131–33. Robert M. Bartlett, M.D., speaking against Proposal for Action, "Freedom of Choice Concerning Abortion," *GS Minutes 1971,* 212.

The proposal on abortion passed, but there were those who spoke out against it. Robert M. Bartlett, a medical doctor from Silver Lake, Ohio, and a delegate from the Ohio Conference, recognized that it was proper for the church to discuss abortion because it "deals with life and death and the creation of life." However, Bartlett laments the lack of theological and scriptural support for the proposal and suggests that the only reasons behind the proposal are selfish. He endorses the "avoidance of unwanted pregnancy," but he opposes "the deliberate interruption of a creative act of God!"

Freedom of Choice Concerning Abortion

A responsible position concerning abortion should be based on a consideration of the rights of the individual woman, her potential child, her family and society, as well as the rights of the fetus.

Theological and Ethical Factors

Standing in the Hebrew-Christian tradition, we affirm God as the Source of life — our life, all life, life to the full. He has called us to share the work of creation with him, giving us the privileges and responsibilities of fellowship in the family and in the wider unities of society. Thus we affirm the freedom with which God endowed men and women, but we affirm and receive this as freedom bound to responsibility. At its best our Western legal tradition, too, has served the dual purpose of protecting human freedom and helping human beings to discharge their responsibilities to one another.

Our religious heritage has also stressed reverence for human life. Accordingly, the enhancement of human life and the protection of the rights of persons, particularly the weak and defenseless, has become an important element in our legal system. It has found expression in laws intended to protect those who cannot protect themselves, such as children, including the unborn. It is neither likely nor desirable that organized society would disavow its responsibility in this regard.

Inevitably, therefore, a judgment will be made or assumed as to when personal human life begins and at what point society has an interest in it and affirms an obligation toward it. Although a form of life exists in the sperm and the unfertilized ovum, a new kind of life emerges at the moment of their union. Many regard conception (up to 72 hours after coitus), others implantation (7 days), as the beginning of an inviolable life. But while such life is human in origin and potentially human in character, the integration of bodily functions and the possibility of social interaction do not appear until later. Alternative candidates for the beginning of significantly human life are the final fixing of the genetic code (3 weeks), the first central nervous system activity (8 weeks), brain development and cardiac activity (12 weeks). Some time after the twelfth week "quickening" occurs; that is, the mother can feel the arm and leg movements of the fetus. "Viability" in the present stage of technology begins between the 20th and 28th week, and the fetus has a chance for survival outside the womb. At some point in the process from conception to birth there comes "a period when a life contains that which is essentially valued as significantly human and should be vested with a sanctity uncompromisable to the interest of lesser claims" (Robert M. Veatch in *Social Action,* March, 1971).

An ethical view does not require an undifferentiated concern for life. It places peculiar value upon personal life and upon the quality of life, both actual and potential. In that light it is understandable that today an increasing number of persons find it difficult, if not impossible, to attribute anything more than the potentiality of human personhood to the embryo in its early stages. The implication is that factors other than its existence may appropriately be given equal or greater weight at this time — the welfare of the whole family, its economic condition, the age of the parents, their view of the optimum number of children consonant with their resources and the pressures of population, their vocational and social objectives, for example.

On the other hand, many would agree that during the later months of a normal pregnancy life should not be interrupted except for the most serious reasons (such as the physical or mental health of the mother, abnormality or disease of the fetus, incest, or rape). This distinction is of the greatest importance. Individuals contemplating an abortion should make a responsible decision early, certainly within the first two or three months.

Legislative Policy

The theological and scientific views on when human life begins are so numerous and varied that one particular view should not be forced on society through its legal system.

Present laws prohibiting abortion are neither just nor enforceable. They compel women either to bear unwanted children or to seek illegal abortions regardless of the medical hazards and suffering involved.

By severely limiting access to safe abortions, these laws have the effect of discriminating against the poor.

The mere liberalization of the laws has not proven to be a viable solution to the problem of illegal abortions. The liberalized laws tend to cause more rigidity and narrowness of interpretation, and, in any case, cannot cover all circumstances in which an abortion may be appropriate.

For these reasons, the Eighth General Synod of the United Church of Christ calls for the repeal of all legal prohibitions of physician-performed abortions. This would take abortion out of the realm of penal law and make voluntary and medically safe abortions legally available to all women. Simultaneously we ask that adequate protection be given to "conscientious objectors" against abortion, including physicians, nurses, and prospective mothers.

Call to Action

In order to give effect to its concern for freedom with responsibility, and acknowledging the church's obligation to aid in the resolution of the problem of unwanted pregnancies, the General Synod of the United Church of Christ takes the following action:

1. The General Synod calls upon the churches of the United Church of Christ and their members to involve themselves extensively in programs which would support repeal of present abortion legislation and to expand their ministries of counsel and concern to all women who have problems related to unwanted pregnancies.

2. The General Synod calls upon pastors, members, local churches, Conferences, and Instrumentalities to provide programs of counseling and education as to the meaning and nature of human life, sexuality, responsible parenthood, population control, and family life.

3. The General Synod calls on pastors, members, local churches, Conferences, and Instrumentalities to support and expand programs of family life and sex education in schools, agencies for adult education, communications media, and other public institutions; and to encourage the extension of information and services related to contraception as instrumental to the prevention of undesirable pregnancies and the achievement of wholesome family life.

4. The General Synod calls on pastors, members, and local churches to offer counseling opportunities and supporting fellowship for persons facing problems of unwanted or ill-advised pregnancies; to assist such persons in making wise ethical decisions regarding their problems; and

to help them find professional assistance if necessary, as through existing noncommercial consultative services.

5. The General Synod urges the Council for Health and Welfare and its member agencies to work for the expansion of family planning services in the communities they serve and to initiate new programs that can serve as models to other hospitals and institutions.

6. The General Synod requests the Division of Health and Welfare and the Division of Christian Education to provide educational resources, consultative services, and training for constituents who wish to sponsor programs which are consistent with this General Synod position.

7. The General Synod calls on pastors, members, health and welfare committees, the Division of Health and Welfare, and other agencies to develop ministries on behalf of disadvantaged and minority groups which would give them freedom of choice in the area of family planning and in the termination of unwanted pregnancies in keeping with this statement.

8. The General Synod calls the above action to the attention of Conferences and Instrumentalities and urges their appropriate staffs to co-operate closely in the implementation of the purposes of this statement.

Against the Proposal Affirming Choice Regarding Abortion

It is proper for a church body to discuss abortion because it deals with life and death and creation of life, and these are within the jurisdiction of the church.

The important issue before us is voluntary abortion of unwanted pregnancies.

I have been disappointed with the scarcity of theological and scriptural support of this action that is proposed. Let me point out some pertinent scriptural and theological observations.

Abortion is not mentioned in the Old or New Testament and so one might assume that it was not practical or it was unmentionable in the Hebrew and early Christian societies.

Scripture indicates that God creates man in his own image, and so man is a creation of God. The commandment, "Thou shalt not kill," comes through loud and clear. Scripture makes many references to Jesus' ministries of healing and mercy but none to his performing an abortion. Can you imagine scripture reading, "And they brought to Jesus many girls and women with unwanted pregnancies. He looked upon them with compassion and caused them all to be aborted. And they fell down at his feet and worshipped him"?

If abortion had been an acceptable practice in the time of Jesus and God had not intervened by means of an angel, Mary might well have had an abortion — at least Joseph planned to put her away privately.

Perhaps you will say abortion was no problem in Jesus' time. I call to your attention that, many centuries before the birth of Christ, abortion was so much a problem in the heathen communities around Palestine that Hippocrates in his code of ethics of medical practice singled out abortion and said he would have no part of it.

The only theological support that I have heard for abortion is that it releases the women from captivity. To me this is a far stretch of the scripture to which it is related.

The theologians tell me the difficulty they have with the abortion issue is the difficulty in defining when human life begins. The only clear-cut moment that can be identified at which human life begins is at the moment of conception or fertilization of the egg. All other points of identification are variable — such points as feeling life, hearing the heartbeat, delivery, severing the umbilical cord, etc.

We hear about elimination of unwanted pregnancy. At least 25 per cent of those of us here in this meeting were unwanted at the time we were conceived and would have been destroyed if voluntary abortion had been the custom of the day.

Every reason that I have heard for abortion of unwanted pregnancy is a selfish one: the unmarried girl or woman who does not want to face the consequences of her act; the mother and father who do not want to share their resources, limited as they may be, with the new child; the mother who is too weary to take care of another child; the woman who is too busy with her social life to have it interrupted with new responsibilities.

I heartily endorse the avoidance of unwanted pregnancy and medical and religious counseling for the distraught and unhappy pregnant woman.

I oppose the destruction of human life and the deliberate interruption of a creative act of God!

87. Reflections on Abortion:
"The Conflict of Moral Presumptions"

(1989)

Lloyd Steffen

Lloyd Steffen (b. 1951) is a UCC minister educated at New College (Florida), Andover Newton Theological School, Yale Divinity School, and Brown University. He was on the faculty at Northland College (1982–90) and has taught at Lehigh University since 1990. Beginning in 1984 Craigville Colloquies on various theological topics were held each year at the Christian campground on Cape Cod (see vol. 7:61). Steffen's paper on abortion was part of Craigville VI (1989): "Human Beginnings: Deciding about Life in the Presence of God." He is the author of Life/Choice: The Theory of Just Abortion *(1994) and* Abortion: A Reader *(1996).*

Abortion and the Conflict of Moral Presumptions

Tempting though it may be to applaud those efforts within the Christian community to reach consensus on so divisive an issue as abortion, it is important that Christians never actually achieve such consensus. The thesis I wish to advance — I would call it the "sustained ambiguity" thesis or the "necessity of uncertainty" thesis — is simply this: that the lack of consensus on abortion within the Christian community constitutes a salutary state

---

Source: Lloyd Steffen, "Abortion and the Conflict of Moral Presumptions," typescript from *Papers of the Craigville Theological Colloquy VI: Human Beginnings: Deciding about Life in the Presence of God* (Craigville, Mass.: Craigville Conference Center, 1989), 20–23.

of affairs while achievement of consensus would represent a triumph of ideological thinking inimical to values to be derived from Christian faith.

Specifically, those who claim certainty on the abortion issue, be they on the side of pro-life or pro-choice, are answering a difficult and ambiguous value question as if it lent itself to resolution with objective certainty, which it does not. Consider how science is used in the abortion debate. Some say science can establish that personhood obtains at the moment of conception, therefore it is immoral to kill a fetus; others say science has failed to establish that a fetus or even a neonate satisfies our criteria for elemental personhood, therefore abortion and even infanticide are permissible. Both positions invoke science as the final arbiter and ultimate authority for deciding questions of value.

Faith is no enemy of science, for both faith and science are truth-seeking enterprises. They do not seek truth in the same realm, however. Science inquires into the realm of nature, seeking to establish what is the case empirically, while faith inquires into the realm of the spirit where freedom is the hallmark and the question at stake concerns meaning and value. Faith seeks to understand the meaning of any given state of affairs that science proposes as factual, and for this reason, faith demands that any interpretation of established facts be critically evaluated and challenged.

The fact is that science cannot determine with objective certainty when the fetus, which is a living biological process, qualifies for the moral office of personhood. Personhood establishes that a living creature can assume the status of a rights-bearing claimant; and because primary among the rights legitimately claimed by persons is a right to continued existence, persons do possess a right to life. For there to be consensus in the religious community, or even in the scientific community, as to when the fetus is a person — the question "When does life begin?" is fundamentally the wrong question — would make it appear that a kind of certainty on this issue is available when it is not. "When is the fetus a person?" cannot be determined by science, only by persons making judgments and operating in accordance with certain values they cherish and wish to promote, believing them to be true and consistent with relevant facts. The kind of factual consensus so important to establishing truth claims in science is not available on the abortion issue, for abortion is essentially a moral problem. Widely shared moral presumptions have created communities of consensus that cannot — and in my view should not — agree with other communities of consensus that take a different view as to what abortion means or which values take precedence.

Communities of consensus have arisen in response to the abortion issue because persons of similar values share a similar interpretation of a factual state of affairs, that state of affairs being that science cannot establish when a fetus becomes a person. Those who have joined a community of consensus on one side of the issue or the other have decided to promote a certain moral presumption — either that the fetus is a person from conception, or that it is not: again, these are value questions not factual questions — and they have sought to advance social policies that would cultivate the particular moral presumptions they honor.

Religious values and faith traditions have influenced how persons enter into communities of consensus on the abortion issue, but, as the fact of wide and deep dissension proves, there is room for division and disagreement even within that community of consensus which is the Church. And it is clear that no single perspective on the abortion issue commands the assent of all Christians. The fact of division within the community of faith means, however, that abortion raises issues involving moral presumptions all Christians ought to hold dear. What is unclear is which presumption ought to take precedence over the other when a conflict between moral presumptions arises. Is the Christian presumption that life, even the life of a fetus, ought to be honored as God's creation and neither needlessly nor directly destroyed the reigning presumption? Or is the presumption that if personhood is not established and the right to life thereby actuated, then human autonomy and the protection of the freedom to decide ought to prevail?

For Christians the debate over abortion comes down to asking which moral presumption important to the faith should take precedence when a conflict arises between them in a situation of objective uncertainty: the value of life or the value of free choice? Of course a conflict between these two values must be established, and sometimes it is not, as in the case of someone seeking an abortion for cosmetic reasons, or because of dissatisfaction with the sex of the fetus, or even as a means of birth control. In such situations the presumption of life would clearly withstand the freedom of choice challenge, since the decision to abort could be shown to be morally trivial; and one cannot, in the Christian faith tradition, end life, human or even potentially human life, for morally trivial reasons.

II

In my view, abortion always involves a conflict between moral presumptions, which is to say that abortion is always a moral problem, to which the division in the Christian community testifies. I make this point because I so often encounter people in my teaching and in my ministry who have come to think that abortion is simply a question one decides one way or the other, as if the status of abortion as a "moral problem" is finally resolvable and therefore non-problematic. I want to preserve the status of abortion as a moral problem so that we might approach this issue in the spirit of faith — with fear and trembling — rather than with the certainty that comes from an easy conscience. If Christians can preserve the conflict between moral presumptions and live with the agony of ambiguity, refusing to treat the abortion issue as if it were an issue in science rather than an issue of faith and values, we might come to recognize that our faith does not decide policy but persons, and that faith offers no easy answers.

Clearly, the killing of the fetus represents a tragic solution to the conflict of moral presumptions; but also tragic is the denial of the freedom to choose when it cannot be shown that the fetus, at least in the first stage of pregnancy, is a person and entitled to claim an irrefutable right to life. My position is that abortion is a human tragedy because what is in conflict is momentous and whatever decision is made reveals our moral presumptions as presumptions. That is, when persons make decisions about abortion, they do so in situations of objective uncertainty; yet, because life and death are involved, human beings proceed as if they had the force of certainty behind them, which they do not. This tragic situation has led me to conclude that at least the conflict between moral presumptions must be preserved so that as Christians, we never assume to be operating in the moral sphere as if we possessed complete knowledge or absolute certainty about the meaning of our deeds and decisions. I speak on behalf of preserving the conflict between moral presumptions and seek to preserve a conflict that we eliminate only at the risk of inviting arrogance, moral insensitivity, religious presumption and finally, self-deception.

It is in the stew of this conflict, which I wish to keep heated and stirred up, that I would offer certain propositions for discussion, indicating also why I believe our presumptions about abortion should fall to the side of freedom of choice rather than accede to person-from-conception thinking.

1. Because a cell may split up to 14 days after conception, it is never clear how many humans will develop from it. Metaphysically, it is inconceivable to me that a fertilized egg that might yet split into multiple human beings could contain one soul that is somehow split or many that are not. For many Christians, the idea of person-from-conception is tied to the concept of the soul that is thought to inhabit the fertilized egg from the time of conception. The twinning phenomenon, however, is a biological process that persuades me that a fertilized egg, because it metamorphosizes, is not even a member of the human species at conception much less an ensouled person.

2. Biology tells us that a fetus is anatomically formed by the third month of gestation, but few organs are histologically differentiated by that time, so that the fetus is still in the state of becoming human rather than being a member of the human species. In other words, the "metamorphosis" so often seen in natural development has not allowed the fetus that is becoming human to claim that it actually is human. A fertilized egg is a product of the species that produces it: it is not thereby automatically a member of the species. A zygote may be on the way to becoming a member of the species without actually being a member, which is to say the fetus develops as a part of a natural process. It seems to me, however, that by the end of the first trimester, an implicit promise has been made to the fetus to continue its life, and that breaking such a promise, while not constituting murder, is a most serious breach of promise keeping and is therefore prima facie immoral.

3. If the fetus is innocent and a person from conception, then it does not seem to me that a woman who gets pregnant by rape can claim that the innocent fetus is an aggressor from whom she needs protection. I do not understand how so many pro-lifers, including the current President of the U.S., can oppose abortion except in the case of rape or incest (or to save the life of the mother). This is logically inconsistent, since they are allowing abortion for an unwanted pregnancy in one case but not in another without explaining how the status of the fetus has sufficiently altered to thereby justify the killing. I hold that people who make such exceptions are inconsistent in allowing choice in some cases where a fetus is not wanted but not in others.

4. The idea that abortions are permissible because a woman has a right to do anything she wants with her body is fallacious. This not only invokes a dualism between mind and body inimical to much feminist philosophical teaching (i.e., inconsistent), but it is one more instance of a domination ethic that is contrary to the dominion-stewardship ethic so central to the Christian understanding of humanity and nature.

5. We Christians need to examine what we mean by the "soul." Our cultural problems with abortion, problems atheistic cultures do not have (e.g., Soviet Union, China), stem from an understanding of the fetus as ensouled, so that the killing of the fetus is killing a person who has been ensouled — which points to an anthropological problem that it is the soul that makes us human. This represents a complete triumph of Greek thinking. Christians, however, are also the inheritors of Hebrew thinking and affirm a bodily resurrection. The point here is that we may not be killing a person with a soul when an abortion is performed, since body and soul may not be so distinguishable as assumed. As Psalm 146 puts it: "When

his breath (spirit) departs he returns to his earth; on that very day his plans perish." If we are not animated by a distinct and survivable immortal soul that inhabits our body, but are our bodies, we need to consider the prospect that when we die we die until such time as we are raised in our bodies, which means that aborting an unformed fetus is not the killing of an ensouled person but the killing of an undeveloped form of life that is on the way to becoming human and on the way to taking hope in the promise of a bodily resurrection.

Given these concerns, I still want to affirm that destroying a fetus, because it is in the process of becoming human and receives tacit protection through a covenant of promise from the mother, ought to command our moral presumptions — not exclusively but in general. Social policy, however, ought to preserve the environment where debate can continue on an issue that cannot be resolved by appeal to objective uncertainty. The morality of abortion is decided by how one settles a conflict in moral presumptions, and I think society ought to provide a context of freedom within which persons on either side of the debate can continue to express the view of their community of consensus. And as a Christian, I want to be able to offer the view of faith which is at least this: that no matter how individual cases of unwanted pregnancy are finally settled, we cannot presume to speak with absolute certainty — only with fear and trembling.

88. Racism and Sexism: *"A Minority Woman's Point of View"*

(1979)

Valerie Russell

Valerie Russell (1941–97) was an African American UCC laywoman who grew up poor in a wealthy Boston, Massachusetts, suburb. She was educated at Suffolk University in Boston and later did graduate work at Columbia University, New York City. After working with the YWCA (1968–73), Russell became assistant to the president of the UCC and coordinator for the Advisory Commission on Women in Church and Society (1973–79). She directed a national conference on the city at Riverside Church (1980–81) and served as the president of the City Mission Society of Boston (1981–91) (see vol. 7:92 for Avery Post's prayer at her installation). She was executive director of the UCC Office for Church and Society (OCIS) (1991–97).

During the 1970s as concerns about racism and sexism led to a General Synod "Pronouncement on Racism and Sexism" (1977) efforts were made to provide a "Resource Packet on Racism and Sexism for Leaders in American Church and Society" (1979). The packet was produced by Valerie Russell, coordinator of the Advisory Commission on Women in Church and Society, and Susan M. Savell, staff for Liberation Church Development of the United Church Board for Homeland Ministries (UCBHM).

Source: Valerie Russell, "A Collective Struggle: A Minority Woman's Point of View," in the *Racism/ Sexism Packet* (New York: Advisory Commission on Women and United Church Board for Homeland Ministries, United Church of Christ, 1979), 1.

A Collective Struggle: A Minority Woman's Point of View

There is a battle now raging about whether or not sexism and racism have real elements in common, and whether or not the collective struggle of one has any real implications for the other. It is my position that the struggle for liberation is a struggle toward a new humanness, and that one dare not happen apart from any other struggle. The seeds which spawn the racist mentality also spawn the sexist mentality, though the results differ in both their historical manifestations and degree of oppression. It is critical to any group of women, working through a Christian perspective toward liberation, that we take a careful look at sexism and racism in order to build an understanding of their similarities and differences. If we are to effect institutional change we need to capitalize upon the similarities but to realistically acknowledge and be sensitive to the differences. This will enable us to build a community of trust with each other and also affirm the nature of pluralism within a context of unity.

WHAT IS RACISM? Any attitude, action or institutional structure which systematically subordinated a person or group because of their color.

WHAT IS SEXISM? Any attitude, action or institutional structure which systematically subordinated a person or group because of their sex.

As we work through these definitions let us begin to look at some of the fundamental similarities in the two problems. One way of doing this is to reflect upon the general nature of oppression and the context which it sets for *human liberation.*

Jürgen Moltmann has pointed out that a succession of freedom movements have expressed the human striving for liberation in Western society. Each new movement has continued the gains of previous ones. "Each one has opened a new front in the struggle for freedom." A staff colleague of mine, Dr. Letty Russell, states in a paper entitled, "Human Liberation in a Feminine Perspective," that "Women belong to one of the groups who find that liberties gained in past revolutions of freedom have not been adequate. As an oppressed majority they point to a basic and persistent form of domination which is expressed in the various social customs regarding the man-woman relationship. As they strive to break the peculiar chains of sexism, they become aware of their solidarity with all those who aspire for full human liberation. Learning from others — they also contribute their own perspective to what is happening in the rapidly changing institutions of society. . . .

"Secondly, HUMAN LIBERATION MEANS NEW CONSCIOUSNESS OF OPPRESSION AND RISING EXPECTATIONS CONCERNING THE FUTURE. Oppressed people begin the process of liberation by negating the negative of the present situation. And it is this discovery that frees them to discover their humanity. . . .

"This is a phenomenon which points to the growing awareness that humanization involves freedom to participate in shaping one's own destiny."

It is precisely at this critical juncture of what Paulo Freire calls "conscientization" that the broad perspective of sexism and racism must converge. It is critical that the *perception of the nature of oppression, and the vision of the new freedom* not be one-sided. For when analyzing the nature of past oppression we quickly realize that part of the disease has been the inherent one-sidedness of the definitions of social reality. Namely, the norms of America, and indeed in most Western thought and historical Christianity, have been set by white, Western, male thinking. The historical struggle which both women and racial minorities have suffered in America is predominately the history of those hang-ups. We have been living out a reality not authentically our own. Yet, through inheritance, assimilation, socialization, seduction, whatever name you call it, the majority of Americans — particularly females — have bought those hang-ups as their own, "lock, stock and barrel." This was particularly true of white women since their physical, social, cultural and economic characteristics most closely resembled the oppressor. Racial groups have always been aware that they have been a part of "the American dream." To Black, Chicana, Asian American, Indian and Puerto Rican women, there is little reason now to believe that suddenly white women, newly aware of their oppression will rise up with a new vision of the future which somehow encompasses more than their historical experience. I am not saying that white women do not have a new vision which is nonoppressive, but it must be defined and demonstrated to be believed. Trust must be earned. *How such trust is earned should be a major focus* for any women's group seeking to deal with questions of liberation. Minority sisters have too bitter a taste in their mouths from the years spent doing white women's housework and child-raising from being constantly demeaned because of white standards of beauty and "gracefulness." Sojourner Truth's now famous poem, "And Ain't I a Woman?" stands as a cry of minority women from the depths of their struggle for acceptance. In their historical eye, the white woman has been their enemy. It is now necessary for white women to prove that just as they will no longer play the pampered soft sex-object role, they will no longer play the role of being the enemy of their minority sisters. The demonstration of this fact, however, will take a determined and intentional effort on the part of all sisters. It is not something which will just "happen." White sisters have to understand this and accept it as reality. One of the reasons that black sisters have been so hostile toward whites in women's liberation is that they have perceived great hostility from white sisters because they have looked upon the good intentions of these sisters with doubt.

I do believe that as white sisters get past the period of exorcism (or expression of rage) to a time when they clearly define their goals, methodologies and value framework, the relationship will, hopefully become more possible. When people are broken open, something new emerges. But what that new will look like is up for grabs in the women's movement. All the input possible must be sought by those from other groupings. None of us can move forward alone. We must seek out new ways of communication and communion so that we can provide some mutual support in the struggle for change.

Finally, white women must realize that minority women are intrinsically bound to the total struggle of a race. The enemy, as stated earlier, is "the white establishment" — not her man. The minority male in America has suffered equally from oppression. In a society which equates manhood with "success" the minority man suffered grave historical injustice. The struggle of minority people is to free themselves mentally and morally from the "oughtness" and oppressive value systems of the mainstream of American life. For many minorities, indeed, the struggle is for actual physical and spiritual survival. These battles cannot be waged by women alone but are intrinsically bound together. Many white sisters have not understood this phenomenon and perceive that minority women are merely perpetuating chauvinism because they have not been so quick to denounce their interdependence with their men. Minority men and women do need to work out new supportive and freeing roles with each other, but that will have to happen within the context of the struggle for justice in America. White women must learn to trust their minority sisters that this is happening and will continue. The process, however, will not often take on the rhetoric, form or methodology of the predominately white "women's lib" movement.

All of us as sisters must become more politically involved in shaping America's new priorities and in reshaping its vision. We must somehow look at our own histories in the collective, as well as personal stories which have shaped our consciousness toward liberation. We must believe in the right and necessity for those collective and personal stories to differ. We must believe that the goals will bring us together out of our diversity. We must believe in the power of healing — that the gaps will be diminished and that our liberation will result in the freeing of the whole human society, because our new consciousness and action toward liberation will empower and bestow dignity, not oppress and deny it. We are not asking for a bigger piece of the American pie, rather we are seeking to formulate a new world.

89. Women and the Church:

The Coordinating Center for Women

(1987)

Immediately after General Synod passed the "Pronouncement on the Status of Women in Church and Society" (1971; see vol. 7:85), president Robert V. Moss appointed a Task Force on Women in Church and Society (1971). During the next few years a newsletter Common Lot *(1972) was launched, and the Antoinette Brown Awards recognizing outstanding women clergy (1973) were established (see vol. 4:77–78 for information about Brown — the first woman ordained within Congregationalism, in 1853). In 1973 the General Synod endorsed the use of inclusive language in future UCC publications (see vol. 7:31). In 1982 a project called United Church of Christ Women in Mission (UCCWM) was developed to increase networking among women throughout the church. The Task Force on Women in Church and Society (1971–75) evolved into an Advisory Commission on Women in Church and Society (1975–79), and finally into A Coordinating Center for Women in Church and Society (CCW) (1979–87). All of these structures were administratively attached to the office of the UCC president.*

The 1987 report of the Coordinating Center for Women (CCW) states: "These structures moved from the earliest mandate to monitor the role and status of women in church and society, through a call for the empowerment of women in a collaborative strategy, . . . to a wide ranging mandate . . . to address the concerns of women and seek strategies to eliminate sexism in church and society."

By 1987 the leadership of CCW called for an end to fifteen years of UCC ad hoc arrangements related to women. It requested that the Coordinating

Source: Excerpt from the "Coordinating Center for Women in Church and Society Report," *GS Minutes 1987,* 121–22.

Center for Women (CCW) be established as "an independent structure that will more adequately meet the needs of the United Church of Christ as it seeks to address the concerns of women through continued advocacy, support, and constituency development." In support of its request it offers theological reflections based upon the biblical text where Jesus liberates the "bent over woman" (Luke 13:10–13).

A Biblical and Theological Perspective

Luke 13:10–13

> One Sabbath Jesus was teaching in a synagogue. A woman there had an evil Spirit that had kept her sick for eighteen years; she was bent over and could not straighten up at all. When Jesus saw her he called out to her, "Woman, you are free from your sickness!" He placed his hands on her, and at once she straightened herself up and praised God. (Good News Bible)

The ministry of Jesus Christ was grounded in words and works of liberation. Jesus brought healing and wholeness to those who were excluded or devalued by the society of his time. With great compassion Jesus reached out to lepers, the physically disabled, the mentally ill; and, in defiance of the customs of his day he reached out to women.

While bringing healing and wholeness to these individuals, Jesus also challenged both the persons and the institutions responsible for their oppression and suffering, and he denied the basic assumptions of his day which perpetuated systems of inequality and oppression. The Church of Jesus Christ, when it has been most faithful to its mandate, has continued to carry on those works of healing and liberation. At times in its history, the Church has suffered from narrowness of vision and profound self-interest. At other times, the Church has worked for freedom and justice with a sense of powerful, self-sacrificing love. In order to maintain the latter, persistent work is needed both within institutional church structures as well as from creative and challenging voices outside that structure.

The bent over woman is a haunting and powerful image. She represents all those who are in pain, all who are oppressed and persecuted. The gospel of Luke tells us that through the healing power of Jesus Christ, the bent over woman was able to stand straight and tall. The healing process which straightened her spine is a scripturally symbolic way of expressing the healing and wholeness which we would desire for all of God's daughters and sons. But the bent over woman is more than a generalized symbol of oppression, as powerful as that image may be. She is also a woman. And she reminds us of the particular call the Church has to address the question of injustices toward women. Within the past 15 years, the United Church of Christ has made great strides in its efforts to recognize the ministries of women. During this period lay women and clergywomen have begun to be included much more fully in the total life of the Church.

Much of that progress toward equality has been achieved through the work of three non-permanent agencies within the United Church of Christ (The Task Force on Women, The Advisory Commission on Women, and the Coordinating Center for Women). Women have been empowered and major changes have taken place in both church and society.

Yet, in spite of gains in equality for women, women in both church and society are still in very marginal positions. Low wages, lack of benefits, inadequate child care, hunger and malnutrition, and inadequate medical care continue to haunt the women of our nation. The number of women and children living in poverty is a frightening and growing reality. Within the church, clergywomen experience difficulty obtaining new placements and laywomen struggle to attain key decision-making positions.

The oppression of women is, and has been expressed throughout history in both church and society by acts of violence and degradation, as well as more subtle forms of subordination. Those subtleties include trivializing women's experience and lives in the church, the workplace and the home; in role stereotyping and language that excludes; in unjust economic systems and inadequate social services to meet women's needs.

Without persistent continuous efforts to challenge its destructive power, sexism will continue to oppress women, and prevent them from experiencing the healing and wholeness which Jesus brought. Their bent over state will keep women from recognizing their gifts and will deny those gifts to the church. In many ways the story of the bent over woman and the assurance that the gifts of the spirit are given by God to everyone express the parameters of our human experience, where we discover both our bent over nature and our gifts. In the fullness of God's vision for us we learn to know and use our gifts wisely, and to increase our capacity to love God and neighbor as we love ourselves.

1 Corinthians 12:4–7

> Now there are varieties of gifts, but the same Spirit; and there are varieties of service, but the same Lord; and there are varieties of working but it is the same God who inspires them all in every one.

> To each is given the manifestation of the Spirit for the common good. (RSV)

The gifts women bring to the church must be accepted, developed and nurtured for the benefit of the whole church. Jesus used the gifts and faithfulness of women to teach and preach and heal. He named their acts of faithfulness and witness as prophecy; he asked them to be his messengers and revealed himself as the risen Christ to the women who were first at the tomb.

Teaching, preaching, healing, prophesy, faithfulness, and witness are all gifts women bring to the mission of the church. The church has not always received those gifts with gratitude and respect. Women also bring to the church gifts of nurture and friendship, living out through its institutions and structures styles of leadership and action which value people and relationships, and affirm the worth and dignity of each person.

God has created women and men in God's own image; from the beginning women and men were created for equality and partnership by a gracious God. The oppression of women is an act of brokenness in our relationship with God who created us to be equal, and because of that brokenness the vision of partnership and wholeness that is God's vision for women and men and for the whole of creation is not fully realized. The church cannot continue to work toward that vision with less than sustained efforts in every setting. Those efforts require an ongoing office or instrumentality to continue the long journey toward God's intended equality for women and men; an arena where women and men each bring their experience, and where each learns to trust the experience of the other in naming the issues that shape reality. Only then, and only together can women and men discern the ways of justice and mutuality which will empower the church to move toward the future where women and men will share their gifts and talents, fully, completely and equally.

Speaking Out on Social Issues

90. Urban Ministry: *"My Visions of a New Jerusalem"*

(1979)

Henry K. Yordon

Henry K. Yordon (b. 1926) is a Congregational Christian/UCC minister educated at Wesleyan University and Yale Divinity School. After serving churches in Waterbury and Southbury, Connecticut (1949–62), since 1962 Yordon spent over forty years as pastor at First Congregational UCC, Norwalk, Connecticut. His commitment to urban ministry illustrates the longstanding work of many United Church of Christ pastors who call the church to actively engage the challenges of urban life driven by the biblical vision of "a New Jerusalem."

My Visions of a New Jerusalem

An urban pastor explains why he believes his parish begins at the pulpit — and extends all the way to city hall

How few of us gathered to protest the governor's paltry proposal for aid to welfare recipients! It used to be the clergy would turn out en masse on behalf of welfare parents. A welfare rally at the capitol was a festive occasion. It was an opportunity to swap tall tales of picketing and protest with priests and ministers from all across the state. This year we had an auxiliary bishop, an elderly black Baptist preacher, the director of a Christian community action program, and myself. Where have all the clergy gone?

Source: Henry K. Yordon, "My Visions of a New Jerusalem," *The Other Side* (July 1979): 38–41.

Many of my fellow ministers have gone from picketing to pastoral counseling. They've hung out the shingle and are practicing transactional analysis for a goodly fee. Others are busily engaged in various strategies for restructuring the congregation. Some are involved in frantic evangelistic efforts.

I am not about to change my way of ministering. It may have been a long drive to the capitol for naught. But I am glad I went and wore my preacher's gown to stand before the governor's door on behalf of the poor. For twenty-eight years this has been the nature of my ministry.

I am a minister who feels called to preach from the pulpit and to administer the sacraments. But I'm called to more than that. I'm also called to be in and out of the mayor's office. I'm called down to the redevelopment agency. I'm called to caucus in a housing project apartment. And I'm called to the press conference on welfare benefits. Yes, I'm called to pray in the sick room and to evangelize at the gas pump. But I am also called to protest from the city hall steps on behalf of black police officers, to picket for a Fair Rent Commission, and to speak a word of encouragement to despairing legal service attorneys. I believe this is all part of my work as a minister in my city.

My flock includes not only those who confess Christ but also all who deny or ignore him. I work at my preaching. For me the eleven o'clock hour on Sunday morning is the most glorious of all the week. The gospel is proclaimed. I visit. I counsel. I pray with a small lay group in the parish hall on Tuesday morning. I hold a Bible study on Wednesday evening, and I meet with a little group around the Lord's table on Thursday noon. None of this is incidental to my ministry. However, I know I am also about the work of ministering when I leave a mid-week service for city hall to protest the closing of a bilingual school.

I believe church politics is more than settling a dispute between the youth group and the ladies' aid. Our worship commission doesn't need the pastor to help decide which choir will sing on the third Sunday. The deacons don't need me to help plan for visiting the sick, developing the confirmation curriculum, or working out the communion schedule. I am needed at the Board of Realtors banquet to inform them of their ministry in this community. You should have seen the heads snap up from the fruit cup when I told them they were ministers. Most think they are in it for the profit. I told them God has a different plan. They are called to welcome Christ in the stranger and to make room for the homeless poor. Perhaps few of the Realtors are Christians. But this invitation to serve may prove to be the seed sown in fertile ground.

When asked to pray over a party given by our city's Community Action Agency, I preached a bit. Everybody was there. Day-care workers, numbers runners, the mayor, state officials, representatives from the Chamber of Commerce and the union halls. They were black and white, Hispanic and Greek. Some work in alcohol rehabilitation and some do pre-trial intervention. Some belong to the League of Women Voters and some to NAACP. I told the party about John's vision in Revelation 7:9 of those "from all nations, and peoples, and tongues, standing before the throne, and before the lamb." I told them we looked a bit like John's vision. We looked as it will look at the Great Banquet.

Then I prayed that our city will be transformed into New Jerusalem. We have the ingredients. Nearly one fifth of us are black. Almost as many are Hispanic. For a time we even had a Costa Rican consulate. It's a stone's throw from Roodner Court Housing Project into exclusive Wilson Point. Some of us ride the commuter train to Wall Street. Others walk around the corner to work at the slipper shop. On a Sunday afternoon in June at Veterans Park, West Indians play cricket and black all-stars hit the hoop. We have soccer in Spanish and Greek. Everybody lives here.

Many consider it faithfully evangelical to pray that a heroin addict on South Main Street become a new creature. But they think it faithlessly activist for a minister to pray that the city take on some semblance of "the city which is to come"! Is it in the Spirit to lay on hands for a back to be straightened or eyes to be opened? Then what about joining hands with hospital workers on a picket line to pray for just and equitable wages? Is that not more than "meddling in politics"?

We are told to ask. I ask. At a kitchen table, I pray for the gifts of the Spirit to help a troubled marriage find new life. The night of a raucous hearing on sex education in our schools, I pray for healing and reconciliation. During angry debates over a holiday for Martin Luther King's birthday, I pray. And I pray believing.

Some might call my parish ugly. But since I "have been born anew to a living hope," that hope has opened the eyes of my heart. I see in this city signs of the kingdom. I see in this city the possibilities of New Jerusalem. A soul is saved, a life is changed, the church rejoices. When I came here in 1962, I wondered if this genteel, rather white Congregational church could possibly take on the whole complexion of the city. Could we ever look like that gathering around the throne? Two years ago on Easter our sexton came to me and said, "I think we are becoming what you want. At the eleven o'clock service I couldn't tell if we were a white church going on black or a black church going on white." If I have not proven to be much of an evangelist, the Lord has used me to gather anew a wide diversity of the saints.

Now I know my boasting is in vain. We don't build the kingdom. We don't pray down New Jerusalem. Jesus said, "It is my Father's good pleasure to give you the kingdom." New Jerusalem is the gift of God. Nothing is really going to happen until the day of the Lord. All I discern is but a foretaste of "the city to come." But God is going to give us the city. God will transform this old town into New Jerusalem. And we've got to act on that faith.

I think I know the reason most of my fellow ministers no longer show up on behalf of welfare parents. It's because they thought we were the ones to transform society and build the city. Apparently they grew tired of having to go back to the capitol year after year. They lost their faith in God's promise. "The poor you will always have with you," Jesus quotes. He is reminding us to keep knocking at the governor's door until the kingdom comes.

My divinity school assistant said, "Before this is over I think I'm going to wind up in jail." I told him, "Now you are getting the message." We live in enemy-occupied territory, not neutral ground. As long as no effort is made to proclaim the gospel throughout the city, the devil may even come to church and make a substantial contribution. But when signs of community appear in a deteriorating neighborhood, the beast is roused. His bulldozer engines roar.

The developers, the planners, the financiers gather with glorious ideas. They want to eliminate Greek and Spanish soccer, West Indian cricket, and downtown basketball from Veterans Park. They intend to transform it into an exclusive multi-million dollar cultural center and convention hall. I will have to cancel Bible class. Can't send a deacon. Have to go challenge the beast myself. I have a sermon to deliver at that public hearing. For I have been called to minister to the entirety of this city. I have been called to act in faith throughout the town, expecting a new Jerusalem.

91. Urban Ministry:

A Born Again Radical

(1982)

DON BENEDICT

Don Benedict (b. 1917) is a Congregational Christian/UCC minister educated at Albion College (Michigan) and Union Theological Seminary in New York. His life work has been committed to creating and sustaining Christian ministry and social justice in cities. Along with several other people, Benedict was involved in the founding of the East Harlem Protestant Parish (New York) (1947), the West Side Christian Parish (New York) (1952), and the Inner City Protestant Parish (Cleveland) (1952–60). He was executive director of the Community Renewal Society (Chicago) (1960–82). In his autobiography, Born Again Radical *(1982), Benedict reinterprets the phrase "born again" to insist that finding new life in the gospel of Jesus Christ leads to radical involvement in social change. "The radical is deeply committed to liberating the victims and confronting oppressors in the name of justice."*

SOURCE: Don Benedict, *Born Again Radical* (New York: Pilgrim Press, 1982), 219–22.

A Born Again Radical

Jesus wept over the city saying, "Would that even today you knew the things that make for peace! But now they are hid from your eyes."

I refer to this association of knowing and feeling when I call myself a "born-again radical." For me, "born again" means both being born into a world of poverty and suffering and also feeling what it means to be despised and rejected; and "radical" pertains to the root. The radical person gets at the roots, searches out the source, cause, or principle.

I do not see how one could be "born again" in this sense without being radical. This would mean seeing and feeling with those who suffer injustice without the disposition and the determination to uproot the causes of evil. To be born again is to manifest more than a passion of sympathy. It is to be more than a tender-hearted spectator who weeps at the personification of tragedy, tosses money to the beggar in the street, and then goes to dinner. Jesus wept, but he was also radical. The radical is deeply committed to liberating the victims and confronting oppressors in the name of justice.

For me, rebirth happens daily. Because progress is slow and the evil remains, one must be born again, not once and for all, but continually to an unfinished task. Paul wrote, "I die daily in Christ." To die daily in Christ is to be reborn again each day to deeper engagement.

Wherever there is individual human suffering, especially in poverty, I find the strongest appeal to both the priestly and prophetic aspects of Christian ministry. The two functions become correlative, one acting in compassion, the other impelled to speak out for justice. Compassion expressed only as pity or paternalism is like love without justice, a pale imitation of the real thing. In true compassion there is partnership, solidarity, and identification.

Some say we can come to faith only through worship. I came through my concern for the unemployed and the alienated, through understanding the deadening weight of ghetto existence on young people, comprehending the effects of dilapidated housing on family life, witnessing privation, discrimination, and violence. I have found worship more significant in times of struggle, more a celebration of the power of God. A great moment was the time of prayer with all the tenants in the freezing building before we went to the housing authority. Another was the time when I was in solitary, utterly alone with my inner conflict. And I remember one night in Newark when several homeless men and women were with us for dinner. They were moved because we had taken them in, and soon there was a general spirit among us, a feeling of jubilation and a kind of paean that seemed ready to burst into a *Te Deum* of friendship. It was almost as if we were drunk, yet we had nothing intoxicating to drink. Suddenly, everyone seemed to come alive; we began to talk and to share some of the most meaningful experiences of our lives. I remember saying afterward that it had been a kind of upper-room pentecostal experience.

For all who think and act in the light of the world as it is, there is a connection between the gospel and politics, and between the gospel and democracy. Certainly today no one would say that economic well-being should not be an important goal. The problem is not economic feasibility as a rule in itself but the absence of democracy in determining it and the narrow extent in applying it. What is economically feasible for one segment may not be economically feasible for others or for the whole society. In fact, it is almost certain not to be. Democracy, when it takes precedence, can be the correcting principle. Christianity looks at decisions from the standpoint of those who will be victimized. And democracy, in guaranteeing for the victims a right to speak and participate politically, educates the whole society in self-discipline and justice, and looks to informed human reason for decision. These victims must be heard. They must be brought into the process. I see no solution being formulated within either capitalist or communist ideologies. I think more solutions will be found in moves toward decentralization and alternate technology geared to the human scale. That is why it is so important to search for local neighborhood initiatives using such technologies, and also for worker-owned structures like cooperatives, and to match such economic control with moves toward neighborhood governance and political communities where individual voices speak with effect. As an ideal, we seem to subscribe to a faith in political democracy but not in economic democracy.

Therefore I believe the Christian should be informed and involved in politics, although this is not to imply that Christians possess better remedies for the problems of poverty and racism than are offered by those outside the church. In political work, as Christians, they do not properly come into a group and say, "We have arrived with the answers." In a community organization they do not always identify themselves, but in working with other people, who may or may not be Christians, they bring a great sense of judgment that comes from their opposition to idolatry and their faith and hope in a perfect kingdom of God which always stands in judgment over human institutions. As Christians, they are continually confronted with the radical dimensions of their faith.

While the individual Christian often takes a partisan stand, I believe that the church itself, as a whole, should do so only in some great extremity. Its position transcends any particular side of a controversy. The church should reach through to the moral imperative, continually pointing to a higher justice and calling for still better solutions. The great danger is insulation. Captivity of the church by the middle and upper classes is potentially fatal; it means nothing less than the absence of the living Christ and the emptiness of the claim to be a center for caring and redemption.

As a community of the faithful, the church can move away from internal institutional aggrandizement toward a role of servanthood in a world seen as the arena of God's activity. Perhaps more functional congregations will arise, organized around questions of justice, devoting themselves to service through action and reflection. But structure is not the primary consideration. New living structures will emerge only insofar as they are expressions of a new response to Christ's call; and a new understanding of the word and the sacraments will emerge only out of the encounter with the world.

I know that some individuals reject any thought of participating in politics, and others take positions on certain issues that they defend as absolutes. Although the goal of the born-again radical Christian — achieving liberty and equality for the poor, oppressed, and rejected — is in a sense absolute, all who pursue the goal should be prepared for argument, discussion, and compromise with regard to the means of achieving it. One model only of perfection exists in the history of the world, incarnate in Jesus Christ.

92. Installation Prayer:

City Missionary Society of Boston

(1981)

Avery Post

During the nineteenth century, Congregationalists in many northern cities founded city mission societies to address the needs of poor immigrants and urban problems. Over the years many of these organizations became strong activist agencies for social and political justice.

In 1981 when Valerie Russell (1941–97), an African American UCC laywoman, was installed as president of the City Mission Society of Boston, she asked her longstanding friend and president of the United Church of Christ, Avery Post, to offer the Installation Prayer (see vol. 7:88 for more information about Valerie Russell).

Avery Post (b. 1924) is a Congregational Christian/UCC minister who was educated at Ohio Wesleyan University and Yale Divinity School. After serving pastorates in Vermont, Ohio, Connecticut, and New York he was president of the Massachusetts Conference UCC (1970–77). In 1977 he became the fourth president of the United Church of Christ, serving three four-year terms (1977–89).

Source: Avery Post, "Prayer at the Installation of Valerie Russell, President, City Missionary Society of Boston," May 10, 1981 [typescript, UCC Archives, Post Papers, box 2, file 3].

Prayer at the Installation of Valerie Russell

O God of all creation and of all history, we give you thanks for this tender moment in which you are trespassing quietly and surely upon our vulnerability, stalking us with your mercies and your heart of grace, unstopping our ears for the beautiful and terrible word of justice, and calling us to a new moment of history in the long struggle toward the humanness that you have ordained, for which you suffer.

Do not spare us, O God, on a joyous and demanding afternoon. Subvert our defenses. Address our pride. Expose the thinness of our commitment. See that we are both limp and liberated before your sovereignty. Baptize us afresh into the death and resurrection of the Lord Jesus. Know that we are standing in the need of prayer, and cause us to fall toward your forgiveness. Do not spare us, dear God, on a joyous and demanding afternoon.

In the spirit, with our thoughts long, we are engulfed in the story of mission, even as we pray. You are a missionary God and your people a missionary people. The Church exists for mission; and out of all that both resists and yields to mission, you have persevered, O God, in this city and this society and this fragile globe, so that we are surrounded now by a great crowd of mothers and fathers, sisters and brothers, who in this place and in every place have lived for the mission, compassionately, devotedly, impatiently, courageously. Overwhelm us, O God, with that impinging community of saints, and especially the host of people who in the name of Jesus Christ and the City Missionary Society of Boston have done Godly and human work in this city for more than a hundred and fifty years.

O God of all pilgrimages, migrations and settlements, we pray for this dear city of Boston and all of its people. We are here this day in your Name for all the people. We pray for justice in the streets and in the neighborhoods. We pray for those victimized by oppression, political expediency and the apathy of the powerful. We pray for the city's leaders, that they may be preoccupied with the social good, governed by principle, and selfless for the sake of all and especially those in pain, poverty and alone. We give thanks for all communities of people in this city and region bent upon justice. Deliver this people, O God, from the temptations and sins of racism, sexism, classism, elitism. And keep us, O God, helpless lovers of this city that we are — from the subtle snares of romancing with this beloved town, as segregating ourselves from all that is unromantic here and in urban America.

You move us, O God, by the way in which you work, and by the way that you raise up leaders from the faith communities, the churches, and nurture, mold and discipline servants of your will to appear in the seasonal springtimes of the human story. So we receive this day, as a gift from your hand, the ministry and leadership of Valerie Russell. We are awed by and thankful for her shaping journey: a committed family, many churches and communities of faith, particular persons (many of them here today), her baptism, her struggle toward faith, her love of freedom and passion for justice, all of her lover's quarrels, mentors, teachers, colleagues, sisters, brothers, the United Church of Christ. And all of this — the gifts of Valerie — are from your hand and we give you thanks.

Put upon her lips, gifted preacher that she is, the ancient and contemporary Gospel of Jesus Christ. Put into the keeping and the stewardship of her person deeds of the gospel. Enlist her warmth in the humanizing of church and society. Use her irritations and impatience as instruments of power and prophetic renewal in a time of surrendering despair. Give her quiet centers from which to sustain her personhood, a life in the Holy Spirit through which gifts will flow for all the people, and life in the Church where she may join in the praise of God, the covenants of mission, and a community of faith. Sustain the lovely rhythms of her life even as she carries great burdens, and grant that her imagining of a more human and just world for us all may not be wounded by all that will frustrate, fatigue and bedevil her.

So, good God, install this dear sister of ours in the office of leadership for which she has been chosen, and may she have grace, mercy, a good time, and peace. Amen.

93. Sanctuary:

A Liturgy

(1983)

David Chevrier

During the 1980s it was estimated that over half a million Salvadorans and many thousands of Guatemalans entered the United States illegally in search of refuge while their homelands were torn apart by war. In most cases the United States government was not responsive to their requests for asylum and many of them were deported. In that situation a handful of North American Christians protested government policies and worked to relieve the suffering of Central Americans, remembering the biblical admonition to provide "cities of refuge" to those fleeing violence.

Wellington Avenue United Church of Christ in Chicago was the first UCC congregation to offer sanctuary to Central Americans seeking refuge from death, torture, or imprisonment. In January 1983 David Chevrier (b. 1938), a UCC minister educated at Dartmouth College and Andover Newton Theological School, who served a church in Vermont and was pastor at Wellington Avenue UCC for over thirty years (1970–2003), reminds the congregation of Jesus' words to Peter, "Feed my lambs." If we truly love Jesus, such a confession means that we are ready to "watch over, care for, feed, and protect the vulnerable of the world," even if it leads to "breaking the law" and "risking the rage of our own government."

Source: [David Chevrier], Liturgy from Wellington Avenue UCC, Chicago, January 9, 1983 [typescript from the church].

Sanctuary Liturgy

Invitation and Call

Come unto me all you who labor and are heavy-laden and I will give you peace. Christ calls us to his Table like a good shepherd calls the sheep to the fold. Like a good shepherd who knows each and every one of the lambs and sheep, so Christ knows each and every one of us by name. Like a good shepherd who makes sure that every lamb and sheep is fed and watered, so Christ provides the Bread and Wine to sustain and fulfill us. Just as a good shepherd builds a "safe place" for the lambs and sheep to rest without fear, so Christ makes a *sanctuary* for us where we can know the Peace of God. Just as the good shepherd stands outside the gate of the fold to protect the sheep and lambs from the ravenous wolves which would slaughter and devour them, so Christ protects us from the forces of evil which seek to destroy our lives.

Christ, the Gracious Host, invites us to come home for refreshment and care, to break bread together, to share the loaf.

A *companion,* quite literally, is a sharer of the loaf. Soon we ourselves will once again become companions, one of another, by sharing the Bread and Wine, the Body of Christ. The El Salvadorans, too, are our companions, which is why it is proper that they are with us to share the Bread. They are our companions just as ultimately everybody on this planet is a companion. In God's eyes there is only one race — the human race.

It is a spiritual fact that all humanity is one. We belong to one another, on every continent and isle, north and south, east and west, all of us — black, white, yellow and red — starved and stuffed, smart and stupid, all three billion of us belong to one another. That's the way God made us. Christ died to keep us that way. Our only sin is that we are constantly trying to put asunder what God has joined together.

Christ is the peace between us . . . and has broken down the barrier which used to keep us apart. . . .

That may sound political, and there will be those who will criticize the church for being too political when we resist those who deny by their words and actions that we indeed are all members of one race — the human race. We need to listen to the words of the gentle Archbishop Oscar Romero. In his homilies he would talk about real life, even if it was controversial. And when people would criticize him for being too political, he would reply, "Brothers and sisters, do not mistake the mission of the church, the preaching of the Gospel, and the work of justice, for a subversive campaign. It is very different. Unless you want to call the Holy Gospel subversive, because it truly challenges the basis of an order that should not exist because it is unjust."

Archbishop Oscar Romero was killed in San Salvador, on March 24, 1980, while celebrating communion. The circumstances of his last moments reflected the essence of his life. Officiating at the funeral of a friend in the small chapel of the hospital where he had ministered to the cancer-ridden poor, he raised the chalice, proclaiming that it was Christ's blood, shed for the salvation and justice of his people. Romero's own blood was then shed as a gunman stepped forward and fired the shots that killed him.

Soon we will be celebrating communion together. Among the theologians there will always be silly talk about transubstantiation and consubstantiation. Please don't look for Christ in the nouns; find him in the verbs: This is my body *broken* for you; this is my blood *shed* for you.

I am glad we are breaking bread with Christ, with each other, and with people all over the world, for we are no longer aliens in a foreign land, but fellow citizens with God's people and part of the household of God.

94. Economic Justice:

"Christian Principles of . . . "

(1987)

Audrey Chapman Smock, Editor

In the early 1980s a group of United Church of Christ theologians began discussions in search of "new economic theories and strategies more faithful to the Gospel." In 1985 the General Synod requested the preparation of a pronouncement containing "an analysis of the global economic crisis from a Christian perspective, an articulation of a public theology of economics, and an appropriate response by the United Church of Christ." When the General Synod voted to affirm the United Church of Christ as a Just Peace Church in 1987 (see vol. 7:64), it also called for economic justice alongside its focus on peace.

In response to these concerns and actions the world issues staff of the United Church Board for World Ministries (UCBWM) coordinated the preparation of a study paper entitled "Christian Faith and Economic Life." The paper was edited by Audrey Chapman Smock, a UCC minister educated at Wellesley College, Columbia University, New York Theological Seminary, and Union Theological Seminary in New York. Smock had worked for the Ford Foundation and done research on east Africa before becoming world issues secretary for the UCBWM (1981–90). In later years she has worked for the American Association for the Advancement of Science (Washington, D.C.).

The "Christian Faith and Economic Life" study paper explores biblical mandates for economic life, sets forth six Christian principles

---

Source: Audrey Chapman Smock, ed., excerpts from "Christian Principles of Economic Justice," chap. 3 in *Christian Faith and Economic Life* (New York: United Church Board for World Ministries, 1987), 8–13.

for economic justice, and provides useful background information about modern economic systems. Its six principles seek to provide a standard against which to measure contemporary economic systems.

The paper was widely circulated and studied, and at the 1989 General Synod a lengthy pronouncement, "Christian Faith: Economic Life and Justice," was passed. That pronouncement was a synthesis of two proposed pronouncements, one of which was based upon the 1987 UCBWM study paper. The 1989 pronouncement was also shaped by feedback from racial and ethnic members of the UCC who argued that "the relationship between racism and economic justice needed further articulation." It was supported by the United Church Board for World Ministries (UCBWM), the United Church Board for Homeland Ministries (UCBHM), the Commission for Racial Justice (CRJ), the Office for Church in Society (OCIS), and the Council for Racial and Ethnic Ministries (COREM).

Christian Principles of Economic Justice

Six Principles

[¶48] To make the transition from the simpler and predominantly rural biblical economies to the contemporary global, complex, and industrial economy, this chapter formulates six Christian principles of economic justice drawn from biblical and theological motifs. Cumulatively these principles articulate the biblical understanding of economic justice in the face of contemporary distortions in economic practice. In so doing they challenge the inadequacies of contemporary economic systems and offer an alternative vision toward which the faith community can move.

[¶49] In our broken and divided world, all institutions and systems are flawed. Nevertheless, human finitude and sin do not mean that all economic systems equally contradict or compromise Christian principles of economic justice. Like human beings, economic systems respond to problems and opportunities in a variety of ways. And, just as persons vary in their gifts and abilities, human institutions and economic systems have differing strengths and weaknesses.

[¶50]The institutions to which the principles will be applied and the specific issues and problems to be considered in this paper are drawn predominantly from capitalist economic systems. This is so because by and large the members of the United Church of Christ, for whose use this paper was written, are part of a capitalistic system. The critical treatment of capitalism in this paper does not imply approval of, or preference for, socialism or state ownership of the means of production. Rather, it reflects a strong sense of responsibility to God and to our sisters and brothers for the justice and faithfulness of the institutions in which we participate. That accountability is even greater within a democratic system in which each citizen retains the freedom to decide and the political voice to challenge false priorities and harmful policies.

[¶51] The biblical vision of an economically just society can be stated in six interrelated principles. These provide both a standard against which to measure contemporary economic systems and a goal inspiring the faith community in its efforts to bring a more just order into being.

1. Fulfilling Basic Material Needs

[¶52] In light of the parable of the great judgment, *a just economic system fulfills the basic material needs of all members of the human community and enhances the life opportunities of the poor, the weak, and groups at the margin of society.* As has already been stated, Scripture confers the role of stewards or economists on members of the faith community, calling us to organize God's gifts so that all persons can lead meaningful lives with their basic needs satisfied. The type of economic institutions and systems established and the policies pursued determine the level of economic productivity and the extent to which the nature of the goods and their distribution contribute to providing the means of life for all persons within the society. With the high level of interdependence within the world economy, national institutions and policies also affect the prospects and well-being of other countries. . . .

2. Economic Democracy

[¶60] *A just economic system is inclusive, involving all people in responsible, participatory, and economically rewarding activity.* Western political democracy is rooted in the covenant tradition of the Protestant reformers. It was the rediscovery of the Old Testament covenant tradition by Calvinist thinkers that paved the way for the emergence of democratic theory.[1] The Hebrew covenant is a life relationship between God and the chosen people established to embody righteousness within the human community. The covenant between God and humanity is a model of relationships among

1. Daniel J. Elazar and John Kincaid, "Covenant and Policy," *New Conversations,* UCBHM, 4, no. 2 (Fall 1979): 5, and Frederic Carney, "Associational Thought in Early Calvinism," B. D. Robertson, ed., *Voluntary Associations* (Richmond, Va.: John Knox Press, 1966), 52.

people, expressed in the covenant of mutual responsibility and commitment. All people are called to participate in, and to share the fruits of, creation and redemption. Those economic conditions that thwart full participation or that generate inequality and injustice therefore are as odious as despotic rulers. Just as governments finally became the property of those who are governed, so the economy belongs to the people who through it are fed and housed and inspired to produce for the needs of their neighbors and for the well-being of the whole community. . . .

3. Human Community

[¶65] *A just economic system builds and enhances human communities wherein people can live with dignity and well-being.* Such communities reflect and preserve the intrinsic worth and sacredness of human beings. They also facilitate expression of the love of neighbor. The community of our concern, the community to which we are responsible, is not limited to our families, our colleagues in life and work, our fellow citizens, our political allies. It extends to all humanity. . . .

4. Human Rights

[¶71] *A just economic system respects the human rights of its members and enhances the level of freedom in the society.* Economy and government are made for people and not human beings for the economic and political systems. As the Pronouncement of the Twelfth General Synod of the United Church of Christ states:

> Human Rights are the gift and demand of God. They have their source in what God has done and is doing in creation, in Jesus Christ, and through the Holy Spirit. Thus, human rights are universal demands. No person, no group, no society is excused from recognizing that other human beings must be treated justly and that societies must be ordered on the basis of freedom and equity.[2] . . .

5. Viable Economic System

[¶76] *A just and viable economic system is based on a responsible and equitable use of the earth's limited resources.* Faithfulness and respect for the Creator entail reverence for the whole of creation. "The earth is the Lord's and the fulness thereof" (Psalm 24:1). The economy of God

---

2. "A Pronouncement on Human Rights," Twelfth General Synod of the United Church of Christ, 1979 (New York: Office for Church in Society, 1979).

encompasses the entire created order, not just humanity. The story of the creation in Genesis states that "God saw everything that had been made, and behold, it was very good" (Genesis 1:31). . . .

6. International Peace

[¶80] *A just economic system promotes international peace and common good.* In the closing years of the twentieth century the challenge is to kindle an awareness that the human family has a common origin and shares a common destiny. As Walter Brueggemann has written,

> The central vision of world history in the Bible is that all of creation is one, every creature in community with every other, living in harmony and security toward the joy and well-being of every other creature.[3]

As Christians we aspire to a new order grounded in God's acts of creating, redeeming, and reconciling creation. . . .

A Call to Hope

[¶87] One major obstacle to economic change is frustration about the possibility of doing anything. Every effort at major reform shows the difficulties. Countless interest groups favor proposed changes, but ask for exceptions in areas affecting them. When all the exceptions are added up, they constitute a massive inertia that prevents significant action. Furthermore, the very real complexity of issues makes it difficult to rally the moral forces of a society which operates most effectively when it has clear and simple issues. All in all, discouragement is as effective as greed in blocking action.

[¶88] The cross of Christ is a constant warning against simple optimism. Jesus prepared his disciples for persecution, not for success. Yet Christians, of all people, have reason to persist in struggles despite discouragement. We believe in God's continuing creative activity in the world. We remember the words of Isaiah of the Exile:

> Why do you say, O Jacob, and speak, O Israel,
> "My way is hid from the Lord,
> and my right is disregarded by God"?
> Have you not known? Have you not heard?
> The Lord is the everlasting God,

3. *Living Toward a Vision: Biblical Reflections on Shalom* (New York: United Church Press, 1982), 15.

> the Creator of the ends of the earth.
> God does not faint or grow weary,
> God's understanding is unsearchable,
> The Lord gives power to the faint,
> and to those who have no might God increases strength.
> (Isaiah 40:27–29)

We are also not alone with our faith. Our hope is fortified by our involvement with the Christian community. With others in the church, we share our visions as well as our struggles and occasional despair.

[¶89] When the church is faithful to Christ's teaching it provides leadership in the quest for economic justice. In recent years, the United Church of Christ has been actively engaged in efforts to promote racial justice, equal rights for women, and world peace. None of these struggles has yet produced a simple success story; all have met frustrations and setbacks. But the church continues its work — and sometimes it makes a difference, but we do not depend on instant success for our hope.

[¶90] Often those who have met the most stubborn forces of history understand the power of hope. James Weldon Johnson, speaking out of the black experience, wrote:

> Sing a song full of the faith
> That our dark past has taught us.
> Sing a song full of the hope
> That the present has brought us.
> Facing the rising sun
> Of a new day begun,
> Let us march on till
> Victory is won.[4]

[¶91] Our God is a God not only of the past and the present but also of the future. What is today need not continue to be. Hungry children can be fed. Resources can be more equitably distributed. God is capable of surprising us, of opening up new possibilities.

4. Eugene D. Levy, ed., *James Weldon Johnson, Black Leader, Black Voice* (Chicago: University of Chicago Press, 1976), 71–72.

95. Advocacy:

Christians for Justice Action

(1982, 1985)

In 1980 James Smucker, conference minister of the New York Conference UCC, and Valerie Russell, former UCC coordinator for the Advisory Commission for Women in Church and Society who was working at Riverside Church in New York City, called a group of UCC activists together. Gathering in New York City for a twenty-four-hour meeting at their own expense, they lamented what they considered rising conservative trends within the UCC and committed themselves to keep justice issues alive and at the forefront of the church's agenda. They formed a new advocacy special-interest group, "Christians for Justice Action" (CJA).

Some people thought that CJA was organized in response to the United Church People for Biblical Witness (UCPBW) (see vol. 7:63 and 7:98), but CJA insisted that was not the case. Without staff and with only small financial contributions sent by seven to eight hundred people on their mailing list, they raise money to do advocacy work on all justice issues at each General Synod. Since 1981 they have put out a semiannual newsletter, publishing a "daily edition" at General Synods. They established the "Burning Bush" award, given to local UCC leaders active in social justice advocacy.

One early participant in CJA remembers its semiannual meetings as filled with "Bible Study, discussion and reflection before addressing business," creating a "real church" for him. CJA felt that the UCC "feared controversy more than it loved justice," and quoting the Bible,

---

Sources: Christians for Justice Action, First membership letter, n.d. [date estimated 1982 by CJA]. [Christians for Justice Action], an excerpt from "The Prophet Speaks to Our Times," *New Conversations* (Spring 1985): 24–25.

"I have seen the affliction of my people . . . " (Exodus 3:7), it set forth a biblical and theological rationale for justice advocacy.

In the 1980s when New Conversations *magazine published an issue on "theological ferment" in the UCC — reprinting many of the key theological documents of the day (see vol. 7:57, 59, 61, and 63) — a working group from Christians for Justice Action gathered for a day in January 1985 to draft its contribution to the theological dialogue. Quoting extensively from Isaiah 58, the authors of "The Prophet Speaks to Our Times" insist that God is always recalling the people to their vocation. The prophet holds up a mirror to the life of God's people, exposing the self-deception of the people and their institutions. The prophet "speaks truth to power." The prophet leads the people to confess that they focus more on the church than the "ministry to which [they] are called in God's world." The prophet demands both justice and mercy.*

"The Prophet Speaks to Our Times" recognizes the tension between advocacy for the poor and the affluence of the UCC, between proclamation and incarnation, but it also celebrates those moments in the history of the UCC when the Spirit makes visible stories of shalom. *It insists that the church "must remain open to the call of the Spirit to cry aloud and spare not." Members of the working group that authored the "Prophet" article were Don Armstrong, Mal Bertram, Bob Lee, Clyde Miller, Valerie Russell, Donna Schaper, and Bill Webber.*

First Membership Letter: Christians for Justice Action

We speak to you, sisters and brothers, as fellow-Christians, members one of another of the United Church of Christ. Like you, we have been called into the church by God and we have pledged ourselves to accept the cost and joy of discipleship in the name of Christ and his cause in the world. We repent of our faithlessness, and we acknowledge that we stand in need of the mercy and grace of God, of a revival of the spirit in our midst, and of a new gift of power to witness boldly.

Nevertheless, at this hour in history, we are saddened by the divisions and inequities that keep nations and races apart. We are alarmed by the amassing of nuclear power, lest it pass beyond our control. We are gravely concerned over the unleashing of national and international corporate power. We are heartsick over the unrelieved plight of the poor and the renewed justification for their exclusion from access to land, tools, and resources. We are enraged by the realities of continued and systematic discrimination against persons for reasons of gender, race, or sexual preference. We remember the relentless demands of our Biblical faith for righteousness and that Christ calls us to join the struggle for justice and peace. We deplore what we believe to be growing distortions of the Biblical message which equates religious faith with either personal salvation or any one economic system, thereby blinding us to the fullness of the Gospel and to economic and political realities.

We intend:

1. To continue to hold aloft the Biblical vision of release to the captives, recovery of sight to the blind, liberation for those who are oppressed, and a day of economic justice;
2. To celebrate our several heritages and our common heritage in the United Church of Christ in which we have struggled for basic human rights through the centuries;
3. To educate ourselves and our church biblically, theologically, and functionally on issues of human justice in this time;
4. To work within the structures of the United Church of Christ to call it to courageous response and bold action in solidarity with the oppressed.

We invite you to join with us in this exploration.

The Prophet Speaks to Our Times

A Concluding Postscript

. . . We will find the true meaning of all these words in our actions together in covenant, as the people of God. In struggle with one another and against the principalities and powers, we will experience profound conflict and healing as a community. We will know what we have known before: our brokenness, defensiveness, fear and self-deception. We will fast in the wrong way and misunderstand the word of God. Fearfully we cling to past assurances. The Spirit will have to call us back to faithfulness again and again. In that constant turning around, we will continue to experience the surprise of God's startling grace which sustains and empowers us through our struggles. We pray to discern God's new truth as revelation continues.

In the telling of our stories and testifying to the breakthroughs of God in our lives, in the listening to the stories the world has to tell, we will be participants in the transformation of both spiritual and physical hungers into the great gift of abundant life. Then we will share the good news of the Gospel with both rich and poor; then the breach will be healed.

When the Bible and our contemporary experience are interpreted in these ways, the task of leadership in the church becomes less a burden and more fully a ministry of promise and hope. Leadership may be bold with a prophetic vision because its journey is shared. It may be bold because God frees us to "sin bravely," to risk being fools for Christ, for God alone is judge. Prudential constraints and institution maintenance are no longer primary concerns. We pray for such leadership in the United Church of Christ to offset our centrist accommodation to politics within the church and world. In this Isaiah vision we are free to accept our mutual responsibility for leadership from which our hierarchies now exclude us.

The biblical vision assumes life in community. In our adherence to the prophetic call, then, the work and leadership of community are shared. Facades of false individual power can be shed. People of color, gays and lesbians, women, young and old, will be intentionally woven into the fabric of leadership. Power will increase for many rather than decrease for some, and leadership will be known by its capacity to include and involve the whole community.

In matters of justice, may we in the UCC always stand in solidarity with the poor and oppressed through reflection, prayer and action. The Isaiah vision, open and forgiving as it is, requires such solidarity for our own wholeness. Jesus chooses to encounter us in a life of such solidarity. Contrary to what our culture prefers from people of faith, this choice will often involve us in direct political action and expressions of outrage against injustice. Such acts may cause division within the church, but such is the nature of biblical witness.

As we seek to be healers of the breach and repairers of streets to dwell in, we who are members of CJA affirm the centrality of Jesus the Christ as our witness. At the same time we affirm that God's Spirit has been and is revealed through many faiths and tongues in every age. Therefore we work with all the worlds God has called into being. As we understand scripture, we must fight the urge to make God too small. Our faith is inclusive and not exclusive.

And thus we return to the cost and joy of discipleship which are the basis for our identity and our mission as the United Church of Christ. God is not finished, and thus we remain open to the call of the Spirit to cry aloud and spare not, to lift up our voices like trumpets and declare to our people, and to ourselves, our transgressions and our hope.

Affirming the Wholeness of Life

96. Social Action and Service: *"Christian Love"*

(1986)

Hobart A. Burch

Hobart A. Burch (b. 1932) is a Congregational Christian/UCC minister educated at Princeton University, Union Theological Seminary in New York, Columbia University, and Brandeis University. After working for the Buffalo, New York Council of Churches (1958–62) and holding several federal government positions (1964–69), he became general secretary for health and welfare of the United Church Board for Homeland Ministries (UCBHM) (1969–74). Later, after serving as executive director of the National Social Welfare Assembly (1974–76), he taught and held administrative positions at the Graduate School of Social Work at the University of Nebraska (1976–2002).

The denominations that came together to form the United Church of Christ, especially the Evangelical Synod of North America before it became part of the Evangelical and Reformed Church had a long history of health and welfare ministries (hospitals and institutions for the ill, disadvantaged, orphaned, and aged). For many years these organizations related to the UCC through the Division of Health and Welfare of the UCBHM. But that relationship ceased to satisfy. In 1983 the General Synod created a Special Advisory Commission Related to Health and Human Services, and in 1985 an independent Council for Health and Human Services Ministries (CHHSM) was established to coordinate health and human services ministries within the United Church of Christ.

Source: Hobart A. Burch, "Christian Love: Social Action and Diakonia," *The Link: Care News from the Council for Health and Human Services Ministries* 3, no. 3 (September 1986).

In spite of organizational difficulties, the United Church of Christ has never wavered in its theological conviction that the church is called to ministries of healing and wholeness by Jesus Christ.

Christian Love: Social Action and Diakonia

The key point is that Christian love, or caring, is total. The ultimate "target" is each individual as a person in his or her own right, and our Christian social concerns as benefiting those individuals:

1. Individuals you personally encounter: as pastor, social worker, deacon, friend, neighbor, family, etc. This includes most of the work of the local congregation and of church-related health and welfare services.
2. Individuals you do not encounter: as in foreign and some homeland missions, civil rights and social justice, welfare rights, peace movements, etc.

The second key issue is how you help. An old public health model is organized around host, agent, and environment. The classic version of this was fighting yellow fever: the host being the individual victim, the agent being the mosquito, and the environment being the swamp. You could help the individual directly by immunization (host intervention), by killing the mosquitoes (agent intervention), or by draining the swamps (environmental).

If your target is emotionally disturbed children you can serve them directly (host intervention), work with their parents (agent intervention), or work for changes in the social environment which generally enhance family life and good parenting (including public education curriculum, full employment, elimination of racial and sexual discrimination which are breeding grounds for problems, etc.).

The theoretical realm of Christian social concern is everything which affects the total well-being of everyone, whether it is called spiritual, social, psychological, emotional, secular, material, or whatever. All is part of God's world and related to God's purpose.

We must "intervene" at all three levels of host, agent, and environment because unlike yellow fever where any one of the methods might solve the problem, no one approach will meet broad human needs all by itself.

1. In a world of sinful saints, no broad social policy or program measure will solve all the problems, so people will always need services and nurture, and some needs can only be met personally anyway.
2. Conversely, no amount of individual remediation can overcome injustice, inequality, war, economic malfunctions, etc.

If this be true, *individually we may follow a vocation which emphasizes only one piece of the total.* Paul says it well in 1 Corinthians. Chapter 12: "Now there are varieties of gifts, but the same Spirit; and there are varieties of service, but the same Lord; and there are varieties of working but it is the same God who inspires them all in everyone. To each is given the manifestation of the spirit for the common good. . . . "

Three strong value positions are corollaries of this:

1. To care about only those whom you personally serve is an egocentric limitation of one's ministry.
2. To support services and oppose social policy and social justice is myopic at best.
3. To care about people as a collectivity but not be concerned with them as individuals is an abstraction, not love. In the Peanuts comic strip, Linus wanted to be a country doctor, but Lucy said he couldn't because he did not love mankind. He said, "I love mankind. It's people I can't stand." Some of my more radical social action colleagues, inside and outside of the church, appear to have lost sight of the individual.

There is no need to illustrate the first two points, since you have probably experienced such attitudes frequently in your everyday encounters.

Several resolutions of the Christian social concerns vocation which are compatible to these interpretations are listed below.

1. If you are in one area, *accept* the others as valid for the Church. (This is minimal, but acceptable.)
2. Be *generally supportive* (not just passively accepting) of those social ministries that aren't your own bag. (How we need and welcome such folk!)
3. Have a *primary area which leads you to secondary action in the other*, such as getting into collective advocacy as an outgrowth of encountering the same problem over and over in different individuals, or being a social actionist informed by personalized caring, or supporting direct

services as a social actionist because of your recognition of the failure of your approach to eliminate the need, etc. (This is the optimum outcome for most caring people.)

4. Combine the two as equal vocations, such as being a social actionist who practices diakonia at home, in the congregation, and in supporting our direct services, or a direct service worker or administrator who is active in social justice and peace causes through church, professional, other channels outside of his basic paid job, or as a program developer in the government, or as a nurturing teacher of social policy, planning, and administration to individual students. (This approach, however, does not often fit both the personality and the opportunity.)

The key is to affirm and spiritually unite health and welfare issues with direct services as part of ONE health and welfare mission. When this occurs, our Christian love can truly be characterized as TOTAL caring.

97. Persons with Handicaps/Disabilities:

Affirming Wholeness

(1977, 1980, 1986)

General Synod, Harold H. Wilke, Dosia Carlson

The affirmation of shalom, of wholeness in the brokenness of our times, has been a major concern of the UCC. Its Council for Health and Human Services Ministries (CHHSM) and the Division of Health and Welfare of the United Church Board for Homeland Ministries (UCBHM) have carried on longstanding ministries of caring. By the 1970s understandings of wholeness changed.

For example, the word "handicap" was originally a sporting term. In the early twentieth century it came to mean "physical disability." During the 1970s many people in the United Church of Christ came to see the word "handicapped" as negative and offensive. For this reason, in 1987 the UCC National Committee on Persons with Handicaps became the UCC National Committee on Persons with Disabilities.

In 1952 Virginia Kreyer (b. 1925) was ordained by another denomination to work at a local Cerebral Palsy Center. By 1971 she had joined a UCC congregation and begun a ministry of education within the United Church of Christ about the needs of persons with disabilities, reminding the church that although it was preaching and teaching it was often ignoring the ministry of healing commanded by Jesus. In 1977 she helped the New York Conference UCC bring a resolution to General Synod on "The Church and Persons with Handicaps." After the resolution passed,

---

Sources: "The Church and Persons with Handicaps," *GS Minutes 1977,* 53–55. Harold H. Wilke, excerpt from chap. 2, "Faith," in *Creating the Caring Congregation* (Nashville: Abingdon Press, 1980), 25–30. Dosia Carlson, "We Yearn, O Christ, for Wholeness," *The New Century Hymnal* (Cleveland: The Pilgrim Press, 1995), Hymn #179. Words Copyright © 1986; rev. 1993 Dosia Carlson. Used by permission.

working with persons with disabilities became a General Synod priority and Virginia Kreyer became a consultant on disabilities ministries within the United Church Board for Homeland Ministries (UCBHM) (1978–95).

Harold Wilke (1914–2003) was an Evangelical and Reformed/UCC minister educated at Eden Theological Seminary, Union Theological Seminary in New York, and Harvard University, and he received a doctorate from the University of Chicago. Wilke was born without arms. As a child his mother said to him: "Harold, you are a boy exactly like your brothers. You only have to work somewhat harder." Although initially he was discouraged from seeking ordination, Wilke eventually served as a local pastor, as a college and hospital chaplain (especially to wounded veterans), and as a denominational executive overseeing the UCC Council for Church and Ministry until the early 1970s. For his service to people with disabilities he was bestowed the "Order of Merit" by the Federal Republic of Germany. In 1975 he founded the Healing Community to help places of worship alter their attitudes and architecture to include the disabled. Wilke wrote that he might be armless, but he was fully armed—armed with the supportive challenging response of his parents and the "everlasting arms" of religious faith— "the spiritual support upholding us all."

Dosia Carlson (b. 1930) is a Congregational Christian/UCC minister educated at Hartford Theological Seminary. After a significant career in education she became an associate minister at the Church of the Beatitudes in Phoenix, Arizona, in 1979. In 1983 Carlson, an accomplished hymn writer, was inspired by a visit of Harold Wilke to her church during the International Year of Persons with Disabilities to write the hymn "We Yearn, O Christ, for Wholeness."

Resolution:
The Church and Persons with Handicaps

Background

One tenth of all Americans are physically and mentally handicapped [Preface, The Rehabilitation Act of 1973 Public Law 92–112] and most are not seen in church because of attitudinal or architectural barriers. Many are confined at home, with relatively few in institutions. This task force asks, on their behalf, the United Church to consider their need for participation within the mainstream of community and church life, and calls for special study and action by the congregations, Conferences and the General Synod.

The church community should focus on the needs of all kinds of disadvantaged persons, especially the handicapped, as voiced in resolutions by several denominations.

The church should support the statement of the World Council of Churches, Nairobi, Kenya, November 1975, which says in part:

> The church cannot exemplify "the full humanity revealed in Christ," bear witness to the interdependence of humankind, or achieve unity in diversity if it continues to acquiesce in the social isolation of disabled persons and to deny them full participation in its life. The unity of the family of God is handicapped where these brothers and sisters are treated as objects of condescending charity. It is broken where they are left out.

The word "handicapped" is defined by the U.S. Department of Health, Education and Welfare to "mean mentally retarded, hard of hearing, deaf, speech impaired, visually handicapped, seriously emotionally disturbed, crippled or other health impaired" persons. (Public Law 91-230 Education of the Handicapped Act.)

Theological Rationale

The Christian church is a community of faith responding to God's healing, reconciling, and empowering work in Christ. The mission of Jesus meant good news for the poor, release for captives, recovering of sight for the blind, and freedom for the oppressed (Luke 4:18). As signs of his ministry Jesus pointed to its gifts for the blind and the lame, lepers, the deaf, even the dead (Mt. 11:4–6). Christ's followers are called to continue the ministry of reconciliation that God carried out in him (2 Cor. 5:18).

Christian faith has always recognized both the glory and frailty of human life. Our glory is that God has created us in the divine image and called us to be his ministers. Our frailty is evident in our dependence in infancy and old age and in our vulnerability throughout all of life.

Christ addresses us in our strength and in our weakness. He reminds us that we human beings need one another. It is our responsibility and our opportunity to strengthen and heal one another within the human family. Especially within the church we recognize that "if one member suffers, all suffer together; if one member is honored, all rejoice together" (1 Cor. 12:26). And the church, in this respect, makes us aware of the kingdom of God, with its claim upon and its promise for all humanity.

Within the human society are some people identified in common language and in public law as handicapped. They bear in evident and painful ways the fragility of all life. The strongest of human beings are at any moment only a microbe or an accident away from the ailments and disabilities that are conspicuous in others. The mingling of strength and frailty in the human race and in every individual are constant reminders of three aspects of our Christian ministry.

First, there is a ministry of the whole church to the handicapped. It is a quite specific continuation of the ministry of Jesus, who healed the sick and who told his followers that their ministry to the sick was a ministry to him (Mt. 25:31–46).

Second, there is a ministry of the handicapped to the church and to humanity. Their presence is a reminder that Christ was a suffering servant, "despised and rejected by men; a man of sorrows, and acquainted with grief" (Isa. 53:3). They are likewise a reminder of Christ's foremost apostle, who when he prayed for relief from his own affliction heard God's response: "My power is made perfect in weakness" (2 Cor. 12:9).

Third, there is a ministry of the church to all those who suffer hardness of heart toward the handicapped. More people than realize it have a hidden hostility toward the handicapped and would even like to blame them for their handicaps, perhaps because they resent the reminder of the frailty of all flesh. To those who think they are well, the church has a ministry of judgment and healing.

Our contemporary society has a special need for the ministry of the handicapped and to the handicapped. This is a success-oriented society. It rejoices — rightly, in part — in the conquest of many ailments that have burdened past generations of humanity. But in its achievements our society often concentrates on health as a norm, at the cost of intolerance of human ailments. It sees suffering as the enemy to overcome, forgetting that suffering may be a means of grace for sufferers and those around them. It often hides away the handicapped or pushes them to the fringes of society, lest they intrude on the superficial happiness of others. It represses the nearness and presence of death.

Sometimes, in a travesty on Christian faith, it even locates human dignity in normality and achievement. Thus even its well-intended compassion for the handicapped is too often a condescending goodness of the well to the ill and disabled rather than a recognition by all of the dignity that by God's grace we share. In traditional Christian faith human dignity has often been described as "alien dignity" — not the dignity of ambitious achievers but the dignity of creatures whom God loves and calls into divine-human community. In that community each of us has the opportunity, as Henri Nouwen puts it, to become the "wounded healer" for others.

As the church learns to recognize human weakness-in-strength and strength-in-weakness, it begins to discover "the cost and joy of discipleship." It finds that the sharing of burdens is the sharing of opportunities. It witnesses to God's gracious love.

Recognizing the distinguished contributions persons with handicaps are making to society in various fields;

Aware of the suffering of persons with handicaps due to rejection and insufficient support;

Cognizant of the wealth of new understandings about societal attitudes toward persons with disabilities;

Observing that a direct result of our high risk technological society is an increasing number of persons with handicaps;

Affirming the need for a positive attitudinal and behavioral response to persons with handicaps;

Acknowledging the vital support and facilitating role the Church could play in their social integration by initiating more empathetic, and creative, ministries with and to persons with handicaps and their families, as in church school curricula, attention to removal of environmental and architectural barriers, provision for regional conferences and retreats, intentional listening to persons with handicaps and honoring their living demonstrations of accomplishment; and *believing* that the unity of the family of God is handicapped where these brothers and sisters are treated as objects of condescending charity and derision, and that the unity is broken when they are left out.

The 11th General Synod of the United Church of Christ therefore, resolves:

1. To undertake at local, association, conference and national levels study of the role of persons with handicaps through groups made up of persons who are handicapped and those who are not. The church at all levels should utilize available resources and information of public and voluntary agencies and determine how best to motivate the caring concern of congregations in order to minister with and to persons with handicaps, and to remove all physical barriers to this end.
2. To encourage the local congregations, associations, conferences, related schools and institutions, and national bodies of the United Church of Christ to implement the full range of professional and non-professional employment of persons with handicaps.
3. To call upon each local congregation of the United Church of Christ to take affirmative action assuring the full integration of persons with handicaps into membership of the Christian fellowship at all levels, encouraging their full participation in the church and society, so that they may realize their full potential.
4. To encourage individuals with handicaps, along with their families, to become part of the ongoing life of the Church. Work may be needed in helping persons with handicaps to grow socially, emotionally, and spiritually, thus acknowledging that both their struggles and gifts are important to the Christian community.
5. To direct the Executive Council to negotiate with the appropriate U.C.C. agencies regarding work with persons with handicaps in order to facilitate the organization of our efforts and to offer a progress report to the 12th General Synod.

Wilke: "Jesus' Word: It's Irrelevant"

The critically important reference to any kind of handicap in the New Testament is the Johannine story of the man blind from his birth (John 9:1–7). In the Goodspeed and Smith translation, it reads:

> As he passed along, he saw a man who had been blind from his birth. His disciples asked him,
>
> "Master, for whose sin was this man born blind? For his own, or for that of his parents?"
>
> Jesus answered,
>
> "It was neither for his own sin nor for that of his parents, but to let what God can do be illustrated in his case. We must carry on the work of him who has sent me while the daylight lasts. Night is coming, when no one can do any work. As long as I am in the world, I am a light for the world."
>
> As he said this he spat on the ground and made clay with the saliva, and he put the clay on the man's eyes, and said to him,
>
> "Go and wash them in the Pool of Siloam" — a name which means One who has been sent. So he went and washed them, and went home able to see.

The following verses indicated the wrangling which went on between him, his parents, and the neighbors, as to what happened, with strong questioning by the Pharisees and the blind man's response, "He put some clay on my eyes, and I washed them, and I can see" (v. 15b).

Later, the Pharisees excluded the blind man from the synagogue. Their charge was, "You were born in utter sin, and are you trying to teach us?" Jesus learned of this and sought him out; after the blind man fell on his knees before him, Jesus said, "I have come into the world to judge men, that those who cannot see may see, and that those who can see may become blind." Some of the Pharisees who heard this asked, "Are we blind too?" Jesus answered, "If you were blind, you would be guilty of no sin, but as it is, you say 'We can see'; so your sin continues" (v. 41).

Throughout the New Testament, Jesus' response to disability and other handicapping conditions is any of these: to heal that condition, to consider it irrelevant, and to seek justice, as in the attempt to change the ritual law on healing.

Let us look at each one of these responses of Jesus in the Johannine story.

The first is the flat denial that sin has anything to do with this handicapping condition. "Neither sinned," Jesus answered, referring to both the parents and to the man himself. It is the most definitive statement we have in the New Testament that sin is not the causative factor in a physically handicapping condition. (There are other statements by Jesus in other situations that imply the relationship of illness and sin, or estrangement from God, and we must consider them later.) This story, the man born blind, carries Jesus' unequivocal and definitive statement that sin did not cause the congenital blindness.

The second response of our Lord is that the blindness is a mark of the Kingdom; it is a sign that God uses persons in specific ways to fulfill the divine intention for the world. In the Goodspeed and Smith translation used here, the phrase is "to let what God can do be illustrated in his case." Jesus dealt with the underlying fact of the situation, namely that the man was blind and that this blindness was not caused by sin. The fact that the man had continued to live in faith (he was a member of the synagogue) that something could be done about himself is the basis for Jesus' phrase, "What God can do . . . in his case." Granted the fact of the illness or in this case the blindness, it is how the person deals with the negative condition that reflects the God-given character of the individual. What God can do in this case where a person, born blind, continues to have faith, illustrates precisely God's intent for every person. How we cope with a situation, how we respond to the low spots and the high spots of our lives, how we seize the opportunity of picking up the rusty blade when the burnished sword is not available to us determines the kind of help God can give us. What God can do is illustrated in the continuing faith of this individual.

A third meaning in this story is of critical importance, and is seen in the fact that there is no hiatus whatever between Jesus' statement that God's strength is illustrated in this man's case and the following phrase, "We must carry on the work of him who has sent me while the daylight lasts." The *we* includes the blind man even before he was healed. We, all of us, must do the work of God.

There is a second parable that defines the place of the handicapped in the life of the Kingdom. It is in the middle of the fourteenth chapter of Luke. We remember the story of a householder who proposed a huge banquet to which he invited his special friends, the affluent and well-to-do. You remember the excuses they gave: "I have bought five yoke of oxen, and I go to examine them" ["I just bought a new sports car, and I've got to try it out"]; "I have married a wife, and therefore I cannot come." The householder, angered, asks his friends to go out into the highways and byways, to bring in the poor and the maimed. Jesus then states, "For every one who exalts himself will be humbled, and he who humbles himself will be exalted" (v. 11). He goes on to say: "Do not invite your friends or your brothers or your kinsmen or rich neighbors, lest they also invite you in return, and you be repaid. But when you give a feast, invite the poor, the maimed, the lame, the blind, and you will be blessed, because they cannot repay you. You will be paid at the resurrection of the just" (vv. 12–14).

The kingdom of God is not complete without the poor and the maimed! And each member thereof is not complete, or has hope of salvation, unless his own lameness or her own blindness, the negative aspects of their lives, are included.

For the Christian community the one lost sheep is the one for whom the Shepherd leaves all the others to save. In Jesus' picture of the Day of Judgment, he expresses the idea that God in Christ comes to the person who visits the sick, the prisoners, and those in need. The nail-pierced hands of Jesus, the stigmata, are the hands of one who cares for the stigmatized, who are in manifold ways pierced by the turned-aside eyes of fellow human beings. In word and action Jesus sets the handicapped directly within the circle of unity of the Christian church.

New Testament theology also builds heavily on the Pauline argument that the individual is made perfect in weakness, that God has chosen the weak of the world to demonstrate life's meanings to the wise and the strong. It is not weakness itself that is to be glorified, but the fact that in weakness one can see clearly God's intent for the world, that is, for the power of Christ to dwell within one.

The doctrine of grace holds that we are accepted into the love, not by our deeds or by our being, but by the grace of God. Thus a person's power, beauty, majesty, and strength all combined cannot save him; salvation comes through grace. Illness, physical handicap, decrepitude, old age, or mental retardation cannot destroy a person in the sight of God; he or she is saved by grace. The condition of everyone of us before God is the same.

There is also the utilitarian question. Why debate theological meanings when these persons are here? We acknowledge their presence among us and indeed see them in us. Without searching for reasons, without attempting to find the cause of evil and illness and pain in the world, we rather ask, What can we do? Jesus' answer at this point is found in his statement to the persons who asked him, "Who sinned, this man or his parents, that he was born blind?" Jesus' response was that neither sinned; then he went on to the next step: within the condition this person has, it is yet his duty and indeed his glorious privilege to praise God.

The messianic feast of Jesus and the "strength in weakness" statements of Paul are cornerstones for the doctrine that within the very nature of the church itself weakness is present, so that God may be glorified.

We Yearn, O Christ, for Wholeness

We yearn, O Christ, for wholeness
and for your healing touch;
too long have we felt helpless;
our burdens seemed too much.
Forgetting all pretenses
we make our pleadings heard,
in hope and expectation
await your gracious Word.

We long to have companions
who travel by our side,
strong friends to call and answer
with whom we are allied;
As we lift up each other
when struggles lay us low,
community develops;
our faith and caring grow.

We need your living presence,
O Christ of Galilee,
a presence that revives us
and sets our spirits free.
No longer are we fearful,
your love pervades each place.
Empower us with courage
to claim your healing grace.

PASSION CHORALE 7.6.7.6.D

98. Human Sexuality:

Definitions and Actions

(1977, 1985)

Edward A. Powers, Editor

In 1975 the General Synod stated, "The United Church of Christ has not faced in depth the issue of human sexuality. Changing morality and ethics within American society present both problems and challenges to the church." It requested the Executive Council "to commission a study concerning the dynamics of human sexuality and to recommend postures for the church." In response the United Church Board for Homeland Ministries (UCBHM) was asked to do the study.

A UCBHM staff team, headed by Edward A. Powers (b. 1927), worked with a diverse group of consultants to explore definitions, provide biblical interpretation, point toward principles of ethical behavior, examine psychosexual development, define public policy issues, and describe the church as a community of grace where human sexuality is acknowledged, judged, and celebrated. Its brief two-page definition of sexuality stands at the core of its study and its 250 pages of information and interpretation are challenging.

Human Sexuality: A Preliminary Study *was presented to the 1977 General Synod, received with appreciation and commended to the congregations, associations, conferences, and instrumentalities of the United Church of Christ for study and response. A study guide was provided.*

The General Synod floor debate and vote to receive the study and commend it to the church for study was sharply divided — 409 for and

Source: [Edward A. Powers], excerpts from *Human Sexuality: A Preliminary Study, The United Church of Christ* (New York: United Church Press, 1977), 12–13, 217–19, 231–32.

210 against. Delegates who voted against the report, being more than 25 percent of the voting delegates, exercised their option "to file a minority viewpoint on the voted issue." Their minority report "Thoughts on Sexuality" (by Martin Duffy) was also commended to the congregations, associations, conferences, and instrumentalities for study and response. Following the General Synod, minority leadership inspired by Barbara Weller, a laywoman from Pennsylvania, organized to bring the sexuality issue back to future synods and to uphold understandings of sexuality grounded in different interpretations of the Bible. Weller and others started a special advocacy group, the United Church People for Biblical Witness (UCPBW). Their concern was homosexuality, but the issues at stake ultimately concerned biblical authority (see vol. 7:63).

In the early 1970s, another special-interest group, founded in 1972 as the UCC Gay Caucus and renamed the United Church Coalition for Gay Concerns and then the United Church Coalition for Lesbian/Gay Concerns, began having pre-synod national gatherings in 1981. The coalition expanded its work to educate and advocate for the acceptance of lesbian, gay, and bisexual persons, encouraging local UCC congregations to declare if they were "open and affirming of all people" (ONA). In 1985 a General Synod resolution, "Calling on United Church of Christ Congregations to Covenant as Open and Affirming," urged congregations to develop covenants of Openness and Affirmation, or pass an Inclusive Non-Discrimination Policy. The coalition provided resources to guide congregations through a self-study process and kept a list of congregations willing to be listed on the UCC Coalition for Lesbian, Gay, Bisexual and Transgendered Concerns "ONA List." By 2000 350 ONA congregations and about a dozen conferences were listed, and many others were supportive, without being "on the list."

Toward a Definition of Sexuality

One's sexuality involves the total sense of self as male and female, man and woman, as well as perceptions of what it is for others to be female and male. It includes attitudes about one's body and others' bodies. It expresses one's definition of gender identity. Sexuality is emotional, physical, cognitive, value-laden, and spiritual. Its dimensions are both personal and social.

A distinction should be made at the outset between sex and sexuality. Sex refers to the physical act of making love, to genital expression. "Sex is, in fact, only a small part of sexuality. . . . Sexuality is, then, an integrated, individualized, unique expression of self."[1]

Sexuality is *emotional.* The infant person experiences what is later understood to be sexuality as it is fed and cuddled, in the sense of warmth or distance between bodies, in comfort or discomfort at wetness or dryness of body, in pleasurable sensations of one's own body. In the early years the child experiences bodily pleasure and discovers sensuality. With the coming of puberty boys and girls experience new awareness of their bodies, other persons, and related emotions. Throughout all of life sexuality deals with one's feelings about self and others, pain and pleasure, distance and closeness, love and hate, physical touching or restraint.

Sexuality is *physical.* It involves touching, physical closeness, and genital sexual expression. It is expressive of the desire for human contact and satisfaction of the need for closeness, intimacy, and physical pleasure. All five senses are involved in one's sexuality.

Sexuality is *cognitive.* Mental attitudes, self-understanding, analyses of human experience and relationships help express who and what persons are as sexual beings. One's understandings of genitalia, coitus, nakedness, other- and same-sex roles affect the body and its sexual expressions. Language is a key part of our sexuality both in naming bodily parts, physical acts, and our own experiences, and in communication with other persons.

Sexuality is *value-laden.* One's sense of the ought, the fitting, the possible, and the communal reflect value systems and ethical structures. Words and concepts such as justice, love, norm, should, and should not are ethical in character and central to a full understanding of sexuality. Values relate both to self-understanding and to expectations of others and of social structures. Values shape how and what persons communicate to one another. One's values determine approaches to honesty, fidelity, promise-keeping, truth-telling, and the purposes of sexual expression.

Sexuality is *spiritual.* The sexual act involves mutual self-giving. The spirit of one person relates deeply to the spirit of another. One chooses to relate to another and to oneself. There is a voluntary surrender of self to another through which a larger unity is achieved without the abridgement of freedom. Elements of transcendence, commitment, being in touch with another and with oneself are involved in one's sexuality and relationships to others as sexual beings. For Christians, sexuality is understood as the gift of God and as a dimension through which the love of God and neighbor is expressed.

---

1. Eleanor S. Morrison and Vera Borosage, eds., *Human Sexuality: Contemporary Perspectives* (Palo Alto, Calif.: Mayfield Publishing Company, 1973), ix.

Sexuality is *personal.* Each person is a sexual being on her or his own terms. In that sense one's sexuality is unique, one of a kind. "Our sexuality belongs first and foremost to us. It is pleasure we want to give and get. It is vital physical expression of attachments to other human beings. It is communication that is fun and playful, serious and passionate."[2]

Sexuality is *social.* It involves couples or partners. It has familial and community of caring contexts. Our sexuality has a bearing on the approach of such issues as war, economics, politics, or national priorities. It relates to such social policy questions as rape laws, equality of women and men in matters of employment, guidelines for genetic research, and abortion. It affects cultural understandings of socialization as male and female, the role of pornography, the meanings of marriage and community.

Sexuality is a central dimension of each person's selfhood, but it is not the whole of that selfhood. It is a critical component of each person's self-understanding and of how each relates to the world. . . .

The Church — the Body

How remarkable it is to think that we are called the *body* of Christ. Jesus is called "the Word made flesh." For ancient Hebrews or for modern Christians, to speak of ourselves as Jesus' body is startling but invigorating! We are to embody the being of Jesus. That says two things: We need to understand the person of Jesus and we need to learn embodiment.

John A. T. Robinson, a New Testament scholar, is fascinated with Paul's use of the image of the body. Paul is struck by the nature of human boundedness. "Who will deliver me from this body of death?" Paul asks, in Romans 7:24. Robinson contends that "Paul saw that the Christian gospel . . . [is] very different. For the body is not simply evil: it is made by God and for God. Solidarity is the divinely ordained structure in which personal life is to be lived."[3]

Robinson sees the body as the central concept in Paul's thought about God and humanity. The great themes of the letters are bound together through the use of the body motif:

> It is from the body of sin and death that we are delivered; it is from the body of Christ on the Cross that we are saved; it is into His body the Church that we are incorporated; it is by His body the Eucharist that this Community is sustained; it is in our body that its new life has

2. The Boston Women's Health Collective, *Our Bodies, Ourselves,* rev. ed. (New York: Simon and Schuster, 1976), 38.

3. From John A. T. Robinson, *The Body, a Study in Pauline Theology* (London: SCM Press, 1952), 8.

> to be manifested; it is to the resurrection of this body to the likeness of His glorious body that we are destined.[4]

And Jesus is for real — fully human, fully God, the creeds say. Docetism (from the Greek word meaning to seem) is the heresy which in effect said that Jesus was play-acting — that he didn't need to eat or sleep because he was superhuman. On the contrary, the incarnation means that the Word did become flesh, fully human with desires and hopes and physical needs. What is it to say that Jesus was fully man? What was the nature of his sexuality? Did he get his feelings hurt? Did he wonder about the changes in his body? Did he fight with his parents? What is it to be his body?

The scripture gives us some clues. Jesus seemed at ease with both men and women. He cut through the stereotypes, barriers, and conventions that separated people. There was in his life — as the gospels share it — neither bond nor free, male nor female, for all were one in him. He was the genial guest at a wedding feast. It was he who interceded for an adulterer and prevented harm or possibly death to her.

James Nelson reflects on the meaning of the humanity of Jesus:

> Can you see the truth of your sexuality and your embodiment vindicated in Christ? He is no sexless, docetic apparition, but the enfleshment of God in a man. Can you also see that the gracious word of acceptance frequently comes through the hidden Christ, the Christ incognito? It may be in the ecstasy and playfulness of sexual communion with your beloved. It may be in such a simple act as the spontaneous hand placed on your arm by a friend, but in that moment you were aware of healing — and hasn't the church long known that healing often comes with "the laying on of hands"? And it may not be heresy, either theological or moral, to suggest that grace may be expressed and reunion discovered in the loving touch of your own body.[5]

The whole life of the congregation is judged by the ideal of the Word made flesh. How do we embody the truth of the gospel that in Christ we are all one? How do we demonstrate that we are members one of another? How does the foot know that it has any relationship to the elbow or the knee of Christ's body? How does the body work when some of its members are missing? How is bread broken and life shared in ways that all persons — regardless of orientation, marital status, or life-style — feel they belong?

---

4. Ibid., 9.

5. James B. Nelson, "Reconciliation: The Body of Christ and the Human Body," *Theological Markings* (Spring 1974): 25.

How are the gifts of each person's uniqueness given and received in such a way that we, though many, become one?

. . .

In the final analysis the church is both gift and the bearer of gift. All that we are, including our sexuality, is a gift of God. God loves the world in a way that is fleshly, loving, faithful — forever and ever. In Jesus we are participants in a new covenant of life, of hope, of love, of justice.

We as sexual creatures are created free to use the gifts of life and of sexuality in ways that ennoble and endear — or betray and demean. That freedom is a gift to have, to hold, to express, to share.

We as sexual creatures are made for relationship, for community. The church is that special form of community through which we experience the fullness of grace, God's presence in trial and rejoicing, and the promise of hope, power, and love in its forms of *agape, philia,* and *eros.*

Stewards of the gift of sexuality: that is who we are. Pray God for faithful stewardship!

Calling on United Church of Christ Congregations to Covenant as Open and Affirming

Whereas, the Apostle Paul said that, as Christians, we are many members, but we are one body in Christ (Rom. 12:4–5), and Jesus calls us to love our neighbors as ourselves (Mk. 12:31) without being judgmental (Mt. 7:1–2) nor disparaging of others (Lk. 18:9–14); and

Whereas, recognizing that many persons of lesbian, gay and bisexual orientation are already members of the church through baptism and confirmation and that these people have talents and gifts to offer the United Church of Christ, and that the UCC has historically affirmed a rich diversity in its theological and biblical perspectives; and

Whereas, the Tenth through Fourteenth General Synods have adopted resolutions encouraging the inclusion, and affirming the human rights, of lesbian, gay and bisexual people within the UCC; and

Whereas, the Executive Council of the United Church of Christ adopted in 1980 "a program of Equal Employment Opportunity which does not

---

SOURCE: "Calling on United Church of Christ Congregations to Covenant as Open and Affirming," *GS Minutes 1985,* 74–75.

discriminate against any employee or applicant because of . . . sexual orientation"; and

Whereas, many parts of the church have remained conspicuously silent despite the continuing injustice of institutionalized discrimination, instances of senseless violence and setbacks in civil rights protection by the Supreme Court; and

Whereas, the church has often perpetuated discriminatory practices and has been unwilling to affirm the full humanness of clergy, laity and staff with lesbian, gay and bisexual, orientation, who experience isolation, ostracism and fear of (or actual) loss of employment; and

Whereas, we are called by Christ's example, to proclaim release to the captives and set at liberty the oppressed (Lk. 4:18); and

Whereas, examples of covenant of Openness and Affirmation and Nondiscrimination Policy may be found in the following:

Example 1:
Covenant of Openness and Affirmation

We know, with Paul, that as Christians, we are many members, but are one body in Christ — members of one another, and that we all have different gifts. With Jesus, we affirm that we are called to love our neighbors as ourselves, that we are called to act as agents of reconciliation and wholeness within the world and within the church itself.

We know that lesbian, gay, and bisexual people are often scorned by the church, and devalued and discriminated against both in the church and in society. We commit ourselves to caring and concern for lesbian, gay and bisexual sisters and brothers by affirming that:

- we believe that lesbian, gay and bisexual people share with all others the worth that comes from being unique individuals;
- we welcome gay, lesbian and bisexual people to join our congregation in the same spirit and manner used in the acceptance of any new members;
- we recognize the presence of ignorance, fear and hatred in the church and in our culture, and covenant to not discriminate on the basis of sexual orientation, nor any other irrelevant factor, and we seek to include and support those who, because of this fear and prejudice, find themselves in exile from a spiritual community;

- we seek to address the needs and advocate the concerns of lesbian, gay and bisexual people in our church and in society by actively encouraging church instrumentalities and secular governmental bodies to adopt and implement policies of non-discrimination; and
- we join together as a covenantal community, to celebrate and share our common communion and the reassurance that we are indeed created by God, reconciled by Christ and empowered by the grace of the Holy Spirit.

Example 2: Inclusive Non-discrimination Policy

We do not discriminate against any person, group or organization in hiring, promotion, membership, appointment, use of facility, provision of services or funding on the basis of race, gender, age, sexual orientation, faith, nationality, ethnicity, marital status, or physical disability.

THEREFORE, the Fifteenth General Synod of the United Church of Christ encourages a policy of non-discrimination in employment, volunteer service and membership policies with regard to sexual orientation; encourages associations, Conferences and all related organizations to adopt a similar policy; and encourages the congregations of the United Church of Christ to adopt a non-discrimination policy and a Covenant of Openness and Affirmation of persons of lesbian, gay and bisexual orientation within the community of faith.

99. Human Sexuality: *"Call to Dialogue" and "Now, No Condemnation"*

(1997, 1998)

Conference Ministers, Paul H. Sherry

Throughout the 1990s various issues related to sexuality continued to challenge the churches. General Synod resolutions on abortion, women, and homosexuality both distressed and inspired UCC members, and worried and pleased ecumenical partners. The General Synod and the national leadership of the United Church of Christ did not remain silent on these controversial issues.

On the question of homosexuality, although most UCC people were firm defenders of the civil rights of lesbian, gay, bisexual and transgendered persons, they were divided on the issue of "blessing relationships between same-sex couples and extending to them the same rights and privileges afforded to heterosexual couples." In 1997 thirty-six UCC conference ministers sent a pastoral letter to United Church of Christ congregations, associations, and conferences inviting them to explore their faith in relation to the "meaning of Christian marriage," the blessing of "unions among same-sex couples," and the "honoring of diverse expressions of loving and caring human relationships." The letter is a pastoral call to dialogue about issues of "great complexity and moral difficulty."

Sources: "A Call to Dialogue: A Pastoral Letter from the Conference Ministers of the United Church of Christ," June 4, 1997, a typescript found in "That We May All Be One, Thirty Years of United Church of Christ Social Justice Policy Statements on Lesbian, Gay and Bisexual Concerns" (Cleveland: United Church of Christ, n.d.), 33–34. Paul H. Sherry, "Now, No Condemnation: The Rights of Gay, Lesbian, and Bisexual Persons in Society and Their Membership and Ministry in the Church," A Pastoral Letter to the United Church of Christ, 1998.

About eighteen months later, Paul Sherry, president of the United Church of Christ (1989–99), also wrote a personal pastoral letter to the church— "Now, No Condemnation: The Rights of Gay, Lesbian and Bisexual Persons in Society and their Membership and Ministry in the Church." Sherry (b. 1933) is an Evangelical and Reformed/UCC minister educated at Franklin and Marshall College and Union Theological Seminary in New York. After serving pastorates in Pennsylvania and New Jersey (1958–65), he served on the staff of the United Church Board for Homeland Ministries (UCBHM) (1966–82) and was executive director of the Community Renewal Society (CRS) of Chicago (1983–89).

Sherry explains that his letter reflects his own convictions and hopes, informed by the General Synod and countless conversations with pastors and lay leaders during his presidency. He states that he has become convinced that the discussion about homosexual persons in society and in the ecumenical community, and the frequency of continuing hate crimes required a response. He applauds ongoing dialogue, but he feels that the voice of the UCC is urgently needed, "bearing witness to the belief that God cherishes all and dignifies all, and to our experience of gay, lesbian, and bisexual persons as gifts of God, called with us by their baptism into the fullest participation in God's mission of reconciliation in the world."

A Call to Dialogue

A Pastoral Letter from the Conference Ministers of the United Church of Christ
June 4, 1997

The Church in every generation has been faced with issues of great complexity and moral difficulty that have caused the household of faith to reaffirm the things that bind us together as the Body of Christ. The Preamble of the Constitution of the United Church of Christ reminds us that while the Church "claims as its own the faith of the historic Church . . . ," it also has "the responsibility . . . in each generation to make this faith its own in the reality of worship, in honesty of thought and expression, and in purity of heart before God."

Former generations have had to deal with such social and cultural challenges as the institution of slavery, divorce and remarriage, war and peace, the ordination of women, civil rights, and a variety of other complex issues. Our readings of scripture have resulted in sometimes confusing and occasionally even conflicting interpretations. In each of these points of tension, some of which continue in our midst, we have had to struggle together as a people of God in ways that test our resolve to remain steadfast to both biblical truth and to our faith community. Each issue has tested the Church's ability to speak boldly and to act passionately while remaining in covenant about that which we believe to be true and good. The Church has been most faithful when it has attempted prayerfully to discern the mind of Christ, engaging scripture and our traditions under the guidance of the Holy Spirit.

One challenge facing the Church in our time is the issue of blessing relationships between same-sex couples and extending to them the same rights and privileges afforded to heterosexual couples. It has become a divisive issue in our culture and has split families, churches, and communities into opposing camps. Scriptures are quoted by all sides in this debate, disclosing both the essential truth of the biblical insights and the limited character of our understanding of God's continuing revelation among us.

When we engage this difficult topic, we see human faces, not abstract issues of sexual ethics, theology, or even matters of church order. First of all we see people; we see brothers and sisters, sons and daughters. We see the very neighbors Jesus has invited us to love. Our families often include gay men and lesbians who are baptized in Christ, members of our congregations, struggling and seeking the meaning and expression of covenantal commitment in Christian community.

We who serve among you as Conference Ministers, like the rest of the Church, and, indeed, like the rest of the society, are not of one mind on this issue. Some members of the household of faith believe that same-sex couples ought to enjoy the same rights as heterosexual couples; others disagree. There are those who argue persuasively that the Gospels have nothing to say about the issue of homosexuality and that therefore we should not judge. There are others who point out that Jesus holds the marriage covenant between a man and a woman as sacred. There is room here for open, honest, and loving debate in "honesty of thought and expression and purity of heart before God."

We believe that the Holy Spirit equips the Church to deal compassionately and faithfully with this contentious matter, not because Christians are especially gifted intellectually or rhetorically, but because of the great gift we have in Jesus Christ in whom all things are reconciled to God. We trust that the bond in Christ which knits us to each other is stronger than anything that can divide us.

We therefore invite you, our sisters and brothers in Christ, in the months ahead to engage in thoughtful, sincere, and respectful dialogue with one another. In congregations, Associations, and Conferences, let us explore our faith in relation to these issues: the meaning of Christian marriage, the blessing of unions among same-sex couples, the honoring of diverse expressions of loving and caring human relationships, being guided in all things by the love of Jesus. Above all, may these conversations be ventured in humility and prayer.

Sherry: "Now, No Condemnation"

There is therefore now no condemnation for those who are in Christ Jesus. (Romans 8:1)

In recent months we have witnessed the continuance of hate crimes against gay, lesbian, and bisexual persons, while in the church discussion about their civil rights and the appropriateness of their membership and ministry in the life of the church has intensified. Several denominations in the United States, as well as some churches and bishops around the world, have adopted or reaffirmed policies that exclude gay, lesbian, and bisexual persons from sharing fully in the ministry of the church. Other Christian leaders have harshly suggested that gay, lesbian, and bisexual persons have no place at all in the life of the church and that their human rights do not deserve the full measure of legal protection. In addition, some political leaders, usually claiming religious support, have vigorously opposed efforts to secure these very rights. Sometimes these anti-gay positions have been justified by flawed scientific understandings of the nature of homosexuality. Underlying many of these convictions is the assumption, frequently untested, that the Bible in general, and Christianity in particular, teach that homosexuality is a sin.

In my role as pastor to the United Church of Christ, and in this season of theological reflection on "The Inclusive Church," I offer this Pastoral Letter to remind all of us that the church is to be a place where all are welcomed, where the gifts of all are recognized and received, and where the rights of all are defended and promoted. When so many in our society would reject and exclude, it is critical that we of the United Church of Christ bear witness to the conviction that it is possible to be deeply faithful to the Bible, profoundly respectful of the historic faith of the church and of its sacraments, and at the same time support the full inclusion and participation of all God's children in the membership and ministry of the church. Likewise, there can be no compromise that all persons in this society must enjoy equal protection under the law.

I write in deep gratitude for the journey of discernment and action that the United Church of Christ has taken over the past several decades. For all our difficulties and challenges, I believe the United Church of Christ is uniquely equipped to take on this complex but crucial vocation both in the public arena and among our ecumenical partners. Informed by the actions of several General Synods, by Biblical and theological reflection, and above all by countless pastoral encounters with members of our church, I am convinced that there must be and will be no turning back from our commitment, especially in the face of the current prejudice and misunderstanding prevalent in both the church and the society.

Contrary to what some assume or allege, the conviction of the General Synod of the United Church of Christ, along with the witness of many conferences, associations, and local churches, is not a superficial response to changing cultural norms or an easy reaction to certain social opinions. At their best, our commitments have grown out of a profound reflection on the meaning of our baptism and our participation in the sacrament of holy communion. Our commitments have grown as we have responded pastorally to the needs of many of our members and their families who have been the victims of prejudice or who have experienced rejection in the church.

We have been confronted and gifted by the presence in our church of gay, lesbian, and bisexual Christians who have been baptized in our sanctuaries, confirmed before our altars, and ordained by our associations. We have been confronted and gifted by men and women faithfully attentive to the Word, diligent in their sacramental life, forthright in their Christian witness and compassionate in their service. We have been confronted and gifted by parents and grandparents, sisters and brothers, daughters and sons, faithful members of our church, whose embrace by a loving God has enabled them to accept a gay, lesbian, or bisexual family member, and who yearn for that same loving embrace to be extended by the church to their child, their grandchild, their brother or sister, their parent. We have been confronted and gifted by faithful, mature, and able members who have experienced God's call to the ordained ministry of Word and Sacrament, who have sought and received the recognition and authorization of the church. We have been confronted and gifted by ordained men and women who have served faithfully and well for many years and who now wish to minister among us with renewed vitality openly affirming their same gender orientation. We have been confronted and gifted by gay, lesbian, and bisexual persons who have found love in the physical, emotional, and spiritual embrace of another, and are living in committed covenantal relationships of fidelity and trust which they yearn for the church to bless and the society to respect and protect. And we have been confronted and gifted by members of our church and those of other churches who have known the pain of rejection, the anguish of exclusion, and the fear of abuse, yet who remain faithful to their baptismal vows, seek to be fed at Christ's Table, and desire to be engaged in the mission of Christ's reconciling love in the world.

Confronted and gifted by these baptized persons, members of the United Church of Christ have been challenged to read the Bible again with new eyes and listen to the Holy Spirit with new ears. We have had to reexamine long held assumptions about those few passages of Scripture that appear to speak about homosexuality in the light of transforming interpretations from widely respected Bible scholars and teachers, and we have begun to recognize how our fears of those who are different and our society's deeply entrenched bias against homosexual persons has often distorted and nearly silenced the Bible's liberating and inclusive voice. At the same time, encounters with hurting and excluded sisters and brothers have caused us to look to the whole of Scripture which speaks of a God who continually reaches out for those who are cast out for any reason, those who live at the margins of our lives. We have been reminded of our identity as disciples of the One who often ate with those rejected by the religious norms of the day, the One who sets before us all the Table of God's inclusive love, mercy, and grace.

In these encounters, we have remembered our own history, recalling ways we have been led to expand the church's welcome to others who have been excluded. We remembered the Amistad and the story of our forebears, both enslaved and free, who rejected Biblical interpretations that supported slavery and whose new appreciation for the Gospel's mandate led them to fight for freedom for all. We remembered Japanese Americans driven from their homes during the Second World War, and those of our churches who spoke out for their rights. We remembered many women who refused to submit to a misuse of the Bible that denied them places of leadership or that conspired in their abuse, and who found affirmation and encouragement in our churches, our colleges, and our seminaries. We remembered ancestors of our Hungarian sisters and brothers whose witness to the Reformed faith led to their persecution as galley slaves and martyrs, as well as those who fled oppression in 1956 to find safe haven among our churches. More recently we remembered our church's call for self-determination for Puerto Rican people, the championing of the rights of Chicano farm workers, the call for respect for the dignity of Native

American people demeaned by caricature and stereotype, the recognition of the rights of Indigenous Hawaiians deprived of their land and culture, and solidarity with those who declared that the apartheid system erected and supported by other Bible reading Christians was idolatry, a denial of the very integrity of the church's confession. All of this has helped us discover that our church's concern for the rights and dignity of gay, lesbian, and bisexual people is not a break from our past, or a departure from Scripture, but is informed by our moments of greatest fidelity to the prophetic voice of the Bible and the Gospel's embrace for those who, with Christ, have been despised.

The encounters in our own church with each other over the subject of sexual orientation have not been easy and, for some, remain profoundly disturbing. We have experienced conflict; the covenants that bind us together have been tested. At times we have felt isolated from and misunderstood by some in the ecumenical community. But we have also experienced marvelous surprises:

- the growth and vitality of many local churches that have declared themselves open to and affirming of the gifts of gay, lesbian, and bisexual persons;
- the gracious perseverance of The United Church Coalition for Gay, Lesbian, Bisexual and Transgender Concerns which, for twenty-six years, has been a prophetic presence in our church, clarifying concerns, challenging stereotypes, providing leaders for every setting of the church's life, gently and persistently changing hearts and minds, providing a refuge for those who have suffered wounds of prejudice and exclusion in church and society;
- the gratitude and encouragement of Christians in other churches who have found in our church's journey to new understandings a sign of hope amid discouragement;
- the growing self-esteem of lesbian, gay, and bisexual youth in our church who are able to worship in congregations that respect their full humanity, as well as the heterosexual youth in our churches who have found themselves called to confront the anti-gay prejudice so prevalent in their schools;
- the renewal that springs forth as we discover, again, that we are not trapped by the past but are part of a living tradition that is "reformed, yet always reforming," a people whose only comfort in life and in death is that they belong to Christ.

In these days we dare not be arrogant. The story of our pilgrimage with our gay, lesbian, and bisexual members at times has been marked by hesitation, fear, and frequent failures of nerve. At times prophetic voices, whether heard from inside or from outside the church, have been resisted. We have not always been properly respectful, or sought to understand with sincerity, those sisters and brothers among us who do not share our understanding or conviction or witness. At the same time, we have sometimes failed to recognize how the Bible has been used by some to perpetuate prejudice and to justify violence against homosexual persons.

But in these days we dare not be silent, either. I believe our voice among the churches and within our society is urgently needed, bearing witness to the belief that God cherishes all and dignifies all, and to our experience of gay, lesbian, and bisexual persons as gifts of God, called with us by their baptism into the fullest participation in God's mission of reconciliation in the world. I am convinced this voice will have power insofar as it is a voice shaped by the language of faith and the experience of worship, a voice in which the liberating truth of the Bible can be heard, and the courageous spirit of the saints will be echoed. By that voice, I believe, our churches will be renewed. More importantly, in that voice, I believe, the lonely will be called to companionship, the frightened will find comfort, the abused will know safety, and those sisters and brothers in Christ who have lost hope will rediscover the blessing of their baptism: Child of God, disciple of Christ, member of Christ's Church.

PART VI

Living Out the Unity

On October 21, 1942, when the editors of the *Christian Century* became aware of union conversations between the Evangelical and Reformed Church and the Congregational Christian Churches, they wrote: "It is a significant and heartening fact that these two churches which have had a taste of union want more of it! They are not content to be merely *united* churches, but wish to be *uniting* churches. The impulse for unity, once it has been released in action, tends to take the form of a mission, with the Holy Spirit (which is the Spirit of unity) increasingly in charge."

This statement, quoted in volume 6 of the *Living Theological Heritage,* emphasizes the longstanding commitment to unity that would become vital to the self-understanding of the United Church of Christ. The sense that all Christians are part of one church was deeply embedded in the formation of the denomination, and it has continued to influence the United Church of Christ since 1957.

Louis H. Gunnemann, senior historian of the United Church of Christ, noted in 1987 that during the twentieth century, Christians all over the world were engaged in trying to understand the nature of the church (ecclesiology). Furthermore, most of this effort was focused upon the quest for a visible church that would be biblically, theologically, and experientially faithful (the ecumenical movement).

The founders of the United Church of Christ were active "ecumenists," shaped by the practical approach to church union known as the "Life and Work" movement. Some key UCC leaders also played significant roles in the theologically grounded "Faith and Order" approach to church union. All of them were convinced that when Christians agreed on the substance of the Christian faith and the essential character of the Christian life, church unity in a divided and hostile world was possible. Conversations that led to the creation of the United Church of Christ emphasized the prayer of Jesus "that they all may be One."

A Christocentric approach to church unity was consistent with the global ecumenical movement that launched the World Council of Churches in 1948. It focused upon Jesus Christ "as God and Savior." It encouraged biblical ways of thinking about the church, and eventually it came to emphasize "mission" as a central mark of the church.

In the United Church of Christ this dynamic understanding of "church" remains foundational. It lies behind the United Church of Christ Statement of Faith (1959), with its affirmation of the church as a community living in response to God's deeds. It also reflects the strength of the Reformation heritage, which helped inspire a growing commitment to social justice in the worldwide ecumenical movement.

Some observers have suggested that this pattern of ecumenical thinking caused the United Church of Christ, during its formation and early years, to focus too little upon the *nature* of the church and too much upon the *form* of the church. Yet, although its ecumenical preoccupation with form sometimes overshadowed its theological work, the UCC did not lose sight of its theological vocation.

Deepening Commitment

At the beginning of the UCC, as Congregational Christian and Evangelical and Reformed leaders waited for the resolution of legal questions about their "union," they became engaged in another ecumenical conversation seeking to develop a "Plan for a United Church in the United States." Known as the "Greenwich Conference on Church Union," representatives of at least nine Protestant denominations (including several historic African American Methodist bodies) met as a "Conference on Church Union" under a "divine imperative" for union. Their good-faith efforts, however, came to an end in 1959 after the formation of the United Church of Christ and after the World Council of Churches and the National Council of Churches promised to look more deeply into matters of organic union (see vol. 6:90).

Within a year, however, the vision of the "Conference on Church Union" and some of its proposals were embraced by Eugene Carson Blake in his famous December 1960 sermon in San Francisco's Grace Episcopal Cathedral. Blake invited all denominations that were serious about church union to explore the establishment of a united church, "truly catholic, truly evangelical, truly reformed." His challenge eventually led in 1962 to the formation of a new group known as the "Consultation on Church Union" (COCU), which even recycled the initials of the earlier conference.

For the United Church of Christ participation in the Consultation on Church Union (COCU) was a natural next step. At the 1959 General Synod the United Church of Christ affirmed its devotion to "the oneness of Christ's church" by establishing a permanent Commission on Christian Unity and Ecumenical Study and Service. In 1963 this commission asked the General Synod to authorize a UCC delegation to the Consultation on Church Union (COCU) and to reaffirm "its steadfast purpose to be a uniting church" (see vol. 7:100).

Three years passed and the first work of COCU, *COCU — Principles of Church Union,* was published in 1966. Although official representatives of the United Church of Christ were deeply invested in COCU and stayed involved, by the mid-1960s the challenges of racial unrest facing the United Church of Christ had diluted much of the grassroots interest in church union. David Colwell, the first chairperson of the Commission on Christian Unity and Ecumenical Study and Service, lamented this decline and reminded members that "our claim to faithfulness is not to be seen in our uniqueness, nor in our being different," but in "seeking the wholeness of Christian truth" brought to us in different traditions (see vol. 7:101).

Many local church members were not sure. As the Consultation on Church Union (COCU) continued, the Theological Commission of the United Church of Christ, in consultation with the Commissions on Worship and Christian Unity, responded to *COCU — Principles of Church Union.* The Commission also prepared a short pamphlet, *Toward an Understanding of Local Autonomy* (1969), which was received by the General Synod and commended to the churches for study. The challenge facing the United Church of Christ was how to relate its covenantal congregational polity and its understanding of local autonomy to emerging models of union that maintained the office of "bishop."

The Theological Commission was very careful. It noted that the "episcopal system" was widespread among Christians and that there was nothing in the "ecclesiological theory of the United Church of Christ, which would prevent the adoption of an episcopal system." The question was the character and function of the episcopal office.

Toward an Understanding of Local Autonomy (1969) emphasized that Christian freedom (autonomy — the meaning given here to the word) is not "self-determination at any level of Church life." Rather, the church calls Christians to "mutual care and mutual responsibility under Christ" . . . "exercised in love, not juridically or coercively." In its 1971 report to the General Synod, the Theological Commission highlighted some of its concerns about the proposed COCU structures: Were they past-oriented or future-oriented? Was power in the new church to be exercised "ministerially (persuasion) or magisterially (coercion)"? Were guarantees written into the structures to ensure future flexibility? The United Church of Christ stood ready to reaffirm wider covenantal relationships as vital to the effective mission of Christ's church, but it also sought to defend the importance of Christian freedom (see vol. 7:102).

In response, the Executive Council asked the Commission on Christian Unity and Ecumenical Study and Service to reexamine the "ecumenical stance and commitment" of the church and to prepare a report recommending new "ecumenical strategies for the seventies." Ten years had passed since the United Church of Christ had formally affirmed its ecumenical vocation. The years had been filled with radical change as local churches and pastors responded to racial unrest and rising discontent over the Vietnam War. In many cases these issues had stimulated and enriched grassroots ecumenical collaboration among Roman Catholics, Lutherans, Methodists, Episcopalians, and other denominations.

As far as denominational work was concerned, however, the commission noted that the UCC had sometimes failed to keep its mission witness connected to its vision of church union. The commission was concerned but reported that the "basic mood in the church about ecumenism" was not so much "cynicism and hopelessness," as "frustration and struggle." It concluded its report: "We sense a great willingness to experiment in a wide variety of ecumenical endeavors, to seek new forms and new styles, not only for their own sake, but to build greater trust, to advance the mission, and to serve the deeper needs of all humankind."

Accepting the work of the commission, the General Synod reclaimed the ecumenical calling of the UCC by passing a statement on the "Ecumenical Stance of the United Church of Christ" (1973). The statement affirmed the goal of church union in terms of the union of all humankind. It rejected thinking that separated "mission from unity, or unity from mission." "Unity and mission," it declared, "belong irrevocably together in God's order" (see vol. 7:103).

At the 1973 General Synod the Commission on Christian Unity and Ecumenical Study and Service was renamed the Council for Ecumenism. Councils and commissions for lay life and work, ministry, theological education, theology, and worship were merged to create a single national entity concerned with leadership in the United Church of Christ — the Office for Church Life and Leadership (OCLL).

As the United Church of Christ refined its self-understanding and streamlined its structures, the ecumenical movement was also changing. Some scholars became concerned that the commitment of academic theologians and also of denominations to the unity of the church was declining. Traditional understandings of ecumenical "vocation" were being "replaced by a multiplicity of professions, none of which [was] actually designed to manifest the unity of the church" (see vol. 7:104).

Fortunately, during the 1970s the United Church of Christ was able to sustain and even reassert its ecumenical witness. It stayed the course with the Consultation on Church Union (COCU). It actively participated in several conciliar bodies such as the National Council of Churches of Christ (NCCC) and the World Council of Churches (WCC). It sought to explore a deeper partnership with the Christian Church (Disciples of Christ). And in 1981 it formalized a "full communion" relationship with the Evangelical Church of the Union (EKU) in East and West Germany (see 7:69).

The relationship between the United Church of Christ and the Christian Church (Disciples of Christ) (CC[DoC])began long before 1957 and from 1961 to 1966 the two denominations engaged in formal conversations about union. By the mid-1960s, however, both denominations set aside those conversations and agreed to concentrate all of their ecumenical energy on the Consultation on Church Union (COCU). Unfortunately COCU did not flourish. After ten years the United Church of Christ and the Christian Church (Disciples of Christ) concluded that COCU was a "longer process than originally anticipated." In 1977 the UCC and the CC(DoC) reopened their conversations and in 1979 "covenanted with one another (for a period of six years) to work together toward embodying God's gift of oneness in Jesus Christ." A joint steering committee made up of representatives from both denominations developed a "Covenant Study Packet" (1981) and a working paper entitled "Shared Life: A New Approach to Church Union" (1983). Local churches were encouraged to respond.

Awareness of the covenant between the United Church of Christ and the Christian Church (Disciples of Christ) spread during the years 1979 to 1985, but the response was mixed. Some leaders who came from the Evangelical and Reformed heritage within the UCC were concerned that unilateral UCC-CC(DoC) conversations might compromise the vision of "organic union" within the wider ecumenical movement. Mercersburg theology advocates strongly supported COCU and were troubled by any "unilateral move" toward a special relationship with the Christian Church (Disciples of Christ). Furthermore, discussions about the sacramental theology of the Disciples and their distance from the historic confessions of faith made some people uneasy.

Although a number of cooperative ventures were launched in local and regional settings to help United Church of Christ and Christian Church (Disciples of Christ) members get to know each other, there was resistance within the United Church of Christ. Dissenting groups were concerned that the joint committees and the various actions of the General Synod and the General Assembly were "a creeping movement to union." They worried that "partnership votes" implied a commitment to union "without the clear consent of our churches and various member bodies" (see vol. 7:105).

In spite of these misgivings, when the six years came to an end the joint steering committee reported that both churches were benefiting from increasingly dynamic understandings of unity. They reported that many people were eager to encourage the "mutual sharing of gifts," although they were not interested in "a compromise of theological positions or practices." In reality, most people in the UCC, especially in areas where there were few Disciples' churches, were ignorant of and/or indifferent about this relationship.

Recognizing this mood, in 1985 the General Synod of the United Church of Christ and the General Assembly of the Christian Church (Disciples of Christ) reaffirmed their relationship as an "Ecumenical Partnership." Partnership, they insisted, was something new. It was not church union in the traditional sense. The marks of partnership were: (1) a commitment to "respond together to the mission God has entrusted to the church," (2) a new resolve to do "theological work to equip churches as they grow toward full communion," and, (3) a pledge to engage in "common worship with frequent and intentional sharing in the Lord's Supper/Holy Communion." They reassured people that this new ecumenical partnership would not compete with, but compliment, the ongoing participation of both denominations in the COCU.

While the majority of UCC members remained rather indifferent about the vision of the joint steering committee and the new "Ecumenical Partnership Committee," some local congregations, associations, conferences, and national instrumentalities experimented with common mission, study, and worship. Four years later, building on their "shared life" the two denominations voted a second resolution of "Ecumenical Partnership" (1989). They acknowledged each other as "true churches" and declared that a relationship of full communion "now exists" between them. They committed themselves to nurture a "dynamic and growing relationship," involving "a mutual commitment to grow together toward a vision of the church that enriches our theological traditions, enhances service and mission and deepens worship" (see vol. 7:105).

The "Ecumenical Partnership" with the Christian Church (Disciples of Christ) eventually did lead to some concrete changes in the life of both denominations. In 1993 the General Synod of the United Church of Christ and the General Assembly of the Christian Church (Disciples of Christ) met together in St. Louis, Missouri. In 1995 the General Synod approved changes to the UCC Constitution and Bylaws supporting "mutual recognition and reconciliation of ordained ministries" between the United Church of Christ and the Christian Church (Disciples of Christ). This meant that clergy in both denominations held "partner standing" in each other's churches. Furthermore, building upon longstanding administrative cooperation in their overseas mission work, in 1996 the two churches formally established an independent Common Global Ministries Board (CGM) to guide and staff their global witness.

Beyond this bilateral relationship with the Christian Church (Disciples of Christ), other forms of ecumenical engagement challenged the United Church of Christ. One of the most important was the document produced by the World Council of Churches Commission on Faith and Order on *Baptism, Eucharist and Ministry* (BEM) (1982).

"BEM," as this document is affectionately called, is a carefully developed theological statement about three basic aspects of the Christian faith that often stand as barriers to church unity. Beginning with the First Conference on Faith and Order in 1927, Protestant, Orthodox, and Roman Catholic leaders worked and reworked texts on baptism, Eucharist or the Lord's Supper, and ministry through five decades of dialogue. By the 1960s it began to take shape, and in 1982 at a meeting in Lima, Peru, the Commission of Faith and Order of the WCC determined unanimously that BEM had reached sufficient "maturity" to be sent to the churches for "official response" and "reception." "Reception" invites churches to react to the text "at the highest appropriate level of authority." It does not seek agreement, but asks if Christians from many different traditions can "recognize" in the text "the faith of the Church through the ages."

The theologians and church leaders who wrote *Baptism, Eucharist and Ministry* insist that it is not a "consensus" document. Full consensus comes only after "churches reach the point of living and acting together in unity." Nevertheless, BEM does identify "major areas of theological convergence" among Christians. "Convergence" acknowledges that despite "diversity in theological expression the churches have much in common in their understanding of the faith." It assumes that Christians will increasingly be able to enter into a "process of growing together in mutual trust," and developing "convergences step by step."

The formal action taken by the UCC, "A Response of the United Church of Christ to *Baptism, Eucharist and Ministry*" (1985) was a theological milestone. Drawing upon feedback from a churchwide process designed by the Council for Ecumenism, the 1985 General Synod of the United Church of Christ voted that it could indeed recognize in the BEM text "the faith of the Church through the ages." It raised specific concerns about baptism,

Eucharist, and ministry and made some general comments. It suggested that the language used in the text needed to be "truly inclusive of all the people of God." It asked for more recognition of the tensions involved when united churches struggle "to incorporate diversity within their common life." The responsc to BEM also called for a stronger affirmation of particular churches as they open their lives to the heritages of other churches. The United Church of Christ affirmed BEM as "provocative, useful, helpful and hopeful." It was "amazed at the extent to which some kind of common ground has been staked out." It concluded, "*Baptism, Eucharist and Ministry* holds great promise as a signpost on our pilgrim way toward a deeper understanding and a more faithful embodiment of the one Church of Jesus Christ that is sent to the one humanity that is made in the image and likeness of God" (see vol. 7:106).

Meanwhile, as the United Church of Christ deepened its ecumenical commitments through expanded relationships with the Christian Church (Disciples of Christ), and developed its serious response to *Baptism, Eucharist and Ministry,* it remained active in the Consultation on Church Union (COCU).

COCU — Principles of Church Union (1966) was revised into *A Plan of Union* (1970). In 1971 the General Synod of the United Church of Christ stated its continuing uneasiness with the COCU plan, stating that its assumptions about the episcopate were "greatly at variance with the United Church of Christ." In spite of its wariness, however, the United Church of Christ affirmed its faith that "God can do a new thing in the church." It challenged COCU to explore "local ecumenical groupings." It pressed COCU to envision a union that was more imaginative, marked by passion — a union that would overcome the "divisions caused by war, by racial injustice, and by discrimination against women."

By the mid-1970s COCU began to respond to concerns raised by the UCC and several other COCU partners. It revised its approach to union, admitting the need to let go of "designing church union from the top down," and it moved to promote what it called "living towards union." In 1976 COCU issued an "Alert on the New Church Dividing Potential of Some Persistent Issues," pointing out the divisive nature of four nontheological issues: racism, sexism, institutionalism, and congregational exclusivism. The "alert" was an ecumenical breakthrough, because it suggested the need to blend classic doctrinal issues of faith and order with the activist mission concerns of Christian life and work. It was important for the United Church of Christ because it honored its activist stance, but it also insisted that doctrinal differences had an important place within a united church, even if they were not necessarily preconditions for common life and witness.

The Consultation on Church Union (COCU) continued its work. It produced *In Quest of a Church of Christ Uniting* (1976), revised it several times, and finally sent *The COCU Consensus: In Quest of a Church of Christ Uniting* (1984) to the churches. The *Consensus* document was the theological section of a three-part COCU proposal designed to enable "participating churches to continue on the way toward visible unity." The *Consensus* document focused upon theology, while *Churches in Covenant Communion* (1989) contained resources to support local covenanting and liturgical sharing.

When the General Synod of the United Church of Christ responded to the *Consensus* document in 1989, it was able to "claim" that there was "sufficient theological basis" for the UCC to participate in a new relationship of commitment with the participating COCU denominations. In keeping with the revisions of the *Consensus* document made by COCU in 1988, the UCC no longer understood "covenanting" as an "interim step" toward institutional union. "Covenant communion" was itself a form of church union. Visible unity was no longer defined in organic terms and more in the direction of "communion in sacred things" (see vol. 7:107).

Following the "UCC Response to the *COCU Consensus*" (1989) the Council for Ecumenism invited the UCC to participate in another grassroots process to reflect on the practical components (structures and liturgies) outlined in *Churches in Covenant Communion* (1989). After another six years, in 1995 the General Synod voted to support COCU as a "new ecclesial reality." The 1995 vote on COCU did not involve institutional merger, nor create a new denomination. The denominations that were part of the Consultation on Church Union (COCU) simply moved to forge "new relationships of unity in all things which are essential to the church's life, namely: faith, ministry and mission." Their covenanting was both an *act* and a *process*.

Although the "UCC Response to Churches in Covenant Communion" (1995) was generally positive, the United Church of Christ also revisited the "premier issue" that it had registered concern about in the 1960s and which still faced the UCC in the 1990s: the ministry of oversight. How could United Church of Christ understandings of ordained ministry be reconciled with "the threefold order" of ministry set forth for the Church of Christ Uniting? The UCC admitted that it needed to study the issues of episcopal authority and corporate oversight carefully, even as it affirmed the new vision of church unity emerging from COCU after thirty years.

As the Consultation on Church Union (COCU) evolved into a new entity, "Churches Uniting in Christ" (CUIC), the United Church of Christ remained deeply committed.

The first three decades of UCC ecumenical work (1957–87) were important, but in spite of its rhetoric its ecumenical witness was sometimes uneven and its allocation of resources for ecumenical work consistently thin. Fortunately, by the mid-1980s things began to change. New ecumenical energy flowing from the ecumenical partnership with the Christian Church (Disciples of Christ) (see vol. 7:105), from the "full communion relationship" with the German EKU in both East and West Germany (see vol. 7:69), from the grassroots study of *Baptism, Eucharist and Ministry* (see vol. 7:106), and from engagement with COCU and its *Consensus* document required action (see vol. 7:107). At the 1987 General Synod, in an unprecedented vote, the Synod amended the budget of the national church to provide new funds for ecumenical work by requesting a reduction in the budgets of other instrumentalities. Two years later, the 1989 General Synod, which was the Synod that deepened the "ecumenical partnership" with the Disciples and approved the COCU *Consensus* document, passed a resolution to set up a churchwide consultation to reassess the funding and staffing of UCC ecumenical responsibilities. Among other things, the resolution called for a UCC national ecumenical officer, "Assistant to the President for Ecumenical Concerns," to be filled by January 1992.

Expanding Relationships

During the 1980s the United Church of Christ clarified its theological identity, learned to live with theological diversity, and renewed its commitment to the unity of the church. As a united and uniting church it expanded its understanding of Christ's prayer "that they may all be One."

At the same time the 1980s were also years that stretched and enriched UCC relationships beyond the Christian family. In 1987 the General Synod approved a resolution on "The Relationship between the United Church of Christ and the Jewish Community." The resolution noted with humility that the Christian church, throughout much of its history, had denied God's continuing covenant relationship with the Jewish people and promoted a doctrine that Christianity superseded Judaism. Christian "supersessionism" had "led to the outright rejection of the Jewish people and to theologically and humanly intolerable violence." It stated, "Judaism has not been superseded by Christianity"; Christianity is not "the successor religion to Judaism"; and "God's covenant with the Jewish people has not been abrogated." "God is faithful in keeping covenant." These statements were based on the recognition that although Christians and Jews do not share identical covenants, their God is one and the same. They reminded Christians how the apostle Paul wrote that God has not "rejected" the Jewish people (Romans 11:2), and that Christians cannot know their identity apart from their Jewish roots and their relationship to contemporary Jewish people.

The core of this resolution, "The Relationship between the UCC and the Jewish Community" (1987) was the first time any major Protestant denomination in North America had gone on record in this way. The action of the United Church of Christ surprised many people, however, and generated a great deal of controversy.

Leaders and members of the UCC struggled to understand how Jesus fulfilled the Jewish covenant, but did not replace it. They wondered if Christians should ever seek to convert the Jews. They debated various meanings of "covenant," and they argued over whether justice related to Middle East land was denied when God's covenant with the Jews was affirmed. Most people, however, failed to understand the fuss, assuming that the General Synod resolution simply affirmed what many tolerant Christians had believed all along.

The theological issues raised by this resolution, however, were deeper than most people realized. Within a few weeks after the 1987 Synod a UCC Interagency Task Force on Jewish Christian Relations encouraged the president of the church to convene a "Theological Panel on Jewish-Christian Relations." Christians needed to recognize the ongoing validity of God's covenant with the Jews, but they also needed to reaffirm their conviction that "God changed the course of the world in Jesus of Nazareth." Christians cannot be who they are without "belief in the singular deed God has done to redeem all the world in the life, death and resurrection of Jesus Christ." The Jewish-Christian Theological Panel held hearings around the country and released its "Message to the Churches" in May 1990 (see vol. 7:108).

At almost exactly the same time the General Synod passed another resolution on "The Relationship between the United Church of Christ and the Muslim Community" (1989). Based on the conviction that God's people are called to be "agents of reconciliation, breaking down walls of division nationally, culturally, racially and religiously" (Ephesians 2:11–18), the resolution acknowledged the "lack of understanding in our society about the Muslim community and its religion." It encouraged "members of the United Church of Christ to seek greater understanding about Islam in the society as a whole." It did not cause any controversy, but the United

Church of Christ named the importance of education about Islam and the need to strengthen Christian-Muslim relations (see vol. 7:109).

Even as the United Church of Christ became more intentional about its relationships with Jews and Muslims, it continued to nurture ecumenical conversations within the wider Christian family. By the early 1990s, Reformed-Lutheran conversations that went back to 1962 were bearing exciting new fruit.

Lutheran-Reformed dialogues involved several Presbyterian, Reformed, and Lutheran denominations. Recognizing divisions reflected in the 1529 debate between Zwingli and Luther in Marburg, Lutheran and Reformed Christians sought to heal historical animosities and find contemporary "pulpit and altar fellowship." Unfortunately, in the mid-1980s, even though European Lutheran and Reformed churches had signed the historic "Leuenberg Agreement" (1973), leaving behind centuries of Lutheran-Reformed conflict, some Lutherans questioned the theological substance of the UCC and resisted its participation in North American Lutheran-Reformed conversations. This was ironic, because after 1981 the UCC was in "full communion" with the Evangelical Church of the Union (EKU) in East and West Germany (composed of Lutheran and Reformed congregations), but it had no comparable understanding with Lutherans in the United States (see vol. 7:69).

The first significant U.S. Lutheran-Reformed document was called *An Invitation to Action* (1983). After that, however, steps toward overcoming some of the divisions among Presbyterians and Lutherans put Reformed-Lutheran conversations on hold until 1987. When they resumed UCC participation was still questioned by some of the Lutherans. Fortunately, solid theological presentations by key UCC leaders reassured Lutheran partners and opened the way for another round of theological conversations. Six Lutheran and six Reformed theologians (two of them from the United Church of Christ) dealt with the remaining disputed questions: the so-called "historic condemnations," the nature of Christ's presence in the Eucharist, and predestination. After four years of theological discussion and debate, they came to enough agreement to recommend that the churches enter into a relationship of "full communion."

Together they wrote *A Common Calling: The Witness of Our Reformation Churches in North America Today* (1993). *A Common Calling* spelled out the theological assumptions allowing the Evangelical Lutheran Church in America, the Presbyterian Church (U.S.A.), the Reformed Church in America, and the United Church of Christ to enter into a relationship of "full communion." Their modern "communion" is not marked by uniformity or complete agreement, but by the principle of "mutual affirmation and mutual admonition." Furthermore, instead of saying "if we can agree, then we can be united," it insists that "in Christ we are already one," and "therefore we will join together in our common calling to the world."

To facilitate the reception of *A Common Calling* among the four participating denominations, a *Formula of Agreement* was drawn up, circulated, widely discussed, and voted in 1997 by all four denominations, declaring themselves in "full communion" with one another. "Full communion" was not a merger of church structures, it was an "intimate relationship between churches involving recognition, eucharistic sharing, common action, and on-going theological dialogue" (see vol. 7:110).

For the United Church of Christ the *Formula of Agreement* was a natural step. Colonial German Reformed congregations had a history of cooperation with Lutherans in Union Churches. Congregationalists had collaborated with Presbyterian and Dutch Reformed churches in nineteenth-century missions. The Evangelical Synod of North America was itself a blend of Lutheran and Reformed practices found in the Church of the Old Prussian Union. The UCC vote on the *Formula of Agreement* was anticipated eagerly. As early as 1994 the Mercersburg Theological Forum, dedicated to preserving the legacy of Mercersburg theology and its ecumenical witness (see vol. 7:68), responded with joy to *A Common Calling* and the anticipated vote (see vol. 7:110).

One other form of ecumenical engagement emerged in the life of the United Church of Christ during the 1980s and 1990s — "partnerships in mission." The earliest "partnerships" were between the Presbyterian Church in the Republic of Korea (1983), the Pentecostal Church of Chile (1985), and the United Church of Christ in the Philippines (1987). These churches were theologically progressive in their reading of scripture and courageous in their stand for justice and human rights. By standing in solidarity with them the United Church of Christ lived out its conviction that the church of Jesus Christ was already one.

In the 1990s additional partnerships developed with the Evangelical Presbyterian Church of Ghana (1991), the United Church in Jamaica and the Cayman Islands (1993), the Korean Christian Church in Japan (1995), the United Reformed Church in the United Kingdom (1995), the Council of Churches in Cuba (1997), the Armenian Evangelical Churches in the Near East (1997), the United Congregational Church of Southern Africa (1999), the Protestant Church in East Timor (1999), and the Congregational Christian Church in American Samoa (1999).

Sometimes the UCC entered into partnership in order to support Christians in difficult circumstances; sometimes the UCC celebrated a new relationship replacing the dependencies of mission history. Sometimes "partners in mission" led to contacts with distant churches once or twice a year, and at other times they were enhanced by daily relationships with congregations literally next door (see vol. 7:79). The "partnership in mission" with the Congregational Christian Church in American Samoa is a good example of how "partnership in mission" evolved into a new form of ecumenical witness.

In the nineteenth century the London Missionary Society brought Christianity to the Samoan Islands, and most Samoans became Congregationalists. Therefore, when Samoan immigrants arrived in the United States in the late twentieth century, they felt a strong affinity with the United Church of Christ and its focus upon the local church. UCC Conferences in Hawaii and the Pacific coast region welcomed many Samoan "new church starts." As Samoans organized UCC congregations, they also maintained strong ties with their home church, the Congregational Christian Church in American Samoa. This presented challenges.

The resolution "Partnership in Mission and Ministry between the Congregational Christian Church in American Samoa and the United Church of Christ" (1999) sets forth common understandings of unity, sacraments, mission, ministry, and diversity. It also suggests practical protocols to deal with overlapping judicatories and allegiances affecting Samoan congregations and clergy. It tries to distinguish between "spiritual and cultural ties that have to do with valued heritage and partnership in mission and program" and "ecclesial ties that have to do with accountability and support associated with membership and standing." It established a "Partnership Committee" to monitor and nurture constructive relationships between the two churches (see vol. 7:111).

The United Church of Christ is the product of a vision of Christian unity that flowered in the early twentieth century. After its founding in 1957, the UCC continued to live out its commitment to unity. During the first thirty years of its life, although ecumenical commitment was assumed, it was not always supported adequately or given highest priority. The ecumenical stance of the United Church of Christ insisted that unity and mission were linked together, but in practice UCC passion for unity sometimes faltered because of insufficient funds and staff.

Yet, during this time a small group of leaders managed to sustain UCC participation in many significant ecumenical ventures: the Consultation on Church Union (COCU), partnership with the Christian Church (Disciples of Christ), full communion with the Evangelical Church of the Union (EKU) in East and West Germany, and the UCC response to *Baptism, Eucharist and Ministry.*

During the 1980s as the United Church of Christ experienced theological and ecumenical renewal (see vol. 7:57–65), it studied, debated, and endorsed one ecumenical document after another. It began to see how ecumenical organizations, "full communion," and "partnerships in mission" embodied the mission of the United Church of Christ as a multiracial, multicultural church. It became more theologically self-conscious about its responsibility and more aggressive in its witness for unity and justice.

At the end of the twentieth century, the UCC ecumenical vocation was strong and theologically mature. For over forty years its worship life had been stretched and enriched by an ecumenical liturgical consensus (see vol. 7:29 and 34). Its understandings of the episcopate came to acknowledge legitimate patterns of oversight in UCC practice (see vol. 7:46). Its global ministries were administered through ecumenical partnerships (see vol. 7:79 and 105).

In its social witness the United Church of Christ was often controversial. Its statements and actions, which consistently related to issues where Christians disagreed (such as the role of women, abortion, homosexuality, etc.), had an impact upon its ecumenical journey — attracting some and putting off others. In ecumenical circles the social witness of the UCC both enhanced and troubled its ecumenical relationships. Yet, more than once, leaders in denominations unable to speak out on controversial issues looked to the witness of the United Church of Christ with deep appreciation. Its Reformed emphasis on the sovereignty of Christ over the social order, as well as over the body of Christ (the church), has been a vital gift to the ecumenical movement (see vol. 7:85, 86, 98, and 99).

Jesus prayed "that they may all be one." Consistently, though imperfectly and incompletely, this prayer has accompanied the United Church of Christ throughout its history, grounding its theology and inspiring the church to be ecumenically engaged. Over and over the UCC has been renewed by the inspiration of the Holy Spirit, taking risks and humbly seeking to bring its words and deeds together. It has drawn on the conviction embedded in the Preamble of its Constitution that the United Church of Christ exists "in order to express more fully the oneness in Christ."

Deepening Commitment

100. Christian Unity:
"Report of the Commission on Unity"

(1963)

The United Church of Christ came into being with the vision that it was the first step in a larger ecumenical venture. It enthusiastically joined the conversations of the Consultation on Church Union (COCU) in April 1962 and March 1963. The General Synod report of the Commission on Christian Unity and Ecumenical Study and Service (1963) recognizes the practical reasons for church union, but insists that "obedience to our Lord rather than the desire for efficiency" requires the UCC to seek further union. The General Synod authorized continued involvement in COCU, but also stipulated that "participation in the development of a Plan of Union in no way commits the United Church of Christ to Union under this or any other plan."

Source: Excerpt from the "Report of the Commission on Unity," *GS Minutes 1963,* 37–38.

Christian Unity

Discussion about Christian unity has often tended to center around practical concerns, such as the need of streamlining our operations and the scandal of competitive action in the mission fields both at home and abroad. We have spoken of the things we hold in common and have believed that goodwill and desire were sufficient to bring about a union of the churches for the achievement of certain specific purposes. This aspect of church union is of permanent importance. Nevertheless, we approach Christian unity from yet another point of view.

Christians are constrained to talk with one another by the clear call of their common Lord, Jesus Christ, who is the Head of the Church. Obedience to our Lord rather than the desire for efficiency, vital though efficiency may be, requires us to seek the further union of the Church of Christ that it may be "truly catholic, truly reformed, and truly evangelical." The United Church is called to take with full seriousness the prayer of Jesus as it is found in the Fourth Gospel, "that they may all be one . . . so that the world may believe that thou hast sent me." For us to conclude that the kind of unity to which our Lord refers can be achieved in spiritual terms alone is to beg the question. Spiritual union can have little meaning either for the people of God or for the world when the divided members of Christ's Body take the sacrament in isolation from each other, gather in separate houses of worship, and severally consider themselves to be God's people in a special sense.

The oneness of the Church is given by God through Jesus Christ. The broken state of the Church is a constant judgment upon it, forcing it to look both inward to its own life and outward to the world in which it is set and to which it is called to be a witness.

The story of God's saving redemption includes the fact of death that new life may come through resurrection. The Church as we have known and loved it in its denominational and institutional forms must be ready, in response to its Lord, to lose its life in order that it may find newness of life. That newness of life is essential if the Church is faithfully to fulfill its mission to the world.

As separated Christians discuss the reunion of Christ's Church, words like "renewal" and "reform" inevitably become a part of the conversation. In their own experience the members of the United Church of Christ, coming as they do from several traditions, have already been forced to reexamine and to appreciate those traditions. We are discovering, however, that over against devotion to the past must be placed a new and radical obedience to the Word God is speaking to us in the present. In the tension that ensues, God begins the painful process of reform and renewal. We can best be faithful to the spirit of our past by placing our tradition in the common treasury, so enriching the cause of renewal and reunion.

The United Church of Christ is not interested in church union for the sake of bigness and power; it does not believe that it is called to involvement in a trading venture in which denominations can be put together with as little dislocation and disturbance as possible. The United Church of Christ, confessing its sin, does seek to hear and respond with obedience to the Word that God speaks to us. We believe that the Head of the church calls us to reunion, to renewal, and to the world. In the faith that God speaks a relevant and saving Word to the faithful, the United Church of Christ is ready to lose its life, if need be, that Christ's church may become visibly one. Such readiness is not to be interpreted as a repudiation of our past; it is rather an attempt to learn a fresh openness and faithfulness to the Lord of the church.

In this sense the United Church of Christ declares "its steadfast purpose to be a uniting church." To this end the United Church welcomes opportunities to examine further possibilities of Christian reunion. . . .

101. Reform and Renewal:

"Church Union"

(1966)

David Colwell

David G. Colwell (1916–2001) was a Congregational Christian/UCC minister educated at Yale University, Harvard University, and Yale Divinity School. After military service during World War II he served pastorates in Massachusetts, Colorado, Washington (D.C.), and Washington (state) (1945–82). Colwell was the first chair of the Commission on Christian Unity and Ecumenical Study and Service (1961–69) and was elected moderator of the United Church of Christ. He also represented the UCC as a delegate to the World Council of Churches and as chair of the Consultation on Church Union (COCU).

Colwell's essay on "Church Union" appears in a small book titled Reform and Renewal: Exploring the United Church of Christ *(1966) published by the United Church Board for Homeland Ministries (UCBHM) containing essays by Douglas Horton, Roger L. Shinn, Ruben H. Huenemann, Harlan G. Lewis, and Gerald J. Jud.*

Source: David G. Colwell, "Church Union," in *Reform and Renewal: Exploring the United Church of Christ* (Philadelphia and Boston: United Church Press, 1966), 98–105.

Church Union

It is easy for us in the United Church of Christ to agree with the expressed conviction that a peculiar genius of our church lies in the field of ecumenicity. Our history of deep involvement in both the conciliar and organic-union aspects of ecumenicity over many years — together with the fact that we are a "united" church — commits us to continued ecumenical involvement. The Second General Synod of the United Church of Christ stated:

> As an expression of the devotion of the United Church of Christ to the oneness of Christ's church and of its steadfast purpose to be a uniting church, the General Synod shall maintain a permanent commission to be known as the Commission on Christian Unity and Ecumenical Study and Service.[1]

There is no reason to detract from the enthusiasm for the ecumenical commitment and potential of the United Church, but a word of caution needs to be added. "Genius for uniting" implies that the United Church has already found "the way" to the united church of the future. The solid contributions that we in the United Church can make out of our own experience should not be discounted, but it is both unwise and unhelpful for us or for any other body to assume that the pattern for such a united church already exists, particularly within its own structures.

Merger or Church Union

A clear distinction must be made between merger of the churches on the one hand and true church union on the other. "Merger" is used to refer to that thesis which looks upon the whole process as putting together two existing institutions. This is the process that is normally followed in the business world. The idea is to accomplish a merger with as little dislocation as possible. In this process there is a good deal of negotiating. A certain amount of good, hardheaded negotiation is necessary, of course, but the instruments of the Christian church should be taken seriously. The Christian faith is a religion of incarnation and thus, particularity; it is not a vague, generalized faith. This means, among other things, that from time to time certain institutional forms become necessary, if we are faithfully to carry on with the mission.

---

1. Minutes, Second General Synod of the United Church of Christ (July 5–9, 1959; Oberlin, Ohio), appendix 6, p. 78.

Jesus Christ calls us to reform and renewal in the church, as well as to the manifestation of the oneness that he gives his church. The matters of reform and renewal and the matter of unity cannot be separated.

It would seem, therefore, that the call is to church union, not to merger. In church union we of the United Church are called to seek and receive with expectation and openness the word that the living Lord of the church has to speak to us. If we are to hear and receive this word, it is only at our peril that we make assumptions about our present achievements and condition. Our spiritual forebear John Robinson expressed his faith that the Lord has yet more light and truth to break forth from his holy Word. We can share this faith, for God will give new forms to a truly united and obedient church.

Moreover, if a Christian is seeking church union, he is willing to submit all of his historic and dearly held ideas and convictions to the rigorous judgment of the Holy Spirit. This is always a painful process, for along the way he is forced to accept new truth and to recognize the fact that what is familiar is not always of the esse of the church. It is also difficult because there is always someone standing by who will strongly urge that such reexamination is really disloyal to one's fathers in the faith.

One of the necessary and central tensions of Christian faith is how to maintain the proper relationship between the historic past and the word of the living God for the present. It is through our historic knowledge that we in the United Church know who we are and who God is; it is through our historic rootage that we can receive the word that the living God is speaking to us in this present. But we all must beware lest our history prove to be a deadening trap, which keeps us forever bound in the past or the present.

It is not difficult to agree with the statement that it is sometimes more profitable to talk with those with whom we seem to have great historic differences than with those with whom we share a common heritage. Those who believe they have much in common neglect opening the most dearly held convictions to one another and, much more importantly, opening themselves to the Holy Spirit. When we talk about church union with those with whom we have not shared a "family" heritage, it is necessary to begin again at the roots of faith and reexamine what we had thought to be the absolute and unquestioned truth of God.

Freedom and Responsibility

In chapter 7 the "middle axiom" is introduced, whereby the general theory of unity in diversity can be translated into the actual life of a united church. The idea that freedom and order must be kept in constant tension and balance is sound. Surely we who are in the United Church of Christ are not the only ones among God's people who cherish this need. Maximum freedom and total responsibility under the Holy Spirit in every area and level of the life of the church have been advocated. Most of us will agree with this general proposition. It is in the working out of the relationships, however, that we begin to find both historic differences and present disagreements. There needs to be a greater measure of connectionalism.

One of the present problems facing the United Church, as well as other churches, is that of regionalism. This is demonstrated quite clearly in the involvement of churches in civil rights. It is commonplace for congregations in certain sections of the country to refuse admission to Negroes. It is also a fact that in churches with a highly connectional system the regional unit is almost completely autonomous in certain respects. Furthermore, in the United Church of Christ it is possible for a conference or an association or a local church completely to ignore or frustrate the will of General Synod. (Surely this is only a partial use of proper freedom in Christ.)

The matter of autonomy is one of the serious problems in the life of the churches. The problems arise to a considerable extent because of the operation of the principle of maximum freedom. As has been pointed out, the whole church says to every individual, every part of the church:

> By virtue of the fact that Christ has touched you with his own hand, we regard you as a potential center of creativity, and we beg you to enter into dialogue — within the love of Christ with the church. We believe that the judgment of Christ is both upon the church and upon you, and what we are seeking together is the perfection that is in Christ.[2]

This principle is sound, but it presents grave problems when a part of the church chooses not to accept the will and insight of the whole church. It also largely ignores the nature of man's sin.

Local Units and Total Church

It has been suggested that the relationship of the conferences to the United Church gives a key to the relationship of the various denominations to that total (united) church:

> Denominations as they are known today would not be happy to yield themselves to an absolutism in which idiosyncrasies that they have

2. See page 87 in *Reform and Renewal: Exploring the United Church of Christ* for an essay by Douglas Horton.

> been ready to die for would be lost. But their members might be ready to take their place in a larger church, if they were allowed to continue — though not as a continuing denomination — to hold to anything they felt the Holy Spirit had entrusted to them, as our conferences, associations, and churches are allowed to hold to what they conscientiously feel they must — all under the overarching sky of a really unifying government.[3]

Serious difficulty arises here. First, the analogy breaks down. A conference is a geographical unity; there are no other conferences of the United Church of Christ within its bounds. In a united church, under this proposal, there would be in the same geographic areas a number of denominations, presumably maintaining a real amount of independence. This would accomplish little in terms of one of the most crucial areas of ecumenicity — the local community, where according to the New Delhi statement, "all in each place who are baptized into Jesus Christ and confess him as Lord and Savior are brought by the Holy Spirit into one fully committed fellowship." The fact that all of these structures would be in the same loose church structure would not alleviate the problem in any great measure.

Second, the phrase "to live their own lives" brings to mind what would better be forgotten; namely, the statements, made in the days before the United Church of Christ came into being, that congregations would not be affected at all. At the time, such statements seemed unimportant. But, in the light of subsequent experience and conviction, were they not blasphemy?

It is intolerable that any church or any of its parts should ever seek a condition in which it can lead its own life apart from the life of the whole church — which includes Rome and Eastern Orthodoxy. Where is the renewal and reform, if it is guaranteed in advance that each denomination can go along as it has in the past? The call is to new and radical obedience, not to the perpetuation of divisions and fragmentations even under some kind of overarching government.

We of the United Church can heartily concur with the suggestion that the life of each congregation should be oriented to the church, which is given of our Lord Christ, and the united church that will come to be. Toward this end, study should be continued by the various agencies of the denomination to insure that the materials they prepare are ecumenical in outlook and as faithful as possible to the one holy, catholic, and apostolic church. Our claim to faithfulness is not to be seen in our uniqueness, nor in our being different; it is rather to be seen in our seeking the wholeness

---

3. See Horton, *Reform and Renewal,* 90.

of Christian truth. A part of that wholeness is brought to us in different traditions.

The statement "None of us in the United Church has given up hope of the Consultation on Church Union, which involves our relationship with no less than five other denominations" was written prior to the fourth meeting of the Consultation on Church Union, which met in Lexington, Kentucky, where significant progress was made. A year earlier, after the Princeton meeting, there was discouragement. None of this was present in Lexington. The Methodists had a substantially new delegation present, and this new group brought new life and new hope to all. There was also a new commitment apparent in the Episcopal delegation.

During the meeting in Lexington, the Consultation voted without dissent to bring into being a special commission composed of one from each delegation. This commission is charged with the preparation of an outline plan of union to be presented to the next meeting of the Consultation in May, 1966, at Dallas, Texas. Beyond that, solid work was done at Lexington on the ministry of a united church, truly catholic, truly evangelical, and truly reformed. Now, for the first time, many church leaders have learned to say, "This would not be possible under our present law or procedures, but we are talking about a united church and there it seems reasonable to follow such a procedure." This is not a weakness, which is selling one's tradition into oblivion; rather it is the kind of growth and flexibility that men experience when they face one another under the conviction that God continues to speak a fresh word of truth.

Crucifixion precedes resurrection, and death — in the Pauline sense of being crucified with Christ — is a precondition of the newness of life in Christ Jesus. Participation in this necessary drama of redemption is a live option for the various traditional forms of the church.

102. Autonomy:

"Report of the Theological Commission"

(1971)

*As the United Church of Christ became more deeply involved in the Consultation on Church Union (COCU) during the 1960s the Theological Commission turned its attention to some of the theological issues that invariably emerge in ecumenical conversations. In 1967 it suggested that the president of the church, authorized by the General Synod, send a letter to "member communions of the National Council of Churches, the Roman Catholic Church and other evangelical churches" stating "two marks of [UCC] current life which, if understood by them, may constitute an encouragement to unity"—namely (1) the practice of welcoming "all who profess and call themselves Christian" to the Lord's Supper and (2) the belief that the ordination of ministers in other communions was "sacred and efficacious" (*GS Minutes 1967, *101).*

The Theological Commission also offered a "Comment" on COCU Principles of Church Union *(1966), stressing the concern of the United Church of Christ that the local church be given "its proper place" in the proposed polity (*GS Minutes 1967, *102–4).*

As the COCU continued, the General Synod asked the Theological Commission "to work through a theological statement and definition of the meaning of autonomy at all levels of our UCC church structure." In July 1969 the commission presented a small pamphlet Toward an Understanding of Local Autonomy *(1969) to the General Synod, which approved it and "commended it to the churches for study."*

The Theological Commission was diligent in its work, and for the next two years it focused its discussions on the "doctrine of the church and the

---

Source: An excerpt from the report of the "Theological Commission," *GS Minutes 1971,* Index 17, 9.

concept of ministry." Its General Synod report (1971) summarizes UCC understandings of autonomy and unity and their implications for mission and structure.

Theological Commission on Autonomy

The Seventh General Synod instructed the Theological Commission "to work through a theological statement and definition of the meaning of autonomy at all levels of our UCC church structure as we further pursue the relationship of the local church to the total denomination, and the denomination's relationship to the Consultation on Church Union."

The Theological Commission devoted itself to this task in its annual meeting in March, 1971. It submits the following statement:

> "The freedom recognized in local autonomy is freedom under Christ —and therefore freedom to respond to the demands of Christ."
> (*Toward an Understanding of Local Autonomy,* p. 3)

I. Autonomy and Unity in the United Church

A. It is a misunderstanding and distortion of the meaning of Christian freedom simply to equate it with self-determination at any level of Church life.

B. The notion of autonomy at the local level originally implied mutual care and mutual responsibility under Christ; by extension, Christian freedom in every area of the Church's structure implies the same mutual care and mutual accountability.

C. Mutual care and mutual accountability are to be exercised in love, not juridically or coercively. At the congregational level, "the majority of the adult members determine the corporate life of the group always with due consideration of the will of any minority. When there are differences of opinion which threaten the unity of the local church, it is the responsibility of all to seek for a consensus of the spirit and through study and consultation to seek the wisdom of the wider church. Groups with conflicting views may separate; but that is an extreme step to be taken with sorrow and pain only when no hope for consensus or co-operation seems possible; and even then never without the continuing hope and genuine prayer that the separated may be again united by the Spirit of Christ. The

United Church of Christ believes that this is the best way to translate Christian love into the framework of government" (*Toward an Understanding of Local Autonomy,* p. 4).

In other structures representative of the life of the Church where mission and unity are threatened, Christian freedom implies that the same care and accountability be exercised in an analogous fashion; i.e., by seeking the wisdom of the wider Church through consultation with the national, regional, and local bodies.

II. Implications for Mission

When Christian freedom as spontaneity and vitality has expressed itself in the Church, this has always included expressions in structures additional to local congregations. These structures, like the local congregations, have come as instruments for more effective mission. They have also helped to supplement some of the vision or work of local congregations.

The relation between local congregations and these other structures has been, in some form, a covenant relation: local churches and broader agencies have interacted with tension and consent to implement the mission. All of the parties in the covenant have helped identify parts of the mission. They have also discerned parts of the mission by responding to the Spirit in movements outside the Church.

Even in the New Testament this pattern is found. Even in the New Testament these several forms of the Church came out of cultural conditions of particular times and places. This is true today. It reminds us that all expressions of the mission need to be flexible. They need to be adaptable according to discerned changes in the culture, or according to changed understandings of the covenantal relationships.

III. Implications for Structure

A. Local autonomy in the tradition we represent has to be seen in the context of a covenant relationship, which has mutual responsibility and ministry as its fundamental insight into the gospel.

B. A strong emphasis in our own time has made the covenant an overarching concern in the doctrine of the Church, and it has also become a governing image in the ecumenical vision; e.g., at Amsterdam the foundation message of the WCC spoke of the Churches "covenanting together," and the intention of the UCC to be a "uniting" Church has this concern at its heart.

C. Therefore, autonomy has to be seen in relation to this intention to express mutual responsibility in ministry and mission. It represents the valid emphasis on Christian freedom within the context of Christian love, compassion, and willingness to share our gifts and on the creativity of the church at the grassroots level.

D. If this is a correct reading of our concern, it means that we have serious questions to put both to COCU and to our own agencies and structures, as to how far existing or proposed structures reflect these insights into the gospel. For example:

1. How far are these structures (forms of ministry, etc.) past-oriented or future-oriented?
2. Is power in the Church to be exercised ministerially (persuasion) or magisterially (coercion)?
3. What guarantees are written into the structures that future structures *can* be flexible?

103. Commitment to Unity: *"The Ecumenical Stance of the United Church of Christ"*

(1973)

In 1971 the General Synod asked the Commission on Christian Unity and Ecumenical Study and Service to reexamine the ecumenical vocation of the United Church of Christ and make recommendations for the future. In response the commission developed a statement entitled "The Ecumenical Stance of the United Church of Christ" (1973). The statement contains a "Theological Affirmation and Call" and seven commitments. The United Church of Christ (1) declares its recognition of members and ministers in other Christian churches, (2) pledges itself to strengthen the conciliar movement, (3) looks with favor upon the possibility of Roman Catholic membership in conciliar ecumenical groups, (4) affirms its support of coalitions, consortia, and clusters in ecumenical work, (5) recommits itself to the Consultation on Church Union (COCU), (6) endorses regional and local ecumenical ventures, and (7) states its intention to remain part of the World Alliance of Reformed Churches (WARC).

Source: "The Ecumenical Stance of the United Church of Christ," *GS Minutes 1973,* 58–60.

Ecumenical Stance of the United Church of Christ

Theological Affirmation and Call

Humanity is broken and divided yet one. The Church of Jesus Christ is broken and divided yet one. The ecumenical commitment of the Church to mission and unity is to symbolize through its worship, its communal and structural life, and its work in the world the Christian union which points toward the larger union of creation. Its task is to work in effective mission to heal dehumanizing divisions and to realize more fully the universal human community which is proclaimed in the reality and the hope of the Kingdom of God.

The ultimate personal identity of each individual is that of a human being, created and loved by God, and part of His universal family. Our identities as individual members and as churches in the corporate life of the United Church of Christ are fragmental identities, necessary but provisional. The task our Lord Jesus Christ sets before us is to realize more fully in our churchly symbols, common life, ecclesiastical structures, and mission the ultimate union of creation, to point with gratitude and to participate where possible in those places where God's Spirit is at work in the world making life whole. To the end that the union and wholeness of God's creation may be affirmed, we believe the effective union and wholeness of Christ's Church is intended.

We affirm, therefore, the description of the nature and shape of unity recommended to the Churches by the Third Assembly in New Delhi of the World Council of Churches:

> "We believe that the unity which is both God's will and his gift to his Church is being made visible as all in each place who are baptized into Jesus Christ and confess him as Lord and Savior are brought by the Holy Spirit into ONE fully committed fellowship, holding the one apostolic faith, preaching the one Gospel, breaking the one bread, joining in common prayer, and having a corporate life reaching out in witness and service to all, and who at the same time are united with the whole Christian fellowship in all places and all ages in such wise that ministry and members are accepted by all, and that all can act and speak together as occasion requires for the tasks to which God calls his people."

We call the whole Church and the communion to which we belong to the task of giving full witness to the continuing process of uniting in ways known and to be made known to us.

Ecumenical commitment and involvement, even as all Christian life, involve costs of time, energy, and fundamental risk. Nevertheless, ecumenicity is not an option for us; rather it is a mandate that prohibits a restrictive view that would separate mission from unity, or unity from mission. Whenever we view ecumenicity as mainly cooperative planning and action rather than as the name for those active steps toward the goal of church union for the union of all humankind, we trap ourselves in the false dichotomy of mission vs. unity or unity vs. mission. The goal is the *union* of the Church and the *union* of creation, and mission and unity are the processes to be followed in reaching the goal. We affirm that these belong irrevocably together in God's order.

We confess our need to understand more fully the demands of the gospel in a world of conflicting demands. We need to *clarify* those demands, particularly as they relate to church union and the union of all creation. We need to provide guidelines, in light of the gospel imperatives for mission and unity, for choosing among the various ecumenical models according to their functions.

We believe that such policy and clarity are built on theological foundations.

104. Ecumenical Vocation:

"Ecumenical Theology — Profession or Vocation?"

(1976)

Paul S. Minear

Paul S. Minear (b. 1906) is a Congregational Christian/UCC minister who spent a lifetime in theological education. He taught at Garrett Biblical Institute (1934–44), Andover Newton Theological School (1944–56), and Yale Divinity School (1956–71). From 1961 to 1963 he was director of the Commission on Faith and Order for the World Council of Churches, and in the 1970s he helped to inaugurate a study program at the Jerusalem Ecumenical Institute for Advanced Theological Study (Tantur). His books in New Testament studies were widely respected, especially Images of the Church in the New Testament *(1960). In an article in* Theology Today *(1976) Minear reports on disturbing trends which he believes are changing the work of professors and denominational staff in the ecumenical movement: (1) "the shift in the location of theological work from the realm of the church and its seminaries to the realm of public universities and their departments," (2) "the tendency [of academic theologians] to adopt without modification the prevailing canons of historical and philosophical methodology for the study of revealed Scripture and doctrine," and (3) "the tendency among academic theologians for professional pressures to supplant the vocational." Minear is concerned that each year theological seminary faculty "speak less to the church, and the church listens less to what we say."*

Source: Paul S. Minear, an excerpt from "Ecumenical Theology — Profession or Vocation?" *Theology Today* (April 1976): 66–73.

Ecumenical Theology—Profession or Vocation?

. . . No one should deny that, thus far, university theologians have exerted a positive influence on the emergence of ecumenism. Within the same departments, theologians from different confessions have learned to accept and to cooperate with one another in teaching students from diverse backgrounds. The adoption of laws forbidding discrimination on religious grounds has encouraged broader contacts and associations. Because of the security of tenure, the constant intellectual stimulus, and the occupational freedoms of campus life, theologians so inclined have been able to devote a portion of time and energy to ecumenical activities. Contemporary American schools have developed catholicity of a sort beyond the reach of American churches, since the universities form a "fifth world" culture of their own that quite transcends national, racial, and religious boundaries of the other four worlds. As noted earlier, this culture undermines absolutist claims and encourages relativist concessions among all its citizens, so that resistances to interdenominational dialogue have been reduced. Accordingly, any list of the major participants in the ecumenical movement would include a large sprinkling of academicians.

Having given full credit to the academic world, however, we must note several limitations to this kind of ecumenism. Few universities accept as an essential function the encouragement of Christian ecumenism. Few academicians have accepted the opportunity to share in interconfessional dialogues as more than an interesting and perhaps productive sideline. Their advancement from one professional echelon to another has not been aided by their maverick activity in ecumenical meetings. Most top scholars have reached the top by avoiding excessive involvement in non-curricular matters; not many have given a major portion of time and energy to ecumenism. It could hardly be otherwise, since the hope of our profession is not the same as the hope of our vocation.

I foresee a diminishing level of ecumenical activity on the part of professional theologians. Along with this diminishing level, I foresee certain permanent inhibitions on the depth and seriousness of ecumenical experience as long as the professionalization of the vocation proceeds apace. The academic theologian will probably continue to stress the importance of such agencies as AAR and SBL more than such agencies as NCC or WCC. Confining ourselves to our work as university theologians, then, I think that the trend is definitely *downward* in terms of both the quantity and the quality of ecumenicity. It is possible for a religion department to be staffed with top scholars from many confessions and the total ecumenical result yet be absolutely nil.

What is the prospect if we turn away from the church's academic experts (*periti*) to its priests, bishops, and administrators? Although I cannot speak in this area with the same confidence as in dealing with academic circles, let me hazard the following guesses:

- the professionalization of Christian vocation has proceeded as deeply and as extensively in church administration as in university teaching; certainly the daily schedule of the minister is determined more by professional demands than by vocational pressures;
- ordination has, in effect, become a stage in professional advancement, an accomplishment on which one is congratulated; in services of ordination, no texts are more popular than 2 Corinthians 3–6, but few images of the minister's work are more pervasive than enabler, change agent, managerial specialist, designer of social institutions, facilitator;
- the relative strength of loyalty to immediate existing institutions when contrasted to less immediate ecumenical experimentation is reflected in the number of ecumenical bureaucrats who, when opportunity affords, shift back to denominational bureaus;
- even after seventy years of ecumenical history, there is no recognition, by way of ordination, of that history; no ecumenical agency has the power to ordain; and no denomination in fact can ordain a person to ministry to all Christians in a given locality or to all churches in nation or world;
- the primary role of the apostle in the New Testament period to advance the unity of the church through personal suffering finds no genuine succession anywhere within ordained ministries today.

The rise of ecumenism, has, of course, owed much to many denominational bureaucrats who have developed an ecumenical conscience as a strong avocation, and to some few for whom an ecumenical ministry has constituted their central dominating vocation. But the initial momentum has spent itself. More and more today the professionalized demands of the ministry in the separate denominational bodies are choking off new impulses toward new frontiers. The future of ecumenism cannot thrive so long as it depends upon the residual energies of professors and priestly bureaucrats after they have exhausted themselves in coping with the urgent demands which their respective professions levy on them as paid supporters of existing institutions.

In this regard, as in many others, I am haunted by the chasm between twentieth and first century Christianity. All of our churches verbally accept the normative authority of the New Testament. None of them today is making a vigorous effort to reshape its institutional and its communal life into closer conformity to the revealed Scriptures. I detect virtually nothing in contemporary ministerial structures that betrays a family likeness to the churches of the New Testament, and I detect even less awareness of the anomalies involved in reading the Scripture as Scripture in our services of worship.

We read, for instance, with appropriate dignity and solemn voice, the verses from Ephesians 4:4f.

> "There is one body and one Spirit, just as you were called to the one hope that belongs to your calling, one Lord, one faith, one baptism, one God and Father of us all. . . . "

We read, quite unaware of how far removed is this one calling and its one hope from the callings which we exercise in the church and in the world. That original vocation has been replaced by a multiplicity of professions, none of which is actually designed to manifest the unity of the church. We still await, therefore, the true beginnings of an ecumenical movement that will embody the full sovereignty of the gospel over the church and the emergence of a vocation that can once again penetrate all the professionalisms of the world. Until we are again fully conscious of sharing in a single vocation that is drawn and driven by the one hope, our affirmations of one Lord, one faith, one baptism will sound like tinkling brass. I hope that such an ecumenical movement may emerge in our time, but I think that such a hope is possible today only by imitating the faith of Abraham, who "in hope believed against hope," who believed in "the God who calls into existence the things that do not exist."

105. Christian Church (Disciples of Christ): *"Ecumenical Partnership"*

(1983, 1989)

Committee for a New Alternative,
UCC-CC(DoC) Partnership Committee

Conversation and cooperation with the Christian Church (Disciples of Christ) predated the creation of the United Church of Christ in 1957. In the 1970s and 1980s as talk of "shared life" and "partnership" was formalized some UCC leaders were wary. Some people had been drained by the UCC union and were not ready to imagine expanding relationships. Others were protective of local church freedoms and hesitant about additional obligations. Still others objected to creating a special covenant with one denomination out of their fear that it might undermine multilateral conversations. A small handful resisted because they believed that any arrangement less than full organic union was theologically weak. "The Committee for a New Alternative" is a good example of the type of grassroots movements that organized to stop or slow down agreements with the Christian Church (Disciples of Christ) during the 1980s.

Nevertheless, for ten years a joint steering committee (1979–85) and an ecumenical partnership committee (1985–89) guided the two denominations into deeper and deeper relationship. The resolution on "Ecumenical Partnership" (1989) builds upon the earlier actions of both denominations in 1979 and 1985. It affirms that unity in Christ's church already exists and each church pledges to find new ways to make it visible through common confession, mutual recognition of members, common celebration of the Lord's Supper or Holy Communion, and the mutual recognition and reconciliation of ordained ministers.

Sources: "Committee for a New Alternative" [Response to UCC-Disciples], n.d. [estimate 1983] [typescript]. "Ecumenical Partnership," *GS Minutes 1989,* 56–58.

Questioning a Special UCC-Disciples Relationship

- *Why do we need to concern ourselves with this issue at this time?*

The Twelfth General Synod meeting in 1979 voted that the 1985 Synod should vote to affirm one of three alternatives:

1. "enter into negotiations toward formal union," or to
2. "continue exploration of different forms of cooperation and relationship" or to
3. "discontinue discussions."

Recently, the Joint UCC Disciples Steering Committee has issued a document: "Shared Life: a New Approach to Church Union." This new approach would have various interlockings of the constituent groups before allowing the two denominations the opportunity of fully considering and voting upon the consequences.

This sets in motion a process in which the goal would be formal corporate union between our two denominations. Ultimately each local church would be required to vote "yes" or "no" on the proposed union. Unless a church votes "yes," it would not be included in the new denomination. A vote of "no" or a vote to "abstain from voting" would mean the exclusion of such a church.

Our concern is that this creeping movement to union commits us to union without the clear consent of our churches and various member bodies.

- *What is the new alternative which you suggest?*

A discontinuance of the discussions which have corporate union as their inevitable goal and substitute the active pursuit of cooperative ecumenical partnerships for mission and witness with the Disciples of Christ as well as with other denominations. This would enable us to preserve a unity in our ecumenical relationships without paying the heavy price exacted by corporate unions at Conference, Instrumentality and Synodical levels.

- *What is this "heavy price"?*

  - There is a *time* price. Those of us who have worked on mergers remember the enormous amount of time and energy spent in meetings dedicated to the details of constitutions, headquarters locations, personnel reallocations, theological and ecclesiastical differences, historic patterns of operations and legal co-mingling of assets and liabilities. When one gets down to it "formal union" or "organic union" is in fact "corporate union": the uniting of various autonomous corporations.

- There is a *financial* price. The Lutherans estimate their union will cost 18 million. For us, where would such money come from? The answer is plain: from the resources which now fund our mission and witness at the local, national and world levels. Money which is spent on union is not available for mission.
- There is a *fragmentation* price. Not all of our churches nor of the Disciples would vote "yes" in such a union proposal. In every merger, a considerable number of churches and members are left behind. The history of various mergers within the United States indicates that the new whole is *not* larger than the sum of its parts. Studies demonstrate that merged denominations, 20 years later, are about the same size as the single largest partner before the union. Concomitantly, mission has been diminished rather than increased.
- There is a *loss of identity price*. We have been working for 27 years for the name United Church of Christ to have a specific identity. A new name would mean beginning all over again.

• *What are the benefits of the suggested "New Alternative"?*

- As we do not now work unilaterally in mission and witness, we would be able to *continue partnership,* not only with the Disciples, but with other denominations.
- Our *focus* on the sins of racism, militarism, poverty, dehumanization and injustice as well as our *concerns* to enhance family life; strengthen our ministry with children, youth and adults; extend church development and evangelism — will not be *deflected* by an internal preoccupation with structure and self-definition which is characteristic of corporate union.
- Our *achievements* of finding significant ways of incorporating minority, racial and ethnic groups within our diverse denominational life and leadership would not be lost.
- Our *theological witness* which has unique and important characteristics would continue to be honed and sharpened without being submerged in a lowest common denominator theological compromise.

- *But aren't we called to corporate union by Jesus' prayer that "they may all be one"?*

One's answer to the theological question which the prayer asks is pivotal in this discussion.

We do *not* believe that a single "super" church is *the* answer to the prayer. We do believe that Christians are called to be partners in witness and mission — as we are now with Protestants, Roman Catholics and Orthodox. The unity to which we are called is not a corporate uniformity. For *this time* in our history, we believe ecumenical partnerships represent our best response to the prayer.

- *Are we to be a united and a uniting church?*

We celebrate the road we have traveled during the 27-year marriage of the UCC toward becoming a "united" church. We believe that we will become even more united in the future as we continue to mine the heritage of our past to address the problems of the future. *We need more time* to do this without the addition of a new member of the marriage. We are *now* a "uniting" church as we bring together folk of many different faith backgrounds within our local churches and join hands with other denominations to share in witness and mission.

- *How does this affect our relationship with COCU?*

We believe that a bilateral union would weaken, rather than strengthen the ecumenical witness and dream.

- *Does this mean that you would never favor a corporate union between denominations?*

No. Some point in the future may call for different actions and reactions than we suggest now. We believe that corporate union is the wrong step for *this church* at *this time* in our history. We would leave the future to the future and deal with the present in the present.

- *What do you suggest be done?*

1. Widen dialogue of this issue at every level of the church's life. We call upon clergy and laity in every Conference and Association to create and participate in dialogues in which all sides of the issue may be aired, discussed and debated.
2. Urge Conferences to deal with this issue at their 1984 annual meetings and report their actions to the 1985 Synod.

3. Urge the option of a "yes" vote on this "new alternative" to delegates to the Fifteenth General Synod in 1985.

- *What can I do?*

Write to us . . . to indicate your willingness to create and participate in dialogues within your association and conference.

Resolution on Ecumenical Partnership

WHEREAS, the gospel of Jesus Christ unites Christ's followers in a single community of faith and compels us to make our unity visible so "that the world may believe . . . " (John 17:21, cf. Eph. 4:4–6, 1 Cor. 12:12–26);

WHEREAS, the Christian Church (Disciples of Christ) and the United Church of Christ in our local churches, Regions/Conferences, and in national and international settings are witnessing significant signs of the movement of the Holy Spirit toward unity;

WHEREAS, the United Church of Christ and the Christian Church (Disciples of Christ) have been partners in mission, in worship, and in theological conversation, and have affirmed a Common Vision Statement;

THEREFORE, BE IT RESOLVED, the 17th General Synod of the United Church of Christ, meeting in Ft. Worth, Texas (June 29–July 4, 1989), and the General Assembly of the Christian Church (Disciples of Christ) meeting in Indianapolis, Indiana (July 28–August 2, 1989) make the following mutual declarations:

A. The 17th General Synod of the United Church of Christ (1989) acknowledges and celebrates before God that the Christian Church (Disciples of Christ) is a "true church," an authentic, faithful part of the one, universal body of Christ.

B. The 17th General Synod of the United Church of Christ (1989) declares and celebrates that a relationship of full communion now exists between both our churches, by which we mean that:

   1. Both churches are one in faith, and make common confession that Jesus is the Christ, the Son/Child of the living God (Matthew 16:16, John 11:27);

2. Members of each partner church are members of the one universal church of Jesus Christ and thus are linked to one another as the members of one body;
3. Members share in celebrating The Lord's Supper/Holy Communion in local churches, Associations/Areas, Regions/Conferences, and in national and international settings;
4. Ordained ministers of each partner church are truly ministers of word and sacrament, and
5. Both churches search for mutual ways of manifesting the common mission of witness and service.

C. The 17th General Synod of the United Church of Christ (1989) confesses participation in the sin of church division and commits itself to work, with God's help and together with its partner church, to effect greater unity in the whole church of Jesus Christ.

BE IT FURTHER RESOLVED, the 17th General Synod of the United Church of Christ (1989) encourages study of biblical, theological, and practical implications of full communion and authorizes the Ecumenical Partnership Committee to give guidance to this process.

BE IT ALSO RESOLVED, the 17th General Synod of the United Church of Christ (1989) receives the following paragraphs as commentary on the meaning of full communion.

Commentary

We envision full communion as a dynamic and growing relationship that is more than just accepting one another as we now are. It is a mutual commitment to grow together toward a vision of the church that enriches our theological traditions, enhances service and mission, and deepens worship. We will find diverse expressions of what it means to live in full communion in Christ as we experience life together.

There follows a commentary on the five aspects of the meaning of full communion. It must be understood within the context of our wider ecumenical commitments, especially the World Council of Churches (including its text, *Baptism, Eucharist and Ministry*) and the Consultation on Church Union. The Christian Church (Disciples of Christ) and the United Church of Christ, along with seven other churches in the U.S.A. that are in the Consultation on Church Union, are laboring to achieve covenant communion in faith, sacraments, ministry, and mission.

> "After more than two decades of theological work by officially designated persons responsible to the most authoritative bodies in the several churches, it is now evident that an essential core of theological agreement exists and continues to grow among these churches in matters of faith, worship, sacrament, membership, ministry, and mission."*

1. Common Confession of Christ

Early Christians declared Jesus to be the Christ (Peter in Matthew 16:16 and Martha in John 11:27). Although the church has developed more extensive statements of faith, the Christian community finds its fundamental identity in this confession. In this resolution we begin by proclaiming our common devotion to the God who was in Christ reconciling the world to God's self (2 Cor. 5:19), the One in whom "we live and move and have our being" (Acts 17:28). By it we also declare our rejection of the distortions both of the gospel and of the cultural idols that constantly tempt us.

2. Mutual Recognition of Members

Baptism and membership in the church are inseparably linked. To be baptized into Christ is to become a member of the body of Christ, the church. For two churches mutually to recognize each other's members implies the recognition that the baptism administered by the partner church is a valid sacramental act. Baptism involves the gift of God's grace and the response of faith. Through baptism, all Christians are united by the Holy Spirit in the one universal church. Mutual recognition does not commit either church to give up its normative practices (for Disciples, the dedication of infants and baptism by immersion of those who make a personal confession of faith; for the United Church of Christ, the sprinkling of the children of believing parents, normally followed, at an appropriate age, by confirmation) or the baptism by the sprinkling or immersion of adults. Mutual recognition of members allows for transfer of membership between Disciples and United Church of Christ local churches by letter.

This declaration is a testimony to the growing theological agreement on baptism among the churches, achieved through the ecumenical movement. It is an affirmation that differences of practice need no longer divide the churches. Partnership is therefore a process for moving beyond divisive disagreements and renewing our understanding of baptism, the sacrament of unity.

---

*Churches in Covenant Communion, approved by the 17th Plenary of the Consultation on Church Union (December 1988) and sent to member churches for formal action.

3. Common Celebration of the Lord's Supper/Holy Communion

The most powerful sign of Christian unity is the common sharing at the Lord's Supper/Holy Communion. Through the life, death, and resurrection of Jesus Christ, God has reconciled us to God's self, and offered us a new relationship of love and unity with one another. Celebrating the sacrament together, we are responding as one family with thanksgiving to what Christ has done for us, praying as one people that the Holy Spirit will lead us into deeper truth and unity, and remembering as one pilgrim people the promises of hope and salvation.

While it is already possible for these two churches to celebrate the Lord's Supper/Holy Communion together, this declaration of full communion encourages such common celebration more regularly and intentionally. Congregations that are geographically near each other are urged to find ways to share in the sacred meal together at least once or twice a year, and to consider more frequent eucharistic services. Conferences and regions, associations and areas are encouraged to plan opportunities to join around the Table regularly and so to bear witness to the conviction that the Lord's Supper/Holy Communion is the central event in the church's life. From it all things flow — engaging in mission, caring for the poor, struggling for justice and peace, making real an inclusive life in Christ, yearning for unity.

The United Church of Christ and the Disciples traditionally have had different eucharistic practices in two respects. Disciples congregations make the Lord's Supper the central point of each Sunday's worship, while most United Church of Christ local churches observe the sacrament monthly or quarterly. Nearly all United Church of Christ local churches have ordained or licensed ministers preside at the Table, whereas elders or ordained ministers preside among Disciples. Neither of these differences, however, need divide our two churches at the Table. The theological issues they raise are being explored in our churches and in the wider ecumenical dialogue in the Consultation on Church Union and in the World Council of Churches.

4. Mutual Recognition and Reconciliation of Ordained Ministries

Mutual recognition of ordained ministries (ministers of word and sacrament of the United Church of Christ; ordained elders and ministers of word and sacrament of the Disciples) is intended to acknowledge in the ministries of the partner church the manifest blessing of God and the fruit of the Spirit, and therefore to affirm them as true ministries of the one, holy

Church of Jesus Christ. Reconciliation of ordained ministries is intended to refer to future actions by the churches, both separately and together, whereby their ordained ministries become one ministry of Jesus Christ.

Reconciliation is not intended to mean either that the standard of ministerial training and certification or differences in ministerial practice and placement process must become the same for both churches. Reconciliation means that an ordained minister of one partner church may function, whenever invited, and as established procedures permit, as a minister to the other. Such action of recognition and reconciliation of these ordained ministries is in harmony with the wider ecumenical understandings.

Ordained ministry in these two partner churches is sufficiently similar in form and substance to pose no serious theological obstacle to the mutual recognition and reconciliation of these ordained ministries in subsequent liturgical celebrations.

5. Common Commitment to Mission

Unity and mission are inseparable. If we imagine ourselves to be sacramentally one and do not engage together in mission, we deceive ourselves. Christ calls us to unite in one mission in and to a suffering and divided world. The church is called to visible oneness as a sign, instrument and foretaste of God's saving reconciliation of all things in Christ. In declaring full communion, these two churches acknowledge that they are partners together in God's mission to and for the whole world.

The mission of the church takes many forms. The church engages in mission through worship, through proclamation of the gospel, and through action. In worship, the church recalls and celebrates the mighty acts of God in creation, redemption, and providence. Thus graciously renewed in faith, hope, and love, its people are sent out in the power of the Holy Spirit to be ambassadors, witnesses, and servants of Christ in the world. In proclamation, the church tells the story by which its own life is defined. As it confesses unambiguously the Christ in whom it lives, the church invites all who will to enter its fellowship of life in Christ. In its action, the church embodies God's justice, peace, and love. As the church reaches out to others, both individually and systemically, it manifests God's reconciling purpose and saving reign in all the earth.

In partnership, the Christian Church (Disciples of Christ) and the United Church of Christ fully claim the mission and make deliberate commitment to engage in mission together, wherever and whenever possible.

106. Baptism, Eucharist and Ministry:

"UCC Response to . . . "

(1985)

The Faith and Order Commission of the World Council of Churches (WCC) voted in 1982 to send Baptism, Eucharist and Ministry *to the churches for study, response, and "reception." The Council for Ecumenism of the United Church of Christ encouraged a general response to the document throughout the UCC. It also asked two "closely related" UCC seminaries, six conferences, and four national instrumentalities or commissions to respond. It provided a "Study Guide to* Baptism, Eucharist and Ministry.*" Local congregations and associations were included in the six targeted conferences.*

"The United Church of Christ Response to Baptism, Eucharist and Ministry*" (1985) is based on information received from this sample. The UCC understood that its initial response was only "an early stage in a longer process of study and 'reception'." Therefore, the UCC response is "neither exhaustive in scope nor conclusive in intent." The General Synod (1985) passed the "Response" to celebrate and share "in an ecumenical project that seeks to express in our time what the churches are able to say together concerning baptism, Eucharist and ministry."*

Source: An excerpt from "A United Church of Christ Response to *Baptism, Eucharist and Ministry,*" *GS Minutes 1985,* Appendix 15, 159–64.

UCC Response to Baptism, Eucharist and Ministry

General Observations

Baptism, Eucharist and Ministry, when all its virtues and faults are catalogued, endures as a "provocative, useful, helpful and hopeful" document that leaves us "amazed at the extent to which some kind of common ground has been staked out" within its pages. We find our experience as a "united and a uniting church" affirmed by the kindred struggle for wholeness and inclusiveness that we recognize in the document.

The convergence represented here, welcome and impressive as it is, loses some of its force because the language in which it is expressed is sometimes ambiguous. Nevertheless, we rejoice at the intention of the text to be as comprehensive as possible of diverse Christian points of view. We are mindful, as our own study of the text has demonstrated, that identical terms "are not always understood in the same way by all of us within the United Church of Christ." The burden of clarity placed upon language in an ecumenical text is understandably demanding. The problem of ambiguity could be eased if such terms were briefly defined where they first occur. For example, in the Chapter on Baptism (par. 10), we appreciate the reference to Jesus Christ as our "Liberator," but regret that both here and elsewhere the passing allusions to the language of liberation theology lack substance.

Although the published text is more inclusive with respect to gender than were the earlier drafts, it falls short of what many regard as possible and necessary. This observation is offered not for aesthetic reasons, but because inclusive language with respect to gender is inseparably linked with our ethical commitment to justice for women.

The technical terminology in the text is perceived by some in the United Church of Christ to exclude those who are not theological specialists from full participation in an endeavor that affects the whole people of God. Some feel excluded by the "high church tilt" of the document and by the "ahistorical" vocabulary that is "dogmatic" but ignores our experience in the contemporary world. We recognize in the document a vocabulary more reflective of the patristic and pre-Reformation church than of the church of all the centuries. Without diminishing this heritage, we long for a vocabulary that celebrates the full catholic heritage that we cherish, including the diversity of the New Testament church and the work of the Holy Spirit found in the obedience of reformers to the Word of God in every age.

The relationship between church unity and the unity of humankind, between unity and mission, is an area that concerns us. The document could state that relationship more convincingly. The weight of attention given to issues important to the unity of the church creates the impression that the ministry of the church to broken humanity is not of equal urgency. It is our hope "that historic divisions may indeed no longer impair the church's mission, in the faith that the world's brokenness will be healed through Christ's presence, and that humanity will, through God's grace, be one."

Finally, we rejoice that although the document speaks to us diversely, it speaks powerfully. Some of us would rush to revise every page. Others are able to say immediately, "we identify our faith position so closely with *Baptism, Eucharist and Ministry* that we have not found any major area of disagreement." Within the United Church of Christ, as well as in our ecumenical relationships, *Baptism, Eucharist and Ministry* holds great promise as a signpost on our pilgrim way toward a deeper understanding and a more faithful embodiment of the one Church of Jesus Christ that is sent to the one humanity that is made in the image and likeness of God.

Baptism

Our affirmation of this chapter of the document may be summarized by the observation that "most groups reported that they could live with the whole thing." Questions raised for the sake of clarification center on the following five themes.

We welcome the emphasis on "a new ethical orientation" (par. 4) that is rightly associated with baptism. However, the impact of this emphasis is weakened, especially in the section on "Celebration" (V) where, to us, "a commissioning for ministry seems muted if not lacking." We also question the terms "believers" and "infant" as they are used throughout the text to qualify baptism. The effect of this usage is to suggest that infants and children cannot "believe" in any sense, and that they must await maturity for their experience of a new ethical orientation. The use of the term "installment" (par. 19), creates a similar quantitative and chronological misunderstanding. Although baptism is offered at diverse ages in our church, "we do not rule out the response of faith in infants which may not be articulated but nevertheless is very real."

The document raises two issues for us in relation to the doctrine of the Trinity. The language in the text is clear that baptism celebrates our incorporation into Christ and into his body, the Church. However, we are baptized in the name of the triune God. Could not the text make it more clear that baptism brings us into relationship with "the whole triune community of God"? Further, many in our church who give full assent to the doctrine of the Trinity look to the day when the language used to express what that doctrine intends will be gender sensitive and inclusive.

A question of pastoral care is raised by the treatment of "re-baptism" (par. 13) in the text. Some in the United Church of Christ are concerned that we minister responsibly to those who are convinced that their earlier experience of baptism was flawed in some way. The pastoral care issue would be helped by a clearer statement of objections to re-baptism, and by the offering of appropriate pastoral alternatives that would correspond to expressed personal need.

What is meant by "indiscriminate baptism" (par. 15), and does the use of this phrase adequately take into account that the difficulties to which it points may pertain to baptism at any age? The choice of words is unfortunate. A representative response notes that "God is rather 'indiscriminate' in sending blessings on the evil as well as the good." Our question does not deny that baptism sometimes may be celebrated in a less than fully responsible way in the United Church of Christ. On the contrary, we recognize the constant need for strengthening our ministry of nurture, and suggest that the document express more cogently "the need for life-long education."

While affirming that the sign of baptism is the sacrament of incorporation into Christ and the church (par. 6), some in the United Church of Christ question the making of the "sign" of this incorporation the exclusive criterion for acknowledging membership in Christ's body. Although they can offer no easy solution to the paradox, they affirm that baptism is the biblical sacrament of entrance into the church, while they also affirm that some who publicly confess Christ, but who do not celebrate either of the dominical sacraments, are not only our kindred in the human family, but are our sisters and brothers in Christ.

Eucharist

The General Synod is encouraged by the evidence of convergence in the text on matters that in former times were the occasion for polemical argumentation and division among the churches. We welcome especially the comprehensive inclusion of diverse biblical images that inform our common understanding and practice of Holy Communion. Although we affirm the term "eucharist," we are concerned that the predominant use of this term may emphasize the human response of faith above the initiative of God.

We recognize in the document's breadth of interpretation concerning "the real, living and active presence" (par. 13) of Christ in the sacrament the diversity that we already experience within the United Church of Christ. We are concerned that this presence neither be identified exclusively with the elements of bread and wine nor associated rigidly with any one particular moment in the celebration, but that Christ's presence be understood in relation to the entire eucharistic action.

The treatment of "sacrifice" shows great sensitivity to our belief that Christ's suffering and death on the cross "are not repeated nor prolonged" (par. 8) in the eucharistic celebration. This claim could be strengthened by giving further attention to the biblical image of the eucharist as a meal of the Reign of God. Although this is discussed (sec. E), the weight of the overall treatment of the sacrament emphasizes the propitiatory nature of Christ's death as it is memorialized in the meal. The document would embrace a more biblically balanced understanding of salvation and of the sacrament if the passing reference to Holy Communion as a "foretaste" (par. 6) of Christ's return and of the final Reign of God were made more explicit. The effect of the current text, as one of our theologians comments, makes the eucharist "merely a 'sign of the Kingdom' rather than an actual entrance into the trinitarian history of God's righteousness in the world."

We raise the issue of the sacrament as a meal of the Reign of God out of our concern that the relationship between the eucharist and ethics be made more compellingly clear. We applaud the several references to this relationship (sections D and E), and are challenged by the vision of the eucharist as a call "to be in solidarity with the outcast" (par. 24). Our pursuit of this understanding, as one voice in our midst has noted, holds great promise "for bringing our operational emphases on ethical considerations into the heart of our liturgical practice where they belong."

The questions of whether baptized children may share fully in Holy Communion is currently being explored in our Church (par. 19). Here again, our practice is diverse. There is an increasing willingness to welcome baptized children to the meal if they show interest and are prepared to participate with understanding appropriate to their age. Whether other children, for whom baptism will come at a later age, may also share in the meal, is often raised. The question reflects pastoral considerations which arise when diversity of baptismal practice is common within one and the same congregation. We invite ecumenical dialogue on how this matter is understood and resolved in other Churches.

We note with appreciation the list of various acts that are appropriately included in a full eucharist celebration (par. 27). This list has already influenced liturgical reform currently in process in our Church. We observe that the offering of the gifts of the people is not mentioned, and express our concern that this important participatory act be included in the list.

There is great diversity in the United Church of Christ with respect to the frequency of celebrating Holy Communion. We read with care the admonition that it "is appropriate that it take place at least every Sunday" (par. 31). Our own guidelines for worship concur in making this recommendation. Our published liturgies for Sunday are Services of Word and Sacrament, and are offered with the hope "that our Church will grow into this practice."

However, a weekly celebration of Holy Communion is not our predominant custom. Our study of *Baptism, Eucharist and Ministry* discloses that the frequency is increasing. Resistance to a weekly celebration of the sacrament is based upon a lack of felt need, a fear that familiarity will diminish the meaning of the sacrament, and a concern that the preaching of the Word may be subordinated to the sacramental action. Regretfully, we note that the document is weak in the case that it makes for the importance of the preaching of the Word in the conjoining of Word and Sacrament.

We are challenged by the document to rethink the question of the frequency of the eucharistic celebration. One of our biblical scholars cautions us that "when the decision is made not to celebrate weekly, it must be made with the awareness of what the losses involved in such a decision are."

We receive with appreciation the suggestion that the consecrated bread and wine that remain at the conclusion of Holy Communion be treated with respect. Our study of the document indicates an expressed willingness among us to "consider the consciences of other brothers and sisters" by making provision for all the elements to be consumed. The very act of doing this can be yet another reminder that the eucharistic meal binds us in sacramental solidarity with all who celebrate Holy Communion, even though we do not understand every aspect of it in the same way.

Ministry

The General Synod commends all who labored to endow the Chapter on Ministry with forthrightness, clarity and sensitivity to the distinctions and enduring convictions held in trust by the diverse Churches. It is especially significant to us that the discussion of ordained ministry is placed within the larger ecclesial context of "The Calling of the Whole People of God" (section I), that all ministry is perceived as service through which we "proclaim and prefigure" (par. 4) the Reign of God in a broken world, and that no one particular pattern of ordained ministry is vested with exclusive biblical authorization (par. 19).

Our study, preliminary in nature as it is, indicates that the Chapter on Ministry raises as many critical issues for us as it appears to resolve. Although the text begins with "The Calling of the Whole People of God" (section I), the transition to the comparatively lengthy discussion of ordained ministries is abrupt, grounded more on the tradition of the Church of the second and third centuries than on the New Testament, and appropriates the New Testament witness in a manner that does not communicate a coherent hermeneutical treatment of scripture.

It is particularly disappointing that while other current ecumenical conversations emphasize clearly that all ministry is founded on Christ's one ministry, the document speaks of "a difference between the apostles and the ordained ministers whose ministries are founded on *theirs* (par. 10, emphasis added). This reference and the reference to the "unique and unrepeatable" role of the Twelve Apostles "as witnesses to the resurrection of Christ" (par. 10), demonstrate a double difficulty for us. While we affirm that the role of being a witness to Christ's resurrection is unique and unrepeatable, we also note that founding ordained ministry on the ministry of the Twelve obscures the grounding of all ministry on the ministry of Christ. It also "predisposes the document to exclude the ministry of women," on the basis of gender, "while ignoring the fact that the first resurrection witness were women," at least in the report of Matthew 28:1–10 and John 20:11–18.

This form of reasoning from the Twelve Apostles to the first bishops requires us to leap from chronology to ontology of office and person, and suggests distinctions in dignity and inequality of gender in ministry which we find untenable. Moreover, from a majority of our respondents, including academic theologians, laity and pastors, we have heard emphatically that "the largest obstacle to accepting and affirming the ministry section is its discussion of the ordination of women."

In a strongly worded statement, the representative voice of one of our biblical scholars protests:

> Paragraph 50 of the ministry section is a slap in the face to women who are being denied ordination. This paragraph calls for a re-evaluation of ordination practices which discriminate on the basis of handicap or race, but in paragraph 18, which raises the issue of the ordination of women, there is no similar statement calling for a re-evaluation on the grounds of sexual discrimination.

To this, one of our Conference study committees adds the question, "Is it not just as reprehensible to bar a woman from full ministry as it is to bar men because they are black?"

Statements intended to promote understanding concerning the ordination of women are read in quite another light. We read in paragraph 18, "The Church must discover the ministry which can be provided by women as well as that which can be provided by men." One of our theologians discerns "insult" in this statement because it does not acknowledge that "women have exercised Christian ministry since New Testament times."

We perceive in this issue a subject that needs considerable additional attention. Closer relationships with Churches which do not ordain women will undoubtedly be compromised until this matter is resolved. Our study indicates a willingness to pursue such relationships "with the hope that our policy on this issue will be a witness to other traditions that the ordination of women is a valid expression of the faith."

In relation to the three-fold pattern of bishops, presbyters and deacons, we affirm this venerable configuration of ordained ministry as one of the historic patterns that has flourished, with some diversity, across the centuries. We acknowledge that it endures as the predominant pattern in our day. We also affirm other patterns of ministry, including the ones evident in our own tradition and practice.

There is an openness in our Church to explore the particular value of the three-fold pattern of bishop, presbyter and deacon in the quest for unity among the Churches. Some among us affirm this pattern while raising the caution that throughout the document the "priestly" function of the ordained ministry "so dominates that the prophetic and servant leader functions are lost from view." Some would resist the three-fold pattern out of concern for its hierarchical possibilities, especially in relation to the title and office of bishop. We cannot concur with any understanding of the three-fold pattern that makes the office of the bishop the only "full" ordained ministry of the Church or that places the bishop between Christ and the faithful as an intermediary to whom obedience is due. At the same time, we rejoice that our Calvin Synod has retained the title and office of bishop, in accordance with its own norms, and we welcome a discussion of how the three-fold pattern can be expressed in a manner that fully respects the participation of the whole people of God in the governance and ministry of the Church. Most would agree that "we are a long way" from moving to this pattern in the United Church of Christ. At the same time, we allow that this pattern, fully reformed in accordance with our understanding of the gospel, may in fact express the functions already identified by other terms in our polity. One theologian challenges us: "The United Church of Christ will surely need to come to grips with the fact that in the ecumenical church there will be bishops. It should be engaging its energy not to prevent this, but rather radically to criticize and transform the character of the bishop's office."

We are not unaware, however, that the real issue behind the three-fold pattern of ministry is not "labels," but "the relationship of the bishop to both the other ordained ministers and the laity of the Church." As we witness the three-fold pattern across the centuries, it confronts us less with a matter of "titles" than with "an approach to polity in which authority flows in a different direction than it is deemed to flow in the United Church of Christ." Therefore, only a transformed version of it, consistent with the best insights of our participatory polity, would be workable and welcome among us.

Where the bishop is seen as a servant of Christ and of the Church, as one responsible for "theological spiritual leadership," rather than primarily as an institutional administrator, there is openness to that office. One of our Conferences reports, through its Theological Commission, "We welcome the recovery of the office of bishop," and are convinced that although the three-fold pattern of ministry "would require some adjustments to our Constitution, it demands nothing impossible."

Openness to this pattern, and especially to the office of bishop, would likely be enhanced if greater care were given in the document to the use of certain images and terms. We read in the Chapter on Baptism that Christ is our "Liberator" (par. 10), and in the Chapter on Eucharist, God's servant (par. 21), "presides at" (par. 29) the Holy Meal. However, in the Chapter on Ministry, where ordained ministry is closely identified with Christ's ministry, we read that "the Church needs persons (i.e., ordained ministers) who are publicly and continually responsible for pointing to its *dependence* on Christ" (par. 8, emphasis added), and who "call the community to *submit*to the authority of Jesus Christ" (par. 11, emphasis added)." The bishop is described as one called to "preside *over* the celebration of the eucharist" (par. 20, emphasis added). The move from Christ the servant who is our Liberator to notions of dependency and submission mediated by the clergy, who do not preside at, but over, the sacraments, is hardly a matter of neutral semantics. It is a move, likely not intended, that raises anew the suspicion that hierarchy is nearby when the three-fold pattern of ministry is present. This is unnecessary and unfortunate. A reformed three-fold pattern of ministry could with integrity be as constitutionally accountable as any other form of ministry practiced in the United Church of Christ or elsewhere.

We raise a concern about the office of deacon and the ministry of the laity. It appears to us that the functions of deacons and the laity are so similar as to render the distinction meaningless. The identity of deacons is not clear, and the treatment of the ministry of the laity is alarmingly weak. We urge further development of both subjects, and register our dismay that the disproportionate attention given to ordained ministry suggests that the calling of the whole people of God to service is not truly a calling to "ministry."

Finally, although we affirm the value of the three-fold pattern of ministry, we cannot regard it as belonging to the esse of the Church. Saying this does not diminish our regard for it. Rather, it makes us mindful, as the document itself states, that there is a place in the Church for the prophetic voice (par. 33), and that hearing that voice often requires that we be open to "unusual ways" and "the special ministries" (par. 33) that God, from time to time, may call forth from the pilgrim Church as it journeys in faith toward the city not made by human hands, eternal in the heavens, whose builder and maker is God.

Conclusion

In answer to the four specific questions placed before us by the Faith and Order Commission, the United Church of Christ, in the context of the Report above, offers this summary response.

I. The extent to which the United Church of Christ can recognize in this text the faith of the Church through the ages.

We affirm, with respect to the issues to which it speaks, that we recognize in *Baptism, Eucharist and Ministry* an expression of the faith of the Church through the ages. We applaud the diversity blessed by the text and, with the qualifications cited in our Report, find the United Church of Christ affirmed as one manifestation of Christ's universal Church.

II. The consequences your church can draw from this text for its relations and dialogues with other churches, particularly with those churches which also recognize the text as an expression of the apostolic faith.

We affirm that *Baptism, Eucharist and Ministry* provides our Church with an invaluable instrument for pursuing our commitment to be "a united and a uniting Church." The convergence represented in the text, though by no means complete, affords us a clarity of focus that challenges us to share more generously the ecclesial gifts that we have come to cherish, and to cherish more graciously the ecclesial gifts offered to us by other Churches.

III. The guidance your church can take from the text for its worship, educational, ethical, and spiritual witness.

We affirm that *Baptism, Eucharist and Ministry* addresses issues with which we are dealing constantly in our Church as we seek to witness to the gospel in the face of the demands of a changing world. The convergence represented in the text, as our Report shows, offers us guidance as we study and reform our celebration of the sacraments and all other worship. It places before us the challenge to look again at our commitment to Christian education and nurture for persons of all ages, and to reflect upon the effectiveness of our education for ecumenism in all parts of our Church, including our seminaries. It calls us to hold in closer relationship our ministry of nurture and our ministry of prophetic servanthood in the cause of peace with justice throughout the world. It raises with new poignancy the essential place of spiritual formation of an order that will sufficiently equip us for faithfulness in the struggle with all unfaith that assaults the Reign of God in human history.

IV. The suggestions your church can make for the ongoing work of Faith and Order as it relates the material of this text on *Baptism, Eucharist and Ministry* to its long-range research project "Towards the Common Expression of the Apostolic Faith Today."

We affirm that the convergence represented *in Baptism, Eucharist and Ministry* requires further development if it is to make an enduring contribution to this research project. We cite in our Report a number of issues that concern us. We repeat here, briefly and for identification only, several issues that carry special urgency for us.

In general, we urge:

- greater care, throughout the document, for the use of language that is truly inclusive of all the people of God.
- a more explicit recognition of the pain and promise that accompany the tensions inherent in the struggle of united and uniting churches to incorporate diversity within their common life.
- a stronger affirmation of the particular heritage of each church and of the capacity of each church, without compromising the integrity of its own historical witness, to be enriched by opening its life to the heritage of other churches.

In the Chapter on Baptism, we urge:

- a clearer understanding of and a stronger commissioning for the ministry of all Christians.

In the Chapter on Eucharist, we urge:

- a clearer statement of Holy Communion as a meal of the Reign of God, by which we are nourished for ethical obedience as servants of Jesus Christ who is the source of peace with justice.
- a more substantive treatment of the parity of the preaching of the Word with Holy Communion in the conjoining of the two in one full service.
- an openness to diverse terms for the meal in order to show that the full meaning of the sacrament is not exhausted by the term "eucharist."

In the Chapter on Ministry, we urge:

- a much stronger explication of the founding of all ministry on the ministry of Christ, including the diverse ministries of the laity, and a more positive statement of the complementarity of distinctive ministries within the one Body of Christ.
- a more sensitive treatment of the serious theological and justice issues involved in the discussion of the ordination of women.
- a clearer affirmation, in the Chapter on Ministry, of the diversity of patterns of ministry blessed by the Holy Spirit, and a greater care in the use of language that might imply that hierarchy and the three-fold pattern of bishop, presbyter and deacon are inextricably related.
- a more balanced presentation of the functions of all ministry, especially the functions of the ordained ministry, with respect to the prophetic and servant leader roles in relation to the priestly role, as all three roles are exemplified in the prophetic, priestly and servant leader ministry of Jesus Christ.

107. Consultation on Church Union (COCU): *"UCC Response to the* COCU Consensus*"*

(1989)

From the 1960s through the 1980s the United Church of Christ sent representatives to the Consultation on Church Union (COCU). By 1988 the COCU Consensus: In Quest of a Church of Christ Uniting *(1984) had been amended to become the* Churches in Covenant Communion: the Church of Christ Uniting. *Its Part I, "The Covenanting Proposal," affirms that "covenanting" did not require a change in "present church structures or of denominational names." It is "not only a step on the way to union" but "an authentic form of union." Second, the UCC also recognizes that action on the* Consensus *document requires more than a commitment to "study and reception" similar to the "UCC Response to* Baptism, Eucharist and Ministry*" (1985) (see vol. 7:106). Embracing the* Consensus *document calls for a "number of deliberate actions by the participating churches." When a church claims the* Consensus *document it indicates its readiness "to participate in a new relationship of commitment with the participating churches which is not yet full organic union, but which is far more than a consultative relationship." Third, the UCC is ready to recognize that the* COCU Consensus *document is an expression of the "Apostolic faith, order, worship and witness of the church," and that it can anticipate the "Church Uniting which the participating bodies by the power of the Holy Spirit wish to become, and that it was a sufficient theological basis for the covenanting acts and the uniting process proposed" by the consultation. By the late 1980s a consensus was "emerging" among a group of churches on a "pilgrimage of faith and reconciliation."*

Source: An excerpt from "United Church of Christ Response to the *COCU Consensus: In Quest of a Church of Christ Uniting," GS Minutes 1989,* Appendix F, 149–53.

UCC Response to the *COCU Consensus*

Our Response

The General Synod of the United Church of Christ responds to *The COCU Consensus: In Quest of a Church of Christ Uniting* aware of the fundamental commitment of the United Church of Christ to Christ's prayer "that they may all be one." We recall that the Basis of Union which guided our parent denominations during the formation of the United Church of Christ affirmed devotion to "one God, the Father of our Lord Jesus Christ, and our membership in the holy catholic Church, which is greater than any single Church and than all the Churches together." Our founders stated "that denominations exist not for themselves but as parts of that Church, within which each denomination is to live and labor and, if need be, die" (Preamble to the UCC Basis of Union).

The United Church of Christ came together in 1957 assuming a theological consensus, embracing different church traditions, practicing diversity in the sacraments, and recognizing variety in ordained ministries. In our thirty-year history there have been many expressions of our commitment to unity through outreach and mission.

The United Church of Christ has been part of the Consultation on Church Union from the beginning. We admit that during some of those years the UCC grassroots understanding of, and zeal for COCU has been minimal. More recently, however, the emerging ecumenical vision of "living our way toward unity" through covenanting, which is now informing COCU's work, is changing this situation. As a United Church, which was officially constituted before it had developed its Statement of Faith, we are a people who know how to live on theological pilgrimage. We find images of journey and process in keeping with our experience as a church.

At the same time, as we approach the Consensus document we are distressed when other churches (and some within our own church) perceive the document affirmations as a way of imposing a uniformity that tolerates no disagreement in Christ's church. As Roger Hazelton, UCC theologian, has helped us to understand, "consensus theology" is constructive, not dogmatic, or even apologetic. It is theology which seeks to give "new visibility, new embodiment to the Church that lives in the midst of the churches." Instead of "searching for some least common denominator, consensus theology keeps in view the unity of faith which can reform and renew the churches" (Roger Hazelton, "Consensus Theology:

Reflections on the COCU Experience," *Andover Newton Quarterly,* XII:1, p. 10).

During the past few years the UCC Council for Ecumenism has invited conferences, instrumentalities and local churches to study the Consensus document and to share their judgment as to whether the United Church of Christ can "claim" the document and recognize in it "an expression" of the Apostolic tradition, an anticipation of the Church Uniting it wishes to become part of, and a "sufficient theological basis for the covenanting acts and the uniting process proposed at this time by the Consultation." Such responses, within the United Church of Christ, are necessarily uneven. Nevertheless, they reflect our ecclesial journey.

Following the outline of the document we have summarized the reactions of these groups in hopes that these insights will illuminate our common pilgrimage.

I. Why Unity?

There is a general appreciation within the UCC for the image of church as a "family created by God in Christ out of all the tribes and nations and peoples." Understanding the church as a sign to the world helps to counteract thinking about "ecumenism as merely a cooperative enterprise which we engage in for purely pragmatic ends." Study groups agree that the biblical exegesis done in the first chapter provides a strong foundation.

UCC people are especially enthusiastic over the assertion that the task of unity today requires the resolution of "Contemporary Church-Dividing Issues," as well as old division. In this matter, it is noted that the Consensus document sets an agenda which moves beyond the perspective of *Baptism, Eucharist and Ministry.* Groups report that the church must be increasingly sensitive to issues of racism, sexism and prejudice against persons with disabilities. One group suggests that the "Alerts" appendices ought to be shared in connection with the Consensus document. Another group proposes an additional "church-dividing issue": class. "Divisions caused by economic and cultural differences are very real, and challenge our predominantly middle-class churches. . . . Inclusiveness ought to be for all, not just against sexism and racism." There are still other contemporary "church-dividing issues": fundamentalism, biblical inerrancy, and methods of church growth. Although historic theological divisions are not the predominant concern of UCC people, the COCU covenanting process has the potential to help us heal not only these, but contemporary divisions within, as well as between our churches.

II. Unity: A Gift to Be Made Visible

The UCC agrees that ecumenical growth preserves heritage and tradition and embraces new commitments through repentance and conversion. It is important that change not be imposed from the outside. It is also important to remain open to new manifestations of Christ's church.

Study groups celebrate the seven characteristics "fundamental to the quest for the visible unity of a Church Uniting which is truly catholic, truly evangelical and truly reformed" (II.6). They suggest that "Denominational barriers have already begun to break down in the eyes of the laity," and therefore, church leaders need to "face up to the similarities in denominations." However, they raise concern about "non-Christian allies in mission" (II.6.b), asking "how do we maintain our necessary evangelical witness in the midst of interfaith dialogue and action?" Finally, they affirm the vision of openness sustained in the Uniting Church by vigilant conscience, and authority balanced by accountability" (II.6.g).

III. Toward a Church Catholic, Evangelical, and Reformed

There is general affirmation of this chapter. Within the UCC we work hard to embrace evangelical and reformed traditions. The four marks of a church truly reformed — pilgrimage, judgment, servant and renewal are especially well stated (III.13.a–d). We applaud the efforts of the Consensus document to overcome the "triumphalism" of contemporary American church life.

Study groups recognize that those of us rooted in the 16th century Protestant Reformation can benefit from attempts to make the Church Uniting more catholic. However, they raise two concerns with this chapter: first, the emphasis on treasuring "essential institutions," and "being unashamed to venerate these visible and human institutions," as the means by which the church "lives in Christ" (III.6), comes, as one group put it, "dangerously close to the worship of graven images."

Secondly, many UCC groups are deeply troubled by the section on corporate discipline (III.7.d). They find the tone of this material goes too far. It sounds threatening. They write, "While we generally affirm the recovery of corporate discipline as a mark of the church truly catholic, we are also reminded that the potential for abuse is a real danger. As the procedures for corporate discipline are specified in the Church Uniting, we trust that the desire for maintaining order and wholeness does not lead to a sacrifice of proper freedom or an inhibition of the unpopular though prophetic witness."

IV. Membership

Few UCC people have any problems with this chapter. In fact the vast majority of our members already assume "mutual recognition of membership" based upon baptism in any Christian communion. Comment is made that many UCC people would "be shocked" to discover that this is not already a "given." "On this point, our members have moved well beyond official ecclesiastical ecumenism."

Within the UCC there are diverse practices surrounding baptism. The openness of the Church Uniting to various bonds or marks of Church membership is in keeping with UCC practice whereby each local congregation manages its own affairs and "admits members in its own way" (UCC Constitution, para. 15). Although baptism is a basic bond of unity, it is often combined with "owning" the particular covenant of that congregation.

One group raises concern about the place of children in relationship to membership. There is need for the idea of "developmental membership," but it is not clear how that combines with some of the marks of membership (IV.9). There may also be a problem with respect to handicapped and disabled persons who cannot "make public statements" or "participate in the life of the world." In this regard, it is helpful to read in the text that "the Church Uniting will receive into membership persons with developmental or accidental disabilities whose only response in faith may be spiritual or mystical, but in the sight of God real and dynamic" (IV.6).

Finally, the challenge to take the nurturing of members more seriously in the Church Uniting is applauded. Yet, it remains unclear, writes one group, what "the recovery and clarification of Christian discipline entails." Again there is a UCC uneasiness with phrases like "discipline" and "safeguarding."

V. Confessing the Faith

Tensions within the United Church of Christ over our own "theological identity" are evident in the UCC response to this chapter. On the one hand there are those who lament that the "tilt" of the Consensus document towards the Apostles' and Nicene Creeds "leaves little room for other witnesses, such as the UCC Statement of Faith." They ask, "how can we make the faith our own if we are tied to ideas and language that are not our own?"

In spite of the section on "Mission as Confession" (V.15–16), many UCC people believe that the Consensus document does not fully explore the fundamental relationship between theology and mission. We appreciate that such statements as "formal assent to a creed cannot substitute for personal commitment" (V.10). We seek to relate confession to faithful living. In the Preamble of the UCC Constitution we affirm "the responsibility of the Church in each generation to make this faith (that of the ancient creeds and the insights of the Protestant Reformers) its own in reality of worship, in honesty of thought and expression, and in purity of heart before God."

On the other hand, other study groups think that by acknowledging the two ancient creeds as the significant and authoritative grounding for our common faith, the Church Uniting can help UCC people claim identification with pre-16th century traditions. They state, "Our people in the pews need to hear that, because then we can understand better the causes of our most ancient and painful divisions. . . . " We must learn to appreciate "the giftedness of Roman Catholic, Orthodox, and other Eastern Rite Christians, as well as the giftedness within our own Reformation Tradition."

Along the same lines, one group feels that the statement "Confession of faith takes place not only, or even primarily, in the setting forth of doctrinal confessions, but also in the forms and acts of public worship" (V.14) goes too far. It is "an unwarranted diminishment of the place of the formal theological enterprise."

Overall, UCC people have a keen appreciation for the way in which the chapter centers confession upon scripture, distinguishes between Tradition with a capital "T" and tradition with a lower case "t," and charges the churches to be responsible guardians of creeds, confessions and covenants. The practice of the United Church of Christ is to speak of these things as "testimonies" rather than "tests" of faith. Furthermore, some groups urge that more sensitivity to the work of the Holy Spirit is needed to temper what they regard as the "legalistic overtones" of creeds, confessions and covenants.

Finally, the UCC struggles daily with "Inclusiveness as Confession." We remain committed to address the "contemporary wrongs which alienate people from themselves, from their neighbors, from the created order of which they are a part, and from God" (V.17). Standing up against "prejudice, hatred, false nationalism, or discrimination based upon supposed social, racial, mental, physical, or sexual superiority" is our calling, even as we disagree with each other regarding the meaning of these obligations.

The majority of UCC people ask if the Church Uniting, in accepting "Inclusiveness as Confession" and affirming the diversity, equality and dignity of *all* persons, will really uphold that commitment. Will it be able to identify itself with persons who are victims of some form of "prejudice, hatred, false nationalism, or discrimination based upon supposed social, racial, mental, physical, or sexual superiority" (V.18), for whom justice has often been thwarted? A sizeable number of UCC people have come to believe that Christians are called, in the words of paragraph 19, to "support *them* in their struggle, . . . to express the love of God for all people and to eliminate the idolatry which is implicit in every kind of human discrimination" (Italics added).

Some UCC people, however, believe that although no one is to be denied a participating life in the Church Uniting, "certain behaviors should not be accepted, affirmed or tolerated." They cannot agree that "Congregations, individuals, or groups of Christians who *exclude* (italics added), exploit, or patronize any of their sisters or brothers, however subtly, offend God and place the profession of their faith in doubt" (V.19). They believe that certain behaviors and lifestyles are "abominable" and "outside the gates" and, therefore, deserving of exclusion (Leviticus 18 and Revelation 22).

VI. Worship

The discussion of worship in this chapter is solid. The UCC incorporates a great deal of diversity in its worship and we are finding that the ecumenical movement and various forms of liturgical renewal already encourage "convergence rather than diversity in the sacramental practices of our churches." Recent change has led us to greater common practice, not less. This is reflected in our recently published *Book of Worship.* In the future, "One might argue that the real question is whether the Church Uniting will encourage enough diversity."

The following sentiment is typical, "Our group is hopeful that our common worshipping life can grow and that each of our respective traditions can nourish one another's. We believe that the chapter lifts up that hope, and yet respects the need for all of us to be comfortable in the style of worship that we choose."

For some UCC people there is a tension between COCU's strong commitment to inclusiveness and the assumption in Chapter VI that the particular words "Father, Son and Holy Spirit" will be used in Baptism (VI.12). It should be noted that the UCC *Book of Worship* retains the traditional language of the baptismal formula but places it in the context of diverse and rich images of the feminine in God and the place of women in the history of salvation. Comment is made that the Consensus document moves the sacraments from "an emphasis on personal relationship to a more ecclesiastical or mystical interpretation" (VI.16–17). Still others remain troubled by the implication that there might be more than the two biblical sacraments in the future Church Uniting (VI.19).

Whereas there is appreciation that all three traditional terms are used to refer to the sacrament of the table (Eucharist, Lord's Supper and Communion), there is concern that a service of worship without the sacrament is "judged inferior." If the sacrament, which "stands at the heart of the Church's worship," is "understood as including the preaching of the Word" (VI.15), "what is the status of worship where eucharist is not celebrated?" What is the integrity of the sacrament in "churches where the celebration of eucharist is not considered the essential core of worship?" "What about those denominations where lay persons preside at eucharist?" As one study group concludes, "It is important to guard against presumption and exclusivity at this point."

VII. Ministry

The chapter on Ministry contains sections which are keenly appreciated within the United Church of Christ and sections which raise deep hesitations about UCC participation in the Church Uniting. We realize that it is only a "sketch," pointing "toward an ordering of ministry which is different from that now found in any of the participating church bodies." We want to believe that "There is room for the participating churches to grow together in unforeseen ways as they work out the implications of the covenant" (A Note on the Function of Chapter VII in the Covenanting Process, p. 39).

The outline of the chapter is sound, beginning with the "Ministry of Jesus Christ and the Ministry of God's People" and affirming that "The ordained and lay ministries of the Church are differing forms of the one ministry of Christ that is shared by the whole People of God" (VII.21). UCC people especially affirm the understanding that all ministries (including lay ministries) should be "at once personal, collegial, and communal." As a church, we affirm "constitutionally and canonically" ordered ministries, but we are reminded that not all valid ministry is so constituted. The Holy Spirit sometimes surprises the church.

UCC study groups also welcome the definition of the ministry of lay persons as foundational to all ministry in the church. We agree that "lay" should not mean "not ordained." "Lay status in the Church is not a residual status, . . . " something "left over" when we finish dealing with clergy. The ministry of lay persons is "the primary form of ministry apart from which no other Christian ministry can be described" (VII.25). Lay persons are called to ministries of "witnessing to the Gospel in worship and in the world, seeking justice and reconciliation in the world, bringing the world before God, providing pastoral care for persons, serving the cause of unity, and participating in governance" (VII.26, a–f).

However, it is the material in the sections on the "Ministry of Ordained Persons" where UCC people have problems. They cannot understand why the Church Uniting should follow the "one ordering" of ordained ministry, the threefold ministry of bishop, presbyter, and deacon, which has "emerged as predominant" (VII.39). As one group put it, "Quite frankly, the threefold pattern of ordained ministry does not excite us. While nothing about it represents an insurmountable problem neither does it represent to us a helpful advance or encouragement."

Others completely reject any notion of threefold ministry, because "The normative character of the three-fold pattern is based on a selective and arbitrary reading of history and scripture and seems designed rather to appease those who already follow this pattern than to be a true and accurate embodiment of the faith we proclaim." Another response argues, in accepting this "The UCC would be surrendering our understanding of the practice of our church, . . . the practice of both 'given' and 'negotiated' authority on the basis of covenant, not by virtue of titles and office." Some point out that the place of specialized ministries, such as Christian education, is unclear in the threefold pattern.

Nevertheless, other study groups made an effort to "appreciate" the fact that churches do need persons who in different ways express and perform diaconal, presbyterial and episcopal functions (VII.42). For example, within the UCC there is interest in recovering the pastoral nature of the office of conference minister, which is "often experienced as largely managerial or administrative." Perhaps, they suggest, "the traditions and experiences of those churches which have retained or recovered the office of bishop largely devoted to a pastoral and teaching role would be of help to us." Other groups admit that even the use of the word "bishop" leads to "serious problems" in the United Church of Christ, except in the Calvin Synod where it is in use. It is noted that much of the language around ordained ministries in the Consensus document is more "ontological" (i.e. "authority . . . rooted in Jesus Christ" [VII.32]) than functional. By contrast, the language used most frequently in the UCC regards ordained ministry as called forth by functional need, at the same time that it is grounded in the call of God through baptism. Within the UCC ordained, commissioned and licensed ministers are created when the church "recognizes that God calls certain of its members to various forms of ministry in and on behalf of the church for which ecclesiastical authorization is required" (UCC Constitution, para. 18).

Finally, UCC study groups do not understand the need for diaconal ministry, in view of the fact that many of its responsibilities are presently carried out by laity. They want to know how deacons will relate "to laity on the one hand, or to clergy, on the other?" "Will the laity's role be downplayed?"

General Observations

The United Church of Christ agrees that the Holy Scriptures are of central importance in the life of the church. We find the use of "inclusiveness" as the guiding principle in the church's theological work an important witness. We believe that openness leads to authentic renewal and reformation.

As a united and uniting church, the UCC seeks to be a community of suffering and service, of faith, hope and love which carries the oneness we know in Christ to all people. Building upon the "evangelical" and "reformed" legacy of the 16th century Reformation, we are in the process of rediscovering our "catholic" roots through participation in the contemporary ecumenical movement. Many of us believe that the prayer of Jesus, "that they may all be one," must remain central to our identity. It is so important, one study group affirms, "that even the most treasured elements of particular traditions should not be held in such high or selfish regard so as to impede the higher good of our emerging unity."

However, there is also a feeling in various places within the UCC that the COCU covenanting process is "too much tinkering with ecclesiastical machinery and not enough dynamic action in mission." There is "a vagueness in the document that fuels disagreement and misunderstanding." Some UCC people find it easier to sense an "impatience" with the process, than any "deep wells of commitment to the long and difficult process of bringing change."

Many UCC people also react negatively to the language of the document. They find it heavy handed. Reuben A. Sheares, II, former executive director of the UCC Office for Church Life and Leadership, has helped us recognize the fact that the United Church of Christ works on a "soft verb system." Generally speaking, strong verbs, such as "demands" or "requires," do not appear in UCC vocabularies. The UCC system uses "soft verbs"; the General Synod "requests," or the Board for Homeland Ministries "urges," "calls upon," etc. There are very few "musts." As we continue our COCU journey the UCC will be more at home with a "covenanting process" which reduces all coercion, be it through words or practices (Reuben A. Sheares, II, Perspectives on the Polity of the United Church of Christ, 1987).

Conclusion

In answer to the request of the Consultation on Church Union that the United Church of Christ by formal action recognize in *The COCU Consensus: In Quest of a Church of Christ Uniting* three things, we respond as follows:

1. The United Church of Christ affirms that it finds in the Consensus document "an expression, in the matters with which it deals, of the Apostolic faith, order, worship and witness of the Church."

   Commentary: Although parts of the document are more in keeping with UCC understandings of theology and mission, no parts of the document fail to point toward a fuller confession of our common faith which can emerge out of life together within one ecclesial fellowship.

2. The United Church of Christ finds in the Consensus document "an anticipation of the Church Uniting which the participating bodies, by the power of the Holy Spirit wish to become."

   Commentary: Admitting that its passion to be a united and uniting church is always tempered by human fears and limitations, the UCC views its entire history as an ecumenical journey.

3. The United Church of Christ finds in the Consensus document "a sufficient theological basis for the covenanting acts and the uniting process proposed at this time by the Consultation."

   Commentary: It applauds the theological environment which provides the context for this emerging consensus, and in keeping with the Preamble to its Constitution, the United Church of Christ "acknowledges as its sole Head, Jesus Christ, Son of God and Savior. It acknowledges as kindred in Christ all who share in this confession."

Expanding Relationships

108. Jewish-Christian Theological Panel: "A Message to the Churches"

(1990)

The Theological Panel on Jewish-Christian Relations was appointed in 1987 to study and interpret the General Synod resolution "The Relationship Between the United Church of Christ and the Jewish Community" (1987). It was made up of nine UCC panelists and three consultants from the Jewish community and the Arab Christian community. The panel held three hearings on the resolution (Columbus, Ohio; Boston, Massachusetts; and Berkeley, California) and read extensively in the literature related to Jewish-Christian dialogue. It also responded to papers on several disputed questions: the meaning of "covenant" to Jews and Christians, the relationship between covenant and land, the understanding of Christ in connection with the Jewish people, the question of conversion, church statements on "supersessionism" and "anti-supersessionism," and Arab-Israeli issues. It listened to specialists and crafted a message to the churches. Its "message" sought to clarify the continuing commitment of the Church to its defining belief in Jesus Christ, alongside its conviction about the unbroken covenant of God with the Jewish people. It also recommended a continuation of the "mode of conversational theology" it found fruitful in its inquiry. Members of the panel were: Kenneth Smith (chair), Donald C. Armstrong, Thomas E. Dipko, Peter B. Doghramji, Martin Duffy, Gabriel Fackre, Louis Gunnemann, André LaCocque, and Sharon H. Ringe.

Source: Jewish-Christian Theological Panel, an excerpt from "A Message to the Churches," May 1990, *New Conversations* (Summer 1990): 5–7.

Jewish-Christian Theological Panel

Affirmations

1. The new context for the very old question of the relation of Jews and Christians is the epochal event of the twentieth century. "After Auschwitz" the world looks different. The Holocaust has sent Christians back to their texts and traditions to re-examine their theology and to ask about their own complicity in the anti-Semitism that gave rise to this horror. The *Shoah* has also sensitized us to the continuing and sometimes growing virulence of anti-Semitism and anti-Judaism in our country and other parts of the world.

The formation of the state of Israel in 1948 is also a new setting for examining old ideas. Some see the state of Israel in the context of God's promise of land to the descendants of Abraham and Sarah; some view it as a haven for victim people; some judge the creation of the state as the expropriation of a country belonging to others and the occasion for continuing victimization of others; and others see some validity in these and other views. This new political fact colors all we have to say on the subject of the resolution.

The same new political fact also causes us to look again at relationships among Jews, Christians, and Muslims who live in the land of Israel-Palestine. The brokenness of those relationships in the present configuration of political power underlies the Uprising. That event also has changed the way the world looks and feels, and it focuses for us the theological question of the role of all of Abraham's descendants according to the promises of God in the outworking of God's purposes. The importance of this development has been brought home to us with special poignancy through the witness of Middle Eastern Christians.

The outpouring of theological commentary on all these events since World War II represents a new framework for viewing the place of the Jewish people in God's plan of salvation. This vast literature includes a spate of official church documents calling for a reconsideration of traditional theological opinion on the relation of the Christian faith to the Jewish people, and with it the rejection of the view that Judaism has been superseded and invalidated by Christianity.

As a church whose Constitution calls us "to make the faith its own in each new generation," and whose Reformation founders pressed us to let "new light and truth break from God's holy Word," we believe that these events and developments compel a new perspective on our faith, and call us to new duties.

2. The deeper understanding of God's Holy Word to which we are being called in today's context is expressed in the New Testament reference to the chosen people cited by the Synod Resolution: "The gifts and call of God are irrevocable" (Romans 11:29). As we walk Paul's own path of struggle with the place of the Jewish people in the purposes of God after the coming of Christ (Romans 9–11), we affirm with the apostle that God has not abrogated their covenant. Such an irrevocable call, with its supporting gifts, contradicts the supersessionist view that God has rescinded the covenant with Israel. We believe that to deny God's irrevocable covenant with the chosen people has led and continues to lead to the "teaching of contempt" for Jews, with its horrifying results. We reject that view and call the members of the United Church of Christ to search their hearts and Scriptures for a deeper understanding of God's unbroken relationship with the Jewish people of today.

3. In the same breath in which Paul affirmed God's unswerving covenant with the Jews, he also declares that "faith comes from what is heard, and what is heard comes by the preaching of Christ" (Romans 10:17). He believed with all his heart that in Jesus, the Jew, a radical new event had taken place: "God shows his love for us that while we were yet sinners, Christ died for us" (Romans 5:8).

The conviction that God changed the course of the world in Jesus of Nazareth is the basis of our covenant as the United Church of Christ. As our Statement of Faith expresses it, we believe that "in Jesus Christ, the man of Nazareth, our crucified and risen Savior, [God] has come to us and shared our common lot, conquering sin and death. . . . " We cannot be who we are without this belief in the singular deed God has done to redeem all the world in the life, death, and resurrection of Jesus Christ. We celebrate this good news in Christian worship, proclaim it in word, and share it in deed.

Our deep belief in the God of love and justice known in Torah and the prophets, and manifest in Jesus Christ, as the gospels attest, is what presses us to be in solidarity with Jews, and all others, in their suffering, and to be self-critical about our teaching and actions toward this covenant people.

4. Our commitment to the particular act of God in Christ is a word we hold as firmly as our avowal of God's unrescinded covenant with the Jewish people. When we hear this twofold word, we overcome a distorted picture of the New Testament.

To affirm that "God was in Christ reconciling the world . . . " (2 Corinthians 5:19) and to affirm, simultaneously, that the "gifts and call of God" to the Jewish people are "irrevocable" (Romans 11:29) is to witness to the faithfulness of God. We have examined a variety of ways of interpreting this double affirmation, and are drawn to some and reject others. Our affirmation both of the continuing covenant of God with the Jewish people and of fulfillment of God's promises in Christ appears to be a paradox. Yet through this double affirmation we are invited into a deeper understanding of our faith. We welcome, therefore, the General Synod resolution as an opportunity to explore once again the richness and complexity of Christian faith. To that end, we provide study materials and further commentary for the use of our denomination.

5. Biblical formulations of God's covenant with the Jewish people include the promise of land. God's concrete gift of land to one people is a symbol of God's grace in giving the earth to all people. The fulfillment of the promise of land is tied to the people's faithfulness and the doing of justice in the land. Some Jews and some Christians consider the creation of the contemporary state of Israel to be the fulfillment of this promise. We do not see consensus in the United Church of Christ or among our panelists on the covenantal significance of the state of Israel.

We appreciate the compelling moral argument for the creation of modern Israel as a vehicle for self-determination and as a haven for a victimized people; we also recognize that this event has entailed the dispossession of Palestinians from their homes and the denial of human rights. Successive General Synods of the United Church of Christ have asserted that both Israelis and Palestinians should enjoy the right to self-determination in their lands, and that both people are entitled to security and justice. In view of their complicity with past injustices to both peoples, Christians of the West bear a special responsibility to work for a resolution of the Israeli-Palestinian issue that assures the human rights and dignity of both peoples.

In the land called Holy, prophets heard the word of God and, Christians believe, the incarnation of God's love took place. Can not the Holy Land become for our time a symbol of hope, a community of all believers, a wellspring of peace for the whole world?

Invitation

In our hearings and our studies, we have learned of countless ways in which the United Church of Christ can implement the purpose of the General Synod resolution and our own convictions as stated above. Instead of detailing these here, we are preparing supportive materials.

As one hearing testimony expressed it, we must "unleash imagination in our pursuit of ways of witnessing as Christians to the continuing covenant of God with the Jewish people."

Our own experience has convinced us of one sure way of pursuing this goal. It reflects the very premise of our Church, as a "united and uniting" community of faith. We believe that the right context for an understanding of the issues, and action upon them, is a forum of different voices. As a Panel we are very diverse in background and perspective. Understanding came hard, and agreements were modest. The grace of accord does not come cheap. Yet there is a joy as well as a cost in this kind of covenanted life together. We, therefore, recommend our own mode of conversational theology, with the kind of diverse voices heard in our forum. It has made possible this message of shared conviction and direction. Come with us on this journey, trusting the promises of our covenant God.

109. Muslim-Christian Relations:

"The Relationship between the United Church of Christ and the Muslim Community"

(1989)

General Synod

The relationship between the United Church of Christ and the Muslim community was initially tied to the work of the American Board of Commissioners for Foreign Missions (ABCFM) in the Middle East during the nineteenth century. It was a relationship sometimes filled with misunderstanding and arrogance. After 1965, when Muslim immigration to North America increased dramatically, the United Church of Christ began to reconstruct its relationship to Islam. In 1989 the General Synod passed a resolution on "the Relationship between the United Church of Christ and the Muslim Community" encouraging UCC members to expand their understanding of Islam.

Source: Resolution "The Relationship between the United Church of Christ and the Muslim Community," *GS Minutes 1989,* 61–62.

The Relationship between the United Church of Christ and the Muslim Community

Theological Rationale

God calls the people of God to be agents of reconciliation, breaking down walls of division nationally, culturally, racially, and religiously (Eph. 2:11–18)

Historical Background

The advent of Christianity in human history in the first century A.D. was preceded by Judaism which shares a common heritage and a context for understanding the New Testament. Islam, the third of the Abrahamic and monotheistic religions, was developed in the 7th century of the Christian era. The Old and New Testament interpretations do not require reference to Islam for Christian understanding and thus Christians have traditionally understood little of the faith and beliefs of Muslims.

Therefore, despite worship of the same God, recognition of common prophets, a shared vision of God's justice, righteousness, compassion and presence in the world, Christians and Muslims have had a history of intolerance, vilification and hostility in word and action as exemplified in the characterization and writings of theologians and scholars beginning with contacts in the seventh century, in wars often explained as religiously stereotyping common in the present.

Further, with the presence of growing Muslim populations and communities in the United States, American Christians have the opportunity to broaden their experience, revise attitudes and enrich theological perspectives of their faith in the context of Islam and the witness of Muslims.

Summary

Faced with the recognition that history extends forward as well as backwards from the crucifixion (in the words of Pilgrim's pastor, John Robinson, "God has yet more truth and light to break forth from His word") and that Christians have often ignored and been openly hostile to the revelation of God to Muslims, we ask for open hearts and minds as we as Christians learn about and support Muslims in their faithfulness in affirming the same God and our common prophets, as we discover in Islam a perspective on our beliefs and traditions and we rejoice in sharing with

Muslims a hope in the principle of justice and righteousness and a belief in the peace of submission to God.

Text of the Resolution

WHEREAS, the God we worship is the God of all creation, and

WHEREAS, we recognize that we share a common tradition of revelation through God's prophets as told in sacred scripture, and a common belief in the compassion, justice, authority and presence of God in human life and society, and

WHEREAS, there exists a lack of understanding in our society about the Muslim community and its religion, and

WHEREAS, injustice and intolerance exist because of this lack of understanding;

THEREFORE, BE IT RESOLVED, the 17th General Synod of the United Church of Christ encourages members of the United Church of Christ to seek greater understanding about Islam in the society as a whole.

FURTHER, the 17th General Synod of the United Church of Christ encourages the Synod to support this resolution, and

1. Calls upon the Office for Church in Society, the United Church Board for Homeland Ministries and the United Church Board for World Ministries to give the highest reasonable support to the work of the Office of Christian-Muslim Relations of the National Council of Churches of Christ in the U.S.A. and to urge the National Council of Churches of Christ in the U.S.A. to increase its emphasis on the work of that office, and
2. Calls upon the subject instrumentalities to coordinate with other denominations and/or other groups who are presently engaged in dialogue with the Muslim community, and
3. Calls upon the subject instrumentalities to identify educational resources for use in local churches to increase understanding of the Muslim community and to foster open dialogue, and
4. Calls upon all local congregations and regional judicatories of the United Church of Christ to actively engage in dialogue with the Muslim community in order to establish relationships of trust and cooperation and to participate in joint witness against all injustice in our local communities and in the world.

110. Lutheran-Reformed Dialogue:

Formula of Agreement *and* *Mercersburg Theological Forum Response*

(1996, 1994)

The results of the first round of Lutheran-Reformed dialogue (1962–66) were published in Marburg Revisited *(1966). Reports on the second and third rounds of dialogue (1972–74) and (1981–83) appeared in* An Invitation to Action *(1983). The fourth round (1988–92) produced* A Common Calling: The Witness of Our Reformation Churches in North America Today *(1993). These theological conversations built upon understandings developed between Lutheran and Reformed churches in Europe (the Leuenberg Agreement, 1973) and the work of a joint international commission of the Lutheran World Federation (LWF) and the World Alliance of Reformed Churches (WARC) —* Toward Church Fellowship *(1989).*

The Formula of Agreement *summarizes a 1997 action taken by four denominations: the Evangelical Lutheran Church in America, the Presbyterian Church (U.S.A.), the Reformed Church in America, and the United Church of Christ. The four churches declare on the basis of* A Common Calling *(1993) that they are in "full communion" with one another.*

Incorporated into the Formula of Agreement *(1997) is a paragraph from the Lutheran-Reformed* Invitation to Action *(1983), endorsed*

Sources: Excerpts on "Full Communion" and "Mutual Affirmation and Admonition" from *Formula of Agreement* between the Evangelical Lutheran Church in America, the Presbyterian Church (U.S.A.), the Reformed Church in America, and the United Church of Christ on entering into full communion on the basis of *A Common Calling*. Published in pamphlet form by the Lutheran-Reformed Joint Coordinating Committee, 1996, 3–6. "Response to *A Common Calling,*" The Mercersburg Theological Forum, April 22, 1994; revised, December 2, 1994.

previously by the UCC General Synod. It affirms fourteen shared traditions as understood within each Church's respective polity, including the ancient creeds, justification by faith, the authority of Scripture, the real presence of Christ in the Lord's Supper and the priesthood of all believers. The fourteen points had all been presupposed in its predecessor document A Common Calling *(1993).*

The core of the Formula of Agreement *(1997) outlines seven ways in which "full communion" is understood. It lifts up "mutual affirmation and mutual admonition" as new ways for Reformation churches to relate to each other. It recognizes that essential conditions for full communion have been met with regard to theological understandings of justification, the sacraments, ministry, and church and world. Continuing areas of diversity are no longer "church-dividing," and all traditions know that they "need each other in order to discern God's gracious promises and obey God's commands." Historic condemnations found in Lutheran and Reformed history "no longer apply to the contemporary doctrinal position of the assenting churches." Even different understandings of the presence of Christ in the sacraments are recognized as complimentary, "further deepening our common experience and expression of the mystery of our Lord's Supper." All of the churches "claim the saving power of God's grace as the center of their faith and life." The* Formula of Agreement *(1997) is grounded in the ecumenical conviction that "there is no turning back, either from the goal of visible unity or from the single ecumenical movement that unites concern for the unity of the Church and concern for engagement in the struggles of the world."*

Soon after the publication of A Common Calling *(1993), a Mercersburg Theological Forum (1994) sponsored by a group within the United Church of Christ committed to preserving the ecumenical insights of nineteenth-century Mercersburg theology (see vol. 7:68) responded positively to the ecumenical vision of* A Common Calling *and its recommendations.*

Formula of Agreement

Full Communion

The term "full communion" is understood here to specifically mean that the four churches:

- recognize each other as churches in which the gospel is rightly preached and the sacraments rightly administered according to the word of God;
- withdraw any historic condemnation by one side or the other as inappropriate for the life and faith of our churches today;
- continue to recognize each other's baptism and authorize and encourage the sharing of the Lord's Supper among their members;
- recognize each others' various ministries and make provision for the orderly exchange of ordained ministers of word and sacrament;
- establish appropriate channels of consultation and decision-making within the existing structures of the churches;
- commit themselves to an ongoing process of theological dialogue in order to clarify further the common understanding of the faith and foster its common expression in evangelism, witness, and service;
- pledge themselves to living together under the gospel in such a way that the principle of mutual affirmation and admonition becomes the basis of a trusting relationship in which respect and love for the other will have a chance to grow. . . .

Mutual Affirmation and Admonition

A concept identified as early as the first Lutheran-Reformed Dialogue became pivotal for the understanding of the Theological Conversations. Participants in the Dialogue discovered that "efforts to guard against possible distortions of truth have resulted in varying emphases in related doctrines which are not in themselves contradictory and in fact are complementary . . . " (*Marburg Revisited,* Preface). Participants in the Theological Conversations rediscovered and considered the implications of this insight and saw it as a foundation for the recommendation for full communion among the four churches. This breakthrough concept, a complementarity of mutual affirmation and mutual admonition, points toward new ways of relating traditions of Reformation churches that heretofore have not been able to reconcile their diverse witnesses to the saving grace of God that is bestowed in Jesus Christ, the Lord of the Church.

This concept provides a basis for acknowledging three essential facets of the Lutheran/Reformed relationship: (1) that each of the churches grounds its life in authentic New Testament traditions of Christ; (2) that the core traditions of these churches belong together within the one, holy, catholic, and apostolic church; and (3) that the historic give-and-take between these churches has resulted in fundamental mutual criticisms that cannot be glossed over, but need to be understood "as diverse witnesses to the one gospel that we confess in common" (*A Common Calling,* 66). A working awareness emerged, which cast in a new light contemporary perspectives on the sixteenth-century debates.

> The theological diversity within our common confession provides both the complementarity needed for a full and adequate witness to the gospel (mutual affirmation) and the corrective reminder that every theological approach is a partial and incomplete witness to the gospel (mutual admonition). (*A Common Calling,* 66)

The working principle of "mutual affirmation and admonition" allows for the affirmation of agreement while at the same time allowing a process of mutual edification and correction in areas where there is not total agreement. Each tradition brings its "corrective witness" to the other while fostering continuing theological reflection and dialogue to further clarify the unity of faith they share and seek. The principle of "mutual affirmation and admonition" views remaining differences as diverse witnesses to the one gospel confessed in common. Whereas conventional modes of thought have hidden the bases of unity behind statements of differences, the new concept insists that, while remaining differences must be acknowledged, even to the extent of their irreconcilability, it is the inherent unity in Christ that is determinative. Thus, the remaining differences are not church dividing.

The concept of mutual affirmation and admonition translates into significant outcomes, both of which inform the relationships of these four churches with one another. The principle of complementarity and its accompanying mode of interpretation make it clear that in entering into full church communion these churches:

- do not consider their own traditional confessional and ecclesiological character to be compromised in the least,
- fully recognize the validity and necessity of the confessional and ecclesiological character of the partner churches,

- intend to allow significant differences to be honestly articulated within the relationship of full communion,
- allow for articulated differences to be opportunities for mutual growth of churchly fullness within each of the partner churches and within the relationship of full communion itself.

A Mercersburg Response to *A Common Calling*

We affirm the seven statements from the recommendations of *A Common Calling: The Witness of our Reformation Churches in North America Today.* In the spirit of "mutual affirmation and admonition" (paragraph 7), for consideration we offer the following:

- We understand "rightly preached and . . . rightly administered" (paragraph 1) to mean that Christ imparts himself through the Word and Sacrament, to which we respond in faith. We look for the signs of this in the common liturgical expression we have inherited through the historic church.
- By virtue of their baptism (paragraph 3), the people of God are called to ministry (paragraph 4). Those who are ordained are set apart to equip the saints through preaching the gospel, administering the sacraments, and embodying the way of Christ. We understand this to be a life-long calling.
- By virtue of their baptism, all are called to witness and to serve (paragraph 6), because to be in Christ is to have Christ in us. Our service is a joyful response to this state of being in Christ.
- We affirm the significance of the Reformation confessional statements in the on-going ecumenical dialogue. We look forward to conversation about how they are understood and how they function in contemporary church life.
- We recognize that this common expression of witness and service has resulted in diversity, challenge and even conflict, not only *among,* but also *within* our traditions. While we may have to accept these differences, we must not allow them to become a denial of our common being in Christ.

111. Samoans:
"Partnership in Mission and Ministry . . . "

(1999)

General Synod

In 1984 the Congregational Christian Church in American Samoa expressed a desire to be in closer relationship with the United Church of Christ. In 1996 the General Assembly of the Congregational Christian Church in American Samoa adopted a resolution approving a relationship with the United Church of Christ as "mutual partners in God's mission." During 1997 and 1998 representatives of the two churches met "to discuss the nature of the proposed partnership and to develop a theological foundation for the partnership." In November 1998 a consultation was held in Hawaii and a statement of "Partnership in Mission and Ministry" was approved. This statement is the basis for the formal partnership between the United Church of Christ and the Congregational Christian Church in American Samoa that was voted at General Synod (1999).

Source: Excerpt from a Resolution on "Partnership in Mission and Ministry Between the Congregational Christian Church in American Samoa and the United Church of Christ," *GS Minutes 1999,* 71–73.

Partnership with the Congregational Church in American Samoa

Foundational Affirmations

Unity

In our common confession of Jesus Christ and in our baptism, we celebrate that we are children of God, disciples of Christ, and members of the Church of Jesus Christ. Responding to this shared confession and baptismal identity, obedient to Christ's prayer "that they may all be one that the world may believe," and accepting mutual responsibility to bear witness in our world to the Good News of Jesus Christ, the Congregational Christian Church in American Samoa and the United Church of Christ enter into a Partnership in Mission and Ministry agreement, giving expression to our unity in Jesus Christ.

Sacraments

This Partnership celebrates the truth that we share a common sacramental life. We recognize the baptism of each church as baptism by water and the Holy Spirit into the one Church of Jesus Christ. We invite each other to the common Table as we celebrate Christ's presence in Holy Communion. In this shared sacramental life, we receive the grace of God and the renewing power of the Holy Spirit. We covenant to seek opportunities to gather at Table and Font.

Mission

This Partnership celebrates the truth that we participate together in the one mission of God. We will support one another in this common responsibility and will extend support to one another through the ecumenical sharing of resources and people. We will encourage each other in the proclamation of the Gospel, invite people into discipleship and will work together for justice, peace and the integrity of God's creation. We covenant to identify appropriate means of consultation and decision-making within the existing structures of our churches so that our partnership in mission can grow.

Ministry

This Partnership celebrates the truth that all members of the church, by virtue of baptism, are called to ministry in Christ. We recognize that lay and ordained ministries requiring authorization are full and valid ministries and we will seek to discover ordered ways by which the ministers of one church may serve effectively, when invited, in the partner church. We covenant to extend honor and respect to those our partner church has authorized for lay and ordained ministry.

Diversity

This Partnership celebrates the truth that our two churches share a common faith. We have received the faith of the Apostles through diverse histories, cultures and traditions. We each claim the responsibility to make this historic faith our own in our differing historical and cultural contexts. Through this rich variety of theological expression, liturgical style and church governance, we recognize in our Partnership that the faith that has nurtured, sustained, and challenged each of our churches is one faith in Jesus Christ. We believe that God intends our differences to be enriching rather than dividing. We covenant to share in teaching and dialogue to encourage mutual enrichment, nurture and growth with full regard for the self-determination of our churches.

Related Recognitions

This Partnership is a way for both churches to be enriched as we share together in faithfulness to God's mission as churches in partnership with each other. It is not a merger of the two churches.

Knowledge and Appreciation

This Partnership recognizes that Partnership is advanced by greater knowledge about and appreciation for each other. Interpretive materials need to be developed by appropriate persons or units within each church. While interpretive materials can be of interest to an even wider constituency, those materials need to be distributed in such a way that the Congregational Christian Church in American Samoa (CCCAS) and the Samoan constituency within the United Church of Christ (UCC) receive both sets of interpretive materials at the same time. The materials will help local churches and their leaders and members better understand their own church and begin to understand the partner church as descriptions of history, ecclesiology, governance, structure, mission, program and ethos are characterized.

Role of Regional Judicatories in Mission

This Partnership recognizes that, where there is significant overlap of congregations and of Districts and Sub-Districts of the CCCAS with United Church of Christ congregations comprised of Samoans within Associations and Conferences of the United Church of Christ, the need for knowledge about and appreciation for the partner church is critical for the success of the Partnership. Knowledge and appreciation of each other fosters a greater likelihood of partnerships in mission and program within overlapping judicatory boundaries and effort that is more regional or global in character. Judicatory leadership in both churches plays a crucial role in brokering and interpreting how regional, national and global mission concerns, program possibilities and resources of each church can be understood, joined and utilized.

Authorization for Ministry

This Partnership recognizes that ministries on behalf of each church for which authorization is needed have similarity and distinguishing factors. Both churches authorize persons for ordained ministry. The CCCAS also authorizes persons to serve as Lay Preachers and the United Church of Christ authorizes persons to serve as Commissioned Ministers or as Licensed Ministers. The Authorizing processes are different in that there is a single national authority for granting authorization in the CCCAS, the Committee of Elders, and that in the United Church of Christ such authority is regional with Associations granting authorization. While honor and respect must be accorded to the authorizations for ministry in each church, the Licensed Ministry of the United Church of Christ and the Ordained Ministry of the CCCAS are different, as are the Lay Preacher and the Licensed Ministry of our respective churches.

Protocol

This Partnership recognizes the need for leadership of the CCCAS and United Church of Christ, in conjunction with appropriate partners within the structures of each church, to assure the presence of appropriate and mutually-respected protocols for the temporary reception of an ordained minister of one church to serve in the other. Should an ordained minister or a local church seek relocation in the partner church, relocation or reception is not to proceed without awareness of both churches. Once relocation of a local church or ordained minister takes place, issues of covenanted ecclesial accountability and support need to be clearly understood and honored.

Ecclesial, Spiritual and Cultural Ties: Accountability for Ministry and Support

This Partnership recognizes that there are cultural and spiritual ties among local churches and authorized ministers of the CCCAS and the United Church of Christ that are Samoan by heritage. Local churches and authorized ministers are encouraged to have clear ecclesial ties, holding authorization or standing in one or the other church while, at the same time, having spiritual and cultural ties to both churches. Spiritual and cultural ties have to do with valued heritage and partnership in mission and program. Ecclesial ties have to do with accountability and support associated with membership and standing. When ecclesial ties include dual affiliations, issues of accountability and support need to be clearly understood among all parties so as to avoid confusion.

Partnership Committee

The Partnership recognizes the need to have a Partnership committee comprised of representatives from both churches to provide leadership to our Partnership in Mission Agreement. This committee will meet at least once a year to advance the relationship and the partnership. The committee's mandate will be reviewed by the two churches after six years and may be renewed. The committee will monitor efforts on behalf of the Partnership as being faithful to the agreement and its recognitions as well as the adequacy of the Partnership as a faithful expression of life together in the Church of Jesus Christ. The committee will report its findings and offer suggestions growing out of ongoing experience to the leadership of both churches on an annual basis. The committee will also plan consultations that bring together a larger group to address issues that benefit the faithfulness of the Partnership. The Partnership Committee will be composed in equal numbers of not less than five or more than ten members from each church.

PART VII

Aspiring to Be a Multiracial and Multicultural Church

The Preamble to the Constitution of the United Church of Christ challenges future generations of UCC members to remember that the UCC was created "in order to express more fully the oneness in Christ of the churches composing it." But what does this mean? Is "oneness in Christ" a unity of denominations, a unity of beliefs, a unity of structures, a unity of witness, a unity of members? In twentieth-century ecumenical history, the search for a unity of "faith and order" and for a unity of "life and work" has called Christians not only to believe, but also to live, to act and to organize together in fresh, imaginative and unprecedented ways.

"Christian unity" is grounded in biblical convictions that the God in whom we place our hope and trust is creator of the whole universe and that under Jesus Christ, the head of the church, the ancient dividing walls of hostility are broken down and there are no more divisions (see Ephesians 2:14 NRSV). The Church seeks to claim God's faithful promise of "a new heaven and a new earth" (Revelation 21:1 NRSV).

This biblical message of unity in Christ is central to the United Church of Christ. At the same time the UCC has also been influenced by the growing diversity of North American society. Since the new immigration laws of 1965, political and social life has become increasingly concerned about social equality and religious freedom. Tolerance and dialogue are highly valued. Christians now worry more about religious bigotry and arrogance than they do about heresy and dissent. Religious diversity, once considered a threat to purity and orthodoxy, is sought out and even considered a virtue.

Yet, social and political trends do not explain the vocation of the United Church of Christ. Its aspiration to become a multiracial and multicultural church is deeply rooted in the biblical message that God calls the church to be one community of many races and cultures, accessible to all. Its calling is not simply a response or adaptation to demographics and social change.

Embracing Diversity

During the 1960s, the life of the United Church of Christ was dramatically shaped by Jesus' teaching about love of neighbor and by the prophetic tradition in Scripture. As the "racial crisis" exploded across the nation, the energy of the church and many of its commitments focused on justice issues (see vol. 7:14–22). By the 1970s, African American members, nurtured in congregations with roots in Congregational and Afro-Christian history, gained considerable prominence and great influence in the United Church of Christ.

The diversity of the entire nation was changing. In 1965, laws designated to limit all but European immigration ended, opening the country to new arrivals from the Middle East, the Pacific, Asia, and Latin America. By the mid-1970s, with rising numbers of minority churches and caucuses enriching its life, the United Church of Christ began to speak about the gift of diversity as an asset. Celebrating the marvel of its unity in Christ, it affirmed in fresh new ways the observation of the apostle Paul that where the Church is inspired by the Spirit of God, "there are varieties of gifts, . . . varieties of service, . . . varieties of activities, but it is the same God who activates all of them in everyone" (1 Corinthians 12:4–6 NRSV). "Every person's and every people's experience of the whole and of the holy is, at best, only a part of reality." "[T]he whole community is enriched by the shared witnessing and expanded experiencing of the parts." The "whole is more than the sum of the parts." UCC leaders sought to empower diverse groups in the church and uphold patterns of ministry based upon "self-determination." They believed that by "empowering" minority congregations and caucuses the United Church of Christ was becoming more faithful to the gospel of Jesus Christ (see vol. 7:112).

In local UCC congregations, when people were invited to talk about what it meant to be Christian in a diverse society, they found the issues extremely complex. Differences of class, race, ethnic tradition, age, and gender were obvious. Many people believed that the gospel challenged them to erase those divisions in the church of Jesus Christ. Diversities of sexuality, politics, and theology, however, were more problematic. Although local UCC members were generally proud that their church encouraged variety and openness, some members wondered about the limits of diversity (see vol. 7:113).

Minority congregations and caucuses continued to form, and in 1983 the General Synod created the Council for Racial and Ethnic Ministries (COREM). COREM provided a central forum where racial and ethnic groups could develop their common agenda, collaborate with program and mission bodies, discern ways to make their gifts available to the church, and advocate for common concerns.

Discussions about pluralism and diversity persisted. A Committee on Pluralism was created by the Executive Council to answer the question "What kind of church do we want the United Church of Christ to be?" It produced a working paper "Toward a Theological Framework for Pluralism" that was shared with the 1985 General Synod. At the same time new affinity and advocacy groups emerged out of the theological ferment of the 1980s, each seeking to emphasize a specific tradition, a forgotten authority or a new challenge (see vol. 7:57–77).

Finally, in 1993 the General Synod answered the question. It called upon "the United Church of Christ in all of its settings to be a true multiracial and multicultural church," confessing and acting out its faith "in the one sovereign God who through Jesus Christ binds in covenant faithful people of all races, ethnicities and cultures." For the United Church of Christ this answer was a response to the times, but it was also a natural extension of its birthright conviction about Christian unity. Jesus had prayed "that they may all be one" and in answer to that prayer the United Church of Christ accepted the challenge to be "One" — a church open to all people (see vol. 7:114).

In the years that followed the "Multiracial and Multicultural resolution" many efforts were made to explore and explain the nature of diversity and/or pluralism. Daniel F. Romero, writing for the Pluralism Working Group of the United Church Board for Homeland Ministries, prepared a foundation paper/pamphlet entitled *Our Futures Inexplicably Linked: A Vision of Pluralism* (1994). It asserted that people of diverse racial, ethnic, cultural, and religious backgrounds are living in closer proximity, making everyone more interdependent. It suggested that the "myths of white, male, or even Christian superiority" have been exposed and everyone is challenged to take more seriously the claims of those who see the world through other eyes.

The preface to *Our Futures Inexplicably Linked,* written by Michael Kinnamon, a Christian Church (Disciples of Christ) theologian who served on the Pluralism Working Group, summarized the main points of the paper. "Pluralism is not simply a synonym for diversity"; it accepts diversity as a source of enrichment rather than a threat. Pluralism is not the opposite of wholeness, but central to wholeness because it values particularity. Pluralism is not synonymous with tolerance, because it sometimes must say "no" to forces that limit. Pluralism involves relating to others on the basis of their own self-definition; it requires a lifestyle of dialogue; and it denies the privilege of any single voice. Pluralism is a commitment of the whole church, yet pluralism is always lived out in local congregations. The good news is that Christ has broken down the dividing walls of hostility and is calling the church to witness to God's intended wholeness for all creation (Ephesians 2:14). Pluralism points "beyond itself to the Source of all unity and the Author of all diversity."

Receiving the Gifts of African Americans

The commitment to become a "multiracial and multicultural church" did not happen overnight. It was the result of a process that took over thirty years. In 1963 as the Fourth General Synod convened in Denver, national unrest over racial issues was high. To provide more racial balance, ten leading UCC African American clergy were invited to attend the 1963 Synod as honorary delegates (voice without vote).

The black clergy were eloquent, and the president of the church, Ben Herbster, spoke about the growing "racial crisis" and Christian responsibility (see vol. 7:17). In a dramatic vote the 1963 General Synod established a "Committee on Racial Justice Now," charged to institute a broad program to eliminate racial segregation and discrimination in church and society. In the years that followed, a network of advocacy groups for racial justice developed: Ministers for Racial and Social Justice (MRSJ) in 1966 [later known as Ministers for Racial, Social and Economic Justice], the United Black Churchmen in 1970 (UBC) [later known as United Black Christians], and the Organization of Black National UCC Staff in 1971. Although only about 3 percent of the members of the United Church of Christ were African American, it was a new day (see vol. 7:21).

The United Church of Christ forged a bold commitment to recognize African American leaders and to promote racial justice. At the 1967 General Synod in Cincinnati, due to the efforts of the MRSJ, an African American pastor named Joseph Evans was nominated from the floor and elected secretary of the denomination. In 1969 African American UCC leaders insisted that James Forman be allowed to speak to the General Synod about the controversial "Black Manifesto" with its request for reparations to support black economic development. Throughout the 1970s and 1980s the United Church of Christ pressed for justice for the Wilmington 10 and spoke out repeatedly against racism (see vol. 7:82–84).

The journey of African Americans from slavery to equality in society and from second-class status to full humanity in a multiracial and multicultural church continued. Remarkable theological and cultural resources sustained blacks through difficult times and continued to nurture a vital Christian faith. The words of the stirring and beautiful "Black National

Anthem" offered poetic phrases that preserved the memory and named some of the basic theological convictions held by African Americans (see vol. 7:115).

African Americans were also inspired by the story of the Amistad rebellion of 1839, when a group of Africans mutinied a slave ship to gain their freedom. After the ship was intercepted by government authorities, the status of the Africans was tested in a legal case that went all the way to the U.S. Supreme Court, while African Americans and white Congregationalists worked together for their cause. One hundred and fifty years later African American theologians developed a new framework for thinking about their faith known as "black theology." Black theology, "God-talk rooted in the realities of slavery, racism, and discrimination," asked two questions: "What was God doing while blacks were undergoing slavery?" and "What is God doing now as blacks struggle for equality, justice, parity, power, and identity?" (see vol. 7:116).

Even as black theology enriched the thinking of many African Americans, in local congregations people "kept the faith," sustaining their Christian identity through "prayer, music and shared experience in worship." Parents and grandparents passed their faith on to the next generation by helping young African Americans discover and learn about "slave resistance," giving kitchen table admonitions that reminded everyone "to be thankful to God for all the blessings received," and addressing practical questions, like "How do I survive from day to day?" (see vol. 7:117).

From 1957 to 1999 fifty-five new African American congregations joined the United Church of Christ. The largest congregation in that group, and the largest congregation in the denomination by the end of the century, was Trinity United Church of Christ in Chicago. Founded in 1962 with fewer than 100 members, Trinity UCC had grown to 10,377 members by 2000. After the assassination of Dr. Martin Luther King Jr. in 1968, the congregation drew up an original and contemporary statement of purpose emphasizing that it was "not ashamed of the gospel of Jesus Christ" and did not "apologize for its African roots." After ten more years it adopted a "Black Value System" that became the basis for a vital program of black worship and social outreach (see vol. 7:118).

African American contributions to the life of the United Church of Christ have brought vitality, spiritual depth, and joy to the church. However, the theological and biblical substance of the African American church, nurtured through suffering and marked by its devotion to Jesus, has brought a particular integrity to the United Church of Christ. As the United Church of Christ seeks to move toward its vision of becoming a multiracial and multicultural church, it is learning to honor the witness and the faithfulness of African Americans who are devoted to the church and its ministry.

Receiving the Gifts of American Indians

Another kind of strength, dignity, and faithfulness is found among indigenous peoples who are part of the United Church of Christ. Called American Indians or Native Americans, diverse nations of indigenous peoples occupied the land long before Spanish and Anglo-Christians came to the North American continent. These peoples offered hospitality to colonial immigrants, but were forced to sustain many indignities and injustices perpetuated in the name of Christianity. The history of broken promises made to indigenous tribal nations and the human misery sustained among Indian peoples is one of the world's great human tragedies. At the same time, many indigenous peoples also embraced the gospel of Jesus Christ.

Historically, UCC mission work among American Indians took place in New England; in Tennessee, Georgia, and Alabama; in Minnesota, Nebraska, and the Dakotas; and in Wisconsin. The Dakota Association was founded in 1872; the Fort Berthold Council of Congregational Churches began in 1876; and in Black River Falls, Wisconsin, the mission and school that led to the HoCak United Church of Christ dates from 1884. Today these geographic areas remain as important units of ministry within the United Church of Christ Council for American Indian Ministry (CAIM). [Note: The United Church of Christ uses the language "American Indians." However, "indigenous peoples, communities, or nations" as well as "native Americans" is also appropriate.]

Shortly after the formation of the United Church of Christ, ministry among indigenous peoples, which had been lodged in the United Church Board for Homeland Ministries (UCBHM), left the Board to become independent. In 1970 the Council for American Indian Ministry (CAIM) was incorporated in the state of North Dakota, and in 1971 the General Synod recognized the council as "the principal agent for distributing resources for Indian ministries" and for representing "the Indian constituency within the United Church of Christ."

CAIM was and is unique. From the beginning all of its work was planned and implemented totally by American Indians, putting to an end the exclusion of the "American Indian from the management of his [or her] own affairs." In 1971 the General Synod also voted to designate the Sunday before Thanksgiving as American Indian Sunday (see vol. 7:119).

Most of American Indians, served by CAIM, attended churches on Indian reservations. By the 1970s, however, only 30 percent of the Indian population remained on reservations, and more and more native peoples were moving to cities. Recognizing this fact, in 1981 the All Nations Indian United Church of Christ was founded in Minneapolis. As the first urban American Indian congregation in the United Church of Christ All Nations is an ecumenical, interfaith, multiracial, and multicultural congregation. Worship begins with the traditional "smudging" of the congregation from the smoke of burning sage, and many other multicultural songs and prayers are offered. All Nations UCC, however, is a Christian congregation committed to healing the past and maintaining culturally sensitive worship and ministry in the present among all people.

New patterns of thinking about ministry for and with American Indians slowly matured in the United Church of Christ. In the 1980s, CAIM, trying to engage the UCC in Indian ministry, presented a plan of action to the General Synod. The pronouncement "A United Church of Christ Ministry with Indians" (1987) noted that "several contemporary theologies have affirmed that God has a preferential option for the poor and the oppressed." "If that be the case," it continued, "God must have a deep preference for the American Indian people." Highlighting needs and spelling out various responses, the pronouncement reaffirmed the commitment of the United Church of Christ to American Indian Ministries (see vol. 7:120). Over the next decade several other General Synod resolutions sought to carry out that commitment by challenging the "Negative Stereotyping of Native Americans" (1991) and questioning national plans for the observance of "the 500th Anniversary of Christopher Columbus' so-called discovery of America" (1991).

Being an American Indian in a predominantly Anglo-Christian society and in a denomination with deep European roots has challenged Indian UCC leaders to reflect sincerely about their faith, to explore the vast richness of their cultures, and to present it to the United Church of Christ to enrich theological discussion. For example, when Native Americans are "designated servants" by the church and the world and given duties that are "menial and tolerated," it has sometimes become harsh and difficult for them to accept the gospel invitation "to be God's servant in the service of others." Indigenous communities of faith give thanks for the One who bent down with towel and basin to wash the disciples' feet, but they know this service only takes place authentically "in communities of equals [where] people can perform menial tasks for one another with honor." Unfortunately, Native Americans who have "internalized oppression," "must decolonize" their lives and "unlearn some of what the missionaries taught" in order to be "equals in the household of faith." They see perceptively the biblical truth that those with power and authority are called to share, so that everyone in the church will be "enabled to choose servanthood in the manner Jesus intended" (see vol. 7:121).

In the closing decades of the twentieth century American Indians have sought to recover the uniqueness and beauty of many tribal traditions, blending these with Christian elements and their native heritage when appropriate. They have been eager to enrich the church in authentic ways, but they have remained cautious that their spirituality may be exploited just as their lands and their people have been violated in defiance of the teachings of Jesus (see vol. 7:122).

Yet, for many indigenous people, living in two cultures is a central part of their spirituality. In the HoCak community "faith involves an awareness of the spiritual force and living in harmony with it." "Faith is an understanding of this interconnectedness, an awareness of the nuances of our actions. Our faith reminds us that we are a part of a larger, global world, where Sunday morning rituals extend to the love we carry all throughout our week." Whereas the Anglo North American culture has a language (English) that is "precise" and unambiguous, native cultures have languages with more levels of meaning to nourish spiritual connections. Sometimes, when languages fail, only the "living message of the community itself" can express the "spiritual connectedness of all things" (see vol. 7:123).

It is impossible to make universal generalizations about the United Church of Christ and American Indians of many nations. There is a strong missionary heritage and a European perspective that for more than 250 years often justified, in the name of Christianity, the annihilation of Indian peoples, religions, and cultures. The combination of immigrant attitudes of entitlement and missionary assumptions of superiority led to the tragic unintentional and intentional devastation of entire civilizations.

At the end of the twentieth century Native American leaders, and many other members of the UCC, agreed that the longstanding assumption that it is impossible to be Christian and Indian at the same time is false and does not serve the church or Indians well. This false assumption has meant that American Indians "have not indigenized, contextualized, [or] formulated [their] own expression of the faith, nor developed [their] own local theologies." As the new century begins, UCC American Indian leadership is challenging Indian people to "engage the gospel from the Indian experience" and asking for "support and encouragement" from the large Euro-American majority in the church. It is also appealing to other people of color to recognize and respect each other's needs so that each will be able to find his or her own way to be part of the "one and many" in the United Church of Christ (see vol. 7:124).

American Indian contributions to the life of the United Church of Christ remain deeply abiding, significant, and challenging. The theological perspectives of American Indians promise to enrich the life of the church even further, claiming new attention and respect for the cultures of many nations grounded in the land and sensitive to the environment and their communities. Their contributions continue to produce a heritage profound in its wisdom and trusting of a grace nurtured in the presence of a vale of tears. As the United Church of Christ seeks to move toward its vision of becoming a multiracial and multicultural church, it is learning to support the witness and faithfulness of American Indians who are devoted to the church and its ministry.

Receiving the Gifts of Pacific Islanders and Asian Americans

In many ways the story of the indigenous people of Hawaii follows the same tragic pattern of conquest by the Europeans on the mainland of the United States. The earliest recorded contact of the Western world with Hawaii was in 1778 by the English explorer, Captain James Cook. The Hawaiian Islands, called the Sandwich Islands after the Earl of Sandwich, became a watering and resupply base for traders who plied the vast Pacific. Within a few decades Hawaiian life changed radically. "As the influence of the *haoles* — Caucasians of Northern European origin, mostly from the United States — continued to permeate island life, demoralization and disease reduced the Hawaiian people from a vibrant 300,000 to little more than 40,000 . . . " [Lawrence H. Fuchs, *Hawaii Pono: A Social History* (New York: Harcourt, Brace & World, 1961)] (see vol. 5:24).

By 1810 the separate island kingdoms had been conquered and united as one nation by King Kamehameha the Great and an era of peace set in. Into these peaceful islands the first Christian missionaries came in 1820 (see vol. 5:21). They were inspired by a young Hawaiian, Henry Obo'okia or Opukaha'ia, who had found his way to New England, had come under the influence of Timothy Dwight, president of Yale University, and become a Christian. He dreamed of taking his new religion back to his people, but he died of typhus fever before he could fulfill his dream. The missionaries were sent by the American Board of Commissioners for Foreign Missions (ABCFM), now the Wider Church Ministries of the United Church of Christ. They preached the Christian message first at the site of what is now the Kawaiaha'o Church, the mother church of Hawaii. They brought not only the gospel, but education and the printing press, and they challenged the unscrupulous practices of the sandalwood traders.

By 1852 the Christian church in Hawaii had flourished and matured to the place where it became a missionary sending community itself, carrying the gospel further west to the Micronesian Islands. And by 1863 the church had matured to the point where the American Board of Commissioners for Foreign Missions declared that Hawaii was no longer a "mission field" and turned over the life of the mission to the Hawaiian Evangelical Association. Hawaiian Christians had flourished and developed their own blend of indigenous vibrant church life that reflected the Aloha spirit of the people along with a pious devotion to the Bible.

Unfortunately, in 1893, *haole*-dominated business interests in the islands engineered, with the support of the U.S. Navy, the overthrow of Queen Liliuokalani, the reigning monarch of the Hawaiian people. The queen was deposed and imprisoned. She was a devoted Christian and one of the remarkable stories emerging from this deplorable situation was the word that the queen forgave those who deposed and imprisoned her. In place of the monarchy a republic, dominated by the United States, was established. In 1900 it became a territory of the United States and in 1959 the fiftieth state. One hundred years later, in 1993, the United Church of Christ offered a formal apology for the ways in which the missionary-descended leadership of the Congregational Church had been complicit in the overthrow of the queen (see vol. 7:125).

During the exciting and tumultuous times leading up to the overthrow and the years following, the Aloha spirit of Hawaiian Christianity prevailed. Not only were mainland "foreigners" welcomed, but as immigrant laborers were brought in from China, Japan, Korea, Portugal, and the Philippines to work on the plantations, the Hawaiian church initiated and supported ministries to them. The Chinese mission began in 1868, the Japanese mission in 1892. A small band of Portuguese became a part of the Congregational Church in 1891. Around 1911 the Congregational Board began a ministry among the Filipinos. Congregational churches on the islands affirmed the diversity of languages, ways of worship, and church life, and at the same time upheld the unity of Christ's church. As new churches were established, the Congregational mission flourished. They were confident that Jesus Christ "never meant everyone to be alike" (see vol. 7:125).

Alongside these developments in Hawaii, beginning in 1853 Congregationalists began new forms of outreach to Asian immigrants arriving in California. The American Missionary Association (AMA), founded to serve the needs of freed slaves and other people of color in 1846, began its ministry among Chinese people in San Francisco in 1853. The Congregational Home Missionary Society (CHMS) launched a San Francisco ministry among the Japanese in 1899. These organizations along with the Board of Home Missions of the [German] Reformed Church in the United States worked with Asian immigrants in California during the first half of the twentieth century. The first Reformed mission among the Japanese began in San Francisco in 1910. After World War II the Congregational Christians tried to "integrate" Japanese people into Anglo churches. This tactic, however, was a failure, leading to flourishing Japanese American congregations in other denominations and a declining Japanese American presence among Congregational Christians.

At the time of the formation of the United Church of Christ in 1957, Pacific Islander and Asian American congregations in the UCC were predominantly Hawaiian, Chinese, and Japanese. Since that time there has been a surge of Filipino congregations (from six to fifteen congregations) and Samoan congregations (from four to fifty-four congregations). Most recently more attention is being given to recent immigrants from the Micronesian islands.

The events of the 1960s and the rise of "black pride" among African Americans had a significant impact on how other ethnic minority peoples saw themselves and their place in the United States. As the UCC tried to respond creatively to the black revolution, other ethnic minorities began to see a new place for themselves in the larger society and in the church. It is an interesting fact that the first executive of the "Committee on Racial Justice Now" (1963) was a Japanese American.

By the early 1970s the Japanese American Council of the UCC took the initiative to organize an Asian American caucus. In April 1974 "Pacific and Asian American Ministries (PAAM)" was founded, and it was recognized as a special-interest group at the 1975 General Synod. PAAM set forth many organizational objectives, as well as stating its intention to promote research about "Asian theology and the unique insights of the heritage of Asians and Hawaiians, etc., for better understanding of the faith" (see vol. 7:126).

In 1979 a resolution on "Racism in the UCC" was presented to the General Synod. It was introduced with a statement that Pacific and Asian Americans "add colorfulness to the United Church of Christ" and ensure that the UCC "will truly be a rainbow in all aspects of life." Leaders of PAAM insisted that "the ultimate will of God is a united church in which all persons are One." Because "in Christ there is no East nor West, nor white nor Black, nor Yellow nor Brown. We are all intended to be One within the fellowship of the church." Sometimes there are situations when God's will becomes "contingent upon the circumstances," but circumstantial activities must always be used to serve the "ultimate will of God" (see vol. 7:126).

PAAM leaders played a key role in the formation of the Council for Racial and Ethnic Ministries (COREM) in 1983 and called the UCC to have compassion for the increasing numbers of immigrants from Asia and the Pacific islands in a resolution in 1985. Early in the 1980s a key PAAM leader preached at General Synod, challenging the whole United Church of Christ to recognize that "the world of the white male control and domination" had collapsed. Asians and Pacific Islanders do not want to be "troublemakers," but they know that the church needs to draw from "fresh and sometimes radically different perspectives" and from "people of different histories," in order to be able to "more adequately witness to Christ and humanity" (see vol. 7:127).

Finally the General Synod adopted a major pronouncement, "A United Church of Christ Ministry with Pacific Islanders and Asian Americans" (1989). The pronouncement lamented the "model minority" myth that implied that Asian Americans had "overcome the bondage of racial discrimination." It spelled out the needs of new immigrants and called on the church to "receive these peoples." It also noted that the various religious traditions represented in Asian American and Pacific Islander populations have "a spirituality which can inform and enrich Christianity" (see vol. 7:128).

Asian American theology is extremely diverse, given the many cultural traditions involved. However it is always "born out of a struggle between the culture of ancestry and the culture of America." It often reflects a tension between "openness and triumphalism; family and individualism; weakness and strength" (see vol. 7:129).

Throughout the 1980s and 1990s Pacific Islanders and Asian Americans pressed UCC General Synods to pass resolutions on the "Redress/Reparation to Japanese Americans" (1981), "Compassion for Asian and Pacific Islander Immigrants" (1985), "Reaffirming Solidarity with our Brothers and Sisters in the United Church of Christ in the Philippines" (1989), "Expressing Solidarity with the Chinese People [at the time of the Tiananmen Square uprisings]" (1989), and "Implementation of Reconciliation with the United Church of Christ and Native Hawaiians" (1995).

Pacific Islanders and Asian Americans "live in the context of two cultures, two histories and two languages." The pressures for assimilation are great and efforts to preserve ethnic roots difficult. Many Pacific Islanders and Asian Americans find the biblical story of "Israel as sojourner" helpful because it encourages them to see their experience "in the light of God's pervasive activities in the world" (see vol. 7:130).

Pacific Islander and Asian American contributions to the United Church of Christ have been substantial. The church has been blessed by the wisdom of native Hawaiian culture. It has also benefited greatly from the spiritual legacies and the theological openness of Asian and Pacific cultures, as well as from the Christian hope of people nurtured through times of great joy and deep sorrow. As the United Church of Christ seeks to move toward its vision of becoming a multiracial and multicultural church, it is learning to accept the gifts and the faithfulness of Pacific Islanders and Asian Americans who are devoted to the church and its ministry.

Receiving the Gifts of Hispanics

The earliest European immigrants to settle the Western Hemisphere were Spanish speaking. In recent years the U.S. census began defining all Spanish-speaking immigrant people as "Hispanic." Hispanics are Mexicans and Mexican Americans in the Southwest; Puerto Ricans in Puerto Rico, New England, and New York City; Latinos/as in Chicago; and Cubans in south Florida. By the end of the twentieth century many immigrants from the Caribbean, Central America, and South America are also called Hispanic.

Members of these communities in the United Church of Christ have varied opinions about this language. Some prefer to be known as Latinos and Latinas, others are comfortable with Hispanic. All of them recognize that the Council for Hispanic Ministries (CHM) represents their interests within the United Church of Christ.

The story of Spanish-speaking churches and members in the UCC has beginnings in both Mexico and Puerto Rico. The American Board of Commissioners for Foreign Missions (ABCFM) began work in Guadalajara, Mexico, in the 1870s, organizing Mexican Congregational Churches. When Mexicans moved north during the first half of the twentieth century, Mexican mission congregations were founded in California, Texas, and New Mexico. By 1999 there were twenty-one predominantly Spanish-speaking congregations in ten mainland United Church of Christ Conferences.

In 1899 the Congregationalists from the American Missionary Association (AMA) began work in Puerto Rico. In the 1930s the Iglesia Evangélica Unida de Puerto Rico (United Evangelical Church of Puerto Rico) was organized, and in the 1960s the IEUPR voted to become a conference of the United Church of Christ. There were fifty-eight UCC congregations in the Puerto Rican UCC Conference in 1999. UCC Spanish-speaking congregations, mostly rooted in Mexican and Puerto Rican culture, made and continue to make important contributions to the United Church of Christ (see vol. 7:131).

The relationship of the United Church of Christ to the growing numbers of Spanish-speaking people in the United States has evolved slowly. It has been supportive of ecumenical and social justice movements involving Latinos/as, but it has been rather slow in developing leadership and local congregations. In the 1960s the UCC was an active supporter of the National Farm Worker Ministry (NFWM) through the National Council of Churches of Christ (NCCC), helping farm workers "organize to overcome their powerlessness and achieve justice, equality and freedom." The United Church Board for Homeland Ministries (UCBHM) made substantial financial commitments to the NFWM, and various votes of General Synods and the UCBHM endorsed boycotts of grapes, lettuce, Gallo wine, Chiquita bananas, and Campbell soups. Olgha Sierra Sandman, a UCC laywoman, worked for thirty years with the National Farm Worker Ministry. Many UCC people will never forget the 1973 General Synod in St. Louis, when ninety-five volunteers chartered a plane and flew to California's Coachella Valley to stand in solidarity with Cesar Chavez and the predominantly Mexican United Farm Workers as they protested low wages and poor working conditions.

The United Church of Christ also offered support to Puerto Rican activists imprisoned for challenging what many consider unjust laws perpetuating the "colonial policies" of the U.S. government related to Puerto Rico. Alejandrina Torres, a UCC pastor's wife imprisoned for sixteen years, benefited from the support of UCC people throughout her incarceration. She was pardoned by President Clinton in 1999.

In 1975 the General Synod took action to formally recognize the Council for Hispanic Ministries (CHM), stating that the church had "too often been ignorant of, or insensitive to, the spiritual and social needs of Hispanic communities in our country." In 1977 another resolution was voted, restating needs and promising action while the Spanish-speaking population of the country and the United Church of Christ continued to grow.

The 1970s were marked with a new excitement about what was known as "liberation theology" emerging in Latin America. There, Roman Catholic and Protestant theologians cultivated a new dialogue between church and society, focusing upon issues of transformation and liberation for poor and oppressed people. Local groups of Christians were encouraged to read the Bible from a liberation perspective. Jesus Christ "was rich, yet for (our) sake he became poor, so that by his poverty (we) might become rich" (2 Corinthians 8:9). And because "Jesus associated his mission with the poor," the plight of the poor "profoundly affects the identity of the church." Liberation theologians insisted that the church is "called to bear direct witness against the scandal of poverty" and to "live in the spirit of humility, openness and dependence on God" (see vol. 7:132).

Although some church people heeded these words, most remained unaware of the needs of Hispanic churches mainly located in the midst of poor barrios. In 1983 when the Council for Racial and Ethnic Ministries (COREM) was formed, the Council for Hispanic Ministries (CHM) was a member. In 1985, once again the General Synod passed a resolution on "Hispanic Concerns."

Ten years had passed since the first General Synod resolution on Hispanics in 1977; the years had been filled with many words but little action. Finally in 1987 the leaders of the CHM forced the issue at the General Synod. First, they proposed a pronouncement, "The Hispanic Ministry of the United Church of Christ" (1987). It quoted from the prophet Amos, "Let justice roll down like waters and righteousness like an everflowing stream" (Amos 5:24). It noted that language barriers were part of the problem, but that the United Church of Christ had not been successful in meeting "the basic needs of Hispanics," nor in "attracting increasing numbers of Hispanics into the United Church of Christ" (see vol. 7:133).

After the pronouncement was approved, as the General Synod moved to vote on a "Proposal for Action," the president of the Council for Hispanic Ministries read a statement chiding the United Church of Christ for its "neglectful response over the past ten years." He noted that "justice does not happen in a vacuum. It happens in the midst of acts of justice and not through the meaningless rhetoric of your deliberations." Joined by a group of CHM leaders on the podium, he concluded with the words, "our soul is hurting and our hearts are broken. . . . " "We will return to hear your response to our claim for justice," and then he "walked out" of the General Synod with members of the Council for Hispanic Ministries and their supporters.

Needless to say, this attracted the attention of the delegates. Intense meetings were held, and within a few hours the president of the church and many of those who had walked out returned to the floor of the Synod. They reported that the hurt had been real and the conversations honest. All were bound together with renewed commitment to enable the United Church of Christ to do God's mission, "not the Hispanic mission," but "the mission of God." The church of Jesus Christ is One, there is no salvation "unless you have it in community" (see vol. 7:134).

The role of Spanish-speaking leaders and congregations in the United Church of Christ improved after 1987, but life in the United Church of

Christ remained difficult. At a "Latino Summit" held in Chicago in 1994 one speaker stated that "socially marginalized individuals" do not "fit the religious requirements of the English speaking congregations." Theology and worship needs are different. "What we [Latinos and Latinas] represent in God's Immediate Realm has been rejected by the institutional church." Therefore, participants in the Summit were invited to respond to God's calling as they understood and appreciated it and to liberate themselves from "the assimilated status that forces us to accept the dominant ideology" (see vol. 7:135).

Spanish-speaking leaders and members in local congregations wrestled with this challenge. In seminaries some Hispanic women (Latinas) stretched the insights of liberation theology and created a "mujerista" theology that blended together the cultural, religious, and existential experiences of women (see vol. 7:136). Spanish-speaking congregations developed "immigration theology," a theology focusing upon the religious needs of individuals and communities that have traveled from somewhere else to be part of the Christian church in the United States. Their faithfulness involves seeing the transcendent in everyday life and grounding that experience in "culturally specific social contexts." Spanish-speaking local congregations promote an "immigrant folklore" made up of stories with common themes that bind diverse communities together and create "an archive of common experiences from which immigrant theology can draw" (see vol. 7:137).

The contributions to the United Church of Christ of Spanish-speaking leaders and members have been generous and deep. At the same time the Hispanic or Latino/Latina experience in the UCC has been uneven. General Synod promises have not always been kept, and some of the diverse needs of Spanish-speaking communities have been ignored. Nevertheless, the spiritual vitality and theological integrity of growing Spanish-speaking congregations remain vitally important. As the United Church of Christ seeks to move toward its vision of becoming a multiracial and multicultural church it is learning to honor the witness and faithfulness of Hispanics/Latinos and Latinas who are devoted to the church and its ministry.

In the 1970s an article in *A.D. Magazine* labeled the United Church of Christ "a beautiful, heady, exasperating mix" (of mostly English and German-Swiss traditions) (see vol. 7:53). The "mix," however, was much more complex. Volumes 1–6 of the *Living Theological Heritage of the United Church of Christ* highlight pre-1957 materials related to African Americans, American Indians, Pacific Islanders and Asian Americans, and

Hispanics. In addition, the faith and practices of German-speaking immigrants from Russia, Hungarians, and Armenians have further enriched theological traditions in the UCC.

In 1993 the General Synod "called upon the United Church of Christ in all its settings to be a true multiracial and multicultural church." This church "confesses and acts out its faith in the one sovereign God who through Jesus Christ binds in covenant faithful people of all races, ethnicities and cultures." It "embodies these diversities as gifts to the human family and rejoices in the variety of God's grace" (see vol. 7:114). In 1957 the Preamble to the UCC Constitution stated that the United Church of Christ is called into being "in order to express more fully the oneness in Christ of the churches composing it" (see vol. 7:8). Led by the Spirit, by the end of the century the founding UCC vision of "church unity" had expanded to embrace the spiritual and theological gifts of many people and many traditions. Aspiring to be a multiracial and multicultural church, led by the One who was crucified and yet lives, the United Church of Christ has developed a wider understanding of the oneness promised in the gospel. It is discovering new ways to confess with Paul, "We who are many, are one body in Christ, and individually we are members, one of another" (Romans 12:5).

Embracing Diversity

112. Responding to Change:
"Empowering Minority Churches and Caucuses"

(1977)

Scott Libbey

Scott Libbey (b. 1929) is a Congregational Christian/UCC minister educated at the University of Iowa and Chicago Theological Seminary. After serving as a pastor in Iowa (1954–59) he became director of Christian education and youth ministry for the Iowa Conference UCC (1959–61) and director of educational programming for the United Church Board for Homeland Ministries (UCBHM) (1961–69). He served as conference minister of the Nebraska Conference UCC (1969–71), conference minister of the Iowa Conference UCC (1971–85), and executive vice president of the United Church Board for World Ministries (UCBWM) (1985–94).

In 1977 when United Church of Christ national and conference leaders gathered in Florida for their annual midwinter meeting Libbey made a presentation on the responsibility of the church to the growing numbers of minority congregations in the UCC. Several pages of typewritten notes found in the UCC archives capture the essence of his message.

Source: Scott Libbey, notes and outline of "Empowerment of Minority Churches and Caucuses," presented to the Management Team, Winter Park, Florida, February 10, 1977.

Empowering Minority Churches and Caucuses

I. Introduction — The Importance of Empowerment

- The understanding of empowerment and finding routes to faithful empowerment within the Church — is one of the most important concerns we can face this week.
- Empowerment is cheapened if we think of it in sociological and organizational terms only.
- Empowerment has to do with the wholeness of being and needs, within the life of the Church, a radical theological understanding.
- Empowerment, so understood, addresses access to the necessary resources for the maturing and interrelationship of a whole personal existence.
- Empowerment relates to history, self-understanding, relationships with others, perception of self in the world, and access to pathways for acting out one's appropriate role in life.
- A deepened understanding of roots could put us in touch with many dimensions of empowerment.
- A for instance is found in the powerful line of Kizzy's "Sam isn't like us. Nobody ever told him where he come from and he don't have no dream about where he might be going."
- The Christian faith, with its understanding of humanity and creation, is foundational to our maturing in empowerment.

II. Toward Images of Empowerment

- Empowerment is a means to an end — not an end in itself.
- Empowerment is the gift of God's grace, not the product of human ingenuity.
- Empowerment for a person and people is made up of several independent and inter-related qualities of being human.
- Empowerment brings together the resources to know who we are, where we have been, where we are going — and provides pathways to share creatively in the journey.
- The resources for empowerment do not belong to one people. In the language of faith these resources belong to God and are to be responsibly available for all of his people. When one or more peoples block

the equitable access to the resources of power for others — they are, in fact, perpetrating evil upon their victims and upon themselves.

III. The Value of "Pluralism" in the United Church of Christ

- When we talk about the distinctive characteristics of the United Church of Christ we almost always mention our "pluralism."
- The assertion is that there is an advantage, a strength — found in sharing in a fellowship which has this diversity in its fellowship.
- Having pluralistic constituencies within the United Church of Christ is an asset.
- Every person's and every people's experience of the whole and of the holy is, at best, only a part of reality.
- We participate in a form of heresy when we isolate our own particular discernments and call them God.
- Any people is involved in faithlessness when (as Whites, or Blacks, or Asians, or Indians, or Hispanics, or — others) they speak and act as though their partial and parochial experience were the universal norm of reality.
- Pluralism is an asset, then, when the depth of experience of each part of the whole community is enriched by the shared witnessing and expanded experiencing of the parts. Thus we will find that the whole is more than the sum of the parts.
- Thus, in the United Church of Christ, we need each other — but each must be empowered to be in their own integrity and to be in the integrity of community.

IV. The Structural Obstacles for Empowerment within the United Church of Christ

- The United Church of Christ is composed of local churches, associations, conferences, and the General Synod.
- Our history demonstrates that an organization structured upon these parts — with such a small percentage representing the minority racial groups and churches — builds in obstacles for empowerment.
- Across the years the structure had manifested a strong tendency to keep the minority constituencies present, but relatively powerless with

decisions about mission, program, evangelism, education, social action — retained neatly within the regular structures and majorities of the church organization.

- The statistical data about the minority presence in our 'pluralism' would suggest that some four to five percent of the total delegation at the General Synod would be made up of minorities — and the structure will move ahead with the insights, experiences, and biases of the majority.
- We must build a creative tension into the life of our structure which will honor and empower the minority presence — and provide access for the whole church to mature in faithfulness.

V. Guidelines for Empowerment within the United Church of Christ

- Recognize that every racial minority church and caucus is different and do not assume that all must be related to within the life of the church within the same pattern.
- Guidelines may be identified that are a beginning clue for what constitutes the basis of empowerment.
- These guidelines would include, at least:

(1) There is empowerment present when the commitment of the United Church of Christ to a ministry with a people, is clear, consistent and intends continuity.

(2) There is empowerment when the shape and form of that ministry with a people is premised upon unalterable self-determination.

A. *Self-determination would include access to the power to identify goals and objectives, plan strategies, and effect implementation for programming — choosing and shaping the presence and participation of partners in the ministry.*

B. *Self-determination is present when there are resources available to be used at the discretion of the people.*

C. *Self-determination is present when there is a structure provided, or an organizational vehicle, some scheme of organization which will facilitate the people's own deciding and acting.*

D. *Self-determination is present when there is an acceptance and participation within the life of the whole Church of a system of mutual accountabilities.*

E. *Self-determination is present when the climate for self valuing for this people within the whole community builds their capacity to act with integrity.*

(3) There is empowerment when there is an access system for this people to participate, responsibly and appropriately, within the major structures of the United Church of Christ.

113. Confronting Change: *"Being Christian in a Pluralistic World"*

(1980)

Chicago Theological Seminary Faculty

As theological concerns increased in the early 1980s, the Office for Church Life and Leadership (OCLL) invited the faculties at several United Church of Christ seminaries to stimulate theological conversation by preparing papers on various topics. Chicago Theological Seminary was invited to write a paper on "pluralism." The faculty took the opportunity to survey local congregations in the Chicago area and prepared a candid report on the ways in which UCC members respond to questions about diversity.

Source: Chicago Theological Seminary Faculty, an excerpt from "Being Christian in a Pluralistic World," a working paper, n.d. [early 1980s], typescript, 12–13.

Being Christian in a Pluralistic World

Issues for Reflection

The practices and patterns embodied in the lives of these UCC churches will be interpreted in a variety of ways, depending upon one's criteria for evaluation. Some will seek more inclusivity; others will seek less, and still others may think the limits to diversity are appropriately embodied in the life and work of one or more of these congregations.

The group at the urban black former CC church affirmed that " . . . in Christ there is no slave, free, no male or female, no homosexual or heterosexual, no rich, no poor, no educated or uneducated, no European descent or African descent, but all are one in Christ Jesus."

As an ideal, the group in the town and country former CC congregation noted: " . . . all members of the group expressed that there should be no limit in the range of diversity [within the congregation]." This view was qualified in the discussion, but they did affirm it as an ideal.

The group at the suburban former E & R church observed:

> A great majority of the people in our church either live in the neighborhood or are attracted to the church by the way we express our faith. These two factors determine the nature of our congregation. We would hope the denomination would provide for a wide variety of diverse churches. All of these churches should be free to determine their own nature within the areas they serve.

A person in the group at the large suburban former CC church commented on her perception of the denomination:

> The UCC as a whole is very tolerant and encourages diversity. Perhaps that is why people sometimes leave the denomination — it is too open. Some people simply don't want the freedom to act; they want to be told what to do. Conversely, there are several members of our church who were under the "safe harbor" approach and who decided to break out in order to have independent and individual thinking. That's why they're here.

All of these observations point up the dilemma of the limits of diversity within a local congregation and within the denomination.

Some of the questions emerging from the consultation for the life and work of the denomination include:

1. What are the limits to theological diversity that can be or ought to be sustained in a local congregation? In the denomination as a whole?
2. What are the limits to involvement in public policy issues that can be or ought to be sustained in a local congregation? In the denomination as a whole?
3. Who speaks for the church? What are the warrants to which spokespersons may appeal for their authority? What is the appropriate style of ministerial leadership in the local congregations depicted here?
4. How can congregational life and work be structured to take account of the factors disclosed in this consultation?
5. What are the strengths and weaknesses of congregational polity in relation to the factors disclosed in this consultation?
6. What relation ought to exist between local congregations, associations, conferences, and denominational agencies and instrumentalities?
7. What can congregations that are relatively homogeneous internally contribute to addressing the social, economic, political, cultural, and religious problems created by diversity in international, national, and denominational life?
8. What do the contrasts between former CC and former E & R congregations mean for the future of the denomination?
9. What life style alternatives can or should be sustained in a local congregation? In the denomination as a whole?
10. What stance is appropriate toward other Christian bodies? Toward non-Christian religious bodies?
11. What limits do or should exist to ethnic and racial diversity within a congregation? In the denomination as a whole?

114. Seeking Change:
"A Multiracial and Multicultural Church"

(1993)

General Synod, James L. Forbes

During the 1960s African Americans became a creative presence in the United Church of Christ, leading to the establishment of the Committee on Racial Justice Now in 1963, Ministers for Racial and Social Justice (MRSJ) (later renamed Ministers for Racial, Social and Economic Justice) in 1966, and the establishment of a permanent national instrumentality — the Commission for Racial Justice (CRJ) in 1969 (see vol. 7:21). In the 1970s additional racial and ethnic advocacy groups were formed: United Black Churchmen (UCB) (later known as United Black Christians) in 1970, the Organization of Black National UCC Staff in 1971, the Council for American Indian Ministry (CAIM) in 1971 (see vol. 7:119), Pacific Islander and Asian American Ministries (PAAM) in 1974 (see vol. 7:126), and the Council for Hispanic Ministries (CHM) in 1977 (see vol. 7: 133–34).

By the early 1980s there was a growing awareness of shared agendas and an increasing desire for all of these groups to work together. Therefore, in 1983 the General Synod created the Council for Racial and Ethnic Ministries (COREM). COREM provided a central forum where racial and ethnic organizations and special-interest groups could develop their common agenda, collaborate with program and mission bodies, discern ways to make their gifts available to the church, and advocate for shared goals.

Sources: Statement of Christian Conviction of the Proposed Pronouncement Calling the United Church of Christ to Be a Multiracial and Multicultural Church, *GS Minutes 1993,* 39–40. James L. Forbes, an excerpt from a Bible study, "A Church for All People: Becoming a Multiracial and Multicultural Church" (Cleveland: United Church of Christ, 1995), 5–6.

As the years went by the rapidly changing demographics of the country and the increasing diversity of UCC congregations, alongside the longstanding theological conviction that the church is called to be "one" in Jesus Christ, pressed the United Church of Christ to develop a new understanding of itself. In 1993 a General Synod pronouncement "Calling the United Church of Christ to be a Multiracial and Multicultural Church" was passed, naming theological and sociological realities that were challenging the United Church of Christ to become a multiracial and multicultural church, accessible to all.

James L. Forbes (b. 1935) is an African American Baptist/UCC minister educated at Howard University, Union Theological Seminary in New York, and Colgate Rochester Divinity School. After serving pastorates in Virginia and North Carolina (1960–75), including campus ministry at Virginia Union University, Forbes returned to Union Theological Seminary in New York to teach homiletics (1976–89). In 1989 he became the senior minister of Riverside Church in New York City. Forbes led Bible study at the 1995 General Synod, reminding Synod delegates that the church described in Acts 2 was already a "multiracial and multicultural church."

Statement of Christian Conviction of the Proposed Pronouncement Calling the United Church of Christ to Be a Multiracial and Multicultural Church

A. The Nineteenth General Synod calls upon the United Church of Christ in all its settings to be a true multiracial and multicultural church. A multiracial and multicultural church confesses and acts out its faith in the one sovereign God who through Jesus Christ binds in covenant faithful people of all races, ethnicities and cultures. A multiracial and multicultural church embodies these diversities as gifts to the human family and rejoices in the variety of God's grace.

B. The Nineteenth General Synod recognizes the following as marks of a multiracial and multicultural church:

   1. CONFESSIONAL: A multiracial and multicultural church is called by God through Jesus Christ to acknowledge and confess its sins of racism and to repent and refrain from all acts of racial discrimination and bigotry.

2. THEOLOGICAL: A multiracial and multicultural church affirms Christian unity while celebrating the theological and liturgical richness that arises from its racial and ethnic diversity.

3. MISSION: A multiracial and multicultural church is called to participate in God's mission of doing justice, loving kindness and walking humbly with God through Christ in all communities with all peoples in all places.

4. INCLUSIVE MINISTRY: A multiracial and multicultural church uses an inclusive and equitable procedure for the calling, placement and standing of ministers in the church while providing equal access to employment in all settings of the church: locally, regionally, nationally, globally and ecumenically.

5. RACIAL JUSTICE STRUCTURE: A multiracial and multicultural church has a full-time national racial justice agency that seeks to coordinate programmatic strategies and involve the entire membership of the church in making racial justice a reality in church and society.

6. MONITORING BODY: A multiracial and multicultural church has a racial and ethnic body to monitor all settings of the church on issues of racial and ethnic inclusivity in the ministry, mission and programs.

7. PROPHETIC ADVOCACY: A multiracial and multicultural church engages in effective prophetic advocacy and public policy development on the issues of racial, social, economic and environmental justice with particular concern as to how these issues impact the quality of life of people of color communities.

8. MULTILINGUAL: A multiracial and multicultural church supports the development and dissemination of multilingual resources for use throughout the church and facilitates the translation of all official church documents such as the constitution and bylaws, creeds or statements of faith into languages that are spoken fluently in the local churches.

9. AFFIRMATIVE ACTION COMMITMENT: A multiracial and multicultural church affirms a commitment to accomplish specific affirmative action goals and objectives.

10. CHRISTIAN EDUCATION, EVANGELISM, AND NEW CHURCH DEVELOPMENT: A multiracial and multicultural church develops, supports and implements strategies concerning evangelism and new church development in racial and ethnic communities; challenges and

invites every member of local congregations to move beyond traditional comfort zones in living out God's multiracial and multicultural mandate; and prepares Christian education resources relevant to the diversity of racial and ethnic Christian faith traditions and cultures within the church.

11. SEMINARY TRAINING: A multiracial and multicultural church encourages related seminaries to develop curricula and educational programs for the training of ministers to include awareness and knowledge concerning the diversity of cultural heritages and theological traditions of the racial and ethnic constituencies of the church.

12. FAITHFUL AND EQUITABLE STEWARDSHIP: A multiracial and multicultural church plans and implements strategies to help ensure and promote a faithful and equitable stewardship and sharing of the financial resources of the church in regard to the empowerment of all local churches, and in particular the empowerment of local racial and ethnic congregations that have been marginalized due to racial discrimination in society.

Bible Study
The Origins of the Vision:
Acts 2:1–21 [Pentecost]

The Commentary and Implications from the text. . . .

The strangeness of our agenda, as a group of people coming together in 1957, was that you were gone [*sic*] to come together pulling people from various heritages and that you were gone to be committed to being a church for all people. The major motif in the organization will be "uniting." That was simply smart on your part because you understood that Jesus had made very few requests for Himself. But at the end he did put in one or two requests: "Lord make them one that the world might believe that you have sent me." So, you very smartly understood that if you were engaged in fulfilling the last will and testament of Jesus, Jesus would find some way to get you funded and sustained into your organizational possibilities.

The United Church of Christ was as radical in what it was attempting to be and do as were the events in this text. Something moved deeply like a mighty burning fire, not characterized by open forest fire, but the controlled slow combustion of the determination to just keep on keeping on until the accumulated wisdom of a tradition would cause the church to fulfill the promise that Jesus had made, "that we might be one." As I look at the text, I realize that everybody there was filled with the Holy Spirit.

Now, I understand that anyone who is in the body of Christ is indeed anointed with the Spirit. Therefore, from my Pentecostal background, I affirm that as any one of my Pentecostal brothers or sisters is filled with the Spirit, so are you! That means your heart has been made available to the living Christ. You were willing to accept the invitation into divine human communion. In a way appropriate to who you are, you realize and accept the Spirit. God has honored you with the Spirit by bringing you this far from the very beginning, as a design in the mind of God, "in my mother's womb you were knitting me together."

A little later on, everybody heard people speaking in their own language. Namely, divine presence made communication possible across the various boundaries of our language heritage. That's true. We've been fed by many different kinds of people. What we in the United Church of Christ are trying to do is so weird. I like to remind you that this Multiracial/Multicultural Pronouncement is a most aberrant form of social consciousness if you measure it statistically. Most people don't really try to go across various boundaries. So you must be drunk to be trying to do this. But Peter stands up and says, "Indeed, these are not drunk as you suppose, for it is only nine o'clock in the morning" It's too early.

But God said, in the last days I'm gone to raise up the people and they're gone to be together across all sorts of boundaries and barriers. In those days, in community, all God's people will experience the Spirit operating through them in regards to God's larger plan. Demographics notwithstanding, sons and daughters, young men and old men, both men and women, I will pour out my Spirit even to those who have been disenfranchised. They will be bearers of the evidence of my Spirit and they will all be able to call upon the name of the Lord and shall be brought into wholeness.

That's what I think the statement is about. The Multiracial/Multicultural Pronouncement is an attempt of the United Church of Christ to live into its origin in the first place, insofar as we are part of the Christian faith. This attempt is thoroughly biblical.

Receiving the Gifts of African Americans

115. Black National Anthem: *"Lift Every Voice and Sing"*

(1921)

James Weldon Johnson

James Weldon Johnson (1871–1938) was an African American poet, lawyer, educator, and diplomat. He earned two degrees at Atlanta University and became a public school teacher and principal in Jacksonville, Florida. He was secretary of the National Association for the Advancement of Colored People (NAACP) for fourteen years. As a university teacher and prolific writer he is known for a novel, The Autobiography of an Ex-Colored Man *(1912); a collection of poetry,* God's Trombones: Seven Negro Sermons in Verse *(1927); and* Along this Way: The Autobiography of James Weldon Johnson *(1933).*

Johnson and his brother, John Rosamond Johnson (1873–1954), wrote the words and music for "Lift Every Voice" for schoolchildren to sing at a celebration on Abraham Lincoln's birthday, February 12, 1921. It later became the official song for the NAACP and is considered by many African Americans to be the "Black National Anthem."

"Lift Every Voice and Sing"

Lift every voice and sing, till earth and heaven ring,
ring with the harmonies of liberty;
Let our rejoicing rise, high as the listening skies,
let it resound loud as the rolling sea.
Sing a song full of the faith that the harsh past has taught us,
Sing a song full of the hope that the present has brought us;
Facing the rising sun of our new day begun,
let us march on till victory is won.

Stony the road we trod, bitter the chastening rod,
felt in the days when hope unborn had died;
Yet with a steady beat, have not our weary feet,
come to the place for which our people sighed?
We have come over a way that with tears has been watered,
We have come, treading our path through the blood of the slaughtered,
Out from the gloomy past, till now we stand at last
where the white gleam of our bright star is cast.

God of our weary years, God of our silent tears,
God who has brought us thus far on the way;
God, who by your might, led us into the light,
keep us forever in the path, we pray.
Lest our feet stray from the places, our God, where we met you,
Lest our hearts, drunk with the wine of the world, forget you;
Shadowed beneath your hand, may we forever stand,
true to our God, true to our native land.

116. Black Theology:

"The Unfinished Agenda"

(1989)

Barbara J. Essex

Barbara J. Essex (b. 1951) is an African American UCC minister educated at Northwestern University and Garrett-Evangelical Theological Seminary. She served on the staff of Trinity United Church of Christ, Chicago (1979–83) (see vol. 7:118). After doing interim ministry in Chicago (1985–86) she became secretary for racial and ethnic ministries for the United Church Board for Homeland Ministries (UCBHM) (1986–91). During the 1990s she was an adjunct faculty member at Hartford Seminary, an executive for the Presbytery of Chicago, an instructor at the American School, Lansing, Illinois, and administrative director for a national leadership program sponsored by Hartford Seminary and Pacific School of Religion. In 1999 she became minister and coordinator of community life at PSR. She is the author of Bad Girls of the Bible: Exploring Women of Questionable Virtue *(1999).*

Essex explains the connection between black theology and the Amistad *incident in the nineteenth century. She argues that black theology is "the philosophical framework for examining the past, present, and future of Black African-Americans."*

Source: Barbara J. Essex, an excerpt from "The Unfinished Agenda: One Continual Cry: Aspects of Black Theology in the Context of the Amistad Rebellion," *New Conversations* (Winter–Spring 1989): 45–46.

The Unfinished Agenda

> *"Wicked people want to make us slaves but the Great God who made all things raise up friends for Mendi people, he gave us Mr. Adams that he may make me free. . . . "* (Kali, *Amistad* captive)

This statement by the African captive, Kali, is the one continual cry of African-Americans since arriving upon these shores as slaves. The *Amistad* incident highlights some important aspects of modern Black Theology. The *Amistad* captives wanted to be free and to return to their homeland. In the midst of their captivity, they recognized their common lot, and they knew the importance of working together despite their differences in language and backgrounds. The reality of the slave trade made them sisters and brothers and unified them in a special way.

The Black American experience is the odyssey of a people and a great adventure of the human spirit. No American can understand her/himself or this country without a serious confrontation with the multifaceted images of Black life. The notion of a Black Theology is not a creation of the twentieth century. Indeed, efforts to evoke loyalty, pride, identity and spirituality date back to the very beginnings of the slave trade. Sengbe and his fellow captives expressed in poignant terms the cry of Africans in the American Diaspora: liberation!

Even before their actions, Blacks were living the roots of Black Theology.

Black Theology is the philosophical framework for examining the past, present, and future of Black African-Americans in the United States. It is rooted in the Black Church. This discussion is based on the following assumptions:

- that the "Black Church" refers to the institutions within the Christian faith;
- that each indigenous group must define and refine its own theology; that is, any group that is spatially and/or socially isolated must write its own theology;
- that Christianity is essentially a religion of redemption and liberation;
- that Christianity is fundamentally different from white American Protestantism;
- that theology is shaped and influenced by an understanding of culture and history; that is, there is a historical context for theology; and
- that theologizing is dynamic because God continues to reveal God's self in history.

"Black Theology," as a methodology, implies inherent unity and oneness. However, it is not a monolith; its perspectives run the gamut from ultra-liberal to ultra-conservative.

In the midst of the diversity, however, there is an undergirding unity. Black Theology is God-talk rooted in the realities of slavery, racism, and discrimination. Black Theology is the attempt to articulate and clarify the African-American community's understanding of God's presence and promise in the midst of a dehumanizing experience. In addition, it is an attempt to explicate the goal to which God is directing creation. Black Theology seeks to answer two questions:

- What was God doing while Blacks were undergoing slavery? and,
- What is God doing now as Blacks struggle for equality, justice, parity, power, and identity?

By necessity, Black Theology has a double thrust; it looks *back* to historical events for meanings, and it looks *forward* to the future with its creative possibilities. Black Theology seeks to understand life's truths in the midst of life's paradoxes. It is not an end unto itself; rather, it is faith seeking understanding and understanding requestioning faith.

Black Christians have always sought to expound, interpret, and apply the content of the Christian faith to the specific context of oppression in the United States. Because slaves were not permitted to learn to read or write, Black God-talk, until recently, has been largely an oral theology embedded in songs, prayers, and sermons. Their meanings are rooted in both African *and* American soil. . . .

117. African American Faithfulness: *"The Power of the Faith Community"*

(1997)

Leslie Carole Taylor

Leslie Carole Taylor (b. 1959) is an African American UCC minister educated at Grinnell College and Chicago Theological Seminary. Before seminary she worked in communications in Detroit, Michigan (1981–84), and in the late 1980s she was part of the national UCC staff for the Coordinating Center for Women (CCW) (1988–90) and the United Church Board for Homeland Ministries (UCBHM) (1990–97). Since 1997 she has served various Ohio churches in interim ministry and been spiritual director for Epiphany Ministries of Ohio, Inc. working with incarcerated and institutionalized youth. When she wrote "The Power of the Faith Community" (1997), sharing out of her personal faith journey, she was pastor of Grace United Church of Christ, Columbus, Ohio.

The Power of the Faith Community: An African American Perspective

A Living Faith

The debate over slavery and religion between white people and the impact of religion on black people are major aspects of the social and cultural experience of slavery. If slaves could be baptized, then they were human

Source: Leslie Carole Taylor, an excerpt from "The Power of the Faith Community: An African American Perspective," in *Habits of Faith* (Cleveland: United Church Board for Homeland Ministries, 1997), 50–53.

beings after all; if they were less than human they should not be brought into the "kingdom of God." So as slaves were baptized or got access to the Bible (which, of course, meant they could read), they took on a new social and cultural identity. In addition to worshiping with their masters in some cases, slaves were able to express their identity in developing their own forms of worship and devotion.

Thus, the church and religion provided the main basis for the independent development of black social life: (1) to deal with the Bible, someone, usually an African American minister, had to read; (2) to deal with religion meant that African American people developed and/or reinforced values that dictated forms of family life, interpersonal relations, and a general sense of justice. In other words, religion was the moral basis for the development of the first forms of education and indigenous forms and values regarding family life.

Many African Americans mark the beginning of their Christian pilgrimage with baptism or, in the case of infant baptism, with the day of their confirmation. Because many African Americans come to the United Church of Christ through other denominations, it is important to recognize the role of the church as the teacher of faith in the beginning of life. Church is more than the building. Church for African Americans is a part of our whole life, individually and collectively/communally. Our faith life is a part of our life at home, at work, at play.

Jesus loves me! This I know, for the Bible tells me so.
Little ones to Him belong; they are weak, but He is strong.

Many children learn at the kitchen table the first lesson of faith — to be thankful to God for all the blessings received. The first prayer we learn is a blessing for a meal; the second, the prayer before bedtime. The message, spoken or unspoken, is to begin and end the day in prayer. One of the first songs children learn is "Jesus Loves Me!" This daily message of unconditional love is repeated on Sunday morning in Sunday school and in morning worship where the Word is heard, prayers are prayed, the songs of the faith are sung in call and response.

It is in church that children see their parents in a different light. It is in church that janitors and domestic workers become trustees or deacons and provide Communion preparation. It is in church that the children see their schoolteachers are also the teachers of the faith, that the music teacher and the choir director are the same person. The children see their self-image affirmed and learn the subtle message that no matter what the "world" says about the role their parents play in society, in church they and their parents are someone special. In church, they are the children of God, and no one can tell them anything different. In turn, the children learn their first leadership skills in church — singing, acting in pageants, performing in music recitals, public speaking, etc. Children are affirmed. In church, self-esteem is raised each time society tries to tear it down. In church we can expect dignity. In church we are special.

Sometimes I feel discouraged and think my work's in vain,
but then the Holy Spirit revives my soul again.
There is a balm in Gilead to make the wounded whole.
There is a balm in Gilead to heal the sin-sick soul.

My Grandmother Taylor always told me, "Pray for what you need and want or something better. You never want to limit God's blessings or the opportunities God will place in your life." As we grow into adulthood, there are moments when life seems to be more than we can bear, when our Christian values seem meaningless in our day-to-day lives. We are faced with racism — overt, institutional, and internalized racism. We are sometimes faced with economic difficulties, with unemployment or underemployment. Our family members may be confronted by chemical dependency or by physical or mental health concerns. We may be faced with the death of a child, a sibling, or a parent. No matter what it is in life, we all face difficult moments. The question is, what makes the difference? How do we hold on to our faith in these moments of crisis?

I believe the answer lies in the messages we learned as children growing up in the church. Just as we learned to be thankful for the blessings we received, in the same way we learn we should not complain about hardships. God is with us in the midst of our storms. As children, we heard the stories of the faith, repeated week in and week out — the stories of liberation, the stories of God's intervention, the stories of answered prayer. We recall those stories and learn from the elders how to stand by the God who has never let us down. That may be fairly easy for many church members who grew up in the church — those with an unquestioning faith.

What about those of us who came to "the throne of grace" as adults? Where is our pool of spiritual resources from which we can draw? I maintain the pool is the shared experience of the Gospel.

For adult converts, it was generally a crisis which brought most of us to the church in the first place. It is through the power of shared concerns expressed in prayer that the healing begins. It is through the sharing of experiences with the saints — the members new and not-so-new, younger and older. It is in the power of the stories of how God has been present with our ancestors, our elders, and each of us. It is through the tears of the weary that strength to go on is realized. It is through those sighs too deep for human words that the prayers of the faithful are able to come forth. It is through the music of the faith — the spirituals, the hymns, the anthems, the gospel music. It is through the music and the prayers that the troubles of the world and the burdens we face are given voice. It is in the music of the church and the way in which the Holy Spirit moves in and through us that we find the courage and strength to face tomorrow.

When we come to the church, we are not looking for the answer to the question, "What happens when we die?" Certainly, that is one question, but I maintain it is not the question. The question I think most people come to have answered in church is, "How do I survive from day to day? How do I face the rising costs of living and the shrinking amount found in my paycheck? How do I face the violence in my home? My neighborhood? My city? How do I cope when everything around me tells me I am destined to fail?" These are the questions. The answers are found in listening carefully to the shared wisdom of the community of faith, in the lived experience of the elders. The answers are found in the Word of God, for it is a word that can be trusted. It is in the church that we share each other's burdens and celebrate each other's joys.

The church provides a venue for leadership development, survival support, and active resistance for political change. When African Americans read the stories of the Exodus, of oppression and persecution, we read our story. It was the power of faith, prayer, and song that allowed nine young African American teenagers to integrate Central High School in Little Rock, Arkansas. The stories and practice of the faith are what sustained civil rights leaders like Rosa Parks, the Rev. Dr. Martin Luther King, Jr., and the Rev. Dr. Andrew Young. Andrew Young, a UCC clergyperson and civil rights leader, tells the story of a march that was supposed to take place one day. Dr. Martin Luther King, Jr., was in jail. Everyone gathered at a church to prepare to march to the jail. When they arrived in front of the jail, they were met by a sea of red fire trucks, attack dogs, and police officers with billy clubs drawn. Dr. Young stood looking at the impenetrable wall of men, machines, and animals. One of the older women in the group of protesters suddenly suggested they all get on their knees to pray. The group began to kneel and pray. Someone started to sing "I will not be moved." Just as Moses used his staff to part the Red Sea, this song and these prayers parted the sea of red fire trucks and the protest march could continue, without any violence. That is nothing short of the power of God. In the face of the impossible, God is always able.

It was the power of faith, prayer, and song that provided strength, courage, and guidance to all the people, well known and little known, who struggle every day to bring about justice.

118. Vital Congregational Life:

Trinity UCC

(1971–81)

Trinity United Church of Christ on the south side of Chicago began when several small struggling black congregations merged in 1962. By the late 1960s, however, it was down to eighty-seven members. A small core of lay members, under the leadership of Vallmer E. Jordan, drew up a statement of purpose to guide them in selecting a new minister.

Jeremiah A. Wright Jr. (b. 1941) became the pastor of Trinity United Church of Christ in 1972. Wright is an African American UCC minister educated at Virginia Union University, Howard University, University of Chicago Divinity School, and United Theological Seminary of the Twin Cities. Under his leadership Trinity UCC has developed a strong understanding of itself as "unashamedly Black and unapologetically Christian." Inspired and empowered by this creed, in 1981 it drafted, discussed, and adopted a "Black Value System." Trinity UCC maintains a dynamic worship program, attracts strong leadership, and serves the needs of thousands of African Americans as the largest congregation in the United Church of Christ.

Source: "Mission Statement" and "Black Value System" from Trinity United Church of Christ, Chicago [from website].

Trinity UCC Mission Statement

Trinity United Church of Christ has been called by God to be a congregation that is not ashamed of the gospel of Jesus Christ and that does not apologize for its African roots! As a congregation of baptized believers, we are called to be agents of liberation not only for the oppressed, but for all of God's family. We, as a church family, acknowledge that we will, building on this affirmation of "who we are" and "whose we are," call men, women, boys and girls to the liberating love of Jesus Christ, inviting them to become a part of the church universal, responding to Jesus' command that we go into all the world and make disciples!

We are called out to be "a chosen people" that pays no attention to socio-economic or educational backgrounds. We are made up of the highly educated and the uneducated. Our congregation is a combination of the haves and the have-nots; the economically disadvantaged, the under-class, the unemployed and the employable.

The fortunate who are among us combine forces with the less fortunate to become agents of change for God who is not pleased with America's economic mal-distribution!

W. E. B. DuBois indicated that the problem in the 20th century was going to be the problem of the color line. He was absolutely correct. Our job as servants of God is to address that problem and eradicate it in the name of Him who came for the whole world by calling all men, women, boys and girls to Christ.

Black Value System

Trinity United Church of Christ adopted the Black Value System in 1981. It was written by lay persons of Trinity under the leadership of Vallmer Jordan.

We believe in the following 12 precepts and covenantal statements:

1. Commitment to God
2. Commitment to the Black Community
3. Commitment to the Black Family
4. Dedication to the Pursuit of Education
5. Dedication to the Pursuit of Excellence
6. Adherence to the Black Work Ethic
7. Commitment to Self-Discipline and Self-Respect
8. Disavowal of the Pursuit of "Middleclassness"
9. Pledge to make the fruits of all developing and acquired skills available to the Black Community
10. Pledge to make the fruits of all developing acquired skills available for strengthening and supporting Black institutions
11. Pledge allegiance to all Black leadership who espouse and embrace the Black Value System
12. Personal commitment to embracement of the Black Value System

Receiving the Gifts of American Indians

119. Council for American Indian Ministry: *American Indian Sunday*

(1971)

Mrs. Dale [Adele] Little Dog

Mrs. Dale [Adele] Little Dog (b. 1926) lives on the Standing Rock Sioux reservation. She is a member of Elk Horn United Church of Christ in Little Eagle, South Dakota. Little Dog was a representative of the Council for American Indian Ministry (CAIM) at the 1971 General Synod. In that year, the United Church of Christ recognized the Council for American Indian Ministry (CAIM) as an independent agency to oversee "the field of Indian work" within the United Church of Christ. As part of a plenary "Unitary Program Presentation" on racial justice, various speakers from African American, American Indian, and Spanish-speaking communities spoke to the General Synod. Following a short film clip from the movie The Last of the Comanches, *Little Dog requests the General Synod to designate the Sunday before Thanksgiving as American Indian Sunday.*

Source: [Adele] Little Dog, Little Eagle, South Dakota, requesting support for American Indian Sunday, *GS Minutes 1971*, 176–77.

An American Indian Perspective

For many Americans the only Indian they ever see is a dead Indian on the late TV show. I am Mrs. Dale Little Dog, a member of the Standing Rock Sioux Tribe from Little Eagle, South Dakota, representing the national Council for American Indian Ministry. We may be the original Americans but we are also the invisible Americans, being tucked away in remote areas called reservations and only paraded before the public in horse operas and tourist centers selling blankets.

The image of the American Indian as a dust-biting savage is changing. We are not of the past, playing that assigned role, for today the American Indian has the internal fortitude to stand up for what he wants. The scene today is dominated by grim statistics, the most shocking in the nation revealing socio-economic and political injustices. We Indians often hear the words "Indian problems." Most of these problems have been created for us by others, as in the cases of alcoholism, family disorganization and juvenile delinquency. With the introduction of certain beverages on our reservation and the destruction of our extended family relationships, these problems arose.

We have been the objects of systematic oppression, systematic destruction, subtle discrimination, and exploitation to an extent that has been unbearable. For generations we have been taught in our educational system to completely ignore our way of life because it is different from the dominant culture which we are coerced to learn in a comparatively short period of time. The attempts to missionize, civilize and assimilate the American Indian into another culture has met with many obstacles, mainly the American Indian himself, who has resisted endlessly to join the melting pot, to join the mainstream, to join the great society.

We must be aware that most of his cultural bearings are in direct conflict with that of the dominant culture.

For example, his value of co-operation conflicts with competition. His value of generosity conflicts with that of rugged individualism. Other comparisons can be made, but the most significant conflict, I believe, concerns that of the value of respect for the wisdom of elders. This has been replaced by different decision-makers, Indian experts and Indian studies programs, all initiated by others. The greed for land base and the intolerance for Indian culture combined into one has driven the American Indian into an intensively developed realm of poverty from which he has never recovered. We have so often experienced programs that were developed, implemented and evaluated for us with a continuous, unbroken narrative of policies and promises disorganizing, contradictory, duplicating, and absolutely unrealistic, often changing abruptly, before we were aware of their existence; or to go further, ineffective programs continued endlessly, disguised by terminology we fail to understand, to the extent that allocations were completely wasted.

The exclusion of the American Indian from the management of his own affairs has been illuminated in the United Church of Christ. The organization of the Council for American Indian Ministry and its auxiliary organizations is indeed a tremendous historical step. It is time we embarked upon a completely new course of action to ensure racial justice; however, we must include other things, such as representation, or should I say more representation, on the Executive Council. I am very happy to say that the paternalistic approach which prevailed for generations, encouraging complete dependency, robbing of dignity, is on its way out — not without resistance, however, on our more local levels. Our needs are many, with leadership and economic development high on our priority list. Like many other minority groups in America we must interact with the great society, but the interaction will continue to be at a low ebb if our leadership and our economy are not developed. Special projects for these must be developed and initiated, implemented by the Indians themselves for they know their needs. This will help create a better understanding, a better relationship for all of us. I wish not to impose an impossible task or an impossible request but I believe that concentrated efforts on the part of Indian leaders and their people and people like you in the audience who are not appalled at the enormity of the task will assist us in developing leadership and economy.

Every Christian has a service to perform. Let's find that particular task, accept it and prepare for it and do it for the glory of God and his Kingdom. Your willingness to involve the American Indian has been exhibited. Your willingness to treat him as an equal is indicated by your past devotion and support, yet the request must come in the behalf of the Council for American Indian Ministry and our people, a group of people constantly searching for identity: I request that the Sunday before Thanksgiving of each year be designated as American Indian Sunday so that we would receive special funding for special projects.

120. Supporting Indigenous Peoples:

Pronouncement on Ministry with Indians

(1987)

General Synod

The General Synod of the United Church of Christ has repeatedly spoken out on issues related to American Indians. After recognizing the Council for American Indian Ministry (CAIM) in 1971, it reaffirmed its commitment to CAIM and authorized financial support in 1973, 1975, and 1979 through a special American Indian Sunday offering, and later through the Neighbors in Need offering. Unfortunately, the situation of indigenous peoples did not improve. Finally, the General Synod passed a comprehensive pronouncement, "A United Church of Christ Ministry with Indians" (1987), and a detailed "Proposal for Action" (1987). At the end of the pronouncement the General Synod made a commitment to four specific "directions for a ministry to, with, and from American Indians." The church would (1) develop new indigenous Indian churches; (2) focus on faith development, children and youth, clergy recruitment, community service, and alcoholism/substance abuse; (3) offer continuing education and support for pastors; and (4) create alliances to support political, economic, and cultural justice for Indians.

The pronouncement was followed by two additional votes: First, a "Proposal for Action" that spelled out an implementation strategy, including funding and the role of other instrumentalities. And second, "A Statement to the United Church of Christ and the Indian Community of the United Church of Christ Expressing Penitence and the Hope of Reconciliation" (1987). In adopting this last statement the General Synod

---

Source: "Excerpts from the Pronouncement: A United Church of Christ Ministry with Indians," *GS Minutes 1987,* 40–41.

recognized its "responsibility—as part of the dominant culture—for the ongoing injustice and religious imperialism that have been so disruptive of the inherent values of Indian life and culture." The General Synod sought "reconciliation," affirming its support of indigenous peoples in their "struggle to reclaim cultural traditions."

A United Church of Christ Ministry with Indians

Summary

A growing concern over both the substance of the United Church of Christ mission with regard to Indian people and issues, and the mechanisms for implementing the mission led to a thorough review by the Executive Council. The situation of United Church of Christ Indian local churches was deteriorating, ordained pastoral leadership was becoming rare, and it was not clear what the major policy goals were. Additionally, the justice issues were not being adequately addressed, particularly in view of the apparent backing away by the federal government from its obligations originally defined by various treaties and other agreements. This Pronouncement reaffirms the General Synod's commitment to a mission with Indian people, identifies basic policy goals for the mission, affirms support for Indian justice issues through treaty observance and meeting of basic needs, and identifies the Council for American Indian Ministry as the primary body (the whole United Church of Christ is responsible) to plan for Indian ministry in the United Church of Christ.

Background

The Executive Council consultation reviewed the history of The Council for American Indian Ministry from its beginning. The twenty-three Indian churches now have become twenty-four with the addition of All Nations Indian United Church of Christ in Minneapolis, an Indian New Initiatives in Church Development new church. In reviewing the situation in the communities where United Church of Christ Indian congregations are located, the Consultation found that reservation conditions remained about the same, while serious attrition has worked away at the churches.

The following observations attempt to provide a context for the United Church of Christ mission with American Indians today.

1. Unemployment in the communities where our United Church of Christ congregations are located ranges usually from 70% to 90%. Rural poverty, without economic development, produces a despair that leads to other problems.

2. Alcoholism, and other forms of substance abuse (including inhalant abuse), has touched every family, and about 90% of individuals in the communities. Children are becoming addicted sometimes as early as their fourth or fifth year.

3. The Spiritual devastation that resulted from the multi-dimensioned experience of genocide which has been followed by policies and laws that continue oppression created a despair, a spiritual vacuum, high suicide rates (particularly among children and teens), and a seriously low sense of self-worth. Indian reaction has been a slow, but authentic, renaissance to value Indian traditions, and to indigenize non-native religions.

4. There are concerted efforts by varieties of groups receiving support from various governmental agencies to abrogate treaties, hunting and fishing agreements, Indian health programs and other parts of decisions made with the federal government in exchange for land through treaties. Jurisdictional disputes have developed. Some long-time observers diagnose a growing racism in and around the Indian communities of the reservations. In some places the conflict has not been far from open violence.

5. The heritage of the mission movement which founded the Indian churches has a profound ambiguity. While it did leave the heritage of the faith, it used what has been described as a "hardware" approach, insisting that Euro-North American culture was a necessary part of the Gospel and so Indian ways had to go. Leadership development that could lead to self-determination has never been a component of the Indian mission. From the 1960s with a few notable exceptions, most congregations have had to rely for leadership on lay licensed ministers or clergy (sometimes not ordained) from other denominations. Ordained clergy who served were usually overcome by the isolation and hopelessness of the setting, and they left after short pastorates. The exclusive use of licensed ministers has become a strategy of attrition.

6. The communities where our United Church of Christ congregations are located may be the only authentic poverty culture for a whole people in our church. The combination of all the above means there is no such thing as a self-supporting Indian congregation. Indian people

are prisoners of their reservation environment, bound by the unbreakable bindings of Bureau of Indian Affairs (BIA) regulations and laws. Poverty, leadership issues, deep-seated conflicts within the congregations all point to the need for an effective intervention in the present policies.

7. The legal history between the United States and the various Indian nations is much too complex and long to attempt to summarize here. Indians do not have many of the rights guaranteed through the Constitution. The Tee-Hit-Ton Doctrine illustrates the legal issue. "In the Tee-Hit-Ton Doctrine, the Supreme Court ruled that the United States government is free to take or confiscate Indian land without due process of law and without fair-market compensation."[1]

Biblical, Theological and Ethical Rationale

> I have seen the affliction of my people who are in Egypt, and have heard their cry because of their taskmasters; I know their sufferings, and I have come down to deliver them out of the hand of the Egyptians, and to bring them up out of that land to a good and broad land, a land flowing with milk and honey. . . . " (Exodus 3:7–8)

> When he saw the crowds, he had compassion for them, because they were harassed and helpless, like sheep without a shepherd. Then he said to his disciples, "The harvest is plentiful, but the laborers are few; pray therefore the Lord of the harvest to send laborers into his harvest." (Matthew 9:36–38)

The text from Exodus may seem ironic, for this text has been used to begin a series of historical analogies which eventually led to a justification of manifest destiny. Manifest destiny became the heretical rationalization which led to the genocide of the Native people, their culture and their ways. And yet, it also describes the experience of Indian people today, suffering under the taskmasters of the dominant culture which expects assimilation, of the law which finds ways to approve of taking land and other benefits away from Indian people, and of the grinding boots of poverty and racism. Deliverance from all of these is the imminent hope of Indian people.

Several contemporary theologies have affirmed that God has preferential option for the poor and the oppressed. If that be the case, God must have a deep preference for the American Indian people today. Just as Christ

1. Robert T. Coulter, "The Moral Crisis of the Law," *Church and Society* (January/February 1985): 26.

has compassion for the crowds, the Church must have a compassion for Indian folk who appear harassed, hopeless and helpless. The call is as loud today as ever: there is overwhelming work to be done in Indian communities, but there are too few laborers. Christ calls, and the United Church of Christ is in a position to provide a response.

"Thus a scan of Jewish history in the Old Testament reveals a dialectic between . . . elect status as God's chosen people and humble awareness of one's solidarity with the entire human family."[2] The contemporary church struggles with the same dialectic between feeling itself to be the body of the elect, yet constantly called to the depth and breadth of its mission with American Indians. The theological implications of the genocide have scarcely been assessed — by those in the dominant culture.

Indian people need the love of God's creativity, the United Church of Christ has the resources to renew the mission, and the people of this nation have serious theological work to do.

Statement of Christian Conviction

The General Synod reaffirms the commitment of the United Church of Christ to American Indian Ministries. The General Synod calls for instrumentalities and conferences:

- to affirm support for Indian congregations,
- to provide for competent and faithful pastoral ministries,
- to support the observance of Indian treaties.

The General Synod requests all parts of the United Church of Christ to urge the federal government to maintain its historic obligations to the Indian people, particularly in relation to Indian health, and to support the fight for justice by the various Indian nations as specific issues emerge from time to time that threaten their integrity, and due process is ignored. . . .

2. Donald Senior and Carroll Stuhlmueller, *The Biblical Foundation for Mission* (Maryknoll, N.Y.: Orbis Books, 1983), 320.

121. Preaching:

Servanthood

(1993)

Rosemary McCombs Maxey

Rosemary McCombs Maxey (b. 1945) is a member of the Muscogee (Creek) Nation of Oklahoma and the first American Indian woman ordained in the United Church of Christ (1987). She was educated at Oklahoma Baptist University, Southwestern Baptist Theological Seminary, and Lancaster Theological Seminary. She served as pastor of Mt. Tabor United Church of Christ, Rocky Ridge, Maryland (1986–97). Maxey is a recipient of the Office for Church in Society (OCIS) Just Peace Award (1993) and the Antoinette Brown Award (1997). Throughout her ministry she has worked diligently for Indian peoples in the UCC and been deeply involved in the Council for American Indian Ministry (CAIM), serving as its chairperson (1998–2000). Maxey preached "God's Gift: Welcomed as Servants" based on John 13:5–15 at the 1993 General Synod in St. Louis, Missouri.

Source: Rosemary McCombs Maxey, "God's Gift: Welcomed as Servants," sermon at General Synod, July 19, 1993 [typescript provided by the author].

God's Gift: Welcomed as Servants

Scripture: John 13:5–15

The Confirmation Class of 1993 of the Mt. Tabor United Church of Christ in Rocky Ridge, Maryland, sat across the table from me last Winter as we began Unit III of *Confirming Our Faith.* Using the tried and true pedagogical method of hunt and read, we propped our heads on our hands and looked for verses of scripture that answers the question, "Who is Jesus Christ?" Reading from page 66, I said, "Jesus lived his whole life in service to others, even giving his life on the cross. Let us look at the distinctive way in which Jesus served."

"Ho-hum," they said.

They read the scripture that we have just heard and I presented a concise summation to these two, young, white, male soon-to-be patriarchs of the church who passively sat before me. "As an action of love, a humble service, and as an example for disciples to follow Jesus washed the disciples' feet."[1]

"Yuck," they replied. "Wash stinky, smelly feet? Me? No Way." They folded their arms across their chests and looked down at their books as if they had reached total clarity about all aspects of this story of Jesus; his relationship to them; and about the extent to which they could benefit from Jesus' example.

In my mind, I went back to the time when I was their age and attending the Weogufkee Indian Baptist Church, a small, rural church in Oklahoma where the membership consisted of Muscogee (Creek) people like myself.

The day I recall is a hot summer day with dry, dusty, gusty winds. The non-Indian missionary serving our tribe was preaching about Jesus washing the disciples' feet. Staring down at our own dusty feet, we sat motionless before him with our arms across our chests.

The missionary preached loudly. "You Creeks need to have your feet washed by Jesus." He spoke with the same definitiveness as my young confirmands. Telling us who Jesus was, he presumed who we were and judged the condition of our feet which needed washing.

"You Redskins have been doing your ceremonial stomp dances and you got your feet dusty and dirty," he yelled. "You Young Braves have been out chasing girls, and you are plagued with evil thoughts. You old chiefs and squaws have been practicing your heathen ways and using Indian

---

1. Gerard Sloyan, *Interpretation: A Bible Commentary for Teaching and Preaching, John* (Atlanta: John Knox Press, 1988), 168.

medicine. Your hearts are as black as those colored people down the road." He continued. "You NEED to have your feet washed by Jesus. In fact, you NEED your whole body washed, scrubbed clean."

The missionary's tone turned somber. He concluded his powerful sermon saying that total purification is the proper disposition for all who believe in Jesus.[2] He offered an invitation, an altar call, in behalf of Jesus. A bench, an anxious bench, was placed before us so that we heathen savages might repent, repent from following ancient traditions and customs that purified us and kept us in touch and in tune with the Creator and the natural world.

Recalling this day, and all other days that this missionary preached for us, I remember no one accepting his invitation. But after each service, we church members lined up, shook his hand, thanked him for coming and invited him to stay for dinner. "Be sure and eat now," the elders would say as they offered him the first plate of food. After he had eaten he was warmly escorted to his pick-up truck and encouraged to visit us again.

Without words, we Muscogee (Creek) people made our own statement about who we were in relation to Jesus' example, the nature of the footwashing, the questionable value of servanthood.

Looking back at my childhood memories, back at the two confirmands from my church and now looking at you, seated across the tables from one another, arms folded, and looking at the theme "God's Gift: Welcomed as Servants." I wonder what thoughts and feelings cross your minds and hearts. "Welcomed as Servants?"

Do you hear the invitation? Do you believe the welcome? If so, what concept of servanthood is implied in the invitation? Is this invitation good news? . . . "to be God's servant in the service of others"? Does the welcome create the space where we can relive the example of Jesus, the empowered teacher, as a willing servant among equals?

For some of us, our experience of the bearers of God's gift of welcome to servanthood has lead us to *lament* the concept. Our experience of servanthood has been to become load bearers, gun bearers, body washers, clothes washers, dishwashers — designated by others as servants.

Many of us recognize that we have been servants *designated* by the church and the world. Native Americans frequently see churches and governments freely utilize our land bases, desecrate our sacred sites and ceremonies, and deny religious freedom. Christians and churches steal our ceremonies for personal use in worship and recreation. Many support the

2. Ibid.

audacious display of Native Americans as mascots for sport teams, automobiles, aircraft, margarine, chewing tobacco. They tell us we are being honored.

My friends, Designation is not a welcomed invitation to servanthood.

Native Americans are not the only ones who lament designated servanthood. Past and present discriminations have bound all of us and caused us to feel unwelcomed and tolerated! The performance of our duty is menial and tolerated! Our presence is trivial and tolerated!

Until we become sovereign, equal partners in the community of faith, instead of designated servants, the footwashing exercise is mere protocol and most demeaning.

If mutual and reciprocal footwashing is to occur among members in the United Church of Christ, we must know who Jesus is; we must know who we are; and we must *know who we are among.* Do not confuse the three as we share good news of God's gift of welcome.

Jesus says he is the sovereign one. He told the disciples, the commissioned 70, and others that he is word, light, life; both example and the sacrifice of God's redeeming love in the world. Jesus told them to accept God's love and go about being ministers, also offering words of eternal life, giving drinks of living water, sharing light with the world. Jesus taught that the ideal was a world where wholeness could be experienced cosmologically and his loved ones were parts of it, sharing in the wholeness, mutually and reciprocally.[3]

The disciples believed him and internalized this concept of equality. All of the disciples, converts who were Jewish, Gentile, even despised Samaritans, men and women were all equal, recipients of the same mission, same Spirit, same power to forgive sins that Jesus had. The community of equals loved Jesus and he loved them.[4] They were Jesus' family and in his family setting on that Maundy Thursday when he washed their feet.

Jesus was *able* to wash all of the disciples' feet, including Judas, because he was sovereign. He was *able to choose* his mode of example, because he was among a community of friends, a group of equals.

Recall the Jewish practice of footwashing. A good host provided this service for guests through a designated servant, the household's slave. Jewish slaves were excused from doing this chore if a Gentile slave was available. When neither was, women performed this duty.

In the Upper Room, Jesus hosted his last meal for his diverse but equal new family. Picture it: A male host who taught the new converts that they

---

3. G. W. MacRae, *Invitation to John* (Garden City, N.Y.: Doubleday Image Books, 1978), 170.
4. Elisabeth Schüssler Fiorenza, *In Memory of Her* (New York: Crossroad, 1987), 325.

were equal in God's eyes; yet he needed to honor the footwashing tradition of his culture.

Around the room, the Jewish converts looked to the Gentile converts and they looked to the Samaritans. Men were looking to the women. Nobody moved. There was no one low enough to perform this menial task. They were all equal now!

So, Jesus waited for the teachable moment . . . the middle of the meal to perform his obligatory duty as host. He didn't ask his mother to do this, or one of the women disciples. He did it himself.

In the performance of his duty, Jesus *chose* this love-action, this servant thing, so he could model for those like himself a lesson they could learn. Those who were male members of the dominant race at that time, in a patriarchal setting, *could* wash the feet of those made equal by God's gift of welcome. In communities of equals, people *can* perform menial tasks for one another *with honor.*

This exemplary footwashing story, often told to us with compelling flourish, exposes several things about who we are or what we think. Some among us, as ministers with power and authority, laud Jesus' acts of humility and servitude, as long as Jesus or someone else is the designated servant. They loath servanthood for themselves and discriminate against those who eke out an existence in the service of others. Sometimes, in their missionary zeal and judgement they want to wash whole bodies when they should be washing only the feet!

Those in hierarchical structures are challenged to be measured by the ability to relinquish power and domination; and identify equally with those created beings who occupy the lowest place,[5] washing their feet, not their whole bodies.

On the other hand, designated servants resist servanthood because we have been conditioned to believe that our servitude will be rewarded in the sweet by and by if we accept this low experience without regard for equality.

We who have internalized oppression must look at the model again. We must decolonize our lives, unlearn some of what the missionaries taught us, throw off the domestication of church and government so that we are *better* participants as equals in the household of faith.

We are not mere servants in the home of the host. Rather we are vital, equal, sovereign partners in the household of faith where Jesus becomes our brother and participates in the struggle for equality with us and washes our feet for us.

---

5. Ibid., 148.

With Jesus, our Sovereign brother, willing servant/empowered teacher, we are brought into the status of equality, where there is no racism, prejudice and inequity. Therefore, designated servant, *reject* the imposition of judgement that our whole bodies need washing when Jesus is washing only our feet.

This model set by Jesus challenges all of us. It calls on all of us to self examination and introspection to redefine who we are in relationship to Jesus and to one another.

Now, let us all remember who we are among.

In Jesus' time, Jesus and his movement offered an alternative interpretation of the Torah which opened up access to God for everyone beyond those members of the elect people of Israel, and especially for those who because of their societal situation had little chance to experience God's power in Temple and Torah.[6] Are we presumptuous enough to reject the example of Jesus?

We are all called to deepen our understanding of who we are among. The missionary who visited my Muscogee community didn't see who he was among because he looked with unloving, unknowing eyes. My young confirmation class had not learned enough nor matured enough to see who they are among. Most of us are ill equipped to look at and know who we are among. We are quick to judge with unloving and unknowing eyes. We use familiar and narrow portions of scriptures as justification for distorting images of God's created ones rather than following Jesus' example in embracing all.

This story of the footwashing reminds us of the ideal balance of love and service among spirit filled, empowered equals. We must discover and rediscover each other as equals. *We have power that must be shared, sovereignty that must be honored, and needs that must be met.* If those with power and authority share it with us and we who are often marginalized can experience the welcomed partnership and *IF* we are *enabled to* choose servanthood in the manner Jesus intended, then we will truly receive God's gift of welcome.

---

6. Ibid., 141.

122. Spiritual Traditions:

Rituals and Music

(1995, 1842)

Traditional, Joseph R. Renville

The spiritual legacy of native Americans is both a gift and a challenge. On the one hand, when American Indians are able to incorporate indigenous tribal traditions into Christian worship, as is done at the All Nations Indian UCC in Minneapolis, the theology and religious practices of the church are enriched and native traditions honored. On the other hand, American Indians are sometimes forced to protect their tribal rituals and practices from exploitation and distortion by those seeking New Age spirituality, or trying to claim Indian identities.

Indigenous peoples in the United Church of Christ are finding new ways to share authentic aspects of their cultures in appropriate settings, and preserve the integrity of those traditions. Liturgies such as the "Native American Blessing" offered during the Sunday Festival Service of Word and Sacrament at the 1995 General Synod greatly enrich the worship of the church.

One of the most well-known American Indian hymns is the "Dakota Hymn," written by Joseph R. Renville (1779–1846), the son of a French-Canadian trader and a Dakota mother. It continues to be greatly revered by the Dakota people and sustained them during times of great injustice and persecution.

Renville was a committed Christian, and the words of his hymn, based on Jeremiah 10:12–13, first appeared in the Dakota language

Sources: "Native American Blessing," from the "Festival Service of Word and Sacrament," General Synod, Sunday July 2, 1995. Joseph R. Renville, "Wakantanka Taku Nitawa" (Many and Great, O God, Are Your Works), *The New Century Hymnal* (Cleveland: Pilgrim Press, 1995), Hymn #3.

in a words-only hymnbook Dakota Dowanpi Kin *(1846). Later his adaptation of a native melody (Lacquiparle) for the hymn appeared in* Dakota Odowan *(1879). In 1930 Francis Philip Frazier (1892–1964) paraphrased the first and last stanzas of Renville's Dakota text into English for a 1930 YWCA national meeting.*

Native American Blessing

Great Spirit, you have always been, and before you no one ever was. There is no other one to pray to but you. Everything that you see, everything has been made by you. The stars all over the universe you have finished. The four quarters of the earth you have made. The day, and everything in the day, you have created. Great Spirit, lean close to the earth so you may hear the weak voice that we send.

Prayer of the 6 directions:

To the West — where the sun sets. A place to remember the things that should disappear in our lives, such as fighting and jealousy, envy and conceit, selfishness and lack of trust in our God. Recall the deaths in life's journey. God be with them and be with us.

To the North — the direction of the hard piercing winds. What are the hard things you have suffered through? Think of the courage needed to accept the jolts that come along with the joys of everyday living. God gives strength to endure the north winds. Thank you, God, for suffering through them with us.

To the East — The sun rises in the East. Thank you, God, for births, for new beginnings, for new jobs, new friends, new challenges. For newness in our hearts, thank you!

To the South — the direction bringing the warm breezes of life. Thank you God for the warmth of love, especially children's experiences of their parents' love. For the warmth and love of friends, for the joy and peace brought to our lives by those we love and by those who love us. Thank you God.

To the Sky — raise your eyes and hands in celebration in all that lifts you in joyous resurrection (fun, blessings, vacations, visits from family and friends, dancing, singing). Thank you God for the happiness that comes out of sorrow and the new life that has come out of old.

Finally, to the Earth—bow your head and cast your eyes down, to be humbled by Mother Earth. Remember to be grateful to the creator who brings so many good gifts from her. Everything we have is a gift from God. Creator, we thank you for the gifts and talents you have given each of us. We ask you to help us use them wisely.

Hear us, four quarters of the world. Relatives are we! Give us the strength to walk the soft earth, a relative to all that is. Give us eyes to see and strength to understand. Only with your power can we face the four winds.

Great Spirit, all over the earth, the faces of living things are all alike. Look upon the faces of children without number and with other children in their arms, so they may face the four winds and walk the good road to the day of quiet.

This is our prayer. The voice we send is weak, yet with earnestness we have sent it. Hear us!

"Wakantanka Taku Nitawa" (Many and Great, O God, Are Your Works)

Wakantanka taku nitawa tankaya qa ota;
Mahpiya kin eyahnake ca, maka kin he duowanca,
Mniowanca sbeya wanke cin, hena oyakihi.

Woehdaku nitawa kin he minagi kin qu wo;
Mahpiya kin iwankam yati, wicowaste yuha nanka,
Wiconi kin he mayaqu nun, owihanke wanin.

Many and great, O God, are your works,
Maker of earth and sky;
Your hands have set the heavens with stars,
your fingers spread the mountains and plains.
Lo, at your word the waters were formed;
deep seas obey your voice.

Grant unto us communion with you,
O star a-biding One;
Come unto us and dwell with us:
with you are found the gifts of life.
Bless us with life that has no end,
eternal life with you.

123. The Faithfulness of Indigenous Peoples: *"Honoring Spiritual Connections"*

(1997)

René Whiterabbit

René Whiterabbit Cutinella [Ttaa Ttoo Nik Winga] (1962–2000) was a member of the HoCak Nation, Buffalo Clan. She graduated from St. Olaf College and United Theological Seminary of the Twin Cities. She was part of the third generation of the Whiterabbit family to enter the Christian ministry. During her short ministry she served as Associate Executive Director of the Council for American Indian Ministry (CAIM) and frequently provided important leadership at the HoCak UCC in Black River Falls, Wisconsin, and the All Nations Indian UCC and Mayflower UCC in Minneapolis. Her reflections about the faithfulness of indigenous peoples, in Habits of Faith, *published by the United Church Board for Homeland Ministries, show how the rich tribal traditions of native peoples enable her to affirm the "spiritual connectedness of all things."*

Source: René Whiterabbit, an excerpt from "Honoring Spiritual Connections: A Native American Faith Journey," in *Habits of Faith* (Cleveland: United Church Board for Homeland Ministries, 1997), 40–46.

Honoring Spiritual Connections: A Native American Faith Journey

Aho, my name is René Whiterabbit. I am also called *ttaa ttoo nik winga,* first buffalo woman, member of the HoCak Nation, buffalo clan. I am mother of Morgan and partner of Steve. I am daughter of Ron and Roberta, granddaughter of Mitchell and Camiele, Murry and Lilac, and Helen and August.

In the HoCak community, we believe in the balance among all life forms. Faith involves an awareness of the spiritual force and living in harmony with it. When we honor the spirit all around us, there is honor and integrity in our interactions. Faith is to honor the spiritual essence that exists in everything. I cannot reduce faith to a simple act or ritual or discipline. Faith is an understanding of this interconnectedness, an awareness of the nuances of our actions. Our faith reminds us that we are a part of a larger, global world, where Sunday morning rituals extend to the love we carry all throughout our week. It is knowing in my soul that I am never only an individual. There is a larger community of which I am part and I am never alone. I am not René Whiterabbit, *ttaa ttoo nik winga,* without the identity of my community.

The Discipline of Language

The life of the community is the most fundamental of the disciplines of faith. The language of the community, in turn, plays a primordial role in the various expressions of our faith. So first I want to speak of the importance of language for all our disciplines of faith. Indeed, language itself is a discipline, in the sense that it "helps us establish, order, foster, and express our growing priority relationship with God, through Jesus Christ," as J. Mary Luti writes.

I am fortunate to have two communities to assist me in balancing my perspectives. I have been raised and taught in two cultures. One culture is technically and mechanically oriented and has a language very useful for talking about technical, mechanical, and even economic issues. I have the words in English to explain in a clear concise manner how a dollar can leave my pocket and eventually influence the interest rate. One of the strengths of the English language is its ability to describe the nuances of this technical world. It is similar to one of the strengths of the Yupick and Jupick languages, in which there are at least twenty-four words to refer to different types of snow, whether thin brittle snow or heavy slushy snow or some other kind of snow. When talking about the frozen tundra it is a gift to have the Yupick and Jupick languages on which to draw.

Today I finished preparing and sharing a sermon with the theme "Circle the World with Love." It was in the reflection on God's love that I found a context for speaking about disciplines that have shaped my faith journey. As a member of the HoCak Nation, I have learned that the spiritual relationships that are recognized in my community are connected deeply with God's love. These relationships have profound implications for our faith journeys as we walk this earth.

The word "love" has been used to describe many forms of relationships. How does divine love differ from human love? Using only the word "love" to describe the relationship and feelings between my son and me is limiting. How can I express that eternal, subtle, protective, caring feeling that he is an extension of my own body and self? Or what words can I use to describe love for a partner? This is different from the love or the depth of care for my child. The word "love" is also used to describe ice cream or pets or the world around us. It isn't unusual to say something like, "I love how the snow looks so beautiful as it freshly blankets the ground." We stretch the word "love" to have a variety of meanings.

The HoCak tradition, which has five levels of language, acknowledges and uses language to express the spiritual nature of all living beings, including the earth. The HoCak language distinguishes between my "love" for my son and my "love" for my partner. In the HoCak language, the level of word that I choose provides an insight into the intensity of my feeling. For example, if I am recognizing the bond between human beings and other creatures of the world I will honor that relationship by using language that encompasses the spirit of the creatures. So when I want to describe the relationship I have with my pet turtle, there are words to express the spirit of that relationship.

In the HoCak nation, there is a special language for children. This is helpful because some HoCak words are difficult to pronounce. This special language is not "baby talk" but a language that recognizes children's time in life. When adults or elders use this language in relation to themselves, it speaks volumes about their need for nurturing. When my Auntie was nearly comatose from diabetes she asked for her NaNé (mother). This word signaled all the comforting that we had been trying to give her was not the same as what her mother would have been able to give her. There was a nurturing in her mother's touch that she needed.

There is a particular language in my community to speak with the one who is most precious to you, a language that marks a special connection. The connection may be limited to a particular time or may exist across the days, yet it exists for that moment. Words spoken in that language are treasured, words held within the heart.

It is often difficult for me to speak in English about the spirit and the spiritual connection between all of us. Language itself limits my expressions of faith. There are not a lot of words in English to mark the differences in the feelings we have for each other. There are not a lot of words to express a force greater than ourselves. I know a man whose job is to care for plants in the offices of big corporations. He wanted to explain to me the connection he felt with those plants, but he struggled with the language to use in speaking about it. As he entered one of the sites to care for the plants, he said he suddenly became aware that the plants knew he was there to take care of them. The lack of vocabulary in English to describe this experience may indicate a lack of value the community places on this type of spiritual connection. If the community valued the spiritual connection, the man could celebrate this event as a most precious time. Instead, he is cautious about sharing.

Our practice of church rituals demonstrates the importance of language for the disciplines of faith. For example, when we are baptized into the church in the ritual of cleansing by holy water, we are called beloved and recognized as beloved children of God. We are recognized as most precious ones, loved by God the Creator. Being beloved by God has a depth and intensity that is difficult to speak about without indicating the nuances of the type of love we are experiencing. How do we share the intensity of the connection that exists, as the man tried to share the intensity of his connection with the plants?

Spiritual Connections

Using only the written or spoken language is limiting in a discussion of love. Reflecting upon my mother's love for me or my partner's love for me, I realize words aren't sufficient. Body language, respect, trust, actions often speak what words cannot. HoCak teachings have helped me know the importance of watching the movement of a person around the community and then listening to that person's words to fully understand the meaning of the message. The HoCak community teaches that actions reflect beliefs. Words are complementary to actions. This insight is based on a deep appreciation of interconnected parts of the self and the extension of this appreciation to the larger community. The emphasis is on the community rather than the individual. . . .

124. Theology:

"An Indian Perspective on the United Church of Christ"

(2000)

Norman W. Jackson

Norman W. Jackson (b. 1929) is a Congregational Christian/UCC minister educated at Hartford Theological Seminary. He is generally thought to be the first American Indian to obtain a graduate theological degree in the UCC. Jackson was conference minister of the Kansas-Oklahoma Conference UCC (1974–78), executive associate to the president of the United Church of Christ (1978–85), executive director of the Council on American Indian Ministry (CAIM) (1986–89), and conference minister of the Hawaii Conference UCC (1989–96). He also taught at Eden Theological Seminary and at United Theological Seminary of the Twin Cities.

Jackson has consistently challenged the United Church of Christ to take its American Indian ministry seriously. He has also encouraged indigenous peoples to claim the legitimacy of their own local theologies. His essay on "An Indian Perspective on the United Church of Christ" appears in a special issue of New Conversations *(Spring 2000) on the theme "American Indians in the United Church of Christ: Nurturing Our Spirituality Across Many Cultures."*

Source: Norman W. Jackson, "An Indian Perspective on the United Church of Christ," *New Conversations* (Spring 2000): 52–55.

An Indian Perspective on the United Church of Christ

In response to the invitation to write a letter to the United Church of Christ from an Indian perspective, my first imperative is to state unequivocally that I do not speak for all Indians any more than you could speak for your racial ethnic group. But, I have had some experiences in this church in local, conference, national, and theological education settings that have fed my perceptions about Indians and the UCC.

However, I will share by quoting liberally from various sources, in part to give authority to some of the points of view that may be new to people. Also, I will be limiting my remarks as much as possible to the United Church of Christ and our churches.

First, to European Americans:

The Missionary Heritage

It has become commonplace to understand the missionary heritage with Indians as, at best, ambiguous. Consider it this way: Indian Christians have been asked to accept a theological/faith perspective for Christianity which legitimated and justified our genocide.

For instance: Lewis Hanke, in a small document entitled "Aristotle and the Indians," quotes from the minutes of a town meeting in Massachusetts, in 1640:

1. *The earth is the Lord's and the followers thereof.* VOTED
2. *The Lord may give the earth or any part of it to his chosen people.* VOTED
3. *We are his chosen people.* VOTED

> Here, in these ludicrous minutes, is an illustration of how our Pilgrim forebears used Covenantal theology to justify their attempt to exterminate the Indians. This is not an illustration of human frailty! Rather, it is an illustration of a group of highly ethical representatives of civilization, chartered by the English crown, holding a covenant with Almighty God as the New Israel, with a mandate to occupy the land and exterminate the barbarous savages in the process. And, they (or shall I say 'we') did it in good biblical conscience.[1]

1. Alfonso A. Román, "The Making of a Character: A Reflection on the American Missionary Association and the Indian Work," Presented to the 100th Anniversary of the Dakota Association, June 11, 1988, p. 4. Emphasis added.

It may be difficult to read this material, but [Alfonso] Román goes on to ask:

> Surely, one of the questions the United Church of Christ must ask itself is: what tragic flaw in that belief system known as Reformation theology could have permitted these people to do what they did and do it in the name of God? It is a question directed not solely at the past. It is a question of crucial importance for our time as well (Don Gall, Marginal Religion among the Lakota Sioux).[2]

George Tinker's judgment is that:

> John Eliot, the highly publicized Puritan missionary to Indian peoples in Massachusetts and the most renowned of the early missionaries in what is today the United States — if not the most successful — comes out of a much discussed historical context . . . the beginnings of the fundamental attitudinal structures that underlie Indian-white relationships in North America, even to the present day, can be traced to the first English colonies of which Eliot was a part. Moreover, the basic outlines of the Euroamerican missionary profile are already clearly evidenced in Eliot, and this combination of immigrant attitudes of superiority and missionary profile makes Eliot an interesting test case for my thesis. To wit, *in Eliot we witness the intentional erosion of Indian culture along with its results, the unintentional devastation of those peoples, all accomplished by thorough confusion of gospel and culture.*
>
> This chapter *will demonstrate Eliot's participation in the full range of what I have identified as cultural genocide in all its social, economic, political, and religious aspects.*[3]

Here are a few of John Eliot's own words:

> As for these poore Indians, they have no principles of their own, nor yet wisdome of their own, (I mean as other Nations have).[4]

Or, a little closer to our UCC Indian congregations,

---

2. Ibid., 4.

3. George Tinker, *Missionary Conquest: The Gospel and Native American Genocide* (Minneapolis: Fortress Press, 1993), 21. Emphasis added.

4. Quoted from ibid., 21.

> WHERE CUSTER FAILED, RELIGION SUCCEEDS
> Kindness Is a Great Civilizer,
> "What military tactics failed to do, religious work did with love." These were the words of Reverend C. L. Hall, pioneer missionary and a prominent figure in North Dakota history, in recalling the events *in subjugation of the Indians* — The significant phase in this missionary's life is the contrast between himself and Custer. Both men started out at the same time with practically the same object in mind: to subdue the Indians — but with totally different weapons.[5]

The above references are separated by about two and a half centuries — centuries during which European invaders, through a variety of means, essentially genocided a people.[6] The Manifest Destiny doctrine widened the legitimization of "the invasion of America."[7] That there appears to be little cognizance of this genocide on the surface of the American conscience testifies to the adequacy of the various rationales for this destruction. When I hear Paeans of patriotic praise to the United States as a wondrous nation of immigrants molded from the wilderness I am reminded of this absence of cognizance.

And Now . . .

Located where poverty, disease, isolation, and the inadequacies of the Bureau of Indian Affairs (schools, hospitals, etc.) are endemically ubiquitous, UCC Indian congregations simply do not have the resources to pay fully for pastoral leadership, let alone develop the kind of missional stance their communities absolutely need. From the perspective of a comfortable white middle class life, deprivation characterizes reservation life.

There are Indian folk alive in our churches today who recall being told that one cannot be both Indian and Christian at the same time. You must choose. Using tribal language brought physical punishment. Expressing the faith could only be done in anglo, not Indian, culture. That tradition continues to permeate many of our congregations so much so that a woman

5. From *100 Years at Ft. Berthold: The History of the Fort Berthold Indian Mission 1876–1976,* compiled by Rev. and Mrs. Harold W. Case (Bismarck, N.D.: Bismarck Tribune, 1977), 95. Emphasis added.

6. I refer the reader to Ronald Takaki's *A Different Drummer: A History of Multicultural America* (Boston: Little, Brown, 1993) for a historical description of how Europeans and Euroamericans dealt with all non-whites. Indians were not the only victims of missionary exuberance and manifest destiny.

7. Francis Jennings, *The Invasion of America: Indians, Colonialism, and the Cant of Conquest* (New York: Norton, 1975). Though an older work, this book covers material not often taught in public school history classes, and explores some long-held beliefs about the reality of the European invasion of the Americas.

at our Convocation stated she could not seek ordination because her ordained grandfather told her that ordained ministry was no place for an Indian woman.

I believe Indian people must acknowledge the ambiguity of the missionary heritage, particularly that part which censures Indian culture. Some time ago, I wrote:

> Of the peoples who have received the gospel from Europeans in the past 500 years, American Indians are among those who have not indigenized, contextualized, formulated our own expression of the faith, nor developed our own local theologies. For the most part, Indians in the United States have imitated their missionaries in leadership style and followed rather docilely the polity imposed on them. Worship tends to reflect the tradition of the denomination, including the ethnic flavor of that denomination, more than the specific Indian culture of the tribe involved.[8]

Indian people must engage with the gospel from the Indian experience of genocided history, exiled in our own homeland, culturally pluralistic, and virtually without resources.[9] We need support and encouragement for this essential task.

We could use pastoral help from non-Indians, but the deep cultural realities along with historically bred distrust requires any non-Indian to be idiosyncratic and filled with *chesed* to receive immediate acceptance as a pastor — though it is possible after time and testing for some to make it. Unfortunately, few non-Indian folk like this receive Calls from God to go to Indian country. But even the best cannot do the Indian theological task.

And So . . .

To the 93% Euroamerican United Church of Christ I say, "Listen up! Read, understand, and internalize the history of your church and nation-state. Participate with us in God's mission so that we may all address the injustice, heal the broken people and ecology, and learn to speak with one another with trust." I cannot help but believe soul work must be done by Americans relative to the genocide that has been, and continues to be, legitimized by the cross, sword, flag, and cash register. We probably cannot help you with that task.

---

8. Norman W. Jackson, "Native American Theology and the United Church of Christ," *Prism* 5, no. 1 (Spring 1990): 67.

9. Gaming has not solved the economic development conundrums in Indian Country, nor is it likely to.

Do not leave us alone under the guise of self-determination. Not only should you hold us accountable for the *Neighbors in Need* money you send us, but you are a part of it. You have a part of God's mission in Indian country, and we must all prayerfully discern what that is.

No, it will not be easy. There are many prejudgments to overcome. There is absence of understanding. There is a culturally congenital need to deny and avoid historical realities. There is a will to invisibility. There is a desire to blame. But, it seems to me, dealing with those alienating walls of hostility is what the basic gospel is about — to liberate and redeem us from all that stuff — so that "justice (will) roll down like waters, and righteousness like an ever-flowing stream."

And, to Other People of Color in the UCC

We share with you the experience of having been marginalized by the dominant culture. We all know that. So, it would seem natural for all of us to join easily into coalitions of justice and development seeking. I just wish we knew each other better, knew the idiosyncrasies of each others' ways, the depth and uniqueness of each others' cultures, so that our natural self-interests could be more readily organized.

We are the smallest organized racial ethnic caucus in the UCC, and we probably have the fewest intrinsic resources. Our reservations routinely have from 40–80% unemployment, off in isolated places where resources like education, medical support, and economic development are difficult to maintain. But, for many Indian folk, that is home, where our people are, our families, and those with whom we share our culture. We do not do well, often, in urban environments which tend to dilute our cultures and force us into an individualism that is alien to our natures.

We differ from you. We are indigenous to this land, now exiles in our own land. The most obvious theological difference would be in the notion of liberation theology. For us, it is difficult to see the Exodus paradigm without completing it with the Conquest — that biblical narrative which was used to justify invasion of our lands and eradication of us as a people. We are in the midst of constructing our own, probably based on a form of creation theology, so be patient with us.

We celebrate your achievements. And, we know that our destiny, like it or not, is in many ways tied with yours as the dominant culture decides how it is going to handle becoming less than the majority in the coming thirty years. We support you and affirm you.

Let Indians decide who is "Indian" enough. It is ironic to be judged by you in ways similar to the dominant culture's.

There is a phrase — beige — that has made the rounds in recent years. As often as not, one that is disparaged. That is the color given to those of us who are the products of interracial marriage. According to all that I read, this group is growing and growing like the proverbial "Topsy." We are all going to have to deal with this one, soon.

In Conclusion

Well, my sisters and brothers in the UCC, I call on you to envision that Pentecost community, that new humanity in Christ, that will bring us all into the yearned for community where we are both one and many.

Receiving the Gifts of Pacific Islanders and Asian Americans

125. Hawaiian Traditions: *Music and Metaphor*

(1893, 1961)

Queen Liliuokalani, Abraham Akaka

Queen Liliuokalani (1838–1917) reigned as queen of Hawaii from 1891 to 1893. In 1893, when some of the wealthy business leaders from the United States objected to her efforts to restore some of the power of the monarchy, her government was overthrown, and she was put in prison. Later she made several trips to the United States, but was unsuccessful in regaining the Hawaiian throne. By 1900 Hawaii had become a U.S. territory.

The Christian piety of the queen led her to write a hymn of forgiveness for those who had brought about the end of her reign. It is much revered by many Christians in Hawaii and customarily sung to those departing the islands. The English translation explains the meaning, but Hawaiians request that the hymn not be sung in English.

Abraham Akaka (1917–97) was a native Hawaiian Congregational Christian/UCC minister who graduated from the University of Hawaii and Chicago Theological Seminary. He served as the pastor of the Kawaiaha'o United Church of Christ in Honolulu for forty years (1944–84). The Kawaiaha'o Church, located across the street from the historic Iolani Palace, is considered Hawaii's Mother Church. It was built of coral blocks between 1836 and 1842. Akaka offered the ukulele image of the Christian community in one of his meditations as chaplain at the 1961 General Synod.

Sources: Queen Liliuokalani, "O Kou Aloha No" (The Queen's Prayer), *The New Century Hymnal* (Cleveland: Pilgrim Press, 1995), Hymn #580. Abraham Akaka, excerpt from a meditation on "Covenant," *GS Minutes 1961*, 78–79.

"O Kou Aloha No"
(The Queen's Prayer)

O kou aloha no A ia ika Lani,
A o kou oiai'o, He hemolele ho'i.

Kou noho mihi ana A pa'ahao la,
O oe ku'u lama kou nani, ko'u ko'o.

Mai nana 'ino 'ino Na hewa o kanaka,
Aka, e huikala, a ma'ema'e no.

Nolaila e ka Haku Malalo okou eheu
Ko makou maluhia, a mau loa aku no.

[Note: This translation is not intended to be sung.]
Your love is in heaven and your truth so perfect. I live in sorrow imprisoned; you are my light, your glory my support. Behold not with malevolence the sins of humankind, but forgive and cleanse. And so, O Lord, beneath your wings be our peace forever more.

Four Strings on the Ukulele

. . . Our Lord bids us now to "Go and tell all my children" by word and example — "You are many nations, but I call you to one Kingdom; you are many races, but I call you to one Brotherhood; you are many cultures, but I call you to one Life; you are many religions, but I call you to the Lord and Light of Life — even Jesus Christ." He calls us to tune up the world that the wilderness might break forth into singing.

Our Lord never meant everyone to be alike. There are four strings on this instrument (holds up ukulele). Instead of "My dog has fleas," we might call these four strings "white, black, yellow, brown," or "Evangelical, Reformed, Congregational, and Christian." But each is under the demand to tune itself to Christ, until his law is written in its heart — tune itself to what it ought to be as white, or black, or yellow, or brown . . . or as Evangelical, Reformed, Congregational, Christian. Only then will the wilderness break forth into singing. The heavenly instrument is the harp — in which every one of the many strings is in tune with Christ. But for now, and on this new altar that our Lord has caused us to erect on our pilgrimage from Chaldea to Canaan, the ukulele must suffice.

When, through covenant people, Hawaii began to know of Christ, there bubbled up in the soul of a Hawaiian named Kalaina a song called "He Kulanakauhale Omao" or the City of God. The words describe a green city — through which the healing streams of water flow — in which all people know the Lord and dwell together in peace. And no matter how much this story is told and sung, it will never grow old.

126. Organizing:

Pacific Islander and Asian American Ministries

(1974, 1982)

PAAM, Mineo Katagiri

On June 9, 1973, key Asian American leaders in the San Francisco area from the Sycamore Congregational UCC in El Cerrito and the Council of Japanese Congregational Churches convened a group to discuss the idea of an Asian caucus in the UCC. Plans were expanded at the 1973 General Synod later that month. Within a year about one hundred representatives of the Chinese, Filipino, Hawaiian, Japanese, Samoan, Korean, and various Southeast Asian communities assembled for a "National Conference on Asian-American Concerns" in San Francisco (April 19–21, 1974). At that meeting the name "Pacific Islander Asian American Ministries" (PAAM) was chosen.

The "Resolution to Organize" shows that the group had very practical goals — to develop (1) peoples, (2) communities, (3) the United Church of Christ and (4) Christian mission outreach programs and strategies. The leaders of PAAM petitioned the Executive Council of the United Church of Christ for recognition as a special-interest group, and that status was formally voted at the 1975 General Synod. PAAM argues that Pacific Islander and Asian American churches need to be taken seriously, that they continue to be victims of racism, and that their rich heritages are not

---

Sources: "Resolution to Organize" Adopted 4/20/74, National Conference on Asian American Concerns, San Francisco, April 19–21, 1974, and a Petition to the Executive Council of the United Church of Christ for Recognition as A Special Interest Group [typescript]. Mineo Katagiri, excerpt from a "Charge to the New PAAM Executive Committee Officers," Friday, July 30, 1982 (transcribed from tape) [typescript].

being affirmed in the United Church of Christ. PAAM played a key role in the development of the General Synod resolution on "Racism and the United Church of Christ" (1979).

Mineo Katagiri (b. 1919) is a Japanese American Congregational Christian/UCC minister who grew up in Hawaii and was educated at the University of Hawaii and Union Theological Seminary in New York. After pastorates in Hawaii (1945–59) he served in campus and urban ministry in Seattle, Washington (1959–70). He was executive assistant to UCC president Robert V. Moss (1970–75) and conference minister of the Northern California Conference UCC (1975–85). When new officers of PAAM were installed at their annual meeting in 1982, Katagiri charges the new Executive Committee to see their work as supported by the "circumstantial will" of God.

Resolution to Organize

The peoples with which the group will be concerned shall include those of Chinese, Filipino, Hawaiian, Japanese, Samoan, Korean, Southeast Asian and other ancestries.

Purpose

I. Development of Peoples

A. To secure funding and initiate programs to develop leadership, lay and professional, within the Asian American and Pacific Islander churches in the UCC.

B. To encourage the nominating committees at all levels of the church to seek persons from the Asian American and Pacific Islander constituency for membership and leadership on boards and committees.

C. To examine the unique situations and meet the needs experienced by Asian-American and Pacific Island youth as a result of the multicultural situation in which they are set.

II. Development of Communities

A. To identify strengths and weaknesses in Asian American and Pacific Islander ministries and formulate and implement remedies.

B. To address the conflicts and problems faced by Asian Americans and Pacific Islanders who experience multi-cultural conflicts and ambiguities.

C. To research Asian theology and the unique insights of the heritage of Asians and Hawaiians, etc., for better understanding of the faith.

D. To encourage cooperation with other Asian American and Pacific Islander congregations and with other denominational Asian caucuses.

III. Development within the United Church of Christ

A. To secure necessary funding for programs to strengthen our churches from our own constituency and churches, and from conferences and national agencies.

B. To formulate and petition the appropriate UCC instrumentalities to adopt policies based on self-determination with reference to Asian American and Pacific Islander needs and concerns:

1. Ministerial education
2. Lay leadership development
3. Christian education programs and publications
4. Mission

C. To cooperate where appropriate with other UCC ethnic caucuses: Blacks, Native Americans, etc.

D. To enable the development of a new and truer image of Asian Americans and Pacific Islanders through the use of the various media within UCC.

E. To represent the concerns of this Conference to all levels of the United Church of Christ:

1. To act as liaison between Asian American and Pacific Islander churches and the appropriate agencies of the church.
2. To provide a forum for ministerial concerns and a vehicle for presenting these concerns to the appropriate agencies of the church.
3. To be supportive of appropriate actions or positions initiated by local churches.

IV. Development of Christian Mission and Outreach Programs and Strategies

Because the following alternative proposal was not adequately discussed, it was agreed by community consensus that the Organizing Committee will consider and incorporate parts of the following resolution into the above resolution which was adopted.

WHEREAS, THERE IS AN ABSENCE OF LEADERSHIP DEVELOPMENT AND TRAINING PROGRAMS FOR LAY PEOPLE AND PASTORS IN THE PACIFIC BASIN,

WHEREAS, THERE IS AN ABSENCE OF PACIFIC BASIN PEOPLE'S REPRESENTATION ON BOARDS OF UCC,

WHEREAS, THERE IS AN ABSENCE OF ADEQUATE RESOURCES FOR IMPLEMENTING THE MISSION FOR PACIFIC BASIN PEOPLES,

THEREFORE, BE IT RESOLVED THAT THE PACIFIC BASIN PEOPLE'S SPECIAL INTEREST GROUP OF THE UCC BE ORGANIZED FOR THE FOLLOWING REASONS:

1. Organize a structure, i.e., Pacific Basin People's Conference of UCC
2. Call upon the national church, local conferences and associations to elect and select representatives as recommended by Pacific Basin Peoples to the Boards
3. To call upon the Office for Church Life and Leadership to consider and plan for an adequate program of leadership development and for training Pacific Basin Peoples.

Charge to PAAM

. . . The theological statement that I want to make is, that in the life of the church these miracles happen when they are in tune with the will of God. Therefore, it is not always the work of us human beings that make these things possible, but because of the soil that has been prepared by God. My own theological affirmation is that in a Christian Church, the ultimate will of God is a united church in which all persons are One. In Christ there is no East nor West, nor white nor Black, nor Yellow nor Brown. We are all intended to be One within the fellowship of the church. That is the ultimate will of God. But, there are circumstances in which God's will is frequently contingent upon the circumstances. Therefore, I believe in the circumstantial will of God. PAAM is a creation which came about in response to the circumstantial will of God. So, in our present context, before the ultimate will of God can become a reality in the Christian church in America, the circumstantial will has to be taken seriously.

We human beings, you see, are not always given the opportunity to deal with the ultimate. We are of the earthy in this life, and this life is full of contingencies. We have to discover the circumstantial will of God for us as we journey through this life. Therefore, I want to affirm that the circumstantial will of God at a given moment in history is as important as our allegiance to the ultimate will of God, but our circumstantial activities must always be used as an understanding of that ultimate will of God. In this sense, the sins of our fathers and mothers are always cast upon the children.

I have over the years not been able always to contain my anger at the mission boards. Because of this history, I am angry, but I am also forgiving of that history.

One of the reasons for the smallness in number of Asian and Pacific Island churches in the United Church of Christ is precisely because the Home Missionary Board, as well as the Foreign Board of Missions, were racist in their understanding of their tasks. They were racist in their organization, and racist in the way they went about doing their mission. We inherited that, so part of our job is to help in the process of reconciliation so that the ultimate can become a reality. . . .

127. Preaching:

On Being Troublemakers

(1981)

Teruo Kawata

Teruo Kawata (b. 1927) is a Japanese American Congregational Christian/UCC minister who grew up in Southern California and experienced the World War II hysteria against Japanese Americans. He was educated at Ottawa University, Kansas, University of Chicago, and Pacific School of Religion. After pastorates in southern California and Hawaii (1952–68) he held various conference and national staff positions in the UCC: Hawaii Conference UCC staff (1968–70), Council for Lay Life and Work (CLLW), the Office for Church Life and Leadership (OCLL) (1970–76), conference minister of the Central Pacific Conference UCC (1976–79), and conference minister of the Hawaii Conference UCC (1979–89). In 1989–90 he was University Church pastor and visiting professor at Silliman University, Philippines.

Kawata was consistently involved with the development of the Pacific Islander and Asian American Ministries (PAAM) (see vol. 7:126). His sermon to the 1981 General Synod reminds the listeners that once a person has been claimed by Jesus Christ, there will always be "a restlessness in our bellies with things as they are."

Source: Teruo Kawata, excerpt from a sermon [no title], *GS Minutes 1981,* 134–36.

. . . On Being Troublemakers

. . . In the first 24 years in the life of the United Church of Christ we have been confronted by a world in turmoil — the Vietnam War, the issues of racial justice, the energy crisis, the claims of women and other minorities. In the midst of these we have sought to lift up a vision of justice and peace.

But another thing has been happening in the past quarter to half a century. The world of the white male control and domination has collapsed. And the disintegration of that world is sending shock wave after shock wave across the land of change and reaction. The macho-ism of the white male controlled society is but the last fighting gasp of a dying era. That's why it's so dangerous.

And if the United Church of Christ is to speak the word of life for this uncertain, lost, torn up, frightened world, it will not be enough to continue to speak only from the theological framework that was born out of that culture.

If the United Church of Christ is to witness to Christ and all humanity, its witness will need to come not only from the richness of our reformation history, but also from the theology that is born from the pain and oppression of black peoples and South American peoples. From the experience of Indians and women and Asians. It will need to be global if it will witness to all humanity.

I hope in the coming years we shall have the courage and openness to engage in a theological ferment drawing from fresh and sometimes radically different perspectives that come from people of different histories, in order that we might more adequately witness to Christ and humanity as we move toward the year 2000. . . .

My experience as a Japanese American growing up in Delano, California, has shaped my vision of the Kingdom. My experience is far less than that of my black and Indian brothers and sisters. But let me share, from who I am, that vision of the Kingdom.

My mother and father spoke of how they were laughed at and ridiculed. They were taken advantage of and exploited because they couldn't understand the language and, because they were afraid, they couldn't fight back. They spoke of killings but the killers were never found. In the town where I grew up we couldn't sit in the center section of the theatre. That was for white people. The Japs and Chinks and Mexicans and Niggers had to sit on the side. I remember a time in high school when about four of us were sitting under a tree during the lunch hour. There were many trees on campus. But these white boys came and kicked us out, yelling, "Get out of here, you Japs." Those were terrifying days after the Japanese attack on Pearl Harbor. Do you know what it might feel like to have American soldiers with guns at bay herding you into trains and trucks, standing guard over you as you were trundled off into the dark, not knowing where they were taking you or what they were going to do to you? Do you know what it feels like to be walking down a street in Chicago and have somebody spit in your face and call you a "God damned Jap"? Some of you have been at those places and worse and you know.

But for those who have not been there, will you feel what that does to you?

- You live with fear because you never quite know if and when they might decide to come at you.
- You feel angry, but you dare not show your anger because you know they will beat hell out of you.
- You feel a rage, a helpless, hopeless rage that churns in your belly and you can't do anything about it.

It's out of this place that I come. And wherever there is bigotry and injustice and violations of people I feel the same fear and rage inside my belly.

Can we, will we, feel that rage, that cries out to us, that cried out to us last night when Brother Crimm from the very depths of his soul sang, "I wish I knew how I would feel to be free . . . "? Will you feel that, in the name of God?

Will you feel that rage when our government will turn its eyes away from the gross violation of human rights and will support instead the dictatorship of El Salvador and the Philippines, of South Korea and South Africa? Somehow will you feel that helpless, hopeless rage that churns in the belly when one's humanity is violated?

Will you feel that in behalf of women when they speak to us about the language that excludes them, about our mother-in-law jokes that ridicule them, and the little old lady in tennis shoe image that violates their dignity?

Will we hear when they say to us our employment and economic practices discriminate against them? And, yes, in our churches too that, in spite of all our rhetoric, we continue to act as though a woman does not have the capacity to share with us the incredible good news that God loves us. How long? I call upon my brothers, how long will we continue to deliberately inflict this hurt upon our sisters?

I hope we can be a people who will feel the rage of these and many more who are daily victims of those in power, that we will stand alongside them, that we will embrace them.

Kazoh Kitamori said that God is in pain because the world is in pain. I pray that we, the people of the United Church of Christ, might take upon ourselves the pain of the world . . . in order that the hope and the life which is in Christ might be made flesh in their midst.

If we do that, we'll be called troublemakers, and it's not easy to be troublemakers. But can we not be?

128. The Challenge:

"A Pronouncement on Ministry with Pacific Islanders and Asian Americans"

(1989)

General Synod

The pronouncement "A United Church of Christ Ministry with Pacific Islanders and Asian Americans" (1989) is a comprehensive statement challenging the United Church of Christ General Synod and all UCC instrumentalities, conferences, associations, and local churches: to be instruments for justice to combat racism, to fight against things that make it difficult for Pacific Islanders and Asian Americans to be full citizens and church members, to accept and utilize their gifts, to provide pastoral ministries to them, and to promote affirmative action policies. It outlines the history of Pacific Islanders and Asian Americans in the United States and the ambiguous blessing of the "model minority" myth. In its "Biblical, Theological and Ethical Rationale" it reminds the church of the biblical mandate to welcome the stranger.

Source: An excerpt from a Pronouncement, "A United Church of Christ Ministry with Pacific Islanders and Asian Americans," *GS Minutes 1989,* 89–90.

A United Church of Christ Ministry with Pacific Islanders and Asian Americans

Biblical, Theological and Ethical Rationale

> "By the waters of Babylon, there we sat down and wept, when we remembered Zion. . . . How shall we sing the Lord's song in a foreign land?"
> (Psalm 137:1, 4, RSV)

> "Come, O blessed of my Father, inherit the kingdom prepared for you from the foundation of the world, for I was hungry and you gave me food, I was thirsty and you gave me drink, I was a stranger and you welcomed me, I was naked and you clothed me, I was sick and you visited me, I was in prison and you came to me."
> (Matthew 25:34–36, RSV)

The immigrants from the Pacific Basin countries have come to America for a number of reasons: to escape oppression and poverty; to make a better life for themselves and their families; to escape war; and as refugees. They have come and have met open hostility. They have been the brunt of racism which, against Pacific Islanders and Asian Americans, takes subtle forms (e.g., because they have excelled academically, it is harder for them to get into colleges). The dominant culture pits minority against minority, using the notion that Asian Americans are the "model minority." The violence now has taken the form of beatings and killings. Thus, it becomes difficult for Pacific Islanders and Asian Americans to sing a new song in a foreign land. They sit by the waters of Babylon weeping.

While some Asian Americans have been in America for many generations and some Pacific Islanders have been American for many more generations, they remain oppressed and excluded peoples. The task of the Church is to deal with the racism that continues to oppress peoples who have contributed and can contribute much to this land and the Church. Pacific Islanders and Asian Americans are citizens, yet treated as foreigners. When racism is overcome and Pacific Islanders and Asian Americans are given equal opportunity and dignity, they will be able to sing a new song in a land that is not foreign. The Church needs to address the psychological, sociological and physical violence in American society and particularly to the Pacific Islanders and Asian Americans.

Historically, the Church has been at the forefront of ministry with Pacific Islanders and Asian Americans. But it is still called to minister to the poor, the oppressed and the stranger, to welcome the thousands of immigrants from Pacific Basin nations who come to this land. The Church is also called to receive the gifts of people from these lands. There are many immigrants who come to these shores and need ministries of many kinds, some as basic as learning English. The Church must learn how to welcome and receive these peoples.

While Asian Americans tend to be Buddhist, Shintoist, Taoist, and of other indigenous religions, there is spirituality in their religion which can inform and enrich Christianity. However, ninety percent of Pacific Islanders have embraced Christianity, interpreting this faith in the context of their various cultural backgrounds. While the triumphalism of many Christians may keep them from seeing the beauty and truth in these religions, ministry in the United Church of Christ must be open to learn truth from them.

The motto of the United Church of Christ is "that they may all be one." So it is that the United Church of Christ is called upon to be at one with Pacific Islanders and Asian Americans and to minister with these persons in our churches and in our communities.

Statement of Christian Conviction

Since the 10th General Synod of the United Church of Christ in 1975 acted to support the program of the Pacific Asian American Ministries, the United Church of Christ has on numerous occasions affirmed its concern for issues affecting Pacific Islanders and Asian Americans. General Synod 17 reaffirms the United Church of Christ's commitment to Pacific Islander and Asian American ministries. The General Synod calls for instrumentalities, conferences, associations, and local churches:

- to be instruments for justice which combat racism and violence in all its forms against Pacific Islanders and Asian Americans;
- to continue the fight against powers and principalities which make it difficult for Pacific Islanders and Asian Americans to be fully vested members of the United States of America and the United Church of Christ;
- to affirm support for Pacific Islander and Asian American congregations;
- to discover, accept and utilize the gifts which Pacific Islanders and Asian Americans bring to the United Church of Christ and to the United States of America;

- to provide competent and faithful pastoral ministries in the Pacific Islander and Asian American churches in the United Church of Christ, and
- to promote and implement the Affirmative Action policies of the United Church of Christ in local churches, associations, conferences and instrumentalities, especially toward hiring of Pacific Islanders and Asian Americans.

129. Theology:
Asian American

(1986)

David Hirano

David Hirano (b. 1935) is a Japanese American UCC minister who graduated from Andover Newton Theological School and the School of Theology at Claremont, California. Raised as a Baptist he served in Baptist churches and on the national staff for the American Baptist Churches (1960–74). He was pastor of the Nuuanu Congregational UCC in Honolulu, Hawaii (1974–86), Christ United Church of Christ, Chicago (1987–90), conference minister of the Connecticut Conference UCC (1991–94), and executive vice-president of the United Church Board for World Ministries (1994–99). His article "Theology among Asian Americans in the United Church of Christ" was published during the first year of Prism: A Theological Forum for the United Church of Christ *(the theological journal started by UCC seminaries in 1985). Hirano admits that although it is very difficult to make theological generalizations, it is possible to describe common themes that enrich the faith of Pacific Islanders and Asian Americans.*

Source: David Hirano, excerpt from "Theology among Asian Americans in the United Church of Christ," *Prism* (Fall 1986): 71–74.

Theology among Asian Americans

. . . Asian American theology is born out of a struggle between the culture of ancestry and the culture of America. The struggle is between openness and triumphalism; family and individualism; weakness and strength. These are parts of the conflict that comes from the struggle between the culture of ancestors and the culture of America.

Most Asian religions are accepting of other religions. In an inurnment of the ashes of a young man at the tomb where the cremains were laid to rest, after the Protestant service was read, one of the family members put a rosary around the urn, then when the urn was put into the tomb, incense was passed out and each family member, whatever his or her religion, offered the incense. Here in a microcosm were seen three different ways of honoring the eternal. Such is the Asian way.

In Japanese culture one can be married by a Shinto or Christian minister and buried Buddhist. It is not unusual to find in the same household a butsudan (Buddhist altar), a kami dana (a Shinto god shelf), and a crucifix. A visit to Hawaii shows the ways in which Japanese have tended to syncretize religions: the Church of World Messianity, the Church of Perfect Liberty, and Seicho no ie are examples of Japanese religions which have taken parts of the major religions of the world and each made a religion of its own.

When caught in the struggle between triumphalism and openness, some Asian Americans say with the dominant culture, "Christ is the only way." The author of this article believes in Jesus Christ as the way for him and, while affirming the Trinity, is open to the idea that the Eternal can manifest Himself/Herself in any way that the Eternal may choose.

The serious student of Christianity and Japanese Buddhism discovers many similarities. William Mensendiek, a missionary of the United Church Board for World Ministries in Japan, writes as follows: "About a thousand years ago, the Empress Komyo, in search of enlightenment, became a Buddhist nun. In those days the only place for the poor to bathe, except for rivers and hot springs, was at the temple which is where public baths here began. Her training included bathing one thousand beggars who could not do it by themselves. After helping 999 she saw that the next one was a leper. By then she had learned that the suffering of others was her own. So she didn't hesitate. That leper was the Buddha! Nirvana was achieved."[1]

---

1. William Mensendiek, letter published for April 1986 mailing, UCC United Church Board for World Ministries, New York.

That story can remind the reader of the saying of Jesus: "Truly, I say to you, as you did it to one of the least of these my brethren, you did it to me."

These similarities, as well as differences, have led the author to engage in a serious study of Buddhism, and through that study he has discovered a better understanding of himself. As he studied the religion of his ancestors, he began to see why he thought and behaved in certain ways. While his early Christian training stressed triumphalism, his inner being fought against it. He found a love for himself which no Euro-American theology gave him. Interestingly, through the study of Buddhism, he found a Christian God who loved and affirmed him as an Asian American.

In the conflict between triumphalism and openness the author has found liberation. In the flight from triumphalism the door of faith opened; the Eternal has been experienced in the day-to-day experiences of life; the ways of the ancestors were affirmed; and Christ has become more than the Christ of the Christian way, but the Christ who is made known in different ways to different cultures.

Another struggle, out of which Asian American theology is born, is the struggle between family and individuals. American culture has rightly stressed the individual. The Constitution of the United States makes clear that all persons have a right to life, liberty, and the pursuit of happiness. Asian cultures, however, stress the family as being more important than the individual, and hence comes the conflict.

In a conversation between the author and a psychotherapist from Japan, the therapist told of Japanese young people who became Christians and then suffered nervous breakdowns. As he looked at the cause, it was because the young people, when adopting Christianity, had to leave their families. Religion separated the individual from the family.

In the sixteenth century St. Francis Xavier went to Japan as a missionary and made an amazing number of converts in a very short time. A study of the methods of evangelism leads one to see that St. Francis tried to convert the daimyo, the lord of a village, and with the conversion of the lord came the whole village or clan.

The family is more important to Asian American and Pacific Island cultures than the individual. Families supersede the person, and individual identity is not as important as the family.

The task, then, is to develop a meaningful theology of the family. When the Japanese settled in the Terminal Island area of Los Angeles County, they became a village similar to those found in Japan. They became a large extended family. Even though the Japanese Americans have scattered, they still maintain their ties. The plantation camps in Hawaii similarly developed into large extended family systems, which take care of members at critical times in their lives.

In developing a theology of family, the author believes that the church can become that kind of extended family. The work of Margaret Swain in family clustering helps white suburban churches to become extended families. In Hawaii, where there are already a large number of extended families in churches, the question rises, how does one minister to the extended family?

The conflict between family and individual raises another question. "How does one deal with shame?" Shame is a feeling associated with groups; guilt is highly individual. Shame has to do with identity, while guilt has more to do with the violation of a rule. Although the distinctions between shame and guilt are sometimes hard to see, the feelings are different and it does not help to mix the two.

Guilt requires forgiveness of sins, while shame requires the repairing of a relationship. Guilt has to do with a crime or transgression which no one may know about; shame has to do with the "eyes of the world on me" and "losing face." While shame is a universal feeling, it is more commonly associated with Asians than with Euro-Americans.

Christianity has dealt with guilt and forgiveness. The Christian liturgy includes the confession of sins. Psychology has enabled people to deal with guilt but does not know how to deal with shame. Likewise, Christianity has not dealt with shame.

But when one begins a cursory examination of the Bible, one finds that shame is emphasized more often than guilt. Helen Merrell Lynd in *Shame and the Search for Identity,* after studying a concordance of the King James Bible, observes that guilt does not appear as often as shame.[2] A reading of the concordance of the Revised Standard Version shows a larger number of references to guilt but still there are more references to shame than to guilt.

Although in the English language there are few words that deal with shame, the Japanese have no word for "guilt." In fact the word "sin" in Japanese means an indiscretion and does not carry the weight of "sin" as a transgression against God's law.

Shame is the feeling of unworthiness, of missing the mark. It is a primal feeling that, as Erik Erikson says, comes in the second stage of the "development of man." He says that shame is too quickly subsumed under guilt.[3] Theologically, shame better describes the condition of the human

2. Helen Merrell Lynd, *On Shame and the Search for Identity* (New York: Harcourt, Brace, 1958), 25.

3. Erik Erikson, *Childhood and Society* (New York: Norton, 1963), 252.

being, for shame has to do with identity. It has to do with the family of God and sin.

In the Japanese family the ultimate punishment for shaming a family was banishment. The ultimate way in which shame was resolved was through hara kiri, committing suicide. While shame is very difficult to resolve, Christianity says, "God will never turn God's back on anybody." So the Christian can be certain that God's love will be there for anybody.

In the study of shame, the author's research has discovered that those who have written books on shame have been Japanese, Germans, Jews, women, and those who deal with alcoholics. All these people know what it is to be ashamed. So for the oppressed, the poor, the unworthy, the guilty, the unloved, who feel ashamed, God's love in Christ is one of the ways in which shame may be dealt with.

Dealing with shame lifts up the importance of the group. For Christians it is the church, the community of faith, that embraces the person no matter how unworthy she or he feels. The church needs to become the extended family in which losers as well as winners are welcomed, where the sinner knows that God loves everyone. The church needs to be the community where people can come to be accepted as people and not have to be perfect, where people can be together to cry, laugh, pray, or play without being self-conscious or feeling that they are being judged. Thus the community of believers becomes an integral part of dealing with shame. The community of believers also becomes the locus in which displaced persons can find identity.

From living as a minority in America one sees the strength and power of the majority, and there is a temptation to powerlessness or to join the powerful. Much of Christianity seems to proclaim a God who comes in power and might. To live as a minority in this country is not to fall into either temptation, but to see that Christ is made known in the weakness of humans.

St. Paul writes, "We are fools for Christ's sake, but you are wise in Christ. We are weak, but you are strong" (1 Corinthians 4:10). Jesus ends up with twelve disciples, one of whom betrays him. Jesus is persecuted and crucified, and after the crucifixion is resurrected. In the eyes of the world Christ was a failure, but through the failure came salvation for all.

In the novels of Shusako Endo, a Roman Catholic layperson in Japan, the Christ figure is a person who is weak: Christ is seen in a sickly patient, a homely boy, or a person who is dying. Assuredly, Christ is made known in the ordinary experiences of humankind. More especially, Christ is made known in the weakness of people.

So those who live as a minority in a majority culture do not have to feel powerless or in fact to join the powerful. Though part of a small minority, the Asian American Christian when faithful to Jesus Christ will be an instrument through which Christ is made known.

Asian American theology is still in the process of conception. It is being born out of suffering and struggle, from which emerges the conviction that Jesus Christ is Lord. This affirmation, while the same for all of Christendom, has a unique interpretation for the Asian American.

130. Assimilation:

"The Asian American and Pacific Islander Experience"

(1998)

Rose W. Lee, David Tuiasosopo

Rose Lee (b. 1935) is a Chinese American lay member of the Berkeley Chinese Congregational Church, UCC, Berkeley, California, where she is organist, church clerk, and Sunday school teacher. She is a graduate of the University of California and held employment as a teacher and as an employee of the State of California. She has been active in the Pacific Islander and Asian American Ministries (PAAM) since its beginnings and served as PAAM moderator (1992–94).

David Tuiasosopo (b. 1941) is a Samoan American UCC minister educated at Missouri State University, the University of Washington, and Parkwood University School of Theology in London, England. In 1962 his family started the First Samoan Christian Church in San Francisco. Later he returned to Samoa and started several churches, spent time in Hawaii, and moved to Washington (state). When he wrote this article for New Conversations, *he was a member of the Samoan Congregational UCC, Seattle, Washington.*

Source: Rose W. Lee and David Tuiasosopo, excerpts from "Assimilation and the Asian American and Pacific Islander Experience," *New Conversations* (Winter 1998): 39.

Chinese American and Samoan Perspectives

Life between Two Cultures

As Asian Americans and Pacific Islanders living in the United States, we live in the context of two cultures, two histories and two languages. We often live on the margins of US society, struggling with the tension between preserving customs, values and beliefs of the old country and assimilating into the mainstream. We need to find creative ways to bridge both worlds in order to help our youth affirm their Asian American and Pacific Islander identities in the context of our Christian communities and in the global world. As the late Dr. David Ng of San Francisco Theological Seminary said, we must seek ways to be "open to transformation into persons who will do ministry that is informed by tradition and is inclusive, multicultural, ecumenical and socially conscious TO THE GOSPEL." . . .

Assimilation and the Christian Faith

We, Asian American and Pacific Islanders can read the Bible through the perspective of our racial and ethnic experiences and values. As we study the biblical story of Israel as a sojourner we will find that our experiences may have much in common with the identity of Israel as a sojourner. It reminds us, as Israel was reminded of the importance of remembering our sojourn experience. We can talk of our experiences as a corporate and particular people in the same way that all generations of Israelites talk of their corporate experience as a people. Israel attempted to understand her sojourn experience in the light of God's pervasive activities in the world and let this understanding define its being and behavior. Asian Americans and Pacific Islanders may also look at that way of seeing things for themselves. We can remember and celebrate the past. We can affirm the Asian American and Pacific Islander identity and experience as positive and Christian. We are reminded of God's love for the marginalized, poor, and oppressed and we can appreciate the role of culture and ethnicity as we try to discern God's nature and will as revealed in the Bible. No matter what choices we make — to affirm or to forge new identities, we know that we are all children of God.

Receiving the Gifts of Hispanics

131. Hymns:
Puerto Rican and Mexican (traditional)

Music is an important way for new immigrants to bring a part of their homeland to a new setting and for second-generation U.S. citizens to stay connected to their cultural roots. Consequently when The New Century Hymnal *(TNCH) was being prepared great care was taken to incorporate 33 Spanish-language hymns to serve the needs of the growing number of predominantly Hispanic congregations and to enrich worship in every congregation in the UCC. Also, in 1999 Pilgrim Press published a Spanish hymnbook containing 495 hymns (see vol. 7:7 for a Spanish version of the UCC Statement of Faith).*

As the UCC aspires to be a multiracial and multicultural church, music is extremely significant. "Cristo es la peña de Horeb" (Christ is the Mountain of Horeb) is an anonymous song widely used in Pentecostal churches in Puerto Rico. "Pues si vivimos" (When We Are Living) is a traditional Mexican folk hymn, and its lyrics are based on Romans 14:7–8. A second stanza was added in 1983 by Elise S. Eslinger (b. 1942). Both of these hymns highlight the presence of God in all of life and the importance of Jesus Christ.

Source: Puerto Rican Hymn, "Cristo es la peña de Horeb" (Christ is the Mountain of Horeb), *The New Century Hymnal* (Cleveland: Pilgrim Press, 1995), Hymn #45. Mexican Folk Hymn and Elise W. Eslinger, "Pues si vivimos" (When We Are Living), © 1989 The United Methodist Publishing House (Administered by the Copyright Company c/o The Copyright Company, Nashville, Tenn.). All Rights Reserved. International Copyright Secured. Used By Permission.

"Cristo es la peña de Horeb" (Christ Is the Mountain of Horeb)

Cristo es la peña de Horeb, que está brotando,
agua de vida saludable para ti.
Cristo es la peña de Horeb, que está brotando,
agua de vida saludable para ti.
Ven, a tomarla que es más dulce que la miel,
Refresca el alma, refresca todo tu ser.
Cristo es la peña de Horeb, que está brotando,
agua de vida saludable para ti.

Christ is the Mountain of Horeb which is flowing:
water of life pour forth to heal, to make us whole.
Christ is the Mountain of Horeb which is flowing:
water of life pour forth to heal, to make us whole.
Sweeter than honey is the stream, come taste and see —
Refresh your being, refresh your heart and mind.
Christ is the Mountain of Horeb which is flowing:
water of life pour fourth to heal, to make us whole.

Cristo es el lirio del valle de las flores,
Cristo es la rosa hermosa y pura de Sarón.
Cristo es la vida y amor de los amores,
Cristo es la eterna fuente de la salvación.
Ven, a buscarla cuando en tristeza estés,
Refresca el alma, refresca todo tu ser.
Cristo es el lirio del valle de las flores,
Cristo es la rosa hermosa y pura de Sarón.

Flower of flowers, the Lily of the Valley,
the Rose of Sharon, blooming pure and free for you.
O Christ the pathway of love above all loves
Eternal Fountain of salvation flowing free.
Come seek the One who understands your grief and pain,
Refresh your being, refresh your heart and mind.
Flower of flowers, the Lily of the Valley,
the Rose of Sharon, blooming pure and free for you.

"Pues si vivimos"
(When We Are Living)

Pues si vivimos, para Dios vivimos
y si morimos, para Dios morimos.
Sea que vivamos o que muramos,
somos del buen Dios, somos del buen Dios.

When we are living, it is in Christ Jesus,
and when we're dying, it is in the Lord.
Both in our living and in our dying,
we belong to God, we belong to God.
We belong to God, we belong to God.

Through all our living,
we our fruits must give.
When we are giving, or when receiving,
we belong to God, we belong to God.
We belong to God, we belong to God.

132. Theology:

"The Gospel and the Poor"

(1979)

Orlando E. Costas

Orlando E. Costas (1942–87) was a Baptist/UCC minister born in Puerto Rico who immigrated to the United States at age twelve. He was educated at Bob Jones University, Nyack Missionary College, and Trinity Evangelical Theological Seminary. He returned to his native Puerto Rico and accepted a missionary appointment to teach in Costa Rica (1970–79), taking some time away from Costa Rica to complete his education at the Free University of Amsterdam in the Netherlands and teach at Selly Oak College in Birmingham, England.

In 1980 he returned to the United States to become a professor at Eastern Baptist Theological Seminary in Wynnewood, Pennsylvania (1980–84), and professor and dean at Andover Newton Theological School (1984–87). He died at age forty-five, and his final book Liberating News: A Theology of Contextual Evangelization *(1989) was published posthumously.*

During the late 1970s Costas wrote The Integrity of Mission: The Inner Life and Outreach of the Church *(1979). This book provides a popular interpretation of mission combining "evangelistic, theological, pastoral, ethical and liturgical interests with a holistic view of mission and a contextual biblical methodology."*

Source: Orlando E. Costas, excerpts from *The Integrity of Mission: The Inner Life and Outreach of the Church* (San Francisco: Harper and Row, 1979), 76–78, 83–88.

The Gospel and the Poor

Over the last several years, theologians have paid increasing attention to the place of the poor in the gospel. In one of the most recent studies on this subject, Julio de Santa Ana states that "the poverty and misery in which millions of the inhabitants of our planet lie" is one of "the most dramatic signs that can be taken notice of in a reading of the facts of our time."[1] He then goes on to deal with the challenge posed by the existence of the sociologically poor to those who "profess biblical faith and believe in Jesus Christ as God and Savior in accordance with the Scriptures."[2]

Nearly two thirds of humankind are deprived of the essentials of life. The reason why this constitutes a problem for Christians in general and the gospel in particular is undeniably concerned with the situation of the poor. The gospels not only point out Jesus' personal poverty, for instance, but also emphasize his ministry to those rejected by society. In this, the gospels verify Paul's assertion that although the Lord Jesus Christ "was rich, yet for (our) sake he became poor, so that by his poverty (we) might become rich" (2 Cor. 8:9). And again: "though he was in the form of God, (he) did not count equality with God a thing to be grasped, but emptied himself, taking the form of a servant, being born in the likeness of men" (Phil. 2:6–7).

This stress on poverty in the life and ministry of Jesus coincides with the social teaching of the OT, where the poor occupy a privileged place, and with the poverty program of the early church (e.g., the community of goods depicted in the early chapters of Acts; with the special attention given to widows; with the concern for the poor of Jerusalem reflected in Paul's collection, the insistence on social equality [i.e., on a relation of mutual love and acceptance] in the gathered community of faith and in the personal relationship between believers; and with James' stern denunciation for the oppression of the poor by the rich in the church). Little wonder that the gospel writers take such care to bring out special anecdotes and parables underlying the special relationship between the good news of the kingdom and the poor of the earth. Luke in fact goes as far as stating that they are the heirs of the kingdom: "Blessed are you poor, for yours is the kingdom of God" (Lk. 6:20). . . .

---

1. Julio de Santa Ana, *Los Pobres,* 5. Here Costas is quoting from the Spanish version de Santa Ana's *Good News to the Poor: The Challenge of the Poor in the History of the Church,* trans. Helen Whittle (Geneva: World Council of Churches, 1977).

2. Ibid., 8.

It seems to me that within the framework of the Covenant, the poor are important not just because of their faithfulness to God but because of his relationship with *humanity.* God's relationship with the poor reveals the redemptive quality of his justice, which restores the fallen and heals the bruised (cf. Ex. 22:21; Lev. 19:33; Deut. 27:19). By the same token, the poor disclose the demands of the New Covenant: meekness, openness to God and trust in him alone (Lk. 18:18–25). No wonder, then, that Jesus associated his mission with the poor, the blind, the captives and the oppressed — because they bear the greatest evidence of the tragedy of sin! The gospel is for all those who see themselves as broken and bruised. To them it announces the Year of Jubilee: the new age of God, yes, the liberation of history!

This is why the poor profoundly affect the identity of the church. The church is both a sign of the commitment of God's mission with the struggle of the wretched of the earth and first fruits of the new creation. In the church, there should be room for all types of human beings, but especially for the outcast, broken and marginal of society, because the church is a *paradigm* of the humanity that God is creating through the saving work of Christ, a paradigm realized and made present by the power of the Holy Spirit out of the discordance and deformation of society. The struggle of the poor for liberation from their material oppressive situations should *also* shape the church's struggle given its calling to be a priestly and prophetic community. To fulfill this task effectively, the church must embody the history of rejection, exploitation and domination of the oppressed majorities of the earth; it must participate in their present state of repressed frustrations, silent protests or overt efforts to break the chains of oppression; and it must articulate their future hopes and aspirations. . . .

Whatever else may be said about the salvation of rich and poor in the Bible, one thing remains clear: Salvation comes by way of conversion from sin and self to God and neighbor. Negatively, this implies a disposition to change one's egoistic values, to renounce any pretension of self-sufficiency and to break with any form of oppression. Positively, it means commitment to God's kingdom and its righteousness, total dependence on the Lord Jesus Christ and entrance into a life of liberating service to all human beings in general and to the sociologically oppressed in particular. In this sense, it must be recognized that "while material poverty is condemned as a scandalous condition, nevertheless, it constitutes a privileged path to the poverty of the Spirit, because those who have nothing have less difficulty in humbling themselves before God, than those who have riches."[3]

---

3. Orlando E. Costas, "Mission Out of Affluence," *Missiology* (1973): 413.

The church should be affected both in its self-image and in its lifestyle by the psychological impoverishment of the rich. But it should be particularly affected by the harsh reality of a world broken and divided between a minority of haves and a majority of have-nots and by the struggle of the latter to become free from the bondage imposed on them by the sinful attitudes and behavior of the former. In this context the church is called on to bear a direct witness against the scandal of poverty, whether in its sociological expression or in its psychological manifestation. But it can only bear this witness to the extent that it assumes the identity of the sociologically poor and lives in the spirit of humility, openness and dependence on God. In the words of Gustavo Gutiérrez:

> Only by rejecting poverty in order to protest against it can the Church preach something that is uniquely its own: "Spiritual poverty," that is, the openness of man and history to the future promised by God. Only in this way will the Church be able to fulfill authentically — and with any possibility of being listened to — its prophetic function of denouncing every injustice to man. And only in this way will it be able to preach the word which liberates, the word of genuine brotherhood.[4]

4. Gustavo Gutiérrez, *A Theology of Liberation* (Maryknoll, N.Y.: Orbis Books, 1973), 302.

133. Hispanic Ministries:

"Biblical, Theological, and Ethical Rationale"

(1987)

General Synod

The 1985 General Synod of the United Church of Christ called on the Executive Council of the UCC to convene a special consultation to consider the future of Hispanic ministries throughout the church and to bring recommendations to the 1987 General Synod. The consultation prepared a lengthy pronouncement and a proposal for action. In its "Background Statement of Significance and Rationale" the pronouncement presents information about the rapid growth of Spanish-speaking people in the United States and the inadequate response of the United Church of Christ to this changing situation. Recognizing that some UCC members who speak Spanish are members of integrated congregations, it laments the fact that as a denomination the United Church of Christ has only nineteen Hispanic congregations. Although twenty-one of the thirty-nine UCC conferences report some sort of involvement in Hispanic ministries, only ten maintain direct work among Hispanics. "The truth is," the statement concludes, "by and large Hispanics in the United Church of Christ are a largely voiceless and powerless ethnic minority."

In its "Biblical, Theological, and Ethical Rationale" the pronouncement reminds the church of the prophetic call to justice and summons the UCC to "extend existing and initiate new ministries to Hispanic people at every level of church life."

Source: "Biblical, Theological, and Ethical Rationale," from the Pronouncement on "The Hispanic Ministry of the United Church of Christ," *GS Minutes 1987,* 45.

Biblical, Theological, and Ethical Rationale

"Let justice roll down like waters and righteousness like an everflowing stream," said the prophet Amos (5:24) over 700 years before Christ. This call to justice was picked up and repeated by nearly every Hebrew prophet who followed and was a cornerstone of Jesus' ethic. The fight against injustice and bigotry remains one of the unfulfilled efforts of the Christian church in every generation. The challenge to love one another remains a faith question for the Christian, for "if any one says, 'I love God,' but hates his brother (or his sister), he is a liar; for he who does not love his brother whom he has seen, cannot love God whom he has not seen. And this commandment we have from him, that he who loves God should love his brother also" (RSV: 1 John 4:20f.).

Called to be Christ's servants in the service of humanity (United Church of Christ Statement of Faith), we in the United Church of Christ — like all our brothers and sisters in the faith — are called to have what some have labeled a "preferential option for the poor." That is, we are called to have a built-in affirmative action policy in all we do. If someone is in need, we are to do something about it. If several someones are in need, we are to serve the one most needy because that is what we are called to do. That is what it is to be a Christian.

As an expression of our love, a love that binds us both to God and to all humanity, we are to care for brothers and sisters with equity. In the United Church of Christ, we have formalized this caring in a variety of special ways. This is not to say that we have obliterated successfully the divisions that separate us race from race, gender from gender. But we have acknowledged our commitment to do so. The Council for Racial and Ethnic Ministries (COREM) is but the most recent example of our effort to coordinate this commitment.

During its first thirty years, the United Church of Christ has made numerous efforts to engage in ministries with and to Hispanics. While some of these have been successful in terms of particular individuals, they have not been successful either in terms of changing the basic needs of Hispanics where they have been undertaken nor in attracting increasing numbers of Hispanics into the United Church of Christ. The needs continue, largely unchanged save for the radical increase in the numbers of Hispanic peoples in our society.

One reason for our lack of success is surely the language barrier. English remains for many Hispanics, especially for those who are first generation immigrants, a second language in which communication is, at best, limited. The number of Spanish-speaking pastors and church workers in the

United Church of Christ is minimal. "But how are men (and women) to call upon him in whom they have not believed? And how are they to believe in him of whom they have never heard? And how are they to hear without a preacher?" So queried the writer of the Letter to the Romans (10:14). As Paul said to the Corinthians, "There are doubtless many different languages in the world, and none is without meaning; but if I do not know the meaning of the language, I shall be a foreigner to the speaker and the speaker a foreigner to me" (1 Corinthians 14:10f).

134. General Synod:

The Hispanic Walkout

(1987)

Abraham Reyes, Vilma M. Machín

*The Hispanic "Walk-Out" was a galvanizing moment in the history of Spanish-speaking members and congregations in the United Church of Christ. Although Hispanics admit that after 1975 the Council for Hispanic Ministries (CHM) had been an important "support and advocacy group," "a place to go and be heard," they were not happy. The role of Hispanics in the UCC remained marginal, like "the voice of one crying in the wilderness" (John 1:23 NRSV). They complained, "Our cultures and contexts [are] not taken into account; no written resources to address our specific educational needs [are] available; there [are] not enough Hispanic national staff members who [can] be liaisons to our community. . . . Institutional racism [is] allowing all of these things to happen." [*The United Church of Christ Council for Hispanic Ministries: Past, Present and Future *(1998)]*

After 1987 things began to change. Not only did the dramatic report of Abraham Reyes, CHM president, the walkout that followed and the response by UCC president Avery Post raise awareness, they prodded the United Church of Christ into action. The General Synod voted to establish a UCC Hispanic Ministries Implementation Team (HMIT) (1987).

Abraham Reyes (b. 1937) is a Mexican American UCC layperson who was educated at Lycoming College (Williamsport, Pennsylvania), Springfield College (Massachusetts), New School of Social Research (New

---

Sources: Abraham Reyes, "Statement of Concern by the Hispanic Community," *GS Minutes 1987*, 45–46. Vilma M. Machín, "The Walk In," in *The United Church of Christ Council for Hispanic Ministries: Past, Present and Future* (Cleveland: United Church of Christ, 1998), 13–14.

York), and Columbia University. He grew up in Guadalajara, Mexico, and was formed by the Mexican Congregational Church. He was director of youth work at Riverside Church in New York City (1969–71) and a community organizer with Broadway UCC in New York City (1971–76). He worked for the Young Men's Christian Association (YMCA) in New York and Connecticut in the 1980s and became executive director of the Boys and Girls Clubs of America (1990–2002). Reyes was president of the Council for Hispanic Ministries (CHM) (1985–88).

Vilma M. Machín (b. 1946) is a UCC minister educated at the Evangelical Seminary of Puerto Rico. She was director of Christian Education of the Puerto Rican Conference UCC (1986–89) and since 1989 she has held several different positions in the national offices of the United Church of Christ, including assistant to the president.

Statement of Concern by the Hispanic Community — The Walkout

Mr. President, Mr. Moderator, brother and sister delegates to the Sixteenth General Synod,

In Ames, Iowa, you gave a renewed sense of hope by initiating a study of Hispanic Ministries and needs. Today, we declare that this hope is diminished by what we consider to be a neglectful response to the needs of Hispanics, a true part of our church,

As children of your past missionary efforts, you taught us to believe that in God's kingdom we were all equals. Yet, we note with a profound sense of sadness that the actions of the predominant society continue to keep us apart on account of our inequality. And we cry with pain when the key leadership of our church makes no intentional effort to redress this injustice.

We call ourselves a "just peace church." And as you are well aware, justice does not happen in a vacuum. It happens in the midst of acts of justice and not through the meaningless rhetoric of your deliberations.

Our people are those who live in the abandoned cities of this land, where you have yet to demonstrate a renewed sense of justice.

Our mothers and fathers are those who cry for a tomorrow when their children cannot be denied by the society that you represent intentional access to systems that empower.

Our people are those brothers and sisters in their beloved country of Puerto Rico who struggle to sever the chains of oppression from the capitalistic nation of which you are citizens.

This church is called by God to do this mission. Not when it is painless or when your own human existence remains unchanged. There is no witnessing or cost of discipleship in the comforts of pagan and luxurious temples. God has called the church to missions in spite of your rules and parliamentary requirements.

The Resolution for action that will come before you expressed what we believe to be just the beginning for Hispanics. However, our church's neglectful response over the past 10 years has now compelled us to conclude that nothing, or very little, will be done.

Our soul is hurting and our hearts are broken! It is, therefore, with a profound sense of corporate loss that we must leave you now! We will return to hear your response to our claim for justice.

[The Hispanic delegation walked out of the Public Auditorium.]

The Walk In

On June 29, 1987, Dr. Avery Post and Mr. Abraham Reyes walked into the Synod Hall accompanied by the council members and their supporters. All delegations and the general public received this group of brothers and sisters with a standing ovation, applause, and a song.

Dr. Avery Post made the following statement:

> A few hours ago, this community of persons left the plenary of the General Synod, called by the Spirit and became one with those whom they asked to join them. Those who were also called by the Spirit, became a community of pain, of deep hurt, and of healing and reconciliation. We faced together, in historic ways, the need for the UCC and for this General Synod to be a truly inclusive community of mission. We faced prayerfully, but also with tears, how the hurt is to any community in our Church, particularly to our Hispanic brothers and sisters. We face the need in support of the pronouncement. Essentially, in support of the essence of the proposal for action, that both the pronouncement and proposal for action be most seriously and responsibly responded [to] by the whole UCC. All of our conferences, congregations, instrumentalities, other bodies, this General

> Synod and the Executive Council. And we've reached, with prayer and hard work, a healing suggestion for all of us, and a leadership suggestion. I ask you to listen to my brother Abe Reyes from the Council.

Abraham Reyes's statement was as follows:

> Time to build. I looked into my pain and saw the hurt. I looked into your face and saw our God. We come back to you with faith, and a spirit of reconciliation, to call each other to do our mission. It isn't my mission, it isn't the Hispanics' mission, nor your mission; it's God's mission. A time to build, a time to heal. An opportunity for not only empowering a given community, but empowering our own existence. You cannot have salvation, unless you have it in the community. In that spirit we return to you with a new vision that a new tomorrow has broken. Thank you.

135. THE LATINO/A SUMMIT:

"Our Response to Christ Is Different"

(1997)

ALFONSO A. ROMÁN

Alfonso A. Román (b. 1936) is a Puerto Rican UCC minister who was educated at the Evangelical Seminary of Puerto Rico and the New School for Social Research in New York. From 1980 to 1990 he was on the staff of the United Church Board for Homeland Ministries (UCBHM). He was also chair of the Council for Hispanic Ministries (CHM) and co-chair of the Hispanic Ministries Implementation Team (HMIT).

The United Church of Christ Latino Summit (La Cumbre Latina) was held in April 1994 in Chicago. Representatives from twenty-two congregations in the United States, eighteen representatives from the Puerto Rico UCC Conference, and thirty-three staff members from the national offices of the United Church of Christ attended. Román's speech challenges UCC Hispanics to recognize that their response to the gospel of Jesus Christ is different and that it is time to build a future based on that "difference."

SOURCE: Alfonso A. Román, "Our Response to Christ Is Different," *New Conversations* (Winter 1997): 30–36.

Our Response to Christ Is Different

"The stone that the builders rejected has become the chief cornerstone. This is the Lord's doing. It is marvelous in our eyes. This is the day that the Lord has made; let us rejoice and be glad in it."
Psalm 118:22–24

According to the Gospel (Matthew 11:2–6), while John the Baptist was in jail, he sent some of his disciples to find out if Jesus was the Messiah. According to the text, Jesus answered: *"Go and tell John what you hear and see: the blind receive their sight, the lame walk, the lepers are cleansed, the deaf hear, the dead are raised, and the poor have good news brought to them. And blessed is anyone who takes no offense at me."*

If there is something certain in Jesus preaching, it is the conviction that his mission was related to the liberation of marginalized and disenfranchised people in his society. If there is something clear about his early disciples, and about the initial followers who became members of the early faith communities, it is that most of them came precisely from those classes. Jesus' understanding of God's Immediate Realm (God's Kingdom) challenged the institutionalized, ritualistic, and social values of Hebrew society of his time, and advanced a different relationship between God and human beings. The socially marginalized are the ones who really receive the advantages of God's Immediate Realm, not those who because of their religious or social position "have arrived," "belong," or "are inside."

After several centuries as a result of the alliance between the institutionalized church with the secular powers, the promises of God's Immediate Realm were identified with the wealth and power of the dominant classes, and the institution-church became the guarantor of the secular power. The institution-church in the U.S. at present is impotent and incompetent to defy those powers, and self-destructs through its irrelevance, lack of evangelistic passion among the blind, the lame, the leper, the deaf, the dead and the poor. The institution-church has lost the ability to proclaim the liberating message to the marginalized people.

This is the historical context in which we, the Latinos and Latinas who are members of the United Church of Christ must affirm and practice our faith in Jesus the Christ as our Lord and Redeemer. Christ is calling us Latin Americans who are living in the U.S. to participate in God's Immediate Realm banquet, totally unconstrained of the political and power structures of the dominant society. The Christ who is calling us, and the One who we are ready to serve is different.

God's Immediate Realm Is Different to Us Because We Conceive Humanness Differently

God's Immediate Realm, according to the Gospels, is like a king preparing a wedding celebration for his son . . . (and) "Those slaves went out into the streets and gathered all whom they found, both good and bad; so the wedding hall was filled with guests" (Matthew 22:10).

In our Latino communities, the independent Christian congregations grow and develop with many socially marginalized individuals who obviously do not fit the religious requirements of the English-speaking congregations. As Latinos our perception of God's will is different, and how to worship God is also different.

The economic, social and cultural reality of the "Latinos y Latinas" in the U.S. is diametrically different to the dominant class' reality. The institution-church's worship experience and its notion of discipleship reflects the social and cultural idiosyncrasy of that dominant class. Therefore, our worship experience and our Christian discipleship is different.

From Exclusion to Affirmation

As descendants of the Mexicans and Spaniards, the residents of the lands that became the southwestern states during the conquest by the Anglo-Saxons were forced to assimilate by the dominant culture. The loss of the Spanish language as well as many of the traditions and values that esteemed a more humane quality of life created a different personality. At the same time, the members of the organized religious congregations established different standards and practices. Economic, cultural, and religious exclusion further created marginalization.

In the last decade, there have been two significant sociological phenomena. First, the Chicano cultural revolution during the 1960s and 1970s transformed the docility of the Mexican, Indigenous and Spanish descendants who lived in the southwest states of the U.S. La Raza's affirmation generated new opportunities and cultural creativeness that allowed the people to compete with the Anglo-Saxon dominant culture.

The second phenomenon was the massive influx of Latin American sojourners to the U.S. As a result of U.S. colonial policy towards Puerto Rico since the turn of the century, there has been a constant flow of Puerto Ricans moving back and forth. The impact of U.S. politics towards the Central (civil strife and ideological conflicts) and South American (dictatorships and oligarchies) countries also catalyzed another influx of low-income people seeking freedom and better economic opportunities.

The cultural affirmation of people of Latin American ancestry in the U.S. in the last few decades is a collective demonstration for communities that are struggling to become free from the cultural, political, and economic oppression imposed by the U.S. and other European capitalist, industrialized nations. The irony is that the marketing and advertising systems of the multinational corporations have recognized that presence and affirmation. They have created opportunities to take advantage of the economic potential that we Latino(a)s represent.

Unfortunately, the ecclesiastic response is different. The Roman Catholic Church has been more receptive than the Protestant denominations in creating conditions of inclusivity where Latino(a)s can express their spiritual sensitivity. Similarly, the charismatic and Pentecostal movements have grown significantly in our low-income communities. Yet, the Latino(a)'s spiritual expression is ignored in the policies and practices of the historic Protestant churches. That is the same attitude that permeates the political processes and government services that negate the quality of life we deserve.

Faith Settings and Practices of the Latino(a)s

The United Church of Christ does not differ much from other U.S. denominations of predominant European ancestry. In their institutional practice, they have excluded Latino(a)s. Their dominant theology, worship tradition, evangelistic emphasis, and social concern do not include Latino(a)s spirituality and life experiences. What we represent in God's Immediate Realm has been rejected by the institution-church.

Given that reality as Latino(a)s, we must determine how are we going to practice and proclaim our faith. First, we must understand that with the UCC's national structure's sluggishness, the lack of pluralistic vision of the Conferences and Associations, and the exclusionary routine of non-Latino congregations, we must respond to God's calling as we understand and appreciate it.

In not recognizing Christ in the people who suffer, who are mistreated and marginalized, and to speak on behalf of the Latino Christians without including them in the fundamental institutional decisions is really the rejection of God's call, and the avoidance of responsibility of participating as guests in God's Immediate Realm celebration. God is calling us, the Latino(a)s in the U.S., to participate in the struggles of the powerless and marginalized and to become collaborators in God's new creation.

Secondly, it is imperative that we liberate ourselves from the assimilated status that forces us to accept the dominant ideology. Such negative adjustment denies our authentic identity and surrenders us to the scheme of those whose culture, language, and emotional and affective vitality is different from ours. Such abdication is manifested in an alienating religious and spiritual practice for those who have already been alienated and marginalized by the dominant economic and political powers.

Since the UCC does not manifest an attractive spirituality to the Latino community, it can't expect a significant Latino engagement. That is the reason why our membership in the UCC is so minimal. The Latino(a)s' Christ dwells outside of the UCC.

The Latino Summit: An Invitation to the UCC

The Latino Summit celebrated in Chicago in 1994 was an attempt to convey to the UCC our perception of Christ and God's Immediate Realm. We examined the political, economic, and social context in which most of Latino and Puerto Rican congregations grow and develop. We affirmed our faith in Jesus Christ who transforms the power exerted by those who keep us economically and politically powerless, impotent to a power of love which unites us in one single family.

We also affirmed our Latino diversity and celebrate the gifts God has given to us and to our communities, but most importantly, we committed ourselves to respond to God by:

- option for an effective integrated evangelism
- option for social justice
- option for the poor
- option for redemptive and culturally rich worship experience
- option for an affirmation of our racial and cultural "mestizaje"
- option for the universal priesthood of all believers
- option for the empowerment of women and youth
- option for an ecumenical incarnation in our communities

We were called to the Summit to explore and design strategies to develop Latino(a) leaders in the church and society to change the unfairness and oppression of that society. That model requires an effective collaboration of national instrumentalities, conferences, associations, theological schools and Latino(a) leaders.

As God spoke to Jesus in the transfiguration mount, God spoke to us, and called us to descend to the valley where our people live. We were revived by the Holy Spirit, ready to minister acts of justice and mercy and to share the vision of a redeemed and liberated society.

The United Church of Christ has refused to hear and honor our vision and proclamation. The builders of the institution-church rejected our stone. Nevertheless, God has acted among us; let us rejoice and be glad in it. God has called us to the wedding celebration. God's slave went out into the street of our "barrios" and gathered all who they found, both good and bad, so the wedding hall could be filled with our people.

136. Hispanic/Latina Faithfulness:

"Actos de Fe/Acts of Faith"

(1997)

Lillian Valentín de Rico

*Lillian Valentín de Rico is a Puerto Rican UCC minister who served as part-time associate conference minister for the Sacramento Valley association in the Northern California Conference UCC (1997–2000). In 2000 she became pastor of the Loomis Basin Congregational UCC in Loomis, California. In her essay "*Actos de Fe */Acts of Faith: A Hispanic/Latina Understanding," which appeared in a pamphlet on spiritual life or* Habits of Faith *published by the United Church Board for Homeland Ministries (UCBHM), de Rico gives a brief description of "*mujerista *theology" (women's theology). Later in the essay she explains how prayer, worship, and rituals are concrete "acts of faith" in the* mujerista *Latina community.*

Source: Lillian Valentín de Rico, an excerpt from "*Actos de Fe*/Acts of Faith: A Hispanic/Latina Understanding," in *Habits of Faith* (Cleveland: United Church Board for Homeland Ministries, 1997), 31–35.

Hispanic/Latina Understanding: Theological Backdrop

In 1988 Ada María Isasi-Díaz, a Cuban-American theologian, and Yolanda Tarango, a Catholic nun, sparked a new dawn of sorts by giving birth to *mujerista* theology. Although *mujerista* theology is unapologetically a theology that speaks to the Hispanic/Latina lived experiences of women in the churches in the United States, it can also enlighten the larger church on various issues, community and faith being two of those issues.

Ada María's theological articulation is predicated on three basic perspectives: cultural, religious, and existential. *The cultural perspective* emphasizes that not only in the church but also in general it is the woman who carries with her the responsibility to transmit, teach, and nurture the propagation of cultural values. Furthermore, she states, "adapting the description of one of the models suggested by H. Richard Niebuhr regarding the relationship between Christ and culture, Hispanic women feel no great tension between their religion and the world." The teaching of cultural mores and norms is therefore also religious and spiritual. Through this transmission of culture the woman gestates healthy and viable members of society, who can thus also be healthy and viable members of the body of Christ, the church. While seeking ultimate freedom from the bondage of social and sinful oppression the *mujerista* does not consider herself free unless her entire community is free. The *mujerista* sees ultimate freedom as the "kin-dom" of God, all God's children living free of oppression in one accord, all in relationship with God and equal relationships with one and other.

The religious perspective seems to stress that the innermost fibers of the Hispanic/Latina are religious. We are a hybrid of many ethnicities that carry with them a high religious component to everyday life. In some combination Hispanic/Latinas are Spanish, Amerindian, and African. This is what we call our *mestizaje,* the result of the mixture of these ethnicities that make us who we are. Each of these three ethnicities have their own very distinct cultural norms and mores that are fundamentally religious. The Spanish during the time of the *conquista* brought with them Catholic influences with such historical and social significance that the very structure of many colonized Spanish countries was based on church structure. The Amerindian culture is rich with religious significance; the Siboney, Araucano, Taino, Maya, and Aztec Amerindians, among others, have left great temples and pyramids that the world still marvels over. African slaves brought to the shores of Latin America by the Spaniards carried with them their religious beliefs and sacred rituals and practices.

Mujerista Christianity is indeed a mixture, a fusion of different religious strands. For the Protestant *mujerista,* central in the fusion is the belief in Christ as the Savior and redeemer of the world.

The existential perspective focuses on the preoccupation of the Hispanic/Latina with surviving in our world today. There are many forces that the Hispanic/Latina faces daily that could destroy not only her but her community. Street violence, drugs, and poverty are some of the obvious. The Hispanic/Latina is constantly in the struggle for being, the struggle for continuing to survive and live in a society that offers little hope for survival. It is in this existential struggle that the *mujerista* draws on her faith. Through the Bible, the example of Jesus, the promise of liberation for the oppressed and captive, and the lived testimonies in their own communities, the mujerista lives with the hope of survival and the promise of eternal life for God's kin-dom. A key phrase for the *mujerista* is *la vida es la lucha* — life is struggle.

137. Immigrant Theology:

"Theology in Context"

(2000)

Enrique Armijo

Enrique Armijo (b. 1973) is a Hispanic American UCC lay member of Iglesia Unida de Cristo in Chapel Hill, North Carolina. He attended law school having done documentary work, oral history, and civil rights investigation. In his master's thesis for the Folklore program at the University of North Carolina Armijo did an ethnographic study of a new Hispanic Protestant congregation, Iglesia Unida de Cristo, sponsored by the United Church of Chapel Hill, a large Anglo congregation in that university-dominated city. Armijo argues that the shared experience of immigration, common to almost all of the members of Iglesia Unida de Cristo, gives Spanish-speaking immigrants from many different nationalities a common theological framework. He suggests that this emerging "immigration theology" is producing a church that is "uniquely Latino and uniquely Protestant."

Source: Enrique Armijo, an excerpt from "Towards a Definition of Theology in Context," in "Un Nuevo Pueblo: An Ethnography of a Hispanic Protestant Community of Faith," Master of Arts thesis, University of North Carolina, 2000, 26–31.

Towards a Definition of Theology in Context

Unlike liberation theology, which is partly informed by Latin American militancy in the face of political and economic colonialism, the defining act of immigration theology is the movement itself — a profound, shared suffering felt on the intimate level, that leads the individual to leave her home country to seek out a better life. Rather than relying on Scripture as justification for revolution and reversing the structure of the existing social order, as the liberationists propose, parishioners at Iglesia Unida experience the convergences between Scripture and liturgy thematically, where Bible stories, songs and sermons relate in dialogue with the experience of being an immigrant, of suffering and struggle. and of faith as a guide in the newly refashioned life. The Biblical precedent promises eventual deliverance and success for those who keep themselves open to God's word, presence, and influence in the time of adjustment.

Interpreting theology in light of immigration requires that we consider Scripture — including the Exodus, the Sermon on the Mount, and references to land the Israelites left behind — from a culturally specific frame of interpretation. But rather than interpreting Iglesia Unida Protestantism as culture, therefore minimizing its transcendent elements, we should interpret the culture of the church, and all that occurs in it, as religious.[1] The ties between present experience and sentiments and the universal themes in Scripture and liturgy allow Iglesia Unida culture to be considered as religious and as contextual, and establishes culture as that which shapes the dialectic frame between the congregants' lives and God's influence.

While the feeling in theology can and should never be totally dissected from the act for the sake of analysis, it is important to consider theology's expressive modes and nature in order to better understand its function. As theologian and anthropologist David Maldonado reminds us, theology is, after all, human activity, and although its themes reflect a relationship with a spiritual world, its practice originates within human experience; consequently, it takes the shape of those who develop and practice it, "in concrete localities and situations."[2] Theology, Maldonado says, reflects

---

1. For an interpretation of the particularities of ethnic culture as religious, see Robert Orsi, *The Madonna of 115th Street: Faith and Community in Italian Harlem, 1880–1950* (New Haven: Yale University Press, 1985).

2. David Maldonado Jr., "Doing Theology and the Anthropological Questions," *Teología en Conjunto,* ed. José David Rodríguez and Loida I. Martell-Otero (Louisville: Westminster John Knox Press, 1994), 98–112.

> the particulars of those engaged in doing theology, an articulation of Christian faith as practiced and experienced in individuals or groups in human contexts.[3]

This conception of theology requires an acknowledgement of the social facet of religious experience, where the key relationship not only rests between the individual and God, but also involves a group articulation of community concerns, needs, beliefs, and relations. The parishioners' contexts are the realities within which "faith is known and religious life is experienced." Such theology speaks to the conditions under which its practitioners live, and offers them rules and relief in dealing with the hardships relevant to that particular life.

As Pastor Maria Teresa implies in Chapter 1, a church without articulated faith is "a recreational center with a supportive counselor." To propose that the theology practiced at Iglesia Unida is context-specific to experiences of immigration felt both by the individual and by the community, we first have to establish theology as speaking on two complementary levels: 1) to the individual's relation to the world in which she lives, as Maldonado articulates above; and 2) to the community's relation to God and each other.

These two levels are in constant and consistent relation, enacting a functional dialectic between what Peter Beyer, in an essay considering globalization's effects on religion, terms the central religious dichotomy: immanence/transcendence. Beyer writes:

> The immanent is the whole world, the whole of perceptible reality, all meaning communicable among human beings. . . . The transcendent, as the polar opposite, serves to give the immanent whole its meaningful context. In this sense, it acts as the condition for the possibility of the immanent. The central religious paradox lies in the fact that the transcendent can only be communicated in immanent terms, and this by definition: communication on the basis of meaning is always immanent, even when the subject of the communication is transcendent. . . . [Religious communication and symbols] always point radically beyond themselves. [They deal] simultaneously with the immanent and the transcendent.[4]

Beyer considers this relationship between this world and another a "paradox" which lends meaning to human communication, a functional

3. Ibid.
4. Peter Beyer, *Religion and Globalization* (London: Sage Publications, 1994), 5.

system by which religious communities negotiate "the root indeterminability of all meaningful human communication, and which offers ways of overcoming or at least managing this indeterminability and its consequences."[5] This methodology follows in a long line of a pathological interpretation of religion, where the worldly and the spiritual are surgically separated, or placed in opposition to each other, in order to better understand religious function. But if we accept faith as the primary part of this social dialectic, consider religious communication as inherently immanent yet in perpetual dialogue with the transcendent, and localize the transcendent as not beyond the reach of the immanent, but expressed within it, we can consider theology not just as serving social functions (such as establishing community, addressing core problems in human life, and confirming elemental moral rules of human conduct), but also as a mode of offering access to communication with a transcendent ever-present. Church members at Iglesia Unida see proof of the transcendental in the everyday: in the way that prayers have helped them find employment or complete a dissertation; in the way God may help a family member successfully cross the river into the United States; in the way they feel the blessings of the service. The theology of church service is a channel through which believers can communicate with God and bring their individual beliefs into a shared social setting, reporting on those transcendent experiences with those who have felt, or seek, those same touches of grace. Social piety exists in this context-specific theology, but not apart from the transcendent nature and expressive relation with the spirit that is at the heart of worship at Iglesia Unida and in all religion. In interpreting the theology of a community in such transition, I've tried to resist the urge to relegate faith as only a mode through which community is shared, but rather consider it as the foundation upon which community is being built.

Theology *is* in part social practice, but that practice is grounded both in culturally specific social contexts and in relation to a real, transcendent world, with the proof of the latter's existence as certain as the former, expressed and made real in communal language. There may be context specific frames of interpretation in the theological language at Iglesia Unida, but that language articulates themes and issues that speak to spiritual concerns as well as to worldly ones. When the *Pastora* or a parishioner makes reference to movement and displacement in the Bible and its relevance to the immigrant experience (such as one guest preacher's declaration that "like Abraham, we leave our families to come to unfamiliar places"), he

5. Ibid.

quickly brings the presence of God into the frame (with "but like Abraham, we leave with the faith that God will be with us. Because he has promised that he will be with us").[6]

To consider the way that expressed theology takes the shape of the communities in which it is enacted, it may be worthwhile to think of theology as an articulated language, as Maldonado says, informed by the particularities of the communities in which it occurs. If context is the painting, then language is the paint — the latter the channel through which the former communicates, the tool that makes meaning of what is being communicated. Language shapes theology the same way it shapes context, and language maximizes its effect in particular contexts by taking their shape. It is also perfectly able to articulate issues and concerns that lie beyond that context, while still working within those context-specific systems. By considering the processual nature of the language of worship — not just the Spanish language, in our case, but the liturgical language, the language of fellowship, the language of support and participation — then we can consider theology from a context-specific perspective without divorcing it from or setting it in paradox to its transcendent nature. These systems of language simultaneously shape and take on the shape of context, emergently creating and following rules of context-specific communication. And theology at its most effective, to repeat, operates within these rules, while at the same time maintaining an open channel of dialogue with the transcendent in order to fulfill its own immanent needs and transcendent destinies. A Bible translated into Spanish, for example, speaks of the same episodes of and testimonies to faith as a Bible in English or, for that matter, in the original Greek. Meaning and interpretation, however, are determined in large measure contextually. The immanent world and the transcendent one, like language and context, are in constant dialogue; one informs understanding of the other.

Immigration as Sustaining Narrative and Bases for Common Understanding

In emergent immigrant communities, where so many members of the population foreground memories of recent arrivals in their personal histories, immigration stories become, like language, a common characteristic. Immigration creates a new folklore, one of escape and readjustment, and, in the case of immigration theology, eventual renewal. These are the experiences that most recently arrived Latinos have in common. Among

6. Hector Velasco, Sermon, Iglesia Unida de Cristo, Chapel Hill, North Carolina, July 6, 1999.

the many functions this immigrant folklore serves is the creation of an archive of common experiences from which immigrant theology can draw. These context-specific texts represent what Jose Limón, in the context of Mexican-American Southern Texas, calls "sustaining narratives" — a shared sense of lived experiences that deepen the common identities of both immigrant and parishioner.[7]

Despite labels like "Latino" or "Hispanic," which may imply a homogeneity within the immigrant community, it is important to keep the diverse nature of United States Hispanicity near the front of our interpretive frame. The services at Iglesia Unida maintain the continuity of the shared experience across many different nationalities, backgrounds, and professions: Mexican, Colombian, Peruvian, Anglo, African-American, Indigenous, European; dishwasher, doctoral student, consultant, housekeeper. Building the theology around the shared experience of immigration allows it to speak to many of the parishioner's current contexts, teaching the manner in which to negotiate this period of cultural transition, and using the morals of Scripture and the epiphany of Pentecost as proof of the eventual deliverance for the community who follows the Christian path. The theology therefore references the themes in the sustaining narratives of the parishioners, and reinforces the shared nature of those themes through participation and performance.

7. José Limón, *Dancing with the Devil: Society and Cultural Poetics in Mexican-American South Texas* (Madison: University of Wisconsin Press, 1994), 112.

PART VIII

Restructuring for God's Mission

The Church of Jesus Christ has a long, rich theological heritage found in many Orthodox, Roman Catholic, and Protestant communities. As a "communion of saints" rooted in baptism; sustained, nourished, and challenged in the eucharist and the proclamation of the Word; and entrusted with the bold yet servant task of bearing witness to the gospel to the end of time, it carries on that heritage. Ordinary people who compose the church have been gathered into congregations, large and small, urban and rural, famous and unknown, scattered across the continents and the islands of the seas. These gathered faithful are summoned by the Holy Spirit of the Triune God to live in covenant, to work and suffer together, embracing a unity that wraps its arms around the marvelous diversities and variety of gifts that are present in the life of the church.

The United Church of Christ, like the prior denominations that came together to give it life, has been sustained from one generation to the next by the grace and benevolence of God, taking on different shapes, forms, and structures as new insights and challenges appeared. Repeatedly it has sought to bear witness with a unified voice to the wondrous fact that in Jesus Christ, the eternal Word of God has become flesh and dwelt among us. In the relatively few years since its founding in 1957, the United Church of Christ has adapted its life to the changing cultures around it, opened itself to the fresh "truth and light yet to break forth out of God's holy Word" anticipated by John Robinson, and rooted itself a living theological heritage. There are times when the life of the UCC has been contentious, politicized, and fractious. At other times it has stumbled and lost focus, but the United Church of Christ has not lost heart. In its most faithful moments it has continually attempted to rethink its calling in terms of a biblically based theology of the church (ecclesiology) and in terms of God's mission in the world.

Rethinking Church and Mission

When the United Church of Christ came into being in 1957 there were many structural and organizational challenges facing the young denomination. National instrumentalities needed to be created and merged; conferences, synods, and associations explored new ways to share their life and work; and congregations sought to understand how local identity and autonomy were to be enhanced and protected in the new church. Only the abiding conviction that Jesus Christ, Head of the church, had called them to be "one" sustained their spirits.

The 1960s were filled with social challenges that consumed the United Church of Christ and dramatically shaped its character, yet constitutional and structural issues persisted. In 1961 a Long Range Planning Committee compiled a list of issues likely to confront the church in the coming decade, some of which involved church order. In 1967 and 1969 a Committee on Structure drafted and revised a "Statement of Purpose and Mission for the UCC" and named ongoing organizational problems that continued to undermine its common life (see vol. 7:11).

The United Church of Christ has consistently fretted and fussed over structures during its entire history. For some people structures stand at the heart of the Christian church. Only with the right structures can God and the gospel be well served. For other people, excess energy expended on church structures is a distraction and even a sin. There is so much to be done in the world, they argue, that spending time on internal organizational issues is irresponsible. Both of these perspectives are alive and well in the United Church of Christ.

From 1957 to 2000 structural and organizational concerns came and went with predictable regularity. Committees were formed, reports prepared, advice heard, and changes made. Over the years the General Synod and national offices made numerous adjustments, realignments, and additions — some even requiring constitutional amendments. From 1973 to 1987 actions were taken to establish the Commission for Racial Justice (CRJ), the Office for Church Life and Leadership (OCLL), the Office for Church In Society (OCIS), the Council for Racial and Ethnic Ministries (COREM), the Council for Health and Human Services Ministries (CHHSM), and the Coordinating Center for Women (CCW).

Location is another issue that has troubled the United Church of Christ. In 1957 the national offices of the General Council of the Congregational Christian Churches were in Boston and the national offices of the Evangelical and Reformed Church were in Philadelphia. In 1963 the General Synod voted to authorize the Executive Council "to establish the National

Headquarters of the United Church of Christ in New York City." By the 1970s escalating costs and the fact that New York seemed too distant for many local people reopened the question. Therefore, in 1979 the General Synod initiated a study related to the location of the national offices. After ten years, much discussion and two committees, in 1989 the General Synod voted to purchase a building and relocate the UCC national offices to Cleveland, Ohio.

During the relocation discussions there were many people who believed that changing the location of the national offices only addressed some of the challenges faced by the UCC. They argued that constitutional structures themselves were inhibiting the effectiveness and faithfulness of the United Church of Christ. Therefore, in 1987 the Executive Council appointed an Advisory Commission on Structure to look into the situation. Two years later it reported back with seven observations: (1) The UCC needed to work on its "ecclesiology" (its understanding of the nature of the church) and "what structural forms best express that understanding." (2) The management and coordination of programs were weak. (3) The ecumenical commitment was strong but underfunded. (4) The office of the president needed to be strengthened. (5) Money was available, but unequally distributed among national bodies. (6) Relationships between conferences and national bodies and between the various national bodies were unclear. (7) There was a proliferation of structures in the national offices. In response, in 1989 the Advisory Commission on Structure was reconstituted as the General Synod Committee on Structure and charged to go deeper into the "major problems related to our current structure."

At the beginning of its work the General Synod Committee on Structure asserted that "The structure of any church must be based on a clear understanding of the nature and purpose of the church, rooted in Holy Scripture, the history of the church, sound theology and the ongoing movements of the Holy Spirit" (Report on Restructure, 1995). Consequently, it focused its work by looking at the church's essential nature and purpose. The committee produced two working papers, affirming the idea that "the church is called by God to be engaged in God's mission," and that "all settings of the church are interdependent" — related to each other, to other Christians, to all humanity, and to the entire universe.

In 1991 the committee developed a background paper, "United Church of Christ Ecclesiology." Beginning with the affirmation that Jesus Christ is the head of the church, it states that the church has four purposes: "To proclaim the gospel to all the world. To gather and support communities of faith in their celebration and mission. To labor for the creation and increase of God's realm of justice and love in the world. And to manifest more fully the unity of the church, all humankind, and the whole creation." In order to do these four things the church "orders" its life in three ways: by encouraging members, authorizing leaders, and enabling all parts of the church to maintain responsible covenant relationships (see vol. 7:138).

A second document, which came to be known as the *Missio Dei* paper, asserts that mission is "derived from the very nature of God." Mission is not an activity of the church; it is an attribute of God. Mission is "a movement from God to the world" and the church is "an instrument for that mission." The "Mission of God," the committee asserted, should provide the basic framework for the structure of the United Church of Christ (see vol. 7:139).

In its 1992 response to the work of the committee the Executive Council urged the General Synod Committee on Structure to move forward. It encouraged the Committee (1) "to use its understanding of mission to shape its recommendation regarding the function and structure of national bodies" and (2) "to expand the scope of its study to include all settings of the United Church of Christ recognizing the interactive nature of all systems and the sought-for covenantal relations of all settings of the UCC."

Revitalizing Structures

Over the next three years the General Synod Committee on Structure continued to ask, "What would the church be like and what should it be doing if it was mission driven?" The committee developed certain principles to guide its thinking about structure: UCC ministry is local, regional, national, and worldwide. The local church is the basic unit of mission. All of the settings of the church are interdependent. The UCC is part of the wider body of Christian believers around the world. The UCC recognizes and values "the diversity of the human community as a gift of God" and seeks to "embody that diversity and be inclusive of all people" (Report on Restructure, 1995).

Furthermore, the committee took seriously the need to develop structures that would enhance relationships within and between the national offices and instrumentalities, the conferences, the associations, and the local churches. In 1993 it made a report; in 1995 it presented a proposal; and in 1997, after some revisions, the required constitutional changes were voted by the General Synod and sent to the conferences for ratification. Finally, in 1999 the General Synod voted on new bylaws, officers, and budgets, and a "new structure" went into effect July 2000.

The core of the new structure blends ten earlier structural units within the national setting of the United Church of Christ into four "covenanted ministries" designed "to work in partnership with and to assist and encourage Local Churches as they engage in God's mission." Instead of a hierarchical organizational chart, a five-member Collegium of Officers and a Mission Planning Council provide leadership. Expanded patterns of representation at the General Synod and on the Executive Council reflect the commitment of the United Church of Christ to be "attentive to the Word," "inclusive of all God's people," "responsive to God's call," and "supportive of one another" (see vol. 7:71). They also promote the aspirations of the United Church of Christ to be a "multiracial and multicultural church" (see vol. 7:114).

In its reports the General Synod Committee on Structure argued that the changes it proposed would cultivate "a more effective, efficient, and faithful way of being 'church' together." The new structure has "a kind of 'dynamic flow' or aliveness which makes it seem more like an organism than . . . an organization." The committee admitted that no structure is perfect, but confessed, "We believe that the risen Christ calls the United Church of Christ to new expressions of ministry and mission in every age." It suggested that the new structure was "marked by simplicity and flexibility and shaped for faithfulness. . . . " It hoped that a "new culture" would be created in Cleveland, a culture that would eventually enrich the whole church (Report on Restructure, 1995).

At the heart of the new structure is the theological concept of "Covenant," long an important idea in Reformed theology. Article III of the new constitution states that "As members of the Body of Christ, each expression of the Church is called to honor and respect the work and ministry of each other part." Although local churches, associations, conferences, ministers, the General Synod, and the Covenanted Ministries exist in "free and voluntary relationships with each other," they are also chided to nurture each other in "covenantal relationships" (see vol. 7:140).

During the development of the restructuring proposal many people were inspired. They liked the reminder that the church needed to overcome its preoccupation with *its* mission and focus upon *God's* mission. Mission was no longer "out there or over there"; mission happened in every setting of the church. They were pleased that the new structures took relationships seriously. As each setting of the church participates in the "one" mission of God, each setting is called "to order its life in ways supportive of other settings."

There were other people, however, who were deeply troubled by the restructuring proposal. They questioned the assumption that national policy makers give "substance and direction to God's mission," when "we already have a structure 'built for mission' called the Local Church." They disputed the idea that the various settings of the church (such as the General Synod) "become a church in themselves." If the local church is still the "basic unit" of the UCC, all other structures are "derivative" and cannot have authority over local churches, not even "covenantal authority" (see vol. 7:141).

Although most UCC members were indifferent or ambivalent about the new structure, many national staff and leaders felt that it was time for a change. A Transition Coordinating Committee (TCC) and a Constitution and Bylaw Revision Team guided the church into the new era. Early in 1997, at the request of the TCC, a small Think Tank was convened to talk together about the theological foundations for the new structure. John Thomas, later elected president and general minister of the restructured church, but at that time assistant to the president for ecumenical concerns, summarized their conversation. The church exists for mission; structures of the church exist to serve God's mission; there is one mission and it belongs to God; and faithful structures are marked by covenantal life (see vol. 7:142).

In the midst of structural and organizational change it is difficult to evaluate results. Some things done for organizational reasons may be theologically thin, and some things done for theological reasons may be organizationally ineffective, yet many members of the United Church of Christ agree that "structures embody spiritual realities." "The way we do things *re-presents* our faith and our vision for the world." People, inside and outside the United Church of Christ, recognize that relationships between the church and the world are changing. Old ways of ordering the church "have unraveled" and God is "mixing things up." It is important for everyone to "attend to the disarray in the current church situation," and "rebuild the church for this new day." In the face of these challenges, the new structures of the United Church of Christ are judged to hold great promise (see vol. 7:143).

The United Church of Christ is a united and uniting church. Jesus prayed "that they may all be one," and the United Church of Christ lives in the light of that prayer. As it has matured and evolved since 1957, it has sought to be, despite its sin and the temptation to compromise its faith, a vibrant united church, engaging the world in the name of Jesus Christ, supporting faithful members, doing significant theological work to reclaim its vocation, and attempting to make a difference in society. It has claimed its defining commitment to unity through landmark "full communion" agreements and partnerships. It has also embraced the goal of becoming a multiracial and multicultural church, restructuring itself for God's mission. As it moves into the future it is grateful for the grace of God in strength and weakness, in faith and unfaith. The United Church of Christ knows that God remains a "God of change and glory." Inspired by its Trinitarian faith it celebrates the Divine mystery that there are "many gifts, one Spirit, one love . . . one Giver, one Word, one Spirit, one God known in many ways" (see vol. 7:144).

Rethinking Church and Mission

138. Background Paper: *"UCC Ecclesiology"*

(1991)

The Advisory Commission on Structure (1987–89) concluded that there was "a lack of clarity and common understanding in the United Church of Christ about the nature and purpose of the church." Therefore, after the Advisory Commission was asked to continue its work as the General Synod Committee on Structure (1989), it began by "looking at our ecclesiology, our understanding of the church's essential nature and purpose." An Ecclesiology Subcommittee (Clyde Steckel, Nancy Elsenheimer, C. Shelby Rooks, and Horace Sills) asked Clyde Steckel to develop a draft paper entitled, "United Church of Christ Ecclesiology." It was reviewed by a group of ten "ecclesiology consultants" and endorsed by the Committee on Structure (January 2, 1991). The "ecclesiology paper," along with the Missio Dei *paper, are basic theological documents that guided the United Church of Christ through restructuring in the 1990s.*

United Church of Christ Ecclesiology

I. The Nature of the Church

"The United Church of Christ acknowledges as its sole Head, Jesus Christ, Son of God and Savior. It acknowledges as kindred in Christ all who share in this confession" (Constitution, Preamble 2).

Source: Clyde Steckel (for the Committee on Structure), "Background Paper: United Church of Christ Ecclesiology," from the *Report on Restructure, GS Minutes 1997,* F1–F7 [dated January 2, 1991].

This confession expresses the foundational nature of the church. The United Church of Christ derives this confession from the biblical testimonies of the mighty acts of God in creating the universe, entering into covenants with humanity in the first human ancestors, symbolized by Adam and Eve in the garden, with the people of Israel through the covenant with Abraham, in the liberation of Abraham's descendants from slavery in Egypt and their formation as a people of Torah at Sinai, by sending these people prophetic messages calling for repentance and a return to God's covenant, in promising a messiah who would renew the nation and the whole world, and by the incarnation of God in Jesus Christ fulfilling the promises of old and in forming the church as God's faithful communities of witness and service, awaiting joyfully the promised fulfillment of humanity and of all creation. The United Church of Christ believes that these biblical testimonies are authoritative for its faith and life and while it acknowledges the authority of the ancient ecumenical creeds along with its Reformation and contemporary statements of faith, these are always to be understood as grounded in the biblical witness.

In this biblically grounded confession of the sole headship of Jesus Christ, the United Church of Christ also declares:

> that all who share this confession do so by the gracious, universal and inclusive *calling* of the God known in Jesus Christ. In the words of the UCC Statement of Faith: "God bestows upon us the Holy Spirit, creating and renewing the church of Jesus Christ, binding in covenant faithful people of all ages, tongues and races. God calls us into the church . . . " (Statement of Faith).

> that "the Word of God in the Scriptures, and . . . the presence and power of the Holy Spirit . . . " (Constitution, Preamble, 2) are the continuing *foundation* of the life and mission of the church.

> that " . . . the faith of the historic Church expressed in the ancient creeds and reclaimed in the basic insights of the Protestant Reformers . . . " (UCC Constitution, Preamble, 2) is part of the *essential* nature of the church.

> that relationships in the church are to be *covenant relationships,* which means that all these relationships are grounded in God's gracious calling and that they are vitally important and serious responsibilities. "In mutual Christian concern and in dedication to Jesus Christ, the Head of the Church, the one and the many share in common Christian experience and responsibility" (Constitution IV, 14).

Thus the most fundamental documents of the UCC, the Constitution and the Statement of Faith, set forth this denomination's beliefs about the nature of the church, as a covenant community of Christ's people called to faithful mission in the world. By these authorities of Word, Spirit, the faith of the historic church, and the covenant of "common Christian experience and responsibility" (Constitution, Preamble, 2), the church declares that it is one and whole, that it remains in faithful continuity with the apostolic faith of the ancient and ecumenical church, and that unity is fundamental to its nature. These traditional "marks of the church" derived from the ancient creeds — one, holy, catholic and apostolic — are understood by the United Church of Christ as expressions of four basic purposes which have increasingly come to characterize its life: to proclaim the gospel to all the world, to gather and support communities of faith in their celebration and mission, to labor for the creation and increase of God's realm of justice and love in the world, and to manifest more fully the unity of the church, all humankind, and the whole creation.

II. The Purposes of the Church

In the course of its history, the United Church of Christ has developed clarity and agreement about these four purposes of the church by its efforts to state its understanding of the character and mission of the church in its most basic form. Among these statements are the following:

> The Constitution says that the purposes of the church include "Christian worship . . . the furtherance of Christian fellowship, and . . . the ongoing work of Christian witness." (IV, 8)
>
> *The Statement of Faith* states that we are called into the church " . . . to accept the cost and joy of discipleship, to be servants in the service of the whole human family, to proclaim the gospel to all the world and resist the powers of evil, to share in Christ's baptism and eat at his table, to join him in his passion and victory."
>
> *A Statement of Purpose and Mission of the United Church of Christ* adopted by the Committee on Structure in 1966 declared that it is the purpose of the church "to be His [*sic*] witnesses, to proclaim the Gospel, to make disciples of all nations, and to work for peace in the world, for justice among men, and for the acknowledgement of God's sovereignty over all. . . . "
>
> *The Statement of Mission* adopted by General Synod Sixteen in 1987 claims that " . . . we seek within the church universal to participate

in God's mission and to follow the way of the crucified and risen Christ. Empowered by the Holy Spirit, we are called and commit ourselves to praise God, confess our sin, and joyfully accept God's forgiveness;

- to proclaim the Gospel of Jesus Christ in our suffering world;
- to embody God's love for all people;
- to hear and give voice to creation's cry for justice and peace;
- to name and confront the power of evil within and among us;
- to repent our silence and complicity with the powers of chaos and death;
- to preach and teach with the power of the living word;
- to join oppressed and troubled people in the struggle for liberation;
- to work for justice, healing and the wholeness of life;
- to embrace the unity of Christ's church;
- to discern and celebrate the present and coming reign of God."

These statements can be summarized in the four basic affirmations cited earlier, namely, that the church is:

A. to proclaim the gospel in all the world;

B. to gather and support communities of faith in their celebration and mission;

C. to labor for the creation and increase of God's realm of justice and love in the world;

D. to manifest more fully the unity of the church, all humankind, and the whole creation.

A. To proclaim the gospel in all the world.

The church's apostolic vocation is to proclaim the gospel, the good news of God's reconciling and saving justification and sanctification in Jesus Christ. This is the good news of God's universal and inclusive love in creation, in the incarnation, ministry, crucifixion and resurrection of Jesus Christ, in the gift of the Holy Spirit and the Spirit's many gifts, in the promises of renewal and fulfillment in human history and all creation. This witness occurs as the scriptures are read, studied and preached; as the sacraments and liturgies of the church are celebrated; as Christians witness through deed, word and prayer in all realms of society; as Christians invite others to respond to the gospel by joining the gathered life of the church.

B. To gather and support communities of faith in their celebration and mission.

These gathered communities of faith — local churches and other expressions of the whole church — are nurtured through the work of the word and Spirit in preaching, worship and the sacraments; in education and fellowship; in the mutual love and encouragement shared among all the faithful; in providing material and other resources to maintain the church and its mission in the world; in caring for the leadership and organizational structures required to sustain the gathered life of the churches; and in manifesting its multicultural, multiracial and inclusive character in each local church and in all other expressions of the church.

C. To labor for the creation and increase of God's realm of justice and love in the world.

The gifts of God's justice and love in the world require discernment and proclamation; participation in political and economic life; in government, business, education, the arts, health care, agriculture, science and technology — in all human activity — for the sake of the human fulfillment they bring, and in order to prevent their use in any way which diminishes or destroys the integrity of creation. These same gifts require witnessing against idolatries of race, gender, nationality, sexual orientation or ethnic background. God's gifts of justice and love also require advocacy for the poor and oppressed and the affirmative inclusion of all people in the community of the church. And these same gifts require making common cause with movements for the transformation of individuals and the structures of society in keeping with the vision of God's universal realm of justice and love.

D. To manifest more fully the unity of the church, all humankind, and the whole creation.

The United Church is a "united and uniting church" (By laws, V.230), believes that God both gives and intends such unity, and that all Christian communities are called to seek greater ecclesial unity. This unity is manifested through responsible and mutually accountable relationships among local churches, Associations, Conferences, the General Synod and its related bodies; through participation in ecumenical organizations at the local, regional, national and global levels; through movements for church union, partnerships, and other kinds of committed relationships on every continent. It is strengthened also through dialogue with other historic religions, particularly Judaism and Islam, where Christians share a significantly common faith heritage. Such dialogue is based upon mutual respect, clarity and conviction about one's own faith stance, the commitment to speak and listen respectfully, and the conviction that each participant has something to give and receive in the dialogue. The commitment of the United Church of Christ to the unity of all humankind is expressed through its advocacy of a just peace for all the peoples and nations of the world, as well as its care for the victims of abuse and oppression. And its commitment to the unity of the whole creation is expressed in its commitment to the protection and enhancement of the national environment against threats to its integrity.

III. Ordering the Ministries of the Church

Church "order" refers to those ways in which churches organize their institutional structures and offices in order to carry on their mission in the world, trusting that God guides the process of ordering the church. The United Church of Christ orders its ministries in three ways:

1. by encouraging and supporting the ministry of each member;
2. by authorizing and setting apart some members for special ministry; and
3. by placing the various bodies of the church in responsible covenantal relationship with each other.

A. The ministry of all:

"The United Church of Christ recognizes that God calls the whole church and every member to participate in and extend the ministry of Jesus Christ by witnessing to the Gospel in church and society. The United Church of Christ seeks to undergird the ministry of its members by nurturing faith, calling forth gifts, and equipping members for Christian service" (Constitution, V, 1 7). This affirmation of the ministry of all members of the church is expressed in the sacrament of baptism and the way it represents the gift of particular ministries as well as the gift of a new identity as one whom Christ has claimed in love.

This affirmation of the role of the church in "nurturing faith, calling forth gifts, and equipping members for Christian service" finds contemporary expression in the remarkable ecumenical convergence articulated in *Baptism, Eucharist and Ministry* (Ministry I., 1–6) and in *The COCU Consensus* (VI., 1–26),

B. The ordering of ministerial leadership in the church:

"The United Church of Christ recognizes that God calls certain of its members to various forms of ministry in and on behalf of the church for which ecclesiastical authorization is required. Recognizing God's call, the ecclesiastical authorization is granted by an Association through the rite of ordination, through commissioning, licensing, granting ordained ministerial standing and other acts of authorization" (Constitution, V., 18).

This list of authorizing actions and the offices to which they relate all express the conviction of the United Church of Christ that God calls some members of the church to these offices for the sake of the mission of the church and its leadership needs. The authorization to preach and preside at sacramental celebrations, to be a pastor and teacher of the church, to exercise pastoral leadership is of crucial importance for the life and mission of the church.

The designation of these leaders is conferred by the church and always remains the authorization of the church, not the office or the person. The spiritual gifts, education, skills and experience required of these leadership offices are examined and attested by the church, but authorization for leadership is *granted* only by the church.

The need for these authorized leaders is finally validated by their ability to enable and strengthen the mission of all God's people in the world. When the servant church is able to proclaim the gospel in all the world, gather and support communities of faith, labor for the increase of God's realm of justice and love in the world, and manifest more fully the unity of the church, all humankind and the whole creation, then the church can give thanks with joy to the God who has called us in Jesus Christ through the power of the Holy Spirit.

C. The ordering of the church for ministry:

The United Church of Christ believes that local churches, called by the sole head of the church, Jesus Christ, are the basic units of the whole church. "The basic unit of the life and organization of the United Church is the local church" (Constitution, IV, 7). These local churches have their life in a joyful, mutually accountable covenant relationship with other local churches, Associations, Conferences and the General Synod and its related bodies. "The local churches of the United Church of Christ have, in fellowship, a God-given responsibility for that Church, its labors and its extension, even as the United Church of Christ has, in fellowship, a God-given responsibility for the well-being and needs and aspirations of its local churches" (Constitution, IV, 14).

The United Church of Christ believes that all these expressions of the church — local, regional, national, worldwide — in covenantal relationships of mutual accountability, have authority in their own spheres, and constantly seek to serve and faithfully represent all parts of the church. "Actions by, or decisions or advice emanating from, the General Synod, a Conference or an Association, should be held in the highest regard by every local church" (Constitution, IV, 16).

While the autonomy of the local church is constitutionally guaranteed ["The autonomy of the local church is inherent and modifiable only by its own action" (Constitution IV, 15)], and the responsible exercise of the autonomy of all other expressions is similarly guarded, this protection is not understood as a warrant for any local church or other expression of the church to ignore its covenantal relationships in the wider church. Indeed the radical freedom inherent in the principle of autonomy requires all the more faithful attention to the connectedness through covenant entailed in this understanding of relationships in the church.

On the continuum of organizational forms seen in church history, these affirmations locate the United Church of Christ within both congregational and presbyterial polities. Though the United Church of Christ does not have episcopal offices, except for the bishop of the Calvin Synod, the functions of episcopacy [pastoral oversight, authoritative teaching, maintaining the unity of the church and apostolic continuity] are carried out by congregations, clergy, denominational staff members and the whole church. The office of conference minister, more than any other in the United Church of Christ, represents the performance of these episcopal functions. This polity is covenantal, where biblical and theological understandings of covenant express the mutual obligations of every part of the church to give and receive counsel, and to take seriously actions by other parts of the church. This polity is also covenantal in its understanding that the God known in Jesus Christ creates and sustains the covenant.

IV. For Further Discussion

In its brief history the United Church has sought to maintain a lively and creative tension and balance in the midst of many conflicting currents of contemporary church life. The United Church of Christ understands that faithfulness to the authority of the scriptural Word and traditions of the church requires answering the call to mission in the midst of pressing social and personal issues which are more complex and daunting than human imagination can grasp. And yet many voices are raised which seem to be saying that scriptural authority and mission are somehow in mutual opposition, that one must choose whether to go "back" to a more centered ecclesial authority or "forward" into a more risky fragmentation in the name of radical solidarity with the poor and the oppressed.

The United Church of Christ understands that the ordering of the church always lies in creative tension with freedom of conscience and the free movement of the Spirit. And yet voices are heard insisting that particular institutional forms and offices have an absolute character which must not be questioned, even in the name of greater Christian unity or a more effective exercise of the church's mission. At the same time others insist upon the freedom of the individual conscience in these same absolute terms.

The United Church of Christ understands that leadership requires both the gifts provided by the Holy Spirit and the kind of formation which comes through meeting educational and authorizing requirements. But voices are heard which call all formal educational and authorizing procedures into question because of their bondage to the dominant culture. And other voices lament the numbers of older and otherwise nontraditional seminarians called by the Spirit to church leadership, for the sake of restoring a quality of leadership which is feared to be slipping away.

And the United Church of Christ understands that the justice call for solidarity with the poor and oppressed can find effective expression only when it maintains and strengthens viable institutions for mission. For some, however, this call for radical solidarity means abandoning existing institutional structures altogether, in the hope that new structures will not fall captive to the dominant culture. Others want to avoid the searching reexamination of comfortable and privileged positions which such solidarity requires.

As it seeks to uphold these affirmations about the church and to be instructed by all its voices clamoring for attention, the United Church of Christ seeks the guidance of Jesus Christ, the great Head of the whole church, confident that in following Christ the United Church of Christ will continue to make significant contributions to faithful mission in the world and to the unity of the church.

January 2, 1991

139. Background Paper:

"*The* Missio Dei"

(1992)

Having concluded that there was "a lack of clarity and common understanding in the United Church of Christ about the nature and purpose of the church," the Advisory Commission on Structure (1987–89) was asked to continue its work as the General Synod Committee on Structure (1989). It asserted its belief "that to design a structure for the 21st Century for the United Church of Christ meant to design a structure to serve mission." Alongside ecclesiology, the committee's views on mission became a matter of first priority and the Executive Council urged the committee "to use its understanding of mission to shape its recommendation regarding the function and structure of the national bodies" (October 1992). Without hesitation the committee proposed "that Missio Dei, *a broad perspective on mission, form the missional base for the proposed structure."*

Source: Background Paper: "A Mission Framework for the General Synod Committee on Structure," from the *Report on Restructure, GS Minutes 1997,* E2–E4.

A Mission Framework for the General Synod Committee on Structure

Introduction

From the beginning the Committee on Structure believed that to design a structure for the 21st Century for the United Church of Christ meant to design a structure to serve mission. Therefore, presenting the Committee's understanding of the nature of mission became a matter of first priority. The Executive Council concurred. In October 1992, the Executive Council urged the Committee

> to use its understanding of mission to shape its recommendation regarding the function and structure of the national bodies;

Mission as Missio Dei

The Committee proposes that Missio Dei, a broad perspective on mission, form the missional base for the proposed structure.

We begin with the conviction that the mission is God's mission. Mission is "derived from the very nature of God."[1] The two word phrase, *Missio Dei,* describes this understanding of mission. David J. Bosch says it this way:

> *In the new image mission is not primarily an activity of the church, but an attribute of God. God is a missionary God. "It is not the church that has a mission of salvation to fulfill in the world; it is the mission of the Son and the Spirit through the Father [sic]*[2] *that includes the Church's" (Moltmann). Mission is thereby seen as a movement from God to the world; the church is viewed as an instrument for that mission. The church is there because there is mission, not vice versa.*[3]

Bosch indicates that a broad spectrum of Christians, including conciliar Protestantism, Eastern Orthodoxy, evangelicals, the Second Vatican Council, have embraced this understanding of mission.

---

1. David J. Bosch, *Transforming Mission: Paradigm Shifts in Theology of Mission* (Maryknoll, N.Y.: Orbis Books, 1991), 390ff. Beginning on page 389 Bosch outlines the concept of Missio Dei, describing it as it developed this past half century, and how it contrasts to previous theological expressions of a mission.

2. Note here: the full understanding of the Trinity is used here. It is not Christ's mission or the Spirit's mission but the mission of the fullness of God. Use of the word "Father" reflects the quote from Jürgen Moltmann in the Bosch text.

3. Bosch, *Transforming Mission,* 390.

1 Peter 2:9[4] provides a Biblical model for Missio Dei. It proclaims the church is the one sent, not the sender. "Since God is a missionary God, God's people are a missionary people."[5] An ecclesiology which emerges from this conviction describes the church as essentially missionary. First, the mission; then the church as the instrument of mission.

The Structure Committee's understanding of mission which shaped its work on structure is that of Missio Dei, of the church brought into being to do God's mission. There is one mission, and that is God's mission.

Implications

Missio Dei provides the basis framework for the structure of any church. For instance:

1. The phrase "oneness of mission" used in the General Synod Committee on Structure Principles document refers to Missio Dei. The church is responding to what God did in Jesus Christ to change everything. Lesslie Newbigin reminds us that mission began with an explosion of joy. When the early apostles testified to a New Reality, people around then would ask, "What is going on?" The answer was always what God had done in Jesus Christ, Missio Dei. Newbigin claims " . . . the great missionary proclamations in Acts are not given on the unilateral initiative of the apostles but in response to the questions asked by others, questions prompted by the presence of something which calls for explanation."[6]

2. The church, created by God for mission lives its vocation only when it is engaged in mission. Missio Dei implies that a theology of mission precedes a theology of the church. God called the church to *do* mission. Ecclesiology defines and orders the church *for* mission.

3. While there is one *Missio dei,* there are many "missions,"[7] that one mission assuming as many expressions as there are theological perspectives. Proclaiming one mission, Missio Dei, may place mission

4. "But you are a chosen race, a royal priesthood, a holy nation, God's own people, in order that you may proclaim the mighty acts of him who called you out of darkness into his marvelous light." *New Revised Standard Version of the Bible.*

5. Bosch, *Transforming Mission,* 372. Here Bosch identifies that ecclesiology does not precede missiology. He cites Barth and Hoedemaker in describing this theological development.

6. Lesslie Newbigin, *The Gospel in a Pluralistic Society* (Grand Rapids and Geneva: Eerdmans/WCC Publications, 1989), 117–19. (The quotation is on page 119.)

7. This document deals with the language confusion of "mission" and "missions" by using "mission" to refer to one mission, God's mission. "Missions" refers to the expressions of mission in various settings by different structures.

in its proper context, but it does not answer the questions about what faithful mission will look like.

4. The Committee on Structure can design a structure built for mission, but the policy makers will give substance and direction to the mission. The structure cannot guarantee that any particular mission will be implemented in the future. Policy and program people make those decisions.

   Therefore, the content of mission is placed in the hands of the General Synod and the elected members of the Ministries.

The United Church of Christ has four settings[8] which live in a constructive relationship between Covenant and Autonomy rather than juridical authority. It is essential to develop clarity of function for each setting as well as the functional relationships between the settings.

The following can be said about each setting:

1. Each setting exists for mission (*Missio Dei*) and participates in being the Church. [Note: In the original this point is misspelled "Mission Dei," a fact noted in vol. 7:141.]

2. Each setting is responsible for implementing Missio Dei that faithfully expresses its own responsibility for mission which, at the same time, honors the Covenant with the rest of the UCC.

3. Each setting of the church (local church, association, conference, General Synod and its instrumentalities) should serve at least three functions in the new structure: 1) engage in mission which expresses its purposes in the larger system; 2) worship, and nurture of its members through word, sacrament and praxis; 3) provide appropriate resources and services to other parts of the church, the substance arrived at collaboratively.

Missiological Structural Principles

Finally, a framework for mission emerging from Missio Dei combined with contemporary understandings of the nature of mission suggests several principles.

---

8. The four settings are: (1) local churches, (2) associations, (3) conferences, and (4) the national settings of the General Synod and its instrumentalities and bodies.

1. It is no longer theologically appropriate to continue a dichotomy between ecclesiological and mission structure. All ecclesiological entities exist because of mission, and mission bodies need the nurture of the spiritual life, and the ordering of the Church as the body of Christ.
2. While the content of mission is to be framed by policy-makers, there are numerous theological resources for interpreting Missio Dei. Bosch describes mission as mediating salvation, the quest for justice, evangelism, contextualization, liberation, inculturation, common witness, as done by the whole people of God.[9]
3. The changing nature of the world and church imply the mission frontier is no longer "out there," but rather, wherever "two or three people are gathered together" in God's name. Mission frontiers are within each local church, in the local community, across the nation, and throughout the world. The local church has become a recognizable and primary base for mission, and national bodies and conferences will need to understand the partnership relationship with local churches and direct energies and resources to participate in local missions as well as their own unique missions. In like manner, local churches will need to understand and support missions undertaken by other settings of the church.
4. Geography, alone, does not provide an adequate rationale as a base for organizing for mission.

In Conclusion

The church exists for mission; mission is local and worldwide; structure cannot guarantee specific thrusts of mission, but it can enhance it.

---

9. Bosch, *Transforming Mission,* 393–503.

Revitalizing Structures

140. A New Old Framework: *"Covenantal Relationships"*

(1987, 1997, 1997)

Max Stackhouse, General Synod, Bill Hulteen

The idea of "covenant" is deeply embedded in Reformed understandings of human community. Max L. Stackhouse (b. 1935), a UCC minister educated at DePauw University and Harvard University, has taught at Harvard University (1965–67), at Andover Newton Theological School (1969–94), and at Princeton Theological Seminary since 1994. In Public Theology and Political Economy: Christian Stewardship in Modern Society *(1984) Stackhouse examines ten themes "appropriate to the content of public theology": creation, liberation, vocation, covenant, moral law, sin, freedom, ecclesiology, and trinity. He suggests that all of these themes illustrate "key elements" for the "renewal of public life" and argues that covenant provides the "shared framework of common moral obligation" to enable humans to "form communities of mutual responsibility."*

When the United Church of Christ named the central theological concept behind its restructuring in the 1990s it chose "covenant." A new Article III, entitled "Covenantal Relationships," is now found in the UCC Constitution: "The United Church of Christ is composed of . . . ," "the various expressions of the church relate to each other in a covenantal manner."

William A. Hulteen Jr. (b. 1936) is a UCC minister educated at Boston University and Boston University School of Theology. After serving

---

Sources: Max L. Stackhouse, an excerpt from *Public Theology and Political Economy: Christian Stewardship in Modern Society* (Grand Rapids: Eerdmans, 1987), 26–27. "Article III," Constitution and Bylaws of the United Church of Christ, 1999. *General Synod Minutes 1987,* 34. Bill Hulteen, an excerpt from "United Church of Christ Covenantal Polity," October 1997 (typescript).

pastorates in Massachusetts (1965–72) he joined the staff of the Ohio Conference UCC (1972–74). In 1975 he moved to the national UCC Office for Church Life and Leadership (OCLL), serving for twenty-five years (1975–2000) and ending his career as its executive director (1988–2000). Reflecting on the importance of the new Article III on "Covenantal Relationships" in the 2000 proposed UCC Constitution, Hulteen insists that the United Church of Christ has already become comfortable with describing its structure as "covenantal polity." The UCC is "in covenant with God." UCC people are "in covenant with each other and God." The substance of covenantal polity names "parties relating to each other," describes "a particular manner of relating," characterizes "the identity and ends to which those relationships are given," and becomes "an instrument for the ongoing generation of conjoined commitments and activity." Covenantal polity understands authority, responsibility, accountability, and boundaries in new ways.

Stackhouse on Covenant

Closely related to vocation is [another] theme indispensable for a public theology: *covenant.* Covenant responds to the question of *how* we humans are to form communities of mutual responsibility as we live out our vocations. People require one another to be whole, and persons in community require a shared framework of common moral obligation that provides the principles by which to structure these relationships.

In the biblical tradition, covenant is seen as a gift of God that bonds the human will to God's justice and to the neighbor in structures of mutual accountability. Historically, "covenant" is the core of the prophetic tradition and has been in contention with two other major understandings of human relatedness — one patriarchal, the other contractual. In patriarchalism it is presumed that some by nature have the right and duty to dominate others in a universe that is inevitably hierarchical. One finds patriarchy in all caste societies, in some theories of marriage, and in many paternalistic condescensions of daily life. It is also frequent in fundamentalism. In contractualism it is presumed that there are no objective — and certainly no absolute — moral guidelines for ordering human relations. Thus humans construct religions, theologies, ethics, and social forms by acts of will and imagination alone. These artifacts of human creativity can be constantly renegotiated according to the desires and felt needs of the parties involved. At moments of disadvantage, agreements may be broken.

This view is frequent in liberationism. If pursued, patriarchalism leads us to new feudalisms; contractualism, to arbitrary relativism.

Covenant recognizes the need for different levels of accountability in social relationships. It has structures of authority, but it calls leadership to regard, serve, and care for those in lower positions. Covenant also recognizes the role of voluntary choice and human agreement, but it sees the basic terms within which viable agreements are made as set by a higher law than we can fabricate out of arbitrary human will or calculate by the changing perceptions of advantage. In short, covenant holds that God sets forth terms and limits for our lives together, and that whatever authority we have and however we exercise our wills, we are to be subject to these terms. There are, as it were, objective mandates for living that require fidelity, obedience, and a willingness to live lovingly with those whom we at times cannot stand. Christians hold that particular covenants in our lives occur in a context that extends, finally, to all humanity, for we are bonded together in a mutuality of existence not of our own construction. Covenant is thus the community-ordering side of vocation.[1]

Constitution of the UCC
Article III

Within the United Church of Christ, the various expressions of the church relate to each other in a covenantal manner. Each expression of the church has responsibilities and rights in relation to the others, to the end that the whole church will seek God's will and be faithful to God's mission. Decisions are made in consultation and collaboration among the various parts of the structure. As members of the Body of Christ, each expression of the church is called to honor and respect the work and ministry of each other part. Each expression of the church listens, hears, and carefully considers the advice, counsel, and requests of others. In this covenant, the various expressions of the United Church of Christ seek to walk together in all God's ways.

---

1. See Joseph L. Allen, *Love and Conflict: A Covenantal Model of Christian Ethics* (Nashville: Abingdon, 1984).

God Does Not Coerce, God Invites

God invites and does not coerce a people to be in covenant with God and each other. As God does not coerce, neither is coercion an instrumental characteristic of covenantal polity. Free willing of commitment to be and remain in covenant with God and each other is a hallmark of covenantal polity in which the unity of all is fostered by community in Christ.

Saying this is a reminder of the stellar work of Robert Paul in his *Freedom with Order: The Doctrine of the Church in the United Church of Christ.*[2]

Any study of the history of church governance is cognizant of times when the vested or assumed power of a few or of the state in relation to religion has been coercive and to the advantage of those in control. It is no wonder that United Church of Christ polity abhors coercive activity, no matter its form of approach or source.

At the same time, though, it is important to acknowledge that significant discourse and dialogue need to be regularly present. They provide for the sharing of both insight and conviction with testimony being subject to challenge or acceptance with neither fear of reprisal nor reward of favor. The absence of such testimony provides a vacuum in which unfaithful notions go unnoticed and bland sameness becomes a touchstone for lackluster and incomplete unity. Vigorous testimony participates in and enlivens the development of a polity that invites but does not coerce.

The offering of testimony is, at times, confused with *speaking for* or as *binding upon.* This confusion is understandable in that many persons contend with hierarchical organizations in day to day life, organizations in which *speaking for* or something being *binding upon* is a reality. But that is not the way of the United Church of Christ. A seldom used example is that no local church speaks for or holds its statements or actions as binding upon other local churches, associations, conferences, or the General Synod. Expressions of the church can and need to offer testimony that can be considered and joined, but assent is willful. Somehow, the United Church of Christ needs to help itself and others "get it."

Covenantal polity needs to take seriously the presence of autonomy with hospitality on behalf of the contribution of invitation and not coercion to the healthy presence of such a governance.

The work of Donald Freeman is a helpful place to begin in the development of a constructive understanding of autonomy in the life of the United Church of Christ. "Every unit of the church," says Freeman, "while in

2. Robert Paul, *Freedom with Order: The Doctrine of the Church in the United Church of Christ* (New York: United Church Press, 1987).

covenant with the other units, has a non-transferable responsibility to discern and respond to the call of God to it — God's will and way for it — in its time and place."[3] Doing so places autonomy within a positive context of responsibility and does not limit its presence to the reductionism of "freedom from." Autonomy has, in this responsibility-oriented understanding of it, a responsible "freedom to" quality. As the "nontransferable responsibility" to which Freeman alludes is acted out, autonomy is not a fence, but becomes a threshold for entering into a covenantal behavior in which testimony is offered, expected, considered, and even joined.

Hospitality, understood here as a spiritual discipline, has to do with an abiding sense of engaging and welcoming the other, knowing that the other can be a source of insight into the ways and will of God. Hospitality is crucial given the multifaceted presence of diversity within the unity of the body of Christ. Instead of "you can't tell me," hospitality looks forward to considering and learning from and with the other. Tonalities of anticipation and humility keep pretentiousness and shallow stereotypes at bay and replace them with disciplined and hospitable openness to the gifts of insight and conviction being offered by and coming from others.

---

3. Donald Freeman, "Autonomy: An Interpretation for the United Church of Christ," *Prism* 11, no. 2 (Fall 1996): 24–25.

141. Critique:

Concern about Restructuring

(1997)

James L. Haddix

James Haddix (b. 1946) is a UCC minister who was educated at the University of Missouri (Columbia), Boston University School of Theology, and Boston University. He was a pastor in New Hampshire (1969–89) and since 1990 has been a pastor in Bangor, Maine. Haddix has been deeply involved with the Congregational Christian Historical Society and the UCC Historical Council. As information about the restructuring design emerged after 1995, Haddix and others raised objections to restructuring on theological and ecclesiological grounds. In a letter to Paul Sherry immediately prior to the 1997 General Synod Haddix argues that the thinking about Missio Dei *is "terribly flawed." He questions the use of Karl Barth's theology of mission as interpreted by the UCC restructuring documents and challenges the assumption that any structure other than the local church can define or have its own mission in Christ's church.*

Source: Excerpts from a letter written by James L. Haddix to Paul H. Sherry, dated June 11, 1997.

Dear Paul,

. . . As you know, I raised objections to restructuring (on theological and ecclesiological grounds) at the Synod in St. Louis. The proposed revisions to the Constitution and the related theological and ecclesiological documents have done nothing to allay my reservations.

The so-called *missio Dei* is terribly flawed. It seems to have been presented in a consciously dishonest way (more on that below). However it was presented, *missio Dei,* as used in UCC documents, is a vehicle for radical pluralism, not for covenantal theology. The authors of the documents try, but they fail, to have it both ways. One cannot have a covenantal theology and a radical (and possibly non-Christian) pluralism. This might serve certain agendas of the national offices, but it does not serve the churches or the mission of God.

I know that the theory underlying this is that the national offices have their own, unique mission (though it is part of *missio Dei*), just as local church[es] have their own things to do (as part of *missio Dei*). And the parts are 'in covenant' with each other because of *missio Dei.* But *missio Dei* is really divisive and not unifying because it is an expression of secularism and a radical independence of various "missions." . . .

For us, the teaching office of the church resides in the local congregation (and, as you well know, this is not just "congregational" polity! it applies across the traditions that have shaped the UCC). The local church is the basic unit, the self-sufficient entity (self-sufficient only as the Spirit of Jesus Christ resides in her and guides her life) through which mission occurs. The church, as the one sent by God, seeks out the lost, the least, and the last. The people of the nations are "baptized in the name of the Father and of the Son and of the Holy Spirit," and are taught "to obey everything [Jesus] has commanded" in and by the church.

In our tradition, local churches, desiring to broaden their own mission of baptizing and teaching, created other structures to extend the influence of the churches in national and international ways. The church (as the one sent) also sent its own to continue to plant other churches. These churches, among the far-flung nations, would then continue the mission of Christ in their own times and places. This was, in part, a response to the insight and questions in Romans:

> For, "every one who calls upon the name of the Lord will be saved." But how are people to call upon him in whom they have not believed? And how are they to believe in him of whom they have never heard? And how are they to hear without a preacher? [Rom 10:13–14]

For us, the mission of Christ, while arguably deriving from God's nature (though not an attribute of God upon which God is dependent in His own being), is carried on in the world through the church. Most particularly this mission calls the nations into the new people established by Christ so baptism and teaching can come to all. In this local churches obey God's command for them as those He sent out. It is here where much in the national restructuring plan falls down.

The national committee on restructuring at best defines mission as *Christian good works.* The content of those works is to be determined by policy makers who address specific needs (works to be done). There may be a question about what "faithful mission will look like." While many may agree with mission as good works, I think it is a benighted definition and fraught with mischief. We need to be very careful here.

At its worst . . . Well, take this statement for instance:

> "While there is one *Missio Dei, there are many 'missions,' that one mission* assuming as many expressions as there are theological perspectives."

Given the amazing variety of theological perspectives (Hindu, Muslim, Taoist, or Wiccan, for instance, to say nothing of the considerable variety available within Christianity itself) what exactly does this phrase mean? Has God's mission anything to do specifically with Jesus Christ and the Christian church? Or do we rather mean that the "good works" of every ostensibly "religious" person in the world is missio Dei? Bosch makes clear that it is the latter.

This is troubling enough, but the next paragraph of the national committee's paper is even more troubling:

> The Committee on Structure can design a structure built for mission, but the policy makers will give substance and direction to the mission. The structure cannot guarantee that any particular mission will be implemented in the future. Policy and program people make those decisions. Therefore, the content of mission is placed in the hands of the General Synod and the elected members of the Ministries.

It seems to me that we already have a structure "built for mission." It is called the church. For us, it has always been the *local church.* Moreover, we already have "substance and direction" for our mission. That substance and direction is not given by "policy makers." It comes from Christ through Scripture. I hope you will read the above paragraphs several times and, as people of congregational tradition standing upon the foundation of the Scripture, try to take in their implications.

Finally, the national committee suggests that there are really four "settings" of the church. The church is not one, it is certainly not local: it has different "settings." There is the local church, the association of churches, the conference (usually a "state" setting made up of several associations), and the General Synod and instrumentalities (or "national" setting). "Each setting exists for mission (*Mission* [*sic*] *Dei*) and participates in being the Church."

This understanding of "church" proclaims a new and profoundly revised understanding for the UCC. This is not merely a restructuring of the "national setting" of the church. By proclaiming "policy makers" as the ones who define the mission of God, we are confronted with a structure that denies Scriptural basis of our own understanding of the church itself.

The national offices become a church in themselves. They use the Scripture (though in a peculiar way) and say that "where two or three are gathered together" there is a church. They are "two or three," the reasoning goes, so they, too, must be a church.

The problem with this is that all the structures beyond local church (which still is the "basic unit" of the United Church of Christ) are *derivative.* They are *creatures of the local churches* and cannot and must not ever have authority over those local churches — not even "covenantal" authority. Neither can they nor must they ever *define the content* of the mission of Christ's church. These extra-parochial structures cannot have "their own unique missions. . . . "

142. New Structure:

"Theological Foundations for a . . . "

(1997)

John H. Thomas

John Thomas (b. 1950) is a UCC minister educated at Gettysburg College and Yale Divinity School. He served churches in Connecticut (1975–81) and Pennsylvania (1982–91). He was assistant to the president for ecumenical concerns (1992–99) and UCC president (1999–2000), becoming general minister and president of the United Church of Christ under the new constitution in 2000. In 1997, in order to help people understand and support the anticipated changes that would flow from the new Constitution and Bylaws, a small "Think Tank" was convened to articulate "Theological Foundations for a New Structure." The group met in March, and Thomas summarizes their work. Members of the "Think Tank" were Paul Sherry, David Hirano, Thomas Dipko, Bill Hulteen, Loey Powell, Mary Ann Neevel, John Thomas, and Robert Witham.

Source: John H. Thomas, "Theological Foundations for a New Structure," part of a paper "Guide to the Proposed Structure for the National Setting of the United Church of Christ," produced by a "think tank" held March 3, 1997, at the request of the Transition Coordinating Committee.

Theological Foundations for a New Structure

The Church Exists for Mission

"The church, created by God for mission, lives its vocation only when it is engaged in mission."[1] This affirmation is the foundational principle of the effort to create a new structure for the national setting of the United Church of Christ. It echoes the words of the First Letter of Peter:

> You are a chosen race, a royal priesthood, a holy nation, God's own people, in order that you may proclaim the mighty acts of him who called you out of darkness into his marvelous light. (1 Peter 2:9, NRSV)

We are chosen as God's own, in order that we may proclaim God's mighty acts. This same theme is central to the United Church of Christ Statement of Faith where we read,

> You call us into your church
> to accept the cost and joy of discipleship,
> to be your servants in the service of others,
> to proclaim the gospel to all the world
> and resist the powers of evil,
> to share in Christ's baptism and eat at his table,
> to join him in his passion and victory.

Indeed, this affirmation about the church and mission is found in the Order for the celebration of Baptism:

> Baptism is the sacrament through which we are united to Jesus Christ and given a part in Christ's ministry of reconciliation.[2]

Chosen for mission. Called to mission. Baptized and given a part in mission. The church exists for mission. This leads us to a related principle:

Structures of the Church Exist to Serve God's Mission

Structures do not exist to serve the church. That is to say, church structures are not in the business of serving themselves. This means that structures

1. "Missio Dei: A Mission Framework for the General Synod Committee on Structure" (1997), 1.
2. *Book of Worship,* United Church of Christ, 135.

must always be evaluated by their effectiveness in serving God's mission. No matter how venerable, how honored, how familiar a structure may be, it must always be open to reformation, reshaping, and renewal in order that it might serve God's mission more effectively and faithfully in a new day. The proposal to reshape the national setting of the church is not a judgment that current or past structures have failed to serve the mission of God faithfully and effectively. Our existing structures have made it possible for the United Church of Christ to be a faithful participant in Christ's ministry of reconciliation and we will remember these structures with gratitude and thanksgiving even as we will cherish the memory of those who were called to minister in and through them over the years. Implementing a new structure is not a repudiation of our past.

Neither is it simply a matter of trying out a new organizational theory or of rearranging existing pieces. There is nothing inherently good in novelty. No, the question we have been trying to respond to during the work leading to the vote of the 20th General Synod, which affirmed the Report of the General Synod Committee on Structure as "a sufficient basis for the restructuring of the national setting of the church," and to the 21st General Synod which will be asked to approve Constitution and Bylaw amendments to implement that restructure, is this: What structures will most effectively and faithfully serve God's mission as we mark the 40th anniversary of the United Church of Christ and prepare to move into a new century? And, if reformation is to be an ongoing mark of the structures of the church, can we create flexible and responsive structures able to serve God's mission in a future we cannot yet imagine?

The church exists for mission. Structures must serve God's mission, not the church. To these two foundational principles, a third can be added:

There Is One Mission, and It Belongs to God

In what has been said above, the phrase "God's Mission" has appeared several times. This is an important understanding that has developed in recent decades, and it helps us see how the restructure of one particular setting of one particular church is of importance to other settings of ministry and to other churches. Put quite simply, to speak of God's mission is to see that "mission is not primarily an activity of the church, but an attribute of God."[3] We often think of mission as a collection of programs, projects, and activities carried out by church members, by local churches,

3. David J. Bosch, *Transforming Mission: Paradigm Shifts in Theology of Mission* (Maryknoll, N.Y.: Orbis Books, 1991), quoted in "Missio Dei," 1.

by associations and conferences, by national agencies and instrumentalities, and by ecumenical bodies. Of course, these activities are crucial. But when we speak of mission in this way, we are tempted to think of "your mission," or "my mission," or "their mission," as if they are unrelated activities, as if we have no responsibility for mission other than that which is "my own."

If, however, there is one mission, and it belongs to God, then each member, and each setting of the church, while carrying out distinctive tasks and responsibilities, shares together in a single mission. We may speak of this theologically by reference to the doctrine of the Trinity: God sends the Son to "share our common lot, conquering sin and death," reconciling the world to God's self. In turn, God "bestows" or sends the Holy Spirit, "creating and renewing the church of Jesus Christ" which is then, itself, sent out to share in the mission of the Son and the Spirit. We are invited to participate in the missionary life of the Triune God.

No longer can we speak of "our mission" as if it belongs only to us, or of "your mission" as if it belongs only to you. No longer is "my mission my problem," and "your mission your problem." We are called instead to a mission that belongs to God, indeed which is the very essence of God, and in which we are given a share. As we share this mission with others, we are called to encourage, support, and challenge each other in faithfulness to God's mission. We can borrow Paul's language when he speaks of the Church as the body of Christ: "The eye cannot say to the hand," "I have no need of you." This understanding helps us see that

Faithful Structures Are Marked by Covenantal Life

Each setting of the church — a local church, association, conference, national ministry, school, college, seminary, health and welfare institution — orders its own life so that it may faithfully participate in the one mission of God. A United Church of Christ theologian recently put it this way:

> Every unit of the church, while in covenant with the other units, has a nontransferable responsibility to discern and respond to the call of God to it — God's will and way for it — in its time and place.[4]

But precisely because it is participating in the one mission of God, each setting is called to order its life so as to be supportive of the other settings in their participation in the same mission of God. The Constitution and Bylaws of the United Church of Christ says it well:

---

4. Don Freeman, "Autonomy: An Interpretation for the United Church of Christ," *Prism* (Fall 1996): 17.

> The Local Churches of the United Church of Christ have, in fellowship, a God-given responsibility for that Church, its labor and its extension even as the United Church of Christ has, in fellowship, a God-given responsibility for the well-being and needs and aspirations of its Local Churches. In mutual Christian concern and in dedication to Jesus Christ, the Head of the Church, the one and the many share in common Christian experience and responsibility.[5]

This covenantal responsibility has always been central to the polity of the United Church of Christ, but it is particularly important today, especially as the national setting of the church considers its responsibility to support local churches in their ministries. Today, mission is no longer merely "foreign" or "overseas." Local churches have "become a recognizable and primary base for mission,"[6] as an intrinsic part of the one global mission of the whole church. In addition to carrying out their own unique ministries, national structures will increasingly need to support local churches as they participate in God's mission in their own communities.

To summarize, we can say that the new structure for the national setting of the church is based on the understanding that

1. The Church exists for mission.
2. Structures of the Church exist to serve God's mission; structures do not exist to serve the Church.
3. There is one mission, and it belongs to God.
4. Faithful structures are marked by covenantal life.

---

5. Constitution and Bylaws of the United Church of Christ, par. 14.
6. "Missio Dei," 3.

143. A New Constitution and Bylaws:
"Achievement and Promise"

(2000)

Peter Schmiechen

Peter Schmiechen (b. 1938) is a UCC minister educated at Elmhurst College, Eden Theological Seminary, and Harvard University. He taught at Elmhurst College until 1985 when he became president of Lancaster Theological Seminary (1985–2002). In his Prism *article "The New Constitution and Bylaws: Achievement and Promise" (1999), although Schmiechen believes that the UCC faces a "spiritual crisis," he argues that structures are important. He applauds the positive steps reflected in the restructuring documents, such as the consolidation of eleven offices into four covenanted ministries. He praises the reaffirmation of the two traditional mandates that have consistently characterized the UCC: ecumenism and social justice. He appreciates the rethinking of the organization in terms of "covenant." He personally celebrates the creation of a Council for Theological Education.*

At the same time Schmiechen also raises questions about some interesting choices and some unfinished business. He observes that relationships between the four covenanted ministries and the General Synod remain ambiguous; that there is no "definition" of a covenanted ministry; and it is not clear how covenanted ministries are both free-standing and part of the church. He wonders how resolutions made by the General Synod, which are only recommendations to local congregations, are able to set official policies for national agencies. He urges that more attention be given to the status of ordained ministry and the relationship

Source: Peter Schmiechen, an excerpt from "The New Constitution and Bylaws: Achievement and Promise," *Prism* (Fall 2000): 33–39.

of the new structures to contemporary changes in church and society. Schmiechen concludes with a hopeful note that the new documents hold promise by drawing upon images of the church that have power to give birth to a new ecclesiology for the UCC.

The New Constitution and Bylaws: Achievement and Promise

Images of the Church

In spite of some interesting choices and unfinished business, the new documents represent a major turning point in the life of the United Church of Christ. There is great promise here because the documents contain several powerful images of the church, which we can now enumerate.

The Confessing Church

At crucial points, the documents offer affirmations regarding God, Christ, the Spirit, and scripture that locate the United Church of Christ on the confessional map. Though brief, these statements are profound and deserve far more consideration than usually received. One of the statements in the Preamble is quite wonderful, though subtle. Paragraph 1 declares that the United Church of Christ was created "to express more fully the oneness in Christ of the churches composing it, to make more effective their common witness to Him, and to serve His kingdom in the world." We do not create the oneness of the church. Our oneness in Christ is a gift from God, which already exists. The church exists by sacramental grace and evangelical preaching.

The Ecumenical Church

This is the first mandate reaffirmed by the new documents. We are by commitment, history, and composition an ecumenical church. Such an existence is precarious and filled with frustration. There is no reason to work at such a project except for the fact that Christ wills that we, who are so different, be united.

The Justice Church

As the second mandate, a passion for justice marks the United Church of Christ, energizes its life, and defines the vision for the future. Like ecumenicity, the documents press issues of justice, peace, and inclusivity at every point.

The Gathered Church

True to the free church, congregational origins of several major branches, as well at the influence of the American experience, the United Church of Christ understands itself as a community of congregations. The congregation is the basic unit of the church. Yet such congregations freely covenant with one another to create unions and partnerships for ministry. Even the new documents list eight councils created by General Synod and seven self-created groups — all with seats on the Executive Council.

The Autonomous Church

The documents retain the affirmation of the autonomy of the local congregation, associations, and conferences. I found no reference to the autonomy of the covenanted ministries, though I have suggested that it may be inferred. I list this image of the church because it is there in the documents. Though many find it to be an invention of 19th and 20th century American individualism — quite contrary to historic Congregational traditions of earlier times — it has become part of the faith and life of the United Church of Christ. The fact that it contradicts the other images listed creates an interesting dilemma for the life and faith of the church.

The Covenantal Church

The new documents appeal to the rich language of the covenant to define relations, expectations and our common life, in spite of the idiosyncratic UCC dogma of autonomy. From Article III until the end, it is clear that these documents envision a church bound by covenantal relations. Here one should note the marvelous constitutional maneuver in paragraphs 17–19 retained from the earlier edition, which builds a fence around paragraph 18 on autonomy. In paragraph 17, the mutual obligations of congregations and other parts of the church are defined in the strongest possible terms. In paragraph 19, local churches are admonished to hold in high regard the actions of associations, conferences, and synod. Though paragraphs 17 and 19 are not new, they take on new force in light of Article III.

The strong covenantal language, along with the connectionalism inherent in the traditions, suggests that the association is really the basic unit of the church — and not the congregation. A congregation only has standing in the United Church of Christ by virtue of being part of an association.

Ministers are ordained and hold standing only through associations. Add to these elements the mutual obligations of paragraph 17, and the result is that a congregation cannot be a member of the United Church of Christ without being in covenantal relations. It will be interesting to see if any association or conference puts this to the test. But the frustration is that, after its role in the Church and Ministry Committee, the association is the weakest part of the church. Somehow we need to examine ways to enliven this part of the structure.

An Emerging Ecclesiology

What then is the ecclesiology that emerges from the documents? Our church is more than a confederation. But it is not easy to find a single phrase to define our communion. Indeed, the United Church of Christ is not easily named by traditional theological or historical categories. The ecumenical vision has produced a gathering of many different traditions at the table. Our affirmation of inclusivity extends the limits even more. We have discovered in some forty-three years that it is possible to live together in the face of considerable variety, difference, and even tension. Perhaps we can find help in understanding such a complicated form of existence by reference to changes in other sectors of the society.

- Unlike business corporations, colleges and seminaries are *loosely coupled.* That is, they combine multiple styles of organization — hierarchical and egalitarian — and make decisions in a variety of ways: appeals to authority and persuasion. In such an organization, members are obligated by organizational charts and structures, yet also free to tell the president what to do.
- The hot topic in many institutions is the creation of operational task forces that bring together people from all over the organizational chart to achieve maximum success. Such operational structures coexist with traditional structures. In the United Church of Christ we see the emergence of such operational forms as the Collegium and Office of Common Services, or even the Executive Council, which bring together officers and representatives to govern on behalf of General Synod. In many respects, operational structures have more power than traditional offices; that may well be true of the new Executive Council — for example, note the extensive list of powers and duties in paragraph 226.
- A final example is our willingness to live with layers of images, practices, and doctrinal traditions. Few persons or organizations achieve

> such single-mindedness and internal consistency that only one thing defines them. The church certainly illustrates an ability to live with layers of traditions and practices. All sorts of things are handed down in Scripture, tradition, hymnals, and liturgies that represent contradictions and tensions. We never completely resolve everything but carry forward much of the old, in spite of our bold declarations to be intentional about things.

The church described by the new documents has a definite character — compared to other traditions — but that character is *loosely coupled,* is as interested in *operational* arrangements as strict organizational charts, and is definitely *layered* with multiple traditions — for example, at least six images of the church, with autonomy and covenant in sharp contradiction. It is a church that claims key Christological images: Head of the Church, Savior, Lord, Son of God, Body of Christ. It shuns hierarchy and affirms a radical egalitarianism born of Baptism and the Lord's Table, which therefore drives it to be ecumenical and inclusive. It wants to affirm logical order and allocate responsibility and power, but it also emphasizes collegial relations. One will not find a simple, single way to describe this church, but it definitely has a constellation of values that give it character, shape, and substance. For this reason it has promise for the future.

The Meaning of Covenantal Relations

That promise, however, will depend on what is meant by covenantal relations and how the church interprets and receives such language. One reading is to see the image as harking back to the covenant theology of the Reformed tradition, revived by 20th-century biblical theology. In the Mosaic covenant, the covenant binds people with God and one another by the gracious action of God. The radical egalitarianism among the human members appeals very much to our culture. But we need to remember that such inclusiveness is only initiated, nurtured, and sustained by the sovereignty of God. In one tradition flowing from the Mosaic covenant, Israel has no king because God is king.

It would be a new day if such a reading were shared by leadership and members. The difficulty is that the Christological affirmations, which transpose the Mosaic covenant into the New Covenant, are primarily in the Preamble and early parts of the documents, with brief references at later points. But not much is said throughout the documents about the meaning of covenantal language, nor is there reference to historic documents that would be guideposts for expounding on this image. The only intermediate norms provided are the often repeated words: mutuality, collaborative, consultative, collegial, and hold in highest regard. Such words give some direction, though they are not entirely clear. Without a definite theological context for such words, a second reading is quite possible. These words represent the key values of contemporary liberal social theory and group dynamics. They are the key concepts for strategies of conflict resolution and organization development by means of group process. They do not, in and of themselves, carry any theological significance.

If the second reading is either intended or used by the church in receiving the documents, then we are back to the dominant American religious practice: religion is a voluntary association of like-minded people. The basic unit of such religion is the individual, who freely chooses to be religious, autonomously decides what to believe and do — for example, shops around — and persists in relations with others only to the extent that they enhance the self or meet self-interests. In this reading, covenant means a contract between human beings on the basis of self-interest. For a long time, we assumed that the church was based on this principle of agreement. In the past thirty years, however, we discovered that we did not agree on very many things. If there is no agreement, what then holds us together? I believe that the church of agreement has failed and is dying. We must admit that we do not agree and that our social processes will not bring us together, no matter how civil they appear. It is at this point that the biblical covenant tradition assumes that community begins by divine initiative — compare the Christological claims in the early sections: Christ is Head, Savior and Lord. Community is, to be sure, nurtured by mutuality, consultation, and collaboration. But such practices are possible only in the context of God's grace and peace, wherein one and all see themselves in the presence of a sovereign God who claims us in spite of our sin.

The promise, therefore, of the new documents is the opening to a biblical understanding of community based on the image of covenant. What is new in the gospel is not our pledge to be collegial but Christ crucified and risen, inviting us to be together at the table. While I believe the writers of these documents know this, the issue is whether all the readers know it? The new documents require a reading informed by a specific theological tradition that is counter-cultural — one that we ourselves resist. Our infatuation with autonomy is not simply our fear of human authoritarianism, but ultimately our fear of God. If we ever entered a real and new covenant, God would change us. The new covenant does require mutuality and respect, but in such a radical form that we usually prefer to qualify it by keeping our distance. Robert's Rules of Order allows us to be in charge.

To say that the new documents require a particular reading of the language pushes us to the importance of shared values and practices within the life of the church. It raises the old issue of worship, preaching, teaching, fellowship, and deeds of justice and grace. Only in a church that knows about covenants, and practices such covenantal relations, will these documents be intelligible. This in turn brings us back to the issue of the current church crisis. The crisis involves decline in numbers and dollars, but also in number of leaders, and generations cut off from any knowledge of the covenantal traditions. The older community of belonging has been replaced by communities based on personal need. The current situation in the church undercuts the shared values and faith in a sovereign God who makes possible covenantal relations. Without a faith and life nourished by the shared values of Baptism and Lord's Table, the phrase "covenantal relations" becomes a group process technique. In this sense, the current church crisis is also a constitutional crisis.

If, then, we want these new documents to build a new structure for our common life, we are going to have to attend to the disarray in the current church situation. There is little in the documents to suggest that our church saw fit to re-organize in radical new ways for this crisis of faith and witness. The documents could just as well have been written for a unified, spiritually healthy, growing church in a stable society. But that does not describe our church or our society. For this constitution to work, we must rebuild the church for this new day. The document is rich in resources and is bold to call us back to the source of our common life and our unity. So let us receive it with gratitude and pledge to "seek God's will and . . . to walk together in all God's ways" (paragraph 6).

144. Many Gifts, One Spirit:
"God of Change and Glory"

(1973)

Al Carmines

Alvin Allison Carmines Jr. (b. 1936) is an ordained UCC minister who was pastor of Judson Memorial UCC (1960–80) and has served Rauschenbusch UCC in New York City since 1980. He has also served as an adjunct faculty member in theater at Columbia University. Carmines was commissioned to write "God of Change and Glory" in 1973 for the Assembly of the Women's Division, General Board of Global Ministries of the United Methodist Church. He wrote the tune to accompany his own words and named it KATHERINE after his mother. It appears in many hymnals under the familiar title "Many Gifts, One Spirit."

Source: Al Carmines, "God of Change and Glory," *The New Century Hymnal* (Cleveland: The Pilgrim Press, 1995), Hymn #177.

God of Change and Glory

God of change and glory,
God of time and space,
when we fear the future,
give to us your grace.
In the midst of changing ways
give us still the grace to praise.

REFRAIN:

Many gifts, one Spirit,
one love known in many ways
In our difference is blessing,
from diversity we praise
One Giver, One Word, one Spirit,
one God known in many ways,
hallowing our days.
For the Giver, for the gifts,
praise, praise praise!

God of many colors,
God of many signs,
you have made us different,
blessing many kinds.
As the old ways disappear,
Let your love cast out our fear.

REFRAIN

Freshness of the morning,
newness of each night,
you are still creating
endless love and light.
This we see, as shadows part,
many gifts from one great heart.

REFRAIN

Tune: KATHERINE

Doxology

This seventh volume of "The Living Theological Heritage" of the United Church of Christ attempts to describe and document the life and witness of the UCC from its birth in 1957 to its restructuring in 2000. It brings together thousands of marvelous stories, fascinating documents, and vivid descriptions of events and persons. It seeks to offer readers a true and accurate picture of the church: its remarkable promise alongside its temptations, evidence of divine inspiration amid its shortcomings.

In earlier Living Theological Heritage volumes efforts were made to reproduce complete documents, and avoid excerpting. In this volume, however, a conscious decision has been made to excerpt rather than exclude. The editors recognize the risk but believe that including illustrative materials from many sources is a more authentic way to show the theological diversity and integrity of the UCC since 1957.

The story of the United Church of Christ is a narrative stretching back through the ages to the birth of the Christian church. Its "living theological heritage" is rooted in the ancient and medieval church, stretched by Reformation turning points, enriched by missionary and ecumenical passions, and faithful to recent justice and peace commitments. Diverse voices further refine its witness to the one Word, Jesus Christ. The UCC celebrates the truth that the love of God gives birth to theological knowledge amid the fragile, incomplete faith of those who seek to follow Jesus. It continues to think, to study, to pray, to serve and bear witness to the gospel from generation to generation.

These almost four thousand pages of commentary and documents are unique in the annals of contemporary Christianity. They offer pastors, teachers, leaders, and members of the United Church of Christ rich resources to nourish faithfulness. As congregations use these seven volumes and grow familiar with their contents, those who have worked for fifteen years to give birth to "LTH" rejoice. They offer these books as a gift to the church in thanksgiving, embracing the future in faith, hope, and love, joining in praise and service to God, who is with the church "to the close of the age."

In response the church gives thanks to these saints:

The original editorial board was made up of C. Shelby Rooks, Gabriel Fackre, William A. Hulteen, Robert P. Noble Jr., Elizabeth C. Nordbeck, Frederick R. Trost, and Barbara Brown Zikmund. With funding from the United Church Board for Homeland Ministries, the editorial board spent over ten years designing the outline for this series, selecting a group of fifteen editors, and engaging with the editors in discussion and debate as each new volume came to life. We give thanks for their love for the church, their patience, good humor, careful work, and scholarship.

Editors

Reinhard Ulrich (b. 1929), editor of Volume 1, "Ancient and Medieval Legacies," is an Evangelical and Reformed/UCC minister who studied at Mission House College, Mission House Theological Seminary (Wisconsin) and the Lutheran School of Theology in Chicago. He served UCC parishes in Wisconsin and in Illinois prior to his appointment as a professor and later an administrator at Lakeland College in Plymouth, Wisconsin (1964–2005).

John B. Payne (b. 1931), editor of Volume 2, "Reformation Roots," is a Christian Church (Disciples of Christ) minister with duel ministerial standing in the UCC. Following studies at Texas Christian University, Vanderbilt University, Harvard University, and Heidelberg University, he taught at Randolph-Macon Woman's College in Virginia and Bradley University. From 1971 to 1999 he served on the faculty at Lancaster Theological Seminary, in Lancaster, Pennsylvania.

Charles Hambrick-Stowe (b. 1948), editor of Volume 3, "Colonial and National Beginnings," is a UCC minister who studied at Hamilton College, Pacific School of Religion, and Boston University Graduate School. He was a UCC missionary associate in Japan (1973–75) and served UCC congregations in Maryland and Pennsylvania (1979–2001). From 2001 to 2004 he served was an administrator at Pittsburgh Theological Seminary. He became academic dean and professor at Northern Seminary (Illinois) in 2004.

Elizabeth C. Nordbeck (b. 1947), co-editor of Volume 4, "Consolidation and Expansion," is a UCC minister who studied at Wellesley College, Harvard Divinity School, and Harvard University. She taught at Keene State College, Vermont (1976–77) and Lancaster Theological Seminary (1978–90), serving as dean of students (1979–81) and academic dean (1981–86). Since 1990 she has been a professor and administrator at Andover Newton Theological School, serving as academic dean (1990–2001).

Lowell H. Zuck (b. 1926), co-editor of Volume 4, "Consolidation and Expansion," is a Church of the Brethren/Evangelical and Reformed/UCC minister who studied at Elizabethtown College (Pennsylvania), Bethany Theological Seminary, and Yale University. He taught at the College of Idaho (1954–55) and at Eden Theological Seminary (1955–94).

Margaret Lamberts Bendroth (b. 1954), co-editor of Volume 5, "Outreach and Diversity," was educated at Cornell University, Trinity Evangelical Divinity School, and Johns Hopkins University. She was an adjunct faculty member at Northeastern University and at Andover Newton Theological School and co-director of the Women and Twentieth-Century Protestantism Project (1995–98). From 1998 to 2004 she was a professor at Calvin College in Grand Rapids, Michigan, and in 2004 she became librarian and executive director of the American Congregational Association in Boston.

Lawrence N. Jones (b. 1921), co-editor of Volume 5, "Outreach and Diversity," is an African American Congregational Christian/UCC minister educated at West Virginia State College, the University of Chicago, Oberlin School of Theology, and Yale University. He worked with the Student Christian Movement (1957–60) and was chaplain at Fisk University (1960–65). He was a professor at Union Theological Seminary in New York (1965–74), serving as dean (1971–74) and then moved to become dean of the School of Divinity of Howard University (1975–91).

Robert A. Schneider (b. 1951), co-editor of Volume 5, "Outreach and Diversity," studied at Davis and Elkins College, Pennsylvania State University, and Harvard University. He served as an interim professor at Andover Newton Theological School (1980–82) and as an adjunct faculty member at Lancaster Theological Seminary (1984) and Elizabethtown College (1984–86). From 1986 to 2004, he served in various teaching and administrative positions at Temple University, where he became assistant vice provost (2001–4). Since 2004 he has been executive associate director of the Middle States Commission on Higher Education, Philadelphia.

Elsabeth Slaughter Hilke (b. 1938), editor of Volume 6, "Growing Toward Unity," is a UCC minister educated at Smith College and Yale

University. She worked and taught for church-related organizations in Europe (1972–79). Since 1979 she has taught at Hood College (1979–82), Western Maryland College (1984), and Frederick Community College (1984–92). In addition, during many of these years she has served as a pastor (interim and called) in nine Maryland UCC churches (1982–).

Frederick R. Trost (b. 1935), co-editor of Volume 7, "United and Uniting," is a UCC minister educated at the University of Michigan, Yale Divinity School, and Heidelberg University. He served as an assistant pastor in the Badische Landeskirche in Germany (1959–60) and as a pastor at St. Pauls UCC in Chicago (1962–81). He was president of the Wisconsin Conference of the United Church of Christ (1981–2001).

Barbara Brown Zikmund (b. 1939), co-editor of Volume 7, "United and Uniting," is a UCC minister educated at Beloit College, Duke Divinity School, and Duke University. She served as interim pastor in several congregations and on the faculty at several colleges (1966–75) before joining the faculty of Chicago Theological Seminary (1975–80). Later she was dean at Pacific School of Religion (1981–90) and president of Hartford Seminary (1990–2000). From 2001 to 2004 she was a missionary associate at Doshisha University in Kyoto, Japan. In 2005 she became a visiting researcher at the Catholic University of America.

As the editors gathered each year to provide supportive suggestions and critique, they were joined and supported from time to time by research assistants and associate editors. George Hing and Bridgette Kelly, archivists of the United Church of Christ, provided additional support. Pilgrim Press publishers Lynne M. Deming and Timothy G. Staveteig, brought irenic and cooperative oversight to the project, and George Graham, Janice Brown, and John Eagleson skillfully managed numerous production details.

Associate Editors

Yvonne V. Delk (b. 1939), associate editor of Volume 7, "United and Uniting," is an African American UCC minister nurtured in the Afro-Christian tradition of the United Church of Christ. She studied at Andover Newton Theological School and at New York Theological Seminary. After ministries of Christian Education in Georgia and Ohio, she joined the staff of the United Church Board for Homeland Ministries as secretary for urban and black church education (1969–76). She was executive director of the UCC Office for Church in Society (1981–90) and of the Community Renewal Society in Chicago (1990–98).

Rosemary McCombs Maxey (b. 1945), associate editor of Volume 7, "United and Uniting," is a member of the Muscogee (Creek) Nation of Oklahoma and is the first American Indian woman ordained in the United Church of Christ (1987). She was educated at Oklahoma Baptist University, Southwestern Baptist Theological Seminary, and Lancaster Theological Seminary. She served as pastor of Mt. Tabor United Church of Christ, Rocky Ridge, Maryland (1986–97).

Teruo Kawata (b. 1927), associate editor of Volume 7, "United and Uniting," is a Japanese American Congregational Christian/UCC minister educated at Ottawa University (Kansas), the University of Chicago, and Pacific School of Religion. After pastorates in southern California and Hawaii (1952–68) he served on the staff of the Hawaii Conference (1968–70), the Council for Lay Life and Work, and the Office for Church Life and Leadership (1970–76). He was conference minister of the Central Pacific Conference UCC (1976–79) and of the Hawaii Conference (1979–89). In 1989–90 he was University Church pastor and visiting professor at Silliman University, Philippines.

Olgha Sierra Sandman (b. 1927), associate editor of Volume 7, "United and Uniting," is a native of Mexico who became a naturalized citizen of the United States in 1966. She was educated at Escuela Normal Superior in Monterrey, Mexico, and at the Baptist Missionary Training School in Chicago. She was an elementary school teacher in Monterrey (1947–49) and worked with the National Migrant Ministry in Illinois, Texas, and Michigan (1951–57). She directed the Farm Worker Ministry of the Illinois Conference of Churches (1974–92). In 1992–93 she lived in Istanbul as co-founder and director of the Istanbul Inter-parish Immigrant Program.

Research Assistants

Virginia H. Child (b. 1943), research assistant for Volumes 4–7, is a UCC minister educated at Castleton (Vermont) State College, Andover Newton Theological School, and Hartford Seminary. She has served as pastor of churches in Vermont, Maine, Massachusetts, Connecticut, and Michigan. Since 2001 she has been pastor of the Mattapoisett Congregational Church UCC, in Massachusetts.

Theodore L. Trost (b. 1954), research assistant for Volume 5, "Outreach and Diversity," studied at the University of Michigan, San Francisco Theological Seminary, and Harvard University. After completing his graduate studies, during which time he assisted the editors of volume 5, he joined the religious studies faculty at the University of Alabama, Tuscaloosa.

Index

Scriptural Index